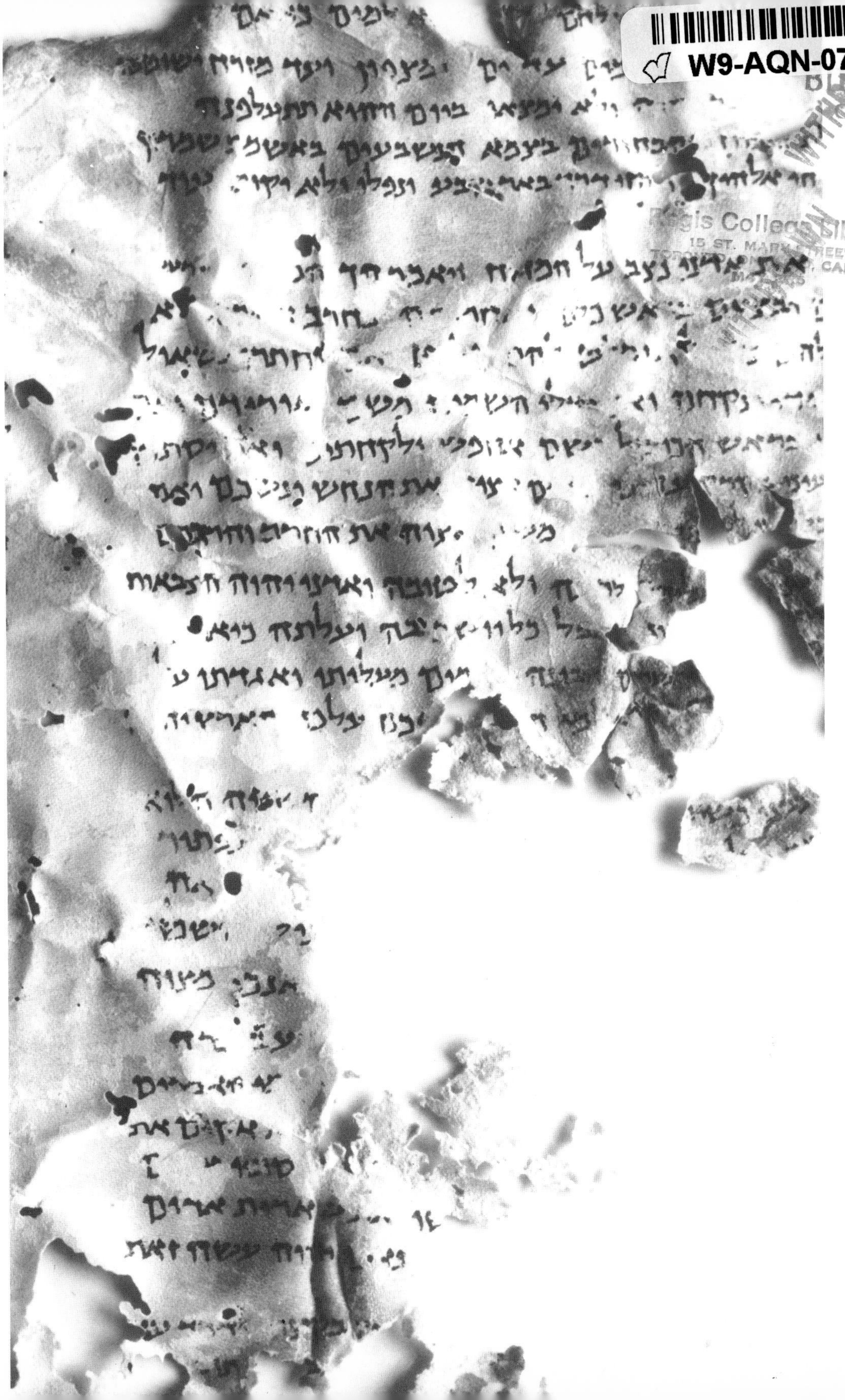

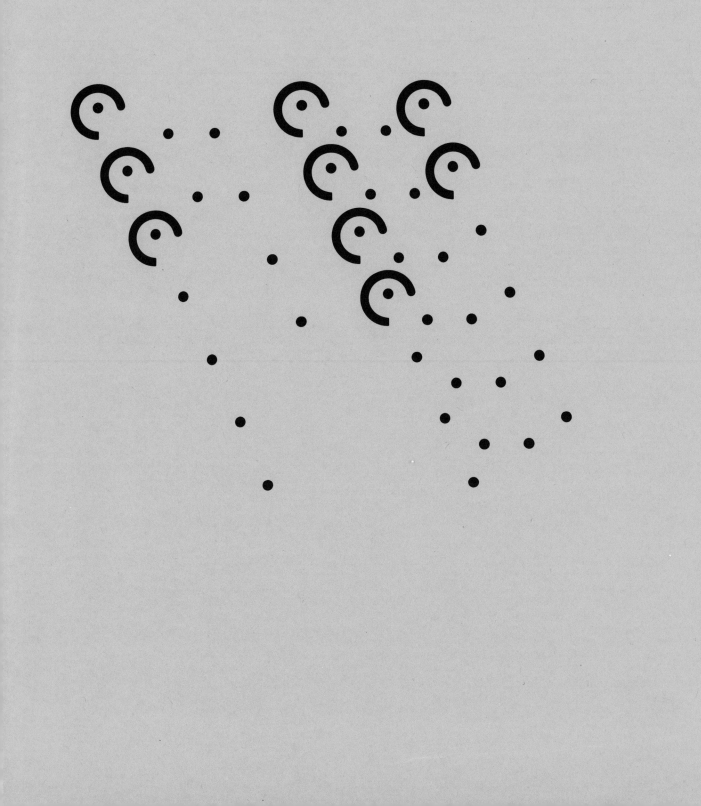

**Hermeneia
—A Critical
and Historical
Commentary
on the Bible**

Joel and Amos

A Commentary on the
Books of the Prophets Joel and Amos

by Hans Walter Wolff

Translated by
Waldemar Janzen,
S. Dean McBride, Jr., and
Charles A. Muenchow

Edited by
S. Dean McBride, Jr.

**Fortress
Press**   Philadelphia

Translated from the German *Dodekapropheton 2 Joel und Amos* by Hans Walter Wolff; 2., durchgesehene Auflage 1975. Biblischer Kommentar Altes Testament, Band XIV/2. © 1969 Neukirchner Verlag, Neukirchen-Vluyn.

Library of Congress Catalog Card Number 75–76932
ISBN 0–8006–6007–2

1–6007 Printed in the United States of America

Type set by Fyldetype, Ltd., the United Kingdom

IN MEMORIAM
MARTIN NOTH

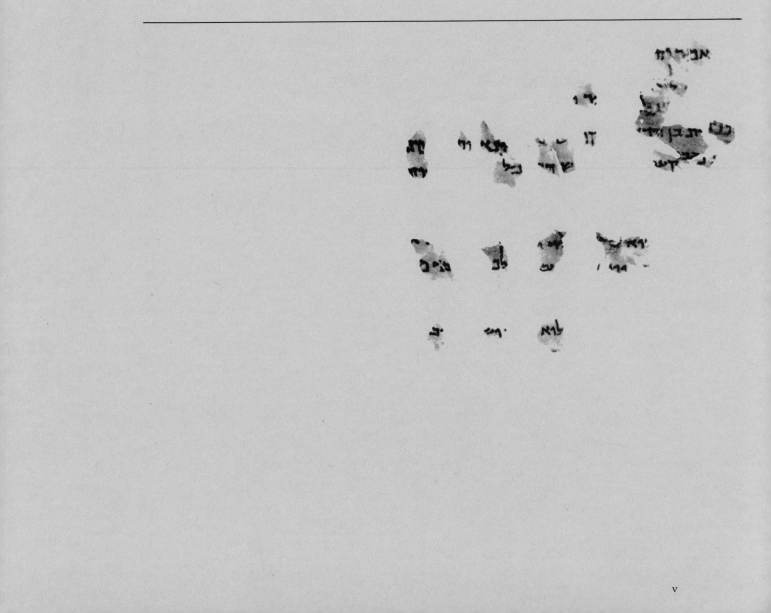

Hans Walter Wolff was born in 1911 at Barmen, Germany, and educated at Bethel, Göttingen, and Bonn. He served as a parish pastor from 1937–1949 and began teaching at the Kirchliche Hochschule in Wuppertal in 1947, where he was professor from 1951–1959. From 1959–1967 he taught at Mainz; since 1967 he has been professor at the University of Heidelberg.

Wolff is the author of numerous books and articles, including his commentary on *Hosea*, which appeared in English in *Hermeneia* in 1974. Other books in English include *Amos the Prophet* (1973), *The Old Testament: A Guide to Its Writings* (1973), *Anthropology of the Old Testament* (1974), and, with Walter Brueggemann, *The Vitality of Old Testament Traditions* (1975). He is an editor of the German series Biblischer Kommentar Altes Testament, in which his volumes on Hosea, Joel, and Amos originally appeared. An additional volume, *Dodekapropheton 3*, is to be published in 1977.

Contents

The name *Hermeneia*, Greek ἑρμηνεία, has been chosen as the title of the commentary series to which this volume belongs. The word *Hermeneia* has a rich background in the history of biblical interpretation as a term used in the ancient Greek–speaking world for the detailed, systematic exposition of a scriptural work. It is hoped that the series, like its name, will carry forward this old and venerable tradition. A second, entirely practical reason for selecting the name lay in the desire to avoid a long descriptive title and its inevitable acronym, or worse, an unpronounceable abbreviation.

The series is designed to be a critical and historical commentary to the Bible without arbitrary limits in size or scope. It will utilize the full range of philological and historical tools, including textual criticism (often ignored in modern commentaries), the methods of the history of tradition (including genre and prosodic analysis), and the history of religion.

Hermeneia is designed to be international and interconfessional in the selection of its authors; its editorial boards were also formed with this end in view. Occasionally the series will offer translations of distinguished commentaries which originally appeared in languages other than English. Published volumes of the series will be revised continually, and, eventually, new commentaries will replace older works in order to preserve the currency of the series. Commentaries are also being assigned for important literature in the categories of apocryphal and pseudepigraphical works relating to the Old and New Testaments, including some of Essene or Gnostic authorship.

The editors of *Hermeneia* impose no systematic–theological perspective upon the series (directly, or indirectly by its selection of authors). It is expected that authors will struggle to lay bare the ancient meaning of a biblical work or pericope. In this way the text's human relevance should become transparent, as is always the case in competent historical discourse. However, the series eschews for itself homiletical translation of the Bible.

The editors are heavily indebted to Fortress Press for its energy and courage in taking up an expensive, long–term project, the rewards of which will accrue chiefly to the field of biblical scholarship.

An initial draft of the translation of this volume was prepared by Waldemar Janzen of the Canadian Mennonite Bible College, Winnipeg, Manitoba. Charles A. Muenchow assisted S. Dean McBride, Jr. in preparing the final version of the translation, notes, and bibliography here presented. For supplying him with a list of translation equivalents for key German form–critical terms, the editor of this volume is indebted to Rolf Knierim and Gene M. Tucker; their suggestions have generally been adopted, though sometimes in modified form. Gary A. Tuttle of Yale University provided valuable assistance in copyediting the volume and in preparing the indices.

The editor responsible for this volume is S. Dean McBride, Jr. of Yale University.

November 1976

Frank Moore Cross, Jr.
For the Old Testament
Editorial Board

Helmut Koester
For the New Testament
Editorial Board

Joel and Amos lie adjacent to one another in the canon. They mark the beginning and the end of written prophecy. The book of Amos is the earliest prophetic work at least a portion of whose written traditions derives from the prophet himself, while the book of Joel was apparently a literary composition from the outset. Amos was the first to proclaim the somber Day of Yahweh, while Joel systematically developed the theme of the Day of Yahweh as a message of judgment as well as of salvation for Israel.

It was possible already in 1963 to publish separately the commentary to Joel. The relatively long interval between the appearance of the first fascicle of the commentary to Amos (1967) and the completion of the work in this year was necessitated by my move from Mainz to Heidelberg. I took the risk of releasing the introduction to the whole commentary along with the initial fascicle. The detailed exegesis of Amos then led me in several lesser though not unimportant places to what I hope are better insights, requiring that slight changes now to be made in the introductory section.

With regard to Joel, I am particularly indebted to Professor Dr. W. H. Schmidt for his valuable help in reading the proofs. For working with me on the commentary to the book of Amos, I am grateful to my capable assistants, Dr. Lothar Perlitt and Dr. Jörg Jeremias, as well as to my students Christof Hardmeier and Gernot Spelsberg. Those who use this commentary have also to thank Mr. Hardmeier for compiling the index.

During the past century alone, how many prominent minds have labored to understand the prophet Amos! How many different conceptions of Amos circulate among us! Of all those spokesmen seized by Yahweh, perhaps none was stranger than he, with his bitter prophecy of the end. Yet the very book named after him already shows how the darkened ember of his proclamations could be rekindled in subsequent decades and even centuries. Only with trepidation does an exegete direct his attention to the man from Tekoa; it is with even greater trepidation that he then releases the results of his effort to expound. In this regard I have in mind not only the many formidable obstacles to understanding and the on-going scholarly discussion of disputed passages. What will stand up to the test? But the other question is much more pressing: to what sort of end does this Amos open our eyes?

June, 1969   *Hans Walter Wolff*
Heidelberg

From the Foreword to the Second German Edition

I owe thanks to Dr. Frank Crüsemann, Jürgen Tubach, and Jürgen Kegler for their help in revising the first edition, and to Mr. Jürgen Tubach and Miss Ellen Widulle for their assistance in proof-reading the second edition. I am particularly indebted to my colleagues Waldemar Janzen of Winnipeg, Canada, who translated this book into English, and S. Dean McBride, Jr., of Yale University in the USA, who is the editor of this volume for the series *Hermeneia* (Fortress Press). Both have placed at my disposal their lists of corrigenda to the first German edition.

June, 1975

H. W. W.
Heidelberg

1. Abbreviations

AASF	Annales Academiae Scientiarum Fennicae
AASOR	Annual of the American Schools of Oriental Research
ad loc.	*ad locum*, at the place or passage discussed
AfO	*Archiv für Orientforschung*
AHW	Wolfram von Soden, *Akkadisches Handwörterbuch* (Wiesbaden: O. Harrassowitz, 1959ff)
AJSL	*American Journal of Semitic Languages and Literatures*
Am	Amos
AnBibl	Analecta Biblica
ANEP	*The Ancient Near East in Pictures Relating to the Old Testament*, ed, J. B. Pritchard (Princeton: Princeton University, 1954)
ANET³	(preceded by name of the translator of text cited or quoted) *Ancient Near Eastern Texts Relating to the Old Testament* (Princeton: Princeton University, ³1969)
AnOr	Analecta Orientalia
AOB	*Altorientalische Bilder zum Alten Testament*, ed. Hugo Gressmann (Berlin and Leipzig, ²1927)
AOT²	*Altorientalische Texte zum Alten Testament*, ed. Hugo Gressmann (Berlin and Leipzig, 1926)
APAW	Abhandlungen der Preußischen Akademie der Wissenschaften, philosophisch–historische Klasse
ARM(T)	Archives royales de Mari (transcription et traduction des textes cunéiformes)
ATA	Altestamentliche Abhandlungen
ATD	Das Alte Testament Deutsch, ed. Walther Eichrodt *et al.*
AThANT	Abhandlungen zur Theologie des Alten und Neuen Testaments
BA	*The Biblical Archaeologist*
BASOR	*Bulletin of the American Schools of Oriental Research*
BAT	Die Botschaft des Alten Testaments (Stuttgart: Calwer)
BBLAK	Beiträge zur Biblischen Landes– und Altertumskunde
BC	Biblischer Commentar über das Alte Testament, ed. Carl Friedrich Keil and Franz Delitzsch
BEvTh	Beiträge zur Evangelischen Theologie
BFChrTh	Beiträge zur Förderung christlicher Theologie
BH³	*Biblia Hebraica*, ed. Rud. Kittel (Stuttgart: Württembergische Bibelanstalt, ³1937)
BHHW	*Biblisch–historisches Handwörterbuch*, 3 vols.; ed. Bo Reicke and Leonhard Rost (Göttingen: Vandenhoeck & Ruprecht, 1962, 1964, 1966).
BHTh	Beiträge zur historischen Theologie
BK	Biblischer Kommentar. Altes Testament, ed. Martin Noth, Hans Walter Wolff and Siegfried Hermann
BOT	De Boeken van het Oude Testament, ed. Adrianus van den Born
BRL	*Biblisches Reallexikon*, ed. Kurt Galling HAT 1/1 (Tübingen, 1937)
BSt	Biblische Studien
BVC	*Bible et vié chrétienne*
BVSAWL	Berichte über die Verhandlungen der Sächsischen Akademie der Wissenschaften zu Leipzig, philologisch–historische Klasse
BWANT	Beiträge zur Wissenschaft vom Alten und Neuen Testament
BZ	*Biblische Zeitschrift*
BZAW	Beihefte zur Zeitschrift für die alttestamentliche Wissenschaft
c.	*circa*
CAD	*The Assyrian Dictionary of the Oriental Institute of the University of Chicago*, ed. A. Leo Oppenheim, *et al.* (Chicago: University of Chicago, 1956ff)
CBQ	*The Catholic Biblical Quarterly*
CD	Cairo (Genizah text of the) Damascus (Document)
Cf.	Compare, consult
chap(s).	Chapter(s)
Chr	Chronicles
CIS	*Corpus inscriptionum semiticarum ab Academia inscriptionum et litterarum humaniorum conditum atque digestum* (Paris: E Reipublicae typographeo, 1881ff)
cj.	Conjecture, conjectured reading
Cor	Corinthians
CTA	Ugaritic texts, cited in accord with the enumeration in: *Corpus des tablettes en cunéiformes alphabétiques découvertes à*

xiv

	Ras Shamra—Ugarit de 1929 à 1939, 2 vols.; ed. Andrée Herdner; Mission de Ras Shamra 10 (Paris: Imprimerie Nationale; Librairie Orientaliste Paul Geuthner, 1963)
CTh	Cahiers Théologiques
Dan	Daniel
DJD	Discoveries in the Judaean Desert
Dtn	Deuteronomy
Dtr	Deuteronomistic Work
DTT	*Dansk Teologisk Tidsskrift*
E	Elohist, Elohistic Work
Eccl	Ecclesiastes
ed.	Editor, edited by
[Ed.]	Editor of this volume of Hermeneia
EHPR	Etudes d'Histoire et de Philosophie Religieuses
esp.	Especially
Est	Esther
et al.	And others
ÉtB	Études bibliques
EvTh	*Evangelische Theologie*
Ex	Exodus
ExpT	*Expository Times*
Ezek	Ezekiel
Ezr	Ezra
f(f)	Designates page(s) or verse(s) immediately following the page or verse cited
fasc.	Fascicle
fig(s)	Figure(s)
FRLANT	Forschungen zur Religion und Literatur des Alten und Neuen Testaments
G	Old Greek version (Septuagint); superscript numerals, letters, and signs are manuscript sigla, etc., cited in accord with *Duodecim prophetae*, ed. Joseph Ziegler; Septuaginta Vetus Testamentum Graecum 13 (Göttingen: Vandenhoeck & Ruprecht, 1963, ²1967)
Gal	Galatians
Gen	Genesis
Hab	Habakkuk
Hag	Haggai
HAT	Handbuch zum Alten Testament, ed. Otto Eissfeldt
HK	Handkommentar zum Alten Testament, ed. Wilhelm Nowack
Hos	Hosea
HS	Die Heilige Schrift des Alten Testaments, ed. Franz Feldmann and Heinrich Herkenne
HSAT	*Die Heilige Schrift des Alten Testament*, 2 vols.; ed. E. Kautzsch and A. Bertholet (Tübingen, ⁴1922–23)
HUCA	*Hebrew Union College Annual*
IB	*The Interpreter's Bible*, 12 vols.; ed. George Arthur Buttrick, *et al.* (New York and Nashville: Abingdon, 1952–

	1957)
Ibid.	*Ibidem*, in the same place or source
ICC	The International Critical Commentary on the Holy Scriptures of the Old and New Testament, ed. S. R. Driver, A. Plummer, and C. A. Briggs
Idem	The same (person)
IEJ	*Israel Exploration Journal*
Is	Isaiah
ITQ	*Irish Theological Quarterly*
J	Yahwist, Yahwistic Work
JAOS	*Journal of the American Oriental Society*
JBL	*Journal of Biblical Literature*
Jer	Jeremiah
Jn	John
JNES	*Journal of Near Eastern Studies*
Jon	Jonah
Josh	Joshua
JPOS	*Journal of the Palestine Oriental Society*
JSS	*Journal of Semitic Studies*
JTS	*Journal of Theological Studies*
Ju	Judges
KAI	Northwest Semitic inscriptions, cited in accord with the enumeration in: *Kanaanäische und Aramäische Inschriften*, vol. 1 (Texte); ed. H. Donner and W. Röllig (Wiesbaden: O. Harrassowitz, 1962)
KAT	Kommentar zum Alten Testament, ed. Ernst Sellin
KEH	Kurzgefasstes exegetisches Handbuch zum Alten Testament
Ken	Hebrew manuscripts collated in Benjamin Kennicott, *Vetus Testamentum Hebraicum cum variis lectionbus*, 2 vols. (Oxford, 1776–1780); superscript numerals designate the manuscript numbers assigned by Kennicott.
Kgs	Kings
KHC	Kurzer Hand–Commentar zum Alten Testament, ed. Karl Marti
KuD	*Kerygma und Dogma*
l(1).	Line(s)
L	Old Latin version (*Vetus Latina*)
Lam	Lamentations
Lev	Leviticus
M	Masoretic text of the Hebrew Bible
Macc	Maccabees
Mal	Malachi
Mi	Micah
Miš.	Mišnah, followed by the title of the tractate being cited
MGWJ	*Monatschrift für Geschichte und Wissenschaft des Judentums*
Mk	Mark
ᴍs(s)	Manuscript(s)
Mt	Matthew
Mur	Wādī Murabbaʿât documents
Mur xɪɪ	Scroll of the Twelve (Minor) Prophets

	from Wādī Murabba'ât		Sirach, Ecclesiasticus)
n(n).	Note(s)	SNVAO 2	Skrifter utgitt av Det Norske Viden-skaps–Akademi i Oslo, II. Hist.–Filos. Klasse
Na	Nahum		
NAB	New American Bible (1970)		
NEB	New English Bible (1970)	Song	Song of Solomon (Song of Songs, Canticles)
Neh	Nehemiah		
N.F.	*Neue Folge*	StANT	Studien zum Alten und Neuen Testament
no(s).	Number(s)		
N.S.	New Series	SVT	Supplements to *Vetus Testamentum*
Nu	Numbers	Syh	Syro–hexaplar version
Ob	Obadiah	*T*	Targum Jonathan (to the Prophets)
OLZ	*Orientalistische Literaturzeitung*	*TDNT*	*Theological Dictionary of the New Testament*, 9 vols.; ed. Gerhard Kittel and Gerhard Friedrich, tr. Geoffrey W. Bromiley (Grand Rapids, Michigan: William B. Eerdmans, 1964–74)
OrAnt	*Oriens Antiquus*		
OTL	Old Testament Library		
OTS	Oudtestamentische Studiën		
P	Priestly Work		
p(p).	Page(s)	ThB	Theologische Bücherei
par(s).	Paragraph(s)	*ThG*	*Theologie und Glaube*
PEQ	*Palestine Exploration Quarterly*	*ThLZ*	*Theologische Literaturzeitung*
PJ	*Palästinajahrbuch*	*ThR*	*Theologische Rundschau*
pl(s).	Plate(s)	ThSt	Theologische Studien
Prv	Proverbs	*ThZ*	*Theologische Zeitschrift*
Ps	Psalms	tr.	Translator, translated by
Q	Qumran documents	[Trans.]	Translators of this volume of Hermeneia
1QH	*Hôdāyôt*, "Thanksgiving Hymns" from Qumran Cave 1		
1QM	*Milḥāmāh*, the "War Scroll" from Qumran Cave 1	[Trans. by Ed.]	Translated by the editor of this volume of Hermeneia
		TrThZ	*Trierer Theologische Zeitschrift*
1QpHab	*Pešer* (commentary) on Habakkuk from Qumran Cave 1	Unpub. Diss.	Unpublished Dissertation
1QpMi	*Pešer* on Micah from Qumran Cave 1	*UT*	(Followed by text name or number) Ugaritic texts as designated in the edition of Cyrus H. Gordon, *Ugaritic Textbook*, AnOr 38 (Roma: Pontificium Institutum Biblicum, 1965)
4QFlor(174)	Florilegium from Qumran Cave 4		
4QPs^a	Psalms scroll, exemplar "a," from Qumran Cave 5		
5QAm(4)	Fragments of scroll with text of Amos from Qumran Cave 5		
		UUÅ	Uppsala Universitets Årsskrift
RB	*Revue Biblique*	v(v)	Verse(s)
rev.	Revision, revised by	*V*	Vulgate translation of Jerome
Rev	Revelation (Apocalypse of John)	*VD*	*Verbum Domini*
*RGG*³	*Die Religion in Geschichte und Gegenwart: Handwörterbuch für Theologie und Religionswissenschaft*, 7 vols. (Tübingen: J. C. B. Mohr [Paul Siebeck], 1957–65)	vol(s).	Volume(s)
		VT	*Vetus Testamentum*
		WA	Weimarer Ausgabe = *D. Martin Luthers Werke. Kritische Gesamtausgabe* (Weimar, 1883ff)
RHR	*Revue de l'histoire des religions*	WMANT	Wissenschaftliche Monographien zum Alten und Neuen Testament
Rom	Romans		
RQ	*Revue de Qumrân*	*WO*	*Die Welt des Orients. Wissenschaftliche Beiträge zur Kunde des Morgenlandes*
RSV	Revised Standard Version (1946, 1952)		
		WuD	*Wort und Dienst*
S	Syriac version (Peshiṭta)	*WUS*	Joseph Aistleitner, *Wörterbuch der ugaritischen Sprache*, ed. Otto Eissfeldt, BVSAWL 106/3 (Berlin: Akademie–Verlag, ³1967)
Sam	Samuel		
SAT	Die Schriften des Alten Testaments in Auswahl übersetzt und erklärt, ed. Hermann Gunkel		
		ZAW	*Zeitschrift für die alttestamentliche Wissenschaft*
SBJ	La sainte bible, sous la direction de l'École biblique de Jérusalem		
		ZDPV	*Zeitschrift des deutschen Palästina–Vereins*
SBT	Studies in Biblical Theology	Zech	Zechariah
SEÅ	*Svensk Exegetisk Årsbok*	Zeph	Zephaniah
Sir	Sirach (The Wisdom of Jesus son of	*ZThK*	*Zeitschrift für Theologie und Kirche*

α′	The Greek translation of Aquila
ε′	The "Quinta" edition
θ′	The Greek translation of Theodotion
λ′	οἱ λοιποί (ἑρμηνευταί) = the later Greek translations
σ′	The Greek translation of Symmachus

2. Short Title List

Alt, *Kleine Schriften* 1–3
    Albrecht Alt, *Kleine Schriften zur Geschichte des Volkes Israel*, 3 vols. (München: C. H. Beck; [1] 1953, [2] 1953 [3, ed. Martin Noth] 1959]).

Alt, "Samaria"
    Albrecht Alt, "Der Stadtstaat Samaria" in *Kleine Schriften* 3, 258–302.

Amsler
    Edmond Jacob, Carl A. Keller, and Samuel Amsler, *Osée, Joël, Amos, Abdias, Jonas*, Commentaire de l'Ancien Testament lla (Neuchâtel: Delachaux & Niestlé, 1965).

Amsler, "Amos"
    Samuel Amsler, "Amos, prophète de la onzième heure," *ThZ* 21 (1965): 318–28.

Bach, *Aufforderungen*
    Robert Bach, *Die Aufforderungen zur Flucht und zum Kampf im alttestamentlichen Prophetenspruch*, WMANT 9 (Neukirchen–Vluyn: Neukirchener Verlag, 1962).

Bach, "Gottesrecht"
    Robert Bach, "Gottesrecht und weltliches Recht in der Verkündigung des Propheton Amos" in *Festschrift für Günther Dehn*, ed. Wilhelm Schneemelcher (Neukirchen: Verlag des Erziehungsvereins, 1957), 23–24.

Barrois, *Manuel*
    Georges Augustin Barrois, *Manuel d'Archéologie Biblique*, 2 vols. (Paris: Éditions Auguste [et J.] Picard; [1] 1939, [2] 1953).

Baumann, "Einzelheit"
    Eberhard Baumann, "Eine Einzelheit," *ZAW* 64 (1952): 62.

Baumgärtel, "Formel"
    Friedrich Baumgärtel, "Die Formel *neʾum jahwe*," *ZAW* 73 (1961): 277–90.

Baumgärtel, "Gottesnamen"
    Friedrich Baumgärtel, "Zu den Gottesnamen in den Büchern Jeremia und Ezechiel" in *Verbannung und Heimkehr: Beiträge zur Geschichte und Theologie Israels im 6. und 5. Jahrhundert v. Chr. (Festschrift für Wilhelm Rudolph)*, ed. Arnulf Kuschke (Tübingen: J. C. B. Mohr [Paul Siebeck], 1961), 1–29.

Baumgartner, "Amos 3:3–8"
    Walter Baumgartner, "Amos 3:3–8," *ZAW* 33 (1913): 78–80.

Baumgartner, "Joel 1 und 2"
    Walter Baumgartner, "Joel 1 und 2" in *Karl Budde zum siebzigsten Geburtstag*, ed. Karl Marti, BZAW 34 (Giessen, 1920), 10–19.

Begrich, *Gesammelte Studien*
    Joachim Begrich, *Gesammelte Studien zum Alten Testament*, ed. Walter Zimmerli; ThB 21 (München: Chr. Kaiser, 1964).

Begrich, "Tora"
    Joachim Begrich, "Die priesterliche Tora" in *Werden und Wesen des Alten Testaments*, ed. Paul Volz, Friedrich Stummer, and Johannes Hempel; BZAW 66 (Berlin, 1936), 63–88 [reprinted in *idem, Gesammelte Studien*, 232–60].

Bentzen, "Ritual Background"
    Aage Bentzen, "The Ritual Background of Amos 1:2—2:16" in OTS 8 (Leiden: E. J. Brill, 1950), 85–99.

Bewer
    Julius A. Bewer, *A Critical and Exegetical Commentary on Obadiah and Joel*, ICC (Edinburgh: T. & T. Clark, 1911).

Bič
    Miloš Bič, *Das Buch Joel* (Berlin: Evangelische–Verlagsanstalt, 1960).

Bourke, "Le jour"
    J. Bourke, "Le jour de Yahvé dans Joël," *RB* 66 (1959): 5–31, 191–212.

Brockelmann, Syntax
    Carl Brockelmann, *Hebräische Syntax* (Neukirchen: Verlag der Buchhandlung des Erziehungsvereins, 1956).

Brueggemann, "Amos 4:4–13"
    Walter Brueggemann, "Amos 4:4–13 and Israel's Covenant Worship," *VT* 15 (1965): 1–15.

Buber, *Kündung*
    Martin Buber and Franz Rosenzweig, *Bücher der Kündung* (Köln & Olten: Jakob Hegner, 1958).

Budde, "Amos"
    Karl Budde, "Zu Text und Auslegung des Buches Amos," *JBL* 43 (1924): 46–131; 44 (1925): 62–122.

Budde, "Geschichte"
    Karl Budde, "Zur Geschichte des Buches Amos" in *Studien zur semitischen Philologie und Religionsgeschichte: Festschrift Julius Wellhausen*, ed. Karl Marti; BZAW 27 (Giessen, 1914), 63–77.

Chary, *Les prophètes*
    Théophane Chary, *Les prophètes et le culte à partir de l'exil autour du Second Temple. L'idéal cultuel des prophètes exiliens et postexiliens*, Bibliothèque de Théologie 3/3 (Tournai: Desclée & Cie, 1955).

Childs, "Enemy"
    Brevard S. Childs, "The Enemy from the North and the Chaos Tradition," *JBL* 78 (1959): 187–98.

Clifford, "Hôy"
    Richard J. Clifford, "The Use of *Hôy* in the Prophets," *CBQ* 28 (1966): 458–64.

Cohen, "Navi"
    Simon Cohen, "Amos *Was* a Navi," *HUCA* 32 (1961): 175–78.

Crenshaw, "Influence"
    James L. Crenshaw, "The Influence of the Wise upon Amos: The 'Doxologies of Amos' and Job 5:9–16; 9:5–10," *ZAW* 79 (1967): 42–52.

Crenshaw, "Theophanic Tradition"
    James L. Crenshaw, "Amos and the Theophanic Tradition," *ZAW* 80 (1968): 203–15.

Cripps
Richard S. Cripps, *A Critical and Exegetical Commentary on the Book of Amos* (London: SPCK, [2]1955–1969).

Crüsemann, *Studien*
Frank Crüsemann, *Studien zur Formgeschichte von Hymnus und Danklied in Israel*, WMANT 32 (Neukirchen–Vluyn: Neukirchener Verlag, 1969).

Dalman, *Arbeit* 1–7
Gustaf Dalman, *Arbeit und Sitte in Palästina*, 7 vols. (Gütersloh: C. Bertelsmann; [1/1, 2] 1928, [2] 1932, [3] 1933, [4] 1935, [5] 1937, [6] 1939, [7] 1942 = Hildesheim: Georg Olms, 1964).

Deden
D. Deden, *De kleine Profeten uit de grondtekst vertaald en uitgelegd*, BOT 12/1 (Roermond: Romen, 1953).

Delekat, "Wörterbuch"
Lienhard Delekat, "Zum hebräischen Wörterbuch," *VT* 14 (1964): 6–66.

Donner, "Botschaft"
Herbert Donner, "Die soziale Botschaft der Propheten im Lichte der Gesellschaftsordnung in Israel," *OrAnt* 2 (1963): 229–45

Donner–Röllig, *KAI*
H. Donner and W. Röllig, *Kanaanäische und Aramäische Inschriften*, 3 vols. (Wiesbaden: O. Harrassowitz; [1] 1962, [2, 3] 1964).

Duhm, "Anmerkungen"
Bernhard Duhm, "Anmerkungen zu den Zwölf Propheten," *ZAW* 31 (1911): 1–43, 81–110, 161–204.

Ehrlich, *Randglossen* 5
Arnold B. Ehrlich, *Randglossen zur hebräischen Bibel: Textkritisches, Sprachliches und Sachliches*, vol. 5: *Ezechiel und die kleinen Propheten* (Leipzig, 1912 = Hildesheim: Georg Olms, 1968).

Eissfeldt, *Kleine Schriften* 1–5
Otto Eissfeldt, *Kleine Schriften*, 5 vols.; ed. Rudolf Sellheim and Fritz Maass (Tübingen: J. C. B. Mohr [Paul Siebeck]; [1] 1962, [2] 1963, [3] 1966, [4] 1968, [5] 1973).

Eissfeldt, *The Old Testament*
Otto Eissfeldt, *The Old Testament: An Introduction*, tr. Peter R. Ackroyd (New York: Harper & Row, 1965) [*Einleitung in das Alte Testament unter Einschluss der Apokryphen und Pseudepigraphen sowie der apokryphen– und pseudepigraphenartigen Qumran–Schriften. Entstehungsgeschichte des Alten Testaments*, Neue Theologische Grundrisse (Tübingen: J. C. B. Mohr [Paul Siebeck], [3]1964)].

Elliger, *Leviticus*
Karl Elliger, *Leviticus*, HAT 1/4 (Tübingen: J. C. B. Mohr [Paul Siebeck], 1966).

Falkenstein–von Soden, *Hymnen*
Adam Falkenstein and Wolfram von Soden, *Sumerisch und Akkadische Hymnen und Gebete*, Bibliothek der Alten Welt. Reihe der Alte Orient (Zürich: Artemis Verlag, 1953).

Fey, *Amos und Jesaja*
Reinhard Fey, *Amos und Jesaja: Abhängigkeit und Eigenständigkeit des Jesaja*, WMANT 12 (Neukirchen–Vluyn: Neukirchener Verlag, 1963).

Fohrer, "Prophetie"
Georg Fohrer, "Prophetie und Magie," *ZAW* 78 (1966): 25–47 (reprinted in *idem, Studien*, 242–63).

Fohrer, *Studien*
Georg Fohrer, *Studien zur alttestamentlichen Prophetie (1949–65)*, BZAW 99 (Berlin: A. Töpelmann, 1967).

Fosbroke
Hughell E. W. Fosbroke, " The Book of Amos: Introduction and Exegesis" in *IB* 6, 761–853.

Fredriksson, *Krieger*
Henning Fredriksson, *Jahwe als Krieger: Studien zum alttestamentlichen Gottesbild* (Lund: C. W. K. Gleerup, 1945).

Frey
Hellmuth Frey, *Das Buch der Kirche in der Weltwende: Die kleinen nachexilischen Propheten*, BAT 24 (Stuttgart: Calwer; 1941, [4]1957).

Galling, "Bethel I, II"
Kurt Galling, "Bethel und Gilgal," *ZDPV* 66 (1943): 140–55; "Bethel und Gilgal II," *ZDPV* 67 (1944): 21–43.

Galling, *Textbuch*
Kurt Galling, *Textbuch zur Geschichte Israels* (Tübingen: J. C. B. Mohr [Paul Siebeck], [2]1968).

Gaster, "Hymn"
Theodor H. Gaster, "An Ancient Hymn in the Prophecies of Amos, "*Journal of the Manchester Egyptian and Oriental Society* 19 (1935): 23–26

Gerstenberger, "Woe–Oracles"
Erhard Gerstenberger, "The Woe–Oracles of the Prophets," *JBL* 81 (1962): 249–63.

Gese, "Beiträge"
Hartmut Gese, "Kleine Beiträge zum Verständnis des Amosbuches," *VT* 12 (1962): 417–38.

Gesenius–Buhl
Wilhelm Gesenius' Hebräisches und aramäisches Handwörterbuch über das Alte Testament, ed. Frants Buhl (Leipzig: [17]1921).

Gesenius–Kautzsch–Cowley
Gesenius' Hebrew Grammar, ed. E. Kautzsch, tr. and rev. A. E. Cowley (Oxford, [2]1910).

Goetze, *Kleinasien*[2]
Albrecht Goetze, *Kleinasien*, Kulturgeschichte des Alten Orients 3/1, Handbuch der Altertumswissenschaft 3/1/3/3/1 (München: C. H. Beck, [2]1957).

Gordon, *UT*
Cyrus H. Gordon, *Ugaritic Textbook*, AnOr 38 (Roma: Pontificium Institutum Biblicum, 1965).

Gottwald, *Kingdoms*
Norman K. Gottwald, *All the Kingdoms of the Earth: Israelite Prophecy and International Relations in the Ancient Near East* (New York: Harper & Row, 1964).

Gradwohl, *Farben*
Roland Gradwohl, *Die Farben im Alten Testament: Eine terminologische Studie*, BZAW 83 (Berlin: A. Töpelmann, 1963).

Gressmann, *Messias*
Hugo Gressmann, *Der Messias*, FRLANT 43 (Göttingen, 1929).

Gressmann, *Prophetie*
Hugo Gressmann, *Die älteste Geschichtsschreibung und Prophetie Israels (von Samuel bis Amos und Hosea)*, SAT 2/1 (Göttingen, ²1921).

Harper
William Rainey Harper, *A Critical and Exegetical Commentary on Amos and Hosea*, ICC (Edinburgh: T. & T. Clark, 1905).

Helck, *Beziehungen*
Hans Wolfgang Helck, *Die Beziehungen Ägyptens zu Vorderasien im 3. und 2. Jahrtausend v. Chr.*, Ägyptologische Abhandlungen 5 (Wiesbaden: O. Harrassowitz, 1962).

Hentschke, *Stellung*
Richard Hentschke, *Die Stellung der vorexilischen Schriftpropheten zum Kultus*, BZAW 75 (Berlin: A. Töpelmann, 1957).

Hermisson, *Spruchweisheit*
Hans Jurgen Hermisson, *Studien zur israelitischen Spruchweisheit*, WMANT 28 (Neukirchen–Vluyn: Neukirchener Verlag, 1968).

Herrmann, *Heilserwartungen*
Siegfried Herrmann, *Die prophetischen Heilserwartungen im Alten Testament: Ursprung und Gestaltwandel*, BWANT 85 (Stuttgart: W. Kohlhammer, 1965).

Hesse, "Amos 5"
Franz Hesse, "Amos 5:4–6, 14f," *ZAW* 68 (1956): 1–17.

Hesse, *Fürbitte*
Franz Hesse, *Die Fürbitte im Alten Testament*, Unpub. Diss. (Erlangen, 1949).

Hillers, "Amos 7:4"
Delbert R. Hillers, "Amos 7:4 and Ancient Parallels," *CBQ* 26 (1964): 221–25.

Hitzig
Ferdinand Hitzig, *Die zwölf kleinen Propheten*, KEH 1 (Leipzig; 1938, ⁴1881 [with Heinrich Steiner]).

Hölscher, *Profeten*
Gustav Hölscher, *Die Profeten Untersuchungen zur Religionsgeschichte Israels* (Leipzig, 1914).

Horst, "Doxologien"
Friedrich Horst, "Die Doxologien im Amosbuch," *ZAW* 47 (1929): 45–54 (reprinted in *idem, Gottes Recht*, 155–66).

Horst, *Gottes Recht*
Friedrich Horst, *Gottes Recht. Studien zum Recht im Alten Testament*, ed. Hans Walter Wolff; ThB 12 (München: Chr. Kaiser, 1961).

Horst, *Hiob*
Friedrich Horst, *Hiob*, BK 16/1 (Neukirchen–Vluyn: Neukirchener Verlag, 1968).

Horst, "Visionsschilderungen"
Friedrich Horst, "Die Visionsschilderungen der alttestamentlichen Propheten," *EvTh* 20 (1960): 193–205

Jahnow, *Leichenlied*
Hedwig Jahnow, *Das hebräische Leichenlied im Rahmen der Völkerdichtung*, BZAW 36 (Giessen, 1923).

Jeremias, *Theophanie*
Jörg Jeremias, *Theophanie: Die Geschichte einer alttestamentlichen Gattung*, WMANT 10 (Neukirchen–Vluyn: Neukirchener Verlag, 1965).

Joüon
Paul Joüon, *Grammaire de l'Hébreu Biblique* (Rome: Institut Biblique Pontifical, ²1947).

Joüon, "Notes"
Paul Joüon, "Notes de lexicographie hébraïque," *Biblica* 7 (1926): 162–70.

Kapelrud, *Central Ideas*
Arvid S. Kapelrud, *Central Ideas in Amos*, SNVAO 2 1956/4 (Oslo.: H. Aschehoug & Co. [W. Nygaard]; 1956, ²1961).

Kapelrud, *Joel*
Arvid S. Kapelrud, *Joel Studies*, UUÅ 1948/4 (Uppsala: A. B. Lundequist, 1948).

Keil
Carl Friedrich Keil, *Biblischer Commentar über die Zwölf Kleinen Propheten*, BC 3/4 (Leipzig, ³1888).

Klopfenstein, *Lüge*
Martin Alfred Klopfenstein, *Die Lüge nach dem Alten Testament* (Zürich: Gotthelf, 1964).

Knierim, *Hauptbegriffe*
Rolf Knierim, *Die Hauptbegriffe für Sünde im Alten Testament* (Gütersloh: Gütersloher Verlagshaus [Gerd Mohn], 1965).

Koehler, *Amos*
Ludwig Koehler, *Amos* (Zürich, 1917: reprinted from *idem*, "Amos", *Schweizerische theologische Zeitschrift* 34 [1917]: 10–21, 68–79, 145–57, 190–208).

Koehler–Baumgartner
Ludwig Koehler and Walter Baumgartner, *Lexicon in Veteris Testamenti Libros* (Leiden: E. J. Brill; 1953, ²1958, ³1967) [references are to the 1953 and 1958 editions unless specifically cited as (³1967)].

Kraus, *Psalmen*
Hans–Joachim Kraus, *Psalmen*, BK 15/1, 2 (Neukirchen–Vluyn: Neukirchener Verlag, ²1961).

Kraus, *Worship*
Hans–Joachim Kraus, *Worship in Israel: A Cultic History of the Old Testament*, tr. Geoffrey Buswell (Oxford: Blackwell, 1966) [*Gottesdienst in Israel. Grundriss einer Geschichte des alttestamentlichen Gottesdienstes* (München: Chr. Kaiser, ²1962)].

Krause, *Studien*
Gerhard Krause, *Studien zu Luthers Auslegung der Kleinen Propheten*, BHTh 33 (Tübingen: J. C. B. Mohr [Paul Siebeck], 1962).

Kutsch, "Heuschreckenplage"

Ernst Kutsch, "Heuschreckenplage und Tag Jahwes in Joel 1 und 2," *ThZ* 18 (1962): 81–94.

Kutsch, "Trauerbräuche"
Ernst Kutsch, " 'Trauerbräuche' und 'Selbstminderingsriten' im Alten Testament" in *Drei Wiener Antrittsreden*, ThSt 78 (Zürich: EVZ–Verlag, 1965), 25–42.

Leahy, "Idea of God"
Michael Leahy, "The Popular Idea of God in Amos," *ITQ* 22 (1955): 68–73.

Lehming, "Erwägungen"
Sigo Lehming, "Erwägungen zu Amos," *ZThK* 55 (1958): 145–69.

Löhr, *Amos*
Max Löhr, *Untersuchungen zum Buch Amos*, BZAW 4 (Giessen, 1901).

Loewenstamm, "Remark"
Samuel E. Loewenstamm, "כלוב קיץ (A Remark on the Typology of the Prophetic Vision [Amos 8:1–3])," [Hebrew] *Tarbiz* 34 (1964–65): 619–22.

Maag, *Text*
Victor Maag, *Text, Wortschatz und Begriffswelt des Buches Amos* (Leiden: E. J. Brill, 1951).

Malamat, "Amos 1:5"
Abraham Malamat, "Amos 1:5 in the Light of the Til Barsip Inscriptions," *BASOR* 129 (1953): 25–26.

Mandelkern
Solomon Mandelkern, *Veteris Testamenti Concordantiae Hebraicae atque Chaldaicae* (Tel–Aviv: Schocken, ⁴1962).

Marti
Karl Marti, *Das Dodekapropheton erklärt*, KHC 13 (Tübingen, 1904).

Mendelsohn, *Slavery*
Isaac Mendelsohn, *Slavery in the Ancient Near East* (New York: Oxford University Press, 1949).

Merx
E. O. Adalbert Merx, *Die Prophetie des Joel und ihre Ausleger von den ältesten Zeiten bis zu den Reformatoren. Eine exegetisch–kritische und hermeneutisch–dogmengeschichtliche Studie* (Halle a.S., 1879).

Michel, *Tempora*
Diethelm Michel, *Tempora und Satzstellung in den Psalmen*, Abhandlungen zur evangelischen Theologie 1 (Bonn: Bouvier & Co., 1960).

Morgenstern, "Amos Studies I–IV," *Amos Studies*
Julian Morgenstern, "Amos Studies I," *HUCA* 11 (1936): 19–140; Amos Studies II," *HUCA* 12–13 (1937–38): 1–53; "Amos Studies III," *HUCA* 15 (1940): 59–304; "Amos Studies IV," *HUCA* 32 (1961): 295–350. "Amos Studies I–III" were reprinted in *Amos Studies*, vol. 1 (Cincinnati: Hebrew Union College, 1941).

Myers, "Date"
Jacob M. Myers, "Some Considerations Bearing on the Date of Joel," *ZAW* 74 (1962): 177–95.

Neher, *Amos*

André Neher, *Amos. Contribution à l'étude du prophétisme* (Paris: J. Vrin, 1950).

Neubauer, "Erwägungen"
Karl Wilhelm Neubauer, "Erwägungen zu Amos 5:4–15," *ZAW* 78 (1966): 292–316.

Nötscher
Friedrich Nötscher, *Zwölfprophetenbuch oder Kleine Propheten*, Echter–Bibel (Würzburg: Echter, 1948).

Noth, *Aufsätze 1, 2*
Martin Noth, *Aufsätze zur biblischen Landes– und Altertumskunde*, 2 vols.; ed. Hans Walter Wolff (Neukirchen–Vluyn: Neukirchener Verlag, 1971).

Noth, *History*
Martin Noth, *The History of Israel*, tr. Peter R. Ackroyd (New York: Harper & Row, ²1960) [*Geschichte Israels* (Göttingen: Vandenhoeck & Ruprecht, ²1954)].

Noth, *Josua*
Martin Noth, *Das Buch Josua*, HAT 1/7 (Tübingen: J. C. B. Mohr [Paul Siebeck], ²1953).

Noth, *Könige*
Martin Noth, *Könige*, BK 9/1 (Neukirchen–Vluyn: Neukirchener Verlag, 1968).

Noth, *World*
Martin Noth, *The Old Testament World*, tr. Victor I. Gruhn (Philadelphia: Fortress, 1966) [*Die Welt des Alten Testaments: Einführung in die Grenzgebiete der alttestamentlichen Wissenschaft*, Sammlung Töpelmann 2/3 (Berlin: A. Töpelmann, ⁴1962)].

Nowack
Wilhelm Nowack, *Die kleinen Propheten übersetzt und erklärt*, HK 3/4 (Göttingen, ³1922).

Oettli, *Amos*
Samuel Oettli, *Amos und Hosea. Zwei Zeugen gegen die Anwendung der Evolutionstheorie auf die Religion Israels*, BFChrTh 5/4 (Gütersloh, 1901).

Oort, "Amos"
Henricus Oort, "De profeet Amos," *Theologisch Tijdschrift* 14 (1880): 114–58.

Osty
E. Osty, *Amos, Osee*, SBJ (Paris: Les Éditions dü Cerf, 1952).

Plöger, Theocracy
Otto Plöger, *Theocracy and Eschatology*, tr. S. Rudman (Richmond, Va.: John Knox, 1968) [*Theokratie und Eschatologie*, WMANT 2 (Neukirchen–Vluyn: Neukirchener Verlag, 1959)].

Posener, *Princes*
Georges Posener, *Princes et pays d'Asie et de Nubie. Textes hiératiques sur des figurines d'envoûtement du Moyen Empire* (Brussels, 1940).

Procksch
Otto Procksch, *Die kleinen prophetischen Schriften vor dem Exil*, Erläuterungen zum Alten Testament 3 (Calw and Stuttgart, 1910).

Procksch, *BH³*
Otto Procksch, Textual notes to "Librum XII prophetarum" in *Biblia Hebraica*, ed. Rud. Kittel

(Stuttgart: Wurttembergische Bibelanstalt, ³1937).

von Rad, *Theology*

Gerhard von Rad, *Old Testament Theology*, 2 vols., tr. D. M. G. Stalker (New York & Evanston: Harper & Row; [1] 1962, [2] 1965) [*Theologie des Alten Testaments*, 2 vols.; Einführung in die evangelische Theologie (München: Chr. Kaiser [1] ³1962, [2] ²1962)].

Rendtorff, *Studien*

Rolf Rendtorff, *Studien zur Geschichte des Opfers im alten Israel*, WMANT 24 (Neukirchen–Vluyn: Neukirchener Verlag, 1967).

Reventlow, *Amt*

Henning Graf Reventlow, *Das Amt des Propheten bei Amos*, FRLANT 80 (Göttingen: Vandenhoeck & Ruprecht, 1962).

Richter, *Recht*

Wolfgang Richter, *Recht und Ethos: Versuch einer Ortung des weisheitlichen Mahnspruchs*, StANT 15 (München: Kösel–Verlag, 1966).

Robinson

Theodore H. Robinson and Friedrich Horst, *Die Zwölf Kleinen Propheten*, HAT 1/14 (Tübingen: J. C. B. Mohr [Paul Siebeck], ³1964).

Rost, "Amos 7:10–17"

Leonhard Rost, "Zu Amos 7:10–17" in *Festgabe für Theodor Zahn* (Leipzig, 1928), 229–36.

Rudolph, *Jeremia*

Wilhelm Rudolph, *Jeremia*, HAT 1/12 (Tübingen: J. C. B. Mohr [Paul Siebeck], ³1968).

Salonen, *Möbel*

Armas Salonen, *Die Möbel des alten Mesopotamien nach sumerisch–akkadischen Quellen: Eine lexikalische und kulturgeschichtliche Untersuchung*, AASF B/127 (Helsinki: Suomalainen Tiedeakatemia, 1963).

Scheepers, *gees van God*

Johannes Hendrick Scheepers, *Die gees van God en die gees van die mens in die Ou Testament* (Kampen: J. H. Kok, 1960).

Schmidt, *Königtum*

Werner Schmidt, *Königtum Gottes in Ugarit und Israel. Zur Herkunft der Königsprädikation Jahwes*, BZAW 80 (Berlin: A. Töpelmann, ²1966).

Schmidt, "Redaktion"

Werner H. Schmidt, "Die deuteronomistische Redaktion des Amosbuches. Zu den theologischen Unterschieden zwischen dem Prophetenwort und seinem Sammler," *ZAW* 77 (1965): 168–93.

Schottroff, *Gedenken*

Willy Schottroff, *"Gedenken" im Alten Orient und im Alten Testament: Die Wurzel zākar im semitischen Sprachkreis*, WMANT 15 (Neukirchen–Vluyn: Neukirchener Verlag, ²1967).

Scott, "Weights"

R. B. Y. Scott, "Weights and Measures of the Bible," *BA* 22 (1959): 22–40 (reprinted in *The Biblical Archaeologist Reader*, vol. 3; ed. Edward F. Campbell, Jr. and David Noel Freedman [Garden City, New York: Doubleday and Company, 1970], 345–58).

Seeligmann, "Gerichtsverfahren"

Isac Leo Seeligmann, "Zur Terminologie für das Gerichtsverfahren im Wortschatz des biblischen Hebräisch" in *Hebräische Wortforschung: Festschrift zum 80. Geburtstag von Walter Baumgartner*, SVT 16 (Leiden: E. J. Brill, 1967), 251–78.

Segert, "*nōqēd*"

Stanislav Segert, "Zur Bedeutung des Wortes *nōqēd*" in *Hebräische Wortforschung: Festschrift zum 80. Geburtstag von Walter Baumgartner*, SVT 16 (Leiden: E. J. Brill, 1967), 279–83.

Sellers, "Stages"

Ovid R. Sellers, "Stages of Locust in Joel," *AJSL* 52 (1935–36): 81–85.

Sellin

Ernst Sellin, *Das Zwölfprophetenbuch*, KAT 12/1 (Leipzig, ³1930).

Sethe, *Ächtung*

Kurt Sethe, *Die Ächtung feindlicher Fürsten, Völker und Dinge auf altägyptischen Tongefäßscherben des Mittleren Reiches*, APAW 5 (Berlin, 1926).

Smend, "Nein"

Rudolf Smend, "Das Nein des Amos," *EvTh* 23 (1963): 404–23.

Speier, "Bemerkungen"

Salomon Speier, "Bemerkungen zu Amos," *VT* 3 (1953): 305–10.

Stoebe, "Amos"

Hans Joachim Stoebe, "Der Prophet Amos und sein bürgerlicher Beruf," *WuD* N.F. 5 (1957): 160–81.

Strobel, "Masse"

August Strobel, "Masse und Gewichte," *BHHW* 2, 1159–69.

Terrien, "Amos and Wisdom"

Samuel Terrien, "Amos and Wisdom" in *Israel's Prophetic Heritage: Essays in Honor of James Muilenburg*, ed. Bernhard W. Anderson and Walter Harrelson (New York: Harper & Brothers, 1962), 108–15

Theis

Johannes Theis, "Der Prophet Joel" and "Der Prophet Amos" in Joseph Lippl and Johannes Theis, *Die Zwölf Kleinen Propheten*, vol. 1; HS 8/3/1 (Bonn, 1937).

Thompson

John A. Thompson, "The Book of Joel: Introduction and Exegesis" in *IB* 6, 729–60.

Thompson, "Locusts"

John A. Thompson, "Joel's Locusts in the Light of Near Eastern Parallels," *JNES* 14 (1955): 52–55.

Treves, "Date"

Marco Treves, "The Date of Joel," *VT* 7 (1957): 149–56.

de Vaux, *Israel*

Roland de Vaux, *Ancient Israel: Its Life and Insti-*

tutions, tr. John McHugh (New York: McGraw–Hill, 1961).

Vila, "dépôt"
André Vila, "Un dépôt de textes d'envoûtement au Moyen Empire," *Journal des Savants* (1963): 135–60.

Wächter, *Tod*
Ludwig Wächter, *Der Tod im Alten Testament*, Arbeiten zur Theologie 2/8 (Stuttgart: Calwer, 1967).

Wanke, "אוֹי"
Gunther Wanke, "אוֹי und הוֹי," *ZAW* 78 (1966): 215–18.

Wanke, *Zionstheologie*
Gunther Wanke, *Die Zionstheologie der Korachiten in ihrem traditions–geschichtlichen Zusammenhang*, BZAW 97 (Berlin: A. Töpelmann, 1966).

Watts, "Amos 5:7"
John D. W. Watts, "Note on the text of Amos 5:7," *VT* 4 (1954): 215–16.

Watts, *Vision*
John D. W. Watts, *Vision and Prophecy in Amos* (Grand Rapids: William B. Eerdmans, 1958).

Weiser
Artur Weiser, *Das Buch der zwölf Kleinen Propheten*, vol. 1; ATD 24/1 (Göttingen: Vandenhoeck & Ruprecht, ⁵1967).

Weiser, *Profetie*
Artur Weiser, *Die Profetie des Amos*, BZAW 53 (Giessen, 1929).

Wellhausen
Julius Wellhausen, *Die kleinen Propheten übersetzt und erklärt*, Skizzen und Vorarbeiten 5 (Berlin: Georg Reimer, ³1898 = 1963).

Westermann, *Basic Forms*
Claus Westermann, *Basic Forms of Prophetic Speech*, tr. Hugh Clayton White (Philadelphia: Westminster, 1967 [*Grundformen prophetischer Rede*, BEvTh 31 (München: Chr. Kaiser, ²1964)].

Westermann, *Forschung*
Claus Westermann, *Forschung am Alten Testament: Gesammelte Studien*, ThB 24 (München: Chr. Kaiser, 1964).

Westermann, "Fragen"
Claus Westermann, "Die Begriffe für Fragen und Suchen im Alten Testament," *KuD* 6 (1960): 2–30

Westermann, *Genesis*
Claus Westermann, *Genesis*, BK 1/1 (Neukirchen–Vluyn: Neukirchener Verlag, 1974).

Wijngaards, "הוֹצִיא"
Joanne Wijngaards, "הוֹצִיא and הֶעֱלָה. A Twofold Approach to the Exodus," *VT* 15 (1965): 92–102.

Wildberger, *Jesaja*
Hans Wildberger, *Jesaja*, BK 10/1 (Neukirchen–Vluyn: Neukirchener Verlag, 1972).

Williams, "Alas-Oracles"
James G. Williams, "The Alas–Oracles of the Eighth Century Prophets," *HUCA* 38 (1967): 75–91.

Wolff, *Amos the Prophet*
Hans Walter Wolff, *Amos the Prophet: The Man and His Background*, tr. Foster R. McCurley (Philadelphia: Fortress, 1973) [*Amos' geistige Heimat*, WMANT 18 (Neukirchen–Vluyn: Neukirchener Verlag, 1964)].

Wolff, *Gesammelte Studien*
Hans Walter Wolff, *Gesammelte Studien zum Alten Testament*, ThB 22 (München: Chr. Kaiser, ²1973).

Wolff, *Hosea*
Hans Walter Wolff, *Hosea: A Commentary on the Book of the Prophet Hosea*, tr. Gary Stansell; Hermeneia (Philadelphia: Fortress, 1974) [*Dodekapropheton 1. Hosea*, BK 14/1 (Neukirchen–Vluyn: Neukirchener Verlag, ²1965)].

Wolff, "Kerygma"
Hans Walter Wolff, "The Kerygma of the Deuteronomic Historical Work" (tr. Frederick C. Prussner) in Hans Walter Wolff and Walter Brueggemann, *The Vitality of Old Testament Traditions* (Atlanta: John Knox, 1975), 83–100 ["Das Kerygma des deuteronomistischen Geschichtswerks," *ZAW* 73 (1961): 171–86 (reprinted in *idem*, *Gesammelte Studien*, 308–24)].

Würthwein, "Amos–Studien"
Ernst Würthwein, "Amos–Studien," *ZAW* 62 (1950): 10–52.

Würthwein, "Kultbescheid"
Ernst Würthwein, "Kultpolemik oder Kultbescheid?" in *Tradition und Situation: Studien zur alttestamentlichen Prophetie, Festschrift für A. Weiser*, ed. Ernst Würthwein and Otto Kaiser (Göttingen: Vandenhoeck & Ruprecht, 1963), 115–31.

Ziegler, *Duodecim prophetae*
Joseph Ziegler, ed., *Duodecim prophetae*, Septuaginta Vetus Testamentum Graecum 13 (Göttingen: Vandenhoeck & Ruprecht; 1963, ²1967).

Zimmerli, *Ezechiel*
Walther Zimmerli, *Ezechiel*, BK 13/1, 2 (Neukirchen–Vluyn: Neukirchener Verlag, 1969).

Zimmerli, *Gottes Offenbarung*
Walther Zimmerli, *Gottes Offenbarung. Gesammelte Aufsätze zum Alten Testament*, ThB 19 (München: Chr. Kaiser, 1963).

van Zyl, *Moabites*
A. H. van Zyl, *The Moabites*, Pretoria Oriental Series 3 (Leiden: E. J. Brill, 1960).

The English translation of the books of Joel and Amos presented in this volume is new, prepared by the translators on the basis of the Hebrew Masoretic text (*M*) and incorporating all of the author's text–critical decisions. The exegetical considerations of the author are consistently reflected, both in the English rendering of the text and in its layout. Words of the translation enclosed within parentheses ( ) amplify the sense of the literal Hebrew, while angle brackets ⟨ ⟩ indicate emendations of *M* discussed in the textual notes. Words and lines of the biblical text enclosed within square brackets [ ] are regarded by the author as secondary interpolations or redactional supplements to the books of Joel and Amos; within these supplements, braces { } enclose segments of text considered to be even later interpolations. Reverse angle brackets ⟩ ⟨ are occasionally used (e.g., Am 6:2, 6b) to set off material less certainly deemed to be secondary.

The translators are also responsible for all renderings of other biblical texts quoted in this volume. In the sections of textual notes, the editor has regularly supplied the English renderings for evidence cited from the ancient texts and versions. In all other cases, the sources of translations of ancient literature are specifically noted.

References to Old Testament passages are given in accord with the standard chapter and verse enumeration of modern printed editions of the Hebrew Bible (e.g., *BH³*); when this enumeration differs from that commonly employed in English Bibles (e.g., RSV and NEB) the latter variants immediately follow in brackets. (It should be noted that brackets are also sometimes used to enclose verse numbers when the author cites biblical texts which he considers to be later interpolations.) In order to avoid undue confusion, a partial exception to the practice of including the variant English enumeration has been made in the commentary to Joel: the variant chapter and verse numbers which exist for the latter half of the book of Joel are cited in brackets in the margins alongside the printed biblical text itself and in the pericope rubrics at the tops of the pages; in the introduction and commentary proper, however, references to the text of Joel are only given using the four chapter division of the Hebrew Bible, since this division corresponds essentially to the author's analysis of the book's structure. (See pp. 8–9, n. 41.)

Ugaritic texts are cited according to the convention of Andrée Herdner (*CTA*), with the designations of the texts in Cyrus H. Gordon's edition (*UT*) following in parentheses.

Recent scholarly works are cited in their published English versions whenever these are available. For the convenience of readers who continue to use the original publications in other languages, the relevant data are retained in brackets following page references to the English versions. In the cases of journal articles and monographs which have been reprinted in volumes of collected essays, the bibliographical references to the latter are cited in parentheses following the page references to the original publications. Quotations from recent literature not available in English translation have been rendered by the translators.

Whenever possible, the author's citations of the scholarly literature have been verified and full bibliographical data provided, though the names of publishers are regularly included only for volumes published during the last thirty years. Otherwise editorial supplementation has been kept to a minimum: in the commentary itself, only rarely have short explanatory notes been added in brackets or new bibliographical items cited. The editor has added to the Bibliography at the end of the volume some new entries, of significant works on Joel and Amos published during the last ten years, but a comprehensive bibliographical up–dating has not been attempted.

The endpapers to this volume display portions of the second century A.D. leather scroll of the Twelve (Minor) Prophets from Cave 2 of *Wâdī Murabbaʿât* (Mur XII). The front endpaper reproduces the fragments of the first three extant columns of the scroll: the small fragment on the right (col. 1) witnesses to the text of Joel 2:20; the major block of fragments exhibit the text of Joel 2:26—4:16 (col. 2), while on the left is preserved a portion of Am 1:5—2:1 (col. 3). The rear endpaper reproduces col. 8 of the extant scroll, attesting portions of Am 8:11—9:15. The photographic prints were provided through the courtesy of Pierre Benoit, O.P., of the *École biblique et archéologique Française* in Jerusalem; they are reproduced with the permission of the Oxford University Press, publisher of the *editio princeps* of Mur XII(88): P. Benoit, O.P., J. T. Milik, and R. de Vaux, O.P., *Les grottes de Murabbaʿât*, 2 vols. ("Texte" and "Planches"), DJD 2 (Oxford: At the Clarendon Press, 1961). (The endpaper reproductions correspond to pls. LVI and LVIII.) Displayed on p. v are fragments of a leather scroll of Amos, dated paleographically to the first century A.D., from Qumran Cave 5 (5QAm): the largest of the fragments attests portions of five lines from Am 1:3–5. The fragments are reproduced, with the permission of the publisher, from M. Baillet, J. T. Milik, and R. de Vaux, O.P., *Les 'Petites Grottes' de Qumran: Exploration de la falaise, Les grottes 2Q, 3Q, 5Q, 6Q, 7Q à 10Q, Le rouleau de cuivre*, DJD 3/Planches (Oxford: At the Clarendon Press, 1962), pl. XXXVI/4.

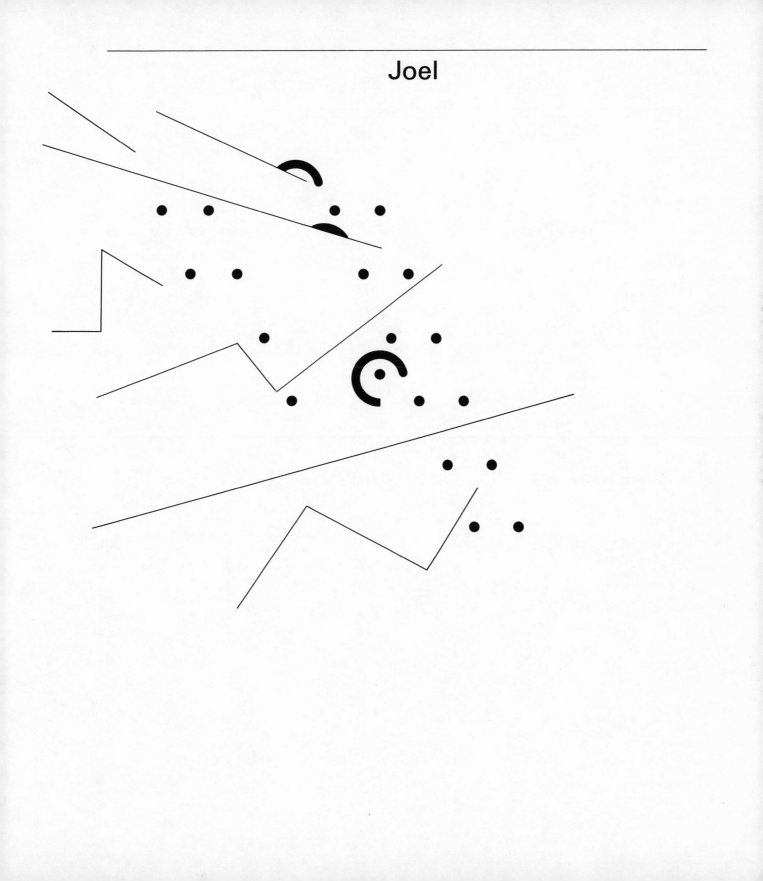

1. The Position of the Book in the Canon

Interpreters were once inclined to associate Joel with the earliest prophets on the basis of the position his book occupies in the canon.[1] This view presupposes that chronological criteria were determinative for the arrangement of the Twelve Prophets, not only in a general way but in the case of each book.[2] Yet the title of Joel (1:1) offered no temporal reference to aid the collectors of the Twelve Prophets.[3] How otherwise should they have known then of the book's origin in the time before Amos? We can scarcely assume they were guided by an examination of the problematical passages which still lead some modern exegetes to date Joel in the time of king Joash at the end of the ninth century B.C.[4]

To the extent that chronological criteria were decisive for the arrangement of the Twelve, they were straight–forward criteria, especially notations of regnal synchronisms. Such data are supplied in the superscriptions to the books of Hosea, Amos, Micah, Zephaniah, Haggai, and Zechariah; and they indeed provide a chronological framework for the collection of the Twelve. But a separate investigation of each of the remaining six books is required to account for its specific placement within the framework. One element of control available to us is the rearrangement of the Twelve Prophets exhibited in the G tradition. G shows a pronounced interest in chronology, as attested, for example, by the placements of Ruth alongside Judges and of Ezra and Nehemiah after the books of Chronicles. But it is precisely in G that we find Hosea, Amos, and Micah grouped together, these being the three books among the Twelve whose superscriptions date their authors to the reigns of eighth century kings. Joel, on the other hand, has been placed in a later position beside the similarly undated books of Obadiah and Jonah. Evidently the G tradition knew of no chronology for Joel which contradicted this rearrangement.

Hence, in view of the absence of chronological data in the book of Joel, those who arranged the Hebrew collection of the Twelve Prophets must have used other criteria to determine its position between Hosea and Amos. These criteria must have been self–evident to them, just as obvious as the temporal references in the superscriptions. Now although the terminology in Joel often recalls other writings included in the Twelve,[5] the most striking resemblances link Joel to Amos. Moreover, these verbal agreements occur at the end of the book of Joel: 4:16aα and 4:18a have their counterparts in Amos 1:2a and 9:13b. This alone would account for the placement of Joel before Amos. Further linkage is suggested by the correspondence between the rubrics in Joel 4:16aα and Amos 1:2a: the arrangers could consider the oracles against the nations in Amos 1:3—2:16 as an elaboration of the judgment announced in Joel 4, particularly since the nations singled out by Joel—Tyre, the Philistines, and Edom (4:4, 19)—reappear in Amos (1:9–10, 6–8, 11–12).

We can see, then, that matters of content dictated Joel's position before Amos, and not some knowledge of the time the book was composed. Here we must

---

1   This view was generally held up to the time of Karl August Credner, *Der Prophet Joel übersetzt und erklärt* (Halle, 1831); to a lesser extent it has been maintained into more recent times.

2   Jerome [in the preface to the *V* translation of the Twelve Prophets, Ed.] reflects Jewish tradition when he writes: "However, in those [cases] where the time [of the prophet] is not stated in the title [of his book], they prophesied under those kings under whom also had prophesied those [prophets] whose [books] preceding theirs have titles" [Trans. by Ed.] (*In quibus autem tempus non praefertur in titulo, sub illis eos regibus prophetasse, sub quibus et hi qui ante eos habent titulos, prophetaverunt*; J.–P. Migne, ed., *Sancti Eusebii Hieronymi: Opera Omnia*, vol. 9, Patrologiae cursus completus, Series Latina 28 [Paris, 1889], 1072).

3   According to Sir 49:10, the collectors' work had been completed by the beginning of the second century B.C.

4   G. Amon, *Die Abfassungszeit des Buches Joel*, Unpub. Diss. (Würzburg, 1942); Miloš Bič, *Das Buch Joel* (Berlin: Evangelische–Verlagsanstalt, 1960).

5   See pp. 5, 10–11.

recognize a common literary development in which considerably more recent, topically relevant material was prefaced to older writing in order to inform its interpretation. This procedure is attested most clearly and extensively in the redaction of the pentateuchal sources,[6] though it is also quite apparent in the redactional process which shaped the prophetic literature.[7] In all likelihood those who arranged the collection of the Twelve wished us to read Amos and the following prophets in the light of Joel's proclamation. For manifest in Joel is a comprehensive view of prophecy closely akin to that governing the prophetic corpus in its final, canonizing redaction.

2. The Time of Joel

In fact Joel is considerably later than his closest neighbors in the canon. Let us take up the problem of dating him by considering first allusions in the book to political events of general historical import.

Joel 4:1–3 assumes the catastrophic fate which began to unfold for Judah and Jerusalem when in 587 Nebuchadnezzar II conquered the city and exiled large segments of the population. This unforgettable, momentous event already belongs to ancient history from Joel's perspective. Thus the Babylonians, whose hegemony had passed to the Persians in 539, are not even mentioned. He refers instead to the shameful abandonment of Judah to foreign nations in general, before whom the land and its inhabitants had for some time lain defenseless. The considerable distance of Joel from the time of the exile is confirmed in passages where the existence of the Temple, rebuilt in the years following 515, is something the prophet takes quite for granted (1:9, 14, 16; 2:17; 4:18). Furthermore, in 2:7 and 9 he makes casual reference to the wall of Jerusalem, implying that the city's fortifications had been restored for some time; the restoration, however, was only accomplished in 445 under Nehemiah's direction.[8] Initially, then, this gives us a *terminus post quem* for Joel in the second half of the fifth century.

Is it also possible to discover a *terminus ante quem*? The statement in 4:17bβ lacks sufficient historical specificity to support the thesis that it recalls the conquest of Jerusalem by Ptolemy Soter in 312.[9] This holds true for the reference to Egypt and Edom in 4:19.[10] On the other hand, the commercial association of the Phoenician cities Tyre and Sidon with the Philistine cities, assumed in 4:4, points to the close of the Persian period.[11] As far as Sidon is concerned, the Persian period already ended in 343, when the city was destroyed by Artaxerxes III Ochus, rather than at the time of Alexander's campaign in 332.[12] It is probable that Sidon was no longer closely associated with Tyre after 343. For Sidon, along with Arvad and Byblos, yielded immediately to Alexander the Great, while Tyre resisted him for seven months, and Gaza for two. The Macedonians, indeed, were able to conquer Tyre only with the assistance of the two Sidonian fleets (with approximately 200 ships).[13] In any case, 4:6 suggests that the events of 332 lie well off in the future. Here the Greeks are portrayed as dwelling at some distance, accessible only through Phoenician–

---

6   Cf. Martin Noth, *A History of Pentateuchal Traditions*, tr. Bernhard W. Anderson (Englewood Cliffs, N.J.: Prentice–Hall, 1972), 11ff [*Überlieferungsgeschichte des Pentateuch* (Stuttgart: W. Kohlhammer, 1948), 11ff].

7   On Hos 1, see Hans Walter Wolff, *Hosea: A Commentary on the Book of the Prophet Hosea*, tr. Gary Stansell; Hermeneia (Philadelphia: Fortress, 1974), xxixf [*Dodekapropheton 1: Hosea*, BK 14/1 (Neukirchen–Vluyn: Neukirchener Verlag, ²1965), xxiv]; on Is 1, see Georg Fohrer, "Jesaja 1 als Zusammenfassung der Verkündigung Jesajas," *ZAW* 74 (1962): 251–68 (reprinted in *idem, Studien zur alttestamentlichen Prophetie (1949–1965)*, BZAW 99 [Berlin: A. Töpelmann, 1967], 148–66).

8   See pp. 43, 46.

9   See p. 82; *contra* Marco Treves, "The Date of

Joel," *VT* 7 (1957): 149–56.

10   See p. 84.

11   See pp. 77–78.

12   Cf. Friedrich Karl Kienitz, *Die politische Geschichte Aegyptens vom 7. bis zum 4. Jahrhundert vor der Zeitwende* (Berlin: Akademie-Verlag, 1953), 181–85.

13   Cf. Ernst Kornemann, ed., *Weltgeschichte des Mittelmeer–Raumes von Philipp II. von Makedonien bis Muhammed*, vol. 1: *Bis zur Schlacht bei Actium* (München: Biederstein, 1948), 109ff.

Philistine mediation. With this we may compare the quite different picture reflected in Zech 9:13 (*M*), where the Greeks have become Jerusalem's proximate antagonists. Now inasmuch as 4:4–8 is a later addition to Joel,[14] an older form of the book must certainly have been extant before 343. Therefore the evidence thus far adduced tentatively establishes Joel in the century between 445 and 343.

The glimpse which the book affords into Jerusalem's internal affairs corroborates this dating. The reins of leadership are held by the elders and the priests: 1:2, 13–14; 2:16–17. This presupposes the political establishment of the postexilic community that Josephus labeled "theocracy," wherein the priesthood exercised governance.[15] The omission of any reference to king and court precludes a preexilic setting: 1:2 explicitly addresses the whole people including its leaders; and 1:5–14 and 2:15–17 unequivocally summon all segments of the population and its leadership, without exception, to make lamentation and penance (cf. Jon 3:6–7). Furthermore, cultic practice of the late postexilic community is definitely indicated by the stereotypical fashion in which reference is made to "meal–offerings and libations" (1:9, 13; 2:14), and by the significance this *tāmîd*–offering has assumed. The designations of the priests as "ministers of Yahweh" and "ministers of the altar" (1:9, 13; 2:17) point in the same direction.[16] Finally, note the casual way the wall of Jerusalem is mentioned in 2:7 and 9.[17] All things considered, the picture of a stable cultic community which emerges from Joel corresponds most closely to the era following Ezra and Nehemiah. This indicates a setting for the book in the second half of the period initially delimited above, i.e., in the first half of the fourth century.

We have already called attention to the import of vocabulary in dating Joel. There are in this regard some striking instances where the book's terminology accords only with the latest literary stratum of the Old Testament. Thus שֶׁלַח ("weapon, missile" 2:8) is elsewhere attested only in Job 33:18; 36:12; 2 Chr 23:10; Neh 4:11 [17], 17 [23]; and סוֹף ("rear, conclusion" 2:20) only in 2 Chr 20:16; Eccl 3:11; 7:2; 12:13. צַחֲנָה ("stench" 2:20) appears also in Sir 11:12 but nowhere else in the Old Testament. Other terms lacking additional Old Testament attestations are very probably late formations: אלה ("to lament") in 1:8; עבש ("to shrivel"), פְּרֻדוֹת ("seed grains"), מֶגְרְפוֹת ("clods"), and מַמְּגֻרוֹת ("granaries"), all in 1:17; and עבט (II: "to change course") in 2:7. The phrases in 2:13b and 14a have exact counterparts only in Jon 4:2 and 3:9. The parallelism of "eastern" and "western" seas is unattested apart from 2:20 and Zech 14:8. The petition "have pity" (חוּסָה 2:17) is otherwise limited to Neh 13:22.

Joel's demonstrable dependence on a sizable number of older prophets is not the least weighty among the factors generally indicating the book's late date.[18] But 3:5 is particularly instructive for establishing a *terminus post quem*: here Joel quotes as Yahweh's word a saying as late as Ob 17a, itself scarcely earlier than the middle of the fifth century. In 2:11 and 3:4 he apparently even cites catchwords from the proclamation of Malachi (3:2, 23 [4:5]). However this may be, it is both clearer and far more significant that Joel, in sharp contrast to Malachi, does not concern himself with the problem of cultic abuses. Priestly ministry and sacrificial practice are firmly implanted in Joel's time. The exertions of Nehemiah and Ezra, we must suppose, have intervened between the careers of the two prophets.

Thus from many sides the evidence directs us to the first half of the fourth century for the time of Joel. The cultic community is well organized. As part of the smoothly functioning Persian Empire, the community is no longer troubled by external unrest. With its theocratic leadership and the canonized Torah to guide it, performing the daily sacrifices, and having purified

---

14 See pp. 74–75.
15 See p. 25 on 1:2.
16 See p. 31 on 1:9.
17 See p. 43.
18 See pp. 10–12.

itself from within of all that was foreign, the community's mood is one of confidence in the inviolability of its own salvation and in Jerusalem's election as the throne of Yahweh's kingdom.[19]

Hence we have confirmed and clarified for ourselves the postexilic dating of the book of Joel, first defended by Wilhelm Vatke in 1835.[20] It has found increasing acceptance since then, in spite of a few voices to the contrary which still defend a dating in the time of king Joash at the end of the ninth century,[21] or in the time of Amos and Hosea,[22] or in the time of Jeremiah.[23]

3. The Book of Joel

Joel research in recent decades has been occupied primarily with the literary problem of the book's unity. This was first questioned by Maurice Vernes in 1872,[24] and carried further by J. W. Rothstein in 1896;[25] Bernhard Duhm in 1911, however, offered the most effective challenge.[26] According to Duhm, an engaging poet has described a locust invasion in chaps. 1—2, while in chaps. 3—4 a synagogue preacher from Maccabean times has developed his eschatology in temperate prose. The preacher incorporated the earlier poetic material into his work by inserting 1:15 and 2:1b–2a, 11b which are therefore extraneous to the original text of chaps. 1—2. With some modifications this thesis of a two–stage formation of the book of

Joel was adopted by many interpreters, Sellin[27] and Robinson[28] being among the most recent to have done so. Nevertheless, doubts about the division of the book into two parts have grown increasingly stronger.[29]

How one views the relationship of chaps. 1 and 2 to each other defines the problem and already determines its solution. Specifically, apart from the Day of Yahweh passages (1:15; 2:1–2, 10–11), we must recognize that the disaster which chap. 2 treats is neither the same as nor even similar to the one portrayed in chap. 1. While 1:4–20 confronts an incipient economic catastrophe, hoping to avert it, 2:1–17 views in the light of this temporary crisis a coming, final catastrophe for Jerusalem, from which at first glance there seems no possible escape (2:3b, 11bβ). This characterization of the relationship is based on the following observations:[30]

a) In the call to communal lamentation, as in the prayers of lament themselves, chap. 1 looks back to calamities that have already set in, and it does so, on the whole, using declarative perfect forms. In contrast, 2:1–17 directs attention exclusively toward calamities yet to come, both in its alarm cry and its call to repentance. The introduction to the call to repentance (2:12 "but even now") and the call itself distinguish particularly between that which was most recently proclaimed (2:1–11) and that which was lamented

19 Cf. 1 Chr 17:14; 29:10–19; 2 Chr 13:(4–5, 8) 10–12.

20 To be sure, Vatke still advocated a fifth century dating: *Die biblische Theologie wissenschaftlich dargestellt*, vol. 1: *Die Religion des Alten Testaments nach den kanonischen Büchern entwickelt* (Berlin, 1835), 462.

21 See above, n. 4.

22 Josef Schmalohr, *Das Buch des Propheten Joel, übersetzt und erklärt*, ATA 7/4 (Münster i.W., 1922).

23 Arvid S. Kapelrud, *Joel Studies*, UUÅ 1948/4 (Uppsala: A. B. Lundequist, 1948).

24 *Le peuple d'Israël et ses espérances relatives à son avenir depuis les origines jusqu'à l'époque persane (Vᵉ siècle avant J.C.)* (Paris, 1872), 46ff.

25 Samuel Rolles Driver, *Einleitung in die Literatur des Alten Testaments*, tr. and annotated by Johann Wilhelm Rothstein (1896), 333f.

26 "Anmerkungen zu den Zwölf Propheten," *ZAW* 31 (1911):187.

27 Ernst Sellin, *Das Zwölfprophetenbuch*, KAT 12/1 (Leipzig, 1922, ²1929, ³1930).

28 Theodore H. Robinson and Friedrich Horst, *Die Zwölf Kleinen Propheten*, HAT 1/14 (Tübingen: J. C.

B. Mohr [Paul Siebeck], 1938, ²1954, ³1964).

29 Ludwig Dennefeld, "Les problèmes du livre de Joël," *Revue des Sciences Religieuses* 6 (1926):26–49; G. M. Rinaldi, *Il libro di Joele tradotto e commentato* (Rapallo, 1938); Kapelrud, *Joel* (1948); D. Deden, *De kleine Profeten uit de grondtekst vertaald en uitgelegd*, BOT 12/1 (Roermond: Romen, 1953); John A. Thompson, "Joel's Locusts in the Light of Near Eastern Parallels," *JNES* 14 (1955):52–55; J. Bourke, "Le jour de Yahvé dans Joël," *RB* 66 (1959):5–31, 191–212; Artur Weiser, *Das Buch der zwölf Kleinen Propheten*, vol. 1; ATD 24/1 (Göttingen: Vandenhoeck & Ruprecht, ⁵1967).

30 For the detailed exegetical arguments, see pp. 41–43.

earlier in chap. 1.

b) While chap. 1 visualizes an extraordinary economic catastrophe brought on by locusts, 2:1–17 no longer mentions locusts but in its alarm cry anticipates a devastating enemy host the like of which has never before been seen (2:2b; cf. 2:6a). Consequently, the prayer in 2:17 never speaks of provisions, as do the laments in 1:16–20, but is concerned instead with the relationship of the world's nations to the people of God, a theme without precedent in chap. 1.

c) Although observations from nature are employed throughout the portrayal of the disaster in chap. 1, to a great extent chap. 2 adopts traditional elements from the descriptions of the enemy in the Day of Yahweh prophecies.[31] To be sure, these latter elements have been highlighted with features inspired by the locust invasion, giving an apocalyptic cast to the eschatological enemy host of the older prophecies.

These observations, which thus far have left out of consideration the Day of Yahweh passages in chaps. 1—2, make it all the clearer that 1:15 and 2:1b, 2a, 11b do not represent extraneous matter. On the contrary, the relationship of chap. 1 to chap. 2, as well as many particular formulations beginning with 1:6a, become intelligible principally on the basis of these passages. An extraordinary economic emergency which Jerusalem faces in the present moment (chap. 1) is proclaimed to be an omen (1:15) that Jerusalem's eschatological destruction, threatened by earlier prophecy and articulated anew by Joel, is near at hand (2:1–11). The unity of the book is therefore prefigured by the distinctive way in which chaps. 1 and 2 cohere in their totality and need not be surmised solely from the continuity of the major eschatological catchwords in 1:15; 2:1–2, 10–11 and 3:3–4; 4:14–16.

Now it remains quite true that 2:18–19a, 21–27 and chap. 1 address the same issue[32]—the economic plight of Jerusalem—about which chaps. 3 and 4 are completely silent. Does this admission necessarily lead us to conclude that chaps. 1—2, since they exhibit a prophecy rooted in its own time, stand in opposition to chaps. 3—4 where a purely eschatological message is unfolded? Surely not. In addition to neglecting the relationship we have described between 2:1–17 and chap. 1, such a conclusion would ignore the bond between the two parts of the book formed by the parallel "assurances of recognition" in 2:27 and 4:17. Furthermore, 2:19b–20 already foretells the reversal of the eschatological disaster.[33] When the book's entire message is taken into consideration, a decisive turning point—not only for the second chapter but for the book as a whole—becomes apparent at the junction between 2:17 and 18. Here there is an abrupt transition, from the preceding cries of lament to the following oracles where divine response to the pleas is assured.[34] The portions of the book on either side of this midpoint form an almost perfect symmetry. The lament over the current scarcity of provisions (1:4–20) is balanced by the promise that this calamity will be reversed (2:21–27). The announcement of the eschatological catastrophe imminent for Jerusalem (2:1–11) is balanced by the promise that Jerusalem's fortunes too will be reversed (4:1–3, 9–17). The call to return to Yahweh as the necessity of the moment (2:12–17) is balanced by the pouring out of the spirit and the deliverance on Zion as the eschatological necessity (chap. 3).

The book, then, very clearly exhibits two major parts. The possibility of understanding it would be foreclosed from the outset were we to attribute the parts to different authors. Only with a perspective

---

31 See pp. 46–48. In a break with exegetical tradition, Luther newly recognized the transition from chap. 1 to chap. 2. In a seminar in 1524, he interpreted Joel 1:4–20 to refer to an actual locust plague, no longer finding there animal–imagery representing nations (see textual note "m" to 2:25). According to Luther, Joel then so obviously speaks of the Assyrian army in 2:11 and 17 that in chap. 2 he had clearly made a transition from the lesser locust plague to "... that total plague which was imminent for the whole population ... brought on by the hand of the Assyrians and Babylonians" [Trans.] (*illam*

perfectam plagam, quae imminebat toti populi ... manu Assyriorum et Babyloniorum facta; *D. Martin Luthers Werke. Kritische Gesamtausgabe* [Weimar, 1889], 13, 71f). Cf. Gerhard Krause, *Studien zu Luthers Auslegung der Kleinen Propheten*, BHTh 33 (Tübingen: J. C. B. Mohr [Paul Siebeck], 1962), 251.

32 See pp. 61–65.
33 See pp. 61–63.
34 See pp. 57–58.

encompassing the whole book are we fully able to comprehend structural configurations whereby emphases on present and future are conjoined: the appeal to the generations incorporated into the solemn pedagogical introduction and didactic admonition in 1:2–3; the narrative frame in 1:4 and 2:18; and the final, great framework of the two–stage self–disclosure oracle with its parallel linking and concluding elements in 2:27 and 4:17.[35] The identity of major catchwords and word groups between chaps. 1—2 and 3—4 further attest to their common authorship:

"sanctify [קדשו] . . . proclaim [קראו]"
   cf. 1:14 and 4:9;
"for the Day of Yahweh is near
[כי קרוב יום יהוה]"
   cf. 1:15 and 2:1bβ–2aα with 4:14;
"the Day of Yahweh is coming
[בוא יום יהוה]"
   cf. 2:1bα and 3:4b;
"darkness [חשך] . . ."
   cf. 2:2 and 3:4;
"to be [one who] escape[s]
[תהיה פליטה]"
   cf. 2:3 and 3:5;
"the heavens and the earth quake
[רעשו שמים וארץ]"
   cf. 2:10a and 4:16aβ;
"the sun and the moon are darkened and the brightness of the stars is extinguished
[שמש וירח קדרו וכוכבים אספו נגהם]"
   cf. 2:10b and 4:15;
"and Yahweh gives forth his voice
[ויהוה נתן קולו]"
   cf. 2:11a and 4:16aα
"the great and terrible Day of Yahweh
[יום יהוה הגדול והנורא]"
   cf. 2:11b and 3:4b;
"gather [קבצו] . . ."

cf. 2:16 and 4:(2), 11;
"the nations [הגוים] . . . my people and my heritage
[עמי ונחלתי]"
cf. 2:17 and 4:2.

But while the basic construction of the four chapters derives from a single author, this does not preclude later literary additions. The clearest case of such an addition by a secondary hand is 4:4–8, where sentence structure and viewpoint set the verses apart from the rest of the book.[36] The apparent addition in 2:26b most likely originated in a copying error.[37] While 4:18–21 gives the appearance of being a secondary expansion of 4:17, it may well have been added later by Joel himself.[38] This may also be the case with shorter insertions such as 2:3bβ and 3:2.[39] On the other hand, there is no compelling reason to regard chap. 3 as a later addition; 4:1–3 is more appropriately linked to 3:5 than it would be to 2:27, and the tradition which Joel here reflects prescribes the connection between 2:25–27 and 3:1–2.[40]

The book's chapter divisions lack uniformity in the texts and versions. Initially Stephen Langton (c. 1205) subdivided the Vulgate text of Joel into three chapters (1:1–20; 2:1–32; 3:1–21). In the fourteenth century this division was introduced also into *G* and most other translations, as well as into the Hebrew Bible where it continued in use through Daniel Bomberg's printing (Venice, 1516–17) of the first Rabbinic Bible of Felix Pratensis. The reorganization of the book into four chapters, achieved by subdividing chap. 2 (1:1–20; 2:1–27; 3:1–5; 4:1–21), first appeared in Bomberg's printing (1524–25) of the second Rabbinic Bible of Jacob ben Ḥayyim; this four–chapter division has since remained the customary one for the Hebrew Bible.[41]

4. The Language of Joel

The distinctiveness of our book's language is best appreciated if we first survey the larger supporting framework of major structural units.

35   See p. 58.
36   See pp. 74–75.
37   See textual note "p" to 2:26.
38   See p. 75.
39   See p. 59.
40   See pp. 60–61.
41   The Luther Bible initially accepted the Vulgate division into 20 + 32 + 21 verses; since the Canstein printings of the eighteenth century we find a division into 20 + 27 + 26 verses. The division of the second Rabbinic Bible into 20 + 27 + 5 + 21 verses was first adopted in the *Probebibel* [literally "Trial Bible" or "Sample Bible"] of 1883 and its revised edition of 1892. Cf. Eberhard Nestle, "(Miscellen, 1.) Zur Kapiteleinteilung in Joel," *ZAW* 24 (1904): 122–27. [The Vulgate division into three chapters has gen-

The opening "call to receive instruction" in 1:2a and the "exhortation concerning transmission" through the sequence of generations in 1:3 set the basic tone of Joel, and betray at the outset a sapiential–didactic proclivity by their interest in the extraordinary as it is mirrored in the comparison of the ages (1:2b).[42] The significance of the commission to pass on news of the event to future generations is not fully clarified in the rest of chap. 1. Such clarification is achieved only when the commission has been informed by all of the book's remaining sections, since they alone reveal the extent to which the present crisis impinges upon the future.

The content of the message to be transmitted is articulated in the form of a great "lamentation liturgy." Its component parts constitute a manual, accommodating everything deemed worthy of notice and promulgation. Yet there is no mistaking the distance between the liturgy as here presented and the actual performance of a lament ceremony. This is made especially apparent by the narrative statements in 1:4 and 2:18 which recount the essential facts concerning not only the terrible current catastrophe but also the subsequent renewal of Yahweh's compassion. Each of these brief reports is then elaborated in a most vivid, superbly artistic fashion in the section of liturgical material which follows it. The two liturgical sections exhibit the typical, primary elements of the conventional lament ceremony: first, the "call to communal lamentation,"[43] expanded into four strophes (1:5–14), followed by cries of lament (1:15–18) and prayers of lament (1:19–20); and, second, the closely associated "assurance oracles answering a plea" with their characteristic features (2:19–27).[44] These major structural parts of a conventional lamentation liturgy have undergone extensive elaboration, and it is only because of the additional content that the liturgy itself becomes worthy of transmission to later generations.

The laments of the initial chapter are first followed in 2:1–11 by a great "alarm cry," which includes a description of the enemy, wherein—after the omens of Yahweh's Day in chap. 1—the inescapable Day of Yahweh itself is announced. In its context this alarm cry performs a function similar to that of the motive-clauses in the call to communal lamentation of chap. 1 (cf. 2:1a with 2:15a). However, this is so only because the alarm is followed by a direct call to a complete return to Yahweh (2:12–17) as the presupposition of a genuine lament ceremony. Thereby the first part of the ancient lamentation liturgy has undergone a unique doubling. In view of the predominating time categories (1:2b, 15; 2:1b, 2a, 2b, 11b) and specific content features, the doubling can only be interpreted as a succession in which the current, temporary crisis is juxtaposed with a calamity announced for the end–time, the two parts exhibiting the appropriately different reactions of lamentation and repentance.

The second major section of the liturgy is developed in a corresponding fashion. Already at the beginning of the supporting "assurance oracles answering a plea" it is likely that a reversal is promised, not only of the food shortage (2:19a) but also of the end–time distress (2:19b–20).[45] Yet in what follows, two differently constructed "assurance oracles answering a plea" (2:21–24, 25–26) stay with the former theme. With 2:27 these assurances of relief from the calamities endured by Jerusalem thus far are transformed into a "self–disclosure oracle."[46] As the continuation shows—already in 2:27b and then through 3:1–5; 4:1ff up to 4:17—it is expanded further into a two–stage self–disclosure oracle.[47] Hence the promised reversal of the current calamities not only forms the basis for the recognition that Yahweh is Israel's God; beyond that, it sustains the certainty that at a later stage (3:1a) Yahweh's final action toward Jerusalem (3:1–5) and the world of nations (4:1–3, 9–17) will be such that his people "will never again be put to shame" (2:27b). The "recognition formula" in 2:27 is therefore the means in the second major section by which the initial

erally been followed in English bible translations—including the Rheims–Douai version (1609), the "Authorized" King James Version (1611), the Revised Standard Version (1952), and the New English Bible (1970). Notable exceptions, following the four chapter division of the second Rabbinic Bible, are the translation of the Jewish Publication Society of America (1917) and the recent New American Bible (1970). Ed.]

42 See p. 26.
43 See pp. 20–22.
44 See p. 58.
45 See pp. 62–63.
46 See p. 58.
47 See p. 65.

assurance oracle answering a plea is expanded to include also the eschatological proclamation. This is manifest first in unconditional announcements of salvation for Jerusalem (3:1, 5) and in motivated threats of punishment against the nations (4:1–3). Thereafter it appears, again with particularly fascinating language, in ironical calls both to battle and to judicial assembly (4:9–14), which provide a splendid counterpart to the alarm cry with its description of the enemy in 2:1–11. And like the alarm cry, the calls proceed into a very similar, often even verbatim description of the signs of theophany (4:15–16; cf. 2:10–11) which characterize the Day of Yahweh. The eschatological message of the second phase is brought to a close in 4:17, which resumes the assurance of recognition from 2:27 and thereby seals the great assurance oracle answering a plea which has been elaborated into the two–stage self–disclosure oracle.

The form–critical analysis of the supporting forms in the book of Joel and their characteristic elaboration not only confirms the book's unity, but at the same time demonstrates that we have before us an artistic literary construction. To be sure, rhetorical forms have been employed almost exclusively: after the pedagogical introduction and didactic admonition, we find the call to communal lamentation, the cries of lament, and the prayers of lament; then the alarm cry with its description of the enemy and the call to repentance; and finally the assurance oracles answering a plea and self–disclosure oracles with their built–in announcements of salvation and punishment and their calls to battle. But in most instances these individual forms have already become visibly detached from their original life–setting, either through artistic embellishment or through different examples of a single form having been combined. The former has occurred in the cases of the four–strophe call to communal lamentation in 1:5–14, the great description of the enemy associated with the alarm cry in 2:4–9, and the two–stage self–disclosure oracle. The latter is evident in the various lament fragments in 1:15–20, the diverse assurance oracles in 2:19–27, and the different calls to battle and judicial assembly in 4:9–14.

Thus the book is essentially a work of literature. In contrast to the speech forms taken up in it (forms at home in the cultus, holy war, and earlier prophecy), the book's sociological function is a sort of "literary opposition" [i.e., a literary critique of prevailing ideologies and institutions]. The book is sustained by an enormous passion for understanding (1:2–3; 2:27; 4:17) in relation to earlier prophecy which had already become Scripture; it engages the task of effecting a revival within the stiffening, religiously self–assured theocratic cultic community.

In its details the language of Joel is determined by the earlier prophetic movement. This will be substantiated step by step in the course of interpretation. Here we wish only to indicate the overall results:

1. On occasion, Joel himself introduces earlier prophetic speech as the word of Yahweh.[48]

2. Whole sentences have been taken over in crucial places: Is 13:6 (as well as Ezek 30:2–3)[49] in 1:15 (cf. 4:14b); Am 1:2a in 4:16aα; and also larger word groups from Zeph 1:14–15 in 2:1–2.

3. A very large number of smaller word groups as well as individual catchwords are embedded in sentences constructed by Joel himself: "all faces are aglow," in 2:6b from Na 2:11b [10b]; "heaven and earth quake," in 2:10a from Is 13:13; "sun, moon and stars" cease to shine, in 2:10b from Is 13:10; the question, "Who can endure Yahweh's great and terrible day?" in 2:11b (cf. also 3:4) from Mal 3:2, 23 [4:5]; the motivation for the "returning," namely, that Yahweh "is slow to anger, and abounding in steadfast love, and repents of evil," in 2:13b as in Jon 4:2; the hope that "perhaps he will turn and repent once more," in 2:14a as in Jon 3:9 (cf. Zeph 2:3); the conception of the enemy from afar as "the northerner," in 2:20 after Jer 1:14–15; 4:6; 6:1, 22 and Ezek 38:6, 15; 39:2; Yahweh is Israel's God "and no other," in 2:27 from Is 45:5, 6, 18, 22; 46:9; Yahweh will "pour out [his] spirit," in 3:1 from Ezek 39:29 (cf. Zech 12:10); the expression "in those days and at that time," in 4:1 as elsewhere only in Jer 33:15; 50:4, 20; Yahweh gathers "all the nations," in 4:2 as in Is 66:18a; (the deeds of the enemies are requited upon their own

---

48 Ob 17 is cited in 3:5. 2:12 is perhaps also a citation; see pp. 48–49.

49 Cf. Zeph 1:7; Ob 15.

heads, in 4:4, 7, as in Ob 15); the summons to prepare for holy war and to advance toward Jerusalem, in 4:9 from Jer 6:4; the battle action is compared to harvesting and pressing of grapes, in 4:13 as in Mi 4:13; Jer 25:30; Is 63:3; 17:5; the catchword "tumult [of battle]" in 4:14 as in Is 13:4; Ezek 7:11–13; 30:4, 10, 15; 39:11, 15; Yahweh dwells "on Zion," in 4:17aβ as in Is 8:18; Jerusalem, as the city of the "sanctuary," is no longer traversed by strangers, in 4:17b as in Is 52:1; ("the mountains will drip with juice," in 4:18a as in Am 9:13; a fountain shall come forth from the Temple, in 4:18b as in Ezek 47:1–12 [cf. Zech 14:8]).

4. Occasionally we find important and rare sentences with a meaning that reverses their original sense, as Is 51:3a in 2:3b, and Is 2:4 (Mi 4:3) in 4:10. This is a sign of the freedom and independence of Joel in his handling of transmitted, prophetic speech.

5. More important than all correspondences of detail is the fact that all important forms of speech employed by Joel, together with their thematic content, are determined by prophetic traditions. The combination of the call to lamentation, "Wail!" (הילילו), which is the key word in 1:5–14, with the exclamation "Alas!" over the Day of Yahweh in 1:15 has Ezek 30:2 for its model.[50] The alarm cry in 2:1–11 corresponds to the cry warning of the enemy from the north (cf. 2:20) in Jer 4:5 and 6:1. In large part the description of the enemy corresponds thematically to the presentation of the Day of Yahweh in Is 13.[51] The elaboration of the self–disclosure oracle into two stages, with a double assurance of recognition, continues forms found in Ezekiel, and in particular the transition from 2:27 to 3:1 is determined by Ezek 39:28–29. The summonses to battle in 4:9–14 have been prompted by the oracles against the nations in Jer 46 and 49—51, as well as those in Ezek 29, 30, 32, 35, 38—39. In view of all this dependence upon the forms of earlier prophecy we need to note again, as an important indication of the independence of Joel, that he can change the party to whom the material is addressed: for example, the oracle against Egypt in Ezek 30:2–3 and that against Babylon in Is 13:6 are turned by him against Jerusalem in 1:15.

On the whole, our detailed comparison leads to the conclusion that there are three tradition complexes which have exerted a determinative influence upon the language of Joel: first, the Day of Yahweh prophecies, especially Zeph 1—2, Is 13, Ezek 30, Ob, and Mal 3; second, and closely related, the oracles against the nations in the book of Jeremiah (46, 49—51) and Ezekiel (29—32, 35); and finally, the prophetic oracles concerning the enemy from the north (Jer 4—6; Ezek 38—39).

The recognition of these influences must not obscure two things:

1. Joel speaks in a way relevant to his time. A new word of Yahweh has been committed to him. The catastrophe of locusts and drought leads him to exhort his contemporaries to reconsider the as yet unfulfilled prophetic word concerning the Day of Yahweh. This former proclamation was now to be recognized by Joel's contemporaries as comprising their cataclysmic fate. The authority for such a current call to return can find its legitimation—apart from the book of Ezekiel—primarily in the Deuteronomic–Deuteronomistic curse oracles (Dtn 28:27, 33, 38, 49–51, 60) and in the Deuteronomistic admonitions to return (Dtn 30:10; 1 Sam 7:3; 1 Kgs 8:48; 2 Kgs 23:25).[52]

2. In spite of his attentive ear for the earlier prophets, Joel largely speaks his own language, with free—often elegant—rhythms that underscore his themes (for example 1:14; 2:9, 20),[53] with concrete images discerned by the keenness of his own eye, evincing his determination to be heard by all (1:5–14; 2:16–17; 4:2–3), and with original metaphors of poetic stature (1:6; 2:4–11; 3:1, 3).

What *function* in the Jerusalem community is reflected by his language? It is undeniable that Joel is close to the priesthood and that he takes up liturgical forms. In spite of this, however, the book on the whole is anything but a document of priestly ministry. Here we are hearing a "literary prophet" in the strictest sense, insofar as he reads prophetic writings and writes prophecy. He belongs to those who study the literary transmissions of the prophets ". . . with the passion of those tormented. They gain from it conclusions that become

---

50 See p. 23.
51 See p. 47.

52 See pp. 48–49.
53 See p. 59.

new revelation for them." [54] He is pursued by the admonition which Is 34 (a chapter to which he relates in several ways) formulates in v 16: "Seek from the book of Yahweh and read: Not one of them shall be missing, . . . for his mouth has commanded, and his spirit has gathered them." Thus we are confronted here with a "learned prophecy" that takes up the received eschatological message with a burning passion for knowledge, and with the help of sapiential training, and gives it new expression in intense expectation of Yahweh's future. Formally, the new dimension lies, first of all, in the fact that the eschatological traditions are incorporated into a time sequence; the starting point for the new proclamation is discovered in the distress of the present time, so that the contemporary generation and its descendants are thereby confronted once again with a call to repentance.

Joel can hardly belong to the circles that take their stand upon the canonized Torah and see in liturgical compliance with it the ultimate will of the God of Israel. Instead, one has the impression that he belongs to those "eschatological groups" [55] who are still expecting completely new acts of Yahweh. In fourth century Jerusalem they constituted a "literary opposition" party to which must also have belonged the author of the eschatological cantatas of Is 24—27, and later, the author of Zech 12—14, as well as (though representing a different wing of the party) the linguistically related author of the Jonah narrative.

5. The Message of Joel

What concerns does Joel raise? His major theme is the Day of Yahweh. No other Old Testament witness gives it as detailed and systematic a treatment as he does. Every section of his book may be understood as a contribution to this theme (1:15; 2:1, 11; 3:4; 4:14). Yahweh's Day is the appointed time of his future acts, by which he brings about the decision between Israel and the world of nations. From its roots in the ancient Israelite war of Yahweh, [56] through its later, widespread appearance in the prophetic eschatology under the catchword "Day of Yahweh," its theme is the decision between Israel and the nations. Two alternatives were available to Joel: the Day of Yahweh could be decisive either for the salvation of Israel or for its destruction. [57] His own contribution consists, first of all, in giving systematic treatment to both alternatives. In the first part of the book (1:4—2:17) he adopts the perspective of prophecy of judgment, according to which Yahweh leads the army of the nations to destroy Israel. In the second part (2:18—4:17 [21]) he adopts the perspective of prophecy of salvation, according to which Israel is delivered by Yahweh from the onslaught of the nations, while the latter are destroyed. By developing the theme in both directions, Joel stands at the threshold between prophetic and apocalyptic eschatology.

When Joel, in the first half of the fourth century, [58] speaks of the Day of Yahweh so extensively and so insistently, he passionately reintroduces for discussion by his contemporaries a theme which, if not forgotten, had at least been largely repressed, especially in the leadership circles of Jerusalem. The restoration of Judah and Jerusalem after the exile (initiated by Zerubbabel and consolidated by the beginning of the fourth century through the efforts of Ezra and Nehemiah) was not accepted by Joel as a wholly valid fulfillment of the word of Yahweh spoken to Israel in the course of history. [59] For, beside the word of the Torah upon which the priestly circles relied, there was

---

54 Gottfried Quell, *Wahre und falsche Propheten: Versuch einer Interpretation*, BFChrTh 46/1 (Gütersloh: C. Bertelsmann, 1952), 133.

55 Otto Plöger, *Theocracy and Eschatology*, tr. S. Rudman (Richmond, Va.: John Knox, 1968), 45, 110 [*Theokratie und Eschatologie*, WMANT 2 (Neukirchen: Neukirchener Verlag, 1959), 59, 134].

56 Gerhard von Rad, *Old Testament Theology*, vol. 2: *The Theology of Israel's Prophetic Traditions*, tr. D. M. G. Stalker (New York and Evanston: Harper & Row, 1965), 119–25 [*Theologie des Alten Testaments*, vol. 2: *Die Theologie der prophetischen Überlieferung Israels*, Einführung in die evangelische Theologie 1 (München: Chr. Kaiser, 5 1968), 129–33].

57 See pp. 33–34.

58 See p. 5.

59 E. O. Adalbert Merx, *Die Prophetie des Joel und ihre Ausleger von den ältesten Zeiten bis zu den Reformatoren. Eine exegetisch–kritische und hermeneutisch–dogmengeschichtliche Studie* (Halle a.S., 1879), 42.

the prophetic word. And from the perspective of earlier prophecy it had to be recognized that the relationship between Israel and the world of nations—as represented by the contemporary Jerusalemite cultic community incorporated into the political framework of a Persian satrapy—was not in keeping with the ultimate will of the God of Israel. To be sure, Joel treats the established worship (with its customs and traditions and the ministry of the priests) as something to be taken for granted and, in itself, unassailable (1:9, 13–14, 16; 2:15–17). However, ultimately he regards it as merely temporary and transient, something that will be overtaken by new, final acts of God, i.e., precisely by the Day of Yahweh to which he redirects attention.

An acute emergency in his own day provides him with a relevant starting point. Although the political conditions in the Persian Empire in that time seemed to be perfectly constant and final, a devastating locust attack and a catastrophic drought (1:4–20) showed that quite extraordinary events were still happening in the history of Jerusalem and Judah (1:2b). Precisely these were to force open the eyes of Jerusalem and Judah and its leadership to the fact that history was still moving toward foundation–shaking changes and that the prophetic theme of the Day of Yahweh had not yet been exhausted. In this respect the locusts are especially important to him because they, as a "nation powerful and beyond numbering," figure as a prototype of the eschatological army of devastation which is to move up against Jerusalem, led by Yahweh himself, on his "Day" (cf. 1:6 with 2:2–11). Beyond the lamentation provoked by the already–present economic emergency, which has to be seen as an omen of the Day of Yahweh, Jerusalem must first of all perceive the new announcement of the final day of judgment. On that day Yahweh will lead up his invincible locust army, thus finally fulfilling the prophetic threats of the "enemy from afar" or "from the north."[60] The extraordinary contemporary event therefore points to the proclamation of a revolutionary final event. This is what Jerusalem's pious, worship–centred self–assurance must recognize. The cultic lamentation over the economic crisis (1:16–20) hence first of all induces

an eschatological alarm (2:1–11). The transition from chap. 1 to chap. 2 should certainly be interpreted in this way.[61] By beginning to compare the times and paying attention to the incisive changes (1:2b; 2:2b), this "learned prophet" again shows himself to stand at the threshold between prophetic and apocalyptic prophecy.

Only a complete "return" can change the Day of Yahweh from a day of judgment into a day of salvation (2:12–13). At the decisive point in the text where he issues the call to "return," Joel shows himself to be a student of the language of the Deuteronomistic theology,[62] while thematically he is especially dependent upon Ezekiel. It is reminiscent of Deuteronomistic language that Joel's exhortation is "to return with whole heart," i.e., to reorient oneself in a genuinely new way towards the coming of Yahweh and not merely to perform a ritual of lamentation anticipating no more than restoration. As to subject matter, however, Joel is heir to Ezekiel. The "return" is based not on the Torah (as in the Deuteronomistic history) but on prophetic proclamation, in this case the eschatological alarm (cf. Ezek 33:1–20; 18:21–32; 3:20–21). Joel assumes once more the office of Israel's watchman, calling the people to return ("but even now," 2:12) in the face of the calamity which he sees moving in upon the land. The distance from Ezekiel can be recognized in that Joel never once describes any guilt from which Jerusalem is to turn away. While the Deuteronomistic historian lamented primarily apostasy from the Mosaic Torah and demanded a turning towards it, for Joel return is necessary because cultic, pious self–sufficiency has caused the prophetic word of the Day of Yahweh, directed against Jerusalem, to go unheard. This calls for a rending of hearts, not of clothes (2:13a). Return essentially means for Joel that one face, on the basis of the prophetic proclamation and with fear and trembling, the completely new acts of God towards Jerusalem. This is his central "kerygma" on the forgotten general theme "Day of Yahweh."[63]

The return which Joel proclaims leaves room for the freedom of Yahweh (2:14). Yet divine compassion prevails, pledged in response to the current economic

60   On the problem of interpreting 2:1–11, see pp. 41–42.
61   See p. 42.
62   See p. 48.
63   We might further remark that the connection between the message of return and the Day of Yahweh

crisis in the "assurance oracle answering a plea" (2:19–27). Moreover this assurance oracle is then taken up (as the opening section) into the great two–stage self–disclosure oracle which comprises the remainder of the book.[64] The reversal of the food catastrophe becomes the basis for the realization (2:27) that the Day of Yahweh itself will bring for Jerusalem fulfillment of the ancient promises of salvation. Whoever is oriented towards the coming God must never expect only restoration. Through the pouring out of his spirit (3:1–2) Yahweh himself will reshape the community into a people united to him in all its members. The present theocratic–hierarchical order will be made obsolete by the concord in his spirit. The cosmic catastrophes become mere signs that, on the great and terrible Day of Yahweh, there will be escape on Mount Zion for all those who, heeding the appeal, will invoke the coming one (3:5). Alongside the sketchy image of the complete renewal and deliverance of Jerusalem, the counterimage of the disintegrating world of nations is juxtaposed in chap. 4. The nations will be doomed because of the injustice they have perpetrated against a defenseless Israel (4:2–3). In a final war of Yahweh, the fate of the nations will be sealed on the plain of judgment (4:9–14). Then Yahweh will settle down on Zion as victor; in his presence his people, who had actually deserved the same punitive judgment (2:1–11), will find refuge and undisturbed peace in the compassionate shadow of the covenant God (cf. 2:13b with 4:17).[65]

Thus a completely new picture of the Zion community (chap. 3) and its worldwide context (chap. 4) is held up before the Jerusalemites of the first half of the fourth century. How different is the present![66] The announcement, newly motivated and rooted in a present divine response (2:19–26), establishes a starting point for the coming acts of God who works "in the midst of Israel" (2:27) in a way that pertains at the same time to Jerusalem and to the whole world. Insofar as Joel distinguishes a preliminary divine response

(2:19–26) from the ultimate time of salvation (3:1–5) and sees the fate of Israel and the whole world of nations linked together in the events of the end–time (commenting explicitly here upon older prophetic utterance [3:5]), we see him once again standing at the threshold between prophetic eschatology and apocalypticism. But he has not crossed that threshold, since he does not establish a time sequence for the various events within the end–time.[67]

We shall summarize to what extent the message of this "learned prophet" has progressed along the way toward apocalypticism:

1. He develops the theme of the Day of Yahweh in all its dimensions, and in doing so he thinks, as a matter of principle, in universal terms. "All the nations" (4:2, 11) are linked together with Israel in the events of the end–time; yet the nations go towards their judgment, while a salutory peace is being prepared for Israel.

2. He exhibits a sapientially inspired interest in the distinction between times (1:2b; 2:2b).[68] In this connection he gives a significant place to natural phenomena within his considerations (1:4–20; cf. 2:10–11; 4:15–16; [4:18]). Above all, he sees the contrast between present and future conditions, but he already knows of a prologue to the future (2:19–27) which functions to gain (divine) recognition.

3. As a learned prophet he is occupied directly (3:5) but, above all, indirectly with the systematic treatment of transmitted prophetic words. He interprets even contemporary events on the basis of earlier prophecy (1:15).

At the same time we must note what still connects Joel with the earlier prophetic movement and distinguishes him from later apocalypticism:

1. To Israel in the present is proclaimed, first of all, a total judgment similar to that announced later for the world of nations (2:1–11).

2. The proclamation has as its starting point not the

---

theme already assures that the call to return in Joel will lack any ethical–moral overtone: from the descriptions of the ancient wars of Yahweh, through Am 5:18–20, and up to Ezek 30 the theme of guilt is not related in a primary way to the Day of Yahweh theme. Cf. Walther Zimmerli, *Ezechiel*, BK 13/2 (Neukirchen–Vluyn: Neukirchener Verlag, 1969), 739.

64 See pp. 58–59.
65 The later additions in 4:18–21 and 4:4–8 variously clarify particular features of chap. 4; see pp. 74–75.
66 See pp. 5–6.
67 Cf. the time determinations in 3:1, 2; and 4:1.
68 See pp. 44–45.

past (camouflaged as future), but decidedly the present.

3. The future stands under the aegis of God's freedom (2:14). The same end–time theophany (2:10–11; 4:15, 16a) can have two entirely opposite effects: destruction of Jerusalem (2:1–9) or judgment on the world of nations (4:1–3, 9–14, [19]) with deliverance and renewal of Jerusalem (3:1–5; 4:16b, 17, [18, 20–21]). At the decisive midpoint of the text, therefore, the contemporary hearer can be called to return (2:12–13).

To this extent Joel does not cease to be a prophet. What is he saying to us today?

1. Israel is awakened from its Torah–contentedness to a life anticipating the coming free acts of God's compassion (2:12–14). It is thus, in Luther's words, "prepared for the future of Christ." [69]

2. The Christ event announced in the meantime has altered Joel's expectation in two ways: (a) The freedom of the compassion of Israel's God has drawn all people from all nations into the deliverance on Mount Zion; (b) for the time being, this deliverance on Mount Zion takes place in the activity of the spirit of the Christ who was crucified and raised again in Jerusalem, and in the word of his witnesses.

3. Where the church after Christ believes herself able to recognize the goal of salvation history in legalistic piety and in hierarchical–liturgical activity, she is therefore in need of the same awakening call as Israel.

4. Unusual present–day threats, especially to her own worship (chap. 1), are to remind her that she has to reckon with the total threat to her existence, a threat that proceeds from her Lord (2:1–11). They are to remind her also, however, that on the basis of the compassion shown already in Christ she is "but even now" called to a total redirection towards the coming reign of the compassion of Christ (2:12–14).

5. After God has in Christ guided the history of Israel to its goal, Joel continues to be a reminder that the reason and goal of the renewal and of the deliverance within a transient world was and remains the transformation of the old and the new people of God in all of its members through the spirit of God himself (3:1–5). [70]

6. Even after Christ one must not forget that salvation history and world history, the history of God's people and that of the world of nations, are correlated. Proclamation of the coming Christ consistently concerns not only the future of the old and the new people of God, but also that of the whole world (2:1–11; 4:1–21). [71]

7. Even after Christ, a deep, momentous chasm cleaves the world. It corresponds to the one which rent ancient Jerusalem at the time of Joel's proclamation: Would the prophet's call be perceived as God's word? Would the coming Lord be invoked and expected through a reorientation of life in its totality towards his anticipated compassion?

In summary, I hear the "learned prophet" Joel say in a world changed since Jesus of Nazareth: Let the catastrophic threats to the present and the future move you to a total reorientation towards the attested and coming compassion of God!

---

69   WA 19, 330; cf. Krause, *Studien*, 298.
70   Cf. Acts 2:1–4, 16–21, 39; and Rom 10:12–13.
71   Cf. Mk 4:26–29; and Rev 14:14–20.

Locusts as Forerunners of the Day of Yahweh

Bibliography

Walter Baumgartner
"Joel 1 und 2" in *Karl Budde zum siebzigsten Geburtstag*, ed. Karl Marti, BZAW 34 (Giessen, 1920), 10–19.

Thérèse Frankfort
"Le כי de Joël 1:12," *VT* 10 (1960): 445–48.

Alfred O. Haldar
The Nature of the Desert in Sumero–Accadian and West–Semitic Religions, UUÅ 1950/3 (Uppsala: A. B. Lundequist, 1950), 56–59.

Ernst Kutsch
"Heuschreckenplage und Tag Jahwes in Joel 1 und 2," *ThZ* 18 (1962): 81–94.

Margarete Plath
"Joel 1:15–20," *ZAW* 47 (1929): 159–60.

Ovid R. Sellers
"Stages of Locust in Joel," *AJSL* 52 (1935–36): 81–85.

M. Sprengling
"Joel 1:17," *JBL* 38 (1919): 129–41.

John A. Thompson
"Joel's Locusts in the Light of Near Eastern Parallels," *JNES* 14 (1955): 52–55.

1

1 The word of Yahweh that came to Joel, the son of Pethuel.[a]

2 Hear this, elders!
Attend, all inhabitants of the land![b]
   Has such a thing[c] happened in your days?
      Or[d] in the days of your fathers?

3 Tell of it to your sons,
   and your sons [e]to their sons,
      and their sons[e] to the following generation!

4 What the biter left, the locust devoured.
   What the locust left, the hopper devoured.
      What the hopper left, the jumper devoured.

5 Awake, drunkards,[f] and weep!
Wail, all drinkers of wine!
   [g]Because of the juice,
      for it is cut off from your mouths.[g]

6 For a nation has come up
against my land,
   powerful and beyond numbering.
Its teeth are the teeth of a lion,
   its fangs the fangs of a lioness.

7 It has laid waste my vine;

a *G* (Βαθουηλ) and likewise *S* and *L* identify the singularly attested name of *M* with that of Bethuel, the father of Rebekah (Gen 22:22–23; 24:15, 24, 47, 50), a name which elsewhere appears only in Josh 19:4 and 1 Chr 4:30. *T* and *V* (*Fatuhel*) as well as *G*[86] support *M*.

b *G*[147] (a 12th century manuscript) renders οἰκουμένην ("inhabited earth, world") rather than γῆν ("land").

c זאת ("this") is here used like כָּזֹאת; cf. 1 Sam 4:7; Is 66:8; Jer 2:10.

d On the disjunctive question, cf. Carl Brockelmann, *Hebräische Syntax* (Neukirchen: Verlag der Buchhandlung des Erziehungsvereins, 1956), par. 169c. ואם for אם is rare and late; cf. Job 21:4.

e–e Textual tradition offers no basis for changing the tricolon into a bicolon by deleting לבניהם ובניהם (as proposed by Sellin, Robinson, and Weiser); the presence of a tricolon in v 4, immediately following, argues against the proposal.

f *G* adds, as an explanatory gloss, ἐξ οἴνου αὐτῶν ("from their wine").

g–g *G* mistakenly construes על־עסיס with יין, rendering οἱ πίνοντες οἶνον εἰς μέθην ("those who drink wine unto drunkenness"); to compensate for the loss of a subject, *G* supplies εὐφροσύνη καὶ χαρά ("joy and

it has broken down my fig tree,
stripped it bare, cast it away;
    its twigs are blanched—white.[h]

8   **Lament**[i] **. . .**
    like a virgin girded with sackcloth,
      because of the husband of her
      youth.[j]

9   **Cut off are meal—offerings and**
    libations
      from the house of Yahweh.
    The priests mourn,[k]
    the ministers of the <altar>.[l]

h $G(\check{\epsilon}\lambda\epsilon\acute{\nu}\kappa\alpha\nu\epsilon)$ reflects contextual accommodation, presupposing that "the nation" (v 6) is the subject of this colon also: i.e., "it has blanched" (הִלְבִּין) for M "they are blanched, made white." Cf. Roland Gradwohl, *Die Farben im Alten Testament: Eine terminologische Studie*, BZAW 83 (Berlin: A. Töpelmann, 1963), 37.

i   There are a number of indications that the text of vv 8–9 was disturbed at an early stage: (1) אֱלִי (feminine singular imperative of אלה = "lament!"?) is a unique form. (2) The imperative lacks a vocative indicating the party addressed (see p. 29 on 1:8). (3) $G\ \theta\rho\acute{\eta}\nu\eta\sigma o\nu\ \pi\rho\acute{o}s\ \mu\epsilon$ ("Wail unto me!") presupposes a longer text than M in v 8a. $\Pi\rho\acute{o}s\ \mu\epsilon$ alone corresponds to the consonantal text of M, though with a different vocalization (אֵלַי); $\theta\rho\acute{\eta}\nu\eta\sigma o\nu$ presupposes a preceding הֵילִיל (cf. vv 5, 11, 13). (4) Two forms in v 9b reflect an uncertain transmission; see textual notes "k" and "l" below. (5) As a report of a mourning by the priests which has already taken place, v 9b seems strange in the context of the exhortations, although it now continues v 9a in an intelligible way, so that v 9b makes appropriate sense in its present location. Most of these difficulties and variants are perhaps explicable if v 9b had originally stood before v 8, its present position following v 9a being the result of early scribal mutilation of the text. (So Sellin; Baumgartner, "Joel 1 und 2"; and Julius A. Bewer, *A Critical and Exegetical Commentary on Obadiah and Joel*, ICC [Edinburgh: T. & T. Clark, 1911].) A suitable reconstruction should recover from vv 9b, 8, 9a and 10 a strophe essentially the same as those in vv 5–7, 11–12, and 13–14. אלי in v 8a may be the mutilated remainder of a second exhortation, a little more of which was still available to G (see above). In vv 2, 5, 11 and 13 a double exhortation is also present in each case; in vv 5, 11 and 13 the second cola contain הֵילִילוּ, which G similarly presupposes in v 8a ($\theta\rho\acute{\eta}\nu\eta\sigma o\nu\ \pi\rho\acute{o}s\ \mu\epsilon$ = הֵילִיל אֵלַי); each colon in the series of exhortations in vv 5, 11 and 13 has a vocative. Combining these observations we may propose the following reconstruction of the bicolon:

אִבְלוּ הַכֹּהֲנִים וְהֵילִילוּ
אֵלוּ מְשָׁרְתֵי מִזְבֵּחַ

Mourn, priests, and wail!
Lament, ministers of the altar!

Yet such a proposal must remain tentative, especially since the simile in v 8 leads us rather to expect a feminine singular addressee.

j   G interprets appropriately $\tau\grave{o}\nu\ \check{\alpha}\nu\delta\rho\alpha\ \alpha\grave{\upsilon}\tau\hat{\eta}s\ \tau\grave{o}\nu\ \pi\alpha\rho\theta\epsilon\nu\iota\kappa\acute{o}\nu$ ("the husband of her maidenhood" = "her first husband").

k $G\ (\pi\epsilon\nu\theta\epsilon\hat{\iota}\tau\epsilon)$ reflects the imperative vocalization אִבְלוּ; cf. the tentative reconstruction in textual note "i" above.

l $G\ (\theta\upsilon\sigma\iota\alpha\sigma\tau\eta\rho\acute{\iota}\omega)$ presupposes מִזְבֵּחַ as in v 13a, in-

rejoicing"), at the end of the clause, borrowing this from 1:16.

10 [m]**The fields are laid waste,**
wilted[n] is the land.
Indeed, the grain is destroyed,
dried up[o] the new-wine,
abated the olive-oil.

11 **Be ashamed,[p] tillers of the soil!**
Wail, vinedressers!
Because of the wheat and because of the barley,
for the harvest of the field is lost.
12 **The vine is wilted,[q]**
the fig tree withered.
Pomegranate, even date palm and apple,
all the trees of the field
are withered away.
Indeed, joy dries up[r]
among the sons of men.

13 **Gird yourselves[s] and lament, priests!**
Wail, ministers of the altar!
Come, pass the night in sackcloth,
ministers of God![t]
For withheld from your house of God,[u]
are meal-offerings and libations.
14 **Announce a holy fast!**
Proclaim a solemn holiday!
Gather the elders,
all the inhabitants of the land,
to the house of Yahweh your God,
and cry out to Yahweh![v]

15 **Alas[w] for the day!**
For the Day of Yahweh is near.
[x]**Like might from the Mighty One it comes.**[x]

16 **Is not food cut off before our eyes,**
joy and rejoicing from our house of God?[y]
17 [z]**The seed grains lie shriveled**
under their clods.[z]
Ruined are the storehouses,
torn down the granaries,
for the grain has withered.

stead of "Yahweh" in *M*. *G* is thereby more congenial to the context (v 9a!). *M* may have been influenced by יהוה in v 9aβ.

m *G* (*ὅτι*) presupposes כִּי at the beginning of v 10a as well as v 10b.

n See Wolff, *Hosea*, textual note "b" to Hos 4:3a.

o The hipʿil of יבשׁ is used here as internally transitive (Robinson); cf. *Gesenius' Hebrew Grammar*, ed. E. Kautzsch, tr. and rev. A. E. Cowley (Oxford, ^{2}1910), par. 53e. So also *G* (*ἐξηράνθη*).

p *G* (*ἐξηράνθησαν*) interprets the form as third plural perfect, continuing the declarative statements of v 10a. And yet *G* renders the parallel element הילילו as an imperative (*θρηνεῖτε*).

q See textual note "o."

r *G* (*ᾔσχυναν*) derives the form from בושׁ. The dual sense "to come to naught"—"to dry up" was probably intended in view of vv 11a and 12a; see p. 32 on 1:11.

s Ken[30] interprets correctly חגרו שׂק ("gird on sackcloth!"); so also *S*. Cf. v 8; 2 Sam 3:31; Jer 4:8; and pp. 32–33 on 1:13.

t *G* (*θεῷ*) presupposes אלהים; *V* (*ministri dei mei*) confirms *M* אלהי ("my God"). V 13b favors the reading of *G*.

u Cf. Paul Joüon, *Grammaire de l'Hébreu Biblique* (Rome: Institut Biblique Pontifical, ^{2}1947), par. 140b; Gesenius–Kautzsch–Cowley, par. 128m.

v *S* presupposes לֵאמֹר, i.e., vv 15–20 are regarded as a quotation of the lament; cf. 2:17.

w *G* repeats the mourning cry three times: *οἴμμοι οἴμμοι οἴμμοι*; so also *V* (*a a a*).

x–x [The English translation of the line approximates the German rendering which Wolff has adopted from Martin Buber and Franz Rosenzweig (*Bücher der Kündung* [Köln & Olten: Jakob Hegner, 1958], 622): "*Wie Gewalt vom Gewaltigen kommt er*." This is an attempt to represent the consonance of the Hebrew: *ûk(ĕ)šōd miššadday yābōʾ*; see p. 34. Ed.]

y See textual note "u."

z–z Cf. Ibn Ezra and Radaq (Gottfried Widmer, *Die Kommentare von Raschi, Ibn Esra, Radaq zu Joel: Text, Übersetzung und Erläuterung, eine Einführung in die rabbinische Bibelexegese* [Basel: Volksdruckerei, 1945], 41ff). Instead of the *hapax legomena* of *M*, *G* has translated more familiar forms: *ἐσκίρτησαν δαμάλεις ἐπὶ ταῖς φάτναις αὐτῶν* = פָּשׁוּ פָרוֹת בְּרִפְתֵּיהֶם (cf. Hab 1:8; 3:17; Mal 3:20 [4:27]) = "the cows stamp about by their manger" (Hebrew: "in their enclosure"). *V* renders differently: *computruerunt iumenta in stercore suo* = (?) עבשׁוּ פְרָדוֹת תחת מַדְמֵנוֹתֵיהֶם (cf. Is 25:10?) = "the beasts of burden rot in their dung" (?). Cf. also *σ'*: *ηὐρωτίασαν σιτοδοχεῖα ἀπὸ τοῦ χρίσματος αὐτῶν* ("the granaries rot away without their oil-coating"). *S* (*wṭwy* = *G* *ἔσκλησαν*) supports *M* (עבשׁו), but corresponds otherwise to *G*. Cf. M. Sprengling, "Joel 1:17," *JBL* 38 (1919): 129–41.

18	ᵃᵃHow the beasts groan!ᵃᵃ
	    The herds of cattle stray about.ᵇᵇ
	        For nowhere is there pasture for
	        them.
	            Even the flocks \<succumb\>.ᶜᶜ
		aa–
		aa
		
		bb
		
		cc
			G: τί ἀποθήσομεν ἐν αὐτοῖς = מַה־נַּנִּיחָה בָהֶם ("What
			shall we store in them?"); the question refers back
			to the storehouses in v 17b. Syh (ἐστέναξε τὰ κτήνη)
			supports M.
			
			G (ἔκλαυσαν) reads the more familiar בָּכוּ, "they
			wept" (cf. 1:5; 2:17).

19	Unto you, Yahweh, I call out.
	        For fire devours the pastures
	        of the range,
	            and flame sets ablaze all the
	            trees of the field.
			אשׁם (qal: "to become subject to punishment"; see
			Wolff, *Hosea*, 89 on Hos 4:15) is not elsewhere at-
			tested in the nip'al. G (ἠφανίσθησαν ["they have
			been obliterated"]) presupposes, as in v 17aβ, the
			root שׁמם and probably read נָשַׁמּוּ (see Wolff, *Hosea*,
			textual note "i" to Hos 5:15b).

20	Even the wild beasts pant after
	    you.
	        For dried up are the torrents of
	        water,
	            and fire devours the pastures
	            of the range.		

Form

After the title (1:1), the book of Joel commences with a stirring summons to hear and promulgate the news of an incomparable event (vv 2–3). In the form of a very terse report the event is initially depicted as a ravaging locust plague (v 4); then its ramifications are unfolded with the aid of an elaborate, exhortative call to lamentation (vv 5–14) and fragments of lament songs (vv 15–20). Here too, at the beginning of the lament (v 15), is explained why news of the incipient disaster must be transmitted through the generations (v 3): it is the harbinger of the Day of Yahweh.

1:1 The basic form of the book's title (v 1) is comparable to Hos 1:1;[1] Mi 1:1; Zeph 1:1; (Jer 1:1 *G*): "the word of Yahweh that came to . . ." (דבר יהוה אשר היה אל). But Joel 1:1 is paralleled only by Jon 1:1 in restricting the particulars given to the names of the author and his father.

1:2–3 The book's opening employs in v 2a the ancient "call to receive instruction" (*Lehreröffnungsruf*), a form especially popular in wisdom circles, used to arouse attentiveness.[2] This introduces a question (v 2b) which seems similarly didactic and impassioned, emphasizing that the event—still to be announced—is something quite unique. In v 3 the significance of what will follow is heavily underscored by the three–part commission to pass on word of it from generation to generation. Apart from the Deuteronomic parenesis, the transmission scheme here articulated reminds us most strongly of the sapiential concern for the ongoing life of tradition, exemplified in Prv 4:1ff and Ps 78:1–8.[3]

1:4 After the momentous introit the prophet comes to the substance of the matter. First, in a tricolon exhibiting precise synonymous parallelism he describes a locust invasion devouring everything before it (v 4). The report's tricolonic structure facilitates its transmission, at the same time dramatizing with climactic force the devastating impact of the locust plague.

1:5–14 There follows an elaborate "call to lamentation." Its framework is revealed in a series of imperatives extending from v 5 through v 14. The strophic structure of the section can be recognized by the introductory prosodic units, each consisting of a bicolon, the two lines of which are formulated in the imperative and include vocatives designating the parties addressed; the parallel cola regularly begin with the command "Wail!" (הילילו; vv 5a, [8a *G*], 11aα, 13aα). Following the introductory prosodic units, each strophe consists of four (vv 11aβ–12) or five (vv 5b–7, 13aβ–14) additional bicola. An analogous strophe—with an introduction phrased in the imperative plus four sets of parallel cola—may be suspected to underlie the faultily transmitted text of vv 8–10.[4] It appears quite probable, therefore, that the section originally comprised a call to lamentation with four strophes. In each of the first three strophes, the "call" proper [i.e., the introductory bicolon] was followed by a statement of motivation beginning with either "because" (על vv 5b, 11aβ) or "for" (כי v 13b). Additional matter in these strophes—some of it also introduced by "for, indeed" (כי vv 5bβ, 6a, 10b, 11b, 12bβ)—elaborates the picture of the disaster. This descriptive material dominates the first

---

1   See Wolff, *Hosea*, 1 [1].
2   See Wolff, *Hosea*, 96f [122f].
3   See p. 26.

4   For an attempt at reconstruction, see above, textual note "i" to 1:8.

three strophes.

Although the final strophe in vv 13–14 begins with a "call" (v 13aα), linking it to vv 5–12,[5] its subsequent format distinguishes it. The portrayal of the disaster, which motivates the call to lamentation and which accounts for by far the major portions of the first three strophes, is here restricted to the third bicolon (v 13b). Conversely, in the final strophe not only the initial bicolon but also the second, the fourth, and the fifth are formulated as imperative calls. In terms of content this means that primary attention has shifted away from the scope of the disaster itself, focusing now on appropriate responses to the crisis. The summons to make lamentation has been defined as a prescription for the observance of ritual acts. The first three strophes, then, function essentially to motivate the lament ceremony, the goal to which we are brought in the final unit.

The Genre "Call to Communal Lamentation"

The communal lament songs have received repeated and thorough form–critical treatment.[6] But thus far little attention has been given to that mode of address which must have preceded the offering of the prayers of lament themselves—when a proclamation was issued, summoning the people to a lament ceremony in the exceptional case of some sudden national emergency, whether it be a threat to the harvest, or war. Joel 1:5–14 is one of the most prominent examples of such calls to communal lamentation. That this speech form had been employed repeatedly since early times is evident from texts such as 1 Kgs 21:9, 12; Am 5:16b; Is 22:12; Jer 36:9; Ezr 8:21; Jon 3:7–8; 2 Chr 20:3. The king could be the initiator of the call[7] and the elders of the city might be those proclaiming it.[8] The use of the divine first person in Joel 1:6 and 7 presupposes the basic form of the messenger speech, also present in corresponding passages (Is 22:12;

32:13; Jer 6:26).

In addition to Joel 1:5–14, the attestations of the genre "call to communal lamentation" are: 2 Sam 3:31; Jer 4:8; 6:26; 7:29; 22:20; 25:34; 49:3; Zeph 1:11; Ezek 21:17 [12]; Is 14:31; 23:1–14; 32:11–14; Zech 11:2. The regularly recurring formal features are: first, the imperative call; second, the vocative used to designate those addressed; and, third, the statement of the cause for the lamenting, introduced usually by "for" (כי)[9] but also by "because" (על)[10] and continued by descriptive clauses.[11]

The most important topics in this call are:
"Make lamentation!" (סִפְדוּ)—
    2 Sam 3:31; Jer 4:8; 49:3; Joel 1:13; cf. Am 5:16; Is 22:12; Zech 12:11–12.
"Weep!" (בכו)—
    2 Sam 1:24; Joel 2:17.
"Wail!" (הילילו)—
    Jer 4:8; 25:34; 49:3; Zeph 1:11; Ezek 21:17 [12]; Is 14:31; 23:1, 6, 14; Joel 1:5, [8a *G*], 11, 13; Zech 11:2.
"Cry out!" (זעקו)—
    Joel 1:14; Is 14:31; Ezek 21:17 [12].
"Rend your garments!" (קרעו בגדיכם)—
    Joel 2:13; 2 Sam 3:31.
"Gird on sackcloth!" (חגרו שׂק)—
    2 Sam 3:31; Is 22:12; Jer 4:8; 6:26; 49:3; cf. Is 15:3.
"Announce a holy fast!" (קדשׁו צום)—
    Joel 1:14; 2:15; cf. 2:12; 1 Kgs 21:9, 12; Jer 36:9; Jon 3:5; Ezr 8:21; 2 Chr 20:3.

In later times it is striking that when the cause is specified we find, in addition to the more specialized terms, the noun "destruction, devastation" (שׁד) and its correlative verb "to destroy, devastate" (שׁדד pu'al) being used quite frequently to describe the general devastation (Jer 49:3; Is 23:1, 14; Zech 11:2; Joel 1:10).

Joel 1:5–14 is not the only example of the genre attesting a strophic construction. Already Zech 11:2 must be considered as having two strophes since all three of the genre's formal features appear twice. Is

---

5   Differently Sellin; Wilhelm Nowack, *Die kleinen Propheten übersetzt und erklärt*, HK 3/4 (Göttingen, [3]1922); Joseph Trinquet, *Habaquq, Abadias, Joël*, SBJ (Paris: Les Éditions du Cerf, [2]1959).

6   Cf. Hermann Gunkel and Joachim Begrich, *Einleitung in die Psalmen. Die Gattungen der religiösen Lyrik Israels*, HK 2/1 (Göttingen, 1933), par. 4; Claus Westermann, "Struktur und Geschichte der Klage im Alten Testament," *ZAW* 66 (1954): 44–80 (reprinted in *idem*, *Forschung am Alten Testament: Gesammelte Studien*, ThB 24 [München: Chr. Kaiser, 1964], 266–305; Hans–Joachim Kraus, *Psalmen*, BK 15/1

(Neukirchen–Vluyn: Neukirchener Verlag, [2]1961), 1i f.

7   2 Sam 3:31; 1 Kgs 21:8; Jon 3:6–9; 2 Chr 20:3.
8   1 Kgs 21:8.
9   Jer 4:8b; 6:26b; 7:29b; 22:20; 25:34; 49:3; Ezek 21:17 [12]; Zech 11:2; Is 14:31; 32:14; 23:1, 4, 14.
10   Is 32:12b–13; לפני is so used in 2 Sam 3:31.
11   Jer 25:35; cf. 2 Sam 1:24; Jer 51:8.

23:1–14 displays five elaborated strophes and therefore stands structurally closest to Joel 1:5–14. With its utterances concerning Tyre, Sidon, and the inhabitants of the seacoast, Is 23:1–14 is probably close to Joel in date as well (cf. Joel 4:4–8); the passage is now usually assigned to the time after the destruction of Sidon by Artaxerxes III Ochus in 343 B.C.[12] The formation of strophes is related to the life-setting of the genre. The one who issues the call cannot simultaneously reach all groups that are to be summoned.[13] Zech 12:12–14 provides evidence that the lamentation is also made in groups (in this case, separately by clans and sexes). Thus Joel 1:5–14 belongs to the latest and expanded examples of the genre "call to communal lamentation." In Is 13:6 and Ezek 30:2–3 the "call to communal lamentation" had already been associated with the announcement of the Day of Yahweh.

Since the cause of the lamentation is accorded especially full treatment in the first three strophes, the passage can perform its function of clarifying the nature of the calamity.

1:15–20 Portions of lamentation as such follow upon the great call. We cannot regard them as developed lament songs; they represent fragments of two lament songs, exhibiting almost exclusively that element of the lament which describes the distress (vv 16–18, 19b–20), without referring to the specific locust plague.[14] The second fragment is formally identified by its opening element (consisting of the invocation of Yahweh's name) as belonging to the lament of an individual: "Unto you, Yahweh, I call out" (v 19a). Yet it expresses nothing other than the troubles of the whole people (cf. especially v 20a). Recently Sigmund Mowinckel has argued against a formal distinction between the "I" and the "we" psalms, maintaining ". . . that there are many communal lament psalms in the first person singular, psalms in which the one who prays is the representative of the congregation, in ancient times the king, and where the calamity is a national one."[15] The first lament song fragment is recognizable as a communal lament by the plural pronouns in v 16. Besides other features, both fragments especially lack two or three elements almost indispensable in the normal Israelite lament song: the petition and the vow, as well as the expression of trust.[16]

The first fragment is preceded in v 15 by a cry of terror, with an unusual formulation for a lament. But is not this cry of terror to be considered a later addition, related (along with the Day of Yahweh comments in 2:1b, 2a, 11b) to a supposed secondary attachment of chaps. 3 and 4?[17] It has been claimed that chaps. 1 and 2 alike originally dealt only with the plague on the land as such. Against these speculations we must consider the following points.

1. This "ah–cry" is indeed quite unusual as an element of a lament song. To be sure, אֲהָהּ ("ah! alas!"), which is first of all a cry of elemental fright,[18] is employed elsewhere to introduce a lament.[19] But this opening usage is always part of the formula "Ah, my Lord Yahweh!" (אהה אדני יהוה),[20] appropriate to the invocation of Yahweh which is an indispensable feature at the beginning of an Israelite lament song.[21] Among the fourteen occurrences of אהה there are only three

12 Cf. Otto Eissfeldt, *The Old Testament: An Introduction*, tr. Peter R. Ackroyd (New York: Harper and Row, 1965), 322f [*Einleitung in das Alte Testament unter Einschluss der Apokryphen und Pseudepigraphen sowie der apokryphen– und pseudepigraphenartigen Qumran–Schriften. Entstehungsgeschichte des Alten Testaments*, Neue Theologische Grundrisse (Tübingen: J. C. B. Mohr [Paul Siebeck], ³1964), 434]; Georg Fohrer, *Das Buch Jesaja*, vol. 1, Züricher Bibelkommentare (Zürich and Stuttgart: Zwingli Verlag, 1960), 239f. On the dating, see above, p. 4 and n. 12 (Kienitz). Differently Wilhelm Rudolph, "Jesaja 23:1–14" in *Festschrift Friedrich Baumgärtel zum 70. Geburtstag*, ed. Leonhard Rost, Erlanger Forschungen A/10 (Erlangen: Universitätsbund, 1959), 166–74.

13 Cf. Is 14:31; Jer 49:3; 22:20.

14 Cf. the corresponding "assurance oracle answering a plea" in 2:21–24; see p. 63.

15 "Review of Diethelm Michel, *Tempora und Satzstellung in den Psalmen* (1960)," *ThLZ* 87 (1962): 36.

16 Cf. Kraus, *Psalmen*, xlv f.

17 Duhm, "Anmerkungen"; Bewer; and Robinson.

18 Ju 6:22; 11:35; 2 Kgs 3:10; 6:5; Jer 1:6.

19 Josh 7:7; Jer 4:10; 14:13; 32:17; Ezek 4:14; 9:8; 11:13; 21:5 [20:49].

20 Cf. Friedrich Baumgärtel, "Zu den Gottesnamen in den Büchern Jeremia und Ezechiel" in *Verbannung und Heimkehr: Beiträge zur Geschichte und Theologie Israels im 6. und 5. Jahrhundert v. Chr. (Festschrift für Wilhelm Rudolph)*, ed. Arnulf Kuschke (Tübingen: J. C. B. Mohr [Paul Siebeck], 1961), 10, 27.

21 Cf. Hermann Gunkel and Joachim Begrich, *Einleitung in die Psalmen. Die Gattungen der religiösen Lyrik Israels*, HK 2/1 (Göttingen, 1933), 121f.

(Ju 11:35; 2 Kgs 3:10; Joel 1:15) unconnected with אדני יהוה. Here too we must consider the single occurrence of the short form הָהּ in Ezek 30:2. The text is especially important since it alone offers an exact parallel to the formulation "Alas for the day" (אהה ליום) in Joel 1:15. It is now necessary to ask whether Joel is concerned to reproduce correctly a lamentation ritual. The observation of the fragmentary character of the lament songs as rendered in vv 16–20 (where they, like the call to lamentation in vv 5–14, serve primarily to describe the disastrous situation) leads one to suspect that this is not the case. This is confirmed by the tone–setting opening address in vv 2–3 which directs all attention toward the uniqueness of a contemporary event. From this perspective the expression "Alas for the day!" in v 15—unusual though it may be in a prayer of lament—must be granted a central place within the present context.

2. The relationship of Joel 1:15 to Ezek 30:2 is not limited to the expression "Alas for the day!" (אהה ליום). Rather, in the Ezekiel text as in Joel there follows a reference to the nearness of the Day of Yahweh as the motivation for the cry of terror. Except in Ezek 30:2 (*M*) the cry is preceded by the exhortation "Wail!"[22] Yet precisely this "Wail!" (הילילו) is the regularly recurring key word of the call to lamentation which forms the preceding section of Joel: vv 5, (8a *G*), 11, 13. It also belongs to the thematic content of the announcement of the Day of Yahweh in Is 13:6 and Zeph 1:11 (cf. Zeph 1:14ff). Thus in grand fashion the call to lamentation in vv 5–14 elaborates the topic "Wail!" within the Day of Yahweh threats.

3. The question which in v 16 introduces the communal lament song fragment ("Is not [הלא] the food destroyed before our eyes?") can hardly be explained on the basis of the formal elements of the lament song. In the latter, הלא may at best introduce a question about Yahweh's action (Ps 60:12 [10]; 85:6–7 [5–6]), but not about the disastrous situation as such.[23] On the other hand, the rhetorical question in v 16 becomes intelligible in connection with v 15 as a confirmation of the lament over a perfectly peculiar day. In Is 23:7, which introduces a strophe, a similar question appears

as the motivation for initiating a lament. In our context the question is stylistically appropriate, continuing the tone–setting pedagogical question in v 2b which stresses the singularity of the catastrophe. V 16 is more intelligible as a sequel to v 15 than it would be to v 14 where the call to lamentation clearly reaches its conclusion.

Thus we have established that there is no reason to remove v 15 from its context. Instead, the whole chapter with its variegated components becomes comprehensible as a unity only on the basis of this cry of terror over the nearness of the Day of Yahweh. In the received tradition—as we glimpse it in Is 13:6; Ezek 30:2; and Zeph 1:11–18—the announcement of the Day of Yahweh had already been combined with a call to lamentation, here in vv 5–14 expanded into a strophic structure. The limitation of the lament song fragments to a description of the calamity (vv 16–18, 19b–20)— like the prominent significance of the same element in the call to lamentation (vv 5b–7, 9a, 10, 11a, 12, 13b)— becomes comprehensible only if the primary interest is not the reproduction of a lamentation ritual but the characterization of an utterly extraordinary contemporary situation. The three–part opening section of the chapter had already underscored the absolute singularity of the present crisis which would still have significance for generations to come.

The prosody of the chapter lacks uniformity. The opening section alone exhibits a completely symmetrical pattern of synonymously parallel members. Two bicola (v 2a, b) are followed by two tricola (vv 3, 4). All of these lines can be read as bearing four stresses, according to the "alternating system" of prosodic analysis;[24] according to the "accentuating system," one has to read vv 2–3 with three stresses per line and v 4 with four stresses per line.

In the call to lamentation the imperatively formulated introductory bicola of the three well–preserved strophes exhibit a strict synonymous parallelism (vv 5a, 11aα, 13aα). In the body of the strophes no consistent poetic structuring can be recognized, even though there is a predominance of prosodic units with clearly synonymous cola: vv 6b, 7a, 7b, 10a, 10b, 12a, 14a. V

---

22   Cf. Zimmerli, *Ezechiel*, 729.

23   As in 1:18, a question about the situation would be introduced by מה ("how? what?").

24   Cf. Friedrich Horst, "Die Kennzeichen der hebräischen Poesie," *ThR* 21 (1953): 97–121.

10b is a tricolon while all the other units are bicola. As a rule the cola bear three stresses, but vv 10a, 10b and 14a have two. The "synthetic" prosodic units seem in some cases to stand under the formal constraint of the genre (vv 5b, 11a, 11b: ... כי ... על; v 13b: כי),[25] and in other cases to function as expansions (vv 12b, 14aβ, 14b). From these findings one can conclude that the call to lamentation is not a poetic work of art. In contrast to vv 2–4, no creative hand can be perceived here. Instead, a block of material has been incorporated which is completely determined by the basic structure of the genre; its poetic components are not constant in the specific application of the speech form, but are accompanied by artless sentences.

The cry of terror in v 15 is a tricolon, like the second half of the opening section (vv 3, 4), but it does not exhibit any strict synonymity.

Synonymous parallels are present in the communal lament song fragment in vv 16–18, with two four–stress cola in v 16, and two three–stress bicola in v 18. The individual lament song exhibits two strophes (vv 19, 20), insofar as there is a correspondence between the invocations by the beasts (v 20a) and by the one who prays (v 19a). The motivating clauses of each strophe display two synonymous four–stress cola, with the last colon of the second strophe repeating the first colon of the first strophe.

Setting

We see no reason to attribute the authorship of the whole chapter to someone other than the Joel named in the book's title. It is easier to understand the absence of the usual chronological information in the title if its writer is identified with the author of what follows,[26] than it would be if we supposed the book to be a later written fixation of what had earlier been promulgated only in oral form. It remains an open question, though, whether Joel himself was also the speaker, especially of that call to lamentation which we find in vv 5–14—i.e., whether he performed a specific function in Jerusalem. The extant composition of pieces which, as forms of speech, have a rather different life-setting in each case, creates the impression of a literary effort.

Among other things it presupposes sapiential training with its concern to transmit tradition, as can be seen in the opening section in vv 2–3. The cry of terror in v 15 has been adopted from Is 13:6 and Ezek 30:2, thus attesting to a preoccupation with older literature.

That our text is temporally far removed from those exilic prophets is shown by the fact that here a functioning temple cultus is assumed (vv 9, 13, 16). Likewise, in this cultus the most important role is played by "meal–offerings and libations" (vv 9, 13) which in this firm pairing belong only to the postexilic period.[27] The interest in handing on tradition through several generations (v 3), related to Ps 78:1–8 and Prv 4:1ff, points to the same period.

From the perspective adopted in the opening section (which refers to later generations), and likewise in the central cry of terror over the nearness of the Day of Yahweh, the chapter directs attention beyond itself (cf. 2:1–2a, 2b, 11; 3:1; 4:1). Conversely, the opening chapter is presupposed in 2:19–26, most clearly in 2:25 (cf. 1:4), and probably also in 4:18 (cf. 1:5, 20). The first chapter, therefore, is correctly understood only in view of its literary connection with that which follows.

Interpretation

■ 1 The prophecy of Joel is called "Yahweh's word" in that comprehensive sense which this label had already acquired in old book-superscriptions.[28] It includes prophetic proclamation about Yahweh (cf. 1:9, 14, 15) and even prayer to him (1:19). To be sure, from its decisive turning point (2:19)[29] on through to the end, the book contains first person address of Yahweh in the basic form of messenger speech, which appears only sporadically before that point (1:6, 7; 2:1).

The name "Joel" is frequent in the Old Testament but, except as the name of a son of Samuel in 1 Sam 8:2, it occurs only in the Chronicler's History. There, of course, the name also designates Samuel's son (1 Chr 6:18 [33]; 15:17), but it further appears: in the tribal genealogies among the Simeonites (1 Chr 4:35), the Reubenites (1 Chr 5:4, 8), the Gadites (1 Chr 5:12), the Issacharites (1 Chr 7:3); later among the Manas-

25 See p. 200.
26 So Weiser.
27 See p. 31 and n. 95.

28 See Wolff, *Hosea*, 4 [2f].
29 Cf. already 2:12.

sites (1 Chr 27:20), among David's heroes (1 Chr 11:38), but especially among the Levites;[30] and finally among the contemporaries of Ezra (Ezr 10:43; Neh 11:9). Joel as a name, then, is better attested in the time of the Chronicler than in any earlier period. It belongs to the type "confessional names" and means "Yahweh is God."

On the other hand, the father's name, "Pethuel," is otherwise unattested. G identified it with the name of Rebekah's father, "Bethuel" (בתואל).[31] The meaning of "Pethuel" (פתואל) has not been fully elucidated.[32] Ludwig Koehler[33] supposes it to derive from p̆etî ʾēl[34] and interprets "Youth of God." A different derivation from the root פתה (qal passive participle, "seduced one of El") is even more uncertain[35] and presupposes that Joel ben Pethuel is a pseudonym with symbolic meaning ("Yahweh–is–God," son of "Seduced–One–of–El"). Already Abraham Kuenen considered the possibility that Joel might be a pseudonym formed by inverting אליה ([= Elijah] "My–God–is–Yahweh").[36] Even though the singularity of the name Pethuel could speak for a symbolic name (whose meaning, to be sure, would remain obscure) this possibility is nevertheless clearly excluded by the frequent occurrences of the name of Joel in the time of our book, a time that certainly must be close to that of the Chronicler's work. It remains most likely that Joel ben Pethuel was the regular name of the author of our book. Further information about his person can be gained only indirectly from his writing. Accordingly, it is certain that he belonged to the Jerusalem community (1:9, 13, 16; 2:1, 15; 3:5; 4:1,

16, 17, 18), but improbable that he is to be reckoned among its priests, about whom and to whom he speaks from a certain distance in 1:9 and 13 (cf. 2:17).

■ 2 Joel demands the attention of "the elders" and of "all inhabitants of the land." The "elders" (זקנים) also appear in the book of Joel in 1:14 (cf. 2:16; 3:1) as the real leadership group. It was not until postexilic times that the elders, who fulfilled merely a subordinate function during the time of the monarchy,[37] regained greater prominence.[38] In connection with the rebuilding of the Temple they are already the responsible representatives of the Jerusalem congregation,[39] a role they maintained, first under the Persian governor[40] until (after the last governor, Bagoas, the successor of Nehemiah) the high priest assumed leadership of the "Council of Elders" (γερουσία).[41] At a later time Josephus calls this constitution a "theocracy." Joel speaks, therefore, during this period. In preexilic times it would be difficult to understand the failure to mention the king and the court, either here, where the concern is emphatically for the whole nation, or elsewhere in the book of Joel (cf. Hos 5:1). Besides the elders, it is of course all inhabitants of the "land" (and not of the "earth"[42]) who are addressed, by which is meant the population of "Judah and Jerusalem" (cf. 4:1), as in 1:14 and 2:1. Joel has no apocalyptic secret to hand on, but like the older prophets makes his proclamation before the entire populace comprising the community and its official leadership.[43] Everyone should attend to what he has to say.

The older prophets also used questions in a didactic–

---

30 I.e., in the tribal genealogies (1 Chr 6:21 [36]); in the time of David, among bearers of the ark (1 Chr 15:7, 11; 23:8) and the treasurers (1 Chr 26:22); and in the time of Hezekiah (2 Chr 29:12 = 1 Chr 6:21 [36]).

31 See textual note "a" to 1:1.

32 Martin Noth, *Die israelitischen Personennamen im Rahmen der gemeinsemitischen Namengebung*, BWANT 3/10 (Stuttgart, 1928 = Hildesheim: Georg Olms, 1966), 255.

33 Ludwig Koehler and Walter Baumgartner, *Lexicon in Veteris Testamenti Libros* (Leiden: E. J. Brill, 1953, ²1958), 786.

34 Cf. "Penuel / Peniel" (פנואל / פניאל).

35 Cf. also Bič, 13.

36 *Historisch–kritisch onderzoek naar het ontstaan en de verzameling van de boeken des Ouden Verbonds*, vol. 2 (Lei-

den, ²1889), par. 68f. Cf. Bewer, 67; Kapelrud, *Joel*, 10.

37 For the end of the period, see 2 Kgs 23:1–2.

38 Cf. Günther Bornkamm, "Πρέσβυς," TDNT 6, 651–61; J. van der Ploeg, "Les anciens dans l'Ancien Testament" in *Lex tua veritas: Festschrift für Hubert Junker*, eds. H. Gross and F. Mussner (Trier: Paulinus–Verlag, 1961), 175–91.

39 Ezr 5:9; 6:8, 14.

40 Ezr 6:7; cf. Ezr 10:8, 14.

41 Josephus, *Antiquities* 12.138–44; 1 Macc 12:6; cf. Kurt Galling, "Judentum, I. Vom Exil bis Hadrian," RGG³ 3, 980.

42 Thus Bič.

43 Cf. Is 1:10; Hos 5:1; Jer 13:15.

sapiential manner, challenging their hearers to reach independent judgment.[44] A new feature in prophecy is the fact that the audience is now called upon to compare a present happening with past events, with the underlying intention that the present situation be recognized as absolutely incomparable (cf. also 2:2b). In a similar way the Yahwist depicted the locust plague over Egypt as something that had never before occurred (Ex 10:6, 14). It is the Deuteronomistic school that first urged a diligent searching of the expanse of time from the creation of man up to the present. In the course of this search, God's speaking with Israel in the Sinai theophany and his elective leading of Israel out of Egypt are to be recognized as an absolutely unique set of events (Dtn 4:32–35). In the lament song of Lam 1:12, Jerusalem's catastrophe in 587 is called a "day of Yahweh's burning anger," and the question is raised whether there is anything with which to compare the sorrows of its inhabitants. Thus it happens on a few occasions that an event of the past is compared with other times. Now, however, Israel—and in view specifically of its present—is drawn into the comparison of the times in order to highlight the inception of the coming Day of Yahweh. In this exhortation to make an evaluative comparison, with the aim of recognizing that which is absolutely new, we have the early signs of apocalypticism (cf. Dan 12:1). From here on the interest in determining the times becomes visible everywhere in the book of Joel: compare 1:15b; 2:1b, 2b, 23b, 25a, 26b, 27b; 3:1a, 2b; and 4:1a, 14b, 18a, 20. Hence also the statements about the nearness of the Day of Yahweh (קָרוֹב) and about ultimacy (לְעוֹלָם) stand out. From the outset the book instructs its readers to take note of the extraordinary phenomena of their time as significant from the vantage point of the God of Israel.

■ 3 Report of these extraordinary phenomena is to be transmitted to the coming generations, as had been done previously with the ancient historical traditions, and as diligently practiced by the Deuteronomic and Deuteronomistic preachers.[45] For since history contained promises of blessing and threats of curse (Dtn 11:19–28), it pertained to coming generations. Just so—that is the colossal affirmation of this early apocalyptic author—the events that have now begun to take place pertain to generations yet to come. This becomes comprehensible only if that which is to be reported comprises not only the current calamity (1:4ff), but also the word of God manifest therein, which is also introduced in narrative style (2:18–19).[46] We find here, therefore, an unfolding of that which concerns the future generations (3:1; 4:1).

Also new in comparison with the Deuteronomic pareneses, it is here not only the immediate future which is spoken of, but beyond it explicitly the third and fourth generations. The development of an unbroken chain of tradents is a sapiential characteristic (cf. Prv 4:1ff). Just as this concern is linked with traditions from salvation history in Ps 78:1ff,[47] it is linked here, in the transition from prophecy to apocalypticism, with the end–time events that have broken into the present.[48] Alfred Jepsen[49] has seen correctly that if one wants to attribute the direct references to the Day of Yahweh and the related passages[50] to a secondary revision, then it is also necessary to attribute the opening section in 1:2–4 to the same apocalyptic author. In such case, however, the remainder of the book falls completely apart. In 1:2–4 we hear the same Joel who first shaped into a unified proclamation the multiplicity of individual traditions appropriated in the book.

■ 4 His starting point is a total economic crisis caused by locusts. Its scope is illustrated by the fact that the locusts, in their various phases of development, have carried out their work of destruction so effectively (cf. 2:25) that it will be felt for years to come.

44 Am 3:3–6; Is 5:4; 28:23–28; Jer 2:10–11; Is 66:8–9.
45 Ex 12:26–27; 13:8; Dtn 4:9; 6:6–7, 20–23; 32:7ff.
46 Cf. Sellin.
47 Cf. Kraus, *Psalmen*, 542.
48 Cf. von Rad, *Theology* 2, 301–08 [314–21], on the sapiential rootage of apocalyptic.
49 "Kleine Beiträge zum Zwölfprophetenbuch," *ZAW* 56 (1938): 86.
50 1:15; 2:1aβ, 1b, 2aα, 10, 11; 3:4, 5; 4:1, 14b, 16aα, 16b, 17b, 18–20.

The Designations for the Locusts

Credner (1831) was the first to maintain that the names for locusts which occur here refer not to different types of insects, but to four developmental stages of the migrant locust. This has been confirmed by Aharoni,[51] Sellers,[52] and Thompson.[53] The designation for locust most often used in the Old Testament is ארבה; it refers to the fully developed, winged migrant locust which can reach a length of almost 6 cm.[54] The Hebrew term carries overtones of the root רב ("great"), suggesting "dense swarm." Up to ten times in a few weeks, the female lays packages of eggs containing about 20 each. The eggs are developed in three weeks, but in winter a diapause usually sets in. ילק ("hopper") probably designates the youngest locust, just hatched from the egg, with wing structures still invisible, i.e., the larva of the first stage (cf. Jer 51:27). חסיל ("jumper") designates the next stage, in which the wing structures are still folded together and enclosed in a sack, but are nevertheless clearly recognizable, the insect having a length of 2–3 cm. (cf. Is 33:4). גזם ("biter") designates the insect with respect to its destructive activity (cf. Am 4:9), since this root in Aramaic, Syriac, and Arabic (ǧzm) always means "to cut." It may well refer to the penultimate stage, therefore, in which the insects are winged, but as yet have not undertaken migratory flight. But it is also possible that גזם is a different designation, alongside ארבה ("locust"), for the fully grown insect, in which case גזם might mean the indigenous, solitary locust, and ארבה the gregarious creature that has flown in from elsewhere. Modern entomologists distinguish five larva stages before the adult stage.[55]

A change in the order of names in 1:4 to agree with 2:25, as proposed by Sellers,[56] cannot be justified by knowledge of the developmental stages, since identification of the Hebrew names with developmental stages represents no more than hypothesis; furthermore, the usage of the designations varies in the Old Testament.

I am indebted to conversations with my zoologist colleague Prof. H. Mislin and the entomologist Dr. Engelmann for the following further clarifications: 1. The different names need not refer to different developmental phases, but can vary, (a) because originally different designations were at home in different regions, without referring necessarily to different insects; (b) because different invading swarms of the same species can be named differently; (c) because the adult form shows differences in color, especially between the gregarious and the solitary forms. 2. The migrant locust does not undergo a metamorphosis as pronounced as those of butterflies, bees, and flies, in so far as it has no dormant pupa stage. Thus it already has a wing structure in the earliest larva stage though, to be sure, this was not recognizable to the ancient observer. One cannot compare the locomotion of the young larvae with the "creeping" of caterpillars; they already "hop" and "jump" like the adult insects. Therefore the translation "creeper" is in no case appropriate.[57] 3. The mode of feeding of the locusts is also basically the same in all phases. (a) Their "biting" is a sharp "cutting." Therefore the translations "gnawer"[58] and "licker"[59] must disappear from our commentaries as inappropriate. (b) Even the larvae do not only eat grass and seed crops, but like the fully grown insects, are already able to devour tree fruits and to strip twigs and shoots (cf. 1:6f).

The four designations attested in Joel 1:4 and 2:25 appear elsewhere in the Old Testament singly or in pairs.[60] As a punishment sent by Yahweh[61] locusts are cause for repentance.[62] They are known in par-

51 Israel Aharoni, *Hā'arbēh* [Hebrew] (Jaffa, 1919), as cited in Gustaf Dalman, *Arbeit und Sitte in Palästina*, vol. 1/2 (Gütersloh, 1928 = Hildesheim: Georg Olms, 1964), 393f.
52 "Stages," 81–85.
53 "Locusts," 52–55.
54 Dalman, *Arbeit* 1/2, 394; and *Arbeit* 2, pls. 75, 76.
55 Tracey Irwin Storer and Robert Leslie Usinger, *General Zoology* (New York: McGraw–Hill. ³1957), 410.
56 "Stages," 82.
57 Cf. still, however, Koehler–Baumgartner. 383.
58 Carl Friedrich Keil, *Biblischer Commentar über die Zwölf Kleinen Propheten*, BC 3/4 (Leipzig, ³1888); Sellin; Johannes Theis, "Der Prophet Joel" in Joseph Lippl and Johannes Theis, *Die Zwölf Kleinen Propheten*, vol. 1, HS 8/3/1 (Bonn, 1937); Hellmuth

Frey, *Das Buch der Kirche in der Weltwende: Die kleinen nachexilischen Propheten*, BAT 24 (Stuttgart, 1941); Weiser.
59 Keil, Robinson, and Frey.
60 Thus 1 Kgs 8:37; Ps 78:46; 105:34; Na 3:15, 17.
61 Dtn 28:38; Am 7:1; Is 33:4.
62 Am 4:9; 1 Kgs 8:37; 2 Chr 6:28.

ticular as one of the last plagues upon Egypt.[63] Nowhere else, however, is there any reference to the destructive work of several developmental stages in succession. In the Yahwistic account of the plagues, the locusts devour what the hail left over.[64] Nowhere else do we find four locust types with different names. Thus it is not surprising that the fourfold enumeration was already regarded in early times as an apocalyptic *topos*, marking the completeness of the report.[65] And yet it is surely amiss to see here images for the political enemies of Israel, or even for the world powers as such, analogous to the four beasts referred to in Dan 7.[66] Already Ephraem the Syrian in his commentary on Joel (c. 350) interpreted the "biter" as Tiglath-pileser, the "locust" as Shalmaneser, the "hopper" as Sennacherib, and the "jumper" as Nebuchadnezzar.[67] The remainder of the chapter shows quite clearly that Joel has in mind damages to the harvest caused by real locusts (cf. vv 5–20). Outside of Israel, locusts are often compared with armies and armies with locusts, but locusts are never symbols for peoples or their rulers.[68]

Even in recent decades it has been experienced how devastating locust plagues in Palestine can be. Gustaf Dalman reports:[69] "In Jerusalem the locusts appeared at that time in flights lasting for hours, like clouds from the northeast and south, from the 22nd to the 27th of March. . . . At the end of May and the beginning of June the first hatching of eggs, deposited by them into the ground, appeared as wingless larvae . . ., which wander about and eat up everything green that they encounter. Wild growth, grain, the leaves of fig trees, vines, even olive trees, everything disappears where they move along. They cover the walls of houses, penetrate to the inside through doors and windows, just as Ex 10:5f assumes. Following a sixfold shedding, the wings appear after approximately two months, and twenty days later they fly on . . ., to invade other regions."

Joel, in his lapidary three–line report, gives expression to the total destruction. One can attempt to explain the four stages something like this: The "biter" (גזם), i.e., the insect that had grown up locally in a solitary fashion, did not devour nearly everything. The actual catastrophe began with the gregarious swarms that in huge numbers flew in (ארבה). Their ample brood hatched a month or two later in the same year, or perhaps in the next spring; in the first (ילק) and the second (חסיל) developmental phases they stripped the land down to the very last remainder. Then the total denudation forced them to move on. According to 2:25 more than the harvest yield of one year is destroyed.[70] Joel uses the factitive perfect (אכל ["to eat, devour"] three times) in his literary presentation, i.e., the grammatical form that highlights the action as such; it is the facticity of the happening that is emphasized.[71] When it is stated three times that even "the leftovers" have been "devoured," this expresses forcefully right at the beginning that attention has been awakened for something extreme, for an eschaton which has entered the field of vision at this point in history.

■ **5** After the forceful presentation of the facts, the call to lamentation shows how strongly people are affected by them. It begins as an awakening call. Until now, the wine of the previous year has robbed the drunkards of their watchfulness.[72] The vocative, as a rule definite (cf. vv 2, 13), stands here without an article, as is also frequently the case elsewhere.[73] Those addressed by this call do not yet see the present reality. Their careless mirth is the drowsiness of sleepers. Only those that have been awakened are able to weep and to wail when they see that they will be without their drink. עסיס is the juice of the new vintage; it is not yet wine in the jug, but rather that which "flows in the vineyards" (4:18; Am 9:13), trampled and crushed from the

---

63 Ex 10:3–19; Ps 78:46; 105:34.
64 On the threefold use of יתר ("to leave over, remain") in Joel 1:4, cf. Ex 10:5, 15.
65 Cf. already Jer 15:2–3; Ezek 14:21.
66 Cf. the reference to four metals in Dan 2.
67 Cf. also Targum Jonathan on 2:25; see textual note "m" to 2:25.
68 On representations of locusts in extrabiblical texts and pictures, cf. Thompson, "Locusts," 54f.
69 *Arbeit* 1/2, 393f (based on Israel Aharoni's description of the locust plague of 1915–16).
70 See p. 64.

71 Cf. most recently Diethelm Michel, *Tempora und Satzstellung in den Psalmen*, Abhandlungen zur evangelischen Theologie 1 (Bonn: Bouvier & Co., 1960), 99, 254.
72 Cf. Hos 4:11; Is 5:11–12.
73 Cf. 1:11; Hos 13:14; Mi 1:2; and Brockelmann, *Syntax*, par. 10.

grapes there in the winepress.[74] It is "cut off from their mouth." Thus the motivation points harshly to the personal reasons for lamentation. Following the locust plague of 1915, wine prices doubled.[75] There is nothing here that would make it necessary to think of the ancient fertility cults;[76] everything becomes intelligible on the basis of a postexilic situation caused by a harvest disaster.

■ 6 The locust plague as the cause of the distress is compared to the advance of a hostile people. In Prv 30:27 this simile is also found, and there the "wisdom" (v 24) of the locusts is seen in the fact that they "march in rank," even though they have "no king." Otherwise Joel's language here is reminiscent of divine speech as it is familiar on the basis of Ezek 38:16 and the threat there of Gog who "came up against my land" (עלה על־ארצי) from the north. This motif, "he comes up against my land," quite clearly prepares the ground for the cry of terror in v 15. That locusts appear "beyond numbering" (Ps 105:34; cf. Ex 10:4–6, 12–15) had been proverbial since ancient times, especially with reference to hostile armies.[77] Similarly, "powerful" (עצום) in this context (as in 2:2, 5) connotes more the idea "multitude" than "power" as such.[78] The destructive power of the locusts is exposed by a comparison of their teeth with "lion's teeth."[79] Job 4:10 also speaks of lion's teeth; they are the weapons without which lions cannot live. Jer 4:6–7 compares the enemy from the north with the lion.[80] "Fangs" (מתלעות)[81] is found only in parallelism with "tooth" (שן): Prv 30:14; Job 29:17; Ps 58:7 [6].

■ 7 The work of the locusts' teeth is portrayed here. The trees, branches, and vines are stripped white of their bark. The shining "shoots" and twigs lie around; "waste" (שמה) means the total devastation, especially by foreign troops (Hos 5:9). "Breaking down" (קצפה) means the mutilation by breaking away of the twigs (cf. Hos 10:7). Just as reference is made to "my land" in v 6, we hear here, in unusual divine speech, of "my vine" and "my fig tree." Thereby reference is made to the special signs of the time of salvation.[82] In this way already in the first strophe the locust invasion is indirectly cited as the end of salvation history so far. Thus vv 6–7 make it clear why the wine drinkers are the first group to be called to lamentation.

■ 8 In the second strophe the group of those addressed can no longer be identified, due to the mutilation of the text.[83] Perhaps "the daughter of my people" (cf. Jer 6:26) is meant collectively; to think of the land (cf. ארצי "my land" v 6a) is less advisable, in view of vv 9a and 10a ("land" אדמה). Here already, by way of comparison, girding with śaq is added to weeping and wailing, as a rite of mourning and repentance.[84] The śaq was a coarsely woven piece of material, generally made of goat's hair and therefore usually black in the Near East. After the rending of the garment (2 Sam 3:31) the śaq was put on the bare body around the hips (Gen 37:34; 1 Kgs 21:27), often covering only the loins; at least it left the chest free for the "beating" which was also a part of mourning practice (Is 32:11–12).[85] In the ancient Near East,[86] just as in ancient Israel, the śaq was worn in situations of personal

---

74 Cf. עסס "to press, crush" in Mal 3:21 [4:3].

75 John A. Thompson, "The Book of Joel: Introduction and Exegesis" in *The Interpreter's Bible*, vol. 6 (New York and Nashville: Abingdon, 1956), 738.

76 Kapelrud, *Joel*; Bič.

77 Cf. Ju 6:5; 7:12; Jer 51:14; Na 3:15–17. The simile is already attested at Ugarit: "Like locusts they tent on the field; like grasshoppers, on the borders of the range" [Trans. by Ed.] (*km 'irby . tškn šd . kšn . p'at mdbr*; *CTA* 14 [= *UT* Krt].192–194, cf. 103–104).

78 Cf. especially Mi 4:3 along with Is 2:4; cf. further Am 5:12; Jer 5:6; Dtn 26:5. On the point, cf. H. W. Hertzberg, "Die 'Abtrünnigen' und die 'Vielen'. Ein Beitrag zu Jesaja 53" in *Verbannung und Heimkehr: Beiträge zur Geschichte und Theologie Israels im 6. und 5. Jahrhundert v. Chr. (Festschrift für Wilhelm Ru-*

dolph), ed. Arnulf Kuschke (Tübingen: J. C. B. Mohr [Paul Siebeck], 1961), 105.

79 So also in Rev 9:8.

80 On 2:20, see pp. 62–63. On the different words for "lion," cf. Friedrich Horst, *Hiob*, BK 16/1 (Neukirchen–Vluyn: Neukirchener Verlag, 1968), 70.

81 Cf. Arabic *lth*, "to bite."

82 See Hos 2:14 [12] and Wolff, *Hosea*, 38 [46].

83 See textual note "i" to 1:8.

84 Cf. Gustav Stählin, "σάκκος," *TDNT* 7, 56–64.

85 See pp. 32–33 on 1:13.

86 Cf. *AOB*, figs. 198, 665; and *ANEP*, figs. 459, 634.

mourning,[87] as well as in those involving communal mourning.[88] It functioned as a visible representation of distress and humiliation. "Rabbi Ḥiyya' ben 'Abba' [c. 300] has said: 'One wants to say with it: Behold, we are accounted like cattle!' "[89] The thought here is that the *śaq* is made of goats' hair.

The simile in which the *śaq* occurs depicts the mourning of a young girl who lost her beloved, prior to marriage. To be sure, most recently it has been held that the terms בתולה and בעל נעורים are mutually exclusive, since the former clearly designates the unmarried "virgin" and the latter is the legal "husband."[90] Therefore, it is claimed, one must think here of the myth wherein the goddess 'Anat mourns the death of her beloved Ba'l.[91] Against this we must note, first, that in Joel's era this myth was hardly so familiar that, given the present wording, the assumed allusion would have been intelligible; second, the two terms may be readily interpreted on the basis of Israelite matrimonial law.

Who is the בעל נעורים?

The expression is unattested elsewhere. בעל immediately suggests the "husband," who, as the legal "owner" of his wife, is called בַּעַל אִשָּׁה (literally "owner of a wife" Ex 21:3), just as the wife, as his property, is the בְּעֻלַת בַּעַל (literally "owned of [by] a husband" Gen 20:3). Given this legal terminology, it seems to be impossible at first that a בתולה—since she is, after all, always an unmarried young woman (cf. Ex 22:15 [16])—should be associated with a בעל. But one must ask here, (1) what בעל נעורים signifies, and (2) what is the precise usage of בתולה.

1. As a parallel to the otherwise unattested בעל נעורים, the Old Testament knows of a אֵשֶׁת נְעוּרִים (Prv 5:18; Is 54:6; Mal 2:14–15). That designation once again seems to exclude the term "virgin" in our

passage. Yet one must remember that "youth" (נעורים) legally means, in similar contexts, the time before marriage (Nu 30:17 [16]; cf. Hos 2:17 [15]), especially the time of betrothal (Jer 2:2). Therefore, אשת נעורים designates the wife as one who was already beloved before the marriage had been concluded. Accordingly, "husband of youth" should mean the husband who was beloved in the time of youth. Roland de Vaux[92] has pointed out that girls in ancient Israel were neither locked up nor veiled, but that there was ample opportunity "for falling in love, and for expressing their feelings," when tending the flocks (Gen 29:6), when fetching water (Gen 24:13; 1 Sam 9:11), when gleaning in the fields (Ruth 2:2f), etc.

2. The בתולה can be that "virgin" who, though not yet initiated into marriage, nevertheless has been acquired as אִשָּׁה by the binding legal act of paying the bridal price, so that to this extent she was already the partner of a בעל. Dtn 22:23–24 witnesses to this identity between a "virgin" (v 23) and a "wife" (אֵשֶׁת רֵעֵהוּ ["his neighbor's wife"] v 24). She is precisely such a fiancée whom the man has already legally "acquired" (ארש) but has not yet brought into his home, not yet "taken" (לקח Dtn 20:7).[93] It follows that the "virgin" can very well be paired with a "husband" at this particular stage, just as she can already be considered as "wife" (אִשָּׁה) after the legal act of the payment of the bridal price.

The בעל נעורים must probably be distinguished, therefore, from the אַלּוּף נְעוּרִים, the "confidant" or "friend of the time of youth," the "beloved" (Prv 2:17; Jer 3:4). Rather, he is that beloved one who has already paid the *mōhar* (the purchase–price of a wife) and has thereby become legally a "husband of a wife" (בעל אשה), even though he has not as yet taken home his wife. To be sure, then, the young woman can already be called "wife" (אשה Dtn 22:24), but just as appropriately she can still be called "virgin" (בתולה Dtn 22:23).

---

87 Gen 37:34; 2 Sam 21:10.
88 2 Sam 3:31; Is 3:24; 15:3; Jer 48:37; Lam 2:10.
89 Babylonian Talmud, Ta'anit 16a, according to Hermann Strack and Paul Billerbeck, *Kommentar zum Neuen Testament aus Talmud und Midrasch*, vol. 4 (München: Beck, 1961), 84 n. 4.
90 Flemming Friis Hvidberg, *Weeping and Laughter in the Old Testament: A Study of Canaanite–Israelite Religion*, tr. Niels Haislund (København: Nyt Nordisk Forlag, A. Busck; 1962), 140–42; Kapelrud, *Joel*, 32; Bič.
91 Cf. *CTA* 5 (= *UT* 67). 6.25–31; translations: H. L.

Ginsberg, *ANET*[3], 139b; G. R. Driver, *Canaanite Myths and Legends*, Old Testament Studies 3 (Edinburgh: T. & T. Clark, 1956), 109.
92 *Ancient Israel: Its Life and Institutions*, tr. John McHugh (New York: McGraw–Hill, 1961), 30.
93 Cf. Wolff, *Hosea*, 52 [63f].

The correspondence of בתולה ("virgin") and בעל נעורים ("husband of youth") points us to a time of love in which separation through death is especially cruel. For the "husband of youth," as "bridegroom," must be distinguished from the אַלּוּף נְעוּרִים, the "friend of youth" before the decisive legal act of concluding the marriage. Death takes place in the brief time span between this legal act of "acquiring" and the act of "taking into the home."[94] In this way the terminological correspondence between בתולה and the בעל נעורים becomes fully intelligible.

At the same time, this clarifies the special character of the simile. The devastating distress, which has befallen the land so suddenly and unexpectedly, demands a lamentation comparable in its intensity only to that of the young woman who has lost the beloved of her youth shortly before marriage. The image underscores the extremely rare nature of the distress over which Jerusalem is to lament.

■ **9** The temple service is endangered. "Meal–offerings and libations" were to be offered twice daily, in the morning and in the evening. For the "meal–offering" (מנחה) flour and oil were needed, while the "libation" (נסך) required wine. Together therefore these represent the products of the land threatened by the locusts. "Meal–offerings and libations" occur in this pairing only in later postexilic texts.[95] "House of Yahweh" (vv 9, 14) and "house of God" (vv 13, 16) correspond to postexilic language usage.[96] Furthermore, "ministers of Yahweh / of the altar" (משרתי יהוה / מזבח cf. v 13; 2:17), in the form of an apposition in the plural, points

to late postexilic times.[97] For Joel the cessation of the *tāmîd*–offering (the "continual/regular sacrifice") is also extremely important in v 13 and in 2:14. With its absence "the blessing" of the God of Israel has also become ineffective (cf. 2:14). Especially affected are the "priests," who mourn even though joy and jubilation ought to prevail before Yahweh (v 16; cf. Dtn 16:11; 26:11). They themselves live on their share of the daily sacrifice (Lev 2:3, 10), but they also can no longer discern the sacrifice as a sign of the saving communion with the God of Israel (Ex 29:42).[98] With the designation "minister" (משרת) Joel depicted the priest not so much as a personal servant of Yahweh (as Ezek 44:15), but rather as an attendant, supervisor, and caretaker of his house. This is shown clearly by the interpretation of the "ministers of Yahweh" (1:9 *M*; 2:17) by means of the designation "ministers of the altar" (1:9 *G*; 1:13). For in Joel's view, after all, it is not Yahweh who lacks the meal–offerings and libations, but the "house of Yahweh" (1:9, 13, 16; but cf. 2:14b).[99] Joel, then, directs special attention to the temple services and the priests, both here and also later in vv 13, 16; 2:17. Yet his attitude to these is quite similar to that displayed toward the wine–drinkers in v 5, and the peasants and vinedressers in v 11. The incipient events also endanger precisely that which goes on in the Temple and in which one finds assurance of salvation.[100]

■ **10** It is of basic importance that Joel has a comprehensive view of the total fate of Jerusalem and Judah. The land, as the ancient and basic gift of salvation

---

94 See the preceding excursus.

95 Cf. Ex 29:38–42; Lev 23:13, 18; Nu 6:15; 15:24; 28:3–9; 29:11, 16–39. The word pair is not yet attested in Ezr 9:4 and Neh 10:34. Cf. on this point Wilhelm Rudolph, *Ezra und Nehemia*, HAT 1/20 (Tübingen: J. C. B. Mohr [Paul Siebeck], 1949), 89f.

96 Cf. Théophane Chary, *Les prophètes et le culte à partir de l'exil autour du Second Temple. L'idéal cultuel des prophètes exiliens et postexiliens*, Bibliothèque de Théologie 3/3 (Tournai: Desclée & Cie, 1955), 127f, 197, 199f.

97 Cf. 2 Chr 29:11; Ezr 8:17; cf. also Chary, *Les prophètes*, 197f.

98 Cf. Gerhard von Rad, *Old Testament Theology*, vol. 1: *The Theology of Israel's Historical Traditions*, tr. D. M. G. Stalker (New York: Harper & Row, 1962), 257 [*Theologie des Alten Testaments*, vol. 1: *Die Theologie*

der geschichtlichen Überlieferungen Israels, Einführung in die evangelische Theologie 1 (München: Chr. Kaiser, ²1962), 255].

99 Cf. L. A. Snijders, "Knechten en Bedienden," *Nederlands Theologisch Tijdschrift* 16 (1961–62): 344–60.

100 Cf. Dan 8:11; 11:31; 12:11.

history—with its yields of "grain, new–wine, and olive–oil" (these appearing in their classic sequence)[101]—is devastated and dried out.[102] This fulfills ancient prophetic threats of judgment.[103] Now the subject is no longer, as in vv 6–7, the locust invasion, but rather a drought which accompanied and intensified that catastrophe. With the loss of the grain, the new–wine and the oil, the products needed for the meal–offerings and libations are lacking (v 9a).[104] A first climax is reached with the conclusion of the second strophe. Externally the alliterations in vv 10a and 10bβ show the intensified passion of speech,[105] rooted in the memory of the classic gifts of salvation and of the prophetic threat of their destruction.

■ **11–12** The third strophe turns to peasants and vine–dressers whose products were already mentioned at the end of the second strophe. "Be ashamed!" (הוביֹשׁו) is just as unique among the calls to communal lamentation as "awake!" (הקיצו) in v 5.[106] This is a sign that the strophic formation does not merely take up traditional material, but has been created by Joel for the occasion at hand. The choice of words may be determined by word play with the hipʻil of יבֹשׁ ("to be dry") in v 10bβ. Lack of a harvest is a disgrace for the peasant, just as childlessness is for parents (Ps 127:3–5), for it is evidence that the blessing has been withdrawn (2:14). "Tillers" (אכרים) and "vinedressers" (כרמים) are

otherwise mentioned together only in 2 Chr 26:10 and Is 61:5, where they are landless agricultural workers.[107] The destroyed yields of their harvest are individually enumerated in long chains: wheat and barley, wine and figs, pomegranates, dates, apples and other tree fruits.[108] Joy withers together with the harvest (cf. Is 9:2 [3]); it gives way to shame. The dual association of הוביש (cf. v 10b with v 11a) is probably intended even though the distinction between "to be ashamed" (הוביש) and "to be withered" (יבֹשׁ qal) makes one think more of shame (as in v 11a). Thérèse Frankfort wants to interpret כִּי causally: the locusts are supposed to have spoilt the peasants' joy in taking care of the irrigation installations.[109] Compare however v 7a; syntactically כִּי has the same emphatic function here as in v 10b and 2:22b.[110]

■ **13** With the fourth strophe the call to communal lamentation reaches its goal, announcing to the priests the exact ritual instructions that are necessary for the lament's implementation. "Gird!" (חגרו) is an ellipsis (just as in Is 32:11b), with "sackcloth" (שַׂקִּים) understood to be the object.[111] Since the chest is bared in the process of putting on the śaq, there follows, in keeping with the ritual, the command "lament!" (ספדו).[112] This command calls for striking one's chest, so as to add one pain to another.[113] The striking is followed by wailing,[114] or crying.[115] In the event of

---

101 Cf. Hos 2:10 [8] and Wolff, *Hosea*, 37 [44].
102 On (ד)שׁד ("devastation, to devastate"), see p. 21.
103 On אמלל / אבל ("to mourn" / "to fade away"), cf. Hos 4:3 and Wolff, *Hosea*, 68 [85]. On יבֹשׁ / אבל ("to mourn" / "to be dry"), cf. Am 1:2. הוביש ("dried up") in the context of the parallelism is to be understood as the hipʻil of יבֹשׁ (cf. 1:12a, 20): so Friedrich Nötscher, *Zwölfprophetenbuch oder Kleine Propheten*, Echter–Bibel (Würzburg: Echter–Verlag, 1948); Deden; and Thompson; *contra* Koehler–Baumgartner, Robinson, and Weiser who read here (as in 1:11a) the hipʻil of בושׁ ("to be ashamed").
104 See p. 31.
105 [In transliteration, the Hebrew reads: *šuddad śādeh ʾābĕlāh ʾădāmāh . . . hôbîš tîrôš.* Trans.]
106 But cf. Is 23:4.
107 Cf. Am 5:16, and Hartmut Gese, "Kleine Beiträge zum Verständnis des Amosbuches," *VT* 12 (1962): 432ff.
108 On this, cf. Martin Noth, *The Old Testament World*, tr. Victor I. Gruhn (Philadelphia: Fortress, 1966),

33ff [*Die Welt des Alten Testaments: Einführung in die Grenzgebiete der alttestamentlichen Wissenschaft*, Sammlung Töpelmann 2/3 (Berlin: A. Töpelmann, ⁴1962), 30f]; and Dalman, *Arbeit* 1/1, 57ff.
109 "Le כִּי de Joël 1:12," *VT* 10 (1960): 445–48.
110 Cf. Wolff, *Hosea*, 135 [173].
111 2 Sam 3:31; Jer 4:8; 6:26; 49:3. Cf. Joel 1:8 and see pp. 29–30.
112 As also in 2 Sam 3:31; Jer 4:8; 49:3; Is 32:12.
113 Cf. Jer 49:3aβ: "scratch yourselves raw!" (?).
114 So also Jer 4:8; 49:3; Mi 1:8.
115 Gen 23:2; 2 Sam 1:12; Ezek 24:16, 23.

especially vehement grief one spends the night in sack-cloth (1 Kgs 21:27; 2 Sam 12:16), also practicing sexual abstinence (Dan 6:19 [18]).[116] The reason for the lamentation given in v 9 is repeated:[117] the daily sacrifice is halted, and, consequently, so too is communion with God.

■ 14 The instructions of v 14 still pertain to the priests. Now however they are no longer concerned with their own exercises of penance, but with those which they are to induce the people to perform. The exhortation "Announce a holy fast!" stands parallel to the following instructions. קדש ("to sanctify") alongside קרא ("to call") expresses the injunction that a cultic act be performed.[118] In this case the cultic act is precisely that of fasting, which usually lasts for one day (Ju 20:26; 1 Sam 14:24), as a sign of submission to the decreed calamity. Along with the fast, rest from all work is prescribed. For עצרה here does not yet mean the "assembly" as such, which is commanded only afterwards, but "withdrawal from work" and thus "solemn holiday."[119] Then, further, the fasting, "festive people" is to be called to the "assembly." Since not only the elders, but "all the inhabitants of the land" are to come into the Temple, the smallness of the postexilic community of Jerusalem and Judah is evident. The purpose of this assembly is the crying to Yahweh always associated with fasting.[120] With the invocation of God, the goal of the summons to communal lamentation has been reached. We sense nothing in Joel of that critical disposition towards the cultus, and especially towards its customary fasting rituals, which we find in Jeremiah (14:12), Trito–Isaiah (58:1–14) and Zechariah (7:5–7). At the same time, though, the instructions regarding the cultus are by no means his real concern. Instead, the great call to communal lamentation only prepares the way for recognition of the significance of the extraordinary hour.

■ 15 The cry of terror—"Alas for the day!"—calls it by name.[121] The hour of extraordinary calamity of the land, caused by the locusts and the drought, is now recognizable as the harbinger of the approaching Day of Yahweh. With the catchword "Day of Yahweh" (יום יהוה) Joel has, after the stirring prelude of vv 2–14, reached his theme proper, which permeates all further parts of the book as its *cantus firmus* (2:1–2, 11; 3:4; 4:14). Nowhere else in the Old Testament is the Day of Yahweh treated in as sustained a way as in the book of Joel.

The "Day of Yahweh"

The expression "Day of Yahweh" (יום יהוה) is attested eleven times in the Old Testament outside the book of Joel, occurring in oracles against Israel (Am 5:18a, 18b, 20; Zech 1:7, 14a, 14b; Mal 3:23 [4:5]; and Ezek 13:5 [referring to a past day]) and against the nations (Is 13:6, 9 [against Babylon in particular] and Ob 15 [against Edom in particular]). Besides these, it occurs five times in the book of Joel alone: against Israel 1:15; 2:1, 11; against the nations 3:4 and 4:14.

In this construct expression "day" (יום) does not mean a definite *extent* of time, but rather a definite *event* in time whose nature is determined by the associated personal name.[122] In this connection "Yahweh" is not the one to whom something happens,[123] but the one who by his appearance and his acting is in complete control of the temporal event. This is made clear by the related designations in twenty–one additional passages which must also be considered: "day for Yahweh" (יום ליהוה) Ezek 30:3; "day for Yahweh of hosts" (יום ליהוה צבאות) Is 2:12; "day of tumult for the Lord Yahweh of hosts" (יום מְהוּמָה לַאדֹנָי יהוה צְבָאוֹת) Is 22:5; "day of the wrath of Yahweh" (יום עֶבְרַת יהוה) Zeph 1.15a, 18; Ezek 7:19; "day of the anger of Yahweh" (יום אַף יהוה) Zeph 2:2, 3; Lam 2:22; 2:1, 21; "day of his burning anger" (יום חֲרוֹן אַפּוֹ) Lam 1:12; "day of Yahweh's vengeance" (יום נָקָם ליהוה) Is 34:8; Jer 46:10; Is 61:2; "day of Yahweh's sacrifice" (יום זֶבַח יהוה) Zeph 1:8; "day of clouds and thick darkness" (יום עָנָן וַעֲרָפֶל) Zeph 1:15b; Ezek 34:12; Joel 2:2; then also "a day of distress and anguish, a day of ruin and devastation, a day of darkness and gloom" יום צָרָה

---

116 1 Kgs 21:27; 2 Sam 12:16.

117 See p. 31.

118 Cf. 2:16; 4:9; Jer 6:4; 2 Kgs 10:20; Ezek 20:20.

119 Lev 23:36; Nu 29:35; Dtn 16:8. On this point, see Ernst Kutsch, "Die Wurzel עצר im Hebräischen," *VT* 2 (1952): 57–69.

120 1 Sam 7:6; Jer 14:12; Neh 1:4; 9:1–4; Ezr 8:21, 23.

121 On אההה ("Ah! Alas!") as a cry of defensive, startled fright, see pp. 22–23.

122 Cf. 2 Sam 23:20 ("day of snow"); Is 9:3 [4] ("day of Midian").

123 Cf. Ob 12; Ezek 21:30 [25]; Job 18:20.

(וּמְעוּקָה יוֹם שֹׁאָה וּמְשׁוֹאָה יוֹם חֹשֶׁךְ וַאֲפֵלָה) Zeph 1:15b, in addition to the earlier phrases from that passage (the last three words are found also in Joel 2:2a, 2b); further, "a day of trumpet blast and battle cry" (יוֹם שׁוֹפָר וּתְרוּעָה) Zeph 1:16a; also "the day of which I have spoken" (הַיּוֹם אֲשֶׁר דִּבַּרְתִּי) Ezek 39:8; "a day for Yahweh is coming" (יוֹם־בָּא לַיהוה) Zech 14:1; and "a day when he fights on a day of battle" (יוֹם הִלָּחֲמוֹ בְּיוֹם קְרָב) Zech 14:3. Of these, the four passages in Lamentations, and Ezek 34:12, refer to the destruction of Jerusalem in 587. Eight of these designations appear in prophetic threats directed against Israel: Is 2:12; Zeph 1:8, 15a, 15b, 18; 2:2, 3; and Ezek 7:19. Five are found in oracles against other nations: Is 61:2 and Ezek 30:3, specifically against Egypt; Jer 46:10 and Is 34:8, against Edom; and Ezek 39:8, against Gog. Finally, Zech 14:1(–3) must be noted as the only passage apart from Joel in which the Day of Yahweh is directed first against Israel and then against the nations.

Zech 14:1, 3 along with Joel 2:1–11; 4:9–17; Zeph 1:15ff; Is 13; 34; and Ezek 30 show quite clearly that the conception of the Day of Yahweh derives largely from the holy war traditions.[124] To these traditions are added certain features of theophany descriptions.[125] All the texts deal at the same time with Israel and the nations, and in all of them the wrath of Yahweh is a decisive feature. The most important difference, which divides the texts into two groups, is that the Day of Yahweh was directed originally against the nations and then against Israel. In the classical examples, drawn from the beginnings of Israel, the "day" is directed against the nations that threaten the people of God.[126] Only later is the "day" turned against Israel which has deserted its God, i.e., against Jerusalem.[127] This reversal occurred with the "threat of judgment" announced by the prophets, which can be seen especially clearly in Is 28:21. And this happened by virtue of the fact that the prophets began to speak of that "day" as a future day. It is in this decisive shift from a salvation-history perspective to one of eschatological judgment that we meet for the first

time the designation יום יהוה in its pregnant form (Am 5:18–20; cf. Is 2:6–22). Only after the fulfillment of the prophetic threats in the catastrophe of Jerusalem is the Day of Yahweh announced increasingly as a day of Yahweh's wrath directed against the nations. The beginnings of apocalypticism exhibited in the Old Testament are distinguished, as far as the Day of Yahweh is concerned, by the fact that they combine the two types transmitted within the received prophetic oracles, i.e., the day of wrath against Israel and the one against the nations. This is what happens in Zech 14 (cf. Ezek 38–39) and above all in Joel 1–4.

In the incipient calamity Joel sees the omen of the final day of judgment against Israel announced by the prophets. The basis for this perception is prepared right from the start by the depiction of the catastrophe as a total and completely unusual one (1:2–4) which endangers cultic communion with God (1:9, 13). Hence also the calamity is portrayed using features analogous to the extant Day of Yahweh threats: the locusts are described in vv 6–7 as the hostile *nation*,[128] and the devastation by drought ("to devastate" שׁדד v 10) already carries overtones of the term "destruction" (שֹׁד).[129]

Therefore: "The Day of Yahweh is near" (קרוב יום יהוה). Joel thus incorporates the decisive and firmly formulated declaration from received tradition. It is familiar from Zeph 1:7, 14; Is 13:6; and Ezek 30:3, and is repeated by Joel in 2:1 and 4:14.[130] In Ezek 30:2–3 it was already connected with the appeal to lamentation and the cry of terror, just as here in vv 15a, 15b; in Is 13:6b it was already connected with the simile which follows here in v 15b. This simile employs a moving and terrifying play on words. The divine name "Shadday" (שׁדי), familiar in Israel through the Priestly Work,[131] resonates with the word שֹׁד (šōd), which

124 Cf. von Rad, *Theology* 2, 119–25 [133–37].
125 Cf. Bourke, "Le jour," 18f; and Ladislav Černý, *The Day of Yahweh and Some Relevant Problems*, Práce Z Vědeckých Ústavů 53 (V Praze: Nákladem Filosofické Fakulty University Karlovy, 1948).
126 Is 9:3 [4] = Ju 7; Is 28:21 = 2 Sam 5:20–25; Zech 14:3.
127 Lam 1:12; 2:1, 21, 22; Ezek 13:5?; 34:12. Only in such reflection upon the catastrophe of 587 does the precise concept of the יום יהוה appear with reference to the past.
128 Cf. Is 13:4ff; Ezek 30:3ff; 38:14ff.
129 Cf. 1:15bβ with Is 13:6b.
130 For the provenance of the exclamation in the ancient wars of Yahweh, see 4:14 and p. 74.
131 Gen 17:1; 28:3; 35:11; etc. On the prehistory of the name ('ēl) šadday, cf. Zimmerli, *Ezechiel*, 238f.

designates violent "devastation" and vehement destructions.[132] This "day" is not yet an accomplished fact, as is the locust invasion and the drought, but it is near; it is in the process of "coming" (יבוא imperfect). It is noteworthy that the declarations taken over verbatim from Ezek 30:2–3 and Is 13:6 are directed there against foreign nations, but here against Jerusalem—Judah, i.e., used in the sense of Am 5:18–20 and Zeph 1:7–18.

■ **16** Joel seeks confirmation from his hearers. To that end he once more emphasizes, in the form of a question, one of the features previously mentioned, the destruction of the daily temple service (cf. 1:9a, 13b). The hallmark of this service was "joy and rejoicing," because in it are celebrated the gifts of salvation and the communion with God to which they attest.[133] It is characteristic of Joel's different disposition towards the cultus that he can take up this word pair which is strictly avoided by Amos, Micah, Jeremiah, and Ezekiel. But the Jerusalem cultus, in which he participates together with his contemporaries, is for him no guarantee of final and ultimate salvation. The present catastrophe was to open the ears of his contemporaries to the transmitted, but as yet unfulfilled prophetic word. Hence his attention is focused not on the question of guilt, but rather on the phenomena of the calamity.

■ **17–18** These are brought into view in vv 17–18 by way of examples. The seed grain has shriveled under the clods of earth. This situation presupposes that the seed had been ploughed under before the beginning of the rainy season, or that it was sown as summer seed into parched land.[134] Here, as in 1:10 and 12, drought is the cause of the distress. The storehouses have fallen apart;[135] the flimsy material from which they were built has been torn down. This is a crass indication of the complete lack of a harvest; no supervisor has looked after the granaries. "Beasts" (בהמה) probably refers here to the domestic animals, distinct from the herds

of cattle named thereafter (cf. Lev 1:2). If so, the large cattle are endangered first. But if even the easily satisfied flocks of small cattle, accustomed to the grass of the steppes, no longer find pastures, then the cause must be a very prolonged drought. Alternatively, one has to think simultaneously here of the locust invasion;[136] for the locust swarms devour absolutely everything they find.[137] Although the formulation is in keeping with the style of the lament, the adoption of received formularies cannot be proved. Just as in the opening in v 16, it seems more probable that we have here an independent formulation born of the situation.

■ **19–20** In contrast, the final section exhibits more traditional phrases: compare Jer 9:9 [10]; 14:5–6; 23:10; Ps 42:2 [1]; 65:13 [12]; and 97:3. Scorching heat and drought are the lament motif. It seems as if here at the end of the section the prophet becomes the first to intone explicitly the lament song to which he has called all groups among the people in vv 5–14 (especially v 14b!), the decisive motifs having already been developed in lament form in the immediately preceding section. Everyman's lamentation here finds preliminary expression.

V 20bβ need not be secondary simply because it repeats v 19bα. The repetition of important phrases is a part of Joel's style (cf. vv 9a, 13b, 16) and is a means of intensification. The phrase repeated here is reminiscent of the devouring fire and the lapping flame in theophany descriptions,[138] such as belong directly to the Day of Yahweh depictions in Zeph 1:18 and Joel 2:3.[139] To this extent even the concluding section still interprets the cry of terror about the approaching Day of Yahweh found in 1:15.

Aim

The introductory chapter of the book of Joel seeks to portray the significance of a quite extraordinary calamity that has befallen the population of Jerusalem and Judah. A terrible locust plague that in several waves

---

132 Cf. Jer 5:6; 48:3.
133 Cf. 1:7a and see above, p. 29; cf. further 2:21, 23. On the history of the word pair "joy and rejoicing," see Wolff, *Hosea*, 153 [197].
134 Cf. Dalman, *Arbeit* 2, 130ff.
135 Cf. Kurt Galling, *Biblisches Reallexikon*, HAT 1/1 (Tübingen, 1937), 492f; and Dalman, *Arbeit* 3, 188ff.

136 Dalman, *Arbeit* 6, 176f.
137 See p. 28.
138 Cf. 1:19b with Ps 50:3; 97:3; 29:7.
139 See p. 44.

afflicted the country for more than a year coincided with a long–sustained drought affecting even the fruit trees and the smaller cattle (1:12, 18). Such a twofold disaster had once been averted by prophetic intercession on behalf of Israel (Am 7:1–6). Now Jerusalem is confronted by the same horror which the locusts once brought upon Egypt (Ex 10). As the Deuteronomic series of curses had proclaimed, the calamities of Egypt have now broken in upon the people of God (cf. Dtn 28:27, 33, 38, 49–51). It is possible that Joel knows this Deuteronomic tradition,[140] but it by no means leads him to admonish the people to listen to the voice of Yahweh in the Torah, as the Deuteronomists had done (cf. Dtn 28:1, 15, 45; 29:28 [29]).

Instead, the calamity stimulates him to give heed to the unfulfilled eschatological prophetic word about the Day of Yahweh. He takes up (1:15) the language of Ezek 30:2–3 and Is 13:6, even though these oracles were directed against foreign nations. He employs them in the sense in which the Day of Yahweh was treated first in Amos (5:18–20) and Isaiah (2:6–22), namely, directed against Israel, and then especially in Zephaniah (1:7–18), directed against Jerusalem. In this way an extremely critical word is spoken in veiled manner against the cultic community of Jerusalem which has constituted itself theocratically.[141] The history of salvation has not already reached its fulfillment in the cultus to which Joel so matter–of–factly assents. A final convulsive event is still to come, namely, that event which the prophetic word of the Day of Yahweh has announced.

Joel recognizes and proclaims as the meaning of the present calamity that it is a harbinger of this "day." Several features show clearly that all statements of this chapter are oriented towards the center in v 15—"For the Day of Yahweh is near; it comes like might from the Mighty One!" 1. The description of the calamity as such dominates the call to communal lamentation (vv 5–14)[142] as well as the subsequent lamentation itself (vv 16–20). The opening section already designates this calamity as a completely unusual and total one (1:2b, 4). 2. The locusts are described in a manner similar to that of the hostile army which the prophets announced for the Day of Yahweh (v 6).[143] 3. An unmistakable accent is placed on the fact that the incipient calamity endangers the daily temple service (vv 9b, 13b, 16).[144] This is an indication that Jerusalem's cultic community as such is not the ultimate goal of God's plans, when seen from the perspective of the God of Israel to whom the prophets give witness. Not until 2:25 is it stated explicitly that Yahweh has sent the locusts as his "great army." 4. From the outset the calamity is endowed with a significance that transcends the present generation. It actually acquires a salvation historical relevance for the future, comparable to the ancient traditions. For that reason the command to transmit news of it is impressed upon the hearers right at the beginning (v 3).[145]

Thus the chapter points beyond its center in v 15 to that which is to follow. For the time being, the present situation of distress leads to the conclusion to cry to Yahweh (vv 14b, 19a), and that in the customary forms of the cultus. In the course of listening to the older prophetic oracles, the extraordinary contemporary happening becomes the occasion for turning to Yahweh as the lord of the present calamity as well as of the approaching day. It gives cause, further, to recognize the present crisis (including the gifts of salvation effective in it) as merely temporary and to become mindful of the word of God concerning the final day.[146]

---

140 Thus Bourke, "Le jour," 15f, 206ff.
141 See p. 25.
142 See pp. 21–22.
143 See p. 29.
144 See p. 31.
145 See p. 26.
146 Cf. Mt 24:32–44, 7–14.

Call to Return Before the Day of Yahweh

Bibliography

J. Bourke
"Le jour de Yahvé dans Joël," *RB* 66 (1959): 5–31, 191–212.

Brevard S. Childs
"The Enemy from the North and the Chaos Tradition," *JBL* 78 (1959): 187–98.

Henning Fredriksson
Jahwe als Krieger: Studien zum alttestamentlichen Gottesbild (Lund: C. W. K. Gleerup, 1945), 28–35.

Ernst Kutsch
"Heuschreckenplage und Tag Jahwes in Joel 1 und 2," *ThZ* 18 (1962): 81–94.

Daniel Leibel
"On יֶעְבְּטוּן (Joel 2:7)," [Hebrew] *Lešonenu* 24 (1959–60): 253.

Samuel E. Loewenstamm
"יֶעְבָּטוּן = יֶעְוְתוּן?," [Hebrew] *Lešonenu* 24 (1959–60): 107–8.

Gerhard von Rad
Old Testament Theology, vol. 2, tr. D. M. G. Stalker (New York and Evanston: Harper & Row, 1965), 119–25 ("The Day of Yahweh") [133–37].

2

1   **Blow the horn on Zion!**
      Sound the alarm on my holy mountain! [a]
         All inhabitants of the land shall tremble.
   For the Day of Yahweh is coming.
      Indeed near is 2/ [b]the dark, gloomy day,[b]
         [c]the day of the dense cloud.[c]
   Like the light of dawn, spread across the mountains,
      (there approaches) a numerous and mighty people.
   Its like has never been from of old.
      And afterwards it will not come again, [d]even unto most distant generations.[d]

3   **Fire devours before it,**
         and flame blazes behind it.
   Like the Delightful Garden is the land before it,
         and after it like a wilderness of desolation.
            Nor is there any escape from it.
4   **Its appearance is like the appearance of horses,**
         like war-horses they run.

a   Sahidic takes note of the speech of Yahweh, not expected in this context, and inserts accordingly: "says the Lord God Almighty".

b–b   Literally "the day of darkness and gloom."

c–c   Literally "the day of the cloud and thick darkness."

d–d   Literally "unto the years of generation and generation [i.e., 'of the chain of generations']."

5
Like the rumbling sound of chariots
    that leap across mountain tops,
like the crackling sound ᵉof a flaming
fire*ᵉ*
    that devours stubble,
like a mighty people
    arrayed for battle.

6
Before it people writhe,
    all faces are aglow.ᶠ

7
Like warriors they run,
    like men of war they scale the wall.
They move ahead each on his way,
    they do not changeᵍ their courses.ʰ

8
No one ⁱpushes asideⁱ the other,
    ʲeach marches in his path.ʲ
ᵏThrough the midst of missiles they
attack,ᵏ
    (their lines) do not stop.

9
They assault the city,
    they storm the wall,
        they scale the houses.
Through the windows
    they enter like a thief.

10
The earth quakes before it,
    the heavens tremble—
ˡwhile sun and moon are darkened,
    the brightness of the stars is ex-
tinguished

11
    and Yahweh lifts up his voice before
his armyˡ—
for exceedingly great is his encampment;
    indeed, mighty is he who carries outᵐ
his word.

e–e Literally "of the flame of fire."

f   Literally "gather glow." G (πᾶν πρόσωπον ὡς πρόσ-καυμα χύτρας ["every face like a scorched (?) pot"]) certainly read פָּרוּר = "cooking pot," and perhaps before it כקיץ instead of קבצו, but is itself difficult to interpret. Did G imagine a "fired" pot or that which had "burnt onto" the pot, or merely the "glowing" of the pot (so also Na 2:11b [10b])? V translates similarly: *omnes vultus rediguntur in ollam* ("every face shall be made like a pot"). G and V, then, have identified פארור with פרור; the boiling pot designates at the same time the boiling heat. Gradwohl (*Farben*, 26) interprets the expression קבץ פארור after Is 40:11: "to pick up the boiling pot" = "to become hot." The interpretation "to gather heat" is more likely.

g   G ἐκκλίνωσιν ("they [do not] bend aside") may quite possibly reflect M. Samuel E. Loewenstamm ("יָצַנְתוּן = יַעֲבְּטוּן?," [Hebrew] *Lešonenu* 24 [1959–60]: 107–8) has pointed out a relationship between עבט and Akkadian *ebētu* "to make crooked, to bend." Julius Wellhausen (*Die kleinen Propheten über-setzt und erklärt*, Skizzen und Vorarbeiten 5 [Berlin: Georg Reimer, ³1898, reprinted 1963]) proposed reading יְעַוְּתוּן (from עות "to be crooked, bent"); Daniel Leibel ("On יַעֲבְּטוּן (Joel 2:7)," [Hebrew] *Lešonenu* 24 [1959–60]: 253) has suggested יַעֲרְבוּן (from ערב "to exchange, pledge"). However, G possibly read יַשּׁוּ(ן), as in Am 2:7.

h   The reference is to fixed marching routes.

i–i Here too G (ἀφέξεται ["keeps apart (from)"], just as θ' (θλίψει) and α' (συντρίψει), may be rendering M (ידחקון; rather than יְרָחֲקוּן as suggested by Otto Procksch in *BH³*, n. "α" to Joel 2:8).

j–j G καταβαρυνόμενοι ἐν τοῖς ὅπλοις αὐτῶν πορεύσονται ("weighed down by their weapons [reflecting כָּבֵד בְּמָגִנָּיו?], they shall move on") is a wide de-parture from M. Nevertheless, since πορεύσονται suggests ילכון in v 8aβ, the G colon is hardly to be considered a variant translation of v 8bα (Merx).

k–k בַּעַד = "distance, separation"; in the construct "[out/in] through." S seems to have read . . . בְּעֹז ("in the strength/might [weight?] of") (Merx, 108). G ἐν τοῖς βέλεσιν αὐτῶν πεσοῦνται ("on their missiles they fall") probably assumes M, since βέλις also renders שלח in Neh 4:17 [23]. T ולאתר דאינון שליחין אזלין קטלין ("and where they are sent, they go [and] kill").

l–l In vv 10b and 11aα circumstantial clauses, recog-nizable by their inverted word order, have been inserted between the presentation of events in v 10a and the motive–clauses in v 11aβ–b; cf. Kutsch, "Heuschreckenplage," 87f.

m   T (עבדי) and σ' (οἱ ποιοῦντες) presuppose plural עֹשֵׂי ("those who perform"), thus designating the "great encampment" in v 11aβ as the executor of the word of Yahweh. G (ὅτι ἰσχυρὰ ἔργα λόγων αὐτοῦ = כִּי עָצְמוּ מַעֲשֵׂי דְבָרָיו ["for the deeds of his words are mighty"]) departs further from M, referring the

Indeed, the Day of Yahweh is great
and very terrible.[n]
And who can endure it?

12 But even now the oracle of Yahweh[o]
(is valid):
Return to me with all your heart,
with fasting, weeping, and mourning!

13 Rend your hearts and not your garments!
Return to Yahweh your God!
For "he is gracious and merciful,
patient and abounding in steadfast
love,
and repents of evil."

14 Perhaps he will turn and repent (of it
once more), and will leave a blessing
behind him,
meal–offerings and libations for
Yahweh your God.

15 Blow the horn on Zion!
Announce a holy fast!
Proclaim a solemn holiday!

16 Gather the people!
Sanctify the congregation!
Assemble the old people!
Gather the children,
even those still sucking at the
breasts!
Let the bridegroom leave his room,
and the bride her chamber!

17 Between the vestibule and the altar let
the priests, the ministers of Yahweh,
weep.
Let them say:
Have pity, Yahweh, upon your people!
Do not hand over your possession to
shame,
that foreign nations should rule[p]
over them.
Why should they say among the
peoples:
"Where is their God?"

statement to the total work of Yahweh proclaimed
in v 10; similarly *S* and *L. V*: *quia fortia et facientia
verbum eius* ("because they are strong and performers
of his words").

n   *G ἐπιφανής* ("conspicuous, epiphanous") interprets
on the basis of homonymy with נראה; cf. Ju 13:6;
Mal 1:14; Zeph 2:11; and also Jean Koenig,
"L'activité herméneutique des scribes dans la transmission du texte de l'Ancien Testament, I," *RHR*
161 (1962): 141–74.

o   *G* adds ὁ θεὸς ὑμῶν ("your God").

p   The interpretation "to mock" (anticipating v 17bβ)
is not found in the ancient translations (*G κατάρξαι*;
V dominentur), but it is known already by Rashi as
well as the majority of more recent interpreters; cf.
Lam 5:8; 2 Chr 7:18; 9:26; 20:6; 23:20.

Form

2:1–11 Chap. 2 begins with a cry of alarm, warning of
the approach of an enemy force, which is immediately
followed by a description of the enemy. In 2:15 the
command to blow the horn on Mount Zion returns to
the theme of 1:5–14 (i.e., the summons to the communal lament ceremony). But this is not the case with
the identical command at the beginning of 2:1, which
(as the following cola clearly indicate) is rather an
order to sound an alarm, comparable to those in Hos
5:8; 8:1; Jer 4:5; and 6:1.[1] The might of the enemy

whose approach is thereby signaled is portrayed in
vv 2aβ–11a. The distinctive feature of this particular
"command to sound the alarm, with description of the
enemy" (*Alarmbefehl mit Feindschilderung*) is that it
incorporates an announcement of the approaching
Day of Yahweh.[2]

It might seem at first glance that a smoother text
would result were we to skip over the stereotyped
reference to the Day of Yahweh in vv 1b–2aα, connecting v 1a and v 2aβ as follows:

1 / Blow the horn in Zion!

1   Cf. Wolff, *Hosea*, 112 [142]; and Robert Bach, *Die
    Aufforderungen zur Flucht und zum Kampf im alttesta-
    mentlichen Prophetenspruch*, WMANT 9 (Neukirchen:
    Neukirchener Verlag, 1962), 19ff.
2   See pp. 43–44.

Sound the alarm on my holy mountain!
    All inhabitants of the land shall tremble.
For there approaches . . . 2aβ/—
    like the light of dawn,
      spread across the mountains—
        a numerous and mighty people.
The inclusion of vv 1b–2a—
    the Day of Yahweh (is coming).
    Indeed near is the dark, gloomy day,
      the day of the dense cloud
—may appear to be secondary, but upon closer inspection it proves to be essential.

For without it one would discover only at the end of the section that the enemy army marching against Jerusalem is Yahweh's army (v 11). Yet what happens "before it" is stated three times previously (vv 3a, 6a, 10a). And these events are understandable only as the effects of Yahweh's appearance with his army,[3] especially since topics from theophanic description are predominant here. This observation alone makes it likely that the announcement of the enemy was, from the very beginning, a proclamation of the Day of Yahweh. Further confirmation lies in the fact that the description of the enemy army appears in all important Day of Yahweh passages (which Joel has demonstrably received from tradition), most clearly in Is 13:2ff and Ezek 30:3ff.[4] In Zeph 1:16 the Day is actually called "a day of horn and battle cry" (יוֹם שׁוֹפָר וּתְרוּעָה; cf. Joel 2:1aα), while immediately preceding this in Zeph 1:15b we find the Day characterized as a "dark, gloomy day, the day of the dense cloud," taken over verbatim by Joel (2:2aα). Thus the linking together of the announcement of the Day of Yahweh with the war–alarm and the subsequent description of the enemy must be explained on the basis of tradition.

The fact that older literary–critical research thought it possible to eliminate the Day of Yahweh passages finds its explanation in the characteristic mode of work of our early apocalypticist who, in part, develops elements of tradition independently (cf. 1:5–14, 15), and in part adopts material verbatim from literary tradition. This creates the impression of a compilation, the same impression we received in chap. 1.

The description of the enemy includes a series of similes in vv 4–7 which has its form–critical model in the announcements of the "nation from afar" (Is 5:26) summoned by Yahweh. These were handed down from older prophecy; in addition to the use of the single simile (Hos 8:1), series had already been formed: Is 5:28–30; Hab 1:8; Jer 4:13; Na 2:5 [4]. Joel not only presents the longest series by far, but exhibits in a preliminary way the style of the apocalyptic vision report. Especially in v 4—"like the appearance of" (כמראה)—Joel has been influenced by the style of Ezekiel (1:13–14, 26–28; 8:2; 10:1; 40:3; 42:11; 43:3), which is found elsewhere in the Old Testament only in Dan 8:15; 10:6, 18. Thus we identify here a late, developed form, as is also the case in the call to communal lamentation in 1:5–14.

2:12–14 A call to repentance, consisting of several member parts, follows immediately, firmly linked to the preceding section by "but even now" (וגם־עתה). It is distinguished from the call to communal lamentation in that it is motivated not by a reference to the calamity,[5] but first by a reference to Yahweh's character and will (v 13b), and second by the prospect of his future action (v 14). The first type of motivation of such a word of admonition belongs to the form of the priestly torah,[6] and the second to its prophetic application (Am 5:5, 15). This word of admonition, then, displays the shape of a later mixed form.

2:15–17 The final series of imperatives corresponds to the basic stock of the concluding strophe of the great call to communal lamentation in chap. 1 (cf. 2:15b, 16aα with 1:14a). But the section shows a threefold development. First it takes up in its opening the alarm cry from 2:1 and is thus linked with 2:1–11, just as are vv 12–14. The call to blow the horn is attested also

---

3   Kutsch, "Heuschreckenplage," 85–88.
4   See pp. 33–34 on 1:15.
5   Cf. the motivation clauses in 1:5–14, and see pp. 21–22.
6   Joachim Begrich, "Die priesterliche Tora" in *Werden und Wesen des Alten Testaments*, ed. Paul Volz, Friedrich Stummer, Johannes Hempel; BZAW 66 (Berlin, 1936), 75–78 (reprinted in *idem, Gesammelte*

Studien zum Alten Testament, ed. Walther Zimmerli, ThB 21 [München: Chr. Kaiser, 1964], 246–49). Cf. Is 1:10–17; Lev 20:7.

in cultic observances,[7] though nowhere else in calls to communal lamentation.[8] Probably, then, this is an echo of 2:1. As to subject matter, this means that the exhortation, proclaimed on Mount Zion, to flee the enemy army of Yahweh is interpreted as a flight toward Yahweh. From Yahweh Israel can escape only toward Yahweh. The second expansion, as compared to 1:14aβ, is evident in the enlarging of the circle of those summoned ("all inhabitants of the land") as far as possible, by naming the smallest infants and those engaged to be married (2:16). Finally, the command "cry to Yahweh!" (1:14b) is documented by a very specific prayer (2:17). In contrast to the lament passages in 1:15–20, this prayer focuses not on the economic distress, but on the relationship to the nations.

The poetic structure is quite varied. Received forms and specific content exert their influence. The alarm cry in v 1a is issued in a synonymous tricolon of three–stress lines; the motivation also initially exhibits three cola (vv 1b–2aα), but of fluctuating length, due to the verbatim incorporation of Zeph 1:14–15. In vv 2aβ–11 the prosodic units, generally synonymous bicola, also vary in line length. In v 2bβ–γ, unusually long five–stress cola portray the expanse of the ages, while short, two–stress cola depict the stormy events in v 9. Cola standing in isolation, like v 3bβ and v 11aα, have an interpretive function in the midst of the description of the enemy.

The call to repentance is regular in structure. Both of its imperative prosodic units make a strong appeal, each attesting a synonymous bicolon (vv 12aβ, 13a); the statement of motivation, on the other hand, exhibits two tricola (vv 13b, 14).

In the concluding call to a ceremony of lamentation, short two–stress commands predominate (vv 15b–16a).

Setting

One's understanding of 2:1–17 as a whole is decided by the question of its relationship to chap. 1. More recent interpretation has found in chap. 2 a description of a locust invasion, just as in chap. 1. The difference is said to lie in the fact that it is the flat land which is threatened in chap. 1, and the city of Jerusalem, in chap. 2;[9] or that in chap. 2 a second locust plague is imminent, caused by the hatching of the brood of the locusts of chap. 1.[10] Against the first proposal it must be pointed out that "the inhabitants of the land" are named in both chapters (1:2, 14; 2:1); that the Jerusalem Temple with its priests is affected in both chap. 1 (vv 9, 13, 16) and chap. 2 (vv 14b, 17); and that the whole region is affected in both chap. 2 (vv 2, 3, 5) and chap. 1 (vv 6–12, 17–20). As far as the second proposal is concerned, chap. 1 already presupposes a total destruction of the harvest by locusts and drought (vv 8–12, 17–18), and 1:4 already reckons with different locust invasions and the hatching of their brood. Now, to be sure, one ought to consider the possibility that 1:4 could be meant as a summary of the events of 1:5—2:17 (the more so since the verse is taken up in 2:25) and that a closer description of the attackers is not given until chap. 2 (vv 4–9), when the subject is the attack upon the city.[11] Above all, the series of similes in 2:4–5 (but also the imagery in 2:7–9) become clearly intelligible if locusts are meant.[12]

Nevertheless, there is an essential difference between the two chapters which must be determined on other grounds:

1. It is out of the question that the same calamity should underlie both chapters.

a) Chap. 1 focuses upon a catastrophe that has already set in, and calls for a communal lamentation over it. The calls, as well as the sentences of lamentation themselves, are rooted in events the effect of which is already felt. By contrast, chap. 2 stands under the aegis of the alarm cry-warning of the enemy who has set out on his way. His army is *still* approaching. In addition to the basic form–critical difference between the call to communal lamentation and the warning cry alerting of the enemy, one must compare

7 Ps 81:4 [3]; cf. Ps 47:2 [1]; Lev 23:24; Nu 10:10.
8 Cf. Hans–Joachim Kraus, *Worship in Israel: A Cultic History of the Old Testament*, tr. Geoffrey Buswell (Oxford: Blackwell, 1966), 66, 211 [*Gottesdienst in Israel. Grundriss einer Geschichte des alttestamentlichen Gottesdienstes* (München: Chr. Kaiser, ²1962), 84, 246].
9 L. H. K. Bleeker, *De kleine Propheten*, Tekst en Uitleg

1/2 (Groningen, 1934); Theis; Deden.
10 Bewer, Sellin, Weiser.
11 Thompson, 743–46.
12 See pp. 45–46.

the predominance of the imperfect forms in 2:4–9 (representing an event in the course of its happening) with the perfects in 1:4–20 (which state facts).

b) The introduction to the call to repentance, with its connecting "but even now" (וגם־עתה 2:12), shows that the occasion for returning, which exists "now," is distinguished from the earlier occasion for lamentation in chap. 1.

c) Both the call to repentance which, as such, has no parallel in chap. 1, and the intensification, which is present in 2:15–17 as over against 1:13–14,[13] points to a calamity that is to be distinguished from chap. 1.

2. The new calamity is no locust disaster.

a) Locusts are not mentioned at all in 2:1–17. They have already receded in 1:8–12.

b) In contrast, the new prayer in 2:17 presupposes that Jerusalem is being overwhelmed by "nations." There is no reference to devastations caused by locusts, in clear contrast to the prayer passages in 1:16–20. It is fire, instead, that devours before and behind the enemy (2:3a); nations writhe under him (2:6a; cf. 2:3bβ); the city with its walls and houses is conquered (2:7–9), even earth and heavens quake, and the heavenly bodies are darkened (2:10).

c) Yahweh is commander–in–chief of the approaching enemy army (2:11). That he leads the locusts was not said in chap. 1 (cf. 1:6–7 and 2:25).[14]

d) In contrast to the locusts of chap. 1, the enemy announced in chap. 2 has not only never appeared in recent generations (1:2b), but never before at all, nor afterwards will he ever appear again (2:2b). The locust disaster was *unusual*, but the new distress to be brought on by the enemy will be *unique*.

3. If this is so, the predicted enemy must be seen as an apocalyptic army.

a) What can be said about the enemy's effects has essentially not been drawn from observations of nature, but comprises traditional elements of the transmitted theophany accounts, of the threats of an enemy from the north, and of representations of the enemy in the prophecies concerning the Day of Yahweh.[15]

b) To be sure, the manner of appearance and the character of the enemy show clear analogies to the locusts. "They represent the enemy in a grotesque enlargement."[16] One must not say, however, that an ordinary army of nations is compared here with locusts, as is the case in Na 3:15, (17) and Jer 51:27;[17] rather, these locustlike apocalyptic creatures (that are, however, never designated as locusts) are announced as the apocalyptic enemy army. Apparently we have here a form prefiguring Rev 9:2–11.

c) Thus 2:1ff depicts neither the same locust disaster as 1:4ff, nor another locust invasion, but intends to announce the imminent onslaught of the overwhelming enemy from afar (or from the north) expected by prophecy. This onslaught, however, has now gained the incomparable character of the Day of Yahweh, interpreted eschatologically. And for its supernatural format the unusual locust invasion in 1:4ff was both harbinger and model.

Consequently, 2:1–17 has its place *after* chap. 1, not only literarily, but also with regard to subject matter. This sequence is irreversible. We have here not a parallel to the temporary distress, but an intensification of it into the ultimate one. To be sure, a linking that would express this is absent. But perhaps one may take note of the speech of Yahweh which appears in the opening lines in a traditional expression ("on my holy mountain" 2:1a).[18] The divine first person speech is not continued, due to the adoption of other transmitted expressions, recurring only once more in connection with the new beginning in 2:12a. It presents 2:1ff as God's answer to the cries of lamentation in 1:16–20. Instead of the answer to a plea, it brings confirmation that the Day of Yahweh itself is now approaching (cf. 2:1b with 1:15).

This chapter also offers only indirect evidence for the time of composition. The fact that the king and his

---

13 See p. 41.

14 See p. 64.

15 Cf. especially Ps 97; Jer 4—6; Am 5:18–20; Zeph 1; Ezek 30; 38—39; Is 13. Cf. also on this point Keil; Hugo Gressmann, *Der Messias*, FRLANT 42 (Göttingen, 1929), 136f; and Kutsch, "Heuschreckenplage," 89–94. See p. 47.

16 Gustav Hölscher, *Die Profeten. Untersuchungen zur*

Religionsgeschichte Israels (Leipzig, 1914), 432. Cf. also Robinson; and especially Fredriksson, *Krieger*, 29–31.

17 Cf. Thompson, "Locusts," 52–54, and *idem*, *IB* 6, 743–46.

18 See p. 43.

court are not mentioned in 2:16–17 (where the various groups of the population are listed), while priests and elders lead the community, definitely indicates a date in the postexilic period.[19] The references to the wall in vv 7a and 9a need not in themselves necessarily point to the time after Nehemiah's building of the wall.[20] In the wider context, however, the mention of the wall twice in quick succession surely presupposes its self–evident existence: Jerusalem possesses defensible fortifications. On the other hand, the chapter's thematic content is clearly indicative of the late postexilic period. The Day of Yahweh, whose depiction in part recalls the exact wording of Zeph 1:14–15 and Is 13,[21] is viewed in a completely new way as far as its scenario is concerned. Sufficient time for considerable ideological development must be assumed. For only so can we account for the older Day of Yahweh *topoi* having been appropriated almost verbatim (and hence probably via literary mediation) while at the same time the enemy army from afar is no longer announced directly and viewed as a human army, as in the older texts, but is anticipated through analogy with a preceding locust invasion. This seems more likely in the later rather than in the earlier Persian period. In this connection the echoes of Mal 3 [3–4],[22] and the close relationship to Jon 3—4[23] are also pertinent.

Interpretation

■1 The שׁוֹפָר is a wind instrument made from a "ram's horn," distinguished from the trumpet by its curved, conical shape.[24] The command to "sound the alarm"

(רוע hipʻil) is probably not meant to be an exhortation to follow up the "blasting" (תקע) on the horns with a general war cry, as in Josh 6:(10, 16,) 20. Instead, it characterizes the horn blowing (in strict synonymity with the preceding colon) as a prolonged, startling, and frightening fanfare (cf. Nu 10:9), in contrast to the signal sounding in connection with festive assemblies (cf. Nu 10:10 with Joel 2:15). Here, then, is a call to alarm in the face of danger from an enemy. Its purpose is not, as in 2:15–17, preparation for the prayer of the fast, but instead, that "all inhabitants of the land shall tremble," i.e., that they shall be anxious for their safety and seek refuge.[25] The call goes forth "on Zion," "on my holy mountain." (Reference to the "holy mountain" as the royal seat of a god is found already in the myth of Baʻl at Ugarit.[26]) In the Old Testament this designation usually occurs in first–person speech of Yahweh.[27]

The alert is motivated ("for" כי v 1b) not by the approach of just any powerful enemy (v 2b); rather "the Day of Yahweh" itself is "coming." "Coming" (בא) in association with "near" (קרוב) is probably to be interpreted as a participle.[28] Ezek 7:7 already attests בא and קרוב side by side in a similar context. Zeph 1:14–16a also associates Yahweh's final day of judgment with the sounding of alarm, calling the Day of Yahweh explicitly a "day of horn–blasting." It belongs to the prehistory of this association that the coming of Yahweh as the judge of the world in Ps 98:6–9 is introduced with the blowing of horns.[29]

Above all, however, the theophany account in the

---

19   See p. 25 on 1:2.

20   Cf. Rudolf Kittel, *Geschichte des Volkes Israel*, vol. 3/2 (Stuttgart, 1929), 605; and Jacob M. Myers, "Some Considerations Bearing on the Date of Joel," *ZAW* 74 (1962): 191.

21   See pp. 46, 47.

22   See pp. 48–49.

23   See pp. 49–50.

24   Cf. *BRL*, 390, 392; and Gerhard Friedrich, "σάλπιγξ," *TDNT* 7, 76.

25   See p. 39.

26   *CTA* 3 (= *UT* ʻnt). 3.26–28:
      btk . ġry . ʾil . ṣpn
         "In the midst of my mountain, divine Ṣapan,
      bqdš . bġr . nḥlty
         "In the 'sanctuary,' the mountain of my possession,

         bnʻm . bgbʻ . tlʾiyt
         "In the sublime place, the height of (my) conquest." [Trans. by Ed.]

27   Cf. Werner Schmidt, "Wo hat die Aussage: Jahwe 'der Heilige' ihren Ursprung?" *ZAW* 74 (1962): 65.

28   Kapelrud, *Joel*, 71.

29   Cf. כי בא ("for he comes") in Ps 98:9; 96:13. In Is 27:13 the connection is already presupposed as self–evident.

Sinai tradition has (in its fusion of the ancient sources) associated the blasting of horns, the dark cloud, and the trembling of the people with the appearance of Yahweh himself.[30] Joel presents the call to sound the horn–blast in the same form in which warning is given of an unnamed enemy in Hos 5:8, and of the enemy from the north (cf. Joel 2:20), whom Yahweh will bring near, in Jer 4:5–6 (cf. Jer 6:1). Thus the association of the ancient warning cry with the threat of a punitive campaign of Yahweh himself already has its prehistory in Hosea and Jeremiah. In the royal songs of Yahweh it occurs in eschatologized form and with reference to the world of nations. In Zeph 1:14–16 this topic was linked closely with the theophany account in the Sinai tradition and for the first time was combined with the catchword "Day of Yahweh" as the day of wrath against Jerusalem. This prehistory is overlooked by the practice, customary for a long time after Duhm, of excising vv 1b–2a.[31]

■ **2** The coming Day of Yahweh is described further as "the dark, gloomy day, the day of the dense cloud," which stands in direct verbal agreement with Zeph 1:15bβ, though from the description there only those features are adopted which in any case had belonged to the thematic content of the Day of Yahweh since Amos ("darkness . . . gloom" חֹשֶׁךְ—אָפֵל Am 5:18, 20). In Ex 10:22 (P?; cf. Ex 10:15 J) "darkness of gloom" (חֹשֶׁךְ־אֲפֵלָה) describes the effect of the locust plague in Egypt. Even clearer is the use of the four–element series to portray the Sinai theophany in Dtn 4:11: "fire . . ., darkness, cloud, and dense (gloom)" (אֵשׁ . . . חֹשֶׁךְ עָנָן וַעֲרָפֶל, cf. Dtn 5:22–23). The older representations do not as yet attest this sequence.[32] The imminent Day of Yahweh corresponds, therefore, to the day of Yahweh's awesome appearance in the past (cf. also Ps 97:2a). In the final analysis, Jerusalem can be threatened only by the God whose will has been proclaimed to Israel. He comes with the enemy army depicted in vv 2aβ–10.

V 2bα provides the subject for v 2aβ.[33] The threat now posed is of a "numerous and mighty people," the description being similar to that of the locusts who have arrived as a "nation powerful and without number" in 1:6a. But we must note that other words are chosen (עם רב ועצום instead of גוי עצום ואין מספר). The influence of the Day of Yahweh tradition is stronger in the description of the coming army than the model of the locust invasion that has already arrived; for it is evident that the idiom recognizable in Is 13:4a, "like a great people" (דמות עם רב), has exerted influence. In v 2aβ it is said that the people "spreads across the mountains like the light of dawn"; even though only the catchword "mountains" appears in Is 13:4, nevertheless this simile also indicates on the whole that more is described here than the locusts of chap. 1. Some have spoken, to be sure, of the reflection of the sun on the wings of the insects;[34] but other interpreters, assuming the phenomenon of ordinary locusts here, have been tempted to conjecture "blackness" (שָׁחוֹר) for "dawn" (שַׁחַר).[35] The context certainly recommends the transmitted wording (cf. v 3a). On the basis of the subject matter one expects the vast expanse of the army and its sudden appearance to be the common denominator of the simile.[36] Moreover, the description of incomparability in v 2bβ constitutes a decided intensification in comparison with 1:2b. To be sure, one can recall the similarly two–part statement of Ex 10:14b (J) ("never before had there been a locust swarm like it, nor ever after shall be again"), in order to confirm that the threatened final catastrophe of Jerusalem is described with features from the Egyptian plague narratives, under the influence of the Deuteronomistic curses (Dtn 28:60). Yet one must not overlook the intensification of the statement in Joel, which places emphasis on the absolute singularity of the approaching Day of Yahweh. "Of old" (עולם) designates the most distant *terminus a quo* conceivable; at no earlier point in time was there

30 Cf. 2:1a, 2a with the corresponding topics in Ex 19:16, 19; and 20:18.

31 See pp. 39–40.

32 Cf. Ex 19:16–19 (JE); 24:16 (P).

33 On the initial position of the simile in the warning cry of the scouts, cf. Hos 8:1a.

34 Karl Marti, *Das Dodekapropheton erklärt*, KHC 13 (Tübingen, 1904); Nowack; Frey.

35 Thus Duhm, "Anmerkungen," 185f; Robinson; and Thompson. The word šĕḥôr means the "blackness [of soot]."

36 Cf. Is 58:8. On the light of dawn that breaks quickly over the horizon, cf. Dalman, *Arbeit*, 1/2, 601.

anything comparable,[37] and ahead to the furtherest generations there will be nothing corresponding to it.[38] This formulation demonstrates that passionate interest in determining the incomparable which apocalypticism developed beyond the sapiential propensity for the ordering and comparing of phenomena.[39]

■ 3 The effect of the army is depicted in v 3. Those who think only of the locusts of chap. 1 have to interpret the "fire" in v 3a as "scorching drought," referring back to 1:19. But were it to devour in front of the locusts, there would remain for them no further destructive work to be performed. Apparently v 3a does not portray a natural event, but rather can only be understood in light of the theophanic tradition in the Day of Yahweh formulations.[40] The emphasis (in contrast to 1:19) upon the fire devouring both "before it" and "behind it" points in that direction, recalling a similar hymnic–eschatological formulation in the royal psalm of Yahweh, Ps 97:3 (cf. also Ps 50:3). Whoever wants to delete the Day of Yahweh passages in chaps. 1 and 2 must be consistent and drop also this sentence,[41] linked to them by its content.[42] In our context, however, the suffixes ("before it," "behind it") must be referred not to Yahweh but to the "numerous and mighty people" in v 2b. The difficulties disappear if we see in this people not the locusts of chap. 1 but the threatening enemy army commanded by Yahweh. That which tradition says of Yahweh's own appearance is here transferred to his coming with his army.[43] The notion of paradise as the "Delightful Garden" (i.e., "Garden of Eden": Gen 2:8, 10, 15; 3:23; 4:16) is taken up again with thoroughness and, for the first time, as a mythological notion by Ezekiel (Ezek 28:13; 31:9, 16, 18); in Ezek 36:35 the comparison with the Garden of Eden (כגן עדן) serves,

as here, to describe the fertile, cultivated land in contrast to that which has been "devastated" (נְשַׁמָּה).[44] Further, in Ezek 36:35 the garden is for the first time drawn into the future expectation of Israel; thereafter, in Is 51:3, it enters especially into the future expectation of Jerusalem (again in form of the comparison "like Eden" כְּעֵדֶן, versus "wilderness" מדבר!). In Joel we see the same formulation with the poles having been reversed. Once more the dependence of Joel on Ezekiel becomes clear, but so too does Joel's great distance from that prophet. Although Joel closely follows the earlier wording, he offers an independent treatment of tradition. While the transformation of the desert into a land of paradise in Ezek 36:35 and Is 51:3 is a saving act of God, the transformation here of the garden of delight into barren steppe is the result of the incomparably forceful incursion of the enemies of Jerusalem, led there on the dark Day of Yahweh. That there is "no escape" belongs to the thematic content of speech concerning the Day of Yahweh (cf. Lam 2:22), just as "escape" (פליטה) appears already in the ancient war terminology (Ju 21:17; 2 Sam 15:14). The certainty that all routes of escape are blocked is, above all, an element of the expectation of the Day of Yahweh since Amos.[45]

■ 4 Following the depiction of its effect, the army itself is portrayed in a series of images. Now more strongly than before, the description of the coming apocalyptic enemies is inspired by the locusts that had already arrived (chap. 1). Yet by "appearance" of horses Joel would hardly have meant the similarity of an individual locust head with a horse's head;[46] for with "horses" (סוסים) and "war–horses" (פרשים) reference is made to the vision of the hostile power as a whole. The common denominator in the simile is the irresistible, superior

---

37   Ernst Jenni, "Das Wort ʿōlām im Alten Testament," ZAW 64 (1952): 225. Cf. Is 63:19; 64:3 [4].

38   See textual note "d" to 2:2.

39   Cf. Dan 12:1. Cf. also 1 QM 18.10, and on this, J. Carmignac, "Les citations de l'Ancien Testament dans 'La Guerre des Fils de Lumière contre les Fils de Ténèbres,'" RB 63 (1956): 381.

40   Cf. Zeph 1:18 with Dtn 4:11; 5:22–26; and Ex 24:17 (P).

41   As Sellin indeed considered doing.

42   Cf. vv 2a, 3a with the reference to ענן וערפל ("cloud and thick darkness") in Ps 97:2, preceding the ref-

erence to "fire" in Ps 97:3.

43   Cf. Kutsch, "Heuschreckenplage," 92f.

44   Cf. in this connection מדבר שממה ("wilderness of desolation") in Joel 2:3, elsewhere attested only in 4:19 and Jer 12:10.

45   Am 5:18–20; cf. Am 9:1; 2:14–15; Is 2:10–21; 13:14–16; Ezek 30:6–9; and Zeph 1:8–13, 18.

46   This similarity is reflected in the names for locusts in German (Heupferd [literally "hay–horse"]) and Italian (cavaletta [literally "little–horse"]).

force which manifests itself in the swiftness and power of war-horses "running."[47] The archaic "energic" ending which we first meet in ירוצון ("they run"), and which is repeated again in v 7, is probably intended to underscore the forceful impact of the event. Horses essentially represent military power (Is 30:15–16; 31:1); they belong particularly to the "nation from afar" (Is 5:26–28), the "enemy from the north" (Jer 6:22–23; cf. Jer 4:13; Ezek 38:4). According to Joel, the locusts are to be recognized as a precedent for the ultimate arrival of that power. Here סוסים is probably a comprehensive concept designating the chariot corps as a whole. Accordingly, פרשים, as a "technical term deriving from the northern Syrian–Aramaic realm," specifies chariot horses.[48]

■ **5** The mighty noise of the rumbling of the chariots itself conveys clearly a tremendous intensification of the buzzing of the wings of the prototypal locust swarms. (The picture in Rev 9:7, 9 was inspired by this text.) When in the simile the hollow, rumbling sound is followed by the bright, rustling crackle of the straw fire, this already conveys accoustically the approach of the apocalyptic enemy army (cf. further vv 6–9). It can be recognized forthwith as a "mighty people," advancing "arrayed for battle" (ערוך מלחמה).[49] Even though the locusts stand in the background as a model, Joel is primarily concerned to describe the threatening army as the fulfillment of the enemy nation proclaimed by prophecy and commanded by Yahweh (cf. especially Jer 6:23).

■ **6** That the locusts as such are by no means meant is shown by v 6. The phrase "before it people writhe [like a woman in travail]" reflects the thematic content of the description of the Day of Yahweh in Is 13:8 and Ezek 30:16, taking up a catchword of the Jeremianic announcement of the enemy from the north (Jer 4:31; cf. Jer 5:3, 22). The singular suffix on מפניו ("before it"), which draws attention alongside the plural verb forms in vv 4–5, 7–8, functions in the corresponding

eschatological royal psalms of Yahweh (Ps 96:9; 97:5) as continuation of the theophany description, bringing Yahweh himself into view.[50] One must in addition take note of Jer 5:22: "Do you not writhe before me?" (אם מפני לא תחילו). Here as in v 3, then, the significance of the apocalyptic army is decisively determined by Yahweh himself (cf. v 11). The motif of faces aglow with intense anguish[51] also belongs to the description of the Day of Yahweh in Is 13:8b, where it is used in the same connection as here.[52]

■ **7–9** In the course of their march the approaching enemies show themselves to be disciplined, irresistible conquerors of fortified cities. The comparison with "warriors" (גבורים) again takes up a topic from Is 13:3. The parallelism of "warriors" and "men of war" (אנשי המלחמה) reappears precisely in the calling up of the army of nations in 4:9. No mention is made at all of the actual destructive activity of ordinary locusts (which wipe out vegetation and therewith the sustenance of men and cattle) even though their ceaseless advance has again served as a model.[53] From the verbal picture the reader perceives that Jerusalem is threatened. The initial איש ("each one") in vv 7b and 8a emphasizes the order, which admits of no exception, of the enemy attack.[54] As ordinary locusts cannot be stopped with missiles, even less so can this apocalyptic army (v 8b). Like the locusts it too forces its way into individual houses, overlooking no window hatch. When fields and trees are eaten bare, the locusts seek out the last human provisions in the houses (cf. Ex 10:6). Yet this feature also serves to show that the threats concerning the Day of Yahweh are now being fulfilled.[55]

■ **10** For two reasons the transition here is quite rough grammatically. In לפניו ("before it") the preceding plural verb forms are again continued by a singular suffix, so that the reader thinks first of Yahweh himself, as in vv 3 and 6. Secondly, there is a final transition now from the imperfects used thus far (which described

---

47   In Job 39:20 the simile is reversed.
48   Kurt Galling, "Der Ehrenname Elisas und die Entrückung Elias," *ZThK* 53 (1956): 134f, cf. 133–35. Cf. 1 Sam 8:11; Na 3:2.
49   Cf. Gen 14:8; Ju 20:20, 22.
50   See above on v 3a. Cf. especially the order of clauses in Ps 97:2–4 with Joel 2:2a, 3a, 6. Cf. Ps 97:5–6 with Joel 2:10.
51   On the expression, see textual note "f" to 2:6.
52   Cf. the sequence of v 6a–b with Is 13:8a–b.
53   See p. 29 on 1:6; on the marching order, cf. especially Prv 30:27.
54   Cf. Brockelmann, *Syntax*, par. 122o.
55   Cf. Is 13:16bα, 21; Zeph 1:13a.

events whose meaning is clarified in connection with vv 1b–3 and 10–11) to forms in the perfect, which substantiate the acts as weighty in their own right.[56] This rough transition leads to decisive statements which are no longer supported by the observation of even the most unusual appearance and behaviour of locusts. The whole cosmos is shaken. V 10a speaks of the quaking of the earth and the heavens in the manner of the theophany accounts[57] which, prior to Joel,[58] had already been adopted in representations of the Day of Yahweh to announce the return of chaos.[59] The darkening of sun, moon, and stars in v 10b carries through the old prophetic motif of the darkness of the Day of Yahweh,[60] in the same manner as Is 13:10.

Comparison of Is 13 with Joel 2:1–11

At this point a coherent comparison of Is 13 with Joel 2:1–11 is useful. We will collate the catchwords and motifs of the Day of Yahweh presentation in Is 13 which recur in Joel 2. In Is 13:3 those called up by Yahweh are designated as his "warriors" (גבורים, cf. Joel 2:7a). A twofold קול ("voice, sound") is used in Is 13:4a, 4b (cf. Joel 2:5a, 5b) to draw attention to the noise of the enemy army which resounds "on the mountains" (בֶּהָרִים, Is 13:4a; cf. Joel 2:2a, 5a). This army also is a "mighty people" (עם רב, Is 13:4a; cf. Joel 2:2b, 5b, 11a). The central verse, Is 13:6 (which Joel has shifted to the center of chap. 1),[61] constitutes proof that the strong contact is not a matter of chance. Corresponding to "they will writhe" (יְחִילוּן) in Is 13:8a, the nations in Joel 2:6a writhe in travail; the view of flaming red "faces" (פנים) in Is 13:8b corresponds to those "aglow" in Joel 2:6b. The motif of the devastation of the earth (Is 13:9b) recurs in Joel 2:3b; the extinction of stars, sun, and moon (Is 13:10), in Joel 2:10b; the quaking of heaven and earth (Is 13:13), in Joel 2:10a; and the despoiling of the houses (Is 13:16), in Joel 2:9. Compare also "to dance" (רקד pi'el) in Is 13:21 with Joel 2:5.

Additionally, we have observed the influence of the language and conceptions of the prophetic threats of the Day of Yahweh found in Am 5:18–20; Zeph 1:14–16; and Ezek 30; of the enemy from the north in Jer 4–6 and Ezek 38–39; of other material from Ezekiel and from the Deuteronomistic sources; as well as of motifs from the royal psalms of Yahweh. But the points of contact with Is 13 are incomparably more intense. In the description of the locusts in chap. 1 a similar influx of traditional material cannot generally be established. Only 1:15 is based on Is 13:6, affirming that the locusts are harbingers of the Day of Yahweh. The threat of that day itself is not made until 2:1–11. The above comparison has established that the Day of Yahweh traditions we discern in Is 13, were determinative for the portrayal in 2:1–11. The prelude of the locust invasion did not have nearly the same uniform impact on the statements. Instead, the unity of the section, especially the juxtaposition of singular (vv 2–3, 6, 10) and plural (vv 4–5, 7–9) phrases, becomes intelligible on the basis of the traditions attested in Is 13.

Yet we must bear in mind that Joel's description of Yahweh's enemy army exhibits a freedom with respect to the sequence of motifs and individual formulations, and that the prelude of the locust invasion has exerted typological influence. The decisive difference from Is 13 is twofold. 1. The message, which was directed there against Babylon, is now turned against Jerusalem. 2. The immediate proximity of the day's fulfillment is verified by the current locust calamity and drought, as the insertion of Is 13:6 in 1:15 shows most clearly.

Using motifs from Is 13:10 and 13, v 10 affirms that the final catastrophe is imminent. When the Day of Yahweh commences for Jerusalem, this will mean the breaking in of chaos. With the shaking of earth and heaven, and with the extinguishing of all the lights of the day and of the night, creation will be reversed. That, however, cannot be accomplished by an ever-so-mighty "military power" (חיל), but only by the commanding voice of Yahweh; yet from him it can be expected with all certainty.

■ **11** After v 11aα the three clauses beginning with כי ("for, indeed") come as a surprise. What do they explain? They can be referred meaningfully only to v 10a, and not to v 11aα. Syntactically this inter-

---

56 On the meaning of the tenses, cf. most recently Michel, *Tempora*.
57 Ju 5:4; Ps 18:8 [7]; 68:9 [8]; 77:19 [18].
58 Is 13:13; cf. Ezek 38:19–20.
59 Cf. Jer 4:23–26; Na 1:5–6. On רעש ("to tremble") as the catchword for the shaking of the world at the return of chaos, cf. Childs "Enemy," 188–90.
60 See p. 44 on 2:2a.
61 See pp. 22–24 on 1:15.

pretation is also demanded.[62] The first two כי–clauses (v 11aβ) express in clear words what was in fact presupposed from the beginning: the "numerous and mighty people" of v 2b is Yahweh's military camp and the executor of his word. "He who carries out his word" (עשה דבר) probably means here performance of the "word" which had come to prophets in earlier times (cf. Jer 1:12), rather than obedience to the command actually being issued by a commander (as in v 11aα). It should be noted how the two adjectives of v 2b—"numerous and mighty" (רב ועצום)—are divided between the two clauses. Yahweh's instrument is that completely irresistible power which convulses the world of nations (v 6) and the cosmos (v 10) as well as Jerusalem. The final כי–clause accounts for the announced and inescapable distress (v 10a), explaining that it signals the onset of the terrible Day of Yahweh which, while known as such, here receives a wholly new proclamation. The Day of Yahweh is already termed "great" in Zeph 1:14; it is called "great and terrible" for the first time in Mal 3:23 [4:5], a description which reappears in Joel 3:4.

The description of the coming Day of Yahweh concludes with a startling question: "Who can endure it?" Even this is not entirely new (cf. Mal 3:2). Yet as an indirect, rousing address to the reader it makes the decisive transition here, a transition that still seems completely excluded at first, since there is, after all, no escape from the irresistible enemy. In the face of the locust calamity already present, Israel has to hear that the Day of Yahweh, announced by the older prophecy, is immediately imminent. But now the concluding question proves to be more than rhetorical.

■ 12 The opening phrase of the section which follows already indicates this: "But even now . . . ." The conjunction must be interpreted as adversative[63] in view of what immediately precedes it. Looking back to the appeals to lamentation in chap. 1, "but even" (וגם) has an additive–intensifying function (cf. 2:3bβ). While the lamentation during the locust calamity was a customary reaction, the possibility of repentance after the announcement of the Day of Yahweh cannot be expected as a matter of course. "Now" (עתה) indicates that the hour is advanced.[64] Behind this statement stands the interest in distinguishing between the times.[65] The divine oracle formula, "oracle / utterance of Yahweh" (נאם יהוה), which is inserted into the opening of the oracle as happens frequently,[66] appears only here in the book of Joel. It underscores at this turning point the fact that to the threat of his army, Yahweh himself adds the following admonition, meant as an invitation. He himself thereby initiates the decisive turn of history. One can take v 12aα as an independent nominal clause: "But even now Yahweh's oracle (is valid): . . . ." If v 12aβ is accordingly introduced as a quotation from tradition, it is no longer disturbing that Yahweh is spoken of in the third person in v 13aβ. It is the message of the Deuteronomistic History which Joel takes up with the call, "Return to Yahweh with all your heart!"[67] From Amos (4:6–11) and Hosea (3:5; 14:2 [1]; cf. Jer 3:10; 24:7) on, returning is known as the saving effect of Yahweh's punitive judgments (cf. Dtn 4:29–31). Moreover, the association of the theme of return with the threat of the Day of Yahweh had already been made before Joel: as to the subject matter, in Zeph 2:3 (without the catchword "return" [שוב], but linked in the same way with the indefinite expectation of deliverance as in v 14), and even more clearly with the announcement of the messenger of Yahweh before the

62 See textual note "l" to 2:10.
63 So Sellin.
64 Kapelrud, *Joel*, 81.
65 See above on 1:2b, 3 and 2:2b.
66 Cf. Wolff, *Hosea*, 41 [49]; and Friedrich Baumgärtel, "Die Formel nᵉᵘm jahwe," *ZAW* 73 (1961): 277–90.
67 Cf. Dtn 30:10; 1 Sam 7:3; 1 Kgs 8:48; 2 Kgs 23:25. Cf. also Hans Walter Wolff, "The Kerygma of the Deuteronomic Historical Work" (tr. Frederick C. Prussner) in Hans Walter Wolff and Walter Brueggemann, *The Vitality of Old Testament Traditions* (Atlanta: John Knox, 1975), 83–100 "Das Kerygma des deuteronomistischen Geschichtswerks," *ZAW* 73 (1961): 171–86 (reprinted in *idem, Gesammelte Studien zum Alten Testament*, ThB 22 [München: Chr. Kaiser, ²1973], 308–24).

Day of Yahweh in Mal 3:1–3, 7.[68] "To return" (שׁוב) means total reorientation toward Yahweh, especially since it is to be effected "with the whole heart," i.e., with the organ of thinking and willing, of aligning one's life.[69] The continuation "and with fasting, weeping, and mourning" seems to be in keeping with the stock of formulas of that time.[70] Joel has no objection to the customary rituals.

■ **13** This verse proves that no stress is placed on v 12b. The rending of one's clothes, which takes place before putting on the *śaq*-garment, is a part of the customary rites of lamentation.[71] The instruction not to do so definitely cannot have the same meaning as the corresponding prohibition in Ezek 24:16–18; yet even if one feels obliged to translate, according to the sense, "rend your hearts and not *only* your garments!" the prophetic criticism of an empty ritualism shows its aftereffect (cf. Jer 4:4). What does Joel have in mind when he demands a reorientation of the direction of one's thought and will, and hence a new orientation towards Yahweh? Neither here nor earlier is there any reference to specific transgressions. Hosea and Jeremiah had first used the verb שׁוב to call for a return to Yahweh from the idols of Canaan (Hos 2:9 [7]; Jer 4:1). Amos (4:6–11), Isaiah (30:15), and Ezekiel (33:9, 15) had employed it to describe a turning away from specific false modes of behavior.[72] As used by the Deuteronomistic historian, however, the verb meant precisely listening to the voice of Yahweh as it had received expression in the Mosaic word of Deuteronomy.[73] In similar fashion Joel recalls indirectly

the prophetic word spoken in earlier times.[74] The cultic community of Jerusalem, which is perhaps already beginning to pride itself on its fulfilling of the Torah, is to stretch forth anew toward the God who does not allow the prophetic word to become void of meaning.

This is also evident from the alteration of the ancient confessional formula added in v 13b. Its elements recur frequently after Ex 34:6–7 (J?).[75] It must be noted nevertheless that the word sequence found in v 13b has an exact parallel only in Jon 4:2.[76] That this agreement is not a matter of chance is shown by the further concurrence of v 14a with Jon 3:9a (cf. Jon 3:10b), but especially by the relationship of thematic contexts: the announcement of the catastrophe awakens repentance in the hearer, and this repentance leads to God's revoking what he had threatened. What was held up before the postexilic congregation in the guise of Nineveh in the book of Jonah, is proclaimed directly to Jerusalem in the book of Joel. The inescapable relationship in vocabulary and themes goes back to a common root. It must be sought where, in the context of discussion about "returning," it is said that God "repents of evil" (נחם על־הרעה), namely, in the Jeremiah traditions[77] and the related Deuteronomic traditions.[78] Here, however, just as in the book of Jonah, the presupposition of repentance on God's part is always "returning" based on the prophetic word. It is exactly the same for Joel: "returning" is expected on the basis of the newly proclaimed prophetic word about the Day of Yahweh. The expression concerning the repentance

---

68 Cf. Mal 3:2a with Joel 2:11; and Mal 3:10a with Joel 2:14b; cf. also Mal 3:23–24 [4:5–6].

69 See Wolff, *Hosea*, 84 [104f]; and Georges Pidoux, *L'homme dans l'Ancien Testament*, CTh 32 (Neuchâtel and Paris: Delachaux & Niestlé, 1953), 25ff.

70 Cf. Est 4:3. On the content, see pp. 32–33 on 1:13–14.

71 See pp. 29–30 on 1:8.

72 Cf. Hans Walter Wolff, "Das Thema der 'Umkehr' in der alttestamentlichen Prophetie," *ZThK* 48 (1951): 129–48 (reprinted in *idem, Gesammelte Studien*, 130–50).

73 Cf. Dtn 30:2, 8, 10; 2 Kgs 17:13; 23:25. Cf. also Wolff, "Kerygma," 96–97 [183 (= *Gesammelte Studien*, 320–21)].

74 See pp. 46–48, and pp. 10–11, 13 of the Introduction.

75 Cf. Ps 86:15; 103:8; 145:8; Neh 9:17. On this cf. also Josef Scharbert, "Formgeschichte und Exegese von Ex 34:6f und seinen Parallelen," *Biblica* 38 (1957): 130–50.

76 In Joel 2:13b and Jon 4:2 alone do we find ונחם על־הרעה ("and repents of evil") as the final element. The sequence חנון ורחום ("gracious and merciful") also appears in Ps 145:8; and Neh 9:17.

77 Cf. Jer 18:7–8; 26:3, 13, 19; 42:10.

78 Ex 32:12, 14; 2 Sam 24:16; cf. also Am 7:3, 6.

of God with respect to the announced judgment interprets the ancient confessional formula anew for the time of the prophetic proclamation of judgment. Earlier, "gracious" (חנון) means the favor and complete goodwill of a superior party who condescends to one who is inferior (Ex 22:26 [27]), while "merciful" (רחום) describes fatherly and motherly care, anxious for the life of one who is helpless and endangered.[79] "Patient" (ארך אפים) means long restraint of anger, whereby anger is removed to a distance because one who might well have reason to be excited takes a "long breath." "Abounding in steadfast love" (רב חסד) designates the wealth of voluntary kindness which through helping–deeds creates community and which keeps faith with a partner.[80] The God of Israel, thus known since antiquity, manifests himself in the time of the prophetic threat of "evil" (רעה)[81] as one who indeed "repents" of it. The confessional formula, thus expanded, motivates the summons to conversion and encourages thereby a new turning toward the God who has been proclaimed.

■ **14** But this must not be misunderstood as a limitation upon the freedom of God. "Who knows?" (מי יודע)[82] is used here, (as in Jon 3:9; 2 Sam 12:22 [cf. Est 4:14]) with that sense which "perhaps" (אולי) has in Am 5:15; Zeph 2:3; Lam 3:29b; and Ex 32:30. This word always designates God's freedom over against those who turn to him, in Zeph 2:3 already in connection with the "turning" provoked by the message of the Day of Yahweh. Joel perhaps emphasizes this divine freedom over against those circles that boast of Jerusalem's election with far too much self–assurance. The "perhaps" of hope is appropriate to the humility of one who prays;[83] in the proclamation of the messenger it underscores the fact that the one called to return stands, for

the time being, under the message of judgment[84] and has to face up to it. That the faithful and merciful God is also free in relation to his own anger ("slow to anger" ארך אפים) is the foundation of the hope expressed in the "perhaps." "He will turn" (ישוב) indicates that human repentance (2:12a, 13a) may lead to a responsive turning on God's part, i.e., precisely that withdrawal of the announced threat which is attested in the Jeremiah traditions. "He will turn and repent" (ישוב ונחם) might represent a shortened form of the Deuteronomistic expression, "Turn from your fierce wrath and repent of the evil" (שוב מחרון אפך והנחם על־הרעה Ex 32:12); yet "he will turn" (ישוב), as a *verbum relativum*, surely means here the return of Yahweh's compassion as in Jon 3:9.[85] The result would be that "he will leave a blessing behind him."[86] The specific formulation recalls "behind it" (אחריו), 2:3. Instead of scorched earth and barren desert, the forgiving God leaves behind "blessing," i.e., a condition that makes life possible, such as is granted when there is grain, new–wine, and olive–oil.[87] Only this grant of life, which has to come from Yahweh himself, makes possible once again "meal–offerings and libations" for the covenant God as a sign of the community of salvation.[88] Through the total threat to its existence Israel has to learn again that it lives by God's compassion, even in its sacrificial cultus. It is the rediscovered prophetic eschatology alone that supports a grateful life of covenant in the Torah.

■ **15** In vv 15–17 there follow the individual cultic instructions for the new turning to Yahweh commanded in 2:12–14, just as in 1:13–14 instructions followed the call to lamentation (1:5–12).[89] With the call to give the horn–signal, the first colon of the alarm cry from 2:1aα is repeated.[90] Flight from Yahweh's

---

79 See Wolff, *Hosea*, 52f [64]; and Alfred Jepsen, "Gnade und Barmherzigkeit im Alten Testament," *KuD* 7 (1961): 261–64.

80 See Wolff, *Hosea*, 52f [64]; Alfred Jepsen, "Gnade und Barmherzigkeit im Alten Testament," *KuD* 7 (1961): 264–71; and Klaus Koch, "'... denn seine Güte währet ewiglich,'" *EvTh* 21 (1961): 538f.

81 רעה is used with the nuance "ruin, disaster" (*Unheil*) in accord with Jer 1:14; cf. Am 3:6.

82 An interrogative form of skeptical wisdom: Eccl 2:19; 6:12; and Jer 17:9.

83 2 Sam 12:22; Lam 3:29b.

84 Am 5:15; Zeph 2:3; Jon 3:9.

85 Cf. the use of שוב in Jon 3:9a, 9b.

86 On the language usage, cf. Ezr 9:8, הַשְׁאִיר לָנוּ פְּלֵיטָה ("to leave us a remnant").

87 Cf. 2:19; Dtn 7:13; 16:10, 15, 17; and Hag 2:15–19.

88 See pp. 31–33 on 1:9, 13.

89 On the interpretation of the verb forms as narrative tenses, see p. 57.

90 See p. 43.

enemy army should lead to seeking refuge with Yah-weh. Instead of the second colon of 2:1aα we find now terminologically fixed directives for a day of fasting.[91]

■ **16** As in 1:14, the determination of a work–free period of fasting is made more precise by the call to assemble for the purpose of prayer, but not by any further ritual instructions (cf. 1:13). In postexilic times "congregation" (קהל) designates the people gathered for worship.[92] "Sanctify" (קדש pi'el) means here: to make complete preparations (Josh 3:5) for worship activity, which involves desisting from work, food, and sexual intercourse.[93] First the "elders, aged" (זקנים) are specifically mentioned. They are not named before the "inhabitants of the land" as in 1:2 and 14, but as the first segment of the congregation of the people, alongside the infants. For this reason the reference here is probably not to the incumbents of an office,[94] but to those who are old.[95] What leads Joel in this passage (in contrast with 1:14aβ) to make the completely unusual, explicit reference to children and infants, bridegroom and bride, as well as to the "old people"? He knows from the words of the prophets concerning the Day of Yahweh that even the children and women will not be spared on that day (Is 13:16; Ezek 30:17–18), and from the Jeremianic traditions, that the joy of bride and bridegroom in particular will be smothered in the hour of Yahweh's judgment (Jer 7:34; 16:9; 25:10). Behind the appeals to infants and bridal couples stands the recognition of the relevance of the prophetic eschatology for all segments of the people; the appeals can hardly be explained from general cultic practice. "Bridegroom" (חתן) and "bride" (כלה), who are to come out of their chamber, designate those who are engaged and are in the process of consummating their marriage vows for the first time. "Room" (חדר) is the

term used also in Ju 15:1; 2 Sam 13:10; 2 Kgs 9:2; and Song 1:4 for the dark inner room in which the couple can be alone.[96] "Chamber" (חפה), also in Ps 19:6 [5], appears in Jewish law as the "usual place of cohabitation with one's wife."[97] Even those are called whom the law exempts from military service (Dtn 20:7; 24:5),[98] for it is not just any war that threatens here, but destruction by Yahweh himself. Therefore the community has to assemble without any exceptions.

■ **17** The final directive pertains to the priests as the spokesmen of the community before God. "Between the vestibule and the altar" (i.e., between the entrance hall of the Temple and the great altar of burnt offering in front of the Temple) they are to make their penitential lament. That is the place where, according to Ezek 8:16 (G and others), twenty men turned their backs instead of their faces to Yahweh.[99] In the Herodian Temple the open space referred to measured twenty–two cubits.[100] Thus a large number of priests found room here to turn toward the sanctuary and thereby toward Yahweh. Murder in this place was a most extreme sacrilege (Mt 23:35). As in 1:15–20, here too the prayer to be said is quoted, but in this case it is a terse and unified petitionary lament. It consists of two petitions, to which are added two motives for Yahweh's intervention. "To pity" (חוס) usually denotes the flowing (of the tears) of the eye, especially in Dtn (7:16; 13:9 [8]; etc.) and in Ezek (5:11; 7:4; etc.), as well as in Is 13:18; it comes to mean compassionate grief as such and can stand in parallelism with "repent, be sorry" (נחם; cf. Ezek 24:14). In this sense it expresses here the expectation of vv 13b and 14a. It does not occur in the laments of the Psalter, but it does appear with the same meaning in Neh 13:22.[101] The priests are to remind Yahweh of his people. In parallelism

91 Cf. 1:14a and p. 33.
92 Ps 107:32; Lev 16:33; 2 Chr 30:2, 4, 13, 17, 23–24.
93 1 Sam 21:6 [5]; cf. Joel 1:13–14 and above pp. 32–33.
94 See p. 25.
95 Cf. Chary, *Les prophètes*, 202.
96 Cf. Gillis Gerleman, *Ruth. Das Hohelied*, BK 18 (Neukirchen: Verlag des Erziehungsvereins, 1965), 98.
97 Miš. Yebamot 3.10, etc. Cf. Dalman, *Arbeit* 6, 35; and Georges A. Barrois, *Manuel d'Archéologie Biblique*, vol. 2 (Paris: A. et J. Picard, 1953), 18.
98 The Mišnah (Berakot 2.5a) even exempts the bride-groom from the evening recitation of the שמע ישראל (i.e., the "Šema'" or "Šema' Israel").
99 Cf. Zimmerli, *Ezechiel*, 220f; and Jer 2:27; 32:33; and 2 Chr 29:6.
100 Miš. Middot 5.1.
101 Cf. Jer 13:14; Ezek 24:14; Ps 72:13; and, especially, Jon 4:10–11.

with "people" (עם) we find "possession" (נחלה); the people of Jerusalem are thus designated as Yahweh's "property." The frequent translation "inheritance" misses both the original sense of the root נחל (as the occurrences of *naḥālum* at Mari show)[102] and the Old Testament usage with respect to the נחלה of God.[103] When would the people of Yahweh, as his property, be handed over to shame? This would be so especially were they to fall into foreign hands. Elsewhere without exception משל ב means "to rule over."[104] This is also how all ancient translations have rendered it. More recent interpretation has deemed it necessary to translate instead "to scorn, mock" because it has been assumed that 2:1ff refers to the same locusts depicted in chap. 1. As soon, however, as one recognizes in the "numerous and mighty people" of 2:2 (cf. vv 5–6, 11) the fulfillment of prophetic threats of a foreign army led up by Yahweh himself, there is no longer any reason to depart from the normal translation. The prayer is to focus on the destruction of the people of Jerusalem as the people of God in the midst of the surrounding nations. Only then does the weight of final lamentation over the mockery of the nations also become intelligible. "Where is their God?"—this question does not pertain to an extraordinary economic crisis, but to the end of the covenant people, and thereby it calls Yahweh himself into question before the nations.[105]

Aim

A startling command to sound the alarm sets the basic tone for the chapter (vv 1a, 15a). Its urgency surpasses that of chap. 1, primarily because the intention is to effect an unreserved change in thinking and willing.[106] Why is it not enough to pray for relief from present calamities? Instead of a favorable response to the earlier pleas, the approach of an even greater emergency has to be announced.

Nor does this announcement actually bring anything new. In different words, which receive their coloring from the locust catastrophe already experienced, it points to the long–proclaimed prophetic message of the Day of Yahweh.[107] It articulates this for those who, even into the time of the disaster's onset, had either ignored the old message or considered it void. The God from Sinai will himself appear anew with an irresistible enemy army. Thus the time of an extraordinary emergency becomes the time to sound the alarm for the final emergency. The prophetic eschatology proves not to have lost its relevance.

In its present form the message is directed exclusively against the people that belong to the sanctuary of Jerusalem. Against those who know themselves to be the people of God (v 17b) the question is hurled: "Who can survive the Day of Yahweh?" (v 11b). Since Amos (5:18–20) and Isaiah (2:9–11) it had been known that there was no escape, no way out of it, unless it be toward Yahweh himself (vv 12–13a).[108] This road, however, cannot be taken with confidence in one's own resolve and in the functioning cultus, but only in the expectation of free, divine compassion (vv 13b–14a).[109] The result is that the demanded reorientation (vv 12b–13a) is nowhere characterized as a turning away from specific social, political, or cultic transgressions. The fact that there is no reference at all in this connection to any sin of Israel has always attracted attention. Not the slightest touch of casuistry and moral criticism can be felt. But what then does "returning" mean? Surely this above all else: to reckon with the God who *has been* proclaimed as the one who *is* to come; to see the goal of God's ways

---

102 Georges Boyer, *Textes juridiques*, ARM(T) 8 (Paris: Imprimerie Nationale, 1958), nos. 11.26; 12.5; and 13.4, 9. Cf. Martin Noth, *Die Ursprünge des alten Israel im Lichte neuer Quellen*, Arbeitsgemeinschaft für Forschung des Landes Nordrhein–Westfalen 94 (Köln: Westdeutscher Verlag, 1961), 18f (reprinted in *idem, Aufsätze zur biblischen Landes– und altertumskunde*, vol. 2 ["Beiträge altorientalischer Texte zur Geschichte Israels"]; ed. Hans Walter Wolff [Neukirchen–Vluyn: Neukirchener Verlag, 1971], 254f).

103 Friedrich Horst, "Zwei Begriffe für Eigentum (Besitz): נַחֲלָה und אֲחֻזָּה" in *Verbannung und Heimkehr: Beiträge zur Geschichte und Theologie Israels im 6. und 5. Jahrhundert v. Chr. (Festschrift für Wilhelm Rudolph)*, ed. Arnulf Kuschke (Tübingen: J. C. B. Mohr [Paul Siebeck], 1961), 142f.

104 Cf. especially Ps 106:41; Dtn 15:6; and Lam 5:8.

105 Cf. especially the following Deuteronomistic passages, linguistically related to our text in many respects: Ex 32:12 and Dtn 9:26–28. Cf. also Ps 44:12–15 [11–14]; 79:4, 10; 115:2; and Ezek 22:4.

106 See pp. 48–49 on vv 12b–13a.

107 See pp. 43–45, 47–48.

108 See pp. 48–49.

not in the functioning cultus of Jerusalem, but to wait, under the proclaimed prophetic word, for him who will show himself to be irrefutably lord in the world of nations. In the present hour it is evident that only by a new demonstration of his mercy can Jerusalem expect to have a future. Since that future now hangs completely in the balance, along with the responsible elders even the youngest and most helpless (Ps 8:3 [2]), as well as those diverted by private joy, are called upon to raise through the mouth of the priests the prayerful outcry of the assembled community (vv 16–17). This outcry can move Yahweh only because he himself has won his people as his possession; and therefore should the foreign nations triumph over Jerusalem, he himself would be called into question by the world of nations.

Under this proclamation of Joel, Jerusalem moved on toward the coming of Jesus Christ. This was the issue that led to division. There were those who continued to seek life in fulfilling the dictates of the Torah; others heard the call of Joel and similar appeals, and looked forward in humility to a new, free act of mercy on God's part. The former fell under the domination of the nations (v 17b), the latter recognized in Christ a heritage of blessing which yielded much more than the continuation of the old worship (v 14).[110]

But in the history of the new Jerusalem, too, the voice of Joel remains relevant. All too frequently a well–functioning churchliness is considered the goal of faith. The word heard concerning the lord and redeemer of all men, concerning his strict judgment on all lukewarmness as well as on all fanatical activity, and the relevance of the fellowship of the crucified with the godless—these should inform faith that looks to the future. The reorientation commanded has lost nothing of its urgency, since it remains true after the resur-

rection of Christ: "Waiting is a mighty deed" (Chr. Blumhardt).

From the perspective of Joel 2:1–17, this first requires of the community the anxious expectation that it itself as one no longer waiting must face judgment, just as the letters to the churches in the Apocalypse of John impress this upon the congregations. The church's name can be erased (Rev 3:5), unless a reorientation toward the word that has been heard begins to reckon with the coming Lord (v 13). If faith does not remain—sustained by the proclaimed word—on the way towards seeing, with hope in the crucified one as Lord of all lords, as peace for all who lack peace, as judge of all who are self–assured, then it will suffer decay and lose its savor. Self–assured and secure churchliness has to experience first, then, that its two last props—the natural craving for piety on the part of weak persons and the political acts of helping that spring from ambiguous interests—can quickly be broken. It can march on into the future only with its eye upon him who has put his seal on Joel 2:13b. For on what basis should Christians be able to say more, with reference to their respective churches, than Joel: "Perhaps he will repent of it once more" (v 14)? Is it not enough today, in the hour when judgment on the house of God comes due (1 Pt 4:17), to accept in the name of Jesus the great offer that Joel voices in the name of his God?—"But even now: reorient yourselves toward me with all your thinking and willing!"

---

109 See pp. 49–50.
110 Cf. already 3:1–2.

New Life for All
Who Call upon Yahweh

Bibliography

Karl Budde
" 'Der von Norden' in Joel 2 : 20," *OLZ* 22 (1919) : 1–5.

Idem
"Der Umschwung in Joel 2," *OLZ* 22 (1919) : 104–10.

Brevard S. Childs
"The Enemy from the North and the Chaos Tradition," *JBL* 78 (1959) : 187–98.

Ernst Ludwig Ehrlich
Der Traum im Alten Testament, BZAW 73 (Berlin : A. Töpelmann, 1953), 140–42.

Albert Gelin
"L'annonce de la Pentecôte (Joël 3 : 1–5)," *BVC* 27 (1959) : 15–19.

Hugo Gressmann
Der Messias, FRLANT 42 (Göttingen, 1929), 137–39.

Alexander Kerrigan
"The 'sensus plenior' of Joel, III, 1–5 in Act., II, 14–36" in *Sacra Pagina : Miscellanea Biblica, Congressus Internationalis Catholici de Re Biblica*, vol. 2 ; ed. J. Coppens, A. Deschamps, É. Massaux ; Bibliotheca Ephemeridum Theologicarum Lovaniensium 12–13 (Paris : Librairie Lecoffre, J. Gabalda et Cie, 1959), 295–313.

Otto Plöger
Theocracy and Eschatology, tr. S. Rudman (Richmond, Va. : John Knox, 1968), 96–105 [117–28].

Cecil Roth
"The Teacher of Righteousness and the Prophecy of Joel," *VT* 13 (1963) : 91–95.

Johannes Hendrik Scheepers
Die gees van God en die gees van die mens in die Ou Testament (Kampen : J. H. Kok, 1960), 223, 290–92.

2

18	Then Yahweh became jealous[a] for his land and felt[a] pity for his people.	a
19	Yahweh answered and said to his people: I am now about to send to you grain, new–wine, and olive–oil, that you can have your fill of it.[b] And I will no more give you over to shame[c] among the nations,	b
20	but I shall drive away the northerner from you and expel him into a land that is parched and desolate,[d] his vanguard into the eastern sea and his rear–guard into the western sea.	c d

a θ' ($\zeta\eta\lambda\acute{\omega}\sigma\epsilon\iota$ ... $\kappa\alpha\grave{\iota}$ $\phi\epsilon\acute{\iota}\sigma\epsilon\tau\alpha\iota$) reads וַיְקַנֵּא ... וַיַּחְמֹל and draws the verse thereby toward the preceding prayer ("and may Yahweh ..."), as does Merx who also reads jussives in v 19 and has the prayer, as a result, with its enclosed speech of Yahweh, extend through to the end of the book. *G*, *T* and *V* confirm *M*.

b   שׂבע, like the other *verba copiae et inopiae*, is construed with the accusative, see Gesenius–Kautzsch–Cowley, par. 117z; Brockelmann, *Syntax*, par. 90d.

c   *T* (חיסודי כפנא) interprets on the basis of v 19a: "the shame of hunger."

d   *G* does not translate ושממה.

His stench shall rise.
  His foul smell shall rise.
    [e]For he has acted great.[e]

21 Fear not, land!
  Be glad and rejoice!
    For Yahweh has acted great!

22 Fear[f] not, beasts of the field!
  For the pastures of the range are green.
  Indeed, the tree bears its fruit,
    the fig tree and the vine give their produce.[g]

23 And (you), sons of Zion, be glad!
  Rejoice in[h] Yahweh, your God!
  For he gives you <food>[i] according to (covenant) righteousness
    and makes rain to fall for you,
    the <early>[j] and the latter rain,
    <as>[k] formerly.

24 The threshing floors shall be full of grain,
  the vats shall overflow with new—wine and olive—oil.

25 And I will restore to you the years that the locust has eaten,
  [l]the hopper and the jumper and the biter,[m]
    my great army,
      which I sent among you.

e–e In *M*, *G* (ὅτι ἐμεγάλυνε τὰ ἔργα αὐτοῦ) and *T* (ארי אסגי למיעבד בישן "... has done much evil") the northerner is the subject of the sentence; the suggestions to insert "Yahweh" from v 21b (Weiser) or to read אַגְדִּיל (Bewer; Sellin; Arnold B. Ehrlich, *Randglossen zur Hebräischen Bibel: Textkritisches, Sprachliches und Sachliches*, vol. 5 [Leipzig, 1912 = Hildesheim: Georg Olms, 1968], 220f) have no basis in tradition. The colon could more easily be seen as an erroneous doublet of v 21b (cf. Joseph Trinquet, *Habaquq, Abadias, Joël*, SBJ [Paris: Les Éditions du Cerf, ²1959]; note vv 26b ‖ 27b, and 4:13aβ ‖ 13bβ); but יהוה is lacking. On גדל hipʿil as a *verbum relativum* with adverbial meaning, cf. Gesenius–Kautzsch–Cowley, par. 114n; in this context the meaning includes the dimension of haughtiness: cf. Ps 35:26; 38:17 [16]; 41:10 [9]; 55:13 [12]; Jer 48:26, 42; Zeph 2:8, 10; Lam 1:9; and Dan 8:4, 8, 11, 25.

f The second person masculine plural sometimes takes the place of the feminine form, especially when the verb stands first; thus also in Ruth 1:8b and Am 4:1. Cf. Joüon, par. 150a; Brockelmann, *Syntax*, par. 50a.

g חיל ("strength, ability"; *G* τὴν ἰσχὺν αὐτῶν ["their strength" = "what only they can"]) stands here as a synonym for פרי ("fruit"); cf. *G*⁴⁶,¹⁰⁶ τὸν καρπόν, and *T* פיריהון.

h *T* (במימרא דיהוה) interprets "in the word of Yahweh."

i *G* (τὰ βρώματα), *L* (*escas*) and *S* (*m'kwlt'*) probably presuppose מַאֲכָל ("food"); cf. אֹכֶל in 1:16 and the exclusive reference of 2:21–24 to chap. 1 (see p. 63). *M* ("teacher" = σ′ [τὸν ὑποδεικνύοντα], *T* and *V* [*doctorem iustitae*]) fits the context less well and may have come about under the influence of v 23b; see textual note "j" and pp. 63–64.

j *M* ("teacher") can have derived from יוֹרֶה ("early rain," thus 34 manuscripts). Rabbinic tradition interprets the early rain as a "teacher": it instructs the people to bring the fruits into the house and to make the roofs watertight; cf. Dalman, *Arbeit* 1/1, 122. The same colon (גשם יורה ומלקוש) stands in Jer 5:24; cf. also Dtn 11:14; both times יורה ומלקוש is a specifying appositive. *G* confirms the correct reading (ὑετὸν πρόϊμον καὶ ὄψιμον).

k *G* (καθὼς ἔμπροσθεν, reflected also in *S* and *V*) presupposes כְּרִאשׁוֹן, which is preferable as a parallel to לצדקה (see p. 64). *M* ("in the first") probably thinks of the first month, Nisan, as does *T* (בירח ניסן).

l According to *G* the four words for locust are uniformly connected by conjunctions. However, we should probably not assume והילק as the original text. The change in sequence alone, over against 1:4, shows that originally only the familiar word for locust was used here; the other designations were added later from 1:4 as (secondary?) apposition.

m *T* (עממיא ולישניא שלטוניא ומלכותא) has already

26	Then you will really eat and be sated,[n] and will praise the name of Yahweh your God, because he has dealt wondrously[o] with you. [And my people shall never more be put to shame.][p]
27	And you shall know that in the midst of Israel am I, and (that) I, Yahweh, am your God, and no one else, and (that) my people shall never—more[q] be put to shame.
3:1 [28]	Afterward I will pour out my[r] spirit on all flesh. Your sons and your daughters will become prophets. Your old men will have dreams.[s] Your young men will see visions.
2 [29]	And even upon the[t] manservants and upon the[t] maidservants I will pour out my[u] spirit in those days.
3 [30]	And I will place portents in the sky[v] and on the earth,[v] blood and fire and mushrooms[w] of smoke.
4 [31]	[x]The sun becomes darkened, and the moon bloody,[x] before the Day of Yahweh comes, the great and terrible one.
5 [32]	And everyone who calls upon[y] the name of Yahweh will be saved.

interpreted the locusts to be "peoples, tongues, governments, and kingdoms," which appears in a concretizing way in a gloss in G^Q (sixth century): αἰγύπτιοι βαβυλώνιοι ἀσσύριοι ἕλληνες ῥωμαῖοι ("Egyptians, Babylonians, Assyrians, Greeks, Romans").

n   אכל ושבע (literally "to eat and to be sated") has become one thought–unit; cf. Dtn 8:10 and Ps 22:27a [26a].

o   לְהַפְלִיא is used adverbially, like הַפְלֵא in Is 29:14 and 2 Chr 2:8 [9].

p   V 26b corresponds verbatim to v 27b. Here as there the preceding form of address is abandoned. Since Wellhausen, v 26b has been considered a secondarily intrusive, erroneously premature conclusion. The sentence is more fitting when attached to the recognition formula in v 27; cf. Is 49:23b; (50:7). T insures the meaning of עמי against a misinterpretation under the influence of v 25 (חיל) by adding בית ישראל ("house of Israel").

q   G (οὐκέτι ["no longer"]) presupposes here, in contrast to v 26b, another עוד, which was probably not original.

r   T makes this more explicit: רוח קדשי ("my holy spirit"). G interprets grammatically under the influence of Nu 11:17, 25 (ἀπὸ τοῦ πνεύματός μου = L [de spiritu meo]): "(shares) of my spirit." α′ and σ′ (τὸ πνεῦμά μου) support M.

s   The effectual object is derived from the same root as the verb ("to dream dreams"); see Brockelmann, *Syntax*, par. 92; and Joüon, par. 125a.

t   T (על עבדין ועל אמהן) does not reflect the definite articles. G corresponds original!y (according to G^{WS*VB}) to M. But the later G tradition generally inserts (cf. Justin, Tertullian, and Augustine) a reinterpreting μου ("upon *my* manservants and *my* maidservants"), as does L (*super servos meos et ancillas meas*).

u   T and G are at variance with M as in 3:1; see textual note "r" above.

v   Later G manuscripts (see Joseph Ziegler, ed., *Duodecim prophetae*, Septuaginta Vetus Testamentum Graecum 13 [Göttingen: Vandenhoeck & Ruprecht, ²1967] 235f) supplement οὐρανῷ ἄνω ("sky *above*") and γῆς κάτω ("earth *below*"), and insert σημεῖα ("signs") before ἐπὶ τῆς γῆς; in this they correspond to Acts 2:19.

w   If תימרה has the same root as תָּמָר ("date palm"), then it means the special "stone–pine form" of, for example, a volcano cloud (Robinson).

x–x   The Hebrew reads: "The sun is transformed into darkness and the moon into blood." The inversion indicates that nothing new has been added, but that v 3 is expanded by a circumstantial clause.

y   קרא ב does not mean "to call with," but "to enter as one who calls into intensive contact with"; cf. ראה ב and שמע ב, where ב also introduces the object in the context of intense personal interaction. Cf. Gesenius–Kautzsch–Cowley, par. 119k; Oskar Grether, *Hebräische Grammatik für den akademischen*

For on Mount Zion and in Jerusalem
there will be escape,
as Yahweh has said,
and among those who survive[z] (are
those) whom Yahweh calls.

Unterricht (München: Evangelischer Presseverband für Bayern, ²1955), par. 89b.

z   *G* (καὶ εὐαγγελιζόμενοι) read וּמְבַשְּׂרִים ("and bearers of good news"); α′ and θ′ (καὶ τοῖς καταλελειμμένοις) support *M*. Noteworthy is *S*: "as the Lord has said to those who survive, whom the Lord appoints." In every respect v 5b gives the impression of being a later addition which was tolerable of various interpretations due to its isolated position after the concluding כאשר אמר יהוה. Sellin tampers extensively with the textual tradition when he reconstructs a *parallelismus membrorum* by transposing ובירושלם from v 5bα to v 5bβ; he claims that it was lost through haplography alongside the graphically similar שרידים in v 5bβ, and was later restored erroneously in v 5bα, while שרידים was filled out to ובשרידים.

Form

The decisive turn of affairs in the book of Joel comes with 2:18. To this point the book has been concerned with the present and future distress of Jerusalem as prelude to the advent of the Day of Yahweh, with the call to repentance being the result. However, from here on only oracles pertaining to the future are collected, oracles that promise new and salutory life for Jerusalem and Judah, as well as the warding off of all their opponents. Within this second major part of the book of Joel there is a significant division after 3:5, since the foreign nations move to the fore thematically only from 4:1 on, the Day of Yahweh then being proclaimed as a day of judgment on the enemies of Jerusalem. In this second section of the second major part there no longer occurs any address to Jerusalem according to the basic form of the "assurance oracle answering a plea" in 2:19—3:5.[1] The first section reaches its conclusion in 3:5 with an "as Yahweh has said," corresponding to the introduction in 2:(18), 19. The Vulgate and, after it, the Septuagint have also linked 3:1–5 closely to 2:18–27, as 2:28–32 in their chapter division.[2]

There is lack of unanimity concerning the exact location of the turning point to the second major part of the book. Budde[3] includes 2:18 (with jussive vocalization)[4] in the prayer of 2:17b, and as a result he has the words of salvation begin only with 2:19. Merx also

included 2:19 with what preceded it, so that then everything following up to the end of the book of Joel would have to be read as the content of the prayer enjoined upon the priests in 2:17. On the other hand, Hitzig[5] wanted to read narrative tenses from 2:17a on, and Bewer even from 2:15 on (as do *M*, *G*, *T* and *V* in 2:18–19). The asyndetically aligned verbal forms in 2:15–16 speak against the latter suggestion; they authenticate themselves as parallels to 1:14 and thereby clearly as imperatives. The imperfects in 2:17 are to be regarded as jussives, since יבכו ("let them weep") in 2:17a continues יצא ("let [him/her] leave") in 2:16b without further caesura. The whole textual tradition argues against a jussive interpretation of 2:19 (Merx), as does also the fact that Yahweh is addressed in the second person in the prayer of 2:17b. Moreover it would be completely unusual to find "oracles answering a plea" of such an extent incorporated in the prayer of lament without another repetition of the complaint or the petition. It remains to consider the proposal of Budde that 2:18 alone be shifted to the prayer, and that because the new mention of Yahweh in 2:19 stands out. But the transition from second– (2:17b) to third–person reference to Yahweh argues against this. "Yahweh" becomes intelligible in 2:19 if 2:18 is regarded as an independent piece of narrative analogous to 1:4, which is then followed by 2:19ff as

---

1   See p. 58.

2   Cf. Noth, *World*, 347f [309], and above p. 8.

3   Karl Budde, "Der Umschwung in Joel 2," *OLZ* 22 (1919): 105f.

4   See textual note "a" to 2:18.

5   Ferdinand Hitzig, "*Die zwölf kleinen Propheten*, KEH 1 (Leipzig, 1838, ⁴1881: [with Heinrich Steiner]).

evidence,[6] with the introduction of the quotation belonging to the evidence.

In the following section varied pieces are quoted, all of them included within a single structural frame as parts of a great "assurance oracle answering a plea" (*Erhörungszuspruch*), based on the turning to Yahweh described in 2:12–17. Comparable to this changeover from a communal prayer of lament to an "oracle of weal" are the transitions in Ps 60 from vv 3–7 [1–5] to vv 8–10 [6–8]; in Ps 85 from vv 2–8 [1–7] to vv 9–14 [8–13]; and in 2 Chr 30 from vv 6–13 to vv 14–17.[7] As the basic element of the oracle answering a plea we usually find divine first–person speech (2:19–20, 25–27; 3:1–3), which mainly conveys a mood of encouragement.[8]

If we observe the change of person between speaker and affected subject, together with the variations in specific themes, six parts can be distinguished: 2:19–20, 21–24, 25–27; 3:1–2, 3–4, 5. הנני (plus participle) at the head of the first utterance (2:19–20) serves as a chief recognition word for the oracle answering a plea, at least after the exile.[9] The content relationships between 2:19 and 1:4ff and between 2:20 and 2:1ff[10] confirm this characterization.

The second piece, consisting of three strophes (2:21–24),[11] is authenticated by the other chief recognition word of the genre of the assurance oracle answering a plea: "Fear not!" (2:21, 22).[12] The assurance is developed by means of elements of the hymn, the call, and the motivation for praise (2:21b, 23–24); a beginning in the direction of this combination is present already in Is 41:14–16 (cf. vv 14a and 16a) and is reflected in the thanksgiving hymn for an answered plea in Ps 118 (cf. v 6 [5] and v 24 [23]). In keeping with the hymnic style, Yahweh is spoken of

not in the first person but in the third, which to be sure happens also in the oracle answering a plea (cf. Ps 85:9–14 [8–13]). Here it seems strange because the third speech (2:25–27) returns to the divine address of 2:19–20.

In terms of content the third speech is connected with the preceding one, but it makes the chain of the consecutive perfects continue into the statement of purpose of the recognition formula: "And you shall know that in the midst of Israel am I, and I, Yahweh, am your God, and no one else" (2:27). Thus we have here an "oracle of divine self–manifestation."[13] This form has already melted into the oracle answering a plea in Deutero–Isaiah (Is 45:2–6; 49:22–26).[14] The typical "and no one else" also shows that Joel takes up Deutero–Isaianic tradition in our passage.[15] Here the "self–disclosure oracle" (*Erweiswort*) no longer concludes with the statement of recognition; instead, the latter element forms a bridge leading to further statements, whereby the simple form is developed into a two–stage self–disclosure oracle. The fulfillment of the preceding assurances should lead to the certain recognition that Yahweh will act dependably with Israel even beyond them.[16] We must note first that the three sayings in 2:19–27 represent on the whole a greatly developed assurance oracle answering a plea, which conveys the impression of a literary composite, due to the seams in the transitions to 2:21 and 25.

This characterization of the section is confirmed by the connection of the sayings in 3:1–5. The introductory "Afterward it will come to pass" attaches them to the foregoing just as clearly as it sets them off from it. Specific marks of the genre of the assurance oracle answering a plea are no longer present; the transforming imprint of the self–disclosure oracle be-

---

6 Similarly 1:5–14; see p. 23.

7 Cf. Wolff, *Hosea*, 119 [151].

8 Note the use of the second person plural in 2:19–20, 25–27; 3:1. Cf. 2 Chr 20:15–17.

9 Cf. Is 58:9; 65:1. Cf. also Paul Humbert, "La formule hébraïque en *hineni* suivi d'un participe" in *idem, Opuscules d'un Hébraïsant*, Mémories de l'Université de Neuchâtel 26 (Neuchâtel: Secrétariat de l'Université, 1958): 54–59.

10 See p. 62.

11 See p. 63.

12 Cf. Lam 3:57 and, on this text, Joachim Begrich,

"Das priesterliche Heilsorakel," *ZAW* 52 (1934): 81–92; reprinted in *idem, Gesammelte Studien*, 217–31.

13 Cf. 1 Kgs 20:13, 28; and also Walther Zimmerli, "Das Wort des göttlichen Selbsterweises (Erweiswort), eine prophetische Gattung" in *Mélanges Bibliques rédigés en l'honneur de André Robert*, Travaux de l'Institut Catholique de Paris 4 (Paris: Bloud et Gay, 1957), 154–66 (reprinted in *idem, Gottes Offenbarung. Gesammelte Aufsätze zum Alten Testament*, ThB 19 [München: Chr. Kaiser, 1963], 120–32).

14 Cf. Walther Zimmerli, *Erkenntnis Gottes nach dem Buche Ezechiel. Eine theologische Studie*, AThANT 27

comes effective now. Only the basic element of divine speech (3:1–3 as in 2:19–20, 25–27)—a common feature of the prophetic oracles of promise in the messenger style generally—and the mode of assurance (second person plural of the affected subjects in 3:1–2) which was sustained in 2:19–27, are continued. Thus the fourth oracle (3:1–2) exhibits the general form of an absolute assurance of salvation, the fifth—immediately attached—that of an announcement of a sign,[17] the sixth—attached with "And it shall come to pass" (והיה) as a new utterance, like 3:1 and 4:18—that of a conditional announcement of salvation.[18] The condition—calling upon the name of Yahweh—with its content references to 2:12–17, ties the last saying into the chain introduced as oracles answering a plea in 2:18–19. Since it is no longer formulated as divine speech, it appeals explicitly to an utterance of Yahweh (3:5b). Thus the character of the oracles concerning the deliverance of Jerusalem as a chain of quotations within the frame of a great narrative context is confirmed.[19]

The recognition that the whole text is literary and composite makes it appear inappropriate from the beginning to attempt to restore, by means of transposition or deletion of "additions," the original text of a uniform, orally proclaimed oracle answering a plea. We have here a composite of oracles answering pleas, proclaimed orally in the days of Joel and referring to the specific initial situation (2:25!), with transmitted oracles of weal that refer directly (2:20; 3:3–4) or indirectly to the renewed threat of the Day of Yahweh (2:1–11). It is the task of the exposition of the text to recognize the connection achieved by Joel.

Thus we cannot accept Sellin's proposal to shift 2:25–27, on account of the divine first person speech, to the position before 2:21–24, especially since 2:21–24 cannot be characterized as a "thanksgiving song."[20] The transposition disturbs the probably deliberate assonance of 2:21b with 2:20bβ, as well as

the connection in content between 2:24 and 2:25. It remains difficult also to deny that sentences like 3:2 belong to an original text of Joel, even though it is obvious that they have the character of supplements; compare "and even . . . in those days" (וגם . . . בימים ההמה), the taking up of the chief catchwords from 3:1, and the absence of the suffixes with the objects. But is not this the way in which Joel himself fits brick upon brick, drawing both on tradition and on his own insight? Cf. "but even" (וגם) in 2:3bβ, 12; "in those days" (בימים ההמה) in 4:1. Something like this is even truer of 3:5. Only 2:26b, as a doublet of 2:27b, probably goes back to a copying error.

The literary character stands against any expectation of a poetic structure. Such can be recognized only in individual pieces. For example, 2:20 stands out with its impressive structure: the announcement of the driving away of the northerner exhibits—after the indirect preliminary announcement in 2:19b—three prosodic units of equal length. The first one begins with two longer synonymous cola, with a slight intensification in the second colon. The second portrays the goal of the destruction in two precisely synonymous cola. The third forms a concluding tricolon; it marks the high point of the threat with two two–stress cola, to which is added synthetically a third, isolated colon as a motivation and a forceful conclusion. Otherwise, beginnings of synonymous parallelism can usually be recognized, most clearly in 2:21–24, without evidence for a strict development of cola and prosodic units. 2:19, 25–27 and 3:1–5 reveal that it is more important to Joel to absorb the tradition into his own contemporary concerns than to achieve poetic form. Yet here, too, various synonymous parallelisms exhibit elevated language, and no less in chap. 3 (vv 1aβ–b, 4a) than previously. Altogether the style of chap. 3 is basically no different than the mixed style of the preceding sections.[21]

(Zürich: Zwingli–Verlag, 1954), 30–32 (= *idem Gottes Offenbarung*, 69–71).

15   Cf. especially Is 45:5–6, 18, 22; and 46:9.
16   For more detailed discussion of the "self–disclosure oracle," see pp. 65, 73–74.
17   Cf. Is 7:14; 1 Kgs 13:3; and Ex 7:3.
18   On the distinction between the announcement of salvation and the assurance of salvation, and their

occurrence side by side, see Wolff, *Hosea*, 47 [57].

19   See p. 57 on 2:18; cf. 1:3!
20   See p. 58.
21   See above.

Setting

The literary setting of our section is inexchangeable and so firmly built into the structure of the book of Joel that it cannot be interpreted without its preceding and following context. Here 2:18 takes up again the narrative tense of 1:4 and makes it understandable that the author is concerned right from the beginning that his story be handed on through the chain of the following generations. Just as the locust plague serves as a reminder of the eschatological day of terror for Jerusalem proclaimed by the prophets, so the report concerning Yahweh's gracious response in the present economic crisis prompts the renewed proclamation of eschatological assurances of salvation for Jerusalem (3:1–5). The connecting link ("Afterward it will come to pass") explains the exhortation to transmit the assurances to the generations to come.

One can ask, to be sure, whether it is not 4:1ff, rather than chap. 3, that should be attached immediately to 2:27, and whether chap. 3 must not be interpreted as a later addition.[22] For just as 2:19–27 proclaims the reversal in the already present economic crisis, 4:1–17 announces the turnabout in the battle of Yahweh and his army of nations against Jerusalem. Also, 4:15 and 16aβ correspond more precisely to 2:10 than to 3:4. Finally, the assurance of recognition in 4:17 appears as a parallel to 2:27. In view of this, one could regard 3:1–5 as a later, explanatory variant to 4:15–16, i.e., as a secondary expansion which would have its counterpart in 4:18–21.

But that leaves open the question why 3:1–5 stands after 2:27 and not after 4:17 or 4:21.

1. It is unthinkable that 3:1–5 should ever have followed the statements of 4:18–21 (which are different in nature) and especially the full assurance of 4:20.

2. The theme of the pouring out of the spirit and the deliverance on Mount Zion in the form extant in 3:1–5 cannot possibly be an explication of 4:15–17, because both the "afterward" of 3:1 and the assignment to "before the great and terrible Day of Yahweh" (3:4b) would become meaningless in that case.

3. Also 4:1 fits better with 3:5 than with 2:27; for 3:1–5 makes clear that "in the midst of Israel"

Yahweh is active and that "his people shall not be put to shame." On the other hand, 4:1ff speaks of Yahweh's acting with the nations and presupposes the deliverance of Jerusalem as an "escape" (3:5) in the midst of a lost world of nations. The eschatological judgment on the nations takes place simultaneously (cf. 4:1, "in those days") with the eschatological deliverance of Jerusalem (3:5), and certainly not with the temporary turn in the economic crisis in 2:19–27.

4. The attachment of the promise of the pouring out of the spirit to the assurance of the new fertility of the land is typical in the tradition and has been adopted by Joel, although he has distended and divided the parts. Thus the promise of the pouring out of the spirit follows upon the promise of the fertile irrigation of the dry land in the assurance oracle answering a plea in Is 44:2–5. Since the reversal of the economic distress has already been proclaimed as the driving out of the "great army" (2:25; cf. 1:6), it is probably the connection of the deliverance of Jerusalem from the foreign nations with the pouring out of the spirit in Ezek 39:28–29 and Zech 12:9–10 which becomes effective here.

5. The recognition formula can no longer be regarded in Joel as a "conclusion which was not expected to be continued."[23] Together with 4:17b, 2:27b already shows that this formula becomes the bridge in a two-stage self-disclosure oracle, a bridge that wants to have the preceding proclamation recognized not merely as a self-manifestation of Yahweh, but as an "omen" for his acts to come. It is significant that the formula appears in this function of transition already in the thematically related oracle of Ezek 39:25–29.

I see no sufficient reason, therefore, to detach 3:1–5 from the transmitted context. In view of the insight we have gained into the manner of working—whereby varied traditions are taken up, joined together and developed—it is also ill-advised to deny Joel's authorship of the chapter, attributing it to a second hand. It is much easier to believe that Joel was the originator of the proclamation of the sequence that starts with the driving out of the locusts and moves on to the pouring out of the spirit and to the eschatological deliverance of Jerusalem than that it derives from a later author,

---

22 Plöger, *Theocracy*, 100–105 [122–28].
23 Plöger, *Theocracy*, 101 [122].

who would probably have formulated chap. 3 in verbal agreement with Ezek 39:28–29 and Zech 12:9–10, and placed it after chap. 4. For Joel—prompted by the calamity that had begun in his time—raises the concerns of received prophetic eschatology, not in slavish dependence, but in a free reinterpretation.

For its dating, the section offers no exact clue. Yet the dependence on older literature and the mode of thought point to the fourth century. Before the author lie the traditions of the school of Ezekiel and those of Deutero–Isaiah; Ob 17a is quoted as a word of Yahweh.[24] Linguistic usage and thematic content belong in temporal proximity with Zech 12:10. Yet this latter text probably already looks back upon events of the time shortly before the turn to the fourth century.[25] The interest in the temporal sequence of the events (2:23b "the former time"; 2:25 "restoring of the years"; 3:1 "afterward"; 3:2 "in those days"; 3:4b "before") and the free incorporation of earlier eschatology into this time sequence show the first steps toward apocalyptic thinking. The sequence comes to grips with an established cultic soteriology. Thus it is characteristic that 2:19–27 does not speak of the renewal of the daily "meal–offerings and libations," which have been made impossible by the calamities of the present (1:9, 13). The blessing as that which makes new life possible, which was asked upon "meal–offerings and libations" (2:14b), takes on instead the form of the pouring out of the spirit, which brings into existence a whole people of prophets (3:1) rather than "ministers of the altar." Here are reflected controversies which are not yet present in the time of Malachi and Ezra–Nehemiah, and which can therefore hardly be dated to a time before the fourth century.

Interpretation

■ **18** Yahweh's response and with it all the following words concerning the future are introduced as his "becoming jealous for his land" and his "feeling pity."

"To become jealous for" (ל קנא pi'el), as a term for the zealous intercession of Yahweh on behalf of his people, is found first in Ezek 39:25 and Zech 1:14; 8:2.[26] In the sense of "saving zeal" this concept has now been detached from the First Commandment and the closely associated cultic usage,[27] but it still posits a sacred contrast; as a rule the nations appear in the same word field (cf. especially Ezek 39:25, 27–28). It is connected with the proclamation of the Day of Yahweh already in Zeph 1:18; there the "Day of Yahweh's wrath" stands parallel to the "fire of his zeal" (cf. Na 1:2). The usage of the word found now in Joel shows the change in the goal toward which Yahweh's day of terror is directed, a change not to be expected from the perspective of 2:1–11, hoped for nevertheless in 2:13–14, and prayed for in 2:17. On account of the reorientation of Israel towards the Day of Yahweh, that day becomes the day of Yahweh's zeal for, rather than against, his people. His "compassion" (חמל) is the cause for the freedom of this great reversal, as it was hoped for in 2:13b–14a with the catchword "to repent of" (נחם). As a term for Yahweh's compassionate interest in the fate of his people and especially of Jerusalem חמל is used, after Jeremiah (13:14), above all in the language of Ezekiel and his school, as well as in lament songs,[28] usually in a negative sense; positively it is still found in Mal 3:17 to express intervention on behalf of a lovable son.[29] All the following words of the book exemplify how Yahweh stands up with zeal for his beloved, helpless land and people, who are powerlessly exposed to the present and future catastrophes.

■ **19** Use of the verb ענה ("to answer") marks the introduction of an oracle answering a plea, in response to a prayer of lament.[30] The promise of "grain, new–wine and olive–oil" points back clearly at first to the calamity described in chap. 1.[31] But, strangely, it does not say that this will make "meal–offerings and libations" possible again.[32] It speaks with compassion only to the fact that people have enough to eat again, and thereby

---

24 See pp. 5–6.

25 Plöger, *Theocracy*, 85–87 [105f].

26 Cf. Zimmerli, *Ezechiel*, 213f. Cf. also the profane use of קנאה for the jealous passion of love in Nu 5:14, 30; Prv 6:34; and Song 8:6.

27 von Rad, *Theology* 1, 208 n. 41 [207, n. 36; 4th edition, 221].

28 Ezek 5:11; 7:4, 9; 8:18; 9:5, 10; 36:21; Lam 2:2,

17, 21; 3:43; Zech 11:6.

29 In Zech 11:5 it is used with reference to a defenseless animal.

30 1 Sam 7:9; Ps 20:2 [1]; 22:22b [21b]; 60:7 [5]; 118:5. On הנני with participle introducing an oracle answering a plea, see p. 58.

31 Cf. 1:10 and pp. 31–32.

32 See p. 31 on 1:9; see also 1:13 and 2:14.

it answers the lament of 1:16a. By contrast, 2:19b already refers back to 2:1–17, as is proved especially by its echoing the prayer in 2:17bα². Chap. 1 said nowhere that the present food shortage would lead to mockery by the nations. Such mockery is rather feared as a result of the attack of the apocalyptic army, threatened in 2:1–11, to which subject 2:20 then directly speaks.

■ 20 The division into verses has unfortunately separated 2:19b and 20. However, with its inverted word order, 2:20a shows that unlike the transition from 2:19a to 19b, a further new act of Yahweh is not being announced, but that the one stated by 2:19b is merely being clarified.

Who is "the northerner"?[33] In more recent times there has been a tendency to see in "the northerner" (הצפוני) the locusts of chap. 1, even though no allusion there suggests this interpretation (cf. also 2:25). Furthermore, the locusts in Palestine came, as a rule, from the east (Ex 10:19) or south.[34] The application of the term to the "north wind"[35] requires textual changes which are without any support in the unanimous textual tradition. Kjeld Jensen[36] has attempted to buttress his tentative suggestion of a Maccabean date for composition of the book of Joel by seeing in the "northerner" Antiochus IV Epiphanes, who according to 2 Macc 9:5–10 was struck by God with severe illness for his threats against Jerusalem, so that "the whole army camp had to bear the stench of his rotting body" (2 Macc 9:9). Apart from the general difficulties in dating Joel so late,[37] 2:20b already makes this identification completely unlikely (even if the eastern sea is taken to be the Indian Ocean).

The designation "the northerner" confirms, on the other hand, the interpretation of 2:1–11 which recognized in the "great and mighty people" the enemy from the north threatened by Jeremiah (1:14–15; 4:6; 6:1, 22) and Ezekiel (38:6, 15; 39:2).[38] The concept of the enemy may have been at home originally in mythic views.[39] Jeremiah sees in him a historical enemy power (as does already Is 5:26–30 in the "enemy from afar"). Does the unique designation "the northerner" (הצפוני), together with the conception that appeared in 2:1–11, indicate a remythologizing as a backlash against prophetic historicizing?[40] Undoubtedly, mythical features are noticeable already in Ezek 38—39 (and Is 13). The rising apocalypticism, which is clearly recognizable in Joel, begins to make use of mythological terminology as code words. This is connected with the fact that it wishes, on the one hand, to take up the prophetic proclamation, but is not able, on the other, to carry out a historical identification. Rather, Joel sees in the natural event of the locust catastrophe a pledge that the prophetic eschatology of disaster will not become void. He can describe its fulfillment only in the form of locust–like apocalyptic creatures, however, and he similarly uses the cryptic term "the northerner," with its mythological ring, for the "last enemy."

The description of the northerner's removal makes use of varied elements. His expulsion into the desert is completed by the drowning of his "vanguard" and his "rear guard." סוף ("end, rear guard") belongs to late Aramaizing language.[41] The sea "in front," the "eastern" one, is the Dead Sea (Ezek 47:18; Zech 14:8); the one "behind" (as one looks east!), the "western" one, is the Mediterranean (Dtn 11:24; 34:2; Zech 14:8). A third way to make his shameful perdition clear is the reference to the rising of the stench of decay (cf. 2 Macc 9:9–10), which stands in embarrassing contrast to his "acting great" (cf. Ezek

33 On the history of interpretation, cf. Kapelrud, *Joel*, 93–108, and especially Aarre Lauha, *Zaphon. Der Nordvölker im Alten Testament*, AASF B/49/2 (Helsinki, 1943).

34 Dalman, *Arbeit* 1/2, 393–95.

35 Karl Budde, " 'Der von Norden' in Joel 2:20," *OLZ* 22 (1919): 1–5; Nowack.

36 "Indledningsspørgsmaal i Joels Bog," *DTT* 4 (1941): 111.

37 See pp. 4–5.

38 See pp. 44–46.

39 Gressmann, *Messias*, 137; Aarre Lauha, *Zaphon. Der*

Norden und die Nordvölker im Alten Testament, AASF B/49/2 (Helsinki, 1943), 53f. In spite of Kapelrud's detailed arguments (*Joel*, 100–08), a precise derivation of the concept from the Ras Shamra texts has thus far not been successfully demonstrated.

40 Childs, "Enemy," 187–98.

41 Cf. Dan 4:8 [11], 19 [22]; 6:27 [26]; 7:26, 28; Eccl 3:11; 7:2; 12:13; and 2 Chr 20:16.

35:13; Dan 8:25aβ).

Thus 2:19a and 2:19b–20, as introductory oracles answering a plea, depict the compassion of Yahweh in its twofold form: first as compassion regarding the distress already at hand, as it appears in chap. 1 as an omen of the Day of Yahweh, and then as the answering of the prayers over the threat of the Day of Yahweh itself in 2:1–17. That which is intimated in the opening oracle is unfolded in what follows:[42] 2:21–27 clarifies the reversal in the present economic crisis (2:19a), and 3:1—4:21 the reversal in the announced eschatological crisis (2:19b–20).

■ **21–24** Here the "land" (v 21), the "beasts" (v 22), and finally the "sons of Zion" (v 23) are exhorted, in three strophes, to fearlessness and rejoicing. An assurance oracle,[43] which states the reason for fearlessness, can at the same time issue a call to "gladness and rejoicing." The word pair "gladness—rejoicing" (גיל—שמח) denotes particularly the joys of harvest.[44] The reasons given become more comprehensive with each strophe. The strophes are not distinguished by addressees, but are meant to be heard all together as a description of the reversal in the calamity. The first reason given, in v 21b, refers back to 2:20b by way of a word play, with a clear transformation of the meaning. Over against the "acting great" of Jerusalem's adversaries it sets the great acts of Yahweh.[45] Vv 22aβb and 23aβb–24 spell out which great acts are meant. They include many references to chap. 1. Just as the addressees "land" (אדמה 2:21, cf. 1:10), "beasts of the field" (בהמות שדי 2:22, cf. 1:20, 18), and "sons of Zion" (בני ציון 2:23, cf. 1:5, 11, 13–14) are those affected by the crisis of chap. 1, the announcement of salvation turns the calamity described there into "gladness and rejoicing" (2:21bα, 23aα, cf. 1:10a, 16b); on

the "greening of the pastures of the range" (2:22aβ), cf. 1:19, 20, (18); on the fruit–bearing of the trees (2:22b), cf. 1:12, 19b; on the "rain" (2:23), cf. the laments over the drought in 1:10, 12, 18–20; on the fullness of the threshing floors and the vats (2:24), cf. 1:5, 17. Thus 2:21–24 shows itself to be an assurance oracle answering a plea which corresponds exactly to the laments in 1:16–20; neither passage mentions the locust plague.

The vigorous capacity of the trees to bear fruit stands for the result, the yield of the harvest.[46] "Sons of Zion" (בני ציון) is found elsewhere only in Lam 4:2 and Ps 149:2. The motive clauses in v 23 (like those in vv 21–22, 24) probably referred originally to the new fruitfulness of the land, and will have dealt with the granting of food and rain.[47] Food "according to righteousness" (לצדקה) is the sustenance appropriate to Yahweh's covenant relationship with Israel.[48]

The "Teacher of Righteousness" in Joel 2:23?

M announces a "teacher for righteousness" in 2:23a, as Hos 10:12 (*M*) does similarly in a comparable context.[49] A related sequence of thoughts is also found in 1 Kgs 8:36.

It has been suspected that the misreading occurred in the context of the Qumran community,[50] and even that the Qumran title was developed from Hos 10:12 and Joel 2:33;[51] Gert Jeremias[52] considers this derivation to be "generally recognized."

It must be emphasized against this that *G* understood both passages altogether differently; in both cases the context shows that *G* is closer to the original text than is *M*.[53] Furthermore, the Qumran texts thus far known never relate the title "Teacher of Righteousness" to Hos 10:12 or Joel 2:23.[54]

It can be concluded, therefore, that the Qumran title originated without reference to Hos 10:12 and

42   Josef Schmalohr, *Das Buch des Propheten Joel, übersetzt und erklärt*, ATA 7/4 (Münster i.W., 1922), 116f.
43   See p. 58.
44   See Wolff, *Hosea*, 153 [197].
45   On the expression, cf. Ps 126:2–3.
46   On חיל ("produce"; literally "strength") in v 22b, see textual note "g" to 2:22.
47   See textual notes "i" and "j" to 2:23.
48   Cf. Hos 10:12 and Is 5:7. Cf. also Wolff, *Hosea*, 185f [240f]; and von Rad, *Theology* 1, 374–76 [372–74; 4th edition, 387f].
49   See Wolff, *Hosea*, textual note "u" to Hos 10:12.

50   Cf. Ovid R. Sellers, "A Possible Old Testament Reference to the Teacher of Righteousness," *IEJ* 5 (1955): 93–95; and Isaac Rabinowitz, "The Guides of Righteousness," *VT* 8 (1958): 391–404.
51   Thus Cecil Roth, "The Teacher of Righteousness and the Prophecy of Joel," *VT* 13 (1963): 91–95.
52   *Der Lehrer der Gerechtigkeit*, Studien zur Umwelt des Neuen Testaments 2 (Göttingen: Vandenhoeck & Ruprecht, 1963), 312, cf. 315.
53   See textual note "i" to 2:23; and Wolff, *Hosea*, textual note "u" to Hos 10:12.
54   Cf. 1 QpHab 2.2; 5.10; 7.4; 8.3; 9.9–10; 11.5;

Joel 2:23. Without further evidence it can not even be claimed that the *M* text of Hos 10:12 and Joel 2:23 originated with the Qumran community; it should be stressed instead "that the expectation of a teacher in the end–time, who would answer all questions, was a quite familiar conception in Rabbinic Judaism."[55] It is telling in this respect that the only passage from the Qumran literature somewhat reminiscent of Hos 10:12 does not even correspond to the text as closely as does one in rabbinic literature.[56] It must also be noted that the Qumran literature usually refers to a מורה הצדק, but never to a מורה לצדקה as does Joel 2:23 (*M*).

Hence the situation remains: 1. The title "Teacher of Righteousness" at Qumran surely did not derive from the original text of Hos 10:12 and Joel 2:23. 2. It is most likely that the *M* text of these passages does not owe its origin to special interests of the Qumran community, seeking scriptural proof for its "Teacher of Righteousness." 3. Instead, *M* is in keeping with the general expectation of a teacher associated with the end–time, current in late Judaism.

The expectation of the "downpour" (גשם), in the form of the "early rain" (יורה), is most lively in November, the time when it is properly due.[57] The "latter rain" is much hoped for in March and even April, so that the summer might not be dry for too long (cf. Am 4:7).[58] The rain is to fall "as formerly,"[59] i.e., as it had when the ancient covenant fellowship was in effect, before the arrival of the calamities. Again Joel shows an interest in comparing the times (cf. 1:2b; 2:2b). *M* בָּרִאשׁוֹן cannot designate an initial time–phase of divine response, to which "afterward" (אחרי־כן 3:1) would then refer back by way of introducing a second

phase;[60] for apart from the position of the word in 2:23b (which does not at all correspond to the construction of 3:1a) בראשון otherwise always means "in the first (month)."[61]

■ **25** After the oracle answering a plea (pertaining to the drought) in 2:21–24, there follows in v 25 a further explication of 2:19a which promises restitution for the locust damages, with clear reference to 1:4. In contrast to 1:4, the enumeration here begins with ארבה, the commonest term for locust, perhaps also designating that type which causes the greatest devastations.[62]

"To restore the years" is a metonymy which recalls the destruction of the harvest yields of several years (cf. Ps 90:15). This clarifies in retrospect the dimension of the catastrophe described in 1:4. "To restore" (שלם pi'el) is an old legal term for the adjustment of damages; it designates the rendering of a substitute payment or of restitution.[63] The locusts appear here as Yahweh's "great army." (חיל should not be taken to refer to the rich yield of future harvests, as in 2:22; the pronominal suffix and the perfect verbal form of the relative clause indicate otherwise. The case here is analogous to that of 1:6, where the harbingers are already referred to using terminology which describes the eschatological military power of Yahweh in 2:11aα.) On the subject matter, compare Mal 3:11–12.

■ **26** The assurance that there will be enough to eat (cf. 2:19a) clarifies the restitution for the lack of harvest yields of bygone years. This restitution will, by its richness, lead again to the praise of the covenant God (cf. already 2:23a). The sequence "eat . . . be sated . . .

---

1 QpMi (14) 8–10; 4 QPs^a (171) 3.15 (to Ps 37:23–24). Cf. also CD 1.11; 6.10–11; 20.1, 28, 32.

55 Gert Jeremias, *Der Lehrer der Gerechtigkeit*, Studien zur Umwelt des Neuen Testaments 2 (Göttingen: Vandenhoeck & Ruprecht, 1963), 287 and, for documentation, 285f.

56 I.e., compare the following: "until he shall arise who teaches righteousness at the end of days" [Trans. by Ed.] (עד עמד יורה הצדק באחרית הימים CD 6.10–11); and "until he shall come and teach righteousness" [Trans. by Ed.] (עד יבוא ויורה צדק; Babylonian Talmud, Bekorot 24a).

57 Dalman, *Arbeit* 1/1, 122.

58 Dalman, *Arbeit* 1/2, 291–94, 302f; R. B. Y. Scott, "Meteorological Phenomena and Terminology in the Old Testament," *ZAW* 64 (1952): 23.

59 See textual note "k" to 2:23.

60 Thus Keil.

61 Gen 8:13; Ex 12:18; Nu 9:5; Ezek 29:17; 30:20; 45:18, 21. On the other hand, for כראשון ("as formerly") cf. Lev. 9:15. On threshing floor and winepress, cf. Wolff, *Hosea*, 154 [198], and below pp. 80–81 on 4:13.

62 See pp. 27–28.

63 Cf. Ex 22:2–4 [3–5]; and Friedrich Horst, "Recht und Religion im Bereich des Alten Testaments," *EvTh* 16 (1956): 49–75 (reprinted in *idem, Gottes Recht. Gesammelte Studien zum Recht im Alten Testament*, ed. Hans Walter Wolff, ThB 12 [München: Chr. Kaiser, 1961], 260–91).

praise" is not to be taken for granted[64] and must therefore be impressed upon the mind occasionally (Dtn 8:10); but Yahweh's new acts will be so startling that the praising of his name as the God of his people cannot but follow (cf. Ps 22:27 [26]). "Wondrously" (להפלא) is used as an adverb which underscores the unusual greatness of his acts, a greatness which can be understood only when one considers God himself (cf. 2:21bβ).

■ **27** The first part of the assurance oracles answering a plea (referring to the reversal in the calamities lamented in chap. 1) reaches its high point in the recognition formula which, when compared to its occurrence in Ezekiel and Deutero–Isaiah, is especially distended here. Thus the reversal of the crisis finds its meaning not within itself, but in a new recognition of Yahweh. He is to be recognized, first, as the God who manifests himself "in the midst of Israel";[65] second, as the covenant God favorably inclined toward his people ("Yahweh, your God" already in 2:23, 26);[66] third, as the "only one," which takes up Deutero–Isaianic language.[67]

The recognition formula does not constitute a conclusion. For the aim of the previously announced response of Yahweh is that he be recognized not only as the God of Israel and the only God, but also as the God who continues to act. Perhaps the unusual formula "in the midst of Israel am I" (בקרב ישראל אני) already points to the fact that he continues to be effective in Israel. V 27b clearly points to the future. The temporary reversal in the calamity is to lead to the recognition that Yahweh's people ultimately will not be destroyed.

This sentence points to the continuation in chaps. 3 and 4,[68] just as it takes up, in terms of subject matter, the prayer in 2:17b and its preliminary answer in 2:19b (–20). In Joel the great capacity of the "self–disclosure oracle" for expansion beyond the recognition formula becomes evident.[69] Not only can it take up once more (with ב plus infinitive construct) that which is to lead to recognition (for example, Ezek 39:28), but it can also accommodate new parts, as happens in Ezek 39:29 with the addition of the pouring out of the spirit, and also here. Thus v 27 does not constitute a conclusion, but a transition in the two–stage self–disclosure oracle (cf. 4:17). The response to Israel's plea concerning its current distress is to lead to the recognition that Yahweh will respond no less wondrously to petition for deliverance from the threatened Day of Yahweh.

■ **3:1** Not only will earlier conditions be restored (v 23), they will be exceeded by a second phase of Yahweh's acting, which will occur "afterward." "Afterward" (אחרי־כן) is a seldom encountered conjunctive formula. It forms the transition to all those further oracles in chaps. 3 and 4 which bring prophetic promises for a more distant time; it presupposes that the preceding assurance oracles of plea–response pertaining to the earlier time have already been fulfilled, confirming the expectation of the much greater future response (2:27). "In the midst of Israel" (2:27) Yahweh is at work, first, through the "pouring out of his spirit." The verb שפך is used for the pouring out of water (Ex 4:9), blood (Gen 9:6), or other liquids. Related to the

---

64   Cf. Hos 13:5–6; and Wolff, *Hosea*, 226 [293f].

65   The expression בקרב ישראל אני ("in the midst of Israel am I") occurs in neither Deutero–Isaiah nor Ezekiel as part of the recognition formula. Cf., however, Zeph 3:15, 17; Hos 11:9; and Mi 3:11. The expression בקרב ישראל ("in the midst of Israel") is attested elsewhere only in Dtn 17:20; Josh 6:25; 13:13.

66   On the "formula of favor" (*Huldformel*), cf. Karl Elliger, "Das Gesetz Leviticus 18," *ZAW* 67 (1955): 23–25; and Walther Zimmerli, "Das Wort des göttlichen Selbsterweises (Erweiswort), eine prophetische Gattung" in *Mélanges Bibliques rédigés en l'honneur de André Robert*, Travaux de l'Institut Catholique de Paris 4 (Paris: Bloud et Gay, 1957), 159 (= idem, *Gottes Offenbarung*, 126).

67   See p. 58.

68   Thus already Christian Gottlieb Kühnöl, Professor of Philosophy in Leipzig, who noted with regard to Joel 2:27: "This thought is only developed further in what follows; it is, as it were, the text upon which Joel comments and which, precisely for that reason, he repeats at the end of his speech as his main thought. Chap. 4:17." ("Über Joel 3:1–5," *Magazin für Religionsphilosophie, Exegese und Kirchengeschichte* [Helmstädt, 1794]: 172f).

69   Cf. Henning Graf Reventlow, *Wächter über Israel: Ezechiel und seine Tradition*, BZAW 82 (Berlin: A. Töpelmann, 1962), 162.

"pouring out of the spirit" is the pouring out of the "heart" (לֵב Ps 62:9 [8]; Lam 2:19) or of the "soul" (נֶפֶשׁ 1 Sam 1:15; Ps 42:5 [4]), connoting an unreserved[70] unburdening of confidences, an open sharing of one's thinking and willing, one's feeling and insight. Yet "spirit" (רוח) is not primarily an organ of cognition (like "heart" לֵב) or of desire (like "soul" נֶפֶשׁ); it is a vital power and will towards action.[71] As such it is not at man's disposal (after all, רוח also means "wind"!); it is given freely by God to sustain human life,[72] or for special mighty deeds[73] and for historical tasks.[74] "Spirit" as vital power is on principle the opposite of the feebleness of "flesh" (בשר Is 31:3). A hymn from Qumran (1 QH 7.6–7) offers us excellent evidence for our understanding of the spirit that is poured out to provide strengthening for the end–time "battles of wickedness": "I thank you, Lord, for you have supported me with your strength, you have sprinkled your holy spirit upon me, that I might not stagger. You have strengthened me before the battles of wickedness." In particular, without the new, restorative, consolidating power of God's "spirit," guilty man is a creature lacking stability (Ps 51:12–13 [10–11]) and incapable of living in accord with the ordinances of God (Ezek 11:19–20; 36:26–27). Seen from this perspective, the pouring out of God's spirit upon flesh means the establishment of new, vigorous life through God's unreserved giving of himself to those who, in themselves, are rootless and feeble, especially in the approaching times of judgment.

The promise of Joel states more precisely for what purpose such "empowering" is given, and to whom it applies. First, in three synonymous, parallel statements which illumine one another, it is affirmed that the pouring out of the spirit will enable prophesying and receiving dreams and visions. Thus Joel has chiefly in view neither the gift of the spirit (with נתן, Ezek 36:26–27) for the purpose of new obedience, nor the pouring out of the spirit (with ערה, Is 32:15; with יצק,

Is 44:3) for the new creation of the people of God. He rather interprets the terse promise of the pouring out of the spirit in Ezek 39:29 (which stands in a related context[75] and also uses the verb שׁפך, in contrast to the other passages adduced for comparison) to announce that the people newly called to life shall be a nation of prophets. What does that mean? It seems that he is not thinking of new prophetic proclamation and, consequently, of a new relationship to the surrounding world. For there is no reference to proclamation, especially since all who are in view shall experience the pouring out. Much less can one think here of a promise of the spirit to Israel for the purpose of effecting the conversion and salvation of the nations of the world.[76] For there is no suggestion of this in 3:1–2, and the broader context explicitly excludes this interpretation. The emphases that become evident in the parallel cola point in another direction. Joel also hardly expects a nation of ecstatics (cf. 1 Sam 10:10–11; 19:20–24). Since the nip'al of נבא in v 1aβ is explained in the following cola (v 1b) only through events that lead to the establishment of a prophetic existence, the verb must be interpreted here to refer not to prophetic expression, but merely to the existence of prophets.[77] If Joel sees prophetic existence as being established through dreams and visions, the Jeremianic polemic against dreamers (Jer 23:25) is apparently completely foreign to him; he is rather influenced in this respect by the Torah, canonized in his time, in which dreams are viewed as a legitimate mode of revelation.[78] It is the relationship to God, then, which has become completely new in the new creation through the pouring out of the spirit.[79] The authorization of prophetic existence does not exclude perception, however, but includes it. Besides Is 11:2, one must note especially that in Joel's period prophetic spokesmen are endowed with speech by the spirit (2 Chr 15:1; 20:14; 24:20); "in the spirit" and in the certainty that "Yahweh is with us!" they confess a fearless confidence

---

70   Cf. Scheepers, *gees van God*, 223.
71   Ju 15:19; Gen 45:27. Cf. Georges Pidoux, *L'homme dans l'Ancien Testament*, CTh 32 (Neuchâtel and Paris: Delachaux & Niestlé, 1953), 22.
72   Is 42:5; Ps 104:29–30; Ezek 37:14.
73   Ju 6:34; 14:6.
74   Jer 51:11; Ezr 1:1; Hag 1:14.
75   See p. 60, point 4.

76   Thus Daniel Lys, *'Rûach'. Le souffle dans l'Ancien Testament. Enquête anthropologique à travers l'histoire théologique d'Israel*, EHPR 56 (Paris: Universitaires de France, 1962), 248.
77   Cf. Rolf Rendtorff, "נָבִיא in the Old Testament," *TDNT* 6, 796–99.
78   Cf. especially Nu 12:6 (J).
79   Cf. Scheepers, *gees van God*, 290f.

in the future acts of God on behalf of his people. Joel probably has in mind a similar confidence, though not their proclamation. Thus he expects the new relationship to God in a form similar to Jer 31:33–34:[80] everyone will stand in a relationship of immediacy to God. Only it is now not the Torah as the will of God for man that forms the content of the knowledge, as in Jer 31:33 and Ezek 11:19–20; 36:26–27, but the prophetic certainty of the coming acts of God on behalf of his people. Indeed, the new prophetic relationship to God is manifest in an authorized calling upon (3:5a) the God who calls (3:5b). From this perspective 3:5a–b is clarified.[81] The expectation is a warning against regarding cultic restoration and life under the canonized Torah in the Jerusalem of the fourth century as the goal of God's ways.

This becomes even clearer when we note for whom the promise is intended. Certainly "all flesh" (כל־בשׂר) can mean the whole of humanity,[82] indeed even animals as well as humans.[83] Yet here it surely means not "the whole world" as such,[84] but "everybody" in Israel, for according to the introduction in 2:19 this oracle also pertains to Yahweh's people, and immediately preceding it the manifestation of Yahweh "in the midst of Israel" has been announced (2:27). Concerning other nations a completely different message is forthcoming (4:1ff). Furthermore, Joel interprets the promise which is meant for the "house of Israel" in Ezek 39:29.[85] Consequently, the oracle uses the style of direct address (as in 2:19–20, 25–27) when it speaks of "your sons and your daughters," of "your old men" and "your young men." The reason "all flesh" (כל־בשׂר) occupies an initial position is twofold: first, because the recipients of the new life with God are in themselves those who are weak, powerless, and hopeless (Is 40:6; 31:3; Ps 56:5 [4]), and second, because it is their totality that is comprehended by the life of hope in God. It is a promise of the fulfillment of Moses' wish in Nu 11:29.[86] The new people of God no longer

recognize privileged individuals. Hitherto there were only exceptional prophetic lives. Reference is made first to "your sons and your daughters," indicating that the nation of the future is meant, and not already the present generation (cf. 3:1a "afterward" [אחרי־כן]), which is rather to transmit the hope (1:3). Moreover, the diminishing of the privileges of the sons is scarcely emphasized; more attention is given to the fact that the "old men"[87] will not be ranked ahead of the young men, nor the young ahead of the old (cf. Mal 3:24 [4:6]). But here, too, it is to be stressed: all will live their lives into the future only on the basis of God's call, and therefore in fearless communion with God.

■ 2 The promise regarding "manservants and maidservants," added by way of intensification, unmistakably introduces into the hope an element of social revolution. The ancient law of God in Israel had already accorded special attention to the rights of male and female slaves,[88] providing that they, too, should freely share the joy to be found in the presence of Israel's God.[89] Beginning with Amos, prophecy had raised its voice on behalf of all who were oppressed and unfree (cf. especially Jer 34:8–22). In the coming age they shall be incorporated fully into the community of the free, by being deigned worthy of the highest distinction along with all the rest.

Thus 3:1–2 announces, as first for a later time, the fulfillment of Ezek 39:29: Yahweh by his power wants to establish life in full community among those who are rootless and feeble. All without exception are to be strengthened in the certainty of God's intercession for his people. Before the wealth of such an outpouring, all distinctions of sex and age recede completely, indeed even the contrasts of social position. Such is the future towards which Israel moves. The receiving of the spirit is the beginning, if "the great and terrible Day of Yahweh" (3:4b) is to pass Israel by.

■ 3–4 In addition, there are cosmic omens. While אות ("sign") need not indicate anything extraordinary,

---

80   Cf. also the "nation of priests" in Ex 19:5–6 (Dtr).

81   See pp. 68–69; cf. also the third passage which, like Ezek 39:29 and Joel 3:1, uses the verb שׁפך in describing the "pouring out" of the spirit, namely, Zech 12:10.

82   Is 40:5; 49:26; Gen 6:12–13.

83   Gen 6:17; 9:11, 16–17.

84   Thus Bewer, 123.

85   Differently A. R. Hulst, "*Kol baśar* in der priesterlichen Fluterzählung" in *Studies in the Book of Genesis*, OTS 12 (Leiden: E. J. Brill, 1958), 47–49.

86   Cf. Nu 11:17, 25; and textual note "r" to 3:1.

87   זקנים is used here as in 2:16, rather than as in 1:2, 14; see p. 51.

88   Ex 21:2–4, 7, 20, 26–27, 32.

89   Ex 20:10; Dtn 5:14–15; 12:12, 18; 16:11, 14.

and פֶּלֶא ("extraordinary thing") need not refer to a sign; מוֹפֵת is that which is completely out of the ordinary and as such has sign character. In the time of Joel the word מוֹפְתִים ("wonders, portents") was known especially as applied to the terrible events associated with the plagues that came upon Egypt.[90] Just as these terrors upon Egypt were signs which preceded the liberation of Israel, "blood, fire, and mushrooms of smoke," and eclipses of sun and moon shall be signs preceding the terrible Day of Yahweh (3:4b) which is now to come upon the world of nations (4:1ff, 12ff, 15ff) and which will, at the same time, bring deliverance to Jerusalem.

The "portents in the sky and on the earth" are developed in chiasmic sequence. Those on earth are noted first: "blood, fire, and mushrooms of smoke" stand for people bleeding to death, and for cities going up in flames; thus the thought is of war and perhaps also of volcanic eruptions.[91] In the sky one is to expect a darkening of sun and moon.[92] That the moon turns "bloody" indicates that the thought here is not, or at least not only, of ordinary eclipses of the sun and the moon, but of times of darkening due to catastrophes. The phenomena are the same as those with which Jerusalem was threatened before the turning point (cf. 2:10); they are familiar from prophecies concerning the Day of Yahweh (cf. 3:4b with 2:11b!). The wonder of the response (2:18–19) to the entreaties (2:17) of those who were aroused (2:12–16) has led to a reversal of the direction of the Day of Yahweh.

■ 5 The linking formula "and it shall come to pass" (וְהָיָה) refers back to the announcement of salvation, and makes the words of Yahweh in the expansion of the assurance of recognition (2:27b) more precise: "my people shall never again be put to shame." In the midst of catastrophes on the earth and in the sky, catastrophes that are portents (3:3–4) for the gift of the new life of communion with God (3:1–2), there will be a place of escape. Joel takes up the traditions of the songs of Zion[93] and the proclamation of Isaiah[94] which received their further development through exilic hope and postexilic proclamation.[95] He does so exactly in that form which is attested for us in Ob 17: "on Mount Zion there will be escape." The inclusion of "as Yahweh has said" at this point shows that we have here a conscious proclamation of transmitted material, and not perchance a new oracle of Yahweh.[96] The ancient place of divine promise will become the final fortress of refuge, and that "for all who call upon the name of Yahweh." "Call by the name of Yahweh" (קרא ב, Ex 33:19) means veneration through worship generally (Gen 12:8), especially the confessing of Yahweh among those of other faiths (Is 41:25; 44:5), worshiping him in the midst of the world of nations (Is 12:4; Ps 105:1; Zech 13:9). Joel can cite this promise insofar as through his exhortations (2:12–17) he has led endangered Jerusalem to a new confession of loyalty to Yahweh.[97]

The conclusion of the verse is difficult. Are "those who survive, whom Yahweh calls" people living in the diaspora (Is 57:19; 66:19; 27:12–13)? Since the sentence gives the impression of being a later addition, this sense as a further expansion of the hopes associated with Zion is perfectly possible. But people "who survive" need not first be called. "Survivor, one who escapes" (שָׂרִיד) is often found in parallelism to "escape, sparing" (פְּלֵיטָה).[98] Thus it is perhaps better to see in the concluding clause a further explanation of v 5abα. Since the combination "on Mount Zion and in Jerusalem" in v 5bα is unusual, "in Jerusalem" might have belonged originally to v 5bβ;[99] yet such a reconstruction remains quite uncertain. As to the subject matter, one can conclude only that v 5bβ probably does not mean Israelites outside of Jerusalem, unless they be those who had fled from the region of Judah into the city (2:1). Nor concerning the future in view here does 4:1–3 offer sufficient cause to think of Israelites living far away. Most likely is meant the same circle of Jeru-

90   Cf. Dtn 6:22; Jer 32:20; 1 Chr 16:12; and Neh 9:10; cf. also Ex 7:3 (P).

91   On תִימָרוֹת ("mushrooms [of smoke]"), see textual note "w" to 3:3; cf. 2:3, 6.

92   Cf. 2:10; 4:15; and also Zeph 1:14–17; Is 13:10; Ezek 32:7–8; Am 8:9. See p. 47.

93   Ps 46; 48; 76; etc. Cf. Kraus, *Psalmen*, lxiv–lxviii.

94   Is 28:16; 14:32; etc. Cf. von Rad, *Theology* 2, 155–

69 [166–79]; and Th. C. Vriezen, *Jahwe en zijn stad* (Amst: Noordholland, 1962).

95   Is 52:1; 60:1–7; etc. Cf. Georg Fohrer, "Zion-Jerusalem in the Old Testament," *TDNT* 7, 312–18.

96   Cf. especially Is 34:16–17; cf. also Dan 9:13; 1 Chr 22:10; 2 Chr 6:10; 23:3; Dtn 6:19; 9:3; Jer 27:13; 40:3.

salemites and Judeans which is addressed throughout the rest of the book.[100] The only difference is that to the narrower designation of this circle in v 5a ("who call upon the name of Yahewh") is added a broader one: "whom Yahweh calls." Just as in 3:1, a new call of election is therefore expected.[101] Is it necessary to surmise here a "conventicle–type limitation" of hope?[102] Zech 13:8–9 speaks explicitly of an exclusion of the saved from a circle of those who will perish; Zech 14:2 refers to the "rest of the people who shall not be exterminated in the city." Here it becomes clear that not merely through physical membership (cf. "flesh" [בשר] in 3:1!) in the people of Jerusalem is deliverance guaranteed, but only by the confession of loyalty to Yahweh, by being responsive to his new call. To this extent v 5 remains in line with 3:1–2. Here as there the stress lies on the fact that "all" (כל in 3:1a and 5a) who await the future from Yahweh will, at the time of the world catastrophe, find refuge in the community of God on Mount Zion.

Aim

The whole section should be understood as an assurance oracle answering a plea (2:18).[103] It responds at the same time to the lamentations over the locust calamity and the drought in chap. 1, and to the call to repentance which the prophet had issued on the basis of the threatened final judgment upon Jerusalem (2:1–17). Both Israel's present situation of distress (2:19a, 21–26) and the imminent danger (2:19b, 20; 3:1–5) are to be turned away. It remains a basic presupposition for understanding the text that we keep in mind both the nature of the present economic distress as an omen of the final blow of destruction which the God of Israel directs against Jerusalem (1:15), and the new re-orientation of the whole of life toward Yahweh as the sole lord of the future of Israel described in the preceding section (2:12–17). The double assurance pertains to the oppressed who see themselves now as being at the mercy of their God, for better or for worse (2:11b, 14, 17).

The pivot is 2:27, whereby the assurance oracle is transformed into a two–stage self–disclosure oracle.[104] Israel is to learn from the aid it receives in the present crisis (2:19a, 21–26) that its God, and no one else, is at work in its midst. Therefore rejoicing and gladness are to be expressed over the new abundance of foodstuffs, because as gifts of the great acts of God (2:21b) they provide cause for praise and for recognition of his covenant faithfulness (2:23, 26–27). Those who experience this are to derive from it the confidence that God's people will not ultimately be destroyed. Here lies the aim of Joel's message. The prophetic promises do not become void for those who stretch forward toward them anew on the basis of the awakening call. The promises are first developed positively in 3:1–5. Transmitted oracles, as we can still recognize them in Ezek 39:29 and Ob 17,[105] are proclaimed anew and expounded. Israel can move toward a future in which God gives the gift of unreserved communion with himself to all, without distinction as to sex, age, and social position. Thus, by his vital power, he creates anew his whole people, enabled as only individuals had been formerly (3:1–2). If God has helped his people through gravest crises, he has done so only in order that they might live with assurance towards this goal, and that they might regard the great world–historical and cosmic catastrophes not as perchance a reason for hopelessness, but on the contrary as an omen of his imminent day (3:3–4). On this day everyone who, struck by the call, expects everything from the name of Yahweh, will be spared in Jerusalem.

The statement in 3:5a that "everyone who calls upon the name of the Lord will be saved" was adopted by the New Testament community, which not only referred it exclusively to the name of Jesus Christ[106] but derived from it the first label for one who is a Christian.[107] For Paul (Rom 10:13), Joel 3:5a is important

---

97 On פליטה ("escape"), see p. 43 on 2:3b.

98 Ob 14; Jer 42:17; 44:14; Josh 8:22.

99 Cf. Sellin; textual note "z" to 3:5.

100 See p. 25 on 1:2.

101 For קרא = "to elect, appoint," cf. Is 51:2.

102 Plöger, *Theocracy*, 104 [126].

103 See pp. 57–59.

104 See pp. 58–60.

105 See pp. 66–68.

106 Rom 10:13–14; Acts 2:21ff.

107 Rom 10:12; 1 Cor 1:2; 2 Tim 2:22; Acts 9:14; 22:16.

documentation that no distinction obtains any longer between Jews and Greeks. He has thereby given a universal interpretation to the "everyone" ($\pi\hat{\alpha}s$) of G, which renders "all" (כל) in 3:5. Joel had no more intended that[108] than he had known the name of Jesus.

Both expanded meanings of this sentence, its reference to Jesus as well as the extension of its validity to all humanity (cf. Acts 10:45), are also found in the Lucan speech of Peter in Acts 2, where now in vv 17–21 Joel 3:1–5a is cited in full, while the important expression from Joel 3:5bβ (interpreted universally through combination with Is 57:19) is cited at the end in v 39. The citation follows G. This is true also of the opening, which is "after these things" ($\mu\epsilon\tau\grave{\alpha}$ $\tau\alpha\hat{\upsilon}\tau\alpha$) in G.[109] For Luke, Pentecost has brought the beginning, not of the end–time but of the new time. Especially with its word concerning the pouring out of the spirit, Joel 3 is used by him as scriptural proof for the early Christian phenomenon of ecstatic speech in the spirit. It accords with the promise that all are in communion with God when Jesus, who was raised by God, pours out the spirit (cf. Acts 2:33 with Acts 2:17).

No interpretation can revert beyond the fact that for Jesus' sake the promise of Joel pertains to all humanity. Little as it is in keeping with Joel's original meaning, it nevertheless clearly lies in the main line of Old Testament expectation (Gen 12:3; Is 2:2–4). This is shown already by the development, only a little later, of the themes of the book of Joel in Zech 14.

Beyond this, the text of Joel may be able to help modern Israel to recognize liberation from horrible calamities as a basis for the hope that God wants to be near to it not only in the regulated order of the Torah, but that he wants to make into a reality the prophetic promise of a new life in unreserved communion with him through the gift of his spirit. Christianity, however, is asked whether it will bring shame or honor to the name of Jesus as it listens to Joel. In many of its members it is ripe for God to lead its enemies against it in order to cast it into perdition (2:1–11). That it can live on (2:18–26), due to the prayers of those who reorient themselves seriously toward the word of Jesus (2:12–17), in spite of gravest crises, is to confirm the certainty (2:27) that "afterward" (3:1) with it too God wants to make his ultimate promise into a reality. Each generation is called to be expectant of the pouring out of the spirit of Jesus, so that the contrasts that rend humanity asunder might be bridged (3:1–2). The world's convulsions are not to mislead Christianity into returning to the human ways of the "flesh"; they should rather be recognized as portents that men may count on the gift of God. For us the traditions of Zion, which are the starting point for Joel in 3:5, are sealed and replaced by that which has been proclaimed through the cross and resurrection of Jesus in front of Jerusalem. The calling upon his name, the confession of loyalty to him who loves the godless, has become the place in which deliverance from strife for the individual can be found, for the living together of the sexes, the generations, and the partners in society, but also for the world of nations as a whole. In this connection the little concluding clause in 3:5bβ (cf. Acts 2:39) remains an ever–present warning to remain expectant of the challenge and the call of admonition of 2:12ff.

---

108 See pp. 68–69.
109 The opening phrase is also transmitted in this form in Acts by codex B; codex D ($\dot{\epsilon}\nu$ $\epsilon o\chi\acute{\alpha}\tau\alpha\iota s$ $\dot{\eta}\mu\acute{\epsilon}\rho\alpha\iota s$ = "in the latter days") must be regarded as secondary. Cf. Ernst Haenchen, "Schriftzitate und Textüberlieferung in der Apostelgeschichte," $ZThK$ 51 (1954): 162; and idem, The Acts of the Apostles: A Commentary, tr. Bernard Noble, Gerald Shinn, Robert McL. Wilson (Philadelphia: Westminster, 1971), 179 [Die Apostelgeschichte: Neu übersetzt und erklärt, Kritisch–exegetischer Kommentar über das Neue Testament 3 (Göttingen: Vandenhoeck & Ruprecht, [13]1961), 142].

The Judgment on the Enemies
of God's People

Bibliography

Robert Bach
Die Aufforderungen zur Flucht und zum Kampf im alt-testamentlichen Prophetenspruch, WMANT 9 (Neu-kirchen: Verlag des Erziehungsvereins, 1962).

Georg Fohrer
"Zion–Jerusalem in the Old Testament," *TDNT* 7, 293–319.

Hugo Gressmann
Der Messias, FRLANT 42 (Göttingen, 1929), 114–16, 139.

J. T. Milik
"Notes d'épigraphie et de topographie palestini-ennes," *RB* 66 (1959): 553–55 ("II.—Torrent des Acacias, Joël, IV, 18").

Jacob M. Myers
"Some Considerations Bearing on the Date of Joel," *ZAW* 74 (1962): 177–95.

Marco Treves
"The Date of Joel," *VT* 7 (1957): 149–56.

4

1 Indeed (it shall be) so! In those days
and at that time,
when[a] [b]I restore the fortunes[b] of
Judah and Jerusalem,
2 then I will gather all the nations
and lead them down [c]to the valley of
Jehoshaphat,[c]
and I will enter into judgment
with them there,
on account of my people and my
possession Israel,
whom they have scattered among
the nations
and have divided up my land,
3 and cast lots[d] for my people
and gave boys[e] for[f] harlots[e]
and sold girls[e] for[f] wine which they
drank.

a   אשר is omitted in some manuscripts (Johannis Bern. de Rossi, *Variae Lectiones Veteris Testamenti*, vol. 3 [Parma, 1786 = Amsterdam: Philo Press, 1970], 185).

b–b   *T* (דאתיב ית גלות ["when I return the captivity"]) and likewise *G* (ὅταν ἐπιστρέψω τὴν αἰχμαλωσίαν) restrict the meaning of the expression שוב שבות, as does already the Qere' (אָשִׁיב); the Masoretes also show a preference for the hip'il in reading this phrase elsewhere, since the transitive meaning of שוב qal gave them difficulties. Cf. R. Borger, "Zu שוב שבו/ית," *ZAW* 66 (1954): 315f; and the Sefire inscription 3.24, on which see below, p. 76, n. 19.

c–c   *T* (למישר פילוג דינא ["to the plain of the judicial decision"]) and θ' (εἰς τὴν χώραν τῆς κρίσεως ["into the country of judgment"]) interpret the proper name. *G*: εἰς τὴν κοιλάδα Ιωσαφατ.

d   ידד qal perfect.

e   The definite forms in the singular are generic: Brockelmann, *Syntax*, par. 21cβ; cf. Eccl 3:17.

f   Since with "to give (over), to sell," the price is indicated by an accusative, ב here introduces that which is acquired; precisely so a' (ἐδίδουν παιδίον ἀντὶ πόρνης ["giving a boy in return for a harlot"]); and, according to the sense, *T* (ויהבו עולימא באגר זניתא ["they gave the boy over as a harlot's hire"] = *S*). *G* (καὶ ἔδωκαν τὰ παιδάρια πόρναις) misinterprets: "they gave the boys to the harlots (= to harlotry)," likewise *L* and *V* (*et posuerunt puerum in prostibulo*), while the identically constructed continuation is understood correctly (καὶ τὰ κοράσια ἐπώλουν ἀντὶ οἴνου = *V*: *et puellam vendiderunt pro vino*).

4 [Furthermore:
What are you to me,
   Tyre and Sidon and all the districts
   of Philistia?
Do you want to pay me back?
   Or[g] do you want to do something
   to me?
Swiftly and speedily I will requite your
action upon your head.

5 Because you took my silver and my
gold
   and carried my goodly treasures
   into your palaces

6 and sold the sons of Judah and the sons
of Jerusalem to the sons of the Greeks,[h]
   in order to remove them from their
   homeland.

7 I am now about to make them set out[i]
from the place
   to which you have sold them,
     and I will requite your action upon
     your head.

8 And I will sell your sons and daughters
by agency of[j] the sons of Judah,
   and they will sell them to the Sabeans[k] {to a nation far off},
     for Yahweh has spoken.]

9 Proclaim this among the nations:
Prepare for a holy war![l]
   Arouse the warriors!
     Let all men of war [m]draw near,
     let them come up![m]

10 Beat your ploughshares into swords
   and your pruning knives into lances!
     Let the weak say: "I am a war-
     rior"![n]

11 <Hasten>[o] and come, all you nations
round about!
   <Gather yourselves>[p] there![q]

g   *V* does not see a disjunctive question (as in *G* and 1:2; Brockelmann, *Syntax*, par. 169c), but lets וְאָם be the opening of an introductory conditional clause to v 4bγ: "if you do something to me, then . . ." (so also Deden). The fact that deeds which have already occurred elicit this oracle speaks decidedly against such an understanding.

h   Bič thinks of יָוֵן (Ps 40:3 [2]; 69:3 [2]) and translates "sons of mire," by which the Egyptians are supposed to be meant. But neither this meaning nor the plural form of the word are attested.

i   Literally "awaken" (*G* ἐξεγείρω), here in the sense of "to set in motion" (*T* "to bring back").

j   *G* (εἰς χεῖρας ["into the hands"]) contradicts the generally instrumental meaning of ביד; "to sell to someone" would require in this context מכר ל; cf. v 6 and v 8aβ. מכר ב means in v 3b "to sell for [in order to acquire] something."

k   *G* (εἰς αἰχμαλωσίαν ["into captivity"]) perhaps presupposes a corrupt text (לַשְּׁבִי or לִשְׁבוּת?; cf. v 1), but has probably been determined in part by the difficulty that the buyer cannot be introduced in the same sentence by both ל and אל. The context (v 6a) makes it appear likely that ל was original; if so, אל־גוי רחוק ("to a nation far off") would be an explanatory gloss. *T* (לבני שבא) as well as α′, σ′ and θ′ (τοῖς σαβαιμ) support *M*.

l   Literally "Sanctify a war!"

m– *G* (προσαγάγετε καὶ ἀναβαίνετε; *G*ˢ lacks καὶ) adjusts
m   to the imperatives of vv 9a, 9bα; the *Vorlage* need not have read נִגְּשׁוּ וַעֲלוּ.

n   *G*: Ἰσχύω ἐγώ ("I am strong"); גבור is likewise rendered with ἰσχύω in Is 5:22 and 10:21. *V*: *fortis ego sum*.

o   Instead of the unexplained *hapax legomenon* of *M* (Arabic *ǧ'ṯ* "to help"), *V* (*erumpite* ["break forth!"]) could reflect חוּשׁוּ (Trinquet) or perhaps עוּרוּ (Wellhausen; Nowack; Sellin; Bach, *Aufforderungen*, 60; Marti; cf. 4:7, 9, 12. *G* (συναθροίζεσθε ["assemble!"]), *S* and *T* read נועו (cf. Am 4:8), not הֵקָּבְצוּ; although there are eleven instances where *G* renders קבץ nip'al with συναθροίζειν, here the form is unlikely alongside קבץ nip'al in v 11aβ, where the root is rendered with συνάγειν, as in 4:2.

p   *T* (ויתכנשון וייתון . . . ויתקרבון) presupposes jussive forms in v 11aα. *G*, however, translates all three verb forms in v 11a as imperatives (v 11aβ: καὶ συνάχθητε; likewise *V*, *congregamini*); because of the following address form (גבוריך) in v 11b one should probably read the imperative הֵקָּבְצוּ here also (Sellin; Robinson; Bach, *Aufforderungen*, 60). *M* "and they shall gather together"; cf. the same transition from the imperative to the jussive in v 9bβ, where—in contrast to this passage—no addressing clause is directly attached, however.

q   *G* (ἐκεῖ) links שָׁמָּה to v 11aβ. *V* supports *M*, but the attachment of "there" to v 11b has become possible only by a misreading of the following word; see textual note "r."

That Yahweh may <shatter>ʳ your
heroes.

12 Let the nations set outˢ and come up
into ᵗthe valley of Jehoshaphat.ᵗ
For there I will sit to judge
all the nations round about.

13 Send the sickle!
For the harvest is ripe.
Come (and) tread!
For the wine press is full.
The vats overflow,
for great is their wickedness.

14 ᵘTumult! Tumultᵘ
in ᵛthe valley of decision!ᵛ
For the Day of Yahweh is near
in ᵛthe valley of decision.ᵛ

15 The sun and the moon are darkened,
the brightness of the stars is extinguished,

16 ʷwhile Yahweh roars from Zion
and raises his voice from Jerusalem,ʷ
so that the heavens and the earth
quake.
But for his people, Yahweh is a refuge,
and a stronghold for Israel's sons.

17 And you shall know
that I, Yahweh, am your God
who dwell on Zion, my holy mountain.
And Jerusalem shall be a sanctuary,
through which strangers will never
passˣ again.

18 And on that day it will come to pass
that the mountains will drip with
juice,
and the hills will flow with milk,
and all Judah's torrents will
flow with water.
For a fountain will flow forth from
Yahweh's house
and it will water the valley
of the acacias.

19 Egypt shall become a desolation
and Edom shall become a wilderness
of desolation
for the violence done to Judah's sons,
in whose land they have shed
innocent blood.

20 But Judah shall be inhabitedʸ for ever,
and Jerusalem from generation
to generation,

21 ᶻ[and I will declare exempt from
punishmentᵃᵃ
their blood which I had not wanted
to declare exempt,ᵇᵇ]ᶻ
since Yahweh dwells on Zion.

r   *T* (תמן יתבר יהוה תקוף גיבריהון [''there Yahweh
will break the power of their warriors'']; similarly
V: *ibi occumbere faciet Dominus robustos tuos*) presupposes either a form of נוח hipʻil, perhaps וְיַנִּיחַ, or
more probably, of חתת hipʻil: וְיָחֵת (cf. Is 9:3 [4];
Jer 49:37; Ob 9!). *G* (ὁ πραὺς ἔστω μαχητής =
הֶעָנִי or הַנֵּח יִהְיֶה גִבּוֹר [''Let the meek become a warrior''], as Zeph 3:12; Zech 9:9; Is 26:6) has probably attempted to guess at the sense of the corrupt
text on the basis of v 10b. *M*, ''lead down thither,
Yahweh, your heroes,'' has probably misread וְיָחֵת
as נחת hipʻil; in this context an addressing of Yahweh is most unlikely. The conception of *M* corresponds to Is 13:3b; Zech 14:5b; 2 Chr 20:22; cf.
1 En 56:5ff and 1 QM 1.10–11.
s   עור nipʻal; cf. v 7 and textual note ''i'' above.
t–t   *T* (as in v 2): ''the plain of the judicial decision.''
u–u   *G*: ἦχοι ἐξήχησαν (''noises reverberate'') = הֲמוֹנִים
יְהֱמָיוּן? Cf. Is 17:12; α′ and σ′ (συναγωγαὶ συναγω-
γαί) as well as θ′ (πλήθη πλήθη) and *V* (*populi populi*)
support *M*.
v–v   *T* (במישר פילוג דינא) translates עמק יהושפט, just as
in vv 2, 12.
w–w   In the original reading of *G*ˢ, v 16α is absent; see
below, p. 81.
x   *S* (''not dwell'') replaces the specific statement of *M*
by a statement contrasting theologically with v 17aβ.
y   *G* (κατοικηθήσεται) and *V* (*habitabitur*) grasp the
sense of *M* as an antithesis to v 19a; cf. Is 13:20;
Jer 17:6, 25b; Ezek 26:20; 29:11.
z–z   A meditation upon דם נקיא (''innocent blood'') in
v 19bβ.
aa   *G* (καὶ ἐκδικήσω [''and I will avenge'']), *S* and *T*
presuppose וְנָקַמְתִּי (or וּפָקַדְתִּי?; cf. Hos 1:4).
bb   *G* (καὶ οὐ μὴ ἀθῳώσω [''and I will not leave un-
punished'']) presupposes at least the root of *M*, even
if it renders the tense as imperfect (וְלֹא אֲנַקֶּה?).
V reads the same verbs (*et mundabo sanguinem eorum,
quem non mundaveram*) in v 21aα and β, and thus confirms the complex sentence of *M*.

Form

Oracles against ''all the nations'' (4:2) ''round about''
(4:11–12) are introduced as motivation (''for'' כי 4:1)

for the deliverance on Zion and in Jerusalem (3:5).
As a continuation of 2:19—3:5 they belong in the total
plan of the book of Joel to the oracles answering a plea

(introduced by 2:18) which respond to the turning commanded in 2:12–17. Yet here, as clearly in chap. 3, the distinguishing marks of actual oracles answering a plea are absent;[1] not even the character of the assurance, which could still be found in 3:1, is retained. Yet the divine speech is continued in the main: 4:1–3, [4–8], 12, 17, [21a].[2]

Divine speech occurs in this context because the sayings of our chapter belong to the broadly developed oracle of divine self–manifestation, formed initially by the assurance of recognition in 2:27 which constitutes a bridge from the promises regarding the present to those for the future. Chap. 4 is also included under the rubric at the beginning of the second colon ("afterward it shall come to pass," והיה אחרי כן, 3:1). The formula "in those days and at that time" (4:1a) refers back to the rubric (cf. 3:2!). The expansion of the first self–disclosure oracle (wherein the oracles answering a plea in 2:19–24 are merged with 2:25–27) leads us in turn to the assurance of recognition in 4:17.[3]

Three pieces belong to the original stock of the chapter:

4:1–3 The linking statement (v 1) is followed by a brief (tricolon) announcement of punishment for "all the nations" (v 2abα), with a longer motivation consisting of six cola.

4:9–14 These verses are a continuation of the announcement of punishment. For it is just here that the important catchwords of 4:1–3 are repeated: "all the nations" (v 2; cf. vv 9, 11, 12); "to gather" (v 2; cf. v 11); "valley of Jehoshaphat" (v 2; cf. v 12); "to enter into judgment" (v 2; cf. v 12). On the whole, this oracle exhibits the form of a "summons to battle" (*Aufforderung zum Kampf*).[4] This is shown most clearly by the imperatives in v 9, but also by the additional exhortations in vv 10, 11, and finally in v 14. The actual summons to battle, whose objective is the battle tumult (v 14a) and the "shattering of the heroes" (v 11b [cj.]), is expanded to include elements such as a court subpoena (v 12) and a call to reap the harvest and tread the wine press (v 13) which underscore the theme of the announcement of punishment. V 14 suggests the possibility that the cry "The Day of Yahweh is near!" was originally associ-

ated with the inauguration of holy war.[5] In 2:1–2 the same cry had initiated the alarm cry on Zion. Chap. 4:9–14 is a perfect counterpart to 2:1–9: there the announcement of the approaching enemy army threatened Jerusalem with destruction; here the same now applies to the nations round about. The summons to battle is an appropriate form by means of which to clarify the beginning of the fulfillment of the announcement of punishment in 4:1–3, just as in 2:1–11 the alarm cry announced the threatening nearness of the Day of Yahweh predicted in chap. 1.

4:15–17 The attachment of the third piece to this chapter is also understandable when comparison is made with chap. 2. In 4:15–16aβ we find 2:10 repeated verbatim, though as now described the direction of the commencing Day of Yahweh is reversed. The breaking in of chaos, which was a threat to Jerusalem in 2:10, now threatens the nations; whereas previously Yahweh uttered his voice at the front of the approaching enemy force (2:11a), now it sounds forth from Zion (4:16a); and whereas in 2:11bβ the continued existence of the people of Jerusalem was thrown completely into question, here in 4:16b that same people has found ultimate refuge. With their description of a positive turn of affairs for Jerusalem, these points of contrast with 2:10–11 comprise a parallel to 3:3–5. Hence with the attached promise of Yahweh's recognition as the saving God of Jerusalem (4:17) the book exhibits a tight compositional symmetry. The actual recognition formula, which brings the two–stage self–disclosure oracle to its objective, is sealed by three concise statements expressing reacceptance.

What follows in 4:18–21 must be regarded as a later addition, and the same is true of 4:4–8.

4:4–8 These verses can be recognized as a later addition by the mere fact that the connection between 4:1–3 and 4:9–17 is interrupted.[6] To be sure, the formulaic link (וגם) "furthermore" is also found in the old book of Joel (2:12), but already in 2:3bβ and 3:2 it was possibly used to introduce later additions. A concluding formula, "for Yahweh has spoken" (v 8b), closes off the insertion.[7] The section exhibits its own language; only through the catchword "to sell" (מכר),

1   See pp. 58–59.
2   Yahweh is referred to in the third person only in the transmitted expressions in 4:11b (cj.), 14, 16a, 16b, [18b].
3   On the development of the oracle answering a plea, see pp. 57–59.

repeated four times (vv 6, 7, 8α, 8β), is it linked with the last colon of the preceding oracle (4:3bβ), where the verb occurs only once alongside synonymous verbs. While the context speaks generally of "all the nations" (4:2, 9, 11, 12), this section specifically addresses Tyre, Sidon, and the regions of Philistia (v 4). Whereas in 4:2–3 Yahweh says "my people," "my possession," and "my land," here we find mentioned the "sons of Judah and the sons of Jerusalem" (v 6; cf. v 8) and "their territory" (v 6b), expressions employed nowhere else in the entire book. Only the other later addition also speaks of "Judah's sons" (4:19; cf. v 8); in 2:23 there is one mention of "sons of Zion." And in 4:16 "his [Yahweh's] people" is termed "sons of Israel." The notion of retribution repetitiously assumes one precise formulation (vv 4b, 7–8) which is conceptually and in substance quite foreign to the context. The rhetorical liveliness, with chains of questions (v 4) and with repetition of words and expressions, is alien to the rest of the book. The sentence constructions are also longer and more frequently interspersed with subordinate clauses than in the material preceding or following, where we mostly find shorter and synonymously parallel cola, composed in 4:2–3 as three tricola. Likewise the chains of exhortations in 4:9–14, with their predominantly two–stress cola, stand out clearly from the prosaic style of the insertion. In 4:15–17 there is a shift to almost patternistic prosodic units with synonymous three–stress cola.

4:18–21 The other later addition, however, the concluding piece in vv 18–21, is related in its basic metrical structure to the original text that precedes it. Yet it does not belong to the book's original version. Even the linking formula, "And on that day it will come to pass" (והיה ביום ההוא), is foreign to the book of Joel,

which surely knows of many ways to link materials. Our formula (used to attach supplemental material more than thirty times elsewhere in the Old Testament)[8] contrasts especially with that formula to which it is most closely related in the book of Joel, in 4:1 ("in those days and at that time"; cf. 3:2). We need to note the use of the expression particularly in Zech 12—14 (chapters that are related to 4:18–21 in content) but also in Is 24, 27 and Ezek 38—39. The collectors of future expectations were very fond of this linking formula. As to subject matter, the reference to specific nations (v 19), Egypt and Edom, sets this passage apart from the main content of the chapter. In vv 20–21b the later addition noticeably echoes the concluding piece in 4:17. Although like 4:8 (cf. 4:6) it refers to "sons of Judah" (v 19) and mentions specific foreign nations, it is hardly possible to attribute it to the same hand as 4:4–8. The foreign nations are different ones; generally also the themes and the language of the two sections differ. Further, meter and word usage show that this later addition imitates the language of Joel, or even derives from Joel's own hand: on "[grape] juice" (עסיס) in v 18aα, cf. 1:5; on "torrents" (אפיקי) in v 18aβ, cf. 1:20; on "Yahweh's house" (בית יהוה) in v 18b, cf. 1:9; on the unique "wilderness of desolation" (מדבר שממה) in v 19a, cf. 2:3;[9] on "for ever" (לעולם) in v 20a, cf. 2:27; on "generation to generation" (דור ודור) in v 20b, cf. 2:2; on v 21b, cf. 4:17aβ.

Setting

We have already established[10] that chap. 4 originally followed chap. 3. The old stock of the chapter does not provide many more clues for determining date than the preceding sections. Once again the fact that Joel makes reference to quite diverse older texts speaks in favor

---

4   Cf. Bach, *Aufforderungen*, 62–66.
5   von Rad, *Theology* 2, 124 n. 39 [136 n. 37].
6   See above.
7   The same formula is attested in Is 22:25; 24:3b; 25:8b; Jer 13:15; and Ob 18. Cf. by way of contrast the formulas in 3:5b ("as Yahweh has said") and 2:12a ("the oracle of Yahweh").
8   Cf. Is 7:18, 21, 23; 10:20, 27; 11:10, 11; 17:4; 22:20; 23:15; 24:21; 27:12, 13; Jer 4:9; 30:8; Ezek 38:10, 18; 39:11; Hos 1:5; 2:18 [16], 23 [21]; Am 8:9; Mi 5:9 [10]; Zeph 1:10; Zech 12:3, 9; 13:2, 4; 14:6, 8, 13.
9   See p. 45.
10   See pp. 60–61.

of a later time. The books of the prophets Amos,[11] Isaiah,[12] and Obadiah[13] are simultaneously at his disposal, or at least the cultic language attested in them is familiar to him. Perhaps traditions of the Chronicler are also presupposed.[14] The broad distension of the recognition formula in 4:17 (cf. 2:27)[15] shows influences of the later layers of the book of Ezekiel. All this, taken together, is not thinkable before the fourth century. On the other hand, the attempt to date the chapter to the early Ptolemaic time, on the basis of v 17bβ in particular (as Treves attempts to do), remains very uncertain, for *literary* influences seem to be stronger here also than those from contemporary history.[16] Approximately the same is true of the later additions concerning Egypt and Edom (v 19). With much greater probability the later addition in vv 4–8 can be assumed to derive from Persian times.[17]

Interpretation of 4:1–3

■ **1** The threat to the nations is attached as a motivation to 3:5.[18] The expression "in those days and at that time" is found elsewhere only in Jer 50:4, 20 and 33:15. In Jer 50:4 the announcement of the fall of Babylon to an enemy from the north is linked with the proclamation of salvation for Judeans; and in Jer 33:15–16 the point of the statement is also the safety and security of Jerusalem. Joel's language, down to its details, is at home in those layers of prophetic tradition which are dominated by the theme "Israel and the nations" and which have as their goal the final restoration of Judah and Jerusalem. "To restore the fortunes" (שׁוּב שְׁבוּת)

expresses this great restoration in the related contexts especially of Zeph 3:20 and Ezek 39:25.[19]

■ **2** When the salvation of Israel is the subject, the fate of the world of nations cannot be left out of the discussion, if one does not want to annul the prophetic tradition.[20] On "to gather" (קבץ pi'el) as a gathering for judgment, cf. Zeph 3:8; Ezek 22:19–20; Hos 8:10; 9:6.[21] The Old Testament nowhere else refers to a "valley–plain of Jehoshaphat." From the fourth century A.D. on, it was sought in the Kidron Valley.[22] But that valley, narrow as it is, is no "plain" (עֵמֶק), but rather a "wadi" (נַחַל).[23] Here the thought is of a spacious area, though framed by mountains, in which a giant assembly for judgment (vv 2b, 12b) and a battle of nations (vv 11, 14) can take place.[24] The name, being symbolic, is completely determined by the significance of the place where Yahweh's act of "judgment" (שׁפט vv 2b, 12b) will come to pass. The prophet knows the geographical location as little as he knows an exact date for the final conflict of Yahweh with the nations. The "valley–plain of Jehoshaphat," just as "the northerner" in 2:20 and the "valley of the acacias" in 4:18b, is a cipher; the use of such was quite popular in the emerging apocalypticism. It is possible that the memory of the battle of king Jehoshaphat, as it may have been known to Joel from the account in 2 Chr 20, could have had a part in determining the expression,[25] but this cannot be demonstrated. Yahweh "leads them down" to their own judgment, just as he led the nations up against Jerusalem (2:11a; cf. 2:25). "I will enter into judgment" (נשׁפטתי), as a nip'al

---

11   Note the use of Am 1:2 in Joel 4:16a.
12   Note the use of Is 2:4b or Mi 4:3b in Joel 4:10; Is 8:18b in Joel 4:17a, [21]; and Is 52:1 in Joel 4:17b.
13   Note the use of Ob 11 in Joel 4:3; Ob 17aβ (*M*) in Joel 4:17.
14   See below on 4:2b.
15   Cf. p. 65 on 2:27.
16   See p. 82.
17   See pp. 77–78.
18   On the linking, see p. 73.
19   On the meaning of the formula, see Wolff, *Hosea*, 123 [156f]. On the formula's linguistic prehistory, see now Sefîre stele 3.24 (*KAI* 224.24), where הֵשִׁיב שְׁבִית ("to cause the restoration of") is attested as a form of the expression used in the eighth century. Cf. textual note "b" to 4:1, and André Dupont-

Sommer and Jean Starcky, *Les inscriptions araméennes de Sfiré (Stèles I et II)*, Extrait des Mémoires présentés par divers savants à l'Académie des Inscriptions et Belles–lettres 15 (Paris: Imprimerie Nationale, 1958), 128. Cf. also Ps 126:1, and Martin Noth, "Der historische Hintergrund der Inschriften von sefire," *ZDPV* 77 (1961): 149 (= *idem, Aufsätze* 2, 189). [Cf. Franz Rosenthal, *ANET³*, 661.]
20   Plöger, *Theocracy*, 39f [52f].
21   Cf. Wolff, *Hosea*, 143, 156 [184, 200].
22   Eusebius, *Onomastikon*; cf. Merx, 197.
23   Cf. Armin Schwarzenbach, *Die geographische Terminologie im Hebräischen des Alten Testaments* (Leiden: E. J. Brill, 1954), 38.
24   On the futile attempts at identification, cf. Gressmann, *Messias*, 115f, 139.
25   Cf. Kjeld Jensen, "Indledningsspørgsmaal i Joels

tolerativum, designates the lawsuit in which Yahweh is at first not the judge, but the plaintiff. This construction also derives from that tradition which was the most important for Joel (cf. Ezek 38:22; Jer 25:31); it is especially suitable here, since the counts of accusation follow. The nations founder because of their injustice against the people and possession of Yahweh. "My people" (עַמִּי) occurs already in 2:27b and reappears in 4:3;[26] 2:27b is now interpreted as being directed at the hostile surrounding world, just as it was directed inward in 3:1–5.[27] As the people of God, Judah and Jerusalem (v 2b) also bear the name "Israel" (cf. 2:27; 4:16). The first count of accusation is the "scattering" of Israel into the world of nations. This rare word (used of the scattering of ashes in Ps 147:16) is elsewhere attested with this meaning only in Jer 50:17 where, in the context of oracles against the nations, the image drawn is of "scattered" sheep. There summarizing reference is made to the deportations, first by the king of Assyria and then by Nebuchadnezzar, the king of Babylon. Joel probably also looks back upon the events of 733, 721, 597, and 586; and above all, of course, upon the dispersion of Judah and Jerusalem. The deportations were the precondition for the new distribution of the soil, now without owner, among the conquerors and the new settlers ("to divide up" חלק).[28] The soil is "Yahweh's land"[29] which he entrusted to Israel. Thus Yahweh is always directly affected by acts of violence on the part of the nations.

■ **3** The rare expression "to cast lots" (ידד גורל) belongs to the tradition of the oracles against the nations. It is found elsewhere only in Ob 11 and Na 3:10. In Ob 11, directed against Edom, Jerusalem is also affected, and there also the deportation precedes. In the judgment against Nineveh in Na 3:10 the lot is cast, as in Joel 4:3, for people; the reference is to the distribution of prisoners of war. The two clauses in v 3b spell out how little value is thereby reckoned to persons: a youth, handed over as a slave, brings a price just enough to

cover the charges for a night with a harlot; the sale of a girl only finances a carousing party.[30] The degradation of defenseless persons to the level of trade items is the final basis for accusation against the nations.

Form of 4:4–8
The later addition proffers a relevant, particular charge. After the linking "furthermore" (וגם),[31] it exhibits in its opening lines the form of a lively legal dispute. "What are you to me?" (מה אתם לי) is the short form of the question "What have you done to me?" (מה עשיתם לי) with which a legal charge begins (Ju 8:1; cf. Jer 2:5, 29; Mi 6:3). A double question (vv 4bα, 4β) elaborates further, leading up to the threat (v 4bγ). The charge is first articulated in vv 5–6; thereafter counteraction is threatened in vv 7–8.

Setting of 4:4–8
The question of dating cannot be decided on the basis of individual pieces of evidence,[32] but must take into account simultaneously the following points: (1) Tyre, Sidon, and the Philistine regions are referred to as acting in concert; (2) the Judeans and the people of Jerusalem were sold to Greeks; (3) the Sabeans appear only in the threat; (4) the piece was inserted later into the context of Joel 4:1–3, 9–14. Now, it is possible to demonstrate (especially by means of the description of the coast found in Pseudo–Skylax) that the Phoenicians and the Philistines constituted a political community in later Persian times, around the middle of the fourth century.[33] Alexander the Great had consequently to break the resistance of both Tyre and Gaza in 332 B.C.[34] That Sidon is not mentioned in the course of Alexander's campaign is explained by the fact that it had already been destroyed by Artaxerxes III in 343.[35] Thus the community of action formed by Tyre, Sidon, and the Philistine cities belongs to the period before 343 (cf. also Jer 47:4). Slave trade with Greece had flourished since the fifth century, but it was especially

Bog," *DTT* 4 (1941): 99–101.
26 Cf. Ezek 38:14, 16; 39:7.
27 On נחלה ("possession"), see p. 52 on 2:17.
28 Cf. Mi 2:4; cf. also Lam 5:2 and 2 Kgs 17:24.
29 Thus already 1:6; cf. 1:7. See p. 29. The first occurrence is Hos 9:3; cf. Wolff, *Hosea*, 154f [199].
30 Dtn 21:14 forbids the sale of prisoners of war.
31 See p. 74.
32 Cf. Myers, "Date."
33 On this see Karl Elliger, "Ein Zeugnis aus der jüdischen Gemeinde im Alexanderjahr 332 v. Chr.," *ZAW* 62 (1950): 63–115, esp. 96–99.
34 Arrian, *Anabasis* 2.24, 27; cf. Zech 9:3–8.
35 Diodorus Siculus 14.45. See p. 4.

in the fourth century that Phoenicia was subject to strong Greek influence.[36] It is true that trade with the Greeks is attested for Tyre in older times as well.[37] But in the earlier period a close political association of Tyre and Sidon with the Philistine cities cannot be demonstrated, which accords with the fact that the list in Ezek 27:12–14 includes not the slightest reference to such an association. That active trade connections between Judah and the Sabeans (to be located in southern Arabia) are unattested after the fifth century,[38] need not argue against dating the threat under discussion to the fourth century, since the Sabeans were well–known in Israel from tradition as "distant people."[39] Nothing worse could happen to those inclined toward Greek ways than that the course of events would take them as slaves in the opposite direction. Since the oracle in 4:4–8 was inserted into a received literary context, a context which according to our other investigations is itself scarcely earlier than the fourth century, we reach the conclusion that the insertion must be dated between 400 and 343. At the same time, the year 343 gives us a *terminus ante quem* for the rest of the book of Joel.

Interpretation of 4:4–21

■ **4** Tyre, modern *Ṣūr*,[40] is named first as the leading city of the Phoenicians. Sidon, modern *Ṣēda'*, situated almost forty kilometers north of Tyre, was originally the most important Phoenician city, so that the Old Testament as well as Homer call the Phoenicians "Sidonians." In the tenth century Sidon fell behind Tyre in prominence, becoming its equal again only in the Persian period.[41] Josh 13:2 also speaks of the "districts of Philistia [the Philistines]" (גלילות [ה]פלשת[ים]), while an enumeration of the Philistine pentapolis follows in v 3:[42] Gaza, Ashdod, Ashkelon,

Gath, and Ekron (cf. Am 1:6–8). Martin Noth[43] surmises that "district" (גלילה), usually translated as "circuit, surroundings," desginates a type of region or countryside. In the fourth century the leading role belonged to Gaza, modern Egyptian *Ġazzeh*. As a trading place of the Arabs, it experienced a peak of prosperity in the Persian period and had minted its own coins since approximately the year 400.[44] The leading city besides Gaza was Ashkelon, modern *'Asqalān*.

The disjunctive question causes one to ask, from the rhetorical standpoint, whether the actions named only later (4:5–6) are thought of as retribution—it being assumed here that the interrogator is not conscious of any guilt on his own part—or whether they do not rather correspond to the willfulness of their perpetrators. Whatever the answer may be, Yahweh, who is still explicitly named as the speaker in v 8b, wants to take vengeance as speedily as possible.[45]

■ **5** Initially cited as actions to be avenged are the taking away of gold and silver and the carrying off of the plundered treasures to the despoiler's own temples or palaces. Here the silver and the gold are regarded as Yahweh's possession (cf. Hag 2:8), as were the land and the people in 4:2–3. It is not necessary in this connection to think of a despoiling of the Temple (2 Kgs 24:13) or a carrying away of sacred implements as in 1 Sam 5:1–2. At least such actions on the part of the Phoenicians and Philistines are not attested. Despoiled private property of individual Judeans or Jerusalemites could also be considered Yahweh's possession (Hag 2:8), insofar as it was the property of the people of God. The despoilers could just as well have used the spoils for "their palaces" as for "their temples"; the Sumerian–Akkadian laonword היכל can designate both

36   Cf. Eduard Meyer, *Geschichte des Altertums*, vol. 4/1: *Das Perserreich und die Griechen: Bis zum Vorabend des Peloponnesischen Krieges* (Stuttgart and Berlin, [4]1921), 129.

37   Myers, "Date," 181–85. Cf. יָוָן ("Javan," i.e. Greece) in Ezek 27:13, 19—in the framework of a list which may derive from the period before 587 and may perhaps have reached the transmitter of the book of Ezekiel by way of Tyrian exiles; so Zimmerli, *Ezechiel*, 661.

38   Myers, "Date," 180f.

39   Cf. 1 Kgs 10:1–13; Jer 6:20; Ezek 38:13; Is 43:3;

60:6; and Job 1:15.

40   Cf. Martin Noth, "Phönizier," *RGG*³ 5, 360–62; and Zimmerli, *Ezechiel*, 601–6.

41   Cf. Zimmerli, *Ezechiel*, 691.

42   Cf. 1 Sam 6:4. On this, see Kurt Galling, "Pentapolis," *RGG*³ 5, 210f; and Herbert Donner, "Philister," *RGG*³ 5, 339–41.

43   *Das Buch Josua*, HAT 1/7 (Tübingen: J. C. B. Mohr [Paul Siebeck] ²1953), 70.

44   Kurt Galling, "Gaza," *RGG*³ 2, 1207f.

45   Cf. Ob 15bβ; Ps 7:17 [16]; 9:16–17 [15–16]. Cf. also Wolff, *Hosea*, 82f [102] on Hos 4:9.

"temple" and "palace."[46] The suffix here speaks more in favor of Phoenician and Philistine "palaces."

■ **6** The sale of Judeans to Greeks[47] is doubly shameful: to do so is not only to treat human beings as trading goods,[48] but—and this alone is specified here—it removes them from their home territory to the world of Greek islands and coast lands beyond the reach of Jerusalem. "Javan" (יָוֵן) for the Greek–speaking regions of the western world and their inhabitants (cf. "Ionians") appears in the Old Testament only in exilic and later texts.[49]

■ **7–8** Nevertheless, Yahweh will help them in distant lands to "set out"; the hipʻil of עוּר means not only "to awaken," but also "to set in motion," "to set marching" (e.g., of soldiers in 4:9; cf. v 12), "to activate." He will use the victims as avengers. The Judeans will become instruments (בְּיַד "by agency of") of the punishing action of Yahweh. It is unique within the Old Testament that the suffering people of God is appointed to inflict, as the instrument of its God, the same sufferings upon its oppressors that it had experienced itself. For here the thought of a synthetic understanding of life, that the evil deed produces its own punishment (i.e., the notion of an "immanent nemesis"),[50] is developed in two directions. First, it is Yahweh who is the subject of the punitive action, and not simply the deed in itself;[51] and second, the one who has suffered from the evil deed becomes the mediator of the punishment. That Israel–Judah should itself become this mediator is something which even the prayer of lament in Ps 137:7–9 does not dare to request. Here it is proclaimed

as Yahweh's threat.[52] Since the guilt is basically identified with the deportation to distant lands, it is the Sabeans who appear in the context of the punishment, people known as merchants since ancient times.[53] They are known as inhabitants of a "distant land" (Jer 6:20), which the gloss[54] then stresses, correctly recognizing the intention of the reference. The punishment transcends the guilt only in that daughters (v 8a) as well as sons (v 6a) are traded. Even before Tyre and Gaza had been conquered by Alexander the Great in 332, Sidon was made to suffer under a punitive expedition of Artaxerxes III Ochus in 343.[55]

■ **9** Unnamed persons are exhorted to announce Yahweh's decrees to the world of nations. The opening in v 9aα indicates that what follows (זֹאת "this") is not intended for Israel. Hence one must not posit two layers in vv 9–14, of which one (vv 9–10, 13–14) would exhort the warriors of God's people to execute judgment upon the nations in the "valley of decision," while the other (vv 11–12) would announce Yahweh himself as judge in the "valley of Jehoshaphat."[56] The parallel appeals to "warriors" and "men of war" remind us of the army which assaults Jerusalem in 2:7. It is true that the forms of address, by which the army of nations is at first summoned to battle, are attested elsewhere when Yahweh summons those who are to march against his enemies. "Prepare for a holy war!" recalls Jer 6:4, where enemies are summoned against Jerusalem.[57] Thereafter follows in sequence the arousing call, the command "to draw near"[58] and to "come up," which traditionally means ascent onto the "mountains of

---

46 See Zimmerli, *Ezekiel*, 220; and Wolff, *Hosea*, 146 [188]. After Ezekiel the term was mostly used in Jerusalem to designate the "Temple of Yahweh" (הֵיכַל יהוה).

47 See pp. 77–78 ("Setting").

48 See p. 77 on 4:3.

49 Gen 10:2, 4 (P); 1 Chr 1:5, 7; Is 66:19; Zech 9:13; Dan 8:21; 10:20; 11:2. On Ezek 27:13, 19, see p. 78 n. 37.

50 Cf. Kraus, *Psalmen*, 61f.

51 So also in 4:4 and 7b, as is most often the case in the Old Testament. See p. 78.

52 Cf. Ob 18; Ps 149:6–9; Mi 4:13; Zech 10:3–5; 12:5–9.

53 1 Kgs 10:2; Ezek 27:22–23; 38:13. On this, see Zimmerli, *Ezekiel*, 656.

54 See textual note 'k" to 4:8.

55 See p. 77.

56 Thus most recently Manfred Weise, "Joelbuch," *RGG*³ 3, 801.

57 Cf. Jer 51:27–28 and Mi 3:5. On this, cf. J. Alberto Soggin, "Der prophetische Gedanke über den heiligen Krieg, als Gericht gegen Israel," *VT* 10 (1960): 79–83; and Bach, *Aufforderungen*, 77.

58 נגשׁ is also used in Jer 46:3 for the advance into battle.

Israel" in the direction of Jerusalem.[59] There is no indication as yet that the invitation to battle is filled with hidden irony.[60] But from v 11b on it becomes clear that this summons must not be understood differently than the one in Is 8:9–10 (cf. Zeph 3:8). The form of the summons to battle is already similarly changed in Jer 46:3–6, 9–10: those who will be vanquished are summoned to battle.[61] The summons in Ezek 38—39 has a similar form. Ezek 38:17 already appealed to earlier prophets. Thus the ironical, artificial formation of the summons becomes intelligible on the basis of the long tradition. The advancing host of nations will founder before Jerusalem.[62]

■ **10** In v 10 the bitterness of the irony can be felt more sharply. For the exhortation to forge farming and vinedressing implements into weapons of war is clearly intended as contrast to Is 2:4 and Mi 4:3. Only if we did not see Joel continually occupied with the appropriation of prophetic traditions could we find here "a proverbial expression . . . used in its original sense."[63] The great oracle about the pilgrimage of the nations, in the course of which the nations find salvation and peace in Jerusalem, has been reformulated into a deployment for war, the end of which is destruction. Those unfit for battle are not forbidden, as one might expect, to boast "I am a warrior!" (cf. Dtn 20:8), as is Moab in Jer 48:14. Those boasting will prove to be the really weak ones, while the opposite will be true of the Jerusalemites according to the comparable tradition in Zech 12:8: "He who stumbles shall be like David."

■ **11** Textually uncertain, v 11 urges all nations to make haste. For they are to gather from their widely diverse locations to the place of destination.[64] That the place (in v 11 "there") is not named until v 12, hardly justifies a transposition of the verses. In any case it is evident

from this point on that several variants of the traditions concerning the judgment of the nations in front of Jerusalem are fused in the composition, variants in which even obscure allusions like "there" (שׁמּה) are immediately understood by the ear attuned to the traditions. According to the text attested by *T*, which is probably the original one,[65] v 11b designates the goal of the military deployment, in complete accord with the picture prepared by the earlier summonses to battle and to the gathering of all the armies of the nations at Mount Zion: "Then he will shatter your heroes!"

■ **12** In contrast, v 12 depicts Yahweh not as warrior, but as judge, taking up the announcement of punishment in 4:2a. Yahweh is enthroned in "the valley of Jehoshaphat"[66] as judge of all the nations, even though "to judge" (שׁפט) here, as in 1 Sam 3:13, clearly acquires the meaning "to condemn, to punish." Yahweh thereby performs the function of the king of the universe (cf. Zech 14:9).[67] The ruler "sits" as judge.[68]

■ **13** With v 13 the picture changes once more: now the military destruction as a punitive action is made clear through reference to harvesting and the pressing of grapes. The same picture is also found in Mi 4:13, in the summons of the daughter of Zion to do battle against many nations.[69] מגל, "sickle," can refer to a vintager's knife.[70] One is inclined here to think of the vintage since בשׁל (literally "to boil," Ezek 24:5) suggests the ripening of grapes (hence the translation "is ripe"; cf. Gen 40:10). The cutting of the grape clusters as well as treading them in the press denotes punishment. The "wine press" (גת) is the upper treading basin of the whole apparatus which is filled with grapes; below it is the "wine vat" (יקב), the trough where the juice that has been pressed-out gathers. The vat can be filled to overflowing (cf. 2:24; Prv 3:10).[71] The over-

---

59 Cf. Ezek 38:9, 11, 16, 18; 39:2.

60 Cf. Bourke, "Le jour," 208.

61 Cf. Bach, *Aufforderungen*, 69f.

62 Is 29:5–8; 17:12–14; Mi 4:11–13; Ezek 38—39; Zech 12:2–6; 14:12–13. Cf. von Rad, *Theology* 2, 156–69, 292–300 [167–79, 305–13].

63 Thus Bach, *Aufforderungen*, 72 n. 1.

64 On קבץ ("to gather") as a technical term in threats of punishment, see p. 76 on 4:2.

65 See textual note "r" to 4:11.

66 On the "valley–plain of Jehoshaphat," see p. 76.

67 Cf. Werner Schmidt, *Königtum Gottes in Ugarit und*

Israel. *Zur Herkunft der Königsprädikation Jahwes*, BZAW 80 (Berlin: A. Töpelmann, ²1966), 36–40.

68 Ps 9:8–9 [7–8]; 122:5. Cf. Jer 26:10b and Ruth 4:2.

69 Cf. Jer 25:30; Is 63:1–6; 17:5. Other metaphors within summonses to military action are attested in Jer 5:10; 50:16, 26–27; on this, cf. Bach, *Aufforderungen*, 64.

70 *BRL*, 475f.

71 See Wolff, *Hosea*, 154 [198] on Hos 9:2.

72 Cf. textual note "r" to 4:11.

full wine press portrays the overabundant measure of the nations' wickedness; the third כי–clause ("for . . ." v 13bγ) interprets the two which precede it (vv 13aβ, 13bα). As Yahweh is the grape treader, his garment can be stained red as blood, like that of the warrior against the nations (Is 63:1–6). Here as in v 9a unspecified persons are summoned. Neither the Jerusalemites (cf. Mi 4:13) nor heavenly beings (cf. Zech 14:5b)[72] are addressed by name. Joel takes up the theme in all its liveliness from tradition, but he avoids anything which might distract from the point that it is Yahweh himself, and he alone, who decides (cf. 4:2, 12b, 17).

■ **14–16** In the thematic portrayal of the battles of the nations, the scene easily shifts from the shouting that accompanies the treading of the grapes in the press[73] to the tumult of the battle itself (cf. 1 Kgs 20:13, 28), a motif which also recurs frequently in the descriptions of the Day of Yahweh.[74] Now the valley of Jehoshaphat, the place of decision (cf. 4:2a, 12), is interpreted as "the valley of decision." The term חרוץ connotes the irrevocably determined sentence of destruction.[75] In its execution the Day of Yahweh now begins (3:4–5), the day that was diverted from Jerusalem (1:15; 2:1, 11) out of compassion (2:13–14, 18–19). To clarify this turn of affairs, v 15 takes up 2:10b verbatim, and v 16aβ takes up 2:10a almost verbatim.[76] Now chaos breaks in upon the world of nations. From the standpoint of textual history[77] we cannot be wholly certain whether the statement in v 16aα was taken up by Joel in the form of an exact quotation of Am 1:2a, or as the phrase had been reinterpreted in Jer 25:30,[78] especially since it breaks up the clauses in vv 15 and 16aβ which are linked by content and on the basis of 2:10. Yet the transformation of 2:10a in 4:16aβ, with the transposition of the subjects in the latter, is most easily accounted for by supposing that v 16aβ was meant from the outset to be a result clause attached to v 16aα. It is true that Joel is generally free in adapting topics of

tradition into his own sentences, but he can also take over two lines literally, especially at decisive high points (as Is 13:6 in 1:15, and Zeph 1:15b in 2:2a). The change of place on the part of Yahweh from the valley of Jehoshaphat (4:12b) to Mount Zion (cf. also 4:17aβ) is best explained if Joel is citing Am 1:2 verbatim. Thus an adoption of Am 1:2a by Joel himself is likely, in the course of which this oracle is turned against the nations (as also in Jer 25:30). In v 16b the consequence for Israel is drawn for the first time since 3:5. Yahweh himself, as the judge of the nations in a criminal court (vv 2, 11b [cj.], 12b, 14b, 16a), is the reliable place of refuge and asylum of his people,[79] the rock castle, fortified beyond conquest, for the sons of Israel.[80] "Stronghold" (מעוז) is elsewhere found in parallelism to "refuge" (מחסה) only in Is 25:4. Those addressed as Yahweh's people are again called "Israel" (as in 2:27; 4:2) though, to be sure, here uniquely "sons of Israel."

■ **17** The new assurance of recognition brings to its goal the eschatological part of the assurance oracle answering a plea introduced in 2:18, the part that began with the first assurance of recognition in 2:27. It is constructed, as in 2:27, with the "formula of favor."[81] The recognition of Yahweh as the Covenant–God of Israel is the final goal of Yahweh's acts with respect to the world of nations. The verse exhibits the basic form of the divine speech which formed the foundation from 2:19 on; it was continued in 4:1–3, was also presupposed in 4:9–13 (as v 12b indicates), and was interrupted only in vv 15–16 by the incorporation of received expressions. The assurance of recognition is articulated in three clauses. First, Yahweh says in the appositive clause of v 17aβ: as the God of the covenant "I dwell on Zion, my holy mountain." This expression (שכן בציון הר־קדשי) has its most precise parallel in Is 8:18, only in Joel the "mountain of Zion" has become the "mountain of my sanctuary" in keeping with the cultic language of the time.[82] The expression of "Yah-

---

73 Is 16:10; Jer 25:30; 48:33; 51:14.
74 See p. 74; and also Is 13:4; Ezek 7:11–13; 30:4, 10, 15; cf. Ezek 39:11, 15.
75 Cf. 1 Kgs 20:40; Is 10:22–23; Dan 9:26–27; cf. also Horst, *Hiob*, 208 on Job 14:5.
76 See p. 74.
77 See textual note "w" to 4:16.
78 Thus Kapelrud, *Joel*, 163f; and Georg Fohrer,

"Zion–Jerusalem in the Old Testament," *TDNT* 7, 316 n. 114.
79 On מחסה ("refuge"), see Kraus, *Psalmen*, 342, on Ps 46:2 [1].
80 Is 17:10; Ps 31:3 [2]; Na 1:7.
81 See p. 65 and n. 66.
82 Cf. Joel 2:1; Ob 16; Ezek 20:40; Is 56:7; 57:13; 65:11, 25; 66:20.

weh's dwelling in the midst of Jerusalem" in Zech 2:14 [10]; 8:3 means, on the other hand, his dwelling among the population; in Joel, however, the place of his sanctuary is thought of as the place of the divine "tabernacling."[83] Only the second sentence spells out that, due to Yahweh's dwelling in the sanctuary of Zion, Jerusalem as a whole[84] becomes "sanctuary," i.e., Yahweh's inalienable possession. Thus is Jerusalem already chosen as "city of the sanctuary" in Is 52:1; according to Zech 14:21 even all the pots in Jerusalem and Judah will be "holy to Yahweh Ṣĕbā'ōt." In both these cases, as well as in Na 2:1 [1:15], a third statement is associated with this, namely, that no unclean and uncircumcised person (Is 52:1), no merchant ("Canaanite," Zech 14:21), no worthless person (Na 2:1 [1:15]) will "pass through" (always עבר) the city. In Joel 4:17 those excluded are called "strangers" (זרים), a designation used for foreigners as those who are outside of the cultus.[85] As to subject matter, then, v 17bβ cites a topic which belongs to the traditional description of the sacred character of the city.

Consequently, one should not attempt to base a dating on this verse, as does Marco Treves ("Date," 153–54). Treves argues that a hostile invasion is meant here. Of the conquerors between 586 and 100 B.C., only Ptolemy Soter (323–285) would be open to consideration. He conquered Jerusalem on a Sabbath in 312.[86] Treves supports his thesis by combining the statements of 4:17bβ and 19, a procedure that is already problematical because of the secondary nature of vv 18–21.[87] He hears the "Never again!" of Joel being exclaimed in view of the assault of 312. But the "never ...again" (לֹא ... עוֹד), which is so important to him, also belongs to the received topics of the description of the eschatological sanctity of Jerusalem, just as "to pass through" (עבר) and the synonyms for "strangers" (זרים): cf. Is 52:1b; Na 2:1b [1:15b]; later also Zech 14:21.

Thus Yahweh's self–manifestation as the God of the covenant is summarized in the assertion that he, as the one present on Zion, appropriates all Jerusalem inalienably to himself and refuses access once and for all to everything pagan. Thereby is highlighted the salvific effect of the judgment on the nations. When Jerusalem is called a "sanctuary," this is meant to stress not so much its cultic purity (thus Zech 14:21), as rather its inviolable assignment to the God of the covenant, making it a refuge and a place of shelter for the people of the covenant (cf. 4:16b and 3:5). In this respect Joel is closer to Deutero–Isaiah (52:1–2; cf. 60:21) than to Zech 14. Those who have completely oriented themselves toward Yahweh's compassion with their thinking and willing (2:12–14) experience once more at the end of the assurance oracle answering a plea that the Day of Yahweh, as a day of judgment, brings their deliverance. In this way it is emphasized—over against the theocratic circles who saw the goal of the ways of God with his people in the already present cultus of Jerusalem[88]—that the future day alone will truly bring Yahweh's reigning presence on Zion as the pledge that Israel can dwell undisturbed.

4:18–21 A common linking formula introduces a later interpretation.[89] One must not understand the concluding passage as though a "lyric picture" were now asserting itself.[90] Instead, wholly in accord with the style of the other labors in the book of Joel, a final theological effort is presented, setting forth two further consequences of the Day of Yahweh whose objective has just been described: Yahweh dwells on Zion in the midst of his people who have been liberated from all the nations round about (2:27; 4:17). This target sentence hence reappears in the section's conclusion, in 4:21b, stating what has once more been explicated.[91] Yahweh's dwelling on Zion in the end–time will have two additional, specific results beyond those proclaimed earlier: first, a paradisal fertility of the land (v 18); and second, political freedom over against Egypt and Edom (vv 19–20).

■18 The reference to the Temple as the source of the

83 On שׁכן ("to tent, dwell, tabernacle"), cf. Arnulf Kuschke, "Die Lagervorstellung der priesterschriftlichen Erzählung. Eine überlieferungsgeschichtliche Studie," ZAW 63 (1951): 84–86; and Werner Schmidt, "מִשְׁכָּן als Ausdruck Jerusalemer Kultsprache," ZAW 75 (1963): 91f.

84 I.e., not only the mountain of Zion as in Ezek 43:12 and Ob 17; cf. Zech 9:8.

85 See Wolff, Hosea, 101 [128].

86 Cf. Josephus, Antiquities 12.1–4.

87 See p. 75, and p. 84 on 4:19.

88 1 Chr 23:25; cf. 2 Chr 6:1 and Neh 1:9.

89 See p. 75.

90 So Weiser.

91 Cf. Curt Kuhl, "Die 'Wiederaufnahme'—ein literarkritisches Prinzip?" ZAW 64 (1952): 1–11.

fountain (v 18b) shows that even the expectation of overwhelming fertility is viewed in light of Yahweh's residing. Hence the reversal in the economic crisis announced in 2:19–26—a reversal which there meant no more than normalization of the food supply—is enlarged to absolutely miraculous dimensions. The conception of the Day of Yahweh as a day of judgment on the nations and a day of deliverance for Israel (4:1–3, 9–17) is thus supplemented by the paradisal motif. For to have found refuge with Yahweh (4:16b) must also mean a surfeit of provisions. Using the same words, Am 9:13bα says that "the mountains drip with juice"; there also the immediately following colon speaks of the "hills," but then departs from Joel in the predicate and even more so in the further continuation. To be sure, the themes in Am 9:13–15 remain related insofar as there also the eschatological expectation associated a paradisal abundance of harvest and political freedom. But the motif of the Temple fountain is completely absent, and the wording of Am 9:13bα coincides with that of Joel 4:18aα only in four cases.[92] Thus Joel takes up catchwords and elements of tradition, incorporating them freely into his own draft. The formulation of the promise of paradise in the three parallel cola in v 18a is reminiscent of the laments in 1:5 and 20—at least with respect to the rare עסיס for "[grape] juice"[93] and the "torrents" (אפיקים) of water. Similarly, the middle colon, which speaks of the abundance of milk on the hills, recalls the distress of the herds of cattle in 1:18. Therefore the extraordinary deprivation will be followed not only by a cessation of want (2:19–27); rather this is merely a pledge that in the end–time there will be an extreme abundance to correspond to the extreme need. Thus the later addition is also determined by the apocalyptic mode of thinking in epochs.

The statement about the Temple fountain in v 18bα is not simply linked in parallel series with the three preceding cola of v 18a. Rather it is substantivized, the finite verb ("goes forth" [יצא]) being placed at the end of the initial colon, while for the purpose of emphasis the "fountain from Yahweh's house" stands at the beginning; an explicating consecutive clause (with converted perfect) follows in v 18bβ. This causal linking of the expectation of the fountain, which becomes a stream, with the expectation of an extraordinary fecundity is prefigured in Ezek 47:1–12.[94] The material dependence of Joel 4:18 on Ezek 47:1–12 is by no means linguistically close. Nevertheless the conceptual difference between v 18b and the related saying in Zech 14:8 is even stronger, for Joel is not yet familiar with the division of the living water into two streams that flow into the eastern and western seas (even though he has mentioned these two seas in 2:20, using exactly the same terms employed in Zech 14:8). Thus the addition to Joel is older than Zech 14. The unique reference to "the valley of the acacias" is independent of the conceptions in Ezek 47. In modern Palestine a comparable designation is found in *Wādī 'eś-Śanṭ*,[95] a valley which, however, leads westward from Bethlehem toward Gath and is already naturally well–watered and fertile.[96] But on the basis of Ezek 47:1–12 we would suppose that Joel 4:18b refers to a valley situated east of Jerusalem. It would be in keeping with this that up to our own time[97] acacias are found in the continuation of the Kidron Valley, the *Wādī 'en-Nār*, which extends through the Wilderness of Judah up to the Dead Sea (cf. Ezek 47:8–9). This large valley–course suits the wide horizon of the expectation which is determined by Ezek 47.[98] The designation "the valley

---

92 Material related in language and subject matter was already known within the ancient Canaanite agricultural cults. As surety that Baʻl is alive, ʼEl perceives in a dream: "The heavens rain oil, the valleys flow with honey" (*šmm . šmn . tmṭrn nḥlm . tlk nbtm*; *CTA* 6 [= *UT* 49]. 3.6–7, 12–13).

93 Elsewhere, apart from Am 9:13, the term is only attested in Is 49:26 and Song 8:2!

94 Ps 46:5 [4] belongs to the broader prehistory of the theme. Cf. Ps 65:10 [9]; Gen 2:10–14; and Is 33:21. On the "spiritualization" of the theme, cf. Ps. 36:9 [8], and also Kraus, *Psalmen*, 343f.

95 So Wellhausen and Bewer.

96 Cf. Gustaf Dalman, "Jahresbericht des Instituts für das Arbeitsjahr 1908/09," *PJ* 5 (1909): 13; and Noth, *World*, 89 [81].

97 Thompson, 760.

98 Cf. Gustaf Dalman, *Jerusalem und sein Gelände*, Schriften des Deutschen Palästina–Instituts 4 (Gütersloh, 1930), 160.

of the acacias" suggests that the valley was particularly lacking in water.[99] Joel, with his own meagre interest in the cultus, would hardly have thought of the fact that the acacia was important for the fashioning of cult objects.[100] Hence the otherwise untraceable, original designation "the valley of the acacias" has above all the status of apocalyptic cipher,[101] which signalizes the miraculous power of fertile life which proceeds from the residence of the God of Israel.

■ **19** The other result of the dwelling of Yahweh in the midst of Israel is the political freedom of the progeny of Judah from their archenemies, Egypt and Edom. Thus the later addition makes concrete what 4:1–3 and 9–14 had developed generally concerning "the nations." In contrast to the later addition in 4:4–8, evoked by a set of contemporary circumstances,[102] it is here probably prophetic tradition which primarily determined the choice of the names. Though Egypt had been an arch-enemy of the people of God since Israel's earliest time,[103] and Edom since the fall of Jerusalem in 587,[104] it is decisive for Joel that both are prevalently mentioned in the Day of Yahweh statements of the prophets.[105] It is here also that the catchword "desolation" (שממה) plays a prominent role (Zeph 1:13; 2:4, 9, 13). The term is most frequently used by Ezekiel (more than twenty times), especially with reference to Egypt in 29:10, 12; 32:15; and with reference to Edom in 35:3, 4, 7, 9, 14, 15. The statement of the guilt is also determined by tradition.[106] Thus this piece of the addition is also determined much more strongly by received prophetic words than by present distress. Joel wants to say once more, by way of a supplement: no prophetic word concerning Yahweh's Day will fail. There is therefore no need to date the oracle to Ptolemaic times on account of a possibly contemporary reference to Ptolemy Soter, especially since similar references to Edom are scarcely supportive.[107] The suffix in בארצם ("in their land") must refer to the Judeans, which is syntactically correct; it becomes in-telligible then especially on the basis of Edom's behavior toward Judah according to Ob 9–14; as for Egypt, one could think of 1 Kgs 14:25–26 and 2 Kgs 23:29.

■ **20, 21b** It is the aim of the punishment of the arch-enemies, Egypt and Edom, that Judah and Jerusalem might look forward to an undisturbed future. "To inhabit" (ישׁב) means here the free, almost sovereign[108] dwelling of the people of God which corresponds to the residing (v 21b) of Yahweh.[109] Where Yahweh has taken up his residence after all the warfare, there his people will also find a homeland that will not be lost. But that will happen only at the future Day of Yahweh, the way towards which leads through the great crisis.

■ **21a** Connection with the catchwords of 4:19b is made by v 21a. The divine speech does not fit the context. It is the aim of this gloss to adduce a final theological clarification. If the Day of Yahweh was announced to Jerusalem earlier (1:4—2:11) as a day of judgment, then that meant precisely that the people of God was "not declared exempt from punishment." But the reversal that has now occurred—whereby Egypt and Edom are punished for their violence against Judah—shows that the sons of Judah are now "declared exempt from punishment" by their God. In the rest of the book of Joel no similar theological trends of thought can be found. They scarcely derive from Joel.

Aim

Only this last chapter of Joel explicitly develops the theme "the people of God and the world of nations." To be sure, intimations of the theme were already present from the first chapter on (cf. 1:6), since the theme does indeed belong inextricably to the message of the Day of Yahweh (1:15). And in 2:1–11 the encoded army of foreign nations, as Yahweh's instrument of judgment, posed a threat. With 2:20 there came, still encoded, the first hint of the great reversal which was already assumed in 3:5. But only in chap. 4 is it

99   So Keil and Marti.
100   Ex 25:10, 23–24; 26:15; 27:1; 30:1. Thus Kapelrud, *Joel*, 170f; and Bič.
101   Cf. p. 76 on the "valley of Jehoshaphat" in 4:2.
102   See pp. 77–78.
103   Ex 1:15ff. Cf. 1 Kgs 14:25–26; 2 Kgs 23:29; and also Wolff, *Hosea*, 145f [187f].
104   Ob 10–14; Lam 4:21; Ps 137:7; Mal 1:3–4.
105   See pp. 33–34. Cf. Ezek 30:3ff; Jer 46:2ff, 10!; Is 34:6ff, 8!.
106   On מחמס ("for the violence"), cf. Ob 10.
107   Treves, "Date," 153f; see p. 82 on 4:17.
108   Cf. Schmidt, *Königtum*, 81f.
109   On the language usage, cf. especially Zech 12:6 and Jer 17:25—in opposition to cities and regions which

made clear by what means Jerusalem will become the place of refuge for those who escape in the midst of a disintegrating world. For "Judah and Jerusalem" are also the anchor point of the theme of this chapter,[110] here specifically as the people and the possession of Yahweh, the God of Israel (vv 2–3, 16–17).

This expresses the fact that the theme "Israel and the nations" is on principle treated as a consequence of the theme, "Israel and its God." Formally, this is exhibited by the sustaining of the divine speech throughout the main strand;[111] as to content, it is shown in that Yahweh announces his own acting primarily as a reversal in the fate of Judah and Jerusalem (vv 1–2, 11, 12, 16). This orientation toward Yahweh becomes inescapably evident when the recognition formula (v 17) marks the actual target of the chapter as the concluding part of a greatly developed two–stage self–disclosure oracle.[112] It is only then that Yahweh is ultimately recognized by his people as the God of Israel. Thus even the later addition concludes by repeating the affirmation of Yahweh's dwelling on Zion (v 21b). This then is the basic tone: Yahweh acts as Israel's God by judging the world of nations. His personal coming and acting (vv 11, 12, 14, 16) are linked inseparably with the complex of themes concerning the "Day of Yahweh" rooted in conceptions of the ancient war of Yahweh.[113] Here, however, it is carried further, in critical conversation with the theocratic theology of priestly circles,[114] to the announcement of the coming personal dwelling of Yahweh on Zion in the midst of his people (vv 17, 21). Thus the statements of 2:27b and 3:1–2, 5 are further developed.

On his day Yahweh proves himself to be Israel's God through his punitive judgment on all oppressors of his people. To the category "oppressors" belong, on principle, "all the nations" (vv 2, 9, 12). The later additions give special prominence to present (vv 4–8) and traditional enemies (v 19). They underscore what is already apparent in the old main strand of the chapter: the nations of the world are impelled toward their destruction precisely because of their transgressions against Israel (vv 2–3, 13). Thus while Israel under the impact of Joel's message awaits the action of its God, it sees itself surrounded by nothing other than a world already given over to destruction. In catastrophic tumults and military deployments (vv 9–14) Yahweh asserts himself as leader and judge.

In the midst of the perishing world of nations, a new and lasting future is prepared for Israel in the precincts of Zion. Yahweh himself is the "place of refuge" there, and the impregnable "stronghold" (v 16b). His city is the inviolable "sanctuary" (v 17b). Yahweh's tabernacling on Zion will bring protection for the whole city area (vv 16–17, 20–21)—and, v 18 adds, a fountain of fertile life for the surrounding regions. In this connection alone is "Yahweh's house" mentioned once more in the book of Joel (v 18b); no longer is it referred to as a cultic place for sacrifice and prayer, as in 1:9, 13–14, 16 and 2:17. Instead, the Temple designates the source of new life which, according to Ezek 47, it represents as Yahweh's Tabernacle.

Thus in this last chapter Joel awakens the hope of latter–day Israel grown tired in its cultus, announcing an intervention of its God into the milieu of the world of nations to effect the total renewal of Jerusalem. Hence earlier prophecy will come to fulfillment.

If Israel awaits the future informed by this word of Joel, it confronts the question whether or not it can see the chapter's basic promise—the promise of God's personal coming and acting, and his tabernacling on Zion—occurring in history in the event of Jesus' fate and in the activity of the spirit through the message of Christ. When the New Testament so attests to this, it appropriately honors that freedom of God to which Joel witnessed when he saw in the locust invasion of his own days the valid omen of the Day of Yahweh announced in prophecy. Israel should take offense neither that the God who comes in Jesus of Nazareth does not

---

have been made uninhabitable, Is 13:20 and Zech 9:5. As a contrasting word, cf. לשממה in 4:19.

110 Cf. the crucial, key declarations in 4:1, 16–17, 20–21.

111 See p. 74.

112 See pp. 81–82.

113 Cf. von Rad, *Theology* 2, 119 [133].

114 See p. 82.

thrust the nations into judgment, but himself bears the guilt of both Israel and the nations; nor that therefore the remark of 4 : 21a includes, at least for the present, Israel's oppressors, gathering around Zion a community out of the whole world.[115]

Around Zion—in the light of New Testament history this means: around the fate of Jesus which was sealed in Jerusalem; around his death as guarantee of God's compassion; and around his resurrection as pledge of new, eternal life. The fulfillment exceeds the promise by far. On the other hand, the light of the promise casts its rays beyond the fulfillment that has taken place. For in the present communion with Christ, security and blessing are still largely hidden under temptations and deprivations. Certainly Joel can open our eyes to many beneficial changes which have occurred in individual lives and in the world of nations through the activity of the living Christ. But as far as the completely new world is concerned—the world that cor-

responds to the inviolable sanctuary of Jerusalem of 4 : 16–17 and the fullness of life which proceeds from the Temple fountain (4 : 18)—the New Testament people of God together with the Old Testament people of God are waiting for a future event which will exceed the bounds of the old expectation (cf. Rev 22 : 1–5).

However, for the New Testament too it is part of the expected future that the sharp sickle will once more pass through the world. Jesus' parable (Mk 4 : 29), as well as the Apocalypse of John (Rev 14 : 14–15, 18, 20; 19 : 15), appropriate the word of Joel concerning the sickle (4 : 13) sent into the harvest of the world of nations. The coming Christ himself will guide it. The word is spoken to us as a warning, insofar as we withdraw from the new order of life which is his compassion. But to all those who can live in an inimical world only by means of this compassion the word is spoken, as once to Israel, for strengthening: the people of God is surrounded only by adversaries who are already on the decline.

---

115 Cf. Luther on Joel 4:2: "He refers everything to the day of the Gospel, not of the Last Judgment" [Trans.] (*omnia refert ad diem evangelii, non extremi iudicii*; WA 13, 83). In his prologue to the book of Joel, Luther comments: "Whatever the ancient fathers understand concerning the Last Judgment, I do not condemn their understanding; but I nevertheless believe that Joel, just as he calls the Christian church the eternal Jerusalem, also calls it the valley of Jehoshaphat, because the whole world is sum-moned toward the Christian church by the word and is judged within it and reproved by the preaching" (WA, *Die Deutsche Bibel* 11/2, 212). Cf. Krause, *Studien*, 323.

Amos

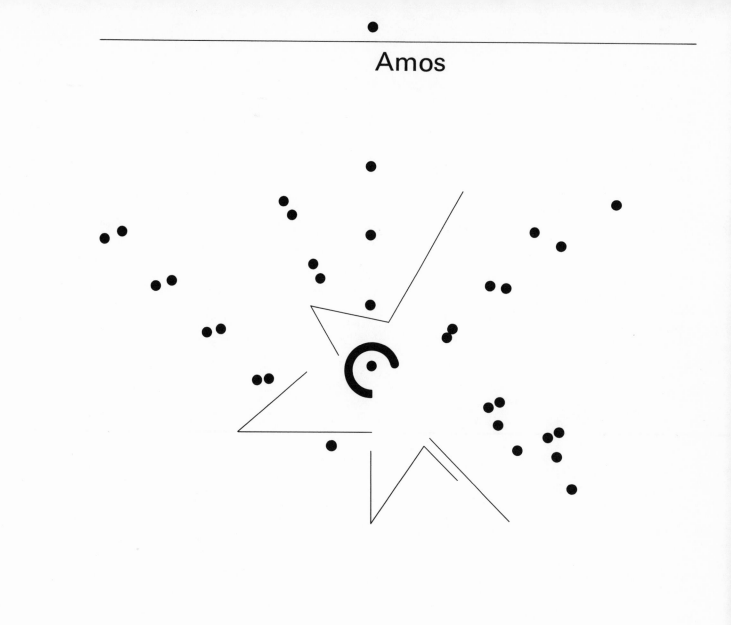

1. The Period

Amos' appearance in Israel during the reign of Jeroboam II (787/6—747/6) is attested by the report that the prophet had announced this king's death by the sword, a threat which Amaziah, the priest at Bethel, conveyed to Jeroboam (7:10–11). The Deuteronomistic redactor of the book's superscription accepted this "dating" and supplemented it, adding the name of Uzziah, the Judean king who had been enthroned in the same year as Jeroboam (1:1b). Since Uzziah became severely ill with leprosy, his son Jotham assumed the responsibilities of government in 757/6. This co-regent is mentioned in Hos 1:1. The fact that he is not designated in Am 1:1 raises the question whether the last decade in the reign of Jeroboam II should even be taken into consideration at all for the time of Amos' appearance. A negative answer is indicated by other considerations.

Amos recalls military successes through which Jeroboam II rounded out the victories of his father Joash (802/1—787/6).[1] It is not certain whether in 6:1 the prophet has in mind army officers who bragged about the conquest of Jerusalem, an event which occurred while Joash still ruled.[2] In 6:13 reference is made to conquests east of the Jordan, and therefore to that territorial expansion of Israel under Jeroboam II associated in 2 Kgs 14:25 with a promise by the prophet Jonah which in turn seems to be reflected in Am 6:14b.

These successes under Joash and early in the reign of his son Jeroboam would have been incredible apart from the changed situation in world politics. During the final third of the ninth century Israel had suffered the powerful onslaughts of the Aramean kingdom;[3] but during the first two decades of the eighth century Aram was subdued by Adad–nirāri III of Assyria (806—783), beginning with his conquest of the capital, Damascus, around 800.[4] This made Israel's expansion possible.

After the death of Adad–nirāri III, however, the power structures shifted again. The kingdom of Urartu, under Argišti I and Sardur III (810—743), gained predominance and kept Assyria so occupied that the Arameans could move freely once again. The advances of Damascene forces into Israelite Gilead, mentioned in Am 1:3, supported by similar incursions of Ammonites (1:13), probably belong to the decades when Urartu was the dominant power. Just as Israel could regain its strength during the two decades that the Aramean kingdom was occupied with Assyria, it was also possible for the Aramean kingdom to recuperate during the following two decades, while Assyria was occupied with Urartu. The allusions to hostile actions east of the Jordan in 1:3 and 13—which do not fit well into the early reign of Jeroboam II, but point with even less likelihood to the ninth century—can easily be understood from the perspective of the time around 760.[5]

This dating is supported by archaeological evidence for an earthquake[6] which may well be identical with the one referred to in 1:1 ("two years before the earthquake"). Perhaps also there is an allusion in 8:9 to the famous eclipse of the sun of 763.[7]

During the period around 760 it is understandable that Amos never refers to Assyria.[8] The large–scale deportations announced in 1:5; 5:5, 27; 6:7; and 7:11, 17 were already known from Urartean practice.[9] It is indicative of Amos' purview that he associates the first deportations geographically with localities in the Aramean kingdom (4:3; 5:27).

After the military successes in the early part of Jeroboam's reign, Israel experienced the period of economic prosperity which is assumed in many of Amos' oracles. Commerce became extremely active (8:5a), and trade was practiced on an international scale (3:9). Deceitful business practices increased profits (8:5b). Building activity flourished (3:15). Houses became more numerous and more substantial than ever before in Israel (3:15b; 5:11; 6:8), and they were elaborately furnished (3:10, 12b, 15b; 6:4a). Viniculture and cattle raising became geared to demanding customers (5:11b;

---

1   2 Kgs 13:24–25; 14:25, 28.
2   2 Kgs 14:13–14; see below on Am 6:1, *ad loc.*
3   2 Kgs 13:7; 10:32–33.
4   See p. 150.
5   See pp. 150–51.
6   See p. 124.
7   See below on 8:9, *ad loc.*
8   See below on 3:9, *ad loc.*
9   See p. 151.

6:4b) since the thirst for pleasure manifest in rollicking feasts had to be accommodated (4:1; 6:4, 6). New music was composed (6:5). Sexual immorality increased (2:7b). The cultus participated in the economic boom: sacrificial offerings proliferated (4:4–5; 5:21–22); the feasts were celebrated with ebullient singing and instrumental music (5:23).

The converse of this development was social upheaval. The rich became richer while the poor became poorer. Such early capitalism quickly led to expropriation of the holdings of the smaller landowners. The ancient Israelite land rights were superceded by Canaanite practice. Slavery for debt took on vicious forms (2:6; 8:6). The socially underprivileged were exploited (2:7a; 4:1; 8:4). Their rights were violated through intimidation of witnesses and bribery of judges (2:7aβ; 5:10, 12).

Thus in the shadow of world politics following the great foreign policy successes of Jeroboam II, luxury and injustice alike abundantly flourished; in the east, border incidents had once again begun to occur. Such is the time of Amos around 760.

2. The Man Amos

When Amos was born and when he died, we do not know. How old he was at the time of his appearance around 760 b.c. remains hidden from us. He had been attentive to affairs faraway (1:3–8; 1:13—2:3; 3:9; [6:2]; 9:7). His verdict concerning Israel was well–founded and conclusive (2:6–9; 5:18–24; 7:11, 16–17). His speech at times took on a sharpness and boldness which appears youthful (4:1; 5:5; 6:12). This and no more can be concluded from his oracles.

The question of how long he was active as a prophet in Israel is also difficult to answer. The view that he made but one speech lasting only twenty to thirty minutes, during a single appearance at Bethel,[10] is completely unlikely. Short, self–contained oracular units are too clearly distinguishable; moreover, at least some of

these become more meaningful when it is assumed that they were proclaimed in Samaria (3:9; 4:1; 6:1). On the basis of 7:10–17 no one contests the fact that Amos also spoke out in the sanctuary of Bethel.

Thus it is likely that he stirred up unrest in at least two localities, and perhaps three, of the northern kingdom, for according to 5:5 it is not impossible that he came to Gilgal as well.[11] And yet we cannot conclude from this that his prophetic ministry extended over a long period of time. The scant allusions to historical events[12] do not allow us to distinguish different phases of his ministry, as it is possible to do in the cases of Hosea, Isaiah, and Jeremiah. However, a few weeks or months will have to be granted, not only to allow for the migratory character of his work, but also to account for two distinguishable literary collections: "the words of Amos from Tekoa" in chaps. 3—6 and the recorded cycles of chaps. 1—2 and 7—9.[13] The early redaction, which connected these two collections in the older stratum of the book's superscription, most probably wanted to date the entire career of Amos "two years before the earthquake," thus assuming that his career had lasted for a period of less than one year.[14]

It is consonant with such a relatively brief, transient appearance that Amos was not a native of the northern kingdom, but a Judean[15] come from Tekoa.[16] Further, he declined to be addressed as a professional prophet, since he made his living raising livestock and as a tender of mulberry trees.[17] As a sheep breeder (and as such to be distinguished clearly from a lowly shepherd) he was probably not exactly poor.[18] His purview is neither that of a common man nor that of a cult functionary steeped in traditions at home within the confines of a sanctuary. If sheep breeding had not been enough to take him into towns and oasis markets to sell animals and wool, then tending sycamores at least demanded a wide range of travel; for that tree does not grow on the hills around Tekoa, but only on the shores of the Dead Sea and the Mediterranean. Thus he became a far–

---

10 Thus Julian Morgenstern, "Amos Studies II: The Sin of Uzziah, the Festival of Jeroboam and the Date of Amos," *HUCA* 12–13 (1937–38): 51 (reprinted in *idem, Amos Studies*, vol. 1 [Cincinnati, 1941], 177).

11 Cf. 4:4.

12 See p. 89.

13 See pp. 107–08.

14 See p. 124.

15 See below on 7:12, *ad loc*.

16 For the location, see p. 123.

17 See below on 7:14, *ad loc*.

18 See pp. 123–24.

sighted, well–informed Israelite. The instruction of ancient Israel, in the form of clan wisdom,[19] had been taught to him by the clan elders in the gate; perhaps this wisdom had been preserved more zealously in Tekoa than elsewhere.[20] In addition, he had brought home from his travels a rich knowledge of events among the neighboring peoples (1:3–8; 1:13—2:3; 3:9; [6:2]; 9:7). Thus he may have come to know the particular ills of the northern kingdom, evident especially in Samaria and Bethel. And yet it was neither his knowledge of Israelite wisdom nor his indignation at past injustices which prompted him to intervene with his word in some chief cities of Israel.

It was the hand of Yahweh which uprooted him temporarily from his familiar realm and made him break the silence of the wise in evil times (5:13). Whenever he reveals the basis for his prophetic appearance, he points exclusively to Yahweh's irresistible insistence. The three passages which especially afford us direct insight into that unique turning point in his life explicitly decline to explain his oracles on the basis of either a conventional office or the tradition. To the priest Amaziah in Bethel he says that it was Yahweh's grasp and call alone which took him away from tending the flock (7:15). To those who attribute his appearance to his own brazen self–will, he directs the question whether then terror at the sudden roar of a lion could be self–willed; it is Yahweh's address that has irresistibly impelled him to make proclamation (3:8). In the cycle of visions he goes into detail to explain how Yahweh has impressed upon him the message of the now imminent end of Israel, a message never heard before (7:1–8; 8:1–2; 9:1–4). That which has been explicated in this threefold manner is confirmed by the individual oracles: It is the announcement of punishment, and not the accusation, which is introduced as Yahweh's word.[21] Amos does not now proclaim judgment as a consequence of legal reasoning, based on the infraction of ancient divine decrees; rather, because he has been constrained by Yahweh to proclaim his judgment, Amos also exposes Israel's guilt as reason for this judgment.

This surprising insistence by Yahweh to issue a threat of punishment is for Amos himself the only important aspect of his life which he conveys to his contemporaries and to posterity, doing so directly or indirectly in almost every one of his oracles. Compared with this, the fact that his language betrays to us the sapiential education of an Israelite with an international purview is of subordinate significance. Both of these factors are made more understandable since the name of his hometown, Tekoa, and his occupation have been transmitted to us. However, we only know all of this because he appeared as the messenger of Yahweh in Samaria and Bethel (and perhaps also here and there in other Israelite localities) during a period of at least a few weeks but scarcely longer than several months.[22]

3. The Language of Amos

The literary tradition hardly allows us to recognize more than two dozen short individual oracles. All the more surprising, then, is the wealth of rhetorical forms which the prophet himself has displayed. We will treat here only Amos' own language; that of those who transmitted and supplemented his work will occupy us in section 5.

First of all, three basic types of speech must be clearly distinguished: (a) The "messenger speech" is strictly tied to the commission from Yahweh and on principle is formulated in the divine first person. Clearly distinct from it is (b) the free "witness–speech," which promotes contact with the listener and by definition introduces Yahweh in the third person. In particular instances free witness–speech may lead up to commission–bound messenger speech, and it is equally possible for stylistic elements of free witness–speech to appear within the formulaic framework of a messenger oracle. The third basic type (c) is that of the "vision report," of which it cannot be said with certainty whether it is rhetorical or literary in origin. Finally, (d) we will have to investigate a number of peculiar elements of speech. Then we will be able to present (e) the forms of composition, and hence (f) gain insight into the creative dynamics of the language of Amos as a whole.

---

19   See pp. 93–100.
20   See p. 123.
21   See pp. 92–93.

22   See the excursus on *The Vocation of Amos*, pp. 312–13.

A. Commission–Bound Messenger Speech

When Yahweh comes to the fore in the messenger speech, it is consistently as the first person speaker. This is a reliable characteristic, though one that is not everywhere apparent. The other characteristic is a framework formula wherein the messenger announces that it is Yahweh who speaks in the first person. The formula is indispensible but variable.

a) The "messenger formula," which derives from the language of diplomatic exchange (cf. 7:11), is used most frequently by Amos.[23] Eleven of his oracles contain the introductory messenger formula "Thus Yahweh has said" (כה אמר יהוה) 1:1, 6, 13; 2:1, 6; 3:11, 12; 5:3, 4, 16; 7:17), and five of these also show the corresponding concluding formula "Yahweh has said" (אמר יהוה 1:5, 8, 15; 2:3; 5:17). The concluding formula alone, without the preceding introductory messenger formula, appears also in 5:27 and 7:3, 6. Only in two of these eleven oracles (5:4–5; 7:17) is the affected party addressed directly; otherwise the party is always referred to in the third person. In seven instances the messenger formula is placed at the head of the entire oracle; four times it appears only at the head of the announcement of punishment (3:11; 5:3, 16; 7:17), but never only at the head of the motivation for punishment. Similarly, the concluding formula is attached only to the announcement of Yahweh's future acts and never to an accusation, a reproach, or a motivation for punishment. This leads to the unambiguous conclusion that the real core of the messenger speech has to be sought in the announcement of judgment.

b) In the book of Amos the "divine oracle formula" ("oracle / utterance of Yahweh," נאם יהוה) in only a few cases goes back with much certainty to Amos himself or to the oldest transmitters of his work (2:16; 3:15; 4:3, 5; [6:14?]; 9:7a).[24] In these instances it always stands at the end of an oracle, in order to distinguish it in a solemn way as speech of Yahweh. It takes the place of "Yahweh has said" (אמר יהוה), which

has a more everyday ring to it.[25]

c) When divine speech is introduced with the "oath formula"—"Yahweh has sworn by" (נשבע יהוה ב)—this intensifies the usual messenger formula (just as does the replacement of "Yahweh has said" [אמר יהוה] by "oracle / utterance of Yahweh" [נאם יהוה] at the end of a unit). Its function is related to that of the messenger formula. For in two instances it only serves to introduce, after a preceding accusation, the announcement of judgment as a divine oracle (4:2; 8:7); in a third instance (6:8) it opens an oracle in which the announcement of punishment and the motivation are intertwined (similar to 1:3, 6, 13; 2:1, 6). Thus the oath formula also fundamentally emphasizes the message of judgment as Yahweh's word and thereby underscores the certainty of judgment beyond any doubt.[26]

d) The "proclamation formula"[27]—"Hear!" (שמע[ו])—commands attentiveness. It does not necessarily (5:1) and not always immediately (4:1; 8:4) introduce an oracle of Yahweh, but it can easily be reshaped (7:16) or expanded (3:1a) for this purpose. The call to "hear," as 7:16–17 shows, is tied less strictly to Yahweh's word of judgment than is the messenger formula, since the proclamation formula opens the whole oracle (together with the motivation for punishment), while the messenger formula introduces only the announcement of punishment (7:17). When the call to "hear" immediately introduces an oracle of Yahweh, the affected party is also addressed in the subsequent speech of Yahweh.[28]

The net result is that the book of Amos formulates approximately twenty old oracles of Amos as messenger speeches. With respect to the divine oracle formulas, as well as in the cases of 7:16 and 8:7, it is no longer possible to distinguish with certainty between what derives from Amos and what belongs to the literary tradition.[29] Approximately half of the oracles of Yahweh are opened with the messenger formula. All the forms of this basic type of messenger speech are in

---

23 On the prehistory of the formula and its use in the book of Amos, see pp. 135–37.

24 See p. 143.

25 Cf. 2:16 with 1:5, 8, 15; 2:3; and 4:3, 5 with 5:17, 27.

26 Cf. further the comments on 4:2, *ad loc.*

27 See Wolff, *Hosea*, 66 [82].

28 Cf. further the comments on 3:1a, *ad loc.*

29 See pp. 108–09.

keeping with the prophet's personal witness, namely, that he was constrained irresistibly by Yahweh himself to undertake the proclamation of his word (3:8; 7:15).[30]

B. Free Witness–Speech

The first characteristic of this type is the absence of all framework formulas that designate Yahweh as the speaker. Within the oracles, Yahweh is referred to only in the third person. Such free prophetic speech occurs either as prologue to an oracle of Yahweh or as an independent unit.

a) Prophetic prologue to the word of Yahweh. We may already recognize this in its tersest form in the proclamation formula in 3:1a: "Hear this word!" Thus the prophet arouses attention, in preparation for the oracle of Yahweh that follows. This appeal recurs verbatim in 4:1 and 5:1. Both oracles show that the appeal need not lead immediately to the word of Yahweh. In 4:1 there first follows instead a detailed characterization of those who are addressed and whose crimes are listed. Only after that is the word of Yahweh issued, separately introduced by the oath formula (cf. 8:4–6 and 8:7). In 5:1 it becomes even clearer that the call is first of all a challenge to hear the prophet's own word ("Hear this word which I take up . . ."); the reference here is to the funerary lament in 5:2 which receives its motivation in the subsequent word of Yahweh (5:3). This combination of the proclamation formula with the prophet's own utterance corresponds to a simple form of "pedagogical introduction" of the wisdom teacher.[31]

Related to this is the call which combines the commands to hear and to testify (3:13a), as well as another which orders witnesses to be assembled so that they may determine the guilt of those (3:9–10 cj.) to whom Yahweh's punishment is then announced in the messenger speech. Here, as apparently also in 6:13, the divine announcement of judgment is motivated first by a free prophetic address and an exposing of guilt. Only in 5:1–2 does the prophetic word anticipate the calamity announced in a messenger speech. In all other cases (3:9–10 cj., 12b, 13a; 4:1; 6:13) the prophet, as witness to the injustice, leads up to the announcement of

punishment in the messenger speech. The *memorabile* in 7:10–17 demonstrates how free prophetic disputation prepares for the proclamation of the messenger oracle (7:17) which forms the climax and conclusion of the disputation. That which, from a rhetorical perspective, stands at the end provides the spiritual dynamic for the whole. In 7:14a Amos is expressly introduced as an autonomous party conversing with the priest Amaziah. He first makes a threefold statement about himself, speaking in the first person (7:14aβ, 14aγ, 14b); he then makes a threefold declaration about Yahweh, referring to him in the third person (7:15a, 15b, 16a). The purpose of this prophetic argument is to report Amos' commission to engage in proclamation, the denial of which (7:16b) motivates the announcement of punishment by Yahweh in the messenger style (7:17).

b) Didactic questions. Disputation concerning the prophet's commission can also appear in an independent sequence of oracles: 3:3–6, 8. A series of questions unfolds. Each one is formulated in such a way that an indissoluble connection between cause and effect cannot be denied. In this way the hearer is brought to the conviction that calamity must also be recognized as the result of Yahweh's acting (3:6b), and the activity of the prophet as the result of Yahweh's speaking (3:8b). In contrast to the messenger address, such disputation which refers to Yahweh in the third person grows out of the denial of the prophetic proclamation and its claim to be speech of Yahweh's messenger. The interrogative style, the series construction, and the method of analogical reasoning are in accord with sapiential instruction and debate.[32]

In 5:20a and 6:[2], 12 paired questions encourage self–judgment. In these cases a pursuit scene (5:19) and subtly devised questions pertaining to animal life which must be rejected as ridiculous (6:12), exhibit a power of conviction spiced with bitter irony. (In contrast to this, the comparison of historical powers [6:2] is sustained by the seriousness of sapiential investigation.) Similar comparative questions have penetrated the style of the messenger speech in 9:7a–b.

---

30 Cf. further the comments on 9:9–10, *ad loc.*

31 See below on 3:1, *ad loc.*, and also Wolff, *Hosea*, 97 [122f].

32 See below on 3:3–8, *ad loc.*

It is not a matter of chance that the didactic questions, are often cast in the style of direct address (6:[2] 12; 9:7a). But even where this style is absent the questions, with their seriate construction, express an almost vehement passion for argument which by no means wants to absolve the listeners from the responsibility of giving their own answers. Stylistically, the didactic questions show most vividly the prophet's tenaciousness, a quality already recognizable in the prologues to the utterances of Yahweh.[33]

c) The "woe–cries," on the other hand, have primarily an objectively didactic sense as far as their original usage is concerned. For in their pedagogical setting they serve as counterparts to the exclamations of happiness appropriate to instruction which teaches the recognition of wrong ways. Within clan pedagogy, the woe–cries belong more to the style of basic catechetical instruction, while the didactic questions encourage those addressed to form their own judgment and to compare even difficult phenomena. But the woe–cries share with the didactic questions the tendency to be constructed in series.

The latter is demonstrated by Amos with his greatest example of this genre in 6:1, 3–6. Alongside this there is a second example in 5:18–20, and perhaps a third, with a mutilated opening, in 5:7, 10.

Besides the tendency to be constructed in series, the characteristic mark of the woe–cries is that "woe" (הוי) is always followed by a plural participle. Direct address is usually not present. Instead, deeds defined in a general way are placed under the woe. There is indeed a violation of style in one particular instance (5:18b) when Amos shifts to direct address in an appended question. Where a regular series follows upon the introductory woe–cry, the further deeds are formulated with alternating participles and finite verbs (6:1, 3–6). The addition of a conclusion, with an explicit announcement of punishment (6:7; cf. [5:11] and 5:19–20), is one of the particular prophetic alterations of the genre (forming the woe–oracle).[34]

Altogether there are far fewer oracles composed as free witness–speeches than there are messenger oracles. Besides the approximately six prophetic oracles that merely prepare for speeches of Yahweh (and thus belong basically with the messenger oracles [a]) there are only four independent disputations in the didactic, interrogative style (b), and two woe oracles, or at the most three (c). But precisely these pieces show the freedom and boldness of the prophet's own initiative, and the wealth of forms in his language. It is not surprising that it was here that the first breakthrough into literary transmission occurred.

C. Vision Reports

The reports in 7:1–3, 4–6, 7–8; 8:1–2 and 9:1–4 were perhaps literary compositions from the outset, though it is possible that they were entrusted orally to a small circle of followers. In any case, in their transmitted shape as autobiographical *memorabilia* they are clearly differentiated both from the forms of messenger speech and from those of free witness–speech. Nowhere else does the prophetic "I" come to the fore in the same way. Only 7:14–15 might be considered comparable; there, however, Amos' autobiographical account belongs to the third–person report of a discussion between the prophet and a prominent listener, who is the subject of the direct address in the following verses (7:16–17). In the vision reports, on the other hand, other addressees recede into the background in the same measure that the prophetic "I" moves to the fore. Although the issue is indeed Israel's fate, not once does Israel figure in the scenes as the recipient of a message which the prophet is being commissioned to deliver, in contrast to the situation as we find it in 1 Kgs 22:20–23; Is 6:8–10; Jer 1:4–10 and Ezek 2:3—3:11. We cannot, therefore, speak of Amos' "*call* visions." Amos remains alone in the face of that which Yahweh shows and tells him. Yahweh grants vision to him, questions him, announces his decision to him. It is to Yahweh that Amos cries out, Yahweh to whom he must give answer. But no commissioning order sends him out among the people of Israel, even though Israel's fate is the sole topic of discussion.

The autobiographical reports exhibit three variations in form. Certainly the vision itself begins each of the five reports, but there is a variation already in

---

33   Cf. further the comments on 9:7, *ad loc.*

34   See the excursus on *Form Criticism of the "Woe–Cries,"* pp. 242–45. On the disputations in 3:12; 4:4–5; and 6:12, see pp. 98–99.

the introduction of the fifth report. While Yahweh is the subject in 7:1, 4, 7 and 8:1 ("Thus Yahweh showed me"), in 9:1 Amos is the subject ("I saw").[35] The second parts of the first four reports are structured as pairs. In the first pair the visions are followed by intercession of the prophet (7:2aβ–b, 5), and in the second pair, by Yahweh's questions concerning the content of the visions (7:8aα; 8:2aα). In the first pair, the third part—the decision of Yahweh—already concludes the reports (7:3, 6). In the second pair, Amos' short answers follow first (7:8aβ and 8:2aβ), and then the concluding words of Yahweh are given (7:8b; 8:2b). In the fifth report, only a lengthy utterance of Yahweh follows the first part, the vision proper. Thus this last report with two parts is preceded by two reports with three parts (7:1–3, 4–6) and two with four (7:7–8; 8:1–2). The reports are developed basically as conversations evoked in the first pair by Amos' intercession, and in the second pair by Yahweh's questions. Just as the vision proper opens each report, the words giving Yahweh's decision always close it. The variants within the five exemplars attest that the selection and the casting of the transmitted forms of the reports were governed by a singular set of experiences.[36]

This third type of speech, the vivid "report" form, illumines on the one hand the passionate language of the free witness–speech and, on the other, the prominent position of irrevocable messenger oracles. Earlier, when treating the first two oracular types, our attention was drawn to the variety of received basic structures and framework formulas. When the vision reports are added to the picture, then we have to reckon with three forces that have influenced Amos' language: transmitted formal material with its basic elements; the audience in each case, and the situation (i.e., the new "life–setting" acquired by a given transmitted form); and the unmistakable individuality of the prophet, who shows himself to be dominated by an irresistible encounter with God. By considering the appropriation of varied language elements and forms of oracular composition, it can further be demonstrated that this third force—the overpowering impact of a revolutionary new insight —forces into its service the shaping powers of the tradition and the situation.

D. Peculiar Language Elements

In his oracles Amos shows himself to be influenced by elements of form which are at home in other speech contexts and which unmistakably shape his messenger oracles and disputation speeches.

a) The "graded numerical saying" is never employed by Amos himself in the way that clan instruction is fond of using it. Amos, of course, did not appear as a wisdom teacher. Yet the cycle of oracles against the nations exhibits in the opening of each oracle an expression which is intelligible only on the basis of that sapiential form of speech: "for three crimes . . . and for four . . ." (1:3, 6, 13; 2:1, 6). The fact that each of the four original oracles against foreign nations focuses on only one crime suffices in itself to establish beyond doubt that we are dealing here with the effects of formative influence from an alien genre. In the original genre, the graded numerical sequence (x and x + 1) begins the synoptic characterization of x + 1 phenomena, wherein the final item of the series often has paramount significance. Amos presupposes that such numerical sayings summarize particular transgressions or crimes. He employs them, however, not for instructional purposes but to motivate Yahweh's irrevocable announcement of punishment. Amos has thereby exchanged the cloak of the clan teacher for that of the prophetic messenger of judgment. This is shown by the first–person speech of Yahweh (which is completely foreign to the numerical saying) and its insoluble connection with the announcement of punishment. The allusion to the numerical saying, as one would allude to familiar instruction, precludes from the outset the possibility that those indicted might excuse themselves on the grounds

---

35 Just as כֹּה הִרְאַנִי יהוה ("Thus Yahweh has shown me") invites comparison with the messenger formula כֹּה אָמַר יהוה ("Thus Yahweh has said"), so too רָאִיתִי ("I saw") in 9:1 recalls the unusual opening of one of the free witness–speeches: ". . . this word which I raise," 5:1.

36 Cf. further the discussion of 7:1–9 "Form," pp. 294–95.

of their ignorance.[37]

b) In the judgment on those who are indicted, a casting in participial style is immediately apparent. The participial forms, always in the plural, occur so frequently and at times so surprisingly, that they too must be explained on the basis of received forms which exert their influence on the language of Amos. The clearest pointer to the generic provenance of these characterizing plural participles is offered by the woe–cries in 5:18, and especially 6:1, 3–6.[38] Thus in the latter text, a single introductory "woe" (הוי) plus adjective is followed by seven cola beginning with plural participles that alternate with cola exhibiting finite verb forms. Now when other oracles frequently begin with simple participles in the plural, it is plausible to assume that this form of characterizing those on whom judgment is passed ought to be understood on the basis of the woe oracles. This is the case especially in 5:7, where interpreters often supply a "woe" (הוי),[39] but also in 6:13, where the continuation shifts to direct address. This use of participles at the beginning of an oracle is related to those participial chains that are attached to a nominal vocative in the opening of an oracle; thus 4:1 exhibits three plural participles. The alternation of plural participles and finite verbs, which we encountered in the woe–cries, occurs within the indictments in 2:7; 3:10b; and 5:12b. The first passage (2:7) even suggests the possibility that the numerical sayings employed at least in part the participial style in their chains, much as do the woe–cries.[40] In any case, the frequency with which plural participles are used to pass judgment on those accused may be explained by Amos here too having adopted a feature from the language of clan instruction.

The situation is different in the case of the singular participles used in the opening of the divine threat of punishment, formulated in the first person: 2:13; 6:8, 14 (cf. 6:11; 9:9; 4:2). Since these are usually introduced by הנה ("hence, so"), a prominent language

element of the vision reports has exerted influence on them.[41]

c) Antitheses occur especially as structural features of admonitory speech (5:4–5: "Seek me . . . do not seek Bethel . . . !").[42] They are widespread in the language of sapiential counseling.[43] A specifically prophetic adaptation is the use of the device to negate the usual relationship between deed and result. While as a rule an incipient result corresponds to the deed which intends it, the prophetic threat sets expected and actual results in sharp contrast to each other (5:11b: "You have built houses of hewn stone, but you will not dwell in them; you have planted delightful vineyards, but you will not drink their wine").[44] The contrasting of God's action and Israel's deeds demonstrates a similar fracture within the framework of the speech of accusation (2:6–8 over against 2:9 [cf. 4:6–11]).

d) Word plays are a further means of inscribing the message poignantly upon ears and consciences. First, the message of the "end" of Israel was impressed upon Amos himself by means of the alliteration קָיִץ—קֵץ (qayiṣ—qēṣ, "summer fruit"—"end"). The announcement of punishment against the "head of the exiles" (רֹאשׁ 6:7) takes up, almost ironically, the claim of those threatened to be the "choicest of the nations" and to use the "choicest oils" (רֵאשִׁית in 6:1 and 6). The impending fate has an exact formal correspondence to the present life–style of those claiming leadership, a life–style whose reality will be blatantly negated by the threatening exilic destiny. Similarly, 5:5b sets present and future in opposition: "For Gilgal will surely depart into exile, and Bethel will come to adversity." The content of the latter element establishes, in a way similar to 6:1 and 3–7, a contrast between the claim inherent in the name "God's house" and the threatening calamity ("adversity"). We are not dealing with a word play here, but we have the beginning of a word alteration which Hosea introduces in the form "house of adversity."[45] Amos himself, in the preceding element of his oracle,

37 Cf. further pp. 137–39.
38 See p. 94.
39 See below on 5:7, *ad loc.*
40 See p. 141.
41 Cf. 7:8 with 7:1, 4, 7; and 8:1! See further the excursus on הנה *in Amos,* p. 142.
42 Cf. further: "Seek good, and not evil!" 5:14a; "Hate evil, and love good!" 5:15a; and 5:24 following 5:21–23!
43 See the discussion of 5:4–5 "Form," p. 232.
44 Cf. further the negations in 2:14–16 and 9:1b–4.
45 Hos 4:15; 5:8; 10:5; 12:5 (G) [4]; see Wolff, *Hosea,* 90 [113].

works with the alliteration of the sanctuary name "Gilgal" and the threat "will surely depart into exile" (גָּלֹה יִגְלֶה, gālōh yigleh).[46] The assonance of the phrase discloses to the ear of the Israelite that the fate which rings forth in the name must of necessity be fulfilled.[47]

e) The rhetorical device of quoting those to whom he is speaking provides yet additional evidence of the prophet's intention, noted earlier, to establish contact with his audience. The account in 7:10–17 offers a pointed illustration of this since the accusation there arises from a disputation with the listener. In the cited injunction against Amos' speaking (7:16), the guilt of the priest Amaziah is substantiated by his own words. In the same way, the citations of those who are being threatened—whether used alone (6:13; 9:10; cf. 8:14), or emphasized at the end of a series of accusations (4:1)—serve to establish guilt. The speakers' own words confirm the justness of the prophet's accusations of uninhibited indulgence ("Fetch that we may imbibe!" 4:1), of self–aggrandizement ("Have we not by our own strength taken Karnaim for ourselves?" 6:13), of self–assurance ("Evil shall not overtake or meet us" 9:10). If 2:12 and 8:5 derive from disciples, then they have employed in the same fashion their master's usage of the quotation to substantiate guilt. Only 5:14b makes use of a quotation ("Yahweh [will be] with you") in order to present an assurance of salvation (here in the form of a demonstration of the linkage between deed and result) as the fulfillment of an expressed expectation. This different function strengthens the doubt whether it is Amos who speaks here, as does the different introduction of the quotation, "and it will be so . . . just as you say" (. . . וִיהִי־כֵן, כַּאֲשֶׁר אֲמַרְתֶּם). In the utterances that are certainly Amos', quotations are regularly introduced with a participial form of אמר (4:1; 6:13; and 7:16; 9:10; cf. also 8:14); in those pieces which are certainly (2:12; cf. 3:1b) or probably (8:5) secondary, the infinitive לֵאמֹר is used.[48] In Amos, therefore, the quotations represent an intensification within the participial style; the function of uncovering guilt, which belongs to the latter, is polemically sharpened: "By your words you will be condemned" (Mt 12:37). The illustration in 6:10 of a scene of calamity by means of a dialogue forms an exception.

f) The richness of imagery shows Amos' desire to communicate clearly, a desire shaped by wisdom. The scope of his comparisons reflects the prophet's breadth of education. Certainly he knows the life of the simple shepherd and his legal obligations (3:12a), and his fear of the lion (3:4, 8; 5:19). Catching birds and other hunting experiences are of course familiar to him (3:5), and from the vantage point of the edge of the steppe he longs for the blessing of streams that flow perennially (5:24). But neither is he unacquainted with scenes from the lives of rich farmers and of prosperous cattle breeders. He is knowledgeable in the breeding of horses and in the work of ploughing (6:12a); he has observed the harvest wagon loaded high, its wheels cutting deep furrows in the soil of the field (2:13). Threshing with modern iron sledges is part of his experience (1:3), and he knows that the fattest cattle are raised in the land of Bashan (4:1). For his similes he similarly draws upon his knowledge of the unusual strength of oaks and the height of distant cedars of Lebanon (2:9), as well as his information concerning the effects of poison and wormwood (5:7; 6:12b). One hears his heart pound when he depicts Israel in the image of the young woman who is stricken in the bloom of her years and for whom the funerary mourning of the clan resounds (5:2; cf. 5:16–17).

In the manifold forms by which the imagery is introduced, the fullness of the prophet's ability to express himself is also revealed. The simple comparison of nouns is carried out with "like" (כְּ 2:9; 5:24). An event described in a sentence is elucidated by a comparable event which is introduced by "just as" (כַּאֲשֶׁר 2:13; 3:12; 5:19; 9:9b). It is typical of Amos, however, that the image as a rule simply takes the place of that which it represents (1:3b; 4:1; 5:7, 20; 6:12b), or it precedes the latter without any formulas of comparison (3:3–6, 8; 5:2; 6:12a, 12b). In this way the language, which is always concrete in any case, not only becomes even more understandable, but is intensified to the point of extreme singleness of purpose (5:2; 3:12; 5:7), and at times even to a shocking sharpness

---

46   In order to reflect the alliteration of the Hebrew, Wellhausen paraphrastically rendered the phrase: "*Gilgal wird zum Galgen gehn*" ("Gilgal will go to the gallows").

47   Cf. also 6:11aβb; see p. 281.

48   See p. 108.

(1:3b; 4:1; 5:19; 6:12b). The images have their function equally in the accusation speech (1:3b; 4:1; 5:7, 24; 6:12) and in the threat of punishment (2:13; 3:12; 5:2, 19–20; 9:9), but also in the disputational clarification of the prophetic self–understanding (3:3–6, 8). Thus Amos misses no opportunity to stimulate the ear and the understanding of his audience.

E. Forms of Composition

The structure of the oracles as rhetorical units documents once again the striving to be clearly understood, the determination to use persuasive language, and above all the dominating significance of the announcement of judgment.

a) The judgment oracle constitutes the basic form of the proclamation of Amos, specifically with the pattern that an indictment precedes the announcement of punishment. More than half of the oracles are so composed. The following methods of conjoining the parts are to be differentiated. The charge of guilt is formulated using עַל ("for, because") plus an infinitive, and the announcement of punishment is attached using either a consecutive perfect form (1:3–8, 13–15; 2:1–3) or a participial construction with הִנֵּה ("hence") as in 2:13–16. Otherwise a conjunction is found only once before the indictment, namely יַעַן ("because") in the insertion at 5:11aα. This יַעַן clause is enclosed within a לָכֵן clause (5:11aβ–b) which establishes connection with the preceding sentences of accusation in 5:7 and 10. "Therefore" (לָכֵן) as a transition to the announcement of punishment is elsewhere attested in 3:11 (after 3:9–10); 5:16–17 (probably making connection with 5:12); 6:7 (after 6:1, 3–6); similarly we find עַל־כֵּן ("therefore") so used in 3:2b (after 3:2a). These approximately ten oracles, which use conjunctions to link the announcement of punishment to a preceding indictment, show impressively that in each case Amos wants to witness to the fact that from the outset Yahweh's judgment is just.[49]

But the same is true in principle of those oracles which combine the two parts only loosely, whether they attach the punishment, using a consecutive perfect (5:7 as also in 1:4, 7, 14; 2:2; similarly 8:14b), or whether they set it off with an oath formula (4:2–3; similarly 8:7 in the oracle 8:4–7, which was probably worked over secondarily).

Only in the oracles added later, in which the language of the pupils cannot be distinguished with certainty from that of the master,[50] do we find the indictment in one instance following the announcement of punishment (9:9–10), and in another framed by announcements of punishment (8:13–14).

If one examines the proportional relationship between the proclamation of punishment and the indictment, the latter is much longer only in 5:7, 10–11 and especially in 6:1, 3–7. By contrast, the judgment speech in 3:13–15 and 5:12, 16–17 is twice as long, and in the four oracles against foreign nations even three times as long as the indictment (1:3–8, 13–15; 2:1–3). Otherwise the two parts are usually balanced. Israel should be informed of its crimes in the same measure that it learns of the response which Yahweh threatens.

b) Special forms. If they have not been abbreviated in the course of literary transmission and if the form–critical delimitation of the speech units is correct, then only two oracles in the book of Amos exhibit an announcement of guilt appearing independently without a proclamation of judgment. They can be designated as "reproaches" proper, especially since in both cases the hearers are directly addressed. But precisely these oracles reflect special forms of tradition. Thus 4:4–5 attests ironized priestly instruction. Its structural elements are exhortations, in the imperative mood, and declarations of purpose and a statement of motive. In the first element, Amos appropriates the traditional form correctly, exhorting his audience to engage in pilgrimages and sacrificial activity (4:4–5a). In using the second element, he already engages in ironical reworking of the form by stating that the purpose of the cultic acts is transgression (the concluding clauses in 4:4aα and 4aβ). The irony is even more fully expressed in the final segment (4:5b), where the self–will of Israel, rather than Yahweh's will, is declared to be the motive for the acts. Thus the priestly torah helps Amos to introduce an impersonal distance into his accusation.

---

49 On the use of כִּי in the transition from accusation to announcement of judgment in 3:14 and 6:14, see below *ad loc*.

50 See pp. 108–10.

The other example, 6:12, bluntly states the charge of injustice: "You turn justice into poison, and the fruit of righteousness into wormwood" (6:12b). But this accusation is made in the light of two preceding questions drawn from animal life (6:12a): "Do horses race over rocky terrain? Or does one plough the sea with oxen?" Hence the prophet adopts the method of the wisdom teacher, who compares human activity with life in nature. A note of mockery is added to the reproach thus constructed: Israel, with its perversion of justice, abandons the order of the universe.

The announcement of punishment is used independently more often than is the accusation; the one threatened is almost always referred to in the third person. Both these features are in keeping with the primacy of the word of punishment within the messenger speech.[51] The independent announcements of punishment also show the influence of unusual forms. In 3:12 a sapiential oracle of comparison declares the hoped-for "rescue" to be evidence of a total loss;[52] again, the cool and factual manner of statement can scarcely hide the biting derision. The utterance of Yahweh concerning the great defeat of Israel (5:3) is preceded in 5:1–2 by a funerary lamentation, which interprets proleptically the threatening course of events as a deadly catastrophe, rather than by the more customary demonstration of guilt. In 6:8–11 the lethal effect of Yahweh's revulsion is presented dialogically in a macabre scene. The supplementary oracles restrict themselves, to a considerable degree, to the announcement and description of the approaching calamity (8:9–10, [11–12]; 9:8a), or to a discussion of it (8:8).

Even the disputations which certainly derive from Amos himself are exclusively bent on effecting the assent of the hearers to the prophetic message of calamity. This is true of the series of didactic questions in 3:3–6 and 8 (with its climaxes in 3:6b and 8b) and also of the elaboration of the woe–cries in 5:18–20 by means of similes and questions concerning the Day of Yahweh. Finally, it is also true of the questions provoking comparison between Israel and the foreign nations in 9:7. These oracular compositions, whether they exclusively attach questions or develop the form of the woe–cry,

do not engage at all in dispute concerning the culpability and the guilt of Israel, but rather are concerned exclusively with the inevitability of the prophet's terrible message.

The composition in 5:4–5 is unique, combining an admonition (5:4b) together with an antithetically juxtaposed warning (5:5a) which is then motivated by a proclamation of judgment (5:5b).[53] One can ask whether the admonition with the assurance of life and the immediately following warning on the theme of pilgrimage ought not to be understood, similarly to 4:4–5, as an alteration of a priestly torah. However, the assurance of life (in the form of a deed—result demonstration in 5:4b) and the antithetic parallelism of admonition and warning remind one more strongly of sapiential thought forms. Above all, unlike 4:5b the conclusion here is not concerned with the will of Yahweh, while it is just that concern which motivates priestly torah. Instead, as the basis for a life or death decision the hearer is confronted with the threatening future in which the sanctuaries will be abandoned to destruction. Hence the brief admonition in 5:4b is now completely overshadowed by the much longer warning, and both of them together are in the end dominated by the threat. Thus the terse, bright opening utterance, which is intelligible on the basis of tradition, is in its further elaboration by Amos completely surrounded by the gloom of approaching judgment.[54]

On the whole it is quite apparent that among the special forms the threat of punishment and the discussion surrounding it are attested much more strongly than the pure reproaches. Even an isolated admonition is dominated by the announcement of calamity. This is in keeping with our earlier discovery that in the developed judgment speech it is predominantly the threat of punishment which is proclaimed as the actual word of Yahweh, and that even the vision reports deal exclusively with the judgment on Israel, and not with its guilt.

c) As far as larger compositions are extant in the

---

51 See pp. 92–93.
52 See below on 3:12, *ad loc*.
53 On 5:6, 14–15 as later interpretations, see pp. 109,

111.
54 See further the discussion of 5:4–5 "Form," p. 232.

book, they demonstrate the power of Amos to use language in preparing for, highlighting, and shaping decisive statements. The cycle of oracles against the nations (1:3–8, 13–15; 2:1–3, 6–9, 13–16) and the visions–cycle (7:1–8; 8:1–2; 9:1–4) constitute our most important evidence.

In both cases the ancient text[55] shows five main parts, of which the last in each instance deviates in form and content most radically from those preceding it. Three stylistic features in particular serve to give shape to these compositions: repetition in the framing sentences and the key sentences, formation of pairs in the first four parts, and building toward the climax in the fifth part.[56] Pair formation and climax can also be observed in the composition of the disputational questions in 3:3–6 and 8.[57] In 4:6–11 there are five members, in each of which the emphatic final sentence is repeated verbatim. But pair formation and climax are not as prominent here as in the other examples. Further observations also make it doubtful that 4:6–11 derives from Amos.[58]

Those oracles which go back to Amos with certainty suffice to show that the forms of composition just pointed out stand in the service of the proclamation of Yahweh's judgmental will. They are perfectly suited to convince the listener that Yahweh is in the right and to provide demonstration of Israel's guilt. That the announcement of punishment is irrevocable is not only directly stated in particular formulas[59] but is also underscored by means of repetition and intensification.

F. The Dynamics of Amos' Language

The basic creative forces in Amos' language can be viewed in their proper interrelationship now that we have surveyed the fundamental literary types, the special elements, and the forms of composition attested in the book.

Especially influential are traditional forms deriving from Amos' cultural heritage, whose provenance we must seek in that form of wisdom which was cultivated within the clans. For the most part only individual elements from the stock of sapiential sayings are incorporated into the prophetic oracles. Merely a few

disputations are shaped completely by that source. It is only when Amos comes to grips with the realm of pilgrimages and sacrifices that he also employs cultic speech forms.

This latter special case may be accounted for by the formative significance of the hearer's situation, which also exerts influence on Amos' oracular patterns elsewhere. The hearer's speech has a direct impact when his own words are quoted. There is an indirect effect upon Amos' language because of the prophet's determination to communicate with his audience, which explains, above all, the prior position of the motivation in the judgment oracles, but also some extremely shocking formulations of the call to hear. These become understandable only in view of the hearer's particular character and his unique situation.

We must look, however, to the realm of prophetic inspiration for the source of the genuinely decisive influence on Amos. Absolutely individual encounters with God moved Amos initially to become a bearer of the word. They are reflected in his direct references to them in disputations and vision reports, and accordingly, in the essential primacy of the concrete announcement of punishment as being the actual word of Yahweh. Demonstrations of guilt and disputations have merely an ancillary function. The irreducible force, which inspirationally overwhelmed Amos, enabled him to reshape received forms with a view toward his directly threatened audience. The characteristic structures of Amos' oracles can be found in no older cultic curse, in no form of the older proclamation of law, in no sapiential instruction. The new forms of his speech can be explained only by the new content of his message.

4. The Message of Amos

If we wish to determine the thematic content of Amos' proclamation, it is first of all necessary to separate out by literary–critical means the material which derives from later hands. In recognizing secondary strata, we must certainly not be guided primarily by differences in content. Initially the issue must be provoked by breaks within the extant literary whole which are also made conspicuous by unambiguous formal differences.

---

55   See pp. 144, 337.
56   See pp. 94–95, 148.
57   See the discussion of 3:3–8 "Form," pp. 181–84.
58   See below on 4:6–11, *ad loc.*
59   See p. 138.

To be sure, differences in content will normally become apparent at the same time. When we present here first the message of Amos himself, we presuppose the literary–critical work which will be summarized in section 5. In order to facilitate there the differentiation between the original proclamation of the prophet and the supplementation and alterations which are the result of the literary development of the book, we present first the former, especially since the uniqueness of Amos' language requires us to seek the new elements in his prophecy.

A. Yahweh

The first answer to the question concerning the proclamation of Amos must be, in keeping with his own perspective, that it is a message from Yahweh. For he himself has basically defined it as such (3:8; 7:15; 7:1–8; 8:1–2; 9:1–4). How does Amos speak of Yahweh?

a) Yahweh is at work with humanity. What can be said of Yahweh is said using verbs. It is striking that Amos eschews all theological concepts. He speaks neither of Yahweh's justice or his faithfulness, nor of his covenant or his law.[60] Not once does Amos use any fixed expression to say that Yahweh is "Israel's God" (or respectively, "thy, his, your, their God"),[61] as do both the older tradition and the prophets who come after him. Nor does he acknowledge any proper analogies for Yahweh, of the sort which Hosea so abundantly presents,[62] even though he frequently offers graphic illustrations of Yahweh's acting.[63] Certain anthropomorphisms appear, but only on the fringes of and in connection with verbal statements: "I will turn my hand against . . ." (1:8), or "I will fix my eye upon them" (9:4; cf. 9:8). Such imagery is used to make explicit the force and inevitability of Yahweh's intervention. As a rule, Amos merely refers to "Yahweh." Perhaps "Lord Yahweh" occurred originally only in the prayerful outcry in the first two visions (7:2, 5);

in most of the remaining cases "Lord" (אֲדֹנָי) is demonstrably a later addition,[64] as is also "[God of] [the] hosts" ([הַ]צְּבָאוֹת] [אֱלֹהֵי]) throughout.[65] In contrast to the liturgy's fullness of affirmation, the most extreme simplicity in speaking of "Yahweh" is Amos' own way to express his deep emotion and reverence. He strictly avoids theological appositions of a nominal or adjectival kind, and likewise shuns all poetical anthropomorphic and theriomorphic similes.

It is in keeping with this simplicity that deities other than Yahweh are not mentioned by Amos a single time.[66] No Baal competes with Yahweh for Israel's affections as we find the situation to be in Hosea. But neither is there a god apart from Yahweh responsible for foreign nations (1:3–8, 13–15; 2:1–3; 3:2; 9:7). It is astonishing how unproblematic this is for Amos, and that he therefore offers no polemic against any cult of foreign gods.[67] That Yahweh is the only God of Israel and of the world of nations is not a theme of his message but its self–evident presupposition.

Given this uncomplicated way of speaking about Yahweh, it is not surprising that the ancient Israelite traditions of salvation history hardly occupy Amos' attention. Only once does he himself make serious reference, in an altogether unconventional form, to the tradition of the giving of the land (2:9).[68] It confirms for him Israel's guilt, since the nation does not, in contrast to its God, take up the cause of the weak and lowly. Moreover, he himself probably also reminded his hearers of the exodus from Egypt (9:7b), but only in order to wrest from Israel any sense of privilege, since similar things can be reported of the Philistines and the Arameans. If Yahweh has chosen Israel before all nations—and for Amos election must be seen in connection with the giving of the land, and not with the exodus from Egypt[69]—then this election establishes, for Amos, only the right of divine judgment (3:2).[70] Thus Amos is remarkably laconic and theologically independent with regard to the traditions of

---

60 Only once, in 4:2, does Yahweh swear "by his holiness."

61 On 4:13 and 9:15, see below, *ad loc.*

62 See Wolff, *Hosea*, xxiii–xxv [xv–xviii].

63 See pp. 97–98.

64 See textual note "o" to 1:8b.

65 See the textual notes on the appropriate passages, and also the excursus on יהוה (אלהי) (ה)צבאות,

pp. 287–88.

66 On 5:26, see p. 112.

67 Cf. Hosea by way of contrast; see Wolff, *Hosea*, xxv–xxix [xviii–xxiii].

68 On 2:10, see p. 112.

69 Cf. 2:9 with 9:7b.

70 On 2:10–12 and 3:1b, see p. 112. It is equally improbable that the enumeration of Yahweh's earlier

salvation history. Only three short sentences recall Yahweh's traditional acts: "Yet I myself destroyed the Amorite on their behalf" (2:9); "You only have I selected from all the clans of the earth" (3:2); and "Did I not bring up Israel from the land of Egypt, and the Philistines from Caphtor and Aram from Kir?" (9:7). Certainly it follows from this that it is precisely through his acts that Yahweh has made himself known to Israel; yet this activity has also embraced the other nations. It is true that the divine acts have demonstrated Yahweh's special willingness to intervene on behalf of Israel (2:9; 3:2). But this only makes imperative a heightened responsibility on Israel's part (3:2), and does not justify any sense of superiority (9:7). Thus the traditions of salvation history are adduced exclusively for the purpose of demonstrating guilt.

b) Yahweh speaks through the prophet. Amos is dominated by his own experiences of God much more strongly than by all Yahwistic traditions. In his disputations he declares repeatedly that Yahweh's speaking has frighteningly and powerfully overwhelmed him (3:8; 7:15). Not infrequently, the divine speaking was preceded by visions (7:1, 4, 7; 8:1; 9:1), but even in these instances the word of Yahweh was always the decisive feature (7:3, 6, 8; 8:2; 9:1aα^2–4). Consequently, most of the oracles are introduced by the messenger formula, "Thus Yahweh has said" (כֹּה אָמַר יהוה),[71] and are concluded by the closing formula, "Yahweh has said" (אמר יהוה),[72] or by the divine oracle formula, "oracle of Yahweh" (נְאֻם יהוה).[73] Is it a matter of chance that Amos himself, when he recalls the earlier acts of Yahweh (2:9; 3:2; 9:7), never speaks of a verbal communication? Such communication is only adduced in secondary passages (2:11–12; 3:7).

Most surprisingly, the oracles of accusation never quote words of Yahweh which derive from the ancient divine law or from a covenant proclamation. Instead, ". . . Israel's actual offences . . . were left to the prophet to interpret."[74] "Thus we see Amos particularly engaged in the task of giving convincing reasons for the coming disaster and, as he goes about his business, we see the man's vitality and intellectual acumen brilliantly at work."[75] If Amos does not use concepts like "Torah" (תּוֹרָה) and "covenant" (בְּרִית),[76] the reason for this is probably not only his reserve toward theological conceptualization. As the genuine word of Yahweh he presents a new message which Yahweh has constrained him to proclaim.[77] What is the new message?

c) Yahweh comes for judgment. With the exception of the isolated reproaches,[78] all the messenger oracles, as well as the disputations (3:6; 5:18–20) and the vision reports, and even the solitary admonition (5:4–5),[79] signal the end of the prior salvation history. At least two thirds of the announcements of punishment attribute the impending end to Yahweh's own intervention, always using the first person of the messenger speech: "I will send fire . . ., I will break . . ., I will cut off" (1:4–5, 7–8, 14; 2:2–3); "I will turn my hand against" (1:8); "I break open" (2:13); "I will requite" (3:2b; cf. 3:14a); "I will wreck" (3:15); "I will pass through your midst" (5:17b); "I will send you into exile" (5:27); "I abhor . . ., I hate . . ., I will deliver up" (6:8); "I will raise up against you" (6:14); "Hence I am setting a plumb line . . ., I will no longer pass him by" (7:8; cf. 8:2); "I will smite . . ., my hand will take them . . ., I will search out and take them . . ., I will command . . ., I will fix my eye upon them" (9:1–4).[80] How incomparably more lively and varied is the way

---

acts of punishment in 4:6–11 derives from Amos himself; see pp. 111–12.

71 See p. 136. The oath formula "Yahweh has sworn" (נִשְׁבַּע יהוה) replaces the messenger formula in 4:2; 6:8; and 8:7.

72 See p. 139.

73 See p. 143.

74 von Rad, *Theology* 2, 134 [145].

75 *Ibid.*, 132 [142f].

76 On "covenant of brothers" (בְּרִית אַחִים) in 1:9, see pp. 159–60.

77 See pp. 91–93.

78 See pp. 98–99.

79 See p. 99.

80 Cf. further the following oracles which have been at least partially reworked: 4:12; 7:9; 8:7, 9–10, 11–12; 9:8, 9.

in which the prophet proclaims those acts of Yahweh's judgment which are coming upon Israel, as compared to his treatment of Yahweh's past deeds! Here Amos seems to be completely involved in that which has been revealed to him. Usually the results of Yahweh's act, as well as the act itself, are described. A historical agent is designated only rarely and imprecisely (3:11; 6:14). Only in a small number of the oracles (3:11; 4:2–3; 5:3, 5, 11; 6:7; 7:11, 17; 8:13–14) is the judgment proclaimed without an explicit testimony to the intervention of Yahweh. It is fully characteristic that the last three vision reports proclaim the approaching judgment in the final analysis always as the relentless, intrusive presence of Yahweh: "I will no longer pass him by" (7:8; 8:2); "I will fix my eye upon them for evil and not for good" (9:4). It is in keeping with this that in 5:16–17 the great funerary lamentation about to break forth is motivated only by the concluding sentence in 5:17b: "I will pass through the midst of you."[81] Death is brought to Israel not by Yahweh's absence, but precisely by his undesired new advent. To have sought Yahweh and inquired of him, whether voluntarily or from distress, would have brought life (5:4).

Thus Amos never speaks of Yahweh as such, but only of Yahweh's dealings with humanity, of his speaking to and through the prophet, and in all this, especially, of his advent which Israel will experience as a destructive blow.

B. Israel

How does Amos speak of Israel? While Yahweh's "I" dominates all else in the announcements of punishment, details concerning Israel are given, first, in those statements which describe the results of Yahweh's intervention, but especially in the speeches of accusation. Thus the concern is mainly with the future and the present of Israel, and only rarely with its past.

a) Israel's future: "The end has come for my people Israel" (8:2). Everything that is said elsewhere concerning Israel's future is an interpretation of this harshest of statements. In 2:13 and 9:1 an earthquake is apparently announced, which causes a panicked flight of the sort which would also be appropriate in the case of a military catastrophe. War in the land is anticipated in 3:11; 6:14 and 7:17. The war shall end with a devastating defeat (5:3), with the death of the king (7:11), and with a mass deportation (7:11) in which the leaders of Samaria will form the vanguard (6:7). The women of Samaria will be taken into captivity, as will also the chief priest of Bethel (7:17), whose wife will be ravished, and the great cultic congregations of Bethel and Gilgal (5:5, 27). A great dying will come upon the land (5:2–3, 16–17; 6:9–10; 7:17aα^2; 8:3; 9:10). With a measuring line the land will be parcelled out to new settlers (7:17aβ). Yahweh's day becomes a dark, gloomy day with a deadly conclusion for Israel (5:18–20).

In none of the oracles which derive with certainty from Amos is it stated clearly that any hope might still exist, even for a remnant, as a result of repentance and betterment.[82] Only the threat against the sanctuaries Bethel and Gilgal begins with the tradition–linked exhortation: "Seek me! Then you shall live" (5:4–5). Amos probably expected this to be realized as little as he did the precept in 5:24. Over against this isolated glimpse of light stands the long list of utterances which explicitly announce the hopeless end, even for a remnant that might perchance have temporarily survived (9:1–4). Nor will strength, courage, and armaments lead to any escape (2:14–16); even if such effort might succeed once or twice, in the end it is nonetheless futile (5:19). Precisely "the remnant" repeatedly becomes the object of the threat (4:2bβ; 6:10; 8:10bβ; cf. 1:8b). The diminution of the clan levy does not motivate the hope that there might be perhaps a remnant of survivors, but justifies the funerary lamentation for the fallen "virgin Israel" (5:2–3), just as the shepherd might exhibit two splintbones or a tip of an ear merely as evidence of a futile fight against some beast of prey (3:12).

Interpretation dare not evade this sombre, enigmatic conclusion: only once, and then in a tentative way at best, does Amos offer encouragement; nowhere does he kindle genuine hope. On the contrary, repeatedly and with sharpest clarity he announces the

---

81 Cf. also 1:8bα in the oracle against Philistia.
82 On 5:6 and 14–15, see pp. 109, 111.

end of Israel which awaits his contemporaries.

b) Israel's present: "They do not know how to do what is right" (3:10a). This accusation motivates Amos' message of death. The relationship between reproach and threat is distorted if one interprets the message of judgment with its motivation as a veiled form of the call to repentance. That which Amos expects of his hearers is no longer a turnabout, but at best a readiness to listen to the charge as just motivation for the announced dark Day of Yahweh. What does Amos designate as Israel's guilt?

It is an exception when in 3:10, with the help of the wisdom term נְכֹחָה, he epitomizes Israel's guilt as a failure to do what is "right."[83] Much clearer than this is the thrice recurring word pair "justice" (מִשְׁפָּט) and "righteousness" (צְדָקָה). The rule of law and righteous conduct should have the effects of life–giving water (5:24), but the rule of law is turned into poison (6:12), and righteousness is forcibly cast to the ground (5:7). The foundations of ancient Israelite clan life are thereby destroyed. Instead, "proud arrogance" (גָּאוֹן) dominates Israel's way of life.[84] In most instances by far, Amos names very specific transgressions. They become evident especially at three points: in the court procedure, in the accumulation of riches, and in the cultus.

In the court procedure at the city gate every Israelite ought to receive the justice due him. But the prophet must voice his sharp criticism here, for hatred is the reward of anyone who champions the rule of law, or of anyone whose testimony is complete (5:10). Judges accept bribes and hence the innocent are afflicted and the poor especially cannot count on legal redress (2:7a; 5:12). People fall prey to debt–slavery on account of trifles (2:6b).[85]

This is an evil result of early capitalism.[86] Therefore Amos condemns the societal life–style of the leading classes even more thoroughly than the judicial process. The wealthy elite reside in luxurious houses (3:12bβ, 15; 5:11aβ; 6:8, 11). They indulge themselves in boisterous feasting, with all imaginable gratification, but at the expense of the poor (4:1; 6:4–6). Amos mentions no other group so often, or by so many epithets, as the "needy" (אֶבְיוֹנִים 2:6; 4:1; 5:12; 8:4, 6), the "poor" (דַּלִּים 2:7; 4:1; 5:11; 8:6), the "oppressed" (עֲנָוִים 2:7; 8:4). Even though "innocent" (צַדִּיקִים 2:6; 5:12), they are at the mercy of the arbitrary expectations and demands of the rich: in the sexual realm (2:7b); in taxation practices (2:8; 5:11); and with respect to all kinds of servile duties (2:7; 4:1; 5:11). The leading circles, however, enjoy an unshakable political and social self–confidence (6:1, 3, 13; 4:1).

The cult merely provides a religious foundation for this arrogance. Cultic activities are determined not, as one might expect, by the search for the way and the will of Yahweh (5:4), but by individual predilections (4:5b): in the enterprise of pilgrimages, in sacrificial practices, in festal banqueting, and in the musical accompaniment of the feasts (4:4–5; 5:21–23). There is no room here for the proclamation of a just order and righteous conduct (5:24). Thus the criticism of the cultus goes hand in hand with legal and social criticism. It may cause surprise that the people, according to Amos' judgment, are doing too much rather than too little for Yahweh. In consonance with his slight interest in theological distinctions, Amos does not conceptually differentiate between the Yahweh of the people, who should be the guarantor of highly valued security, and the Yahweh to whom he himself testifies, the Yahweh who by deed and word has also led into freedom the weak in Israel. In Amos it is largely put like this: Israel's injustice must be sought exclusively in the oppression of the poor. And yet only one side of the matter is thereby expressed.

c) Israel's origin: "You only have I selected . . ." (3:2a). This is the other side of the motivation for judgment, only seldom expressed, to be sure, but unmistakably present. Not only is the approaching end

---

83   See below on 3:10, *ad loc.*, and also Hans Walter Wolff, *Amos the Prophet: The Man and His Background*, tr. Foster R. McCurley (Philadelphia: Fortress, 1973), 24–27, 57–59 [*Amos' geistige Heimat*, WMANT 18 (Neukirchen: Neukirchener Verlag, 1964), 18, 39f].

84   See p. 282.

85   See p. 165.

86   See pp. 89–90.

dictated by current injustice as such, this injustice can also be recognized as rejection of Yahweh's acting and election. The most polished expression of this is found in the oracle of 3:2, which adduces as the sole reason for Yahweh's punitive intervention the election by which Yahweh singled out Israel from all other nations. In the strophe concerned with Israel in the cycle of oracles against the nations, the motivation of punishment—the list of Israel's crimes in 2:9—is followed, as a contrasting high point, by remembrance of Yahweh's intervention during the conquest era on behalf of weak Israel and against the land's exceedingly powerful former inhabitants. If Israel had oriented itself toward the way and will of Yahweh, it would have enjoyed an inviolable existence. That is what the call of admonition in 5:4 presupposes. It is striking that Yahweh, in the words which inform the prophet of Yahweh's verdict and commission, still says "my people" three times (7:8; 8:2; 7:15).[87] Even though Amos never speaks of Yahweh as "Israel's God," it is nevertheless undisputed that those addressed in his proclamation are, by their origin, "Yahweh's people." Only against this background does the revolutionary dimension of Amos' message become completely clear: from Yahweh the end has come upon Yahweh's people. Even as previously the giving of the land and election had been linked together, so now are expulsion and rejection. In summarizing the perspective of Amos, we ought to say no less than this: he must announce the end of the hitherto existing salvation history. That is the provocatively new dimension in his message. The older maledictions did not dare to express this, even conditionally, for Israel as a whole.

C. The Nations

That which Amos has to say about the nations not only supplements but also clarifies the message he delivers from Yahweh to Israel. In addition to the complete judgment speeches directed toward the foreign nations in the cycle of oracles against the nations, statements about the nations appear in both announcements and motivations of punishment within oracles concerning Israel.

a) In motivations of punishment the nations are referred to merely as Israel's adversaries, in conformity with tradition. In 2:9 the Amorites, as the former owners of the land, are called great and strong. As such, Yahweh destroyed them for the sake of Israel. This prior act of Yahweh now confirms the sentence against the great and strong in Israel, who have taken over the role of the land's former inhabitants. The judgment which, according to the tradition, had befallen the old adversary now strikes Israel. In 3:2 "all the clans of the earth" are mentioned, in order to make clear Yahweh's unique election of Israel. Yet it is also the case that the tradition as here adopted no longer serves to denigrate the other nations in comparison with Israel, but is rather used only to underscore Israel's unique responsibility (3:2b). Quite bluntly, 9:7a states that henceforth Yahweh will value Israel no more than one of the most distant and despised nations, the Cushites. The use of the exodus tradition to substantiate Israel's preeminence is invalidated with particular boldness by the claim that Israel's chief enemies, the Philistines and Arameans, similarly experienced Yahweh's guidance (9:7b). Thus the exodus, conquest, and election traditions are assigned a new function in Amos: the possibility of asserting a privileged status among the nations and of expecting special indulgence is wrested from Israel (3:2). Indeed the history of Yahweh's prior dealings with the nations must be considered parallel to the ancient (9:7b) or recent (2:9; 9:7a) history of Israel.

b) In the announcements of punishment against Israel the nations figure as Yahweh's instruments of judgment. But no specific nation is ever named. In 3:11 there is a general reference to an "enemy." In 6:14 is mentioned "a nation" which will afflict Israel, but here, as in most of the other announcements of punishment, Yahweh himself is really the one who leads the foes. According to 9:4, he himself deals with Israel even more harshly than do her "enemies"; while they only deport, he deploys the slaying sword. The direction toward which it is expected that Israel will be deported when the punishment occurs is indicated only generally by place designations from the Aramean

---

87   Cf. also 9:10, [14].

kingdom (4:3; 5:27).[88] Yet the Arameans are not specified as instruments of Yahweh. It becomes clear only that Israel's end is also seen by Amos in the framework of worldwide political upheavals. Just as once, in the granting of the land, Yahweh had singled out Israel from among the nations, so now in expelling Israel from the land he uses the nations of the world to execute his judgment. The nations are at Yahweh's free disposal, both for and against Israel.

c) How completely the foreign nations are associated with Israel before Yahweh is shown most clearly by the oracles against the nations. For Amos, they, like Israel, are guilty before Yahweh because they have mistreated weaker human beings (1:3, 6, 13; 2:1). Essentially, there is no different standard of justice for them than for Israel. Thus it is Yahweh, and not another god, who also proves to be their judge (1:4–5, 7–8, 14–15; 2:2–3). Just as he at one time led the Philistines and the Arameans (9:7b) and judged the Amorites (2:9), so he determines the future of the Arameans and the Philistines, the Ammonites and the Moabites.

Thus the new elements in Amos' message can be summed up in three statements:

1. With unproblematic clarity he testifies to Yahweh alone as the God of Israel as well as of the nations; the origins and future of both are freely determined by him.

2. The message of Israel's full and complete expulsion from the land is an eschatological proclamation insofar as it announces the end of the hitherto existing salvation history and thereby of every privileged position of Israel in history. Israel founders because of its contempt for the rights of the weak as sanctioned by Yahweh.

3. The most surprising consequence is therefore the equalization of the nations with Israel and of Israel with the nations; the nations stand, just as does Israel, under Yahweh's guidance.

The lasting significance of the total proclamation of the prophet is consonant with this:

1. It is a message related to history, in its own way unrepeatable. It bears witness to a God who in his dealings with Israel and the nations brings any re-

lationships which still exist to an irreparable end, and who just as irresistibly establishes new ones. In that Amos' prophetic word announces terror and death, it points toward a wholly unfathomable future. Only the reverse side of salvation as previously experienced becomes visible. Perhaps such voices need be heard at times also in the name of Jesus.

2. Israel founders because in its communal life it fails to match the effort of its God on behalf of the weak. The future of the world of nations is wholly bound up with equity for the oppressed. God desires not self–interested and self–assured religiosity, but rather a humanitarianism characterized by justice and readiness to assist others. Humanity forfeits its future when in the midst of cultic activity it loses sight of God's freedom to act and shrinks back from the grip of his word. In the name of Jesus also the people of God are measured by their efforts on behalf of the oppressed, and the world of nations is judged by its relationship to its weakest members.

3. In that Amos with his message of judgment thrusts Israel back among the nations, there appears here a negative print of Pentecost. The wall between God's people and the nations of the world is already being broken down. The Church will suffer damage if it does not allow to be utterly eradicated that sense of special privilege which, despite Amos, gained strength again in Israel. There are religious privileges which also in the name of Jesus must be revealed as unfounded, even deadly. A reconciled community of nations can come into existence only through recognition that it is first of all a community of those justly condemned. The Church should clear the way among the world's nations for this recognition.

5. The Formation of the Book of Amos

Even a cursory examination of the book of Amos forces one to posit behind it a long history of literary growth. On the basis of mere oral tradition it would be impossible to explain either the interruption of the vision reports, formulated in the first person, by a third–person narrative in 7:10–17, or the insertion of various strophes of a hymn at widely separated points in the

---

88 Cf. the comments on 4:3 and 5:7, *ad loc.*
89 See pp. 117–18.
90 See pp. 93–94.

91 On the divine oracle formula, see the comments on 4:4–5, *ad loc.*, and also the excursus on נאם יהוה *in the Book of Amos*, p. 143.

book (4:13; 5:8–9; 9:5–6). It is scarcely probable that the book attained its present configuration before the postexilic period. Thus even later supplementations, concerned with eschatological salvation theology, can be distinguished clearly enough from a Deuteronomistic hand of exilic times.

Nevertheless, the process of the literary fixation must have begun already in the lifetime of the prophet. To be sure, the initial phases are the most difficult to ascertain. Yet the preliminary investigations of the last decades have opened up new possibilities. By combining analysis of the oldest elements of superscription with observations on the groupings of oracles and reports, we are able to distinguish with a high degree of probability three eighth–century literary strata, all of which for the most part derive from Amos himself and his contemporary disciples. Three additional strata can be recognized as later interpretations by their distinctive language and different intentions. They derive from the following centuries.

A. "The Words of Amos from Tekoa"

Analysis of the superscription in 1:1 indicates that its oldest level can be recognized in the phrase "the words of Amos from Tekoa" (דִּבְרֵי עָמוֹס מִתְּקוֹעַ).[89] If we ask which collection of oracles might have been thus introduced, the indications point to chaps. 3—6. For the oracles in 1:3—2:16 are immediately introduced by the messenger formula as words of Yahweh; hence the initial rubric "words of Amos" characterizes this material no more appropriately than it would the vision reports in chaps. 7—9. On the other hand, many oracles in chaps. 3—6 are exclusively "words of Amos" in the basic form of free witness–speech:[90] 3:3–8; 4:4–5;[91] 5:7, 10–11, 18–20; 6:12. Other units in this section are first introduced by a saying of Amos and then, in second position, present an oracle of Yahweh:[92] 3:1a + 2, 9–11, 13–15; 4:1–3; 5:1–3, 12 + 16–17; 6:1–7, 13–14. Among these are interspersed only isolated sayings which transmit pure oracles of Yahweh: 3:12; 5:4–5, 21–24 + 27; (6:8?). It cannot be clearly determined whether one or another of these oracles may have been introduced here only through the re-

dactional work of Amos' school.[93] Yet the superscription "words of Amos from Tekoa" well suits the basic stock of chaps. 3—6, not only because of the nature of most of the oracles, but also because several individual utterances are introduced directly as "word" (דָּבָר 3:1; 4:1; 5:1) and, at least in 5:1, Amos is explicitly named as the "I" who speaks the "word."[94] Therefore we must also reckon with the possibility that this collection may go back to Amos himself. There can be little certainty as to whether the core of this collection derives from oracles which were proclaimed in Samaria (3:9; 4:1; 6:1) or during an itinerant career, the prophet wandering between Samaria and Bethel (and Gilgal? 4:4; 5:5).

B. The Literary Fixation of the Cycles

The five reports of visions in 7:1–8; 8:1–2 and 9:1–4 must certainly, on the basis of their autobiographical style, be traced to Amos himself. General correspondences as well as similarities of detail contribute to the surmise that the cycle of oracles against the nations was fixed literarily at the same time as the visions: the five–part structuring with the formation of pairs and with the climax being reached in the final part; the repetition of framing sentences and key sentences; the close thematic relationship between the two concluding parts of the cycles (2:13–16 and 9:1–4); and significant minor correspondences, such as use of the concluding formula of the messenger speech, "Yahweh has said" (אמר יהוה 1:5, 8, 15; 2:3; 7:3, 6), which is otherwise unusual in the book of Amos.[95] The redaction which inserted 7:9–17 into the cycle of visions associated the complex with Amos' appearance at Bethel. It is conceivable that Bethel was also the setting for the cycle of oracles against the nations.[96] Perhaps the literary fixation of this material was connected with the banishment of the prophet from Bethel (7:12) and the end of his activity in the northern kingdom. Should the literary uniformity of the recorded oracle cycles lead us to conclude that they, in comparison with the collections of oracles in chaps. 3—6, represent a more advanced stage of literary development? After all, the structuring of free–witness oracles and commissioned messenger

---

92 See p. 93.
93 See pp. 108–11.
94 On the "I" in 5:12, see below *ad loc.*

95 Cf. pp. 100, 148.
96 See p. 149.

oracles in chaps. 3—6 is indeed much looser and un-ordered. The redaction, in any case, attaches the recorded cycles to an already extant collection of "the words of Amos from Tekoa."[97]

C. The Old School of Amos

The first traces of this early redaction are evident in the second relative clause of the present superscription: "which he viewed concerning Israel two years before the earthquake."[98] Unlike Amos himself, the redaction does not use "saw" (ראה 7:1, 4, 7; 8:1; 9:1), but rather "viewed" (חזה 1:1); yet it does link the visions with the "words," though not without some stylistic abrasiveness ("The words of Amos, . . . which he viewed . . .").[99] Hence also the recorded cycles are set as brackets around the "words of Amos from Tekoa," comparable to the method ancient redactors were fond of using to incorporate more recent literary material, with which they were closely associated, into existing works.[100]

This older redaction of the superscription, evident in the second relative clause, can be attributed to the old school of Amos. That we must certainly reckon with such a circle of disciples, concerned with the trans-mission of the master's words, is shown first by the insertion of a third—person report of Amos' experiences (7:10–17) into the first—person reports of the visions. The author must have been an eyewitness, seeing and hearing what he reported. He matches the style and themes of Amos almost exactly.[101] He describes a scene which he could hardly have invented and records a threat against Jeroboam II (7:11) which was not ful-filled and was therefore extended to the "house of Jero-boam" (7:9), since Jeroboam's son Zechariah did in-deed fall by the sword.[102] We must attribute 7:9, if not

to the same hand, at least to the same old school of Amos, for it calls Israel "Isaac" ("high places of Isaac") as is done elsewhere in the entire book of Amos only in the third—person report in 7:16 ("house of Isaac"). Moreover, as in 7:11, the author of 7:9 refers to Jero-boam without citing his father's name; thus he, unlike later redactors, did not find it necessary to distinguish this king as "Jerobaom, son of Joash" (1:1) from Jeroboam I.

Hence this old school of Amos still had at its disposal remembered deeds and sayings of the prophet which were transmitted as part of neither the "words of Amos from Tekoa" nor the recorded cycles. In 7:9–17 it elucidated the first vision, which testified to the in-evitability of the judgment.

This school dealt similarly with the fourth and fifth visions. Syntactically, 8:3 is linked to 8:2 in the same way as 7:9 is to 7:8 (perfect consecutive). On the basis of 8:4–7 it is possible to demonstrate that this school transmitted old sayings of Amos (since the wording of 8:5 and 6a corresponds almost exactly to 2:6b–7a); on the other hand, the passage also exhibits the diver-gent language of the disciples.[103] In 8:8 a threat is presented in the form of a question, such as never occurs in Amos' own oracles, but which is quite intelli-gible if it derived from the discussion of disciples about words of the master. At issue here is the threat of an earthquake; the formulation of the superscription attests that this was a particular concern of the old school of Amos.[104] In 8:9–14 judgment sayings are attached by means of connective formulas which were current in both older and more recent times. On the basis of content, 8:9–10 and 13–14 can be traced back to the old school of Amos, especially since 8:14 clearly alludes to conditions in the northern kingdom.[105]

---

97 On the redactional linkage of the two collections, see p. 288.

98 See p. 120.

99 See pp. 117–18.

100 Cf. the framing of older Pentateuchal material by the Priestly writings, and the "ring-construction" in Is 1—12 around an older core of Is 6:1—9:6.

101 On the threat of deportation in 7:11 and 17, see p. 103. On the introduction of the quotation in 7:16, see p. 97. On the introduction of the oracle of Yah-weh in 7:17, see p. 92. Amos himself, on the other hand, never employs "Hear the word of Yahweh"

(7:16), particularly not before quoting an opponent.

102 Cf. 2 Kgs 14:29 with 15:10.

103 Note the following: "Hear this!" in 8:4, rather than "Hear this word" as in 3:1; 4:1; and 5:1; the in-troduction of the quotation in 8:5a with לֵאמֹר instead of a participle (see p. 97); the oath formula in 8:7a with its curious appropriation of material from 6:8; and the content of the threat in 8:7b which, abandoning concreteness, takes up the vo-cabulary of cultic songs of lamentation (see below on 8:7, *ad loc.*).

The later additions in 9:7, 8a and 9–10 are strongly reminiscent of the themes and the language of Amos himself: 9:7a–b recalls his interrogative style of disputation;[106] 9:8a his threats of deportation;[107] 9:9 his use of graphic language;[108] 9:10 the threat of death[109] and his characteristic way of introducing quotations.[110] But here, too, the disciples' own language can be perceived: in the mixing of the disputational style with messenger speech (9:7a–b);[111] in the repetition here of the root "to sin" (חטא 9:8a, 10a; otherwise rare in Amos) which is closely associated with cultic language;[112] and in the unique final placement of the motivation of punishment in 9:10b.[113]

To summarize our conclusions thus far, the supplementations to the cycle of visions make it necessary to reckon with the literary activity of the old school of Amos. The school promulgated oracles of Amos, and yet its own divergent language can be recognized. In any given instance it is often difficult to distinguish between the *ipsissima verba* of the prophet and the new formulations and supplementations of the disciples.

This being the case, it is reasonable to suppose that we must also reckon with expansions by the school of Amos in "the words of Amos from Tekoa" complex, although it may be impossible to recognize them in every instance. With a high degree of probability, however, the following passages should be attributed to the school, since they lack, in any event, literary–critical continuity with their context. The uniform participial series in 6:1 and 3–6, appropriate to the woe oracle, is disrupted by 6:2. This verse interprets the arrogance

of Samaria's leadership (6:1), employing the interrogative style of disputation and comparison which we have already encountered in 8:8 and 9:7a–b. Then too, 6:6b is a run–on line and, as a negation, it is formally out of keeping with the framework. Moreover, the reference here to the "ruin of Joseph," as is also the case with the content of 6:2, points not to the time of Amos' appearance in the northern kingdom, but rather to later decades.[114]

"Joseph" instead of "Israel" is also found in 5:15.[115] In addition, 5:14–15 together with 5:13 break the continuity between 5:12 + 16–17.[116] Thus 5:14–15 is best understood as a later interpretation of 5:4, linked with the words of Amos concerning behavior "in the gate."[117] Yet basic admonitions here take the place of concrete rebukes. The final clause of 5:4, "then you shall live" (וִחְיוּ), now becomes "that you may live" (לְמַעַן תִּחְיוּ 5:14a). The admonition is motivated not, as in 5:5b, by a threat of judgment, but by the discussion of a possible deliverance of a "remnant of Joseph." The way in which issue is taken with the listeners' hopes,[118] and the uncertainty of the "perhaps" in 5:15b, correspond much more closely to the style of the disciples than to the master's unambiguous message of judgment.[119] That the disciples share with Amos the cultural background of "wisdom" is shown by 5:13.[120]

Finally, the warning attached in 5:5a—"Do not cross over to Beer-sheba!"—can be recognized as a later addition to the preceding warnings against Bethel and Gilgal by the fact that no corresponding threat

104 See p. 117 on 1:1. The phrase "two years before the earthquake" alludes to threats in the recorded cycles (2:13; 9:1); the cycles were linked together with "the words of Amos from Tekoa," which set in the foreground the political catastrophe rather than the earthquake.
105 On 8:11–12, see p. 113.
106 See pp. 93–94.
107 See p. 103.
108 See pp. 97–98.
109 See p. 103.
110 See p. 97.
111 See pp. 93–94.
112 See p. 152.
113 See p. 98.
114 See p. 110.
115 Amos himself never employs this surrogate, which

elsewhere in the book appears only in 5:6; see p. 111.
116 Note the use of "therefore" (לָכֵן) in 5:16a, on which see below *ad loc.*
117 Cf. 5:15a with 5:10 and 12.
118 See p. 97.
119 For details, see below on 5:13, *ad loc.* 5:6 is comparable, both in its tone of warning which arouses hope and in its language usage ("house of Joseph"!); see p. 111.
120 See below on 5:13, *ad loc.* On 6:9–10, see pp. 280–81.

follows in 5:5b. We can understand it particularly well as a supplement of the school of Amos, since Beer–sheba is mentioned also in 8:14 and since this place helps to explain the references to the "house of Isaac" (7:16) and the "high places of Isaac" (7:9).[121]

It may also be asked whether 5:25–26 and 2:10–12 (in the cycle of oracles against the nations) should not be attributed to the old school of Amos. Both passages stand out clearly from their contexts. In their interrogative style of disputation (2:11b; 5:25), in their thematic content (cf. 2:12 with 7:16bα), and in temporal setting,[122] they could belong to the purview of the old school of Amos. Yet I find more convincing reasons for a later dating.[123]

What can be said with respect to the time of the old school of Amos? Apparently it commenced its literary activity only after that earthquake which Amos had threatened. The fulfillment of the prophetic word perhaps effected the combination of the two collections that were already in existence (1:1; 2:13; 9:1). Yet beyond that, the school seems to look back not only upon the death of Jeroboam II, but even upon Shallum's revolt against Zechariah, the son of Jeroboam.[124] To be sure, according to 8:14 the sanctuary of Dan has not yet fallen victim to the campaigns of Tiglath–pileser III in 733. But 6:2 apparently already presupposes the advance of the Assyrians against Syria and, accordingly, also the attempts at forming an anti–Assyrian coalition which occurred in the middle of the third decade of the eighth century. At the very least the "ruin of Joseph" (6:6b), and with it the question of the future for a "remnant of Joseph" (5:15),[125] have become visible on the horizon. Does the unusual appellation "Joseph" for Israel—similar to the use of "Ephraim" in Hosea—already presuppose an endangering of Israelite territories?[126] In any case, the school of Amos was probably active in the generation between 760 and 730; perhaps its major activity coincided with the beginning of the Assyrian crisis for the northern kingdom, around 735.

The place of the school's activity must be sought in Judah, in the realm which was the master's homeland. Would it have been necessary otherwise to call Jeroboam "king of Israel" in 7:10? More remarkable, however, are the designations "house of Isaac" (7:16) for Israel and "high places of Isaac" (7:9) for its sanctuaries, terminology found only in the work of the school. This must be viewed in connection with the mentioning of the sanctuary at Beer–sheba (8:14; 5:5aγ), also found only in this stratum of the book of Amos. Beer–sheba may have been an old cultic meeting place of Israelite and Edomite pilgrims who venerated Isaac as their common tribal patriarch (Nu 20:14; Dtn 23:8[7]). We can only surmise why the clan–wisdom circles around Amos took special interest in such associations and designations.[127] On this basis we can conclude only that the school of Amos apparently made contact with pilgrims to Beer–sheba from the northern kingdom and discussed with them the words of the master. It was probably anticipated that through the agency of such pilgrims the now further explicated prophetic word might be spoken anew in the northern kingdom's hour of crisis.[128]

Given this type of audience, it is understandable that a much stronger interest in cultic issues is shown by the school than by Amos himself. Thus the school is interested in: the role which Amaziah, the priest of Bethel, played in Amos' life (7:10–17); the "high places of Isaac" (7:9); Samaria, Dan, and Beer–sheba (8:14); the problem of rest on feast days (8:5); catchwords of cultic lamentation (8:7b); priestly encouragement (5:14b); and the mentioning of the name of Yahweh (6:10). But here too the threats of deportation (7:11, 17; 9:8a) and the question whether a part of the northern kingdom might survive (5:14–15; 6:2, 6b; 9:10) gain their urgency in view of Tiglath–pileser's advances. We cannot overlook the possibility that older oracles of Amos, in either the cycles or the "words," also re-

---

121 See below.
122 Cf. 5:26 with 2 Kgs 17:30; see below on 5:26, *ad loc.*
123 See pp. 112–13.
124 Cf. 7:9 and 11 with 2 Kgs 14:29 and 15:10.
125 Cf. "house of Joseph" in 5:6!
126 See below on 6:6b, *ad loc.*, and also Wolff, *Hosea*, 164 [212].
127 Cf. Wolff, *Amos the Prophet*, 77–81 [53–55], and be-

low on 5:5, *ad loc.*
128 See below on 7:10–17 "Setting," pp. 308–10.

ceived their present, politically pointed formulation only at the hands of the old school of Amos. Yet in most cases this is quite unlikely in view of the probably original sharpness of the older material.

D. The Bethel–Exposition of the Josianic Age

In 3:14bα we find a later addition, clearly distinguishable from the context. Employing words found in the earlier form of the verse, it interprets the more general threat of the transmitted oracle to mean retribution against the "altars of Bethel." Now there is certainly a clear threat against Bethel (5:5bβ) which derives from Amos himself, according to which "Bethel will become adversity." Furthermore, we know that Josiah destroyed the sanctuary of Bethel (2 Kgs 23:15), and that this cultic–political measure was associated with the appearance of a "man of God from Judah" and was understood as fulfillment of his threat against the altar of Bethel (2 Kgs 23:17; cf. 1 Kgs 13). The Deuteronomistic History has quite probably made use here of popular traditions about Amos.[129]

Such traditions of the Josianic age have found expression in the book of Amos not only in the later addition of 3:14bα (which can be recognized clearly from a literary–critical perspective), but also in several other places which either spoke of Bethel directly, or which, like 3:14, could at least be interpreted easily as referring to Bethel because they mentioned an "altar" in connection with the threat of destruction.

We start with 5:6, for this utterance is attached immediately to 5:5bβ noted above, the single threat by Amos himself against Bethel. In contrast to 3:14bα, however, we have in 5:6 the independent oracle which initially takes up verbatim the admonition in 5:4b, merely transposing it from the messenger style into the disputation style. To this is attached a פֶּן–clause ("lest . . .") which is formulated in a very cumbersome way, changing subject three times. Little is left of Amos' polished language in 5:5. The designation "house of Joseph" reminds one of 5:15 (cf. 6:6b). At the end of the verse, the entire warning oracle is related to Bethel;[130] thus, only the statement of Amos concerning Bethel is taken over from 5:5b, not that concerning Gilgal. This becomes understandable if the supplementary admonition has in view the destruction of Bethel by Josiah.[131] Josiah's cultic policy should be accepted, so that even worse consequences might not ensue for the house of Joseph. The acceptance of the divine judgment on Bethel is solemnized by a hymnic piece which now appears in 5:8–9, probably through a copyist's error having been separated from 5:6 by 5:7, which belongs with 5:10–11.[132]

Another, obviously related hymnic piece is found in 9:5–6. In its position after 9:1–4, it can be understood to have the same function as the hymnic piece in chap. 5, if 9:1 was also taken to refer to the destruction of the Bethel sanctuary and to Josiah's measures.

The first hymnic piece of this kind, however, is found already in 4:13.[133] Can it be explained in the same way? Here a reproach against Bethel precedes (4:4–5) though only at a considerable distance from the hymnic piece. While 4:4–5 is not a threat, apart from 5:5 it is the only utterance directed against Bethel which with certainty derives from Amos himself. In the present text it is followed by an oracle of accusation with five strophes (4:6–11), obviously linked secondarily to 4:5 by "even though I" (וְגַם־אֲנִי) in 4:6. There is nothing comparable to this accusation in Amos' own oracles; thematically it is reminiscent of curse liturgies (such as Lev 26).[134] Here, prior to the positive admonition to

---

129 Thus Eissfeldt, *The Old Testament*, 290 [388]; see below on 5:6, *ad loc.* However, cf. Martin Noth, *Könige*, BK 9/1 (Neukirchen–Vluyn: Neukirchener Verlag, 1968), 295.

130 This is accomplished by means of an interpretive gloss, typically introduced by לְ = "with respect to, concerning." We would scarcely expect the object of the preceding verbs (אכל, "to devour," and כבה piʿel, "to quench") to be attached using לְ; see textual note "p–p" to 5:6.

131 Or, Josiah's destruction of the shrine is at least referred to by the addition of לְבֵית־אֵל ("concerning Bethel")—as an utterance of Amos' school? See p. 109, and the comments on 5:6, *ad loc.*

132 Cf. Friedrich Horst, "Die Doxologien im Amosbuch," *ZAW* 47 (1929): 45–54 (reprinted in *idem*, *Gottes Recht*, 155–66).

133 On the reconstruction of the complete hymn with three strophes, see the excursus on *The Hymnic Passages in the Book of Amos*, pp. 215–17.

134 See the discussion of 4:6–11 "Form," pp. 212–14.

seek Yahweh (5:6), the point stressed is that Israel had not returned to Yahweh in spite of repeated chastisements by him. This accusation is followed in 4:12 by a sentence construction which, exhibiting a convoluted style similar to that of 5:6, has a prosaic and cumbersome effect. Only general reference is made to Yahweh's punitive action, without any more concrete details being provided. All attempts at reconstruction seem unsatisfactory.[135] The "thus" (כֹּה) and "this" (זֹאת) of the indefinite announcement of punishment are most intelligible if they allude to the action taken by Josiah against Bethel. Then the injunction that Israel should prepare to meet its God acquires meaning as a call to acknowledge his just judgment; it thereby appropriately introduces the first strophe of the hymn in which honor is ascribed to Yahweh (4:13). There is nothing in the Psalter corresponding to this hymn, possibly because it associates with Yahweh syncretistic hymnic material from the Bethel sanctuary of the seventh century.

Thus the hymn in 4:13; 5:8–9 and 9:5–6 consists of three strophes, the first or the first two strophes introduced by homilies (4:6–12; 5:6)[136] which seek to relate the oracles of Amos against Bethel (4:4–5; 5:4–5) to Josiah's destruction of the sanctuary. Josiah's measures should be acknowledged, in accordance with 2 Kgs 23:15–20, as the fulfillment of the prophecy of "the man of God from Judah" (1 Kgs 13), and thereby as Yahweh's act. Following upon 9:1, 9:5–6 interprets the prophetic word against a sanctuary as also referring to that event, just as does the supplement in 3:14. In the days of Josiah, then, the book of Amos was searched so thoroughly for references to Bethel, or even merely to an "altar," that no passage was overlooked which lent itself to interpretation in light of Josiah's action. The doxologies allow speculation that the "Bethel–exposition" was associated with a concrete liturgical occasion at the Bethel sanctuary in the third decade before the end of the seventh century.

In addition, I consider it likely that 1:2 goes back to the same Bethel–exposition of the Josianic age. Here, with reference to Amos' own proclamation (and employing the style of the hymnic theophany tradition),

the new judgment of Yahweh is announced as being sent forth from Jerusalem into regions of the northern kingdom.[137] The later Deuteronomistic redaction could not speak of Jerusalem in such a positive manner.

E. The Deuteronomistic Redaction

The initial concern of this redaction is to show that Judah and Jerusalem stand under the just judgment of Yahweh—in the same way as Israel was seen by Amos and his school to stand under Yahweh's will to punish, and especially as Bethel was viewed by the homileticians and liturgists of the Josianic age. This is accomplished by inserting the Judah strophe into the cycle of oracles against the nations in 2:4–5, and by the addition of 3:1b which in essence extends the scope of "against you" (עֲלֵיכֶם) in 3:2b to embrace the "whole family" (therefore including Judah) which Yahweh brought up out of Egypt.[138] Furthermore, 6:1aα and 1bβ can be recognized as Deuteronomistic additions.[139] But the Deuteronomistic school is far too circumspect in its theological work to draw only Judah into the proclamation against Israel.

First, the redaction also incorporates additional oracles against other nations—specifically against Tyre and Edom (1:9–12) which, given the purview of the exilic age, could not be omitted.[140] It further seeks to complete the portrayal of Yahweh's acts in the history of salvation. While in 2:9 Amos mentioned only the giving of the land, the redaction grafts on as supplement reference to the exodus and wilderness traditions (2:10). Then it mentions the sending of charismatics, not without parenetically soliciting the listener's assent to the benevolent deeds of Yahweh (2:11), hence to reprove them for their culpable behavior toward the Nazirites and the prophets (2:12). Thus the question of guilt is considered in the context of salvation history. This is accomplished in the same way in connection with Amos' acute critique of the cult by the addition of 5:25–26. Now the legitimacy of sacrificial worship is tested against the period of "forty years" in the wilderness, which often occupies the Deuteronomists.[141] Here, too, the redaction employs the parenetic style of question and direct address, as in 2:10–12, and fills

---

135 See below on 4:12, *ad loc.*

136 See p. 111, and the comments below on 5:6, *ad loc.*

137 See pp. 121–22.

138 See below on 3:1b, *ad loc.*

139 See pp. 269–71.

140 See pp. 151–52.

out the statement with material from the treasury of Deuteronomistic historical knowledge.[142]

The redaction exhibits a prominent interest in the theological phenomenon of prophecy (cf. 2:11–12). The words of Amos in 3:6b and 8b offer sufficient occasion to formulate a basic theorem on the relationship of prophetic word to historical event (3:7). Yahweh reveals his plan to his servants, the prophets, before he puts it into effect. Here a guiding principle of the Deuteronomistic presentation of history emerged in the course of exegesis of prophecy.[143] It is uncertain whether the threat concerning the hunger for Yahweh's word (8:11–12) also belongs to the Deuteronomistic redaction (cf. Dtn 8:3), or whether it does not rather belong to the old school of Amos.[144]

However, the addition in 1:1 synchronizing the prophet with the history of the Israelite kings, as well as associating him with the sheep breeders—i.e., the final elaboration of the book's superscription—certainly belongs to the Deuteronomistic redaction. Thereby the redaction once again betrays its comprehensive historical interest and its special concern for the phenomenon of prophecy.[145]

As to method, elaborations of the Deuteronomistic redaction are characteristically linked with sentences or semantic contexts, while those of the Bethel–exposition of the Josianic age are merely attached to the catchwords "Bethel" or "altar"; work of the school of Amos never builds upon catchwords, but brings relationships of substance to light.

F. The Postexilic Eschatology of Salvation
After the early postexilic period, when salvation prophecy came to the fore, it was no longer possible to transmit a prophetic proclamation of judgment as one-sidedly harsh as Amos' without adding a new word of salvation (9:11–15). In doing so, the very wording of Amos' own judgment (5:11b) could be adopted, though it had to be transformed into a positive prognosis. Unique assurances of salvation (9:11) stand alongside widely propagated promises (9:15).[146]

Prior to the later utterances of weal at the end of the book, restraints upon Amos' sombre proclamation of calamity are surprisingly rare. The impact is lessened only by 9:8b, an addition which stresses that extirpation from the land does not mean destruction of the people as such. In 5:22aα there is an addition exempting burnt offerings from the rejection which applies to other offerings. In keeping with the postexilic order of worship, the judgment of the prophet (which had become incomprehensible) is here restricted, just as the comparable judgment in Ps 51:18–19 [16–17] is modified by vv 20–21 [18–19]. Similarly, completely contrary to the prophet's intention, the supplement "like David" in 6:5 may be an apology for the invention of musical instruments, in accord with the Chronicler's liturgical sensitivities. Yet, how sparse are such mitigations in the book of Amos compared to the rest of prophetic literature!

On the whole, therefore, the uniquely sombre message of Amos concerning the end of Israel remains unmistakably audible through all layers of tradition. To be sure, the old school of Amos modified it in one instance with the cultic expectation of salvation (5:14–15). The Bethel–exposition and the Deuteronomistic redaction recognize the new relevance of the words of Amos in the seventh and sixth centuries. Only the postexilic theology adds, briefly but distinctly, that Yahweh's sentence of death is not his last word.

---

141 See below on 2:10bα, *ad loc.*
142 Cf. 2 Kgs 17:30 with Am 5:26, on which see also below, *ad loc.*
143 See below on 3:7, *ad loc.*
144 See below on 8:11–12, *ad loc.*
145 See pp. 120–21.
146 Cf. further below on 9:11–15, *ad loc.*

The Title and Motto of the Book

Bibliography

Alfred Bertholet
"Zu Amos 1:2" in *Festschrift G. Nathanael Bonwetsch* (Leipzig, 1918), 1–12.

Miloš Bič
"Der Prophet Amos—ein Haepatoskopos," *VT* 1 (1951): 293–96.

Karl Budde
"Amos 1:2," *ZAW* 30 (1910): 37–41.

Idem
"Die Überschrift des Buches Amos und des Propheten Heimat" in *Semitic Studies in Memory of Rev. Dr. Alexander Kohut*, ed. George Alexander Kohut (Berlin, 1897), 106–10.

Idem
"Zur Geschichte des Buches Amos" in *Studien zur semitischen Philologie und Religionsgeschichte: Festschrift Julius Wellhausen*, ed. Karl Marti, BZAW 27 (Giessen, 1914), 63–77.

Jörg Jeremias
Theophanie: Die Geschichte einer alttestamentlichen Gattung, WMANT 10 (Neukirchen–Vluyn: Neukirchener Verlag, 1965), 12–17, 130–38, 154.

Julian Morgenstern
"Amos Studies I," *HUCA* 11 (1936): 130–40 (reprinted in *idem*, *Amos Studies*, vol. 1 [Cincinnati, 1941], 114–24).

A. E. Murtonen
"The Prophet Amos—a Hepatoscoper?" *VT* 2 (1952): 170–71.

Hans Schmidt
"Die Herkunft des Propheten Amos" in *Karl Budde zum siebzigsten Geburtstag*, ed. Karl Marti, BZAW 34 (Giessen, 1920), 158–71.

Werner H. Schmidt
"Die deuteronomistische Redaktion des Amosbuches. Zu den theologischen Unterschieden zwischen dem Prophetenwort und seinem Sammler," *ZAW* 77 (1965): 168–93.

Stanislav Segert
"Zur Bedeutung des Wortes *nōqēd*" in *Hebräische Wortforschung: Festschrift zum 80. Geburtstag von Walter Baumgartner*, ed. Benedikt Hartmann *et al.*, SVT 16 (Leiden: E. J. Brill, 1967), 279–83.

Salomon Speier
"Bemerkungen zu Amos," *VT* 3 (1953): 305–6.

Hans Joachim Stoebe
"Der Prophet Amos und sein bürgerlicher Beruf," *WuD* N.F.5 (1957): 160–81.

Meir Weiss
"In the Footsteps of One Biblical Metaphor," [Hebrew] *Tarbiz* 34 (1964–65): 107–28.

1   The words of Amos [, who[a] was among the sheep breeders,[b]] from[c] Tekoa, which he viewed concerning Israel[d] [in the days of Uzziah king of Judah and in the days of Jeroboam the son of Joash, king of Israel,] two years before the earthquake.

2   [And he said:

Yahweh roars from Zion
   and raises his voice out of Jerusalem,
then[e] [the pastures of the shepherds wilt[g]
   and the head of Carmel withers.[f]]

a   G (οἳ ἐγένοντο ["which occurred"]) supposes the relative clause to modify "the words," thus making the clause parallel to the following relative clause. V and T support M.

b   G (ἐν νακκαριμ) could reflect a misspelled or misread בַּבֹּקְרִים (cf. 7:14) but more likely resulted from reading ר instead of ד in the transmitted text. α′ (ἐν ποιμνιοτρόφοις ["among sheepherders"]), σ′ (ἐν τοῖς ποίμεσιν ["among the shepherds"]), θ′ (in nocedim, according to Jerome's commentary on the Twelve Prophets) and the remaining Greek witnesses (ἐν τοῖς κτηνοτρόφοις ["among the cattle–keepers"]), as well as S (nqd'), also do not presuppose בּוֹקֵר, a term which in the entire Hebrew Bible is found only in 7:14 and is there translated by G as αἰπόλος ["goatherd"], by α′ σ′ θ′ ε′ as βουκόλος ["herdsman"]. T (מרי גיתין ["owner of herds, cattleman"]) expresses the leadership function of the נקד. Manuscripts of the Lucianic recension and the Catena group exhibit here the town name καριαθιαρ(ε)ιμ (cf. Jer 33:20 G).

c   G[B] and other G[MSS] (cf. Ziegler, *Duodecim prophetae*, 181), render ἐν θεκουε (["in Tekoa"] = בתקוע?).

d   G (Ιερουσαλημ) hardly represents a conscious interpretation in the direction of 2:4–5, as "Jerusalem" occurs otherwise, apart from 2:5, only in 1:2. Probably we have here a scribal error based on easily confused abbreviations (?) (so William Rainey Harper, *A Critical and Exegetical Commentary on Amos and Hosea*, ICC [Edinburgh: T. & T. Clark, 1905], 2; and Victor Maag, *Text, Wortschatz und Begriffswelt des Buches Amos* [Leiden: E. J. Brill, 1951], 1); cf. Is 1:1.

e   The transition from the imperfect in v 2a to the consecutive perfect in v 2b indicates an apodosis (Joüon, par. 119c, i, j), especially after the inversion of the subject in the protasis (conditional clause); cf. Joel 4:18b.

f–f   T (ויצדון מדורי מלכיא ויחרב תקוף כרכיהון) depicts the effect of the divine utterance on "the dwellings of the kings" and "the fortification of their castles."

g   See Wolff, *Hosea*, textual note "b" to Hos 4:3.

Form

In no other prophetic book is the superscription linked by "and he said" (1:2a) to an initial, brief oracle. Nor is there a single subsequent oracle of our book introduced by "and he said" (ויאמר) with Amos as the subject. 1:2 is clearly set off from 1:3—2:16, since in the latter Yahweh is the speaker while in the former he is spoken of; moreover, a connective particle is lacking. The foreign nations theme is not yet intimated.[1] Probably because the superscription and the initial oracle together intend succinctly to inform the reader about the person (1:1) and the message (1:2) of the prophet, the two elements have been fused into an unaccustomed unity.

1   Differently, Aage Bentzen, "The Ritual Background of Amos 1:2—2:16," in OTS 8 (Leiden: E. J. Brill, 1950), 93–96; and Arvid S. Kapelrud, *Central Ideas in Amos*, SNVAO 1956/4 (Oslo: H. Aschehoug & Co. [W. Nygaard], 1956, ²1961), 17–19.

1:1 Tensions and overloading are apparent in v 1, signaling the existence here of literary strata. Already in the first relative clause there is disharmony between the notices regarding the prophet's vocation and domicile. It is probably an impermissible smoothing to translate: "who was among the sheep breeders from Tekoa." If this had been the intended meaning, the place name should rather have been introduced by the phrase "who were of/in Tekoa" (אֲשֶׁר בִּתְקוֹעַ; cf. Jer 1:1).[2] "From Tekoa" (מתקוע) apparently must be connected directly with "Amos."[3] The position immediately following the personal name corresponds to that appropriate for attachment of gentilics ("Amos from/of Tekoa").[4] The gentilic thus seems to have been severed from the personal name by the relative clause "who was among the sheep breeders" (אשר היה בנקדים). This supposition becomes especially compelling when one considers a second, even clearer tension between the two relative clauses. While the first אשר-clause unquestionably has "Amos" as its antecedent, the second probably refers back to the "words of Amos" (דברי־עמוס), since the comparable superscriptions (Is 1:1; 2:1; 13:1; Mi 1:1; Hab 1:1) always specify an object for the verb "to view" (חזה).[5] Two relative clauses with such different antecedents hardly flowed from the same pen. Summarizing the preceding observations, we conclude that the first relative clause ("who was among the sheep breeders") is a later addition.

The hypothesis that an older superscription has been secondarily expanded is confirmed by the rest of v 1. The broad notice "in the days of Uzziah king of Judah and in the days of Jeroboam the son of Joash, king of Israel" sets Amos' utterances in a wide span of time covering roughly forty years.[6] The notice is in accord with the conventional formulas used by redactors who, from a distant perspective, delineate the historical contexts of the prophets.[7] Alongside this broad synchronism stands the unusually precise one: "two years before the earthquake." Here there is still a sense of nearness to the recently experienced event. Hence the following text may initially be considered to have comprised the older superscription: "The words of Amos from Tekoa, which he viewed concerning Israel two years before the earthquake."

The supplemental material which we have identified may also be distinguished as such in that its content could have been derived from the oracles transmitted in the book. That Amos "was among the sheep breeders" could be gleaned from 7:14. The unique word בּוֹקֵר attested there must have been understood in the sense of "shepherd" in connection with the reference to "flock" in 7:15.[8] The term "sheep breeder" (נֹקֵד) was probably more common; it has, at least, one attestation in the Deuteronomistic History (2 Kgs 3:4). The dating of Amos in the time of Jeroboam was dictated by 7:10–11. The book's remaining traditions do not offer any evidence that Amos came "from Tekoa" or that he received his message "two years before the earthquake."

To be sure, the statement of the second relative clause, that Amos "viewed [words] concerning Israel," could be understood as reference to the visions (in chaps. 7–9), even though "to view" (חזה) is used here and not "to see" (ראה) as in 7:1, 4, 7; 8:1; and 9:1. But it is only this second relative clause which links the temporal statement—"two years before the earthquake"—to the old superscription. We must suppose, therefore, that the second relative clause and the concise temporal statement originated together. Now, however, the content of this clause stands in a certain tension with

2   Karl Budde, "Die Überschrift des Buches Amos und des Propheten Heimat" in *Semitic Studies in Memory of Rev. Dr. Alexander Kohut*, ed. George Alexander Kohut (Berlin, 1897), 106–10.

3   Cf. "Ibzan from/of Bethlehem" (אִבְצָן מִבֵּית לָחֶם), Ju 12:8; "Haruz from/of Jotbah" (חָרוּץ מִן־יָטְבָה), 2 Kgs 21:19; "Pedaiah from/of Rumah" (פְּדָיָה מִן־רוּמָה), 2 Kgs 23:36.

4   Cf. "Elijah the Tishbite" (אֵלִיָּהוּ הַתִּשְׁבִּי), 1 Kgs 17:1; "Micah the Moreshethite" (מִיכָה הַמֹּרַשְׁתִּי), Mi 1:1; "Nahum the Elkoshite" (נַחוּם הָאֶלְקֹשִׁי), Na 1:1.

5   The matter is viewed differently by Artur Weiser (*Die Profetie des Amos*, BZAW 53 [Giessen, 1929], 254–255) and Maag (*Text*, 2–3); against their interpretation cf. already G (οὓς εἶδεν) and V (*quae vidit*) [i.e., "which (plural) he saw" rather than "who saw," Ed.].

6   See p. 124.

7   Cf. Hos 1:1; Mi 1:1; Zeph 1:1; Is 1:1; and Jer 1:2; see Wolff, *Hosea*, 3–4 [1–2].

8   Cf. also G αἰπόλος ("goatherd") in 7:14.

the initial segment of the superscription to which it refers: "The words of Amos from Tekoa." That Amos saw "words" is less disturbing in light of Is 2:1 and Mi 1:1, where words are also seen.[9] It is surprising, however, that, according to our relative clause, Amos saw "the words *of Amos*." This is without analogue in other superscriptions, where the object of the vision (when defined by the attachment of a personal name) is exclusively "the word of Yahweh."[10] We must therefore consider the possibility that an older form of the superscription stated only: "The words of Amos from Tekoa." To this was added, first, the second relative clause: "which he saw concerning Israel two years before the earthquake." A final supplementation introduced the first relative clause, "who was among the sheep breeders," and the broad dating–formula ("in the days of . . . king of Israel").

1:2 An oracle expressly introduced as an utterance of Amos is linked immediately to the superscription. It contains two prosodic units, each with two three–stress cola exhibiting synonymous parallelism. The two bicola comprise a strophe with synthetic parallelism. The first bicolon announces Yahweh's action; the second describes its effect. There is no mention of guilt. Since Yahweh is introduced in the third person, the form of speech here does not correspond to prophetic messenger speech. Nor does it suit prophetic disputation speech which, to be sure, also speaks of Yahweh in the third person, but which usually makes a rather lively attempt to rouse the listener by means of a question (3:6, 8) or imperative address (5:18). The oracle under discussion is, in its measured regularity, more akin to hymnic style. Thus it has probably been correctly assigned to the theophany accounts,[11] the origin of which must be suspected to lie in the hymns of the victory celebrations of the old Israelite militia.[12] The first segment of these hymns treats of the coming of Yahweh from Sinai, and the second describes the concurrent effects in nature.[13] In the history of this genre four formal characteristics are attested so persistently that they recur in the oracle under discussion: 1) The divine name stands at the head of the first segment. 2) The place of Yahweh's departure is introduced by "from" (מִן). 3) The effect of Yahweh's coming is portrayed in the second segment, using stative (descriptive) perfect verbal forms. 4) Phenomena of nature are the subjects of the stative verbs in these latter result clauses.

On the other hand, our oracle departs in a fourfold way from the original form of the theophany account: 1) In the oracle nothing is declared about Yahweh using the infinitives (Ju 5:4; Ps 68:8 [7]), participles (Mi 1:3; Is 26:21) or verb forms in the perfect (Dtn 33:2; Ps 46:7b [6b]) so typical of the hymnic theophany account when lauding Yahweh's completed actions. Instead, we find the imperfect used here, describing a present event, as is appropriate to a prophetic announcement of Yahweh's acting.[14] 2) The verbs of the first bicolon do not really portray manifestations of a theophany which, characteristically, would be done by using verbs such as "to go forth" (Ju 5:4; Ps 68:8 [7]; Mi 1:3), "to come" (Dtn 33:2; Hab 3:3; Ps 50:3), "to shine forth" (Dtn 33:2; Ps 50:2), "to descend" (Mi 1:3), "to march" (Ju 5:4; Ps 68:8 [7]). Instead, there is reference here to the "roaring" and the raising of the "voice of Yahweh." To be sure, the second expression—"to raise [one's] voice" (נתן קול)—takes up that feature of the theophany account which describes the divine voice of thunder in the storm.[15] But the expression is here proleptically interpreted as a

---

9   Cf. also Is 13:1 and Hab 1:1; certainly the same relative clause refers to the "vision" of Isaiah in Is 1:1.
10   Mi 1:1; cf. Jer 23:18 *M*.
11   Bentzen, "Ritual Background," 96.
12   Jeremias, *Theophanie*, 142–57.
13   Ju 5:4–5; Dtn 33:2; Ps 68:8–9 [7–8]; cf. Mi 1:3–4; Hab 3:3. Cf. also Jeremias, *Theophanie*, 7–16.
14   Am 1:3a; 3:2b; 5:3; cf. also Hab 3:3 and Ps 50:2–3.
15   The expression appears already in the Ugaritic texts; cf. *CTA* 4 (= *UT* 51).5.70 [*w⟨y⟩tn.qlh.b'rpt*,

"he utters his voice in the stormclouds," Ed.] and Ps 46:7b. Cf. also Ps 18:14 [13]; 104:7; and Is 30:30–31.

lion's "roaring."[16] This simile never appears in older descriptions of theophanies or thunderstorms;[17] moreover, a thunderstorm would not cause drought.[18] Against this we must note that it is precisely in Amos that the roaring (of the lion) is set into parallelism with the speaking of Yahweh to his prophet (3:8). Thus a metaphor used by Amos to comprehend his auditions is introduced into the ancient form of the theophany accounts.[19] 3) The place from which the voice of Yahweh goes forth is neither Sinai (Ju 5:4; Dtn 33:2; cf. Ps 68:8 [7]) nor the heavens (Mi 1:3; Jer 25:30), but Mount Zion (as is elsewhere the case only in Ps 50:2). 4) The disruption of nature leads not to Israel's deliverance (as in Ju 5:4ff; Dtn 33:2ff; Ps 46:7[6]ff; 68:8 [7]ff) but to the ruin of Israel's land (cf. Mi 1:3ff).

The old form of the hymnic theophany account thus accommodates the announcement of an awesomely effective audition of Yahweh. It seems appropriately to have been placed at the head of the book as a motto summarizing the message of the prophet.

Setting

Whether this motto should be associated with the original superscription or one of the later expansions is an issue closely tied to that of the provenance of the literary strata in 1:1.

A consideration of which oracles might originally have been introduced by the core of the book's title—"The words of Amos from Tekoa"—points neither to the "oracles against the nations" in chaps. 1—2, which are introduced by "Thus Yahweh has said," nor to the visions in chaps. 7—9, which either open with "Thus the Lord Yahweh showed me" (7:1, 4, 7; 8:1) or depict Yahweh himself (9:1). In chaps. 3—5, however, oracles occur which in each instance are proclaimed as "word" (דבר 3:1; 4:1; 5:1), though not as Yahweh's word (3:3–8)—or at least not at the outset (4:1; 5:1-2) —but are rather presented as "words of Amos." The woe–cries which begin in 5:7 (cj.), 18 and 6:1 also contain for the most part "words of Amos," in accord with the style of clan instruction.[20] Thus the initial rubric of the book's title may have been attached to a basic stock of oracles in chaps. 3—6. Since at least in 5:1 (12?) the "I" of the prophet appears expressly as speaker of "this word,"[21] it is probable that this collection goes back to Amos himself. Moreover we could then expect that the earliest form of the superscription originated with Amos and those most closely associated with him. "The words of Amos" (דברי עמוס) finds its precise counterpart in the Old Testament only in "the titles of the collections of proverbs that belong to the wisdom of the sons of the east":[22] "the words of Agur" (דִּבְרֵי־אָגוּר Prv 30:1), and "the words of Lemuel" (דִּבְרֵי־לְמוּאֵל Prv 31:1).[23] Egyptian wisdom writings

---

16 שׁאג ("to roar") as in Am 3:4 where, it should be noted, there is also a parallelism between שׁאג and נתן קולו.

17 Its first occurrence is in Job 37:4.

18 Cf. Weiser, *Profetie*, 79f.

19 Cf. Ps 50:3ff; and 76:9 [8].

20 See p. 94.

21 Contrast the use of "and he said" (ויאמר) in 1:2 and 7:14.

22 Berend Gemser, *Sprüche Salomos*, HAT 1/14 (Tübingen: J. C. B. Mohr [Paul Siebeck], ²1963), 103, 107.

23 Cf. further "[the] words of [the] wise" (דִּבְרֵי חֲכָמִים), Prv 22:17; and "the words of Qohelet" (דִּבְרֵי קֹהֶלֶת), Eccl 1:1; note also 2 Sam 20:17 and Job 31:40. On the other hand, דִּבְרֵי יִרְמְיָהוּ in Jer 1:1 means "the history of Jeremiah," analogous to דִּבְרֵי שְׁלֹמֹה ("the history of Solomon") in 1 Kgs 11:41, דִּבְרֵי נְחֶמְיָה ("the history of Nehemiah") in Neh 1:1, and many other examples in the historical writings. Moreover, one should note especially דְּבַר יהוה ("the word of Yahweh") in Jer 1:2 (cf. also

Jer 51:64), on which see Wilhelm Rudolph, *Jeremia*, HAT 1/12 (Tübingen: J. C. B. Mohr [Paul Siebeck], ³1968), 2–4. In light of our completely different analysis of the traditions in Amos, it seems incorrect to suppose with Budde ("Geschichte") that Am 1:1 originated as the introduction to 7:10–17; the second relative clause already indicates otherwise.

bear similar titles.[24] The intellectual affinity of the oldest "writing prophets" with wisdom may likewise account for prophetic oracles becoming literature.

We have recognized the second relative clause to be an older supplement:[25] "which he viewed concerning Israel two years before the earthquake." Its secondary character is also indicated by its close connection with some of the accretions to the basic stock of chaps. 3—6. Primarily, though, this supplement must be associated with the five visions, i.e., the core material of chaps. 7—9. It is this latter material to which the verb "he viewed" (חזה) refers. Now the visions are composed in the first–person style, and therefore they probably go back to Amos himself, but they always denote the visionary experience using "to see" (ראה 7:1, 4, 7; 8:1; 9:1). Consequently, the supplement to the title derives from a redactor who joined the original collection of "the words of Amos" with the five–part cycle of vision reports. The combination "The words . . ., which he viewed . . ." might have seemed particularly appropriate to the redactor in light of 7:8; 8:2 and 9:1. The visions culminate in the viewing of an earthquake.[26] Such an earthquake is also depicted in 2:13–16, at the end of the likewise five–part[27] cycle of oracles against the nations.[28] The dating "two years before the earthquake" in the redacted title becomes understandable only with reference to the corresponding vision and proclamation. Finally, the formal relationship (five strophes) evident between the cycle of oracles against the nations and the vision reports leads us to consider the possibility that the older redaction, to which the second relative clause belongs, simultaneously joined the basic stock of chaps. 1—2 and chaps. 7—9 with that of chaps. 3—6. The terse notice "two years before the earthquake" was unequivocal only

for the generation which had experienced the event. Later on, the addition of a royal name (as in Zech 14:5) would have become absolutely necessary. It was perhaps the occurrence of the earthquake that gave rise to the redactional effort. Since the old redactor specifically remarks that Amos viewed words "concerning *Israel*," the redactional work was probably done in Judah at a time when "Israel" still existed as a state (i.e., prior to 721, if not before 733);[29] the redactor was removed from the date of the prophet's visions by at least two years, but not by much more. The redactional formula, "which he viewed concerning" (אשר חזה על), was appropriated by younger contemporaries of the school of Amos for use with other collections of prophetic oracles, as Is 1:1; 2:1; and Mi 1:1 show.[30]

By the time of the later editors who expanded the book's title, Amos had long belonged to history. In specifying his vocation and placing him in the reign of Jeroboam, they presuppose 7:10–17 to be part of the book,[31] and consequently the literary collection at their disposal at least approximates very closely the book's present shape.[32] The use of "was" (היה) in the first relative clause points to a closed era of the past.[33] Notes concerning vocation do not appear in the titles of prophetic books before Jer 1:1 ("from among the priests"), and thereafter they usually state "the prophet" (הַנָּבִיא).[34] Because of 7:14 our redactor had to disassociate Amos from this latter designation.

The first relative clause may therefore belong to the same redaction in which Amos is dated by means of the type of synchronism preserved in the Deuteronomistic History (2 Kgs 14:28; 15:6). That Uzziah of Judah is not only named alongside of Jeroboam of Israel but is even accorded priority of position suggests that the later redactor worked in Judah. Probably he

---

24 Cf. Hans Wildberger, *Jesaja*, BK 10/1 (Neukirchen-Vluyn: Neukirchener Verlag, 1972), 2; and the more extensive discussion of Siegfried Herrmann, *Die prophetischen Heilserwartungen im Alten Tetament: Ursprung und Gestaltwandel*, BWANT 85 (Stuttgart: W. Kohlhammer, 1965), 21–25, 41.

25 See pp. 117–18.

26 Cf. "earthquake" (רעשׁ) in 1:1 and 9:1.

27 See p. 151.

28 Cf. the wording of 9:1b and 2:14–16! On the interpretation of 2:13 see below, *ad loc.*

29 See pp. 108–11, and Wolff, *Hosea*, 113f [144].

30 Cf., from a later period, Is 13:1 and Hab 1:1.

31 See p. 117.

32 Schmidt, "Redaktion," 170.

33 Cf. Gen 1:2; 2 Sam 3:17; Jon 3:3; and also Brockelmann, *Syntax*, par. 30c, and Joüon, par. 154m.

34 Hab 1:1; Hag 1:1; Zech 1:1.

belonged to those Deuteronomistic circles of the sixth century which, following the destruction of Jerusalem, occupied themselves intensively with the collection of preexilic prophetic oracles. Yet the book's title has not been recast as extensively as, for example, Hos 1:1.[35] This in itself, however, is not sufficient cause to attribute the redaction of Am 1:1 already to the seventh–century Deuteronomic movement, whose redactional work on prophetic oracles proclaimed in the northern kingdom we can recognize in Hos 1:7 and 3:5.[36] While significantly informed by the prophetic spirit, the earlier Deuteronomic movement at the same time held a positive view of Jerusalem as the dwelling place of Yahweh's name. Such a redactor would be quite conceivable during the reign of Josiah (639—609). The very fact that v 2 is directly attached to the superscription could suggest an association with the work of this redactor, but the evidence by no means demands such a conclusion.[37]

1:2 This verse, on the contrary, must be attributed to a Judean redaction which did not yet assume as critical a stance towards Jerusalem as reflected in 2:4–5 and comparable Judean glosses in the book of Hosea.[38]

To be sure, there have been attempts to ascribe this verse to Amos, as does the redactional introduction "And he said" (ויאמר). In support of this it can be argued that "to roar" (שאג 3:4, 8), "to raise one's voice" (נתן קולו 3:4), and "Carmel" (הכרמל 9:3) demonstrably belong to his vocabulary. Moreover, the mention of Carmel seems appropriate to the message of judgment of a prophet sent from Judah into the northern kingdom, and "the pastures of the shepherds" belong to his particular realm of experience. In addition, we could consider whether Jer 25:30b has not

preserved the original wording, since it designates the place from which the voice of Yahweh proceeds as "from on high" (מִמָּרוֹם)[39] and "from his holy habitation" (מִמְּעוֹן קָדְשׁוֹ).[40] In that case it would have to be assumed that "Zion" and "Jerusalem" were only introduced into Am 1:2 by a later redaction on the basis of Joel 4:16 [3:16]. The form–critical link with the theophany accounts in the victory songs and the inversion of the form to foretell disaster[41] could also be supposed to reflect Amos' familiarity with transmitted speech forms and traditions.[42]

But precisely the passages just referred to for comparison indicate how incomparably more polemical and aggressive Amos is, in both his style of speaking and the contrasting content of his speech. With Amos the tone of accusation is ever present, even though in exceptional cases the offense is not specifically named. The situation is otherwise in 1:2. The hymnic style exhibited here is foreign to Amos.[43] Artur Weiser has shown that it is also impossible to comprehend the content of the verse in terms of Amos' "call experience."[44] Amos never threatens Israel with drought; in the report of his second vision he even says explicitly that such will not come to pass. Above all, however, Zion and Jerusalem never figure in Amos' own utterances as the place from which the voice of Yahweh proceeds; nowhere else in the book do they play a role even remotely analogous to the one portrayed in 1:2.[45] In terms of both form and content only Ps 50:2–3 is comparable to our oracle.[46] The description of the theophany of Yahweh in the first part of the psalm, with the following segment portraying its effect, might correspond to Am 1:2, as might also the interpretation of the theophany as the sounding forth of Yahweh's voice (Ps 50:1a, 3aα), its impact being like that of a

35 "The word of Yahweh . . ."; see Wolff, *Hosea*, 3–6 [1–5].

36 See Wolff, *Hosea*, xxxi f [xxvi f].

37 See pp. 112–13.

38 Hos 4:5aβ; 5:5bβ; 6:11a; etc. See Wolff, *Hosea*, xxxii [xxvii].

39 Cf. Am 9:2b.

40 Cf. Am 3:4.

41 See pp. 118–19.

42 Cf. 4:4–5; 5:18–20, 21–24; etc.

43 See pp. 118–19.

44 *Profetie*, 79–83. Against Alfred Bertholet, "Zu Amos

1:2" in *Festschrift G. Nathanael Bonwetsch* (Leipzig, 1918), 1–12.

45 The same holds true for the heavenly places from which, according to Jer 25:30, Yahweh's word issues forth, quite apart from the fact that these designations are most adequately explained as belonging to the time of the redaction of the book of Jeremiah. Moreover, Joel's dependence upon older prophetic books is demonstrable (see pp. 10–11), while it is not readily apparent that the book of Joel has influenced the transmission of Amos.

46 Jeremias, *Theophanie*, 13, 64.

scorching blast of heat (Ps 50:3aβ–b). This psalm, whose later segments are reminiscent of the language and the themes of prophecy, including Amos',[47] could well be attributed to those circles which prefaced our verse to the book of Amos as a motto.[48] H. J. Kraus has shown that many features of Ps 50 point to the time of Josiah.[49] And yet, despite all such possible affinities, it must be noted that Am 1:2 exhibits significant differences of vocabulary and perspective. These variants in 1:2 ("to roar," "pastures of the shepherds," "the head of Carmel") are not attested in earlier theophanic tradition; they are therefore best understood as conscious references to the proclamation of Amos.[50] We assume, therefore, that the Judean redactor tried to summarize the prophet's message, using the familiar cultic style of Jerusalem. This also clarifies his intention, expressed in the introductory "and he said" (ויאמר), to let Amos speak for himself.

This understanding of the hymnic opening, which points to the cultic use of the book of Amos, finds further elaboration and confirmation in the hymnic inclusions and conclusions in 4:13; 5:8–9; and 9:5–6. They exhibit related tendencies in style and content.[51] This hymnic bracketing also substantiates the assumption that the book of Amos had acquired approximately its present shape before the later redaction of the title.[52]

Jer 25:30b and Joel 4:16a [3:16a] make use of Am 1:2a. Jer 25:30 in this regard represents a post–Jeremianic interpretation which has appropriated the transmitted prophetic word.[53] Since Jerusalem and its Temple have in the meantime been destroyed,

Yahweh's roaring voice issues from (the heavenly) "on high" which is his "holy habitation." Here too the impact of the voice is initially felt by "Yahweh's pasture," i.e. by his own people as in Am 1:2, although since Judah is now the referent, regions of the northern kingdom are no longer designated. Then, however, the oracle is directed against all nations (Jer 25:31–33). This latter dimension is presupposed in Joel 4:16a [3:16a], where Am 1:2 has been adopted verbatim (the original wording being once again appropriate in the fourth century).[54]

Interpretation

■1 The book's old core bears the remarkably unpretentious superscription "the words of Amos from Tekoa." Since it is promulgated neither as "vision" (Is 1:1)[55] nor even as "the word of Yahweh" (Hos 1:1, etc.), which designation later traditionalists of prophetic oracles were fond of employing, we may deduce that at the time of composition there was as yet no independent tradition for the literary compilation of prophetic oracles. The form used in the compilation of sayings of the wise has been appropriated.[56]

No other person mentioned in the Old Testament bears the name "Amos." "Amasiah" (עֲמַסְיָה 2 Chr 17:16), a name of thanksgiving meaning "Yahweh carries" or "Yahweh has taken up protectingly into his arms," is comparable.[57] "Amos" (עמוס) would be the appropriate shortened form.[58] In contrast to Isaiah, Hosea, *et al.*, Amos has no recorded patronymic. We cannot conclude from this that Amos was "of lowly

---

47   Cf. Ps 50:7, 9, 17ff with Am 3:13; 5:21–22; 2:6ff; 4:1; 5:10ff.
48   See pp. 111–12.
49   *Psalmen*, 374.
50   See p. 121.
51   Johannes Lindblom, *Prophecy in Ancient Israel* (Philadelphia: Fortress, ²1963), 116–117.
52   See pp. 120–21.
53   Rudolph, *Jeremia*, 166–167.
54   See p. 81.
55   Regarding, חזה see p. 120.
56   See pp. 119–20.
57   Cf. Martin Noth, *Die israelitischen Personennamen im Rahmen der gemeinsemitischen Namengebung*, BWANT 3/10 (Stuttgart, 1928 = Hildesheim: Georg Olms, 1966), 178. Cf. also Ps 68:20; and *CIS* 1, 5732: עמסמלקרת = עמשמלקרת.

58   The possibility of interpreting the name in a passive sense—"He who is carried (by Yahweh)"—cannot be excluded; so Richard S. Cripps, *A Critical and Exegetical Commentary on the Book of Amos* (London: Society for Promoting Christian Knowledge, ²1955), 10; cf. Is 46:(1), 3. However, the Canaanite personal names מלקרתעמס (*KAI* 49.18) and אשמנעמס (*KAI* 64.2; 79.4)—"Melqart / Eshmun has carried"—favor the interpretation given in the text above.

birth."[59] Patronymics are also lacking in the cases of Obadiah, Habakkuk, and Haggai, and especially where the clan home of an individual is designated, as in the cases of Micah (Mi 1:1) and Nahum (Na 1:1). Moreover the names of unquestionably well–known, prominent figures may appear without patronymics, as in the case of king Uzziah (alongside Jeroboam ben Joash) in Am 1:1b.[60] Since it is evident on other grounds that the author of the book's original title cannot have been far removed from Amos himself,[61] the brevity of data given in the title must also be taken as an indication that the distance between them was negligible, if indeed the author and Amos are not identical.

On the other hand, the author's distance from Amos' home seems to have been considerable, not only because Amos proclaimed his message in the northern kingdom, but perhaps also because the earliest collection of his oracles was made away from Tekoa, or at least sought a hearing well beyond the confines of Tekoa. We must look for the location of Tekoa on the eastern edge of the presently rather extensive settlement of *Hirbet Teqū*, perhaps on the little knoll there, where ceramic remains from the Iron I period, as well as from the Early Bronze age, have been found.[62] Tekoa is situated at an altitude of 825 meters, directly south of Jerusalem, approximately seventeen lineal kilometers from the city center.[63] The main traffic artery which runs south to north along the mountain ridge can be reached easily, at a point just ten kilometers south of Bethlehem, after traveling about seven kilometers in a west–north-westerly direction from Tekoa. However there is also a road passing over the "Ascent of Ziz," leading to the western shore of the Dead Sea in the vicinity of *'En Jidi* (En–gedi).[64] The location of Tekoa is exactly on the border between the cultivated land to the west and the steppe, the "wilderness of Judah," to the east.[65] According to 2 Sam 14:2 "wisdom" had a particular association with Tekoa: it is from there that David's general, Joab, has a "wise woman" brought to Jerusalem. The occurrence of the place name in the list of fortresses in 2 Chr 11:5–6 underscores Tekoa's border location. Although the rabbinic and medieval assumption that Amos' home town must be sought in the northern kingdom has indeed been revived in more recent times, there has not been convincing evidence offered in support of it.[66]

Judean Tekoa is well suited to be a place of residence for "sheep breeders." It is probably on the basis of 7:14 that Amos is numbered among them in 1:1.[67] "Sheep breeder" (נֹקֵד) appears elsewhere in the Old Testament only in 2 Kgs 3:4. There it is stated that king Mesha of Moab sponsored sheep breeding on such a scale that he was able to supply the king of Israel regularly with the wool of 100,000 lambs and 100,000 rams. Then too, in a text from Ugarit a *rb nqdm* is mentioned alongside the *rb khnm*.[68] This reference, however, does not even allow us to conclude with certainty that there was at Ugarit a "chief shepherd" who, like the "chief priest," belonged to the temple personnel, the less so since we have another Ugaritic text in which *nqdm* appears in a list following designations of other vocational groups (military classes?) and prior to

---

59 Ludwig Koehler, *Amos* (Zürich, 1917: reprinted from "Amos," *Schweizer Theologische Zeitschrift* 34 [1917]), 35.

60 Cf. also Prv 31:1.

61 See p. 119.

62 Cf. Martin Noth, "Das Deutsche Evangelische Institut für Altertumswissenschaft des Heiligen Landes. Lehrkursus 1956," *ZDPV* 73 (1957): 3–4; and Arnulf Kuschke, "Beiträge zur Siedlungsgeschichte der Biḳā'," *ZDPV* 74 (1958): 9–10. On burial finds, including some from the Iron II period, cf. Paul W. Lapp, "Palestine: Known but Mostly Unknown," *BA* 26 (1963): 124; and Hans Joachim Stoebe, "Das Deutsche Evangelische Institut für Altertumswissenschaft des Heiligen Landes. Lehrkursus 1964," *ZDPV* 82 (1966): 16.

63 Cf. the map 1:100,000, South Levant Series, on which see Noth, *World*, 4 [3].

64 Noth, *World*, 89–90 [82].

65 Martin Noth, "Das Deutsche Evangelische Institut für Altertumswissenschaft des Heiligen Landes. Lehrkursus 1955," *ZDPV* 72 (1956): 33.

66 Cf. Hans Schmidt, "Die Herkunft des Propheten Amos" in *Karl Budde zum siebzigsten Geburtstag*, ed. Karl Marti, BZAW 34 (Giessen, 1920), 158–71; and Salomon Speier, "Bemerkungen," 305–06.

67 See p. 117.

68 *CTA* 6.6 (= *UT* 62).55.

khnm and *qdšm*.[69] To be sure, it is quite possible that at Ugarit, as at Bablyon, sheep breeders were responsible for temple flocks. But must they therefore have belonged to the cultic personnel? Certainly in the case of Amos such a positive conclusion should not be drawn.[70] Yet on the basis of both 2 Kgs 3:4 and the Ugaritic attestations it must be inferred that much more is meant by "sheep breeder" (נֹקֵד) than an ordinary "shepherd" (רֹעֶה).[71] We cannot conclude from Am 1:1, in view of its composition history and the secondary character of the first relative clause,[72] that there were many sheep breeders in Tekoa. Amos was no doubt among the prominent men of the place. Amos' vocation of sheep breeding was considered by the redactor just as noteworthy for an understanding of him as was elsewhere the observation that a warrior and king like Saul had joined the prophets (1 Sam 10:11–12).

"To view" (חזה) refers to the reception of visions. While the common word "to see" can also describe the prophetic visionary experience,[73] חזה is used exclusively to designate the special prophetic mode of seeing and hence the revelatory encounter as such.[74] It is Amos' reception of visions concerning Israel which explains his appearance there; neither a previously held office nor his own will led him to speak. Thus the appellation "visionary" (חֹזֶה) which, according to 7:12, the priest Amaziah uses in addressing Amos seems appropriate.

Uzziah's reign, like Jeroboam's, most likely began in 787/86.[75] Jeroboam II died in 747/46. Although Uzziah lived until about 735, during his latter years he was severely ill and hence the regency in Jerusalem was already assumed by Jotham in 757/56 (2 Kgs 15:5). Since Jotham is not mentioned in 1:1, there is sufficient reason to conclude that the redactors wished to assign Amos' prophetic activity to the first three

decades of the reign of Jeroboam II. Jotham is cited as coregent with Uzziah in Hos 1:1 and Is 1:1 (cf. Is 6:1).[76] Accordingly, Amos must have prophesied in Israel at least five years before the beginning of Hosea's prophetic activity.[77]

According to the older dating, which belongs to the redaction of the superscription promulgated in the generation of Amos himself,[78] the prophet delivered his proclamation "two years before the earthquake." This notice provides indirect evidence that at least the basic stock of oracles[79] included in this redaction originated in a period of less than a year's duration. Now the oracles of Amos already look back on the great military successes of Jeroboam II,[80] and indicate that the ruling classes are enjoying prosperity and security. Already there is need to ward off new border incursions in the Transjordan by the Arameans and Ammonites (1:3, 13).[81] Thus the oracles are most intelligibly dated towards the end of the first three decades of the reign of Jeroboam, that is *circa* 760. Archaeological data suggest the same period. Stratum VI at Hazor shows evidence of destruction caused by a great earthquake, traces of which have also been uncovered in archaeological work at Samaria. Independently of the exegetical considerations noted above, the excavators have dated this earthquake *circa* 760.[82] Centuries later this earthquake is mentioned in Zech 14:5, though probably not independently of the literary tradition in Am 1:1.

■ **2** The introductory hymnic passage seeks to epitomize that which Amos had proclaimed ("and he said" [ויאמר]) and thereby to set the tone for the whole book. While the old theophany accounts began by praising the redeemer, this oracle is a confession of the devastating force of Yahweh's terrifying voice. Amos himself,

69   *CTA* 71 (= *UT* 113).71.
70   Against Kapelrud (*Central Ideas*, 5–7, 69) and others.
71   Cf. Stoebe, "Amos," 166; and the *T* reading cited in textual note "b" to 1:1.
72   See p. 120.
73   Amos himself employs "to see" (ראה) in 7:1, 4, 7; 8:1; 9:1.
74   Cf. Wildberger, *Jesaja*, 5–6.
75   On the problem of the regnal dates of Uzziah of Judah and Jeroboam II of Israel, see Wolff, *Hosea*, 5–6 [4], and Wildberger, *Jesaja*, 3–4.
76   Cf. Ernst Kutsch, "Israel, II. Chronologie der

Könige von Israel und Juda," *RGG*³ 3, 943; and Alfred Jepsen, "Zur Chronologie der Könige von Israel und Juda" in Alfred Jepsen and Robert Hanhart, *Untersuchungen zur israelitisch–jüdischen Chronologie*, BZAW 88 (Berlin: A. Töpelmann, 1964), 38.
77   Cf. Wolff, *Hosea*, xxi [xi].
78   See p. 120.
79   See p. 120.
80   Cf. Am 6:13 with 2 Kgs 14:25.
81   See pp. 150–51.
82   Cf. Yigael Yadin, Yohanan Aharoni, Ruth Amiran, Trude Dothan, Immanuel Dunayevsky, and Jean

in his extant oracles, never spoke so directly of the "[lion's] roar" of Yahweh's voice. He did, however, experience in his own life the irresistible power of Yahweh's address, and he has indeed compared this to the effect of the lion's roaring (3:8). Nor did Amos ever name "Zion" and "Jerusalem" as the place from which the voice of Yahweh went forth. But the transmitters are certain that the God proclaimed in the Jerusalem sanctuary (cf. Ps 50) is identical with the one to whom Amos bore witness. Yahweh's voice is here directed toward neither a particular audience nor an individual messenger in such a way that it might become humanly intelligible, as it is in the oracles of Amos. Rather, it rages inarticulately through the land, immediately wreaking havoc. Just as in the old theophany accounts, the stress lies on the declarative perfects of the result clauses (v 2b), although the use of the present and durative imperfects in the protasis is a departure from the older type.[83] The effect of the word is drought described by the verb יבשׁ ("to wither") as well as by its synonym אבל ("to wilt").[84] The "pastures of the shepherds" belong to the realm of the sheep breeder (1:1). Their drying up takes away his basis of existence. The "head of Carmel" is probably not mentioned primarily as a prominent region of the northern kingdom, but rather because of its plentiful forests, comparable only to areas outside of Palestine, such as in Lebanon.[85] Even today the Carmel Ridge, which south of the bay of Haifa rises to a height of more than 500 meters, is one of the genuine forest areas in the land west of the Jordan; it owes its name to the rich vine-

yards and orchards of its slopes. Shepherds' pastures and the head of Carmel together describe the completeness of the devastation. A drought that makes both forests and meadows die must indeed be of eschatological dimensions. It is the task of the book of Amos to proclaim such an end, and even though the image of drought is not usually employed,[86] the end is always viewed as the consequence of the terrifying voice of Yahweh. It would be misleading to see in the shepherds the leaders of the foreign nations, and in the "head of Carmel" an allusion to the king of Israel,[87] in order so to establish a connection (which is neither formally nor thematically apparent) between 1:2 and the oracles against the nations in 1:3—2:16. Parallel hymnic accounts of theophanies with effects in nature, known now from the ancient Near Eastern milieu, have been compiled by Jörg Jeremias.[88]

Aim

The superscription is free of any theological ambition to present the prophet's word as divine word. Its basic core exhibits an interest in the person and origin of the speaker, without whom the collected oracles would not have been promulgated. The first redaction, which introduces Amos as one who "viewed" words concerning Israel "two years before the earthquake," allows us to recognize that the literary crystallization of the prophetic oracles was prompted in any event by the fulfillment of the prophet's threats; this legitimation apparently strengthened a determination to transmit the oracles. The later synchronization of Amos with

Perrot, *Hazor II: An Account of the Second Season of Excavations, 1956* (Jerusalem: Hebrew University [Magnes Press], 1960), 24–26, 36–37.

83 See p. 118.

84 On אבל ("to wilt, wither"), see Wolff, *Hosea*, 65 (textual note "b" to Hos 4:2) [81]. Ernst Kutsch has shown it to be probable that the connotations "dry up" and "mourn" derive from a common root, meaning "to diminish": "'Trauerbräuche' und 'Selbstminderungsriten' im Alten Testament" in *Drei Wiener Antrittsreden*, ThSt 78 (Zürich: EVZ Verlag, 1965), 35–36.

85 Is 33:9; 35:2; Na 1:4.

86 Cf. only Am 7:4–6.

87 Kapelrud, *Central Ideas*, 19.

88 *Theophanie*, 75–87; cf. also Johannes Lindblom, *Prophecy in Ancient Israel* (Philadelphia: Fortress, [2]1963), 116–117.

the history of the monarchy shows that the words of the prophet were spoken in quiet, prosperous times, which thus suggests that they were meant to be heard not as interpretation of current history, but as harbinger of that which was yet to come. They could therefore claim new attention in Jerusalem and Judah in similar times of the seventh and sixth centuries.[89]

The "motto" was probably formulated in retrospect by the book's tradents; it establishes the basic tone of the prophet's message, employing the hymnic style, perhaps as an overture to the liturgical reading of the Amos–traditions.[90] It professes the drying up of the land to be the effect of that powerful word which found its spokesman in Amos. Every future reader should recognize behind the prophetic oracles here transmitted the devastating power of Yahweh himself.

89 See pp. 111–12.
90 See pp. 121–22.

The Guiltiest of the Guilty

Bibliography

Robert Bach
  "Gottesrecht und weltliches Recht in der Verkündigung des Propheten Amos" in *Festschrift für
  Günther Dehn*, ed. Wilhelm Schneemelcher (Neukirchen: Verlag der Buchhandlung des Erziehungsvereins, 1957), 23–34.

M. A. Beek
  "The Religious Background of Amos 2:6–8" in
  OTS 5 (Leiden: E. J. Brill, 1948), 132–41.

Aage Bentzen
  "The Ritual Background of Amos 1:2—2:16" in
  OTS 8 (Leiden: E. J. Brill, 1950), 85–99.

G. Johannes Botterweck
  "Zur Authentizität des Buches Amos," *BZ* N.F. 2
  (1958): 176–89 (178–81).

Reinhard Fey
  *Amos und Jesaja: Abhängigkeit und Eigenständigkeit des
  Jesaja*, WMANT 12 (Neukirchen–Vluyn: Neu-
  kirchener Verlag, 1963), 44–48.

Hartmut Gese
  "Kleine Beiträge zum Verständnis des Amosbuches," *VT* 12 (1962): 417–24.

Norman K. Gottwald
  *All the Kingdoms of the Earth: Israelite Prophecy and
  International Relations in the Ancient Near East* (New
  York: Harper & Row, 1964), 94–114.

Menahem Haran
  "The Rise and Decline of the Empire of Jeroboam
  ben Joash," *VT* 17 (1967): 266–97 (272–78: "II.
  Historical Background of Am. 1:2—2:6").

Hope W. Hogg
  "The Starting–Point of the Religious Message of
  Amos" in *Transactions of the Third International Congress for the History of Religions*, vol. 1 (Oxford, 1908),
  325–27.

Arvid S. Kapelrud
  Central Ideas in Amos, SNVAO 1956/4 (Oslo: H.
  Aschehoug & Co. [W. Nygaard], 1956, ²1961),
  17–33.

Sigo Lehming
  "Erwägungen zu Amos," *ZThK* 55 (1958): 145–69
  (157–60: "Die Fremdvölkersprüche in Am 1:3ff").

Abraham Malamat
  "Amos 1:5 in the Light of the Til Barsip Inscriptions," *BASOR* 129 (1953): 25–26.

André Neher
  Amos. Contribution à l'étude du prophétisme (Paris: J.
  Vrin, 1950), 49–76.

Henning Graf Reventlow
  Das Amt des Propheten bei Amos, FRLANT 80 (Göttingen: Vandenhoeck & Ruprecht, 1962), 56–75.

Werner H. Schmidt
  "Die deuteronomistische Redaktion des Amosbuches. Zu den theologischen Unterschieden zwi-

schen dem Prophetenwort und seinem Sammler,"
ZAW 77 (1965): 174–83.

Artur Weiser
  Die Profetie des Amos, BZAW 53 (Giessen, 1929),
  85–116.

Hans Walter Wolff
  Amos the Prophet: The Man and His Background, tr.
  Foster R. McCurley (Philadelphia: Fortress, 1973),
  34–44 [24–30].

Ernst Würthwein
  "Amos-Studien," *ZAW* 62 (1950): 35–40.

1

1:3

Thus Yahweh has[a] **said:**

**For three crimes of Damascus
and for four, I will not take it**[b] **back,
[c]because they threshed Gilead**[d]
with iron sledges.[c]

a   While *G* always renders the subsequent occurrences of the messenger formula in the present tense ($\tau\acute{\alpha}\delta\epsilon$ $\lambda\acute{\epsilon}\gamma\epsilon\iota$ $\kappa\acute{\upsilon}\rho\iota o\varsigma$ ["Thus Yahweh says"], 1:6, 9, 11, 13; 2:1, 4, 6; 3:11), it translates here $\kappa\alpha\grave{\iota}$ $\epsilon\tilde{\iota}\pi\epsilon$ $\kappa\acute{\upsilon}\rho\iota o\varsigma$ ("And Yahweh has said").

b   How one translates the hip'il of שׁוּב depends on the interpretation of the suffixed object pronoun. Is the reference here (1) to the turning back of the *Assyrian* invader, as in 2 Kgs 19:7 and 28? (So Hope W. Hogg, "The Starting-Point of the Religious Message of Amos" in *Transactons of the Third International Congress for the History of Religions*, vol. 1 [Oxford, 1908], 325–27). Or is the reference (2) to a return with respect to *Damascus*, more specifically (a) to a restoration of its deported population (1:5b; cf. Job 33:29–30, and the comments of Rashi, Ibn-Ezra, and Kimhi on Am 1:3), or (b) to the granting of a favorable answer to its petitions (Job 35:4; 40:4; see Neher, *Amos*, 50), or (c) to its return to Yahweh, in accord with 4:6–11 (so Morgenstern, "Amos Studies IV: The Address of Amos—Text and Commentary," *HUCA* 32 [1961]: 314)? Or (3) to the averting of the *punishment* subsequently announced in 1:4–5 (so Wellhausen; Cripps; and Buber, *Kündung*, 633: "... kehre ichs nicht ab" ["I will not turn (it) away"])? Or (4) to the recalling of the *word* of Yahweh as such? Only for the last of these possibilities does the book of Amos elsewhere offer close analogies, in 7:2–3, 5–6, 8bβ; 8:2bβ (cf. Nu 23:20; Is 55:11; 45:23). Were we to suppose the suffix refers to the Assyrians or to Damascus there would be no possibility of interpreting all the following strophes in corresponding fashion; apart from 1:15, exile is otherwise nowhere else threatened in these oracles. Were the reference to punishment, a feminine suffix would sooner have been expected (so Is 43:13; 14:27), at least in view of the regularly recurring use of אֵשׁ ("fire"). To be sure, some *G* witnesses here attest $\alpha\mathring{\upsilon}\tau\acute{\eta}\nu$ (feminine singular; likewise *L*: *eam*), while others have $\alpha\mathring{\upsilon}\tauο\acute{\upsilon}\varsigma$ (masculine plural), but the primary *G* tradition is $\alpha\mathring{\upsilon}\tau\acute{ο}\nu$ (masculine singular) (cf. Ziegler, *Duodecim prophetae*, 181).

c–c   One may ask whether in the progression of the oracle 1:3b is not more closely linked to vv 4–5 than to v 3a, since: (1) guilt and punishment are merely al-

4 So I will send fire into Hazael's house,
and it shall devour Benhadad's[e]
strongholds.[f]

5 [g]I will break the bar of Damascus,[g]
and cut off the one who reigns[h]
from Sin Valley[i]
and the one who holds the scepter
from House of Pleasure.[j]
Then Aram's people will be deported to Kir[k]

—Yahweh has said.

6 Thus Yahweh has said:

For three crimes of Gaza
and for four, I will not take it back,
[l]because they deported entire[m] (village)
populations[l]
to deliver them up to Edom.

luded to in v 3a, while in vv 3b and 4–5 they are
elaborated; and (2) the plural suffix in על־דושם
(literally "because of their threshing") is more readily explained by what follows than by what precedes.
Yet as an explication of the "crimes," introduced by
the preposition על־, the infinitival clause is clearly
attached to v 3a.

d   G (τὰς ἐν γαστρὶ ἐχούσας τῶν ἐν Γάλααδ ["the pregnant women who were in Gilead"] = L) and 5
QAm (4) 1, [הרו]ה (M. Baillet, J. T. Milik and
R. de Vaux, Les "Petites Grottes" de Qumran, DJD 3/
Texte [Oxford: Clarendon Press, 1962], 173),
interpret on the basis of 1:13. The reading of T is
more general: ית יתבי ארע גלעד ("the inhabitants
of the land of Gilead"). σ' (τὴν γαλααδ) and V support M.

e   G (Aδερ) reads ר for ד.

f   G (θεμέλια) interprets "foundation walls"; α' and σ'
(βάρεις) "large houses" or "towers"; θ' (τὰς αὐλάς)
"the courts."

g–g   Marti, Morgenstern ("Amos Studies IV," 300, 314)
and others, place v 5aα after v 5bβ, in order to
achieve a strict parallelism of bicola as in 1:8. There
is no textual support for this suggestion.

h   Literally "the one who sits [on the throne]" (see
p. 156); G (κατοικοῦντας) interprets "the inhabitants," contrary to the parallel colon in v 5aγ (cf.
1:8a) and anticipating v 5b.

i   G (ἐκ πεδίου Ων) does not justify Morgenstern's reading בקעת־בעל = Baalbek ("Amos Studies IV,"
314); for Ων in G, cf. Wolff, Hosea, textual note "k"
to Hos 12:5b. α' (ἀνωφέλους) and σ' (ἀδικίας) interpret M: "[valley] of those good for nothing" and
"of iniquity," respectively. Buber (Kündung, 633)
renders "Ebne des Args" ("plain of guile").

j   G (ἐξ ἀνδρῶν Χαρραν) probably read בְּנֵי (Bohairic
translation: e filiis) instead of בית. Χαρραν = חָרָן
(Gen 11:31–32 and repeatedly) for עדן cannot be
explained as due to misreading ד as ר (Harper); it
perhaps reflects a particular tradition which derived
the parallel אֲרָם = Συρία ∥ חָרָן = Χαρραν from Gen
28:5–7, 10, and recalls the capital city of the north
Aramean state Bīt Adini (Malamat, "Amos 1:5,"
26). σ' (ἐξ οἴκου εδεν) supports M. θ' (ἐν οἴκω τρύφης)
and V (de domo voluptatis) interpret M: "house of
indulging." Buber (Kündung, 633) renders "Haus
der Lust" ("house of lust").

k   G (ἐπίκλητος) erroneously reads קריא ("called, appointed, chosen"), used as in Nu 1:16 and 26:9.

l   Literally "because they exiled a whole exile"; for
the "effectual (internal) object" [i.e., cognate accusative construction, Ed.], cf. Brockelmann, Syntax,
par. 92a.

m   G (τοῦ Σαλωμων ["of Solomon"]) misconstrues
שלמה as a proper name. σ', θ' (αἰχμαλωσίαν τελείαν)
and V (captivitatem perfectam) catch the correct sense.

n   According to G (Ακκαρων) and Sennacherib, Taylor
Prism 2.69 (Oppenheim, ANET³, 287; AOT², 353),
the place name was vocalized עֶקְרוֹן ('Aqqārôn) in

7 So I will send fire upon the wall of
Gaza,
   and it shall devour her strongholds.

8 I will cut off the one who reigns
from Ashdod
   and the one who holds the scepter
from Ashkelon.
I will turn my hand against Ekron,[n]
   and the remnant of the Philistines
shall be destroyed
     —[the Lord][o] Yahweh has said.

9 [Thus Yahweh has said:

For three crimes of Tyre
   and for four, I will not take it back,
because they delivered up entire[p] (village) populations to Edom[q]
   and did not remember the covenant
of brothers.

10 So I will send fire upon the wall of
Tyre,
   and it shall devour her strongholds.

11 Thus Yahweh has said:

For three crimes of Edom
   and for four, I will not take it back,
because he pursues his brother with
the sword
   and deadens[r] his pity,[s]
(because) his anger plunders[t] continuously,[u]
   and his wrath is ever alert.[v]

12 So I will send fire against Teman,
   and it shall devour the strongholds
of Bozrah.][w]

---

o   antiquity (Noth, *Josua*, 70).

    This expansion was as yet unknown to G (cf. also
1:5, 15; 2:3), but it is attested in Mur XII (88)
3.25 (see P. Benoit, J. T. Milik and R. de Vaux,
Les grottes de Murabba'ât, DJD 2/Texte [Oxford:
Clarendon Press, 1961], 186), *T*, and *V*. Elsewhere
in the book of Amos אדני appears frequently as an
addition: 3:8, 11, 13; 4:2; 5:16; 6:8; 7:1, 4; 8:1,
3, 9, 11; 9:5; and probably also 4:5 and 5:3.

p   On G (τοῦ Σαλωμων), see textual note "m" above.

q   Robinson's proposal to read לָאָרָם—"for geographical reasons" (so Maag, *Text*, 7)—has no textual
support and merely obscures the dependence of the
formulation on 1:6b.

r   The perfect consecutive is to be understood here in
a frequentative sense (cf. Joüon, par. 119v); literally
"destroys."

s   G^W (a third century MS) translates μήτραν
("womb"), a rendering also considered by Jerome
(*vulvam ejus*) (M. Rahmer, "Die hebräischen Traditionen in den Werken des Hieronymus," *MGWJ* 42
[1898]: 6–7). This has already become μητέρα
("mother") in G^B and, like the G reading in 1:3
(see textual note "d" above), is an interpretation
based upon 1:13. G also glosses ἐπὶ γῆς ("upon [the]
earth"; cf. 5:2), intended perhaps to correspond
to the place designations in 1:3b and 13b (?).

t   The primary meaning of טרף is "to tear apart"
(used especially of beasts of prey; cf. Hos 5:14). In
Job 16:9 (cf. Job 18:4) אַפּוֹ is also found as subject
of the verb. The imperfect consecutive indicates the
change of subject. Since Justus Olshausen (*Die
Psalmen erklärt*, KEH [Leipzig, 1853], 397 on Ps
103:9) it has usually been supposed—with G, S and
V—that Edom is the subject of 1:11b, and that
וַיִּטֹּר is to be read, in accord with S and V (*tenuerit*)
[i.e., the sense of the colon being "(Edom) maintained his anger continuously," Ed.]. In support of
this widely accepted proposal the following may be
noted: (1) טרף occurs far more often than נטר and
thus, as *lectio faciliar*, could be secondary; (2) the
parallelism of נטר with שָׁמַר, corresponding to Jer
3:5; and (3) no change of subject is required. On
the other hand, the following items may be adduced
in support of M: (1) G (ἥρπασεν ["they plundered,
seized"]); (2) the phrase טרף אפו, in which אף is
subject, merits preference as the more difficult and
rarer expression, especially since its feasibility is
attested by Job 16:9, (18:4); (3) in contrast, נטר
אפו is never attested elsewhere as such, but only postulated (cf. Jer 3:5, 12; Na 1:2; Ps 103:9; and
Koehler-Baumgartner, 613); and (4) the syntactical
break—the transition to the imperfect consecutive—
is more readily understandable if it signals a change
of subject; see textual note "v" to 1:11 below.

u   G (εἰς μαρτύριον ["for a testimony"]) erroneously
vocalizes לָעֵד (as in Mi 7:18 and Zeph 3:8).

v   If עברה ("wrath") is the subject of the colon (see
textual note "t" above), then the verbal form of

13   Thus Yahweh has said:

For three crimes of the Ammonites
and for four, I will not take it back,
because they ripped open[x] the pregnant
women of Gilead,
in order to[y] enlarge their own territory.

14   So I ⟨will send⟩[z] fire upon the wall of
Rabbah,
and it shall devour her strongholds,
with fanfare on the day of battle,
with a gale[aa] on the day of the
whirlwind.[bb]

שמר here refers to the careful watching of the plundered booty (// טרף); cf. Ju 1:24; Job 10:14; and
on the latter reference, Horst, *Hiob*, 157. In this case
the consonantal reading שמרה may be interpreted
without difficulty as a third feminine singular perfect. The Masoretic vocalization שְׁמָרָה, instead of
the usual שָׁמְרָה (so also Karl Budde, "Zu Text und
Auslegung des Buches Amos," *JBL* 43 [1924]: 66),
is perhaps to be explained as an example of n^e sīgāh
[i.e., recessive tone; cf. Gesenius-Kautzsch-Cowley,
par. 29d, e, and Joüon, par. 31c; Ed.]. The attempt
to reinterpret the affirmative ה as a third feminine
singular suffix (Gesenius-Kautzsch-Cowley, par.
58g; Joüon, par 6li) contradicts the Masoretic tradition which explicitly wants the ה to be read without *mappîq* (M. Rahmer, "Die hebräischen Traditionen in den Werken des Hieronymus," *MGWJ* 42
[1898]: 7). The generally accepted proposal of
Justus Olshausen (*Die Psalmen erklärt*, KEH [Leip-
zig, 1853], 397) to read שָׁמַר לָנֶצַח finds support for
the ל in *G* (εἰς νῖκος) and *T* (לְאַפְרָשׁ). However,
נצח alone is attested with the same sense ("[for]
ever") in Ps 13:2 [1] and 16:11. *M* can scarcely be
explained as having developed secondarily. Neher
(*Amos*, 49) and Buber (*Kündung*, 634), in contrast to
the majority of recent interpreters, also take אף and
עברה to be the subjects of the cola in 1:11bβ.

w   On the secondary character of 1:9–12, see pp. 139–
40.

x   Elsewhere this connotation is always conveyed by
the pi'el of בקע (2 Kgs 8:12; 15:16; cf. also Hos
14:1 [13:16]; 13:8; 2 Kgs 2:24). But this does not
necessarily mean we should, with Morgenstern
("Amos Studies IV," 315), vocalize בַּקְעָם; see p.
161. In 2 Chr 32:1 the same qal infinitive form connotes the breaching of a besieged town, a meaning
which in Is 7:6 is expressed by the hip'il of בקע.

y   Otto Procksch (*BH*[3], n. "a–a" to Am 1:13), Morgenstern ("Amos Studies IV," 315), and others
adopt a likely shorter reading (להרחיב גבולם) in
order to bring the length of 1:13bβ into conformity
with the final cola in 1:3b and 1:6b; on למען see
textual note "p" to 2:7.

z   Here too, in conformity with all of the other strophes,
ושלחתי is to be read; *M* may be explained on the
basis of Jer 49:2, 27; see p. 161.

aa   *G* (καὶ σεισθήσεται ["and he / she shall be tossed
about"]) presupposes (based on a defective *Vorlage*?)
וְסָעַר; but what is the antecedent of the subject?
The parallelism in 1:14b supports *M*.

bb   *G* (συντελείας αὐτῆς ["her consummation"]) misconstrues the form, vocalizing סוֹפָה.

cc   *G* (οἱ βασιλεῖς αὐτῆς ["her kings"]) must have been
derived from a faulty text (מְלָכֶיהָ?). Manuscripts
of *G* (especially those of the Lucianic group), α´, σ´
and others attest μελχομ (*V*: *Melchom*), as in Jer
30:1, 3 *G* (= Jer 49:1, 3 *M*) and Zeph 1:5—i.e.,
thinking of the god of the Ammonites, they vocalize
the consonantal text of *M* as מִלְכֹּם, in accord with

Then their king[cc] shall go into exile,
  he[dd] and his princes together

    —Yahweh has said.

2

2:1   Thus Yahweh has said:

For three crimes of Moab
  and for four, I will not take it back,
[a]because he burned to lime the bones[b]
  of the king of Edom.[a]
2 So I will send fire against Moab,[c]
    and it shall devour the strongholds
      of Kerioth.
  Then Moab shall die amidst the clash
  (of battle),
    with fanfare,[d] with the blast of
    the horn.
3 I will cut off the ruler from ⟨his⟩[e]
  midst,
    and all ⟨his⟩[e] princes I will slay
    with him

    —Yahweh has said.

---

1 Kgs 11:5, 33 and 2 Kgs 23:13.

dd In light of the reading of מלכם as the name of the Ammonite god (see the preceding textual note), *G* supplies οἱ ἱερεῖς αὐτῶν ["their priests"], following Jer 30:3 *G* (= Jer 49:3 *M*), thus supposing כֹּהֲנָיו in place of הוא. *T* and *V*, in addition to the parallelism מלכם ‖ שריו and the contextual content of 1:13–14, support the more concise, terse text of *M*.

a–a *T* (על דאוקיד גרמי מלכא דאדום וסדינון בגירא בביתיה) interprets the purpose of the burning of the bones of the king of Edom: "Because he burned the bones . . . and used them for plaster on his house"; cf. Neher, *Amos*, 52–53. *V* stresses the completeness of the burning: *eo quod incenderit ossa regis Idumaeae usque ad cinerem* (". . . entirely unto ashes").

b Procksch (*BH*[3], n. "a" to Am 2:1), Morgenstern ("Amos Studies IV," 315) and others suppose on metrical grounds that the name of the king of Edom has been lost here. But also in 1:13b (see textual note "y" above) and 2:6b the cola in the transmitted text do not correspond in length with those of 1:3b and 1:6b; hence any reconstruction based on metrical symmetry remains precarious.

c In 2:1a and 2:2b alike, "Moab" means the Moabite population. The fire is sent against a city in most of the strophes. Therefore Procksch (*BH*[3], n. "a" to Am 2:2) proposed to read בְּעָרֵי מוֹאָב here, and Meinhold (Johannes Meinhold and Hans Lietzmann, *Der Prophet Amos. Hebräisch und Griechisch*, Kleine Texte für theologische Vorlesungen und Übungen 15/16 [Bonn, 1905], 6) proposed בְּקִיר מוֹאָב. The latter suggestion gains plausibility if we suppose the last word of v 2a (הקריות) to be a misplaced supplement to the text, containing the detached word (קיר; cf. Is 15:1) to which the suffix of an original אַרְמְנוֹתֶיהָ (1:7, [10], 14) has been joined, now reinterpreted as the definite article (so also Weiser, and Morgenstern, "Amos Studies IV," 315). However, against the proposal we must note: (1) קיר is not קְרִיּוֹת; (2) in 1:4 also there is no city designated for destruction; and (3) the oracles of Amos regularly mention the "wall" (1:7, 14) of the designated city (i.e., apart from 1:12 which belongs to the secondary portion of the cycle).

d Five manuscripts of *M* as well as *S*, *G*, and *T* attest conjunctive ו here; but the bare apposition is in accord with the style of Amos in 1:14.

e Following Wellhausen, the suffixes have usually been read as masculine: שָׂרָיו and מִקִּרְבּֽוֹ. Manuscripts of the Lucianic and Catena groups, and Theodore of Mopsuestia, presuppose masculine suffixes, but the *G* witnesses otherwise read the suffixes as feminine. *M* treats "Moab" as masculine when it refers to people, and as feminine when it refers to land (Ehrlich, *Randglossen* 5, 230; cf. Wildberger, *Jesaja*, textual note "a" to Is 2:8). Perhaps the feminine suffixes refer to Kerioth (so Amsler, *ad loc.*: Edmond

4 [Thus Yahweh has said:

For three crimes of Judah
     and for four, I will not take it back,
because they repudiate Yahweh's
instruction
         and his decrees they do not ob-
         serve,
     (because) their false (gods)[f] lead
     them astray,
         after which their fathers walked.

5 So I will send fire against Judah,
     and it shall devour the strongholds
     of Jerusalem.][g]

6 Thus Yahweh has said:

For three crimes of Israel
     and for four, I will not take it back,
because they sell[h] the innocent for[i]
silver
         and the needy for[i] a pair of san-
         dals.

7 They[j] <trample>[k] [on the dust of the
     earth][l] upon[m] the head of the poor,
         and they pervert[n] the way (to
         justice) of the oppressed.[o]
     A man and his father copulate with
     the (same) maiden,
         [in order to profane my holy
         name.][p]

Jacob, Carl A. Keller, and Samuel Amsler, *Osée,
Joël, Amos, Abdias, Jonas*, Commentaire de l'Ancien
Testament 11a [Neuchâtel: Delachaux & Niestlé,
1965]).

f This unique occurrence of כְּזָבִים with the connotation "idols" corresponds to the use of הֲבָלִים in the
   Deuteronomistic History (Dtn 32:21; 1 Kgs 16:13,
   26; 2 Kgs 17:15; cf. also Jer 2:5; 8:19; 14:22; Jon
   2:9 [8]; Ps 31:7 [6]). Accordingly G offers equivalent translations here (τὰ μάταια αὐτῶν ["their fol-
   lies"]) and in 1 Kgs 16:13, 36; as well as in 2 Kgs
   17:15 (where, moreover, the Hebrew expression is
   הָלַךְ אַחֲרֵי הַהֶבֶל).

g On the secondary character of 2:4–5, see pp. 139–
   40.

h On the form, cf. Joüon, par. 65b; in view of the
   many parallels there cited for vowel interchange in
   the qal infinitive construct, it is quite improbable
   that מכר should here be read with other than its
   usual sense—i.e., that it should be interpreted in the
   sense of קנה (8:6 = "to acquire") (so Ehrlich, *Randglossen* 5, 230–31; Neher, *Amos*, 54). Cf. also the
   versions.

i בעבור interchanges with בּ *pretii* as in 8:6; cf. Sir
   7:18 (ב) and 38:17 (בעבור). As a generic term, כסף is
   treated as definite (Brockelmann, *Syntax*, par. 21cβ).

j The participial construction here continues the
   words of accusation begun in 2:6b ("because..."),
   just as 6:1b + 3–6 continues the woe-cry in 6:1a; as
   in 6:6a, an imperfect follows.

k שׁאף ("to gasp, pant after") always takes an accusative ("air" Jer 2:24; 14:6; cf. Is 42:14; "shade"
   Job 7:2; "night" Job 36:20), even when it means
   "to ambush, persecute" (Ezek 36:3; Ps 56:2–3
   [1–2]), which meaning must be assumed for M here
   as in 8:4. More probably we should read הַשָּׁאפִים,
   with G (τὰ πατοῦντα ["those treading"]), deriving
   the form from the much rarer root שׁוף I, attested
   only in Gen 3:15. M could then be explained as a
   misreading of an older linear vocalization, in favor
   of the more frequently attested vocable.

l This addition, already underlying G (ἐπὶ τὸν χοῦν
   τῆς γῆς), confirms our tentative interpretation of the
   participle (see the preceding note) by explaining
   that the head of the poor is treated as dirt. But the
   gloss destroys the bicolon and requires an additional
   verb for a smooth reading—which G hence also introduces (καὶ ἐκονδύλιζον = "and who slap"), thereby mitigating the terse original text.

m When used with verbs denoting attack, בּ conveys a
   hostile "against" (Koehler-Baumgartner, 103 #10),
   as in 1 Kgs 2:44b; Nu 22:6; Josh 11:7; and 2 Sam
   18:28; cf. Brockelmann, *Syntax*, par. 106h.

n The sense and usage of the word correspond to 5:12;
   Prv 17:23; 18:5; and Dtn 16:19.

o On the meaning of the word cf. Lienhard Delekat,
   "Zum hebräischen Wörterbuch," *VT* 14 (1964):
   44–45.

p The expression חלל את־שם קדשׁי belongs to the

8

<. . .>^q garments taken in pledge
they spread out
    [beside every altar,]^r
and wine of those mulcted they
drink
    [in the house of their God].^r

9

Yet I myself destroyed the Amorite
on their behalf,^s
    whose height was like the height of
    cedars,
      and who was as strong as oaks;
    but I destroyed his fruit above
      and his roots beneath.

10

[And I myself brought you up from the
land of Egypt and led you forty years
through the wilderness, to possess the
land of the Amorite. /11 And I installed
^tprophets among^u your sons and
^tNazirites^v among^u your youth. Was it
not indeed so, sons of Israel?— utter-
ance of Yahweh. /12 But you made the
Nazirites drink wine, and the prophets
you commanded, 'Do not prophesy!']^w

13

Hence, I break open^x beneath you,^y
    just as the cart breaks open,
      (the cart) which is full of sheaves.

14

Then refuge shall vanish from the swift
    and as for the strong,
      his might shall give no support
        [and the warrior shall not save
        his own life].^z

---

language of Ezekiel (20:39; 36:20–22; cf. Zimmerli, *Ezechiel*, 457, and also 466 on Ezek 20:9) and the Holiness Code (Lev 20:3; 22:2, 32). The use of למען as a means of attachment is also a favorite device in the book of Ezekiel (more than thirty occurrences), though it is even more frequent in the Deuteronomic–Deuteronomistic didactic style.

q *G* does not presuppose על here. The hip'il of נטה is elsewhere used transitively, and not of human beings who "stretch themselves out"; cf. 2:7aβ and 5:12bβ. It is likely that על־ was inserted (to facilitate the semantic connection of v 8a with v 7b) along with the additions in 2:7bβ and 2:8aβ, 8bβ.

r Like the addition in 2:7bβ, the references to cult places in v 8 are interpretations of Amos on the basis of Hosea (e.g., Hos 4:13–14) (Marti; Duhm, "Anmerkungen," 3–4; Albrecht Alt, as cited in Kurt Galling, "Bethel und Gilgal II," *ZDPV* 67 [1944], 37–38). Without them, a bicolon comparable to those in 2:6 and 2:7a emerges. The last segment (v 8bβ) lacks a preposition. Originally these two additions probably belonged together ("beside every altar in the house of their God") and were only secondarily separated.

s Here מִפְּנֵי does not merely have a spatial sense ("in front of") but emphasizes the personal motive, as in Hos 10:15; Gen 6:13; and Dtn 28:20. Following Duhm ("Anmerkungen," 4) the suffix is often read as second masculine plural (מִפְּנֵיכֶם). Yet prior to this, those being accused are never directly addressed; only with the inserted section in 2:10–12 is there a shift to direct address.

t The function of the noun, as the purpose and goal of the verbal action, is introduced by the preposition ל (Brockelmann, *Syntax*, par. 107b).

u מִן is used here in its basic partitive sense "a part of" = "some of," as in Ex 16:27; 17:5; etc. (Brockelmann, *Syntax*, par. 111a).

v *G* (εἰς ἁγιασμόν ["for sanctification"]) probably did not take נזירים as an abstract plural, since it correctly renders the same plural form in 2:12 (and in Lev 25:11); rather, it is more likely that a mutilated text was read as נֵזֶר (cf. Lev 21:12; Zech 9:16).

w On the secondary character of 2:10–12 see pp. 141–42.

x *G* (κυλίω = "I turn, roll") reflects the picture of a rolling wagon, as do also α' (τριζήσω ["I will clatter"]) and *V* (*stridebo* ["I will grind, creak"]). For an interpretation of this difficult Hebrew word as the "digging in" of wheels, "ploughing up" or "tearing open" the ground, see Gese, "Beiträge," 417–24.

y Since up to 2:9 (and also in the continuation of our oracle) direct address is not employed, we must reckon with the possibility that the original reading was תַּחְתֵּיהֶם, the present *M* text being an accommodation to the insertion in 2:10–12, composed in the parenetic style; see pp. 142–43.

z 2:14b and 2:15aβ are probably additions, included in the interest of plerophory, since: (1) their vocabu-

15 He who wields the bow shall not prevail,[aa]
　　[and the swift shall not ⟨save himself⟩[bb] with his feet,][cc]
　even he who guides[dd] the horse shall not save his own life.

16 As for the (most) stouthearted[ee] among the warriors,
　naked he shall flee on that day

　　　　—oracle of Yahweh.

lary has been derived almost entirely from the context; (2) the threefold repetition of (נפשׁו) לא ימלט would be unusual for Amos; and (3) the two sentences disturb the parallelism of the clearly coordinated bicola in 2:14–15, as well as the climactic structure of 2:14–16—the swift // the strong : : the bowman // the charioteer : : the most stouthearted of the warriors.

aa　עמד ("to stand") in the sense of "to have endurance" (2 Kgs 6:31; Ps 33:11; Job 8:15), "to remain alive" (Ex 21:21), "to stand one's ground in battle" (Ezek 13:5).

bb　G (οὐ μὴ διασωθῇ) presupposes a nip'al vocalization, יִמָּלֵט. M has probably been influenced by 2:14b.

cc　See textual note "z" to 2:14.

dd　רכב describes first and fundamentally "driving," and only secondarily "riding"; cf. Kurt Galling, "Der Ehrenname Elisas und die Entrückung Elias," ZThK 53 (1956): 131. See pp. 171–72.

ee　Literally "the one who is strong with respect to his heart"; cf. Brockelmann, *Syntax*, pars. 71a, 77–78. G (καὶ εὑρήσει τὴν καρδίαν αὐτοῦ ἐν δυναστείαις ["and he will find his heart in mighty–deeds"]) misconstrues the initial word (וְיִמְצָא) and must then reinterpret בגבורים with the sense of בַּגְּבוּרוֹת (cf. Na 2:4 [3]). On the attempts at correction within the G tradition, cf. Ziegler, *Duodecim prophetae*, 185–86: G[BC], and V, as well as some other witnesses, add ὁ κραταιός ["the strong one"] before the verb, while the Lucianic witnesses, G[B*] and others also add the negative οὐ μή; the Hexaplaric text (εὑρεθῇ ἡ καρδία ["he whose heart is found"]) restores the correct sense by vocalizing יִמָּצֵא. α' and σ' confirm M.

Form

The strict formal similarities shown by the individual oracles identify our long section as a cohesive unit of tradition. To be sure, the last oracle is much more comprehensive than all the preceding ones, exhibiting new elements of form and content (2:7–8, 9, 13–16), but at no point within it can an incipit, comparable to that in 3:1, be recognized.

A. The Form of the Individual Oracles.

I.
The oracles concerning the Arameans (1:3–5), the Philistines (1:6–8), the Ammonites (1:13–15), and the Moabites (2:1–3) are completely uniform in structure. Each contains these five elements: 1. The formula which introduces messenger speech; 2. The general proclamation of irrevocable judgments; 3. The specific indictment charging guilt; 4. The specific articulation of the announcement of punishment; 5. The formula which concludes messenger speech. The first, second and fifth elements are identically worded in all the oracles, the only exception being the different proper names in the second element. The third and fourth elements exhibit uniformity in syntax and size, as well as largely identical wording in the first bicolon of the announcement of punishment.

1. Within the corpus of the collections of prophetic oracles, the formula which introduces messenger speech—"Thus Yahweh has said" (כה אמר יהוה)—appears for the first time in the book of Amos. Although divine

first person address is common in Hosea,[1] this formula (which is one of the most important aids for determining oracular boundaries and subdivisions) is absent there. It occurs in eleven genuine oracles of Amos (1:3, 6, 13; 2:1, 6; 3:11, 12; 5:3, 4, 16; 7:17) and in three oracles which are later additions (1:9, 11; 2:4). Apart from chaps. 1—2, this formula unequivocally designates the beginning of a new oracle only in 3:12. Otherwise it is preceded by a conjunction, in three cases by "therefore" (לָכֵן 3:11; 5:16; 7:17) and twice by "for" (כִּי 5:3, 4). With the exception of 5:4, the formula introducing messenger speech is thereby specifically attached to the oracular element of the announcement of punishment.

The prehistory of this formula must be sought in the general and widespread practice of message transmission.[2] Gen 32:4–6 [3–5] and Ju 11:14–15 offer vivid illustrations. Here, within the larger framework of accounts describing the sending of messengers, the formula's derivation from the actual commissioning of a messenger is readily apparent. The association in the account itself of the commissioning speech ("X spoke to Y: You shall say to Z") with the messenger speech formula *per se* ("Thus X has said") (Gen 32:5 [4]) is later encountered frequently in Jeremiah[3] and Ezekiel.[4] This association ultimately reflects the style of discourse appropriate to international diplomatic exchange. The ambassadorial style has survived in literary form, especially in communiques such as the letter of Itur-asdu to king Zimri–lim of Mari: "To my lord say: Thus says your servant Itur–asdu."[5] The formula's life-setting in oral communication is quite vividly depicted in the Isaiah–narratives of the Deuteronomistic History. The messenger of Sennacherib calls to the people of Jerusalem: "Say to Hezekiah: Thus the Great King has said" (2 Kgs 18:19).[6] Hezekiah later sends messengers to the prophet Isaiah: "And they said to him: Thus Hezekiah has said . . ." (2 Kgs 19:3). The prophet begins his response: "Say to your master: Thus Yahweh has said . . ." (2 Kgs 19:6). Here the narrative context demonstrates that the prophetic messenger–speech formula originates in the style of general diplomatic communication. The book of Amos itself confirms these findings. The chief priest Amaziah employs the formula when reporting the words of the prophet to king Jeroboam: "Thus Amos has said" (7:11). Even though Amos is here not the sender, nevertheless the use of the formula shows how firmly it was anchored in the general practice of message transmission:

Friedrich Baumgärtel has attempted to determine even more precisely the provenance of the specifically prophetic messenger–speech formula "Thus Yahweh has said."[7] He seeks it in the sacerdotal realm—more specifically, in an oracular ritual connected with the ark. He claims that the divine name "Yahweh Sabaoth" (יהוה צבאות), attached to the ark, occurs particularly in combination with the formula כה אמר.[8] Yet against Baumgärtel's view we must consider, on the one hand, that this combined expression is first attested more than twice in the books of Jeremiah (fifty–five times), Haggai (five times), and Zechariah (seventeen times), whereas in association with the ark traditions it occurs only in

---

1 See Wolff, *Hosea*, xxiii [xiv–xv].
2 Studies during the past half century have amply demonstrated the point, beginning with that of Ludwig Koehler, *Deuterojesaja (Jes. 40–55) stilkritisch untersucht*, BZAW 37 (Giessen, 1923), 102–09; more recently, Claus Westermann, *Basic Forms of Prophetic Speech*, tr. Hugh Clayton White (Philadelphia: Westminster, 1967), 99–115 [*Grundformen prophetischer Rede*, BEvTh 31 (München: Chr. Kaiser, ²1964), 71–82]; cf. Zimmerli, *Ezechiel*, 73.
3 Jer 2:1–2; 8:4; 10:1–2; etc.
4 Ezek 2:4; 3:10–11, 27; etc.
5 As cited by Wolfram von Soden, "Verkündigung des Gotteswillens durch prophetisches Wort in den altbabylonischen Briefen aus Mâri," *WO* 1 (1947–52): 398. Other examples are given by Ludwig Koehler, *Deuterojesaja (Jes. 40–55) stilkritisch unter-*

sucht, BZAW 37 (Giessen, 1923), 102. Note further Georges Dossin, *et al.*, *Textes divers*, ARM(T) 13 (Paris: Imprimerie Nationale, 1964), 23.1–2 and 114.10; on which see Hermann Schult, "Vier weitere Mari–Briefe 'prophetischen' Inhalts," *ZDPV* 82 (1966): 228–32 [cf. William L. Moran, *ANET*³, 624 and 625].
6 Similarly 2 Kgs 18:29, 31: "Thus the king of Assyria has said."
7 Cf. Baumgärtel, "Formel," 277–90; and *idem*, "Gottesnamen," 1–29.
8 *Ibid.*, 20–21.

136

isolated instances.[9] On the other hand, in Amos (where we find the earliest datable occurrences of the messenger–speech formula in significant number) the simpler form "Thus Yahweh has said" (כה אמר יהוה) is attested ten times, in contrast to the single occurrence (5:16) of the expanded form "Thus Yahweh, God of Hosts, has said" (כה אמר יהוה אלהי צבאות). Furthermore, the expansion here is very probably secondary.[10] Thus it is unlikely that Amos borrowed this formula from some cultic oracular style. Moreover, Baumgärtel's designation "oracle formula" (Orakelformel) is not especially apt since the messages so introduced are scarcely ever responses to inquiries.

Our preference for the designation "messenger–speech formula" (Botenspruchformel) also has significance for translation. As has been indicated, the formula is primarily associated with the practice of sending messengers.[11] Its utterance at the time a message is delivered recalls the earlier event of commissioning. Therefore, ordinarily the rendition "Thus Yahweh has said" recommends itself; in 7:11, certainly, כה אמר עמוס must be translated "thus Amos has said."[12]

2. The general proclamation of irrevocable judgment invariably reads: "For three crimes of X and for four, I will not take it back." This first sentence of the messenger speeches summarizes—though somewhat enigmatically—the basis for and the inevitability of impending punishment. The shape of the first segment in particular has obviously been dictated by a firmly established tradition of speech, especially since in each case only one transgression is subsequently treated.

The graduated numerical saying must be presupposed by the reference to "three crimes and four."[13] The graduated numerical saying collocates phenomena, forming a sequence in which their number is preceded by a citation of the next lower number, along with an indication of how the phenomena are associated. Examples range from the numerical sequence one–two (Ps 62:12–13 [11–12]; Job 33:14–15), to the sequence nine–ten (Sir 25:7–11). However, the sequence three–four which appears in Amos is also the one most frequently encountered elsewhere.[14] (Four items can be enumerated on the fingers of one hand, and are thus easily remembered.) Such sayings as these must have been more popular than the literary remains would lead us to suspect. Otherwise, Amos could not have employed graduated numerical sayings with such matter–of–factness.

The enumerated phenomena can, in principle, belong to any realm of life, such as nature (Prv 30:15–16), ethnology (Sir 50:25–26), or theology (Ps 62:12–13 [11–12]; Job 5:19–27; 33:14–15). However, for pedagogical reasons the numerical sequences most often deal with the affairs of human life in community, especially proper and wicked conduct. This is also the case with the only known extra–biblical examples of the graduated numerical saying: one saying of Aḥiqar (6.92–93) designates three modes of conduct which delight Shamash;[15] a Ugaritic saying names three kinds of misdemeanor (at the sacrificial meal) which Baal hates.[16] In the Old Testament, graduated numerical sayings enumerating instances of good behavior[17]

---

9 2 Sam 7:8, and occasionally elsewhere in the older literature.

10 See textual note "hh" to 5:16.

11 See p. 136.

12 Cf. Zimmerli, *Ezechiel*, 73; Westermann, *Basic Forms*, 101–102 [72]; and A. H. van Zyl, "The Message Formula in the Book of Judges" in *Ou Testamentiese Werkgemeenskap in Suid-Afrika: Papers Read at the 2nd Meeting* (Potchefstroom: Rege-Pers Beperk, 1959), 61–64.

13 Cf. Wolfgang M. W. Roth, "The Numerical Sequence x / x + 1 in the Old Testament," *VT* 12 (1962): 300–11; Georg Sauer, *Die Sprüche Agurs. Untersuchungen zur Herkunft, Verbreitung und Bedeutung einer biblischen Stilform unter besonderer Berücksichtigung von Proverbia c. 30*, BWANT 84 (Stuttgart: W. Kohlhammer, 1963); Wolff, *Amos the Prophet*, 34–44 [24–

30]; and Wolfgang M. W. Roth, *Numerical Sayings in the Old Testament*, SVT 13 (Leiden: E. J. Brill, 1965).

14 Prv 30:15–16, 18–19, 21–23, 29–31; Sir 26:5–6.

15 Translations: H. L. Ginsberg, *ANET*[3], 428; *AOT*[2], 457.

16 *CTA* 4 (= *UT* 51).3.17–21; cf. Cyrus H. Gordon, *Ugaritic Textbook*, AnOr 38 (Roma: Pontificium Institutum Biblicum, 1965), 44 (par. 7.9).

17 Sir 25:7–11.

are less common than those listing examples of wicked behavior.[18] Therefore we are not surprised that the graduated numerical sayings used by Amos refer to crimes.

Amos makes use of these sayings, but he does not follow through with them. How are we to explain the fact that in the oracles against foreign nations Amos initially refers to a sequence of three–four transgressions, but then specifies only one? After stating the numbers of phenomena involved (x and x + 1), the regular graduated numerical saying always proceeds to enumerate the larger figure (x + 1) and never merely the smaller number of phenomena (x).[19] And yet the introductory numerical citations in the stricter form of the saying already imply special emphasis on the culminating phenomenon (x + 1). Indeed we are able to demonstrate, from the few graduated numerical sayings preserved for us, that the culminating item is often clearly distinguished from those (x) preceding it. Thus each of the sayings in Prv 30:18–19 and 29–31 presents an initial list of three non–human phenomena, and then adds as fourth in the sequence a corresponding mode of human behavior. More important for our purpose are sayings which enumerate wrong actions in such a way that the final one is singularly climactic.

Sir 26:5–6:
Before three things my heart trembles,
    before a fourth I am very frightened:
Public slander, the rousing of a rabble,
and false witness—
    all these are more pernicious than death.
But a jealous wife creates heartache and woe,
    and the lashing of (her) tongue
    broadcasts to everyone.

Sir 23:16–21 castigates onanism (v 16b) and fornication (v 17), but then it singles out adultery for especially severe condemnation (vv 18–21). In Sir 26:28 emphasis is quite clearly placed on the concluding item:

Concerning two things my heart is grieved,
    but concerning a third my wrath is aroused:
when a man of means is reduced to poverty,
    when men of understanding are treated
    contemptuously;
but when a man turns from righteousness to sin—
    may the Lord prepare him for the sword!

Only the last clause has to do with an actual crime which merits divine punishment.[20] The graduated numerical sayings to which Amos alludes must formerly have been of similar types. He cites explicitly only the last of four crimes, the one which tips, indeed overloads, the scales, rendering Yahweh's direct intervention unavoidable.

It is thus quite evident that Amos fashioned the introductory formal element of our oracles out of generally familiar traditional material which was particularly well suited for oral transmission, since the numerical scheme facilitated memorization. If the genre developed from the riddle, as Eissfeldt assumes,[21] then its catechetical function becomes even more understandable. It, like "the wisdom of the sons of the east,"[22] must have been known not only in Israel, but also among the kindred peoples who were Israel's neighbors. Since we nowhere find our genre attested in cultic texts, and since no trace of it is to be found elsewhere in preexilic literature, it is most likely that Amos here adapted for his own purposes an element traditionally associated with popular wisdom instruction.

The play on the graduated numerical saying is subordinated to the proclamation that the punishment, later to be announced in detail, is irrevocable. "I will not take it back" (לא אשיבנו) strikes a sombre introductory note.[23] This prefatory stereotyped formula, declaring that the impending judgment is irrevocable, provides an initial indication of the incisiveness and inflexible assertiveness of Amos' mode of address. Hos 5:9b is perhaps comparable: "Among the tribes of Israel I proclaim what is sure."[24] But alongside this

---

18 Prv 6:16–19; 30:21–23; Sir 23:16–21; 26:5–6, 28; 50:25–26.

19 Cf. Prv 6:16–19; 30:15–16, 18–19, 21–23, 29–31; Sir 26:5–6.

20 Cf. Wolff, *Amos the Prophet*, 38–42 [26–29].

21 *The Old Testament*, 85–86 [114–15].

22 1 Kgs 5:10 [4:30]; Prv 30:15ff.

23 On the translation of שוב in the hip'il, see textual note "b" to 1:3.

24 See Wolff, *Hosea*, 113 [144].

affirmative concluding formula (phrased in the perfect tense), Amos' veiled, anticipatory imperfect tense—coming at the outset of the messenger speech—is more ominous by far.

As for poetic structure, the prefatory proclamation is formulated as a bicolon exhibiting a progressive parallelism, in which the second line repeats the motivating element ("for, because" [על] with numeral) of the first line and then continues on to state the threat. In the midst of polysyllabic beats, the monosyllabically syncopated "not" (לא) carries the heaviest stress. In a quite formal way the negative plays a dominant role in the book of Amos right from the outset.

3. The specific indictment, charging guilt, corresponds to the syntactical structure of the veiled proclamation; the decisive crime is now first revealed. Specifically, the preposition על is repeated, but this time it is linked to an infinitive construct (describing the offending act) plus pronominal suffix. Syntactically the infinitive clause is more closely connected with the preceding clause than with the following one. The line as introduced by the preposition forms a prosodic unit of five or six beats, again exhibiting a sort of progressive parallelism (this time echoing the whole of the preceding bicolon) which independently proceeds to articulate the charge previously unspecified.

4. The specific articulation of the announcement of punishment follows the charge identifying the decisive crime, and is the goal anticipated in the terse proclamation of irrevocable judgment. Thus the structure of the oracle shows that the prophet announces nothing other than a judgment which is well founded and therefore just. It is this announcement of Yahweh's punishment that finally represents the actual content of the messenger speech, the primary substance to be communicated. Here at last is the word which, according to the prefatory proclamation, Yahweh will not "take back." The emphasis this element receives, as that which is prefigured, and its dominant, culminating

position, mark it as the chief feature of each of the individual oracles. Employing the first–person style of messenger address, the punitive action is articulated in three bicola exhibiting synonymous parallelism throughout[25]—the initial bicolon in each of the four older oracles against foreign nations being worded identically except for the names. Near the end of each oracle those threatened become the subjects of declarative sentences (1:5b, 8bβ, 15; 2:2b). Thus are the consequences of Yahweh's intervention emphasized.

5. The formula which concludes messenger speech repeats "Yahweh has said" (אמר יהוה) from the introductory formula. Both formulas are extrametrical and together frame the five prosodic units of each oracle. (Most of the prosodic units are six–stress bicola; only the second prosodic unit of each oracle is not subdivided into parallel three–stress cola.) Altogether the concluding formula is found in eight authentic oracles of Amos.[26] Strangely enough, it is employed nowhere else in the preexilic prophetic literature. In Haggai, Zechariah, and Malachi it appears quite frequently, but usually in expanded form. Thus the terse concluding formula "Yahweh has said" (אמר יהוה) is to be regarded as a special characteristic of the oldest Amos–tradition which, according to 7:3 and 6, goes back to the prophet himself. It is only used to close the first–person announcements of God's future action, and it thereby serves as a counterpart to the characteristic role of the formula which introduces messenger speech.[27] Thus the formulas which frame the oracles generally function to emphasize that the announced action of Yahweh is the essential content of the messenger speeches.

II.

On purely formal grounds, the four strictly parallel oracles against foreign nations thus far treated (1:3–5, 6–8, 13–15; 2:1–3) can be distinguished from the oracles against Tyre (1:9–10), Edom (1:11–12), and Judah (2:4–5). Only the first two elements (the formula which introduces messenger speech, and the gen-

---

25   Differently, Hans Kosmala, "Form and Structure in Ancient Hebrew Poetry (A New Approach)," *VT* 14 (1964): 429.

26   I.e., in addition to its occurrences in the four older oracles against foreign nations (1:5, 8, 15; 2:3) it appears in 5:17, 27; 7:3, 6; and in expanded form it is found in the secondary conclusion to the book (9:15).

27   See p. 92.

eral proclamation of irrevocable judgment) reappear verbatim in these latter oracles. To be sure, they also introduce the third element (the specification of guilt) with על plus infinitive construct, but the infinitival clause *per se* is shortened, only to be expanded by one (1:9) or more (1:11; 2:4) verbal clauses (exhibiting perfect or imperfect consecutive forms). The fourth element (the announcement of punishment) in the latter group has been reduced in size by two-thirds, repeating in each case only the wording of the first bicolon of the element as attested in the four oracles against foreign nations already treated. The fifth element (the concluding messenger formula) is regularly omitted in the second group of three oracles.

The most striking feature among these formal variations is the elaboration of the indictment alongside the shortened announcement of punishment. The threat of Yahweh's intervention has acquired formulaic brevity; the description of its consequence for those threatened, which is never omitted in the oracles of the first group (1:5b, 8bβ, 15; 2:2b; cf. 2:14–16), is completely absent. The interest has shifted to the specification of guilt. No longer are separate criminal acts simply enumerated; now motives and subjective attitudes are described, with the help of the vocabulary of a specific type of piety. Such weighty differences in language alone make it necessary to draw literary-critical conclusions. In addition, the description of the crime in the oracle against Tyre (1:9bα) repeats almost verbatim the criminal charge made in the oracle against the Philistines (1:6b), while the accusation in the oracle against Edom (1:11bα) is substantially reminiscent of the charges leveled against Damascus (1:3b) and Amon (1:13b), although it is a pale generalization in comparison with the original formulations. Finally, the indictment in the oracle against Judah (2:4b) pertains only to its relationship with God (in contrast even to the oracle against Israel); at the same time the element violates the otherwise

accepted convention of messenger speech (2:4aα, 5) by naming Yahweh in the third person. Hence it is an inescapable conclusion that these three oracles must be considered later additions. This has been recognized with increasing clarity by Wellhausen, Marti, Nowack, Sellin, and Weiser, and has been demonstrated conclusively by Werner H. Schmidt.[28] The opponents of this position[29] have as a rule overlooked the form-critical arguments. Although Reventlow takes note of them, he is able to make his claim for a "uniformity of form"[30] in all of the individual oracles in 1:3—2:5 only by way of a large number of literary-critical emendations. He asserts not only that the "charge in each case originally comprised only a single sentence,"[31] but that "the announcement of punishment in its original form also consisted of a single sentence."[32] On the basis of this he consistently deletes as explanatory glosses the final two bicola (1:5, 8, 14b–15; 2:2b–3) in the announcements of punishment of the oracles against the Arameans, the Philistines, the Ammonites, and the Moabites, as well as all finite verbal clauses (1:9bβ, 11bα²–β; 2:4bα²–β) in the indictments of the oracles against Tyre, Edom, and Judah. These many deletions, without supporting text-critical evidence, are surely too high a price to pay for the uniformity in form of all the individual oracles. The distinctiveness of the two groups of oracles as transmitted is blurred without sufficient cause. In contrast, the isolation of a secondary stratum of three complete oracles is based not only on form-critical analysis of the transmitted text, but can be judiciously supported by linguistic and historical-theological considerations.[33] However, we ought to attribute to the secondary deposit neither more nor less than the oracles against Tyre, Edom, and Judah. Duhm wanted to separate the Philistine oracle (1:6–8) from the original stratum as well,[34] because it supposedly disturbed the "sequence of the threatened peoples."[35] Robinson wants to bracket out the Judah-oracle alone, since he gives major credence only to

---

28   "Redaktion," 174–78.
29   Among them, Karl Cramer, *Amos. Versuch einer theologischen Interpretation*, BWANT 51 (Stuttgart, 1930); and Neher, *Amos*.
30   *Amt*, 62.
31   *Ibid.*, 56.
32   *Ibid.*, 58.
33   Schmidt, "Redaktion," 184–85.
34   "Anmerkungen," 2; similarly Nowack.
35   On the "sequence" argument, see pp. 144–46.

"historical considerations."[36] But the form–critical and linguistic observations advanced above compel us to assign to a secondary deposit no more and no less than 1:9–12 and 2:4–5.

III.

What is the relationship of the oracle against Israel (2:6–16), considered first of all from a form–critical perspective, to the two strata thus far distinguished? At first glance it is apparent that here too only the first and second elements (the formula which introduces messenger speech and the general proclamation of irrevocable judgment) reappear verbatim. However, closer examination reveals that neither the third, fourth nor fifth element differs from its counterpart in the oracles of the original stratum in the way that distinguished the oracles against Tyre, Edom, and Judah. The following special features of the oracle merit comment:

1. The specification of guilt exhibits two types of elaboration. a) Four prosodic units are devoted to enumerating a whole series of criminal acts. The first unit (2:6b) is formulated in accord with the pattern established in the preceding oracles—i.e., with the preposition על plus infinitive construct. The expansion which follows differs in both content and form from the type found in the group of secondary oracles. Here, rather than motives being attributed to particular crimes, additional specific crimes are cited.[37] This extension of the list of accusations exhibits neither perfect nor imperfect consecutive verbal forms; instead, the expansion is introduced by a participial form (2:7a) and is then continued by imperfect verbs. Elsewhere in speeches of accusation Amos displays a similar inclination to use participial forms (4:1aβ–b; 5:7; 6:13; [8:4]). This is especially the case in the woe–cries (5:18; 6:1, 3–6) where, on occasion, the participle may be continued by an imperfect (6:6a). Like the numerical saying, the series of woe–cries enumerates unjust deeds.[38] Moreover, it is probably not incidental

that Prv 6:16–19 preserves a graduated numerical saying in which deeds hateful to Yahweh are enumerated, using participial forms. Hence we may suppose that it was this genre of speech—to which also 2:6a explicitly points—that inspired the use of a participle to introduce an expansion of the indictment. It is therefore unlikely that 2:7 begins a completely new oracle (which perhaps might have been a woe–cry originally) and that the old oracle against Israel is preserved only as a fragment in 2:6.[39] On the contrary, from the standpoint of both style and content the extension of the list of crimes in 2:6b–8 is more clearly patterned after an expanded four–part graduated numerical saying than are all the preceding oracles of Amos against foreign nations, let alone those oracles belonging to the secondary group. We have to do here with a genuine formal development which must be attributed to Amos himself. Metrically, the old text of the section (apart from 2:7b) is structured into bicola exhibiting synonymous parallelism.

b) A second type of elaboration is found in the continuation of the indictment in 2:9, where the accusation is intensified in a wholly novel way by contrasting the deeds of Israel with God's former action on Israel's behalf.[40] An initial four–stress colon identifies God's act, the first–person style effectively emphasizing the role of Yahweh. The magnitude of the event is underscored in the two following prosodic units, each a bicolon exhibiting synonymous parallelism.

In contrast, the verses which follow (2:10–12) exhibit a predominantly prosaic style. There are additional indications of the secondary character of the verses: a shift to direct address is attested by all of them; using traditional language, 2:10 recalls the exodus and wilderness traditions, before coming back in the final clause to the tradition of the granting of the land which alone had been treated in 2:9; and 2:11, which is emphatically parenetic, reverts to the specification of guilt that had been concluded in 2:6b–8. As regards

---

36 Robinson, 76; cf. also Maag, *Text*, 8. See below, pp. 151–52.

37 Only in material that is manifestly secondary to the oracle do we find instead specific charges being elaborated; see textual notes "p" to 2:7bβ, and "r" to 2:8aβ and 8bβ.

38 Cf. Wolff, *Amos the Prophet*, 17–34 [12–23].

39 As supposed by Reventlow, *Amt*, 57–58.

40 See Westermann, "Die Mari–Briefe und die Prophetie in Israel" in *Forschung*, 182; and *idem*, "Vergegenwärtigung der Geschichte in den Psalmen" in *Forschung*, 329 (reprinted from *Zwischenstation. Festschrift für Karl Kupisch zum 60. Geburtstag*, ed. Ernst Wolff [München: Chr. Kaiser, 1963], 275).

content as well, these verses are best explained as later supplements to the oracle.[41] They supply additional historical particulars which reinforce Amos' own intention to display Israel's guilt prominently, not only by elaborately compiling her various crimes but by stressing the saving acts of God on Israel's behalf against powerful foreign nations.

2. On formal grounds alone the announcement of punishment in 2:13–16 must be clearly distinguished from those in the preceding oracles. While in the secondary oracles this element was reduced in size from three prosodic units to one, in the case of the oracle against Israel it has been expanded to five units, consisting for the most part of bicola exhibiting clear synonymous parallelism. The initial unit stands out in many respects. It abandons the stereotyped threat adopted even in the secondary oracles. It displays a rhythmic and stylistic relationship to 2:9a (the statement of God's fundamental salvific action) which, originally, immediately preceded it. Here too the initial prosodic unit consists of a single colon of four stresses. Here too follows a bicolon (only one in this case to be sure!) that employs a simile to elucidate Yahweh's action. Here there is an even stronger initial emphasis upon Yahweh as speaker than in 2:9a. For, while in 2:9 a contrast was drawn between Israel's deeds and Yahweh's former action, now we encounter a wholly new first-person introduction, appropriate to the announcement of the wholly new action of Yahweh. The new act is to be one of judgment, and as such it stands in contrast to the earlier salvific intervention of God.

הנה in Amos

הנה אנכי מעיק ("Hence, I break open") is reminiscent of the construction הִנְנִי plus a participle, which later gained currency as a major formal characteristic of the "oracle answering a plea."[42] Elsewhere in Amos this shorter form, with pronominal suffix, appears in

6:14 and 7:8, while the full form with the independent pronoun "I" (אנכי) recurs in 9:9. הִנֵּה יָמִים בָּאִים ("Hence / so! Days are coming [when . . .]") is found at the beginning of divine utterances in 4:2; 8:11; and [9:13]. It is interesting that the immediate contexts of these latter passages also attest the interpolated or concluding "divine oracle formula" (נאם יהוה) which is similarly present at the end of the section 2:13–16.[43] הנה introduces a third-person reference to Yahweh's action in 6:11 and 9:8 (and in [4:13] as well). וְהִנֵּה occupies a fixed position in the first four vision reports, where it introduces that which Yahweh shows to the prophet (7:1, 4, 7; 8:1), thus functioning in the same way it does in the old dream narratives.[44]

This survey indicates that הנה occurs seven times in Amos at the beginning of a divine utterance (הנה אנכי 2:13; 9:9; הנני 6:14; 7:8; הנה ימים באים 4:2; 8:11; [9:13]), four times in the vision reports as a device to arouse the prophet's attention to that which Yahweh is showing him (7:1, 4, 7; 8:1), and three times in third-person references to acts of Yahweh ([4:13]; 6:11; 9:8). We may conclude from this: 1. הנה in Amos is always associated with Yahweh and his revelatory activity. It calls attention exclusively to *God's* action. 2. A strictly formulaic usage cannot be discerned; in its fourteen occurrences (at least two of which are secondary) it appears in no less than five different combinations. Such linguistic vitality warns against the attempt to see behind Amos' usage a cultic formulary. 3. הנה in Amos is attested significantly often (five times) in the visions. Interestingly enough, it is here too that we discern a shift in the function of הנה, from stressing the content of the vision per se (7:1, 4, 7; 8:1) to emphasizing at the outset of divine speech the self-proclamation of God's impending activity (7:8). The latter function is also attested in 2:13; 6:14; and 9:9; and is similarly apparent in 4:2; 8:11; and [9:13]. In the authentic oracles of Amos, הנה always introduces an announcement of judgment. Thus הנה אנכי and הנני plus participle belong to the prehistory of the subsequently familiar form of the "oracle answering a plea."[45]

In 2:13 הנה signals the beginning of the actual divine message. Whether there is here an accompanying shift to direct address must remain uncertain,[46] es-

---

41 Cf. the carefully detailed discussion of Schmidt, "Redaktion," 178–83.

42 See pp. 57–58, on Joel 2:19; and Wolff, *Hosea*, 36 [43], on Hos 2:8.

43 The divine oracle formula appears as a secondary addition in 6:14.

44 Cf. Gen 28:12 and 37:7. Cf. also Hans Walter Wolff, *Frieden ohne Ende: Jesaja 7:1–17 und 9:1–6 ausgelegt,*

BSt 35 (Neukirchen–Vluyn: Neukirchener Verlag, 1962), 35, 38–39.

45 See p. 58.

46 Despite 4:2 and 6:14. See textual note "y" to 2:13.

pecially since תחתיהם ("beneath *them*") in 2:13a would provide a better counterpart (within the framework of the two contrasting sections) to מפניהם ("on *their* behalf") in 2:9a. Although only one bicolon further describes Yahweh's action in 2:13 (in contrast to the two elaborating bicola which follow the initial colon in 2:9), three additional bicola are attached in 2:14–16, depicting the consequences of Yahweh's action. The recipients of the divine judgment become the subjects of these latter bicola. Thus once again in the Israel oracle a structural element is enlarged; the elaboration of this particular element, while a constant feature of the four older oracles against foreign nations,[47] is uniformly absent in the group of younger oracles.[48]

3. The divine oracle formula, נאם יהוה ("oracle / utterance of Yahweh"), appears in the oracle against Israel in place of the formula which concludes messenger speech, אמר יהוה ("Yahweh has said"), as attested in 1:5, 8, 15; and 2:3. The three younger oracles are without concluding formulas (1:10, 12; 2:5). Why does the divine oracle formula stand at the end of the oracle against Israel, and to whom is its presence to be attributed? These questions can be answered only after surveying all occurrences of the formula in the book of Amos.

נאם יהוה in the Book of Amos

The formula occurs a total of twenty–one times in Amos. It appears thirteen times at the conclusion of an oracle (2:[11], 16; 3:15; 4:3, 5, 6, 8, 9, 10, 11; 9:7, 8, [12]), three times in a medial position (3:10; 6:14; 8:3), and five times together with other formulas as part of an oracular introduction (3:13; 6:8; 8:9, 11; [9:13]). The medial and introductory occurrences can in each case be assigned to later redactional activity (as will be shown in commenting on the individual texts). Even when it stands in final position the formula may be secondary, as it is at least in 2:11 and 9:12. That no less than half of the formula's occurrences in the book were added after the time of Amos

is in accord with the observation that the formula is not frequently attested elsewhere prior to Jeremiah (169 occurrences) and Ezekiel (85 occurrences).[49]

Regarding the remaining occurrences in Amos, it is often difficult to decide in a given case whether the formula belongs to a stage of literary redaction or to an old oracle of Amos. Especially in 9:7 and 3:15 the formula would seem to be an indispensable accompaniment to the oral proclamation of the oracles, since in neither case is the speaker otherwise identified with Yahweh by means of a framework formula. This observation necessitates that we reckon with the possibility that Amos himself may elsewhere have used the formula, albeit only at the conclusion of an oracle. Accordingly, it is probable that the divine oracle formula in 2:16 also derives from Amos himself, especially since the four preceding oracles against foreign nations attributable to him likewise exhibit a concluding formula.

It is possible that the expression נאם יהוה as such either originated with Amos or belonged to the particular stock of traditions upon which he drew. For, the precise expression is not attested in any text securely datable before the time of Amos (Ps 110:1?), nor is it identifiable as belonging to the language of earlier, specifically Israelite cultic proclamation. נאם is associated with human speakers in Nu 24:3–4, 15–16 and 2 Sam 23:1, which is likewise true in the sapiential realm according to Prv 30:1. These references to sayings of Balaam, David, and Agur direct us toward ancient Near Eastern circles of seers and wise men who were already regarded, at least in part, as belonging to antiquity by the eighth century. The formula is found only at the beginning of sayings in the cases just noted. Amos uses the formula exclusively at the conclusion of oracles. With the help of the archaic word נאם ("oracle / utterance") he has created a linguistically novel parallel to אמר יהוה ("Yahweh has said"), the formula which he most often employs to conclude messenger speech. (Or, if he did not coin a new formula it is he, at least, who has demonstrably made ample use of it for the first time.) Using this divine oracle formula, Amos is able to give a striking, indeed ceremonial emphasis to the conclusion of the oracle against Israel, which is the apex of the entire oracular series.

47 See p. 139.
48 See p. 140.
49 Cf. Rolf Rendtorff, "Zum Gebrauch der Formel ne'um jahve im Jeremiabuch," *ZAW* 66 (1954): 27–37, especially 27–28 (reprinted in *idem*, *Gesammelte Studien zum Alten Testament*, ThB 57 [München: Chr. Kaiser, 1975], 256–266); Baumgärtel, "Formel," 277–90; and Westermann, *Basic Forms*, 188–89

[135–36]. On the expansion of the formula, see the excursus on יהוה (אלהי) (ה)צבאות, pp. 287–88.

143

Thus, the divine oracle formula is the last among many enhancements evident in the oracle against Israel. In comparison with the formula which concludes messenger speech, it sustains a more solemn affirmation of the certainty that it is Yahweh himself who confronts Israel through the prophetic oracle. The probability is, therefore, that rather than being redactional, the use of the formula here goes back to Amos himself.

B. The Form of the Composition.

Investigation of the individual oracles has shown that a distinction must be made between the structurally homogeneous oracles against Damascus, the Philistines, the Ammonites, and the Moabites on the one hand, and those against Tyre, Edom, and Judah on the other. The oracle against Israel falls into neither group. The group consisting of three oracles is shown to be secondary by its word–borrowings and its stylistic irregularities, both of which are factors betraying a lack of originality. Even a comparison to the group of four on strictly formal grounds reveals in the group of three a twofold reorientation. This latter group shifts the emphasis of the message from the punishment to the crime. The consequences of the punishment are no longer designated, but the motives for the crimes are specified. The oracle against Israel, on the other hand, stands in a different formal relationship to the original oracles against foreign nations. It exhibits, not a reorientation but an extensive and intensive augmentation. In establishing Israel's guilt, the list of criminal acts is first recited in full, corresponding to the higher value in the graduated numerical sequence. Then, the *proprium* of Israel's guilt is made manifest by juxtaposing an account of Yahweh's former intervention on Israel's behalf. Accordingly, it is all the more strongly underscored that the Yahweh who speaks in the announcement of punishment is now to be the originator of a very different sort of calamity. The ramifications of this are then described in considerably greater detail.

Finally, the formula which concludes messenger speech is not simply omitted, as in the secondary oracles, but it is replaced by the solemn divine oracle formula. These formal connections thus demand that the oracle against Israel be associated with the group of four original oracles against foreign nations.

What is the organizational scheme underlying the composition? The older interpreters thought the sequence of oracles to be a "natural" one[50]—in order, moving from north to south. But in that case the Philistine oracle has to be excluded, without sufficient cause for doing so. The latter oracle can be retained if we suppose the arrangement to have been determined by the military–political plan of the Assyrians as foreseen by Amos.[51] Yet why should the prophet have been governed by such an interest when he does not even mention the Assyrians? Thus Weiser stressed that we must focus upon the composition's conspicuously paramount interest in Israel;[52] this has resulted in the view that psychological considerations determined the sequence of nations, namely that the order reflects the degrees of forceful enmity preceived by Israel among her neighbors. Accordingly, the Arameans and the Philistines should stand at the top of the list. But why are they not then treated at the end of the series, given its tendency toward escalation?

More recent research has been strongly influenced by Aage Bentzen's proposal that the ritual of execration of foreign princes and peoples, attested from the Egyptian Middle Kingdom, ought to be seen as lying behind the oracles against foreign nations in Amos.[53] The Egyptian execration texts of the eighteenth century B.C. are found on pottery bowls, dishes, and pots (at least ten centimeters in diameter) or on clay figurines (31–35 centimeters in height) portraying prisoners kneeling with their hands bound behind their backs. Compactly written horizontal inscriptions cover these figurines from neck to knees, both front and back.[54] Enumerated in this fashion are the names of

---

50   Marti, 158.
51   So according to Wellhausen, 68, 75.
52   *Profetie*, 86–87.
53   "Ritual Background," 85–99. For the texts, see especially the following: Kurt Sethe, *Die Ächtung feindlicher Fürsten, Völker und Dinge auf altägyptischen Tongefäßscherben des Mittleren Reiches*, APAW 5 (Berlin, 1926); Georges Posener, *Princes et pays d'Asie et de Nubie. Textes hiératiques sur des figurines d'envoûtement du Moyen Empire* (Brussels, 1940); John A. Wilson, *ANET*³, 328–29; Hans Wolfgang Helck, *Die Beziehungen Ägyptens zu Vorderasien im 3. und 2. Jahrtausend v. Chr.*, Ägyptologische Abhandlungen 5 (Wiesbaden: O. Harrassowitz, 1962), 49–67; and André Vila, "Un dépôt de textes d'envoûtement au Moyen Empire," *Journal des Savants* (1963): 135–60.

princes, places, and regions in Nubia, in the Palestine–Syria region of Asia, and in Libya, as well as the names of Egyptian rebels (including deceased persons, whose active interference from the realm of the dead was feared). Destructive powers generally, sometimes even deities, are also mentioned.[55] The Egyptian king or a priest would break the vessels or figurines in a ritual act. A mural in the library of Edfu shows a ritual–priest piercing nine figurines of prisoners in one thrust with a sort of barbecue spit.[56] The purpose of the act was, through magic, to render powerless those designated by name. Similar acts of sympathetic magic as practiced in Syria, at precisely the time of Amos, are now known to us from a treaty inscribed upon the Sefîre stele. At the conclusion of the treaty ceremony, the wax figure of a man was burnt or had its eyes gouged out; bows and arrows were broken; a calf was cut up; wax figures of women were stripped, beaten, and abused—all this to demonstrate that, in case of breach of treaty, the same would befall the renegade and his kin.[57] Similar practices are attested for the time around 750 by the treaty between Asshur–nirâri V and Mati'ilu of Bît–Agûsi (Arpad).[58]

Bentzen's reference to the execration texts has received widespread attention,[59] because these documents provide a series of analogies to Am 1–2 not otherwise attested in such combination, either in the Old Testament or elsewhere in ancient Near Eastern sources. In Amos and the execration texts alike (1) peoples and places are designated (2) whose destruction is ordained; (3) their rulers and princes are usually also named; and

perhaps most importantly (4) the execration texts are also directed against Egyptians, analogous to Amos' prophesies against Israel. Bentzen himself places limitations on the comparison. We ought not to suppose, of course, that a magical act[60] per se is reflected in Amos, especially since no mention is made of inscribed pottery vessels.[61] Nevertheless, on the basis of Amos' form of address, Bentzen wants to postulate in Israel a comparable cultic rite (associated with the New Year festival) whose purpose was the execration of the foreign and domestic enemies. Such far–reaching conclusions demand a careful examination of the presuppositions. Do the four points of comparison between Amos and the execration texts noted above suffice to explain the form of composition in Am 1—2? The following factors must be kept in mind:

1. In terms of form the texts cannot be compared at all. The execration texts are merely lists of names (of princes, cities, countries, evil powers); they scarcely exhibit a complete sentence, much less complex oracles.

2. The sequence of those named in the execration texts is said to be determined by the compass directions.[62] Moreover, this arrangement as such is supposed to have magical significance, and to retain even in Amos an effectiveness against peoples "who were not unfamiliar with magical views and acts."[63] Now, the efforts of Bentzen and Fohrer to do so already indicate that a constant sequence—from south, to north, to west, to east—cannot be ascertained in the texts. Such a sequence might at best be recognized in Amos as a modification of the Egyptian one, though the existence

---

Cf. Georg Fohrer, "Prophetie und Magie," *ZAW* 78 (1966): 25–47, esp. 33, 40–43 (reprinted in *idem, Studien,* 242–63).

54 Posener, *Princes,* 17–18. Inscriptions cover only the front of the smaller figurines (14.5 centimeters in height); see Vila, "dépôt," 147. There have also been isolated finds of figurines depicting birds, fish, barks, and the like; see Vila, "dépôt," 158–59.

55 Siegfried Morenz, *Egyptian Religion,* tr. Ann E. Keep (Ithaca, New York: Cornell University Press, 1973), 27 [*Aegyptische Religion,* Die Religionen der Menschheit 8 (Stuttgart: W. Kohlhammer, 1960), 28].

56 Posener, *Princes,* 7.

57 Sefire stele I A 37–42. Cf. *KAI* 222A 37–42; and also the comments of H. Donner and W. Röllig, *Kanaanäische und Aramäische Inschriften,* vol. 2 (Wiesbaden: O. Harrassowitz, 1964), 251. [Cf. Franz Rosenthal, *ANET³,* 660.]

58 11.10–35: Ernst F. Weidner, "Der Staatsvertrag Aššurnirâris VI. von Assyrien mit Mati'ilu von Bît-Agusi," *AfO* 8 (1932–33): 17–26 (text: 18–19). Cf. also Dennis J. McCarthy, *Treaty and Covenant,* AnBibl 21 (Rome: Pontifical Biblical Institute, 1963), 195 [and Erica Reiner, *ANET³,* 532–33].

59 From, among others, Kapelrud, *Central Ideas,* 17–33; Reventlow, *Amt,* 62–75; and Fohrer, "Prophetie," 40–44.

60 Cf. Sefire stele I (*KAI* 222) A 37–42, noted above.

61 Perhaps a remote parallel is to be found in Jer 19.

62 Bentzen, "Ritual Background," 89–90.

63 Fohrer, "Prophetie," 41–42.

of the latter itself remains extremely problematic. Above all, however, more thorough study of the Egyptian texts has demonstrated that no magical conception of the compass points was determinative for the sequence. As Helck has shown, the sequence of names rather accords with the lines of the trade routes.[64] This also explains why, in the Egyptian references to Asia, rulers are named for the more southerly areas, while only cities and regions are identified for the more northerly ones. The execration ritual was probably intended to help safeguard the caravan routes. In any case, the sequence of places is determined not by magical conceptions but by the pattern of road connections.

3. The reason for the Egyptian execrations is obvious, both from the standpoint of the accompanying ritual and from the texts themselves: those named endanger Egyptian interests. Potential and actual rebels and antagonistic forces, both at home and abroad, are to be expurgated. This single, self-evident purpose is made manifest especially by the general, summarizing notices which conclude the lists of names, referring for example to those "who may rebel, who may plot, who may fight, who may talk of fighting, or who may talk of rebelling—in this entire land."[65] In contrast to this, Amos names specific crimes in each oracle. The characteristic wording of the graduated numerical sayings emphasizes from the outset of the oracles that these crimes are the grounds for the divine threats. Moreover, the crimes are not presented as violations of Israelite political interests; such an understanding is never stressed in the indictments, nor can it even be indirectly deduced in isolated cases (2:1). On the contrary, the oracular framework shows clearly that it is Yahweh's will which has been violated; this concern dominates the oracles.

4. Similarly, the threat in Amos against the native population is of a wholly different sort than that in the execration texts. It is Yahweh's will, rather than the interest of the political establishment, which is decisive. Consequently, the oracle against Israel exhibits emphases[66] which are absent in the Egyptian material.[67] To be sure, the names of some Egyptians are preceded by the word mwt = "may he die."[68] Here individual domestic rebels and destructive powers are exorcized, just as are foreign ones. But in Amos, *all* Israel stands under the threat, without any possibility of some escaping (2:14–16).[69] This clearly indicates how completely different are the respective presuppositions and intentions of the two sets of texts.[70]

5. Finally, we have to look more closely at how the actions are effected, more precisely at the respective functions of deity in the texts. In the ritual of execration, humans attempt to shape the course of world events. Amos announces the sovereign activity of Yahweh. In Egypt, as our comparative texts indicate, only occasionally were various gods explicitly invoked and pressed into service;[71] other gods were themselves the targets of execration.[72] In Israel, Yahweh's omnipotent actions are announced to the people; his word alone governs Israel and foreign nations alike.

In light of this list of profound differences, the small number of formal agreements noted earlier scarcely allow us to suppose that Amos had been influenced, even if only indirectly, by an ancient execration ritual. The points of agreement are circumstantial, being quite understandable as independent developments within their respective settings.

Bentzen sought the immediate background for Amos' composition in Israelite cursing ceremonies comparable to the Egyptian ritual.[73] It is true that in certain psalms

64   Helck, *Beziehungen*, 62–63.
65   John A. Wilson, *ANET*[3], 329. Cf. Sethe, *Ächtung*, 42–43, 58–59, 60–62.
66   See p. 144.
67   As already noted by Bentzen, "Ritual Background," 94.
68   Sethe, *Ächtung*, 19, 62–69.
69   Kapelrud, *Central Ideas*, 20.
70   Cf. Fey, *Amos und Jesaja*, 46.
71   E.g., Ḥammu, Šamaš, Sin, Hadad; cf. Helck, *Beziehungen*, 67.
72   So Siegfried Morenz, *Egyptian Religion*, tr. Ann E. Keep (Ithaca, New York: Cornell University Press, 1973), 27, 284n. 59 [27], who follows the interpretation of Georges Posener, "Les empreintes magiques de Gizeh et les morts dangereux" in *Festschrift zum 80. Geburtstag von Hermann Junker*, Mitteilungen des Deutschen Archäologischen Instituts, Abteilung Kairo 16 (Wiesbaden: O. Harrassowitz, 1958), 252–70, esp. 267.
73   Bentzen, "Ritual Background," 91–94.

Yahweh is extolled as judge over all evildoers on earth (Ps 75:11 [10]).[74] Moreover, individual foreign nations may be designated (Ps 76:11 [10] cj.),[75] the grounds for Yahweh's judgment may be specified (Ps 82:3–4), and the divine punishment to be visited upon peoples and princes may be described (Ps 149:7–8).[76] Here we encounter related motifs, informed by the same faith in Yahweh, which stand closer to Amos than do the execration texts; behind psalms preserved in the Jerusalem cult may be discerned Canaanite 'Elyôn (עליון) and 'El traditions.[77] However, apart from the difficulty of dating such psalms and of assigning them to specific cultic occasions, nowhere in them do we find even the slightest basis for supposing the existence in Israel's cult of formularies in which the structure of the individual oracle, the grouping of Israel with foreign nations, and the intensified condemnation of Isarel were comparable to Am 1—2.

Much the same objection must be raised against Reventlow's effort to posit behind Am 1—2 a cursing–ritual associated with a festival proclaiming the covenant.[78] Reventlow pursues further the observations of Bentzen, critically accepting the work of Weiser and Kapelrud, and arrives at the thesis that a "covenant festival" was the life–setting which supported the claim of Yahweh's universal sovereignty. Following Würthwein's and Bach's findings, he bases this thesis on the assumption that Amos, ". . . when making his accusations, had in view the sum total of the generally familiar stock of covenant law . . ."[79] to which the nations were also subjected. While it cannot be denied that the accusations of Amos occasionally resonate with elements of the ancient Israelite law transmitted in the legal codes, there are no linguistic parallels so exact as to permit one to speak of an institutionalized cursing–ritual. Moreover, it is impossible to demonstrate the existence in Israel of a covenantal cult festival in which indictment and announcement of punishment would have been combined in the form of messenger speech,

in which several nations would have appeared together with Israel in a single oracular composition, and especially in which destruction would have been decreed for the totality of Israel, in terms even more forceful than those directed against the surrounding nations. Such a formulary would indeed be highly unlikely since the pre–prophetic cursing–formularies are directed, not against all Israel, but against the specific transgressors of particular laws (Dtn 27:15–26).

The only assured result of the recent research into the provenance of the genre of the cycle of oracles against the nations is the discovery of several isolated formal similarities. For the whole complex and its characteristic features a model has not been discovered nor has even the likelihood of one been established. The dissolution of the composition into individual oracles[80] has proven to be as untenable a solution as the attempt of Würthwein[81] to assign the oracles against foreign nations to an earlier period of Amos' ministry (marked by prophecy of salvation) and the oracle against Israel to a later one (marked by prophecy of judgment). Both attempts only make more complicated the task of accounting for the composition's uniformity, especially since that which the individual oracles have in common is manifestly original.

All possibilities of comparison having been exhausted, how are we to understand the genre of the composition?

1. There emerged here a particular kind of speech not previously heard in Israel. This must once again be strongly emphasized. Certainly we have come to recognize that various traditional elements were here fused into something new, but we must also keep in mind Amos' own sense of having been compelled to do Yahweh's bidding (7:1–8; 8:1–2; 7:14–15; 3:8). Only thus does the intensity and unwavering certitude of Amos in executing his commission to proclaim Israel's end as being the will of Yahweh become understandable. This context explains also the terse form of the

---

74 Bentzen ("Ritual Background," 92–93) cites Ps 75; 76; 82; and 149.
75 Cf. Kraus, *Psalmen*, on Ps 76:11 *ad loc.*; cf. also Ps 60:8–10 [6–8].
76 Cf. also Ps 9:9 [8], 20–21 [19–20]; 96:10; etc.
77 Kraus, *Psalmen*, 199–200; Schmidt, *Königtum*, 39–43.
78 Reventlow, *Amt*, 62–75.
79 *Ibid.*, 75.
80 Robinson; E. Osty, *Amos, Osée*, SBJ (Paris: Les Éditions du Cerf, 1952).
81 "Amos–Studien," 37–38.

messenger speeches, the preponderance of the oracle against Israel, and the subjection to Yahweh's word of all the other nations as well.

2. Foreign nations were necessarily already involved in words and actions of Yahweh in the ancient Israelite exodus and conquest traditions, as well as in the traditions of the early wars of Yahweh. Amos undeniably has these traditions in view (2:9; 3:2). Perhaps the Arameans and Philistines head the list as arch-enemies (cf. 9:7); Ammon and Moab may have been placed together as kindred neighbors (Gen 19:37–38).[82] However, including Israel in the list of these peoples ripe for judgment was unprecedented. Amos boldly does so for the first time, and more than once (9:7; cf. 6:2). Only a recognition of the creative role of Amos explains the formal parallels, with regard to both the opening element and the reasons for punishment, between the oracle against Israel and the oracles against the foreign nations.

3. No other formal element in these oracles appears with such stereotyped regularity as that which designates the crime, repeatedly employing as it does the graduated numerical saying. The use of such a saying reflects the influence of oral traditions of popular wisdom instruction which, like other wisdom material, linked Israel to the surrounding world.[83] To be sure, this recognition of the prophet's cultural antecedents explains neither the terse form of the speech of Yahweh's messenger nor the severity of the announced punishment.[84] But it does explain the international scope of Amos' knowledge and concerns, and it suggests how he could categorically subsume all peoples under the same juridical order. Most important, however, is the fact that the demonstrable affinity between the thought and speech modes of the graduated numerical saying (as well as other wisdom forms similarly characterized by seriatim structure) and our present cluster of homomorphic oracles establishes the form of the latter as a plausible rhetorical possibility.

4. Finally, in addition to the stereotypical features of the oracles, the wisdom tradition accounts for the inner structure of the series. The comparative mode of thinking constitutive of the graduated numerical saying, with its frequent emphasis upon the last item,[85] explains the forcefully intensified variants of the concluding oracle against Israel. The last of the five visions and the final bicola of the didactic questions in 3:3–6+8 stand out in a similar way. Both of these parallels likewise exhibit a tendency for the elements preceding the final one to be arranged by pairs.[86] There is nothing preserved in the liturgical style of the hymns (the use of refrains notwithstanding),[87] much less in other cultic genres, which offers a parallel, especially to the emphatic reorientation achieved in the concluding oracle while preserving the basic structure of the oracles preceding it. The only larger composition from earlier times that might be considered even remotely to approximate the repetitive style and the concluding reorientation is Jotham's Fable in Ju 9:8–15.[88] Though their specific forms and themes differ, the two compositions derive from the same cultural milieu of wisdom. In the composition of his messenger speeches, Amos met the demands of his unique commission by drawing upon the patterns of thought and diction appropriate to the realm of wisdom.

Setting

What was the life–setting of this new pattern of speech? Only for some of the elements incorporated does tradition offer tentative answers. The numerical saying belonged to popular wisdom instruction; announcing the destruction of certain foreign nations had been a function of charismatics at the beginning of the ancient wars of Yahweh; the leveling of threats against individual Israelites for particular transgressions had its place in cultic cursing ceremonies; and the association of specific crimes with specific punishments was appropriate to casuistic legal precedents. But just as the

---

82   Weiser, 136.

83   See pp. 137–38.

84   On this see p. 91.

85   See p. 138.

86   See p. 100.

87   Johannes Lindblom, *Die literarische Gattung der prophetischen Literatur*, UUÅ (Uppsala, 1924), 74. Cf., for example, Ps 46; 67; or the laments in Ps 42—43

and 80.

88   Cf. James Muilenburg, "A Study in Hebrew Rhetoric: Repetition and Style" in *Congress Volume: Copenhagen, 1953*, SVT 1 (Leiden: E. J. Brill, 1953), 88–111 (esp. 103).

formulas framing messenger speech, adopted from the language of diplomatic exchange, now served to articulate a precise, unique commission of Yahweh, so too the new form of speech drew upon popular wisdom instruction to elucidate the grounds for impending punishment. Yet the composition links acute threats against foreign nations with the threat against Israel in a way that would be quite unimaginable in the context of any hypothetical, postulated New Year or covenant festival in Israel. Such a message would have negated the very festival. We must therefore suppose as the life–setting of our cycle of messenger speeches, not an established Israelite institution but rather the circumstantial, unexpected, immediate appearance of an individual prophetic speaker.

Our perspective allows for the possibility that Amos delivered this cycle of oracles on the occasion of a festival assembly. From 1 Kgs 12 : 32 we learn that a Yahwistic festival was celebrated at Bethel in autumn, at the end of the harvest season; Am 7 : 10–17 informs us that Amos made an appearance at Bethel. We do not know whether the leveling of threats against foreign and domestic enemies was a fixed item on the agenda of this festival. Some scholars suspect it was. Be that as it may, the threatening of enemies might have pleased an audience at any time. Hence while Amos no doubt intended the initial oracles of the cycle to be taken seriously, they were also a cleverly devised lure, compelling his audience toward an acceptance of the even harsher message against Israel as Yahweh's word.[89] This oracular composition would seem particularly appropriate at the *beginning* of Amos' career.[90] Later the effectiveness of the surprise element would have been blunted, and we must assume that the composition was intended to be startling, if only because

Amos, as far as we know, never again spoke of the crimes and punishment of the foreign nations.[91]

Can we determine the historical setting of these oracles of Amos? Only the oracles against the Arameans and the Ammonites touch on events that suggest broader historical connections. Both nations are accused of having committed atrocities in Gilead, the region of Israel east of the Jordan (1 : 3, 13); regarding the Ammonites it is explicitly remarked that territorial conquest was their goal.

Hitherto it has usually been assumed that Amos was alluding to events from the last third of the ninth century.[92] Indeed we know that Hazael of Damascus (842–806) had enhanced Aramean power considerably since the final campaign of Shalmaneser III (858–824)—in the twenty–first year of his reign, thus c. 838—against the cities of Hazael "in the land of Damascus."[93] Thereafter both Shalmaneser III and his successor Shamshi–adad V (824–811) had been occupied elsewhere, thus freeing Hazael and his son Ben–hadad to exert military pressure against Israel during the reigns of Jehu (845–818) and his son Jehoahaz (818–802).[94] Israel's troops could not prevent the loss of the whole east Jordan region as far south as the Arnon, which is to say "all the land of Gilead" (2 Kgs 10 : 32–33; cf. 2 Kgs 13 : 7). Hazael appears also to have made an alliance with the Philistines; in any event, c. 815 he expropriated the old Philistine city of Gath, which formerly had been under the control of Judah since at least the time of Rehoboam.[95] The oracle against the Philistines in Am 1 : 6–8 immediately follows that against the Arameans. To be sure, neither Gath nor a relationship with Damascus is herein mentioned, nor is any Israelite or Judean territory identified by name.

89 Weiser, *Profetie*, 103; Rudolf Smend, "Das Nein des Amos," *EvTh* 23 (1963): 410.

90 So Weiser, 134; Deden, 124.

91 See pp. 308–10 on 7 : 10–17.

92 Martin Noth, *The History of Israel*, tr. Peter R. Ackroyd (New York: Harper & Row, ²1960), 248–49 [*Geschichte Israels* (Göttingen: Vandenhoeck & Ruprecht, ²1954), 227]; John Bright, *A History of Israel* (Philadelphia: Westminster, ²1972), 251; Weiser, on Am 1 : 3, 13 *ad loc.*

93 A. Leo Oppenheim, *ANET*³, 280; *AOT*², 343. On the regnal dates of the Assyrian kings, cf. Petrus E.

van der Meer, *The Chronology of Ancient Western Asia and Egypt*, Documenta et monumenta orientis antiqui 2 (Leiden: E. J. Brill, 1955, ²1963), 8. (Leiden: E. J. Brill, ²1955, 1963), 8.

94 2 Kgs 8 : 12; 13 : 3. On the regnal dates of the Israelite kings, cf. Alfred Jepsen, "Zur Chronologie der Könige von Israel und Juda" in Alfred Jepsen and Robert Hanhart, *Untersuchungen zur israelitisch–jüdischen Chronologie*, BZAW 88 (Berlin: A. Töpelmann, 1964), 42.

95 2 Kgs 12 : 18. Cf. Noth, *History*, 238–39 [217–18]. See p. 158.

The juxtaposition of the oracles against Aram and Philistia in Am 1:3–8 thus ought not to be facilely explained on the mere supposition that this reflects the conquest of Gath by Hazael. It is quite improbable that Amos, in the oracle against Aram, would refer to military events which had taken place at least two generations earlier. Moreover, no text gives evidence for a simultaneous territorial expansion by the Ammonites into the territory of Gilead at that time (1:13); the wording of 2 Kgs 10:32–33 excludes even the possibility that such could have occurred. In addition, we otherwise know Amos only as a prophet who speaks out against the misdeeds of his own day.

Above all, however, it must be kept in mind that the Aramean conquests in the region east of the Jordan during the ninth century had been nullified during the first two decades of the eighth century. An indirect ally of the Israelite kings had arisen in the person of Adad–nirāri III of Assyria (cf. 2 Kgs 13:5). In the fifth year of his reign (c. 800) he besieged Benhadad in Damascus and forced him into subjection.[96] Apparently Aramean power was so weakened as a result that Jehoash (802–787) was able, in the course of three battles, to retrieve from Aramean control many cities which Hazael had taken from his father Jehoahaz (2 Kgs 13:24–25). Jeroboam II (787–747) was able to extend the Israelite sphere of control still further, probably even capturing Damascus and Hamath (2 Kgs 14:28). In the first quarter of the eighth century Israel had thus recovered from the defeats of the ninth century. Is it really likely then that Amos, in his indictments of Aram and Ammon, had in mind events prior to the restoration of Israelite power? Might he not well have been referring to events of his own day?

In order to answer this question one has to take note of the change in the international political situation which developed soon after the death of Adad–nirāri III (782). Under its energetic rulers Argišti I and Sardur III (810–743), the kingdom of Urartu (whose center was located in the region of Lake Van) gained supremacy over Assyria.[97] Assyria was under such pressure from all sides that it remains an open question whether, in the battle of 773 between Shalmaneser IV (787–772) and Damascus, the Arameans were being attacked[98] or were themselves the attackers.[99] In any case, Assyria under the following rulers Asshur–dan III (772–754) and Asshur–nirāri V (754–745) was so weakened that the Arameans had ample time to regroup their forces. The re–emergence of Aramean power is indirectly attested by the fact that it was not until 732 that Tiglath–pileser III was able decisively to conquer the kingdom of Damascus. It is quite evident, then, that a conquest of Damascus by Jeroboam II (2 Kgs 14:28) had no lasting consequences. In light of the wider political situation it thus appears feasible, even likely, that during the second quarter of the eighth century the Arameans were again encroaching on (northern) Gilead, where it bordered on their own territory (1:3). For this period there is no textual evidence which contradicts the possibility that the Ammonites may have tried simultaneously to penetrate the southern portion of Gilead (1:13). The Ammonites and the Arameans had already waged a joint campaign against David (2 Sam 10:6–14). However, we are told nothing of such a coalition existing in the ninth century. It would appear justified to assume during the time of Jeroboam II a state of warfare in which success alternated between Israel on the one hand and the Arameans and Ammonites on the other. Such a situation accords well with a date for Amos c. 760[100] and agrees perfectly with his various statements.[101] Hence the allusion to victories in Transjordan (6:13) becomes intelligible alongside the threat that Jeroboam "shall die by the sword" (7:11), and the references in 1:3 and 13 to Aramean and Ammonite incursions. Moreover, 2 Kgs 14:28 implies that Jeroboam II was entangled in difficult military conflicts and was not always the victor (2 Kgs 14:25). If in his oracles against foreign

---

96 A. Leo Oppenheim, *ANET*[3], 281; *AOT*[2], 345.

97 Cf. Albrecht Goetze, *Kleinasien*, Kulturgeschichte des Alten Orients 3/1, Handbuch der Altertums-wissenschaft 3/1/3/3/1 (München: C. H. Beck, [2]1957), 192–200.

98 So André Dupont–Sommer, *Les Araméens*, L'Orient Ancien Illustré 2 (Paris: A. Maisonneuve, 1949), 55.

99 So Simon Cohen, "The Political Background of the Words of Amos," *HUCA* 36 (1965): 153–60 (esp. 158).

100 See pp. 89–90.

101 See n. 99 above.

nations Amos had recalled events of the preceding century, it is most unlikely that in his oracle against Israel (2:6–16) he would have remained completely silent concerning the Israelite counter–attacks under Jehoash and at the beginning of the reign of Jeroboam II. If, on the other hand, Amos was referring to events of his own day in 1:3—2:3, then the entire cycle is in accord with his characteristic method of condemning contemporary abuses, as is pre–eminently the case in the oracle against Israel. Then too the prophet's silence concerning Assyria may be explained as due to the ascendency of Urartu, and we can understand why his threats of deportation single out places in the Aramean kingdom (4:3; 5:27) whose territorial control he supposes to be quite vast (1:5). Furthermore, it is known that not only Assyria, but also Urartu carried out large-scale deportations.[102]

We conclude, therefore, that the Aramean incursions in the Transjordan referred to in 1:3, as well as the Ammonite attempts at conquest cited in 1:13, are better attributed to the second quarter of the eighth century than to the ninth century. Amos' allusions here confirm that he was active in a latter phase of the reign of Jeroboam II when, in addition to a sense of well-being and self–confidence resulting from the successes of the earlier phase, there was also a renewal of crisis in the Transjordan. Thus rather than only seeking to discover confirmations of known historical phenomena in the oracles against foreign nations, they should also be recognized as sources which can be exploited in order to expand our historical knowledge of the time around 760.

In addressing the question of literary promulgation and growth, we should take note of the close relationship between the oracles against foreign nations and the cycle of visions (7:1–8; 8:1–2; 9:1–4). Each of the compositions is comprised of five strophes, the first four of which are structured as pairs,[103] while the fifth exhibits variations on the basic pattern, setting it apart as a climax. In both cases an earthquake is announced in the fifth strophe; at some length and using similar expressions,[104] the impossibility of flight is detailed—not even a remnant can escape.[105] The stereotyped announcement that Yahweh will not turn back his word (1:3—2:6) is clearly illustrated in the sequence of visions. The report of the first two visions that the threatened calamity was taken back (7:3, 6) does not reappear in the latter three. Moreover, 7:3 and 7:6 attest the formula which concludes messenger speech, "Yahweh has said" (אמר יהוה), which also occurs in the older oracles against foreign nations (1:5, 8, 15; 2:3) but is otherwise rare in Amos.[106] These close similarities lead us to suppose that the two cycles were written down at the same time.[107]

The secondary oracles in 1:9–12 and 2:4–5 are so closely related to one another—both in the ways they differ from the older oracles and in their common structure[108]—that one is naturally inclined to attribute them to the same redactor. The shift of emphasis to the specification of guilt, and the terminology employed in the oracle against Judah are reminiscent of the concerns and the language of the Deuteronomistic History (middle of the sixth century). The enlargement of the cycle by introducing oracles against Tyre and Edom recalls the especially emphatic way in which Ezekiel directs threats not only against Tyre (Ezek 26—28), but also against Edom.[109] On the basis of the Ezekiel parallels, the oracles in Amos against Tyre and Edom may be assigned to the period after 587.[110] The redactor of Amos has not introduced an oracle against

---

102 Involving as many as 50,000 people at a time; cf. Goetze, *Kleinasien*[2], 196.
103 See pp. 94–95.
104 Cf. 2:13–16 with 9:1–4.
105 Cf. 9:1aβb with 1:8bβ and 2:14a, 15b.
106 Elsewhere in Amos the formula appears only in 5:17 and 27.
107 Cf. Luis Alonso-Schökel, "Die stilistische Analyse bei den Propheten" in *Congress Volume: Oxford, 1959*, SVT 7 (Leiden: E. J. Brill, 1960), 154–64 (esp. 162).
108 See pp. 139–40.

109 Ezek 25:12–14. Note the position of the threat against Edom, following that against Philistia and preceding those against Ammon and Moab!
110 Cf. Zimmerli, *Ezechiel*, 588–89; a coalition in which Edom, Tyre and Judah appear with Moab and Ammon is already attested in Jer 27:3.

Babylon, just as there is none in Ezekiel, where Babylon is the executor of Yahweh's will.[111] Thus the choices of nations for inclusion in the cycle, as well as language and theology, point to the middle of the sixth century as the time when the secondary oracles were added.[112]

The attempt has been made to attribute the addition in 2:10–12 to the same period.[113] Unlike the oracles in 1:9–12 and 2:4–5, however, the purpose of this supplement is not to add new names to the list, contemporizing the cycle for a new audience. Instead, it is an expansion within the older oracle against Israel, which employs liturgical material to elaborate the backward glance into the history of salvation. There is here a more direct approach to an audience, though this is merely stylistic, achieved by the inclusion of parenetic address. As in the cases of the Judah strophe and the small additions in 2:7bβ, 8aβ, 8bβ the purpose served by the supplement in 2:10–12 is a strictly theological explication of guilt. Therefore its author is undoubtedly related to the larger exilic circle of Deuteronomistic interpreters of the prophetic tradition.

Interpretation

■ **3** Amos speaks as the messenger of Yahweh just as much when he addresses the foreign nations as he does when he addresses Israel.[114] He bases his accusations on transmitted lists of atrocities which may have been familiar in both Israel and the surrounding nations in the form of graduated numerical sayings.[115] For Amos these atrocities represent violations of the universally valid law of his God. The key term designating the punishable offences is פְּשָׁעִים ("crimes").

פֶּשַׁע ("crime") in Amos

פֶּשַׁע is the most important word which Amos uses to designate censurable actions, though elsewhere in the Old Testament the term is used much less frequently than "sin" (חטא) and "iniquity" (עָוֹן).[116] It occurs seven times in authentic oracles of Amos (1:3, 6, 13; 2:1, 6; 3:14; 5:12), and three times in secondary oracles (1:9, 11; 2:4). There are two attestations in Amos of verbal forms of פשע (4:4a, 4b). In contrast, the following have only one attestation apiece in Amos: "transgressions" (עֲוֹנֹת 3:2); "sins" (חַטָּאות in parallelism with פְּשָׁעִים in 5:12); "sinful kingdom" (מַמְלָכָה הַחַטָּאָה 9:8); and "sinners" (חַטָּאִים 9:10). It is noteworthy that the noun occurs only in the plural. It serves as ". . . a legal *terminus technicus* to characterize and summarize particular cases."[117] In Amos these cases exclusively involve infractions of property and personal rights.[118]

Where did Amos get this comprehensive concept? In older epic texts in the Pentateuch it appears in connection with juridical controversies within the clan, such as those between Jacob and Laban (Gen 31:36) and between Joseph and his brothers (Gen 50:17). In the extensive legal corpora of the Pentateuch it is found only once, in Ex. 22:8 [9]. Here, however, we are dealing with a legal "axiom" of an unusual sort, preserved ". . . in a very old formulation which is evidently taken over from pre–Israelite times . . ." since it still contains a reference to "gods."[119] In this passage, as in Amos, פשע is a comprehensive concept for infraction of property rights, of which four specific cases are subsequently enumerated. The preposition in the introductory rubric (עַל־כָּל־דְּבַר־פֶּשַׁע) "for every case of misappropri-

---

111 Cf. Zimmerli, *Ezechiel*, 580, 604–05.
112 Cf. Schmidt, "Redaktion," 174–78.
113 *Ibid.*, 178–82.
114 On the messenger–speech formula see pp. 135–37.
115 See pp. 137–38.
116 Ludwig Koehler, *Old Testament Theology*, tr. A. S. Todd (Philadelphia: Westminster, 1957), 268–72 [*Theologie des Alten Testaments*, Neue Theologische Grundrisse (Tübingen: J. C. B. Mohr [Paul Siebeck], ⁴1966), 158–61].
117 Rolf Knierim, *Die Hauptbegriffe für Sünde im Alten Testament* (Gütersloh: Gütersloher Verlagshaus [Gerd Mohn], 1965), 127.
118 Cf. *ibid.*, 149.
119 Martin Noth, *Exodus: A Commentary*, tr. J. S. Bowden, OTL (Philadelphia: Westminster, 1962), 184 [*Das zweite Buch Mose, Exodus*, ATD 5 (Göttingen: Vandenhoeck & Ruprecht, 1959), 149].

ation") also reminds one of the use of פשע in Am 1:3, 6, etc. While the usage of פשע is thus rare and unusual in the Pentateuch, it appears frequently in older collections of the book of Proverbs. To the seven occurrences of the noun in Amos (or ten, if the secondary oracles are included) there is a correspondingly high number of twelve occurrences in Proverbs.[120] The two occurrences of the verb in Amos are matched by two in Proverbs (Prv 18:19; 28:21). In the whole Pentateuch there is not a single attestation of the verb, while in the Psalter there are but two (Ps 37:38; 51:15 [13])! These statistics alone should suffice to identify the realm of life to which Amos' chief word for sin originally belonged. An analysis of its meaning corroborates our statistical findings. First of all, as in Amos and in Ex 22:8 [9] so too in Proverbs the noun is attested (in the plural as also in Amos) as a comprehensive concept in conjunction with the preposition על (Prv 10:12). More importantly, as in Amos so too in Proverbs the term refers exclusively to transgressions against society: it is used to characterize hatred, quarreling, strife, and robbery as crimes (10:12; 17:19; 28:24; 29:22); it is contrasted with the qualities of love and forbearance (10:12; 17:9; 19:11). In Canaanite texts the word is unattested.[121] In Ugaritic texts it is thus far attested once (pš'), where it stands in parallelism with "haughtiness, arrogance" (g'an).[122]

All this leads to the conclusion that Amos' use of this term reflects his familiarity with the realm of oral clan–tradition, the same realm within which also the graduated numerical sayings served a pedagogical purpose. In view of the concrete actions which he describes with this key term, the translation "crime" seems appropriate. All of the cases specified involve infractions of property and personal rights, deeds which deliberately violate communal standards.[123]

The first oracle deals with the crimes of Damascus. The city stands for its rulers (v 4) and its inhabitants (v 5b). The reference is to the capital of the Aramean kingdom, situated to the northeast of Israel. As an oasis at the southeastern foot of the Antilebanon range, it had developed (perhaps already in the fourth millennium) into a nomad's marketplace and a caravan town.[124] By David's time it had long been the center of an Aramean state. David subjugated it along with other Aramean states (2 Sam 8:3–8; 10:6–19), but it soon regained its independence during Solomon's reign (1 Kgs 11:23–25) and became the hub of a sizeable Aramean kingdom.[125] Under the sovereignty of Damascus, the Arameans were a source of considerable trouble for Israel not only in the ninth century, but also during the reign of Jeroboam II at the time of Amos.[126] Damascus is for Amos a major point of reference in the far–flung network of highways of the ancient Near East (5:27). He is also conscious of the size of the Aramean political conglomerate (1:5a), and he means to include the whole empire when he holds chiefly accountable its nearby capital city, Damascus.

The preliminary reference to Aram's guilt is joined to an ominous declaration that the announcement of punishment to follow is irrevocable. The proleptic suffix ("it") refers to the threat which will not be turned back.[127] This declaration may be connected with the prophetic experience preserved in the cycle of vision reports. Yahweh revoked the two initial sentences he intended (7:3, 6), but subsequently he remained adamant (7:8b; 8:2b; 9:4b). These negative formulations which conclude the latter visions—"I will never again pass him by" (לֹא־אֹסִיף עוֹד עֲבוֹר לוֹ) and "and not for good" (וְלֹא לְטוֹבָה)—explicitly negate the gracious retraction granted earlier. Thus the cycle of visions provides the background against which the stereotyped formula "I will not take it back" (לֹא אֲשִׁיבֶנּוּ) is to be understood.[128] Within the whole Old Testa-

---

120 Prv 10:12, 19; 12:13; 17:9, 19; 19:11; 28:2, 13, 24; 29:6, 16, 22. In the entire Pentateuch the noun appears only nine times, with only four of these being in older Pentateuchal texts; in the entire Psalter it occurs only fourteen times!

121 Cf. Donner–Röllig, *KAI* 3, Kanaanäisches Glossar; and Charles–F. Jean and Jacob Hoftijzer, *Dictionnaire des Inscriptions Sémitiques de l'Ouest* (Leiden: E. J. Brill, 1965).

122 *CTA* 17 (= *UT* 2 Aqht).6.43–44.

123 Cf. Knierim, *Hauptbegriffe*, 177–80, 183.

124 Kurt Galling, "Damaskus," *RGG*[3] 2, 22.

125 Cf. Martin Noth, "Beiträge zur Geschichte des Ostjordanlandes III., Die Nachbarn der israelitischen Stämme im Ostjordanlande," *BBLAK* (= *ZDPV* 68) (1951): 19–36 (reprinted in *idem*, *Aufsätze* 1, 449–63); and *idem*, *World*, 80–81 [73–74].

126 See pp. 150–51.

127 See textual note "b" to 1:3 for the arguments upon which this interpretation is based and for discussion of other views. Cf. also Is 45:23.

128 See p. 151.

ment, only the Elohistic Balaam oracle exhibits a comparably worded expression "and I cannot take it back" (וְלֹא אֲשִׁיבֶנָּה Nu 23:20b) which, since it stands in opposition to a form of the root "to repent" (נחם) in Nu 23:19a, also brings to mind Am 7:3 and 6. There is, in addition, a comparable idea expressed in Is 55:11. In Akkadian prayers the name of a deity is often followed by an appositional clause stating that "his command is not turned away (changed, overthrown)."[129] Yet the similarity of formulation here cannot obscure a fundamental difference. The Akkadian texts presuppose polytheistic thinking, in which a person hopes that the decree of one deity might be rescinded while that of another remains irreversible. The word of the particular deity being invoked is affirmed as intrinsically irreversible. Form–critically these passages are typical of the often hymnically phrased adulation appropriate to invocations in the prayers of lamentation. In those Sumerian and Babylonian hymns in which the deities speak in the first person, statements such as "I will not take it back" have not yet been found.[130] In Amos, on the other hand, Yahweh speaks in the first person through his messenger's address and declares that the divine punishment is irrevocable—not intrinsically (cf. 7:3, 6) but as it is now to be promulgated.

The reason for the punishment is described using the imagery of threshing. The technique by which grain was cut up and crushed gives this metaphor its brutal cogency. Grain was threshed by drawing over it a heavy sledge, the boards of which were curved upward at the front and the underside of which was studded with prongs; the use of iron knives, rather than flint-stones, for these prongs in the iron age significantly increased the efficiency of the sledge. It is this technical advance that Amos has in mind when he uses the imagery to depict cruelties of warfare.[131] Amos may have been prompted to adopt this metaphor because of the way certain prisoners of war were treated (cf. Ju 8:7, 16), but it is not necessary to assume that he was so motivated.[132]

At issue here is warfare in a district. The name "Gilead" probably originally designated the region south of the Jabbok but was later applied to the whole area of Israelite settlement in the Transjordan. South of the Jabbok, Gilead comprised Ephraimite territory, bordering on Ammon in the east (Ju 12:1–6); north of the Jabbok, and especially above ʿAjlūn, it comprised Manassite territory (1 Kgs 4:13), bordering on the Aramean kingdom.[133] It is of this northern Gilead that we must think in connection with the attacks by Damascus.

■ 4 Yahweh announces that it is he who will carry out the punishment. He is the real force behind the impending catastrophes (cf. 3:6; 5:17; 7:9). The threat of being consumed by fire is also directed against Israel, both in the second vision (7:4) and in 5:6. As in these latter oracles, the oracle against Damascus isolates as the particularly important property of fire the fact that it "devours" (אכל).[134] The imagery of devouring fire in our text carries with it the further connotation of Yahweh as a military leader and conquerer.[135] The

129 Cf. the texts cited by Wolfram von Soden, *Akkadisches Handwörterbuch* 1 (Wiesbaden: O. Harrassowitz, 1965), 221 (under *enû* N). E.g., Erich Ebeling, *Die akkadische Gebetsserie "Handerhebung*,*"* Deutsche Akademie der Wissenschaften zu Berlin, Institut für Orientforschung 20 (Berlin: Akademie Verlag, 1953), 30ff, lines 21ff (an entreaty made while "raising the hands" to Gula, the compassionate goddess): "At the word of your exalted command, which is not [changed] in Ekur, and your firm promise, which is not bent, may my angry god return, my angry goddess [turn toward me], the god of my city, Marduk, who has become angry, [may he calm down]. . . ."; and 126–27, l. 36, where, using similar expressions, the goddess Tašmêtum is invoked and entreated to reverse, by means of her own incontrovertible word, the decisions of other deities.

130 According to Wolfram von Soden (by letter).

131 Cf. 2 Kgs 13:7; Mi 4:13; Hab 3:12; and Is 41:15. Cf. also Dalman, *Arbeit* 3, 114; and *BRL*, 137–39.

132 So Hughell E. W. Fosbroke, "The Book of Amos: Introduction and Exegesis" in *The Interpreter's Bible*, vol. 6 (New York and Nashville: Abingdon, 1956), 779.

133 Cf. Martin Noth, "Gilead und Gad," *ZDPV* 75 (1959): 14–73, esp. 60–61 (reprinted in *idem, Aufsätze* 1, 489–543, esp. 532–33).

134 See also 1:7, [10, 12], 14; 2:2, [5]. The same property characterizes the fire which proceeds directly from Yahweh in 1 Kgs 18:38 and Lev 10:2.

135 Cf. Fredriksson, *Krieger*, 93–94.

use of fire in conquering enemy cities, and especially in destroying residential palaces, was accepted military practice in the ancient Near Eastern world. In the text of the treaty between kings Bar–ga'yāh of KTK and Matî'–'el of Arpad, for example, the latter monarch stands under the threat of having both his capital city, Arpad, and himself consigned to flames should he break the treaty.[136] Shalmaneser III, describing his conquest of the residence of Hamath's ruler, reports: "I threw fire into his palaces."[137] It is in keeping with the common practice, then, that the oracle of Amos first of all threatens to set ablaze "Hazael's house" and "Benhadad's strongholds." From the context, "strongholds" (ארמנות) must designate sections of the royal palace, or of the capital city generally, which could easily be defended.[138] Roland de Vaux renders this word as "the keep" (le donjon).[139] The use of the word elsewhere in Amos indicates that "strongholds" also refers to internationally renowned structures (3:9) which served both as secure refuges (3:11) and as treasure houses (3:10). They were thus objects of national pride (6:8). Ludwig Koehler[140] and Victor Maag[141] derive the word etymologically from a verbal root meaning "to throw" or "to shoot" (רמה I), pointing out that the cognate root in Akkadian has preserved the earlier meanings "to lay a foundation" and "to occupy a dwelling." Amos' Israelite contemporaries may well have heard in the word overtones of the similar sounding root רום ("to be high, exalted"), especially since the prophet treated these lofty abodes as physical expressions of haughtiness (3:10–11; 6:8).[142] Thus in destroying these structures Yahweh simultaneously reduces to ruins the self–reliance and wealth of their inhabitants. Archaeology has to date been able to contribute little to a fuller understanding of the nature of these "strongholds." However, Arnulf Kuschke has referred me to the house models from Yemen[143] and to the multi–storied buildings from Ḥaḍramaut which may preserve older building styles.[144]

Amos names as rulers of Damascus the Aramean kings Hazael and Benhadad. The name of Benhadad seems to be attested three times in the succession of Aramean kings. Benhadad I, son of Tabrimmon, ruled at the beginning of the ninth century.[145] He must be distinguished from the enemy of king Ahab of Israel in the middle of the ninth century,[146] who is regularly called "king of Aram" (מלך ארם), a title also borne by the quite possibly identical Barhadad of the Aramaic inscription from 'el–Brej.[147] According to 2 Kgs 8:15, this Benhadad was assassinated by Hazael, whom Shalmaneser III calls "the son of a nobody."[148] A son of this dynasty–founder, Hazael, again bore the old Damascene royal name Benhadad; he is mentioned in 2 Kgs 13:3 and 24, and on the Zakir Stele from Hamath.[149] This latter Benhadad was a contemporary of Adad–nirâri III of Assyria and of the kings Jehoahaz and Jehoash of Israel,[150] which means that his reign extended from c. 806 down into the eighth century. The available sources do not allow us to decide whether it was under his rule that the Aramean state again increased in power,[151] or whether Amos had in mind a Hazael II, a Benhadad IV, or even someone bearing

---

136 Sefîre stele I A 35–38 (*KAI* 222A.35–38).

137 Monolith Inscription 2.89. Translations: A. Leo Oppenheim, *ANET*³, 278; *AOT*², 340.

138 On the palace, cf. 1 Kgs 16:18 and 2 Kgs 15:25; on the capital city, cf. Am 1:7, 10, [12], 14; 2:2, [4] and Ps 122:7; cf. also Prv 18:19.

139 de Vaux, *Israel*, 235–36 [*Les Institutions de L'Ancien Testament*, vol. 2 (Paris: Les Éditions du Cerf, 1960), 41].

140 Koehler–Baumgartner, 88.

141 Maag, *Text*, 125–26.

142 Maag, *Text*, 127.

143 Helmuth Theodor Bossert, *Altsyrien* (Tübingen: E. Wasmuth, 1951), nos. 1275–1278.

144 Daniel van der Meulen and Hermann von Wissmann, *Ḥaḍramaut* (Leiden, 1932), pls. opposite pp. 80, 113, 124, etc.

145 1 Kgs 15:18, 20. Cf. Noth, *Könige*, 338–39.

146 1 Kgs 20:1–34; 2 Kgs 6:24; 8:7, 9.

147 *KAI* 201.1–3; see also Donner–Röllig, *KAI* 2, 203f; and Hans Bardtke, "Benhadad," *BHHW* 1, 215.

148 Basalt statue of Shalmaneser III, 1.25–26. Translations: A. Leo Oppenheim, *ANET*³, 280; *AOT*², 344. On the problems in the identification of Adad–idri with Benhadad II, see Ernst Michel, "Die Assur–Texte Salmanassars III. (858–824)," *WO* 1 (1947), 59; for additional literature, see Hans Bardtke, "Benhadad," *BHHW* 1, 215–16. On the usurper Hazael, see p. 149.

149 *KAI* 202 A 4.

150 See p. 150, and Donner–Röllig, *KAI* 2, 207, 209.

151 See p. 150.

an entirely different name. Just as Tiglath–pileser III still called Israel "house of Omri" almost 150 years after Omri's death,[152] so the Aramean rulers had been known for generations under the dynastic names of Benhadad and Hazael.[153] The fact that the names are mentioned here does not at all preclude the possibility that Amos was referring in 1:3b to contemporary events.[154]

■ **5** In what follows Yahweh is even more clearly portrayed as the military conqueror of Damascus. He breaks the "bar" of Damascus. The reference is to the device by means of which the city gate was secured, a factor in the defense of a city just as important as the fortification of its walls. Even in smaller cities this locking bar was made of bronze or iron (cf. 1 Kgs 4:13). In order to render impossible the pivoting open of the doors of the gate, even from the inside, the bar was anchored at each end in the gate–posts. Nothing short of the impossible feat of a Samson (Ju 16:3), i.e., lifting out the gate–posts together with the doors, could overcome the gate so secured with its bar. Yahweh's superior power "breaks asunder" the bar of Damascus.

After the reference to Damascus, two additional portions of the expansive Aramean kingdom are singled out. Both of these latter are designated only by means of Hebrew epithets, meant to characterize the natures of the districts: "Sin Valley" and "House of Pleasure." The use of such allusive names impedes more precise identifications.

"Sin Valley" (בִּקְעַת אָוֶן) could mean the fertile plateau between the Lebanon and the Antilebanon, which Josh 11:17 calls "the Valley of the Lebanon" (בִּקְעַת הַלְּבָנוֹן). Eissfeldt equated "Sin Valley" with the famous locality of Baalbek in the center of that plateau.[155] However, the name itself suggests a region,

and this becomes even more likely if "House of Pleasure" (or "House of Eden," בית עדן), which stands in poetic parallelism with "Sin Valley," is to be identified with the petty state of Bīt–Adini on the Euphrates, whose capital city of Til–Barsip (now *Tell ʾAḥmar*) was situated on the left bank of the Euphrates somewhat downstream from Carchemish. The references to "Eden" (עֶדֶן) in 2 Kgs 19:12 and Ezek 27:28[156] indicate the same area of northern Syria. It is true that around 856 B.C. this Aramean realm was made into an Assyrian province by Shalmaneser III, but under Šamši–ilu, who demonstrably governed Bīt–Adini for about thirty years (his name is attested for the period 780–752), this territory may well have been attached to the greater Aramean state, Urartu having weakened the hegemony of Assyria.[157] Perhaps it is due to the energetic governance of this "scepter bearer," Šamši–ilu, that Amos mentions the distant Bīt–Adini. Since he also refers to the apparently much closer region of the plateau between the Lebanon and the Antilebanon, he probably intends the two territories to represent the power of the Aramean kingdom, composed as it was of many small, self–governing territories all standing under the hegemony of Damascus.[158] In any case, in the year 733/32 Tiglath–pileser III transformed "sixteen districts of the land of Damascus"[159] into four Assyrian provinces.

Having introduced Damascene royal names in v 4, Amos also refers to the responsible sovereigns in v 5a, though here designating them only by function rather than by personal name. יוֹשֵׁב, on the basis of parallelism alone, must be taken to mean "the one who is enthroned" and not the region's population (for which one would rather expect a plural). The parallel תּוֹמֵךְ שֵׁבֶט ("bearer of a staff," i.e., as an insignia of rulership)

152 A. Leo Oppenheim, *ANET*³, 284; *AOT*², 347.
153 Cf. Cripps, 120.
154 See pp. 150–51.
155 Otto Eissfeldt, "Die ältesten Bezeugungen von Baalbek als Kultstätte," *Forschungen und Fortschritte* 12 (1936): 51–53.
156 Cf. Zimmerli, *Ezechiel*, 657. Cf. also textual note "j" to 1:5, on the G rendering.
157 Cf. Malamat, "Amos 1:5," 25–26; Gottwald, *Kingdoms*, 95–96; and William W. Hallo, "From Qarqar to Carchemish: Assyria and Israel in the Light of New Discoveries," *BA* 23 (1960): 34–61, esp. 44

(reprinted in David Noel Freedman and Edward F. Campbell, Jr., eds., *The Biblical Archaeologist Reader*, vol. 2 [Garden City, New York: Doubleday and Company, 1964], 152–88). See also pp. 150–51.
158 See Albrecht Alt, "Die syrische Staatenwelt vor dem Einbruch der Assyrer" in *Kleine Schriften zur Geschichte des Volkes Israel*, vol. 3, ed. Martin Noth (München: C. H. Beck, 1959), 223–24.
159 Annals 209. Translations: A. Leo Oppenheim, *ANET*³, 283; *AOT*², 347.

unequivocally designates a ruler. Of both it is said that Yahweh will "cut them down" (כרת hip'il) as one cuts down trees (1 Kgs 5:20 [6]).

The Aramean people, on the other hand, are to be deported back to their place of origin, "Kir" (קיר), which according to Am 9:7 apparently had the same historical significance for Aram as Egypt did for Israel. If that is so, then the force of the threat is the complete abrogation of the proud political history of the Arameans. Yahweh will do just this. Amos does not identify the political means by which the threat will be effectuated. But the idea of massive resettlement of conquered populations, though not attested in the Old Testament prior to Amos, must have been known to him. Tiglath-pileser III was not the first to relocate conquered peoples; this had already been practiced by the Urartians, who were ascendant in Amos' time.[160] According to 2 Kgs 16:9, the Assyrians carried out the threatened fate against Aram.

■ **6** Gaza alone is mentioned initially in the oracle against the Philistines, as was Damascus in the oracle against the Arameans. Apparently Gaza was considered foremost among the Philistine cities,[161] even though it was the southernmost of them, situated at the borderland with Egypt (i.e., modern *Ġazzeh*, located about five kilometers from the coast).[162] The indictment specifies deportation of people. At issue here is the practice, associated with war from earliest times in the ancient orient, of enslaving those taken captive.[163] That the deportation here is said to have been "complete" (שְׁלֵמָה) no doubt refers to the total conscription of entire settlements. The captured peoples in this instance were handed over to Edom.

The verb סגר (hip'il) is used to describe the extradition of an escaped slave to his lawful master in Dtn 23:16 [15], and the extradition of refugees in Ob 14. The same usage is attested for Aramaic סכר (hap'el) in the Sefîre treaty texts.[164] Neher has proposed this meaning for סגר in Am 1:6 as well, since nothing is said here of a commercial transaction.[165] But by selecting this verb (which in the qal means "to enclose"), Amos intends to point up the harsh, forceful treatment accorded the captives. There is no indication whatsoever of restoring to the Edomites what is rightfully theirs. On the contrary, it is stressed that the Philistines handed over defenseless people in great number to the mercy of a third party.[166] The wording indicates that Amos is concerned less with how such business was done than with the fact that human beings have been treated as mere objects, involuntarily serving the interests of the powerful. The Philistines have drawn upon their surplus of slaves, accumulated as spoils of war, to supply the needs of the Edomites. The transaction had a strictly economic significance.[167] We can only speculate as to whether the Edomites needed workers in greater numbers for their copper mining and smelting operations on the eastern side of the *Wādī 'el-'Arabah* near *Feinān*,[168] as well as for service in their seaports of Ezion–Geber and Elath on the Gulf of *'el-'Aqabah*,[169] or whether they acted as middlemen for buyers in Africa and South Arabia, being in the position to do so because of their traditional nomadic mobility and access to the Red Sea.[170] It is likely that Israelite (or Judean) villages were hit by Philistine slave raids, for the fighting in the borderland did not cease even after David's victories over the Philistines.[171] In Is 9:11 [12] the Arameans and the Philistines are allied in their oppression of Israel ("in front" and "in the back"). Yet Amos here associates the crime neither with a region (as he does in 1:3) nor a specific place. It is not

---

160   See p. 151.

161   See p. 78, on Joel 4:4.

162   Cf. 1 Kgs 5:1 [4:21] with 5:4 [4:24]; see also Noth, *Könige*, 76.

163   Cf. Isaac Mendelsohn, *Slavery in the Ancient Near East* (New York: Oxford University Press, 1949), 1ff; and 2 Sam 12:31; Dtn 21:10; Code of Hammurabi, pars. 280–81.

164   *KAI* 224.2–3.

165   Neher, *Amos*, 52.

166   See the related use of סכר hip'il ("to give over") in Is 19:4.

167   Mendelsohn, *Slavery*, 92ff, 121.

168   Noth, *World*, 44 [40].

169   *Ibid.*, 79 [72].

170   Cf. Gottwald, *Kingdoms*, 98–99.

171   Cf. 1 Kgs 2:39–40; 15:27; 16:15; 2 Chr 11:8; 2 Kgs 12:18 [17]; 2 Chr 26:6.

injury to Israel but exclusively the sheer inhumanity of the act as such which informs the indictment. Already in the second millennium B.C. clear limits were recognized in the ancient Near East to the arbitrary treatment of slaves, as is evident especially from the Code of Hammurabi and the Nuzi texts.[172] Ancient Israelite law took up this concern and provided its own emphases. It is in Amos that attention begins to be paid to the freedom and dignity of persons as such, a concern which ultimately aims at equality, elevating the slave to the status of brother to the free man.[173]

■ 7 Iniquitous Gaza will be subjected to the same hostile attack of Yahweh as Damascus.[174] Even the fortified wall will not withstand the divine pyrotechnics.

■ 8 Just as other territories of the Aramean kingdom were threatened in addition to Damsacus, so also here are three Philistine cities mentioned in addition to Gaza. In the same words as in 1:5aβ–γ we are told that Yahweh will "cut down" the "enthroned one" of Ashdod and the "scepter bearer" of Ashkelon.[175] Ashdod, modern 'Eśdūd, is situated approximately thirty–five kilometers to the northeast of Gaza and, like the latter, about five kilometers from the coast.[176] Halfway between these two cities lies the coastal town of Ashkelon, modern 'Aśqalān. The location of Ekron[177] has not been determined with certainty; in any case it must be sought inland and to the north rather than to the south of Ashdod. While it was customary for a time, following Alt, to identify Ekron with 'Āqir,[178] more recent investigations make likely its association with the Ḥirbet 'el-Muqanna' situated some twenty

kilometers from the coast, on the latitude of Ashdod.[179] Gath is not mentioned, probably because it was not independent in the days of Amos. After Hazael had seized it from the Judeans (2 Kgs 12:18 [17]),[180] it may have been briefly restored to Judean control under Uzziah (2 Chr 26:6), but at least by 711 it belonged to the realm of Ashdod.[181]

Yahweh's "hand," turned against Ekron, denotes his overwhelming strength. He who is in someone's hand is in his power.[182] Here we meet for the first time the characteristic idea of Amos that it means calamity if Yahweh "turns toward" (שׁוּב hip'il)[183] someone. Equally characteristic is the threat expressed in the final clause, which proclaims destruction even for the "remnant" of the Philistines. Oracles against Israel often conclude with the notice that any remnant which escapes the initial stroke of punishment will inevitably fall under a subsequent blow.[184] Ezek 25:16 returns to the theme of Am 1:8bβ.

■ 9 The oracle against Tyre issues its initial indictment in words almost identical with those used in the preceding oracle against the Philistines.[185] This alone marks the Tyre oracle as secondary.[186] Threats against Phoenicia's leading commercial and maritime city with its island fortress[187] are attested in Israel only after 604 B.C., when Nebuchadnezzar II made his appearance.[188] It is understandable that an exilic author would modify the phrase "to deport into exile" (הגלה גלות), which in 1:6 was used to refer to the carrying off of people into slavery, because in the meantime the expression had come to refer exclusively to the de-

172 Cf. the data collected by Mendelsohn, Slavery.

173 Neh 5:8; Job 31:13–15; 1 Cor 12:13; Gal 3:28.

174 See pp. 154–55, on 1:4.

175 See pp. 156–57.

176 For the excavation results, see David Noel Freedman, "The Second Season at Ancient Ashdod," BA 26 (1963): 134–39.

177 On the original pronunciation 'Aqqārôn (עֶקְרוֹן), see textual note "n" to 1:8.

178 Albrecht Alt, "Das Institut im Jahre 1932," PJ 29 (1933): 13. This identification was still adopted by Noth, Josua, 75.

179 Kurt Galling, "Pentapolis," RGG³ 5, 210.

180 See p. 149.

181 Sargon's "Display Inscription," 104. Translations: A. Leo Oppenheim, ANET³, 286; AOT², 350.

182 Aubrey R. Johnson, The Vitality of the Individual in

the Thought of Ancient Israel (Cardiff: University of Wales Press, ²1964), 56; cf. Dtn 26:8; Is 5:25, etc.; [Is 1:25].

183 Other formulations are employed to express the idea in 5:17b; 7:8b; 8:2b; 9:4b.

184 4:2; 8:10; 9:1; here the "remnant" is always called אחרית; cf. Gese, "Beiträge," 436–37. On the subject, cf. also 2:14–16; 6:9–10; and 9:1–4.

185 See above, p. 157, on 1:6b.

186 See pp. 139–40.

187 See p. 78.

188 Jer 27:3; 47:4; 25:22; Ezek 26:1—28:19; Is 23; Joel 4:4–8 [3:4–8].

portation policies of the Babylonian empire.[189] The Phoenicians themselves did not practice deportation of subject peoples; they merely delivered up (refugees of) the "exile" (גָּלוּת) (cf. Ob 14). From 1:6b the redactor took over the identification of the Edomites as partners in the slave trade, since in his own time they were, of course, a matter of very major concern.[190] In contrast to Amos' practice, the redactor explains why the crime of Tyre was so reprehensible: "They did not remember the covenant of brothers." Prominent biblical usage of the verb זכר ("to remember") is first attested in Deuteronomy (where it occurs 13 times), Ezekiel (9 times) and Deutero–Isaiah (9 times).[191] The expression "to remember a covenant" (זכר ברית) is unattested in preexilic material but is relatively frequent in the Priestly Work.[192] In this expression זכר connotes an "active, not only a reflective attitude," directed toward the "preservation" of the covenant.[193] "Covenant" (ברית) is probably associated etymologically with Akkadian *bi/ertu(m)*, which with lengthening of the second syllable gives rise to the Middle Assyrian *berittu* ("bond, fetter").[194] The word expresses a legal relationship between two parties.[195] The expression "covenant of brothers" used here is unattested elsewhere in the Old Testament and in documents from the ancient Near East. However, brotherhood is mentioned in a stereotyped way in connection with the conclusion of political treaties, as for example in that between Ramses II and Ḫattušiliš III.[196] In the Old Testament, "my brother" occurs as a form of address in the course of negotiations between treaty partners in 1 Kgs 9:10–14 (13!).[197] Those interpreters[198] who want to trace the expression "covenant of brothers" to Amos himself, and who view it as a reference to the relationship of "brotherhood" existing between Tyre and Israel, recall the treaty between Hiram of Tyre and Solomon (cf. 1 Kgs 5:15–26 [1–12]), which had a prior history under David (2 Sam 5:11) and a sequel under Ahab (1 Kgs 16:31). It is more likely, however, that the "covenant of brothers" (ברית אחים) refers to the bond of kinship between Israel and Edom, a relationship canonically expressed in the Jacob—Esau sagas of Genesis.[199] The Deuteronomic writings, to which the indictment in our oracle exhibits a linguistic relationship, explicitly declared Edom to be the "brother" of Israel (Dtn 23:8a [7a]; cf. Hos 12:4 [3]). 1:11, which also comes from the later redactor,[200] confirms this interpretation, since Edom is clearly seen here as standing in a relationship of brotherhood with Israel. Thus the reference in our oracle is not to one particular treaty but to the paradigm of all treaties: the legal consanguineous bond uniting kinsmen.[201] The whole sentence corresponds to the theological and salvation–historical language and thought of circles

189 2 Kgs 24:14–15; 25:11; Jer 24:1; 27:10; 52:30 and elsewhere.

190 See p. 160 on 1:11.

191 Brevard S. Childs, *Memory and Tradition in Israel*, SBT 37 (London: SCM, 1962), 43–44.

192 Gen 9:15–16; Ex 2:24; 6:5; also Lev 26:42, 45; Ezek 16:60. Cf. also Willy Schottroff, *"Gedenken" im Alten Orient und im Alten Testament*, WMANT 15 (Neukirchen-Vluyn: Neukirchener Verlag, ²1967), 202.

193 Schottroff, *Gedanken*, 159–60.

194 Oswald Loretz, "ברית—'Band–Bund'," *VT* 16 (1965): 239–41; and *AHW* 1, 129–30.

195 Wolff, *Hosea*, 50–51 [61–62].

196 In the Egyptian text of the treaty: ". . . that good peace and brotherhood occur between us forever, while he is in brotherhood with me, and he is at peace with me, and I am in brotherhood with him and I am at peace with him forever" (John A. Wilson, *ANET*³, 199). Cf. the Hittite version, Albrecht Goetze, *ANET*³, 201–02. For additional evidence and literature, see Erhard Gerstenberger, "Covenant and Commandment," *JBL* 84 (1965): 40–41.

197 Cf. 1 Kgs 20:32; Gen 13:8; 31:46, 54.

198 So Hitzig; Budde, "Amos," 62–64; and Neher, *Amos*, 52, 66–67.

199 Gen 25—28; 32—33; Nu 20:14. Cf. already Wellhausen, 69–70; also Nötscher; Fosbroke; Zimmerli, *Ezechiel*, 597; and Martin Noth, "Edomiter," *RGG*³ 2, 309.

200 See p. 151.

201 Cf. Gottfried Quell, "διαθήκη," *TDNT* 2, 114; and Koehler–Baumgartner, 26 ("duty towards tribal kinsmen"). Cf. also Jean Nougayrol, *Le Palais Royal d'Ugarit*, vol. 4 ("Textes Accadiens des Archives Sud"), Mission de Ras Shamra 9 (Paris: Imprimerie Nationale, 1956), 133 (17.116.21–22): "Indeed my brother, I and you are brothers, sons of the same man. Since we are brothers, why should there not be good relations between us?" [Trans. by Ed.].

trained in the Deuteronomistic tradition.

■ **10** The announcement of punishment simply repeats the first sentence of the threat against the Philistine cities.[202]

■ **11** Particular expressions in the oracle against Edom identify it also as an exilic addition. To be sure, the relationship between Israel and Edom had been strained since the days of David (2 Sam 8:13–14) and Solomon (1 Kgs 11:14–15), access to the Gulf of *'el-'Aqabah* being an especially frequent point of contention.[203] The same situation prevailed in the days of Uzziah, Amos' contemporary (2 Kgs 14:22). At that time it was admittedly the Judean king who was the aggressor, as he campaigned through the Edomite territory to the east and west of the *Wādī 'el-'Arabah* between the Dead Sea and the Gulf of *'el-'Aqabah*. Thus over the course of centuries Edom's "anger" had grown. However, that Edom "pursued his brother with the sword," together with the statements following this one, is best understood with reference to the period after the Babylonian conquest of Jerusalem in 587; for this period alone are there supporting statements elsewhere. According to Ezek 35:5–6 it was then that the Edomites took their revenge with the "sword" on the defenseless Judeans, while Ob 14 confirms that refugees in particular were those whom the Edomites persecuted, slaughtered, or extradited.[204] Ob 10 and 12 speak of Jacob as "brother," referring to the same situation reflected in our supplementary oracle in Amos.[205] Only in this later period was it especially appropriate to expect that "pity" might be shown by Edom. But

"pity" was suppressed by seething anger, inciting Edom even to "plunder."[206] The latter probably refers to plundering in the destroyed city of Jerusalem (Ob 13; Ps 137:7). Edom's wrath is thus "alert";[207] it acts "continuously,"[208] fueling bitter revenge and spiteful joy over Jerusalem's downfall (Ob 9–14; Ezek 35:15).

■ **12** Here, as in the oracle against Tyre, the announcement of punishment corresponds to what is only the initial bicolon of the same element in the older oracles of Amos himself. The localities designated are Teman and Bozrah. Teman may refer to a region. Wellhausen already observed that "upon the wall" (בְּחוֹמַת, cf. 1:7, 10, 14) is missing here;[209] a simple "against" (בְּ) prefaces the names of countries in 2:2 and 5. Perhaps Teman is also to be understood as referring to a region in Jer 49:7 and 20,[210] though it may be the name of a city as well.[211] Likewise, Bozrah is not only a particular city (*Bṣêrah*) situated on the heights east of the *Wādī 'el-'Arabah*, approximately halfway between the southern tip of the Dead Sea and the Gulf of *'el-'Aqabah*; it is also the name of a larger district within which several towns are located.[212] Teman and Bozrah alike are prominently mentioned among the Edomite localities and regions only in exilic and postexilic texts.

■ **13** In the oracle against Ammon it is again Amos who speaks. He refers to the accused by the usual designation "sons of Ammon." It is exceptional in the Old Testament for "Ammon" (1 Sam 11:11; Ps 82:8 [7]) to be used in the way that Amos, in our series of oracles, speaks of Aram (1:5), Edom (1:6), Moab (2:1), and Israel (2:6).[213] The indictment charges that "they

202 See p. 158, on 1:7.
203 2 Kgs 8:20–22; 14:7, 22; 16:6.
204 Cf. also Joel 4:19 [3:19].
205 See pp. 158–59, on 1:9bβ.
206 See textual note "t" to 1:11.
207 On the form שׁמרה, see textual note "v" to 1:11.
208 On the adverbial use of נצח in the sense of "really, truly" and then "forever," cf. Lienhard Delekat, "Probleme der Psalmenüberschriften," *ZAW* 76 (1964): 288; and L. Kopf, "Arabische Etymologien und Parallelen zum Bibelwörterbuch," *VT* 8 (1958): 184–86.
209 Wellhausen, 70.
210 Rudolph, *Jeremia*, 290.
211 Cf. Gen 36:15, 42; Ob 9; Ezek 25:13; and Zimmerli, *Ezechiel*, 597. Cf. also Nelson Glueck, *Explorations in Eastern Palestine*, AASOR 15 (New

Haven, 1934–35), 82–83; and *idem*, "Three Israelite Towns in the Jordan Valley: Zarethan, Succoth, Zaphon," *BASOR* 90 (1943): 5; Glueck proposes to identify Teman with the site of *Ṭawîlān* in the vicinity of Petra.
212 Jer 49:13; cf. Jer 49:22; Is 34:6; 63:1; Gen 36:33.
213 See Zimmerli, *Ezechiel*, 589–90.

ripped open the pregnant women of Gilead." This atrocity of warfare is attested in the ancient Near East. Tiglath–pileser I (c. 1100 B.C.) is lauded in these words: "He shredded to pieces the bellies of the pregnant, he pierced the body of the weak."[214] Homer also knows of the practice.[215] In the Old Testament such an act is not only anticipated from the Aramean Hazael (2 Kgs 8:12), but is even attributed to the Israelite king Menahem (2 Kgs 15:16). In Hosea 14:1 [13:16] it is used as a threat. The verb בקע employed in these cases[216] is used elsewhere to describe the "ripping apart" of prey by animals (2 Kgs 2:24; Hos 13:8). In contrast to the attitude toward this act of warfare attributed to Tiglath–pileser and Agamemnon (in the *Iliad*), Amos deems it grounds for punishment because it is executed upon defenseless women and helpless unborn. This atrocity was committed as part of a program of territorial expansion. "Gilead" here means the region of Transjordan south of the Jabbok River settled by the tribe of Ephraim.[217] Since the period of the Judges, the Ammonites had repeatedly pushed from the east into the fertile areas of western Transjordan.[218] In the days of Amos they were once again encroaching upon Gilead, encouraged by the neighboring Arameans to the north (1:3).[219] Apparently Jeroboam II was unable to "restore" the boundary between Gilead and Ammon without resorting to warfare (cf. 2 Kgs 14:25, 28).

■ **14** The unexpected variant "so I will kindle" (וְהִצַּתִּי) in the otherwise stereotyped opening of the announcement of punishment ("so I will send" [וְשִׁלַּחְתִּי] in 1:4,

7; 2:2) is in accord with Jer 49:(2,) 27; its appearance here is to be traced to the work of a scribe probably influenced by terminology in the book of Jeremiah.[220] The fire devastates "Rabbah" (רבה), "the great," the capital city of the Ammonites,[221] which was situated on the upper course of the Jabbok in the area of the modern Jordanian capital ʾAmmān. In what follows it is explicitly affirmed that Yahweh, as warrior, kindles the conflagration.[222] The "fanfare on the day of battle" describes the intense shouting of all the combatants (1 Sam 4:5–6), augmented by the blowing of trumpets (Am 2:2). Such a clamor might denote either a signal for attack[223] or the warning to those under attack raised by their own watchmen.[224] Intended here is the noise of the attack,[225] as is shown by the following parallel colon. "Tempest" (סַעַר) can only be understood as a phenomenon accompanying a theophany of Yahweh:[226] it is the lashing, pursuing (Ps 83:16 [15]), even fire–fanning storm (Jer 23:19: "whirling tempest"). סופה designates the destructive "whirlwind" (Hos 8:7) whose effects upon humanity are devastating (cf. Prv 1:27; 10:25). Yahweh, appropriating as his own all of the awesome power attributed to weather deities, brings the whirlwind along with his raging storm.

■ **15** Despite that segment of the textual tradition which assumes the vocalization מִלְכֹּם ("Milkom") instead of מַלְכָּם ("their king"),[227] Yahweh's war is not against gods. Rather it is a human foe who is threatened here, just as in the other oracles of Amos against foreign nations and against Israel. This is clearly supposed by

214 Hartmut Schmökel, *Ur, Assur und Babylon: Drei Jahrtausende im Zweistromland*, Grosse Kulturen der Frühzeit (Stuttgart: G. Kilpper, 1955), 114.

215 *Iliad* 6.57–58: "Of them let not one escape sheer destruction and the might of our hands, nay, not the man–child whom his mother bears in her womb; let not even him escape, but let all perish together out of Ilios, unmourned and unmarked" (tr. A. T. Murray, *Homer, The Iliad*, vol. 1, Loeb Classical Library [Cambridge, Massachusetts, and London, 1924], 266–67).

216 The pi'el is used in 2 Kgs 8:12; 15:16; and the pu'al in Hos 14:1 [13:6]. Whether the qal vocalization accurately preserves the language of Amos cannot be determined; see textual note "x" to 1:13.

217 See p. 154, on 1:3.

218 Ju 11:4–5; 1 Sam 11; cf. Jer 49:1.

219 See pp. 150–51.

220 Cf. Jer 11:16; 17:27; 21:14; 32:29; 43:12; 50:32.

221 2 Sam 11:1; 12:27, 29. To distinguish the capital from other "great" cities, it is also called "Rabbah of the Ammonites" (רַבַּת בְּנֵי עַמּוֹן), e.g., 2 Sam 12:26.

222 See pp. 154–55, on 1:4.

223 1 Sam 4:5–6; Jer 4:19; Ezek 21:27 [22].

224 Only the blowing of trumpets is attested for the alarm, however (Nu 10:9; Hos 5:8). See Wolff, *Hosea*, 113 [143].

225 Cf. Paul Humbert, *La "terou'a": Analyse d'un rite biblique* (Neuchâtel: Secrétariat de l'Université, 1946).

226 Cf. Ps 83:16 [15]; Is 29:6; and Na 1:3.

227 See textual note "cc" to 1:15.

the immediate context. The reading "their king" is required by the reference to "princes" (שׂרים), meaning court and military officials,[228] in the following parallel colon.[229] Hence, as in the case of the Arameans in 1:5,[230] the result of the war of conquest is announced to be the deportation of the king and his bureaucracy. Here also, then, it is for the purpose of historical intervention that Yahweh, in waging holy war, employs the natural forces of fire and storm.

■ **2:1** Threatened next are the Moabites, the kindred of the Ammonites.[231] The main settlements of Moab were located east of the southern half of the Dead Sea, in the area extending from *Šēl Hēdān* and the Arnon (*Šēl 'el–Mōjib*) to the *Wādī 'el–Ḥesā*.[232] The latter, which opens into the southern end of the Dead Sea, forms the natural boundary between Moab and Edom, being quite a deep rift throughout its course.[233] Moreover its fords were protected on both sides by border fortifications.[234] This suggests that armed confrontations must have taken place between Moab and Edom, even though little record of them has been preserved. They are presupposed when Amos accuses Moab of desecrating the bones of an Edomite king. But this allegation is too vague to suppose that the act of violence to which it refers had occurred as a consequence of the campaign which, according to 2 Kgs 3:6–7, Joram of Israel and Jehoshaphat of Judah had conducted through the steppes of Edom—and with the direct support of the king of Edom (2 Kgs 3:9)— against a rebellious Moab.[235] Hostilities between Moab and Edom are probably also referred to in the conclusion of the Mēša' inscription.[236] The information given in the text of Amos does not allow us to date the event in question. In all probability the prophet had in mind some otherwise unknown incident of the quite recent past, and not wars of the ninth century.[237]

Royal bones were burned to lime. This offense against one who is dead forms the counterpart to the outrage against unborn life for which the Ammonites are reproached in 1:13. To the ancients, the bones of a dead person were not merely a reminder of a life that had been. A certain power inhered in them, as is illustrated by 2 Kgs 13:20–21, according to which a corpse was revivified through contact with the bones of Elisha.[238] Still, there is no indication that Amos shares in this magical way of thinking. Perhaps he only echoes the common sentiment that even the corpse of an enemy should be given proper burial.[239] In this case, then, the corpse was violated in an especially offensive way, the bones having been "burned to lime." Death by fire was an ancient form of capital punishment,[240] whose purpose was the total obliteration of evil. If Amos stresses "to lime" (לשׂיד), he surely wants to underscore the totality of the destruction. The corpse was burned so thoroughly ". . . that the bone ashes became as fine and white as powdered chalk."[241] The Vulgate brings out this nuance by specifying that the bones were burned "entirely unto ashes."[242] But since Amos apparently had in mind something especially reprehensible, we must probably follow the Targum in interpreting לשׂיד to mean that the Moabites had

228 See Wolff, *Hosea*, 62 [78].

229 Cf. Hos 3:4; 7:3, 5; 13:10.

230 See pp. 156–57.

231 On the possible compositional significance of this, see p. 148.

232 Cf. further Zimmerli, *Ezechiel*, 593.

233 Martin Noth, "Beiträge zur Geschichte des Ostjordanlandes III," BBLAK (= *ZDPV* 68) (1951): 46 (= idem, *Aufsätze* 1, 519).

234 Nelson Glueck, *Explorations in Eastern Palestine II*, AASOR 15 (New Haven, 1934–35), 104–106.

235 So A. H. van Zyl, *The Moabites*, Pretoria Oriental Series 3 (Leiden: E. J. Brill, 1960), 20.

236 Lines 31–33; cf. Donner–Röllig, *KAI* 2, 179; and also van Zyl, *Moabites*, 143.

237 See pp. 150–51.

238 Cf. Aubrey R. Johnson, *The Vitality of the Individual in the Thought of Ancient Israel* (Cardiff: University of Wales Press, ²1964), 88.

239 2 Kgs 9:34; cf. Amsler, 177.

240 E.g. Gen 38:24; Lev 20:14; and Josh 7:25. Cf. Karl Elliger, *Leviticus*, HAT 1/4 (Tübingen: J. C. B. Mohr [Paul Siebeck], 1966), 276.

241 Gradwohl, *Farben*, 87.

242 See textual note "b" to 2:1.

manufactured from these royal ashes some substance which could be used to whitewash stones (Dtn 27:2, 4) and houses.[243] That such a thing was done to an Edomite king makes it for Amos no less reprehensible than if it had been done to an Israelite. Nor is there the slightest intimation that the Edomites were considered to be allies of Israel.[244] The mere fact that the remains of a human being were so desecrated, that a man had been treated as material, was of itself sufficient cause for Amos' indictment.

■ 2 Again Yahweh will attack with fire. Designated as its targets are, first, the population of Moab,[245] which had been indicted in 2:1, without a specific place being mentioned;[246] and, in the parallel colon, Kerioth. Bernhardt has identified the latter place as modern *Qurēyāt ʿAlēyān*, situated in the eastern part of the fertile plateau of *ʾel–Belqā*.[247] The fact that it is the single Moabite locality to be specified becomes intelligible in light of the Mēšaʿ inscription, which indicates that Kerioth was the site of a venerable sanctuary of Chemosh, the Moabite god.[248] (It is difficult to decide whether the definite article in הקריות originated with Amos or was added by some later copyist.[249]) The threatened punishment is obviously once again military annihilation by Yahweh, for Moab "dies" amidst the tumult of battle. שאון refers to the "uproar" raised by masses of storming troops (Is 13:4) or to the "clash" of an attack on fortified cities (Hos 10:14).[250]

In addition to the general population of Moab, the nation's political leaders are explicitly named (as in 1:5, 8, 15)—though here, to be sure, it is not the king (cf. 1:15) but the שופט, elsewhere usually rendered "judge," who is designated along with the "princes" (שרים). The reference is to the regent, who, while no doubt an arbiter in judicial matters, was empowered to make other sorts of decisions as well.[251] For all purposes, then, the official in question was a king.[252] Moreover, it is a monarchy which, from earliest times, is attested as Moab's form of government.[253] Thus it is emphasized once more by Amos that through Yahweh's war a death blow will be leveled against those who have wantonly violated human dignity.

■ 4 The accusation made against Judah is more extensive than that in any of the preceding oracles; in word count it slightly surpasses even the indictment of Edom (1:11). Qualitatively it is unique as well, specifying no crimes against human beings, but only those committed directly against Yahweh. The stylistic break within the speech of Yahweh—where reference is made to Yahweh in the third person (v 4bα)—forcefully draws attention to this essential character of Judah's guilt.

The phraseology throughout the indictment reflects the language of the Deuteronomistic school. Since the time of Josiah,[254] the school had diligently attended to the "Torah" (תורה) as crystallized in the Deuteronomic law which it considered to be the authoritative instruction of Yahweh. From this perspective Israel's culpability lay in having repudiated (מאס) Yahweh and his words,[255] since the observance of Yahweh's decrees was the chief mandate with which Israel had been charged.[256] The converse formulation of this

---

243 See textual note "b" to 2:1.
244 Cf. Reventlow, *Amt*, 68.
245 Cf. also מואב in 2:2b.
246 See textual note "c" to 2:2.
247 Karl–Heinz Bernhardt, "Beobachtungen zur Identifizierung moabitischer Ortslagen," *ZDPV* 76 (1960): 136–158; and map, 137.
248 Mēšaʿ inscription, ll. 12–13.
249 Compare Jer 48:41 with 48:24. Cf. Karl–Heinz Bernhardt, "Beobachtungen zur Identifizierung moabitischer Ortslagen," *ZDPV* 76 (1960): 144.
250 See Wolff, Hosea, 187 [243]. On "tumult of war" (תרועה), see p. 161, on 1:14b.
251 1 Kgs 3:9; 2 Kgs 15:5; Dan 9:12.
252 Wolfgang Richter, "Zu den 'Richtern Israels'," *ZAW* 77 (1965): 40–72 (esp. 58, 71); and Noth, *Könige*, 51.

253 Nu 23:7; Ju 3:12–19; 2 Kgs 3:4–7; Jer 27:3; and the Mēšaʿ inscription, ll. 1, 23.
254 2 Kgs 22:8, 11; 23:24–25.
255 1 Sam 8:7; 10:19; 15:23, 26; 2 Kgs 17:15.
256 "To keep his statutes" (שמר חקיו): Dtn 4:5–6, 40; 5:1; 6:17; 7:11; 11:32; 16:12; 17:19; 26:16–17; 1 Kgs 3:14; 8:58; 9:4; 2 Kgs 17:37; 23:3. In Deuteronomistic parlance תורה refers to Yahweh's "instruction" as a whole, while חקים means the "decrees" or "statutes" considered individually. Cf. Dtn 4:44–45; 17:19; and also Richard Hentschke, *Satzung und Setzender: Ein Beitrag zur israelitischen Rechtsterminologie*: BWANT 83 (Stuttgart: W. Kohlhammer, 1963), 89, 92.

(v 4bβ) is also typical of the Deuteronomistic school: defection to foreign gods and being led astray by them.[257] Only the word כְּזָבִים (literally "lies") as a designation for the false gods is otherwise unattested in the school's parlance. Elsewhere, following the usage current in Jeremiah (e.g., 2:5), the usual Deuteronomistic surrogate for idol is הֶבֶל (often rendered "vanity").[258] Yet in Jer 10:14–15 the latter already occurs in parallelism with "falsehood" (שֶׁקֶר), and in Ps 62:10 [9] it is paralleled by "lie" (כָּזָב). The Deuteronomistic attitude is clearly stated in 1 Sam 12:21(cf. 2 Kgs 17:15b): foreign deities can neither profit nor save; consequently they deceive. Or, as our Deuteronomistic preacher in Amos expresses it, they are "lies" personified.[259]

■ 5 Because Judah, since the days of the fathers, had followed the deceptively attractive pagan divinities rather than the established word of Yahweh, it receives the same judgment which the crimes of the foreign nations had merited for them. Our Deuteronomist, writing at a time when "the fire" had long since consumed Jerusalem (2 Kgs 25:9), was content to repeat the stereotyped sentence of Amos without elaboration; he confined his eloquence to a disclosure of what he saw to be the fundamental reason his God had sent this punishment (2:4).

■ 6 The final oracle of Amos in this series is directed against "Israel." Does this refer to the state of that name, the northern kingdom? Amos' preceding oracles might initially lead us to suppose so, since in the corresponding formulaic openings of each of them a political entity is identified: Damascus (1:3), Gaza (1:6), the Ammonites (1:13), and Moab (2:1). Furthermore, a national catastrophe is threatened at the end of the oracle against Israel (2:14–16). However, the list of accusations in 2:6–9 is clearly distinguished from the reproaches against the foreign nations by the fact that it does not include war crimes, for which the national leadership would primarily be held accountable. The announcements of punishment against the foreign nations always name those politically responsible,[260] whereas in the oracle against Israel this is nowhere the case.

"Israel" in the Book of Amos

The name "Israel" (ישראל) occurs a total of thirty times in Amos. It stands alone in ten cases (1:1bα[1]; 2:6; 3:14; [4:12a, 12b]; 7:9, 11, 16, 17; 9:7b). The expression "my people Israel" (עַמִּי יִשְׂרָאֵל) occurs four times (7:8, 15; 8:2; [9:14]); "virgin Israel" (בְּתוּלַת יִשְׂרָאֵל) is found once (5:2); "sons of Israel" (בְּנֵי יִשְׂרָאֵל) five times ([2:11]; 3:1, 12; 4:5; 9:7a); "house of Israel" (בֵּית יִשְׂרָאֵל) eight times (5:1, 3, 4, [25]; 6:[1], 14; [7:10b]; 9:9); and "king of Israel" (מֶלֶךְ יִשְׂרָאֵל) appears twice ([1:1bα[2]; 7:10a]). On closer inspection it is apparent that the usage of "Israel," "house of Israel," and "sons of Israel" is not random. The connotation of "house of Israel" is clearest in 7:10b, where the immediate context is concerned with the fate of the "king of Israel" (7:10a; cf. 7:9, 11 and 1:1bα[2]) and, consequently, with the fate of the royal dynasty and the northern state (7:10bβ–γ). But in the remaining seven occurrences as well, "house of Israel" refers to the state of the northern kingdom, with its supporting political (5:1–3; [6:1]) and cultic (5:4, 25; cf. 7:13) institutions, in the midst of the rest of the nations of the world (6:14; 9:9). On the other hand, the simple designation "Israel" appears alongside "my people Israel" (7:15–17; cf. 7:8, 9),[261] thus connoting *the people of God* (cf. 4:12b). This meaning is also implied in 9:7b, where the reference is to God's historical dealings with "Israel"; and in 2:6 and 3:14, which speak of God's plans for "Israel" (cf. 2:9); and in 7:9, 11b, 17b (cf. 1:1bα[1]), where the end of this history is announced. The expression "sons of Israel" has the same connotation as "Israel," the only distinction between them being stylistic: "sons of Israel" usually appears in direct address formulated in the second person plural (2:11; 3:1a; 4:5; 9:7a; the single exception being 3:12), whereas "Israel" always appears as a third person singular referent, except in the case of 4:12 (second person singular).

---

257 Ju 2:11–13; 1 Sam 12:20–21; 2 Kgs 17:15. תעה hip'il ("to lead astray, seduce") is also used in 2 Kgs 21:9 to describe apostasy, while הלך אחרי occurs with this sense frequently, e.g., Dtn 4:3; 6:14; 8:19; 11:28; 13:3 [2]; Ju 2:12; and 2 Kgs 17:15.

258 E.g., 2 Kgs 17:15; see textual note "f" to 2:4.

259 Cf. Martin Alfred Klopfenstein, *Die Lüge nach dem Alten Testament* (Zürich: Gotthelf, 1964), 236–37.

260 1:4–5, 8, 15; 2:3; note the contrast in the secondary oracles 1:10, 12; 2:5.

261 See also the exposition of 7:8, *ad loc*.

Hence also in our passage when Amos says "Israel" he intends to level the following accusations against the people of God. This is made quite clear as the accusation is developed in 2:6b–8, and especially by the contrast drawn in 2:9 between Israel's deeds and the acts of Yahweh. The crimes with which Israel is charged, unlike those leveled against the foreign nations, consist not of war crimes perpetrated against other nations, but rather of transgressions against the harmonious ordering of Israelite communal life. Israel's "war crimes" are acts committed by the powerful in oppressing the poor among their own people. The full list of such crimes is enumerated in four bicola.

1. Sale into Debt–Slavery of the Innocent and the Needy. Here and elsewhere such transactions are designated by the verb מכר "to sell,"[262] the inverse being expressed by קנה "to purchase."[263] Although the practice could involve kidnaping (Ex 21:16; Dtn 24:7), this was not usually the case according to the biblical attestations, that in 2 Kgs 4:1 being especially clear on the point.[264] Since the victim in Am 2:6 is called "innocent" (צדיק), some interpreters have supposed the crime as here charged to involve the bribing of judges.[265] But where bribery is demonstrably in view, Amos employs different language (5:12; 2:7aβ).[266] To be sure, both here and in 5:12 צדיק designates the person guiltless before the law, yet the point at issue is not a judicial sentence passed on the victim, but the fact that he is sold for money. The one who is "innocent" is paralleled by the "needy" (אביון), and the latter term even replaces the former in the closely related oracle in 8:6 (where דַּלִּים // אביון). The stated reason for this selling of human beings was to satisfy creditors demanding monetary compensation for "silver" owed them,[267] or even in lieu of other payment for a mere

"pair of sandals" (which had been stolen, or borrowed and then lost?). The noun נַעֲלָיִם (dual, "sandals") is attested only in Amos, namely here and in 8:6; the use of the dual was perhaps meant to indicate a single pair of sandals.[268] Such a debt is much too insignificant to justify the enslavement of a poor debtor; the אביון is by definition one who is "in need" of help.[269] In the case of the monetary indebtedness, on the other hand, the amount owed need not have been insignificant. Here the seller is accused because he accepted money in exchange for an "innocent" person, which could involve, for example, either someone kidnaped (Ex 21:16; Dtn 24:7) or the son of a debtor (2 Kgs 4:1). It is not possible to conclude from the tone of Amos' accusation that he rejected slavery for debt as a legal institution altogether. Rather his indictment is leveled, on the one hand, against the sale of individuals who were personally innocent and, on the other hand, against the sale of needy persons who had only incurred debt for some minor necessity of life. It is not accidental that "innocent" (צדיק) stands in the first colon while "sandals" (נעלים) emphatically concludes the second. In so far as Amos was at all mindful of the distinction between "casuistic" and "apodictic" laws, one can say at the most that he, in agreement "with one of the fundamental tendencies of apodictic law,"[270] was concerned to restrict liability in the practice of debt–servitude, as it was legitimated in the casuistic law (Ex 21:2–11; Dtn 15:12–19), to those who had themselves incurred heavy debts.[271] Yet Amos' judgment is not rendered on the basis of a selective acceptance or rejection of certain legal traditions. He speaks rather as an advocate for "the rights of the poor and needy" (Prv 31:9), assuming an obligation well recognized in Israel no less than in "the wisdom of the sons

---

262 Ex 21:7–8; Lev 25:39; Dtn 15:12; Is 50:1; Neh 5:8.

263 Am 8:6; Ex 21:2; Neh 5:8; see also textual note "h" to 2:6.

264 Cf. Neh 5:2, 5. See also the texts cited in nn. 262 and 263 above.

265 So Sellin, and Robinson.

266 Cf. Is 1:23; 5:23; Mi 3:11; 1 Sam 12:3; and Ps 15:5.

267 See textual note "i" to 2:6.

268 Joüon, par. 91c.

269 Koehler–Baumgartner, 4–5.

270 Bach, "Gottesrecht," 29. Cf. Ex 21:6 and Dtn 24:7.

271 Cf. 2 Kgs 4:1–7; Lev 25:39–46; and Neh 5:1–13.

of the east.''[272] In view of the formal use in 2:6a of the numerical saying, it seems a likely possibility that the clan wisdom with which Amos was so intimately acquainted may have imposed narrow restrictions on the practice of debt–servitude.

■ 7 2. Oppression of the Poor. The same sapiential regimen of clan life informs not only the participial construction[273] of v 7a, but also the parallel statements about the "poor" (דלים) and the "oppressed" (ענוים). These terms are nowehere paralleled in the legal traditions of the Pentateuch, but they do so appear in the woe–cry of Is 10:2, where the plural forms of the words and the theme of the text are identical with those of Am 2:7. This suggests less that Isaiah was dependent upon Amos[274] than that both prophets drew upon a common stock of sapiential material.[275] The terms עני and דל are used in parallelism to articulate the same concern in the sapiential admonition of Prv 22:22: "Do not rob the poor, because he is poor, or crush the oppressed at the gate!"[276] Moreover the word דל—standing alone as a designation for one who is lowly, weak, helpless—appears nowhere else in the Old Testament with such frequency as it does in wisdom sayings.[277] The antonym of דָּל is "rich" (עָשִׁיר);[278] in three instances the injustice perpetrated against the poor is described as "oppression" or "violation" (עשק).[279] It is in accord with this that Amos' indictment is directed against "those who ⟨trample⟩ upon the head of the poor."[280] The ענוים[281] are those who are "humbled" or "oppressed."[282] Their opposites are not the rich, but the brutal and the arrogant;[283] accordingly ". . . the concept involves a legal assertion."[284] Hence also, then, the expression "to pervert (their) way" (נטה דרך hip'il) is an abbreviated equivalent of "to pervert the courses of justice" (הַטּוֹת אָרְחוֹת מִשְׁפָּט Prv 17:23),[285] the references being, more explicitly, to the judicial proceedings in the city gate (5:12). Not only must the clan elders avoid committing such injustices themselves, they must teach the younger generation to do the same. Instruction of just this sort is found in an apodictic series preserved in the Book of the Covenant (Ex 23:6–8; cf. Dtn 16:19; 24:17), which specifies that justice would be distorted by the toleration of false testimony or bribery (Ex 23:7–8) and the correlative favoring of one party in a dispute over another ("recognizing faces" in Dtn 16:19).

3. Abuse of Maidens. The נערה is generally a young woman, legally a minor, though her status seems less a matter of actual age than of social standing. In our passage "the maiden" is further defined neither as wife nor as sister, nor is there anything which indicates that a female servant is meant.[286] The reproach addresses the case of "a man and his father" consorting sexually with "the (same) maiden," since here the expression הלך אל

---

272 Cf. Ex 23:6–7 and Dtn 15:7–11 with Prv 14:31–32; 19:17; 22:22; 29:14; 31:8–9, 20. Cf. also F. Charles Fensham, "Widow, Orphan, and the Poor in Ancient Near Eastern Legal and Wisdom Literature," *JNES* 21 (1962): 129–39; and Erling Hammershaimb, "On the Ethics of the Old Testament Prophets" in *Congress Volume, Oxford, 1959*, SVT 7 (Leiden: E. J. Brill, 1960), 75–101.

273 See p. 141.

274 Fey, *Amos und Jesaja*, 62–63.

275 Wolff, *Amos the Prophet*, 80–85 [55–58].

276 Cf. also Ps 72:12–13 and 82:3–4.

277 דל is attested thirteen times in Proverbs alone, as compared with only five occurrences in the Pentateuch and two in the Psalter!

278 Prv 10:15; 22:16; 28:11; cf. 19:4.

279 Prv 14:31; 22:16; 28:3. See also Prv 22:22 where גזל = "to rob" // דכא pi'el = "to crush [under foot]."

280 See textual note "k" to 2:7.

281 On the variant forms of the word, see Delekat, "Wörterbuch," 35–49 (esp. 44–46).

282 Root ענה; cf. Ernst Kutsch, עֲנָוָה "*Demut*." *Ein Beitrag zum Thema "Gott und Mensch im Alten Testament*," Unpub. "Habilitationsschrift" (Mainz, 1960).

283 Cf. Prv 16:19; 22:22; 30:14.

284 Arnulf Kuschke, "Arm und Reich im Alten Testament," *ZAW* 57 (1939): 49–50.

285 Cf. Prv 18:5 and Is 10:2.

286 In contrast to the use of "maiden" in, e.g., Prv 9:3; 27:27; 31:15; 1 Sam 25:42; and Gen 24:61. Cf. Maag, *Text*, 175–77.

(literally "to go unto") means nothing less than "to copulate with."[287] Thus in our text, as often elsewhere,[288] נערה simply denotes a marriageable girl. The terminology of our passage and the situation it portrays are unattested in the biblical legal traditions. To be sure, there are apodictic injunctions against a man having intercourse with both a woman and her daughter,[289] or a son with the wife of his father,[290] or a father with the wife of his son;[291] but nowhere do we encounter the prohibition of father and son having intercourse with the same young woman. Casuistic law handles a similar case when it provides that a female house slave shall be elevated to the full legal status of a wife if either the householder or his son has intercourse with her (Ex 21:7–11). Amos, however, is not speaking of a female slave (אָמָה Ex 21:7), but simply of a young woman, one who is not identified more precisely either as a maidservant or a temple prostitute.[292] If it were the "exploitation of her defenselessness and servitude"[293] which made the act reprehensible, this dependence and weakness of the woman ought to have been stressed. The only thing that is emphasized as being reprehensible here, however, is the fact that "a man and his son" consort sexually with "the (same) maiden." In other words the elder, already married, father has intruded upon his son's love affair, and by so doing has turned a young woman into an object for the gratification of forbidden lusts. Thus the clan ethos which Amos affirms guards not only the marital relationship and the legal rights of slaves, but also the very personhood of a young woman, as well as her potential marriageability. It distinguishes at the same time the legal status of the son from that of the father, and in so doing protects the uniqueness of the love relationship. In this respect the case to which Amos

refers is particularly close to that treated in Dtn 22:28–29, interpreted in the light of its correlative in Dtn 22:23–27. By engaging in sexual congress with a young maiden, the young man obligates himself to marry her, while the man's father is prohibited from having intercourse with her, just as he is with his daughter–in–law. Hence what we have here in Amos is, in effect, a radicalizing of the apodictic stipulation in Lev 18:15 (cf. Lev 20:12).[294]

■ 8 4. Exploitation of Debtors. It is only by means of secondary expansions[295] that v 8 has been brought into close thematic association with v 7b (which has also been expanded). Originally two strictly parallel three-stress cola treated the use of pledged items and fines. In wisdom literature the catchwords "to pledge" (חבל)[296] and "to fine" (ענשׁ)[297] occur even more frequently than in the Book of the Covenant and in Deuteronomy.[298] However, the legal tradition in the Pentateuch shows more clearly than the wisdom material the nature of the injustice Amos has in mind. The law codes restrict the taking of items as collateral on the basis of the type of article, the length of time, and the person affected. Hand–mill and grindstone may not be taken in pledge at all, according to Dtn 24:6, since they are instruments essential to life; the cloak (of a poor man) may not be kept as a pledge overnight (Ex 22:25 [26]; Dtn 24:12–13); a widow's garment may not be taken from her (Dtn 24:17). When Amos speaks of "garments taken in pledge," he is referring to items which, in the case of a widow, may not be taken at all, and in any case may not be kept overnight. The "spreading out" (נטה hip'il) of garments, however, surely means the preparation of a place in which to bed down for the night (Ex 22:26 [27]; Dtn 24:12). Amos is thus accusing people of disregarding the laws meant

---

287 Cf. Hos 3:3 cj.; and Wolff, *Hosea*, 56 [70].
288 Gen 24:14, 16, etc.; 34:3, 12; Dtn 22:23–29; Ju 21:12; 1 Sam 9:11.
289 Lev 18:17; 20:14.
290 Lev 18:8; 20:11; Dtn 23:1 [22:30]; 27:20.
291 Lev 18:15; 20:12.
292 Bach, "Gottesrecht," 30–33.
293 Maag, *Text*, 175.
294 On v 7bβ, see textual note "p" to 2:7. The addition perhaps represents an interpretation of v 7bα in the light of Hos 4:14 (see Wolff, *Hosea*, 88–89 [110–11]), but in any case according to the standard of

the Holiness Code (Lev 20:3, etc.). For an exposition, see Zimmerli, *Ezechiel*, 457, 875–76.
295 See textual notes "q" and "r" to 2:7.
296 Prv 13:13; 20:16; 27:13; Job 22:6; 24:3, 9.
297 Prv 17:26; 19:19; 21:11; 22:3; 27:12.
298 Ex 21:22; 22:25 [26]; Dtn 22:19; 24:6, 17. Apart from Am 2:8 the only other occurrences of these words are in Ezek 18:16; 2 Kgs 23:33; and 2 Chr 36:3.

to protect the destitute. The (original) following colon shows even more clearly how Amos empathizes with the plight of debtors. "Monetary fines" (עֲנוּשִׁים) were imposed (עָנַשׁ), for example, on a man who, while scuffling with another man, bumped a pregnant woman so severly that she miscarried (Ex 21:22), or on someone who falsely impugned the virtue of an Israelite virgin (Dtn 22:19). Such fines were meant to make restitution for damages and not to finance drinking bouts (cf. 6:6).

Amos is unfailingly concerned to spread the umbrella of legal protection over the oppressed, even should they be technically guilty. No specific model can be adduced for either the precise wording or the sequence of themes in 2:6b–8. The individual accusations leveled by Amos find only certain conceptual parallels in the older legal tradition. The pattern of a series of four accusations is elsewhere attested only where loosely related themes are handled, as for example, in Lev 19:13–14a. It thus appears that our particular series of accusations in Amos was formulated *ad hoc* and as a reflection of familiar abuses. The traditional clan wisdom seems to have determined both the syntactical structure and the selection of particular themes.[299]

■ 9 In none of the oracles against the foreign nations does the accusation have the cutting edge found here, because only Israel is evaluated in relation to an act of Yahweh. The transitional exclamation "Yet I . . ." sets the previously described behavior of Israel into sharp contrast with the subsequently mentioned deed of Israel's God. In the historical accounts of the Psalter, such a juxtaposition becomes the rule (cf. Ps 106:7–23). Yet Amos contrasts the present violent treatment of the poor in Israel with the historical acts of Yahweh on behalf of the lowly. He mercilessly exterminated the formidable prior inhabitants of the land; "to destroy" (שׁמד hip'il) designates within the context of the Yahwistic holy war the complete annihilation of the enemy.[300] Those who held sway in the land in former times are called "Amorites," just as in Elohistic[301] and later Deuteronomistic usage.[302] The context in Amos does not betray any dependence of the prophet upon the Elohist, nor is there any indication that he adopts the older understanding of the Amorites as mountain dwellers, as distinguished from the Canaanites who lived on the coastal plain.[303] Etymologically "Amorite" (אמרי) is to be derived from *Amurru*, which in Old Akkadian and in Old Babylonian refers to nomads of various origins, and which in Middle and Late Babylonian, as well as in Neo–Assyrian, is a geographical term designating the west in general.[304] It has proved impossible so far to explain how this word made its way into the linguistic usage of Israel.[305] When one recalls that Amos was a Judean, however, it may not be insignificant that isolated older traditions localized the Amorites specifically in the Judean area.[306] It was on behalf of the very Israelites now under indictment that Yahweh had destroyed the Amorites.[307] The latter are characterized as having been particularly tall and strong, a description which underscores the enormity not only of Yahweh's saving act but also of Israel's subsequent depravity as described in 2:6b–8. The height of cedars and the strength of oaks are both proverbial,[308] though it is Amos alone who introduced these similes into the tradition describing the occupation of the land. By so doing he vividly articulated a theme which the Yahwistic spy report in Nu 13:28 presents in different words: "The people who dwell in the land are strong, and the cities are fortified and very large; and besides, we saw the descendants of Anak there." Just this feature of the occupation tradition is prominently displayed in the Deuteronomistic recapitulation in Dtn 1:28, while in Dtn 9:2 the Anakim are described as irresistible giants. This theme belonging to the occupation tradition, literarily transmitted by the Yahwist, originally circulated in the area of Hebron (Nu 13:22) and was associated with the person of Caleb (Nu 13:30). It was thus a familiar Judean tradition[309] which informed

---

299 See pp. 137–38.
300 Josh 11:20; 7:12; cf. 1 Kgs 13:34.
301 Gen 15:16; 48:22; Nu 21:21, 25–26, 31; 22:2.
302 E.g., Dtn 1:7, 19–20; cf. the Deuteronomistic expansion which follows in Am 2:10bβ.
303 Nu 13:29; Dtn 1:7; Josh, 11:3.
304 *AHW* 1, 46.
305 Cf. Martin Noth, "Num. 21 als Glied der 'Hexateuch'–Erzählung," *ZAW* 58 (1940–41): 182–87; and Robert Bach, "Amoriter," *BHHW* 1, 84.
306 Ju 1:34–35; cf. Gen 14:7, 13.
307 On מפניהם, see textual note "s" to 2:9.
308 Cf. Is 2:13, and also Wildberger, *Jesaja*, 109.
309 Cf. the reference to "the Amorite" Mamre in Gen 14:13. See also Martin Noth, *Numbers: A Commentary*, tr. James D. Martin; OTL (Philadelphia:

Amos' affirmation that Yahweh had exterminated those haughty giants.

In v 9b, a further development of the occupation account is introduced by ואשמיד ("but I destroyed")—reflecting the catchword השמדתי in v 9aα—which emphasizes the totality of the extermination. In order to make the point, Amos used a formulaic expression for which there are two other attestations known to us. In Is 37:31 (= 2 Kgs 19:30) those Judeans who survive the invasion of Sennacherib are assured that they will again "take root downward, and bear fruit upward." Similarly, the fifth-century 'Ešmun'azar inscription from Sidon contains a curse formula which threatens desecrators of the king's sarcophagus as follows: "May they have no root down below and no fruit up on top."[310] There are only three insignificant details in which these two texts agree against the form of the expression in Amos: they reverse the sequence "fruit—root" of Amos, both nouns appear without suffixes, and instead of "above—beneath" (ממעל—מתחת) they read "downward—upward" (לְמַטָּ[ה]—לְמָעְלָ[ה]). The image depicted in all three cases is the same, however, corresponding in part to that of the expression "destroy it root and branch." The richness unique to the Hebrew metaphor is that it combines the imagery of both planting and harvesting, imagery which when applied to human beings conjures up images of stability and prosperity. If "fruit" were here meant to refer to descendants, as it does in Hos 9:16 and Ezek 17:9, then the sequence "fruit—root" would be quite difficult to understand.[311] The extermination of the Amorite is thus vividly depicted as an uprooting of lofty trees, and Amos thereby gives an unusually sombre tone to the tradition of the occupation of the land. While this by no means denies the affirmation in v 9a

that the Amorites were banished for the sake of the (weak) Israelites, it serves the purpose of holding up the event as a mirror before guilty Israel. By emphasizing at the end of the retrospect Yahweh's total judgment upon the land's former inhabitants, Amos anticipates the sentence which is to be passed on its present population.

■ **10** The prophet's account of Yahweh's former acts in history stimulated a Deuteronomistic redactor to add the supplements in 2:10–12.[312] The initial ואנכי of 2:9 is also employed to open v 10 ("and I"), while the target of Yahweh's activity in 2:9, "the Amorite" (האמרי), is named again at the conclusion of v 10.[313] This provides a framework into which the exodus and wilderness traditions, unmentioned by Amos, are introduced. While Yahweh remains the speaker (as in 2:9), the Israelites are no longer referred to in the third person but are now directly addressed. (This forceful parenetic style is maintained, employing other means as well, through 2:11–12.)

It is noteworthy that here, in recounting the exodus, the verb עלה (hip'il, "to bring up") is used rather than יצא (hip'il, "to lead out"), since in the Deuteronomic—Deuteronomistic literature the latter verb is far more frequently employed for this purpose.[314] Certainly we find the use of "to bring up" in texts which are unquestionably older, such as Am 9:7 and Hos 12:14 [13], while the book of Deuteronomy employs "to bring up" when referring to the exodus in only one instance (Dtn 20:1), in contrast to the twenty instances in which it so uses "to lead out." Nevertheless it is the Deuteronomic—Deuteronomistic usage of עלה (hip'il) which best accounts for the word choice in our text. Thus we find that "to bring up" is employed: where the gift of the land is included within a retrospective view of the

---

Westminster, 1968), 105–06 [*Das vierte Buch Mose: Numeri*, ATD 7 (Göttingen: Vanderhoeck & Ruprecht, 1966), 91].

310 Franz Rosenthal, *ANET*³, 509; text: KAI 14.11–12.

311 Neher (*Amos*) and Deden take the metaphor to mean "the young and the old," but this interpretation is precluded especially by Is 37:31, as well as Mal 3:19 [4:1]. Cf. further, H. L. Ginsberg, "'Roots Below and Fruit Above' and Related Matters" in *Hebrew and Semitic Studies Presented to G. R. Driver*, ed. D. Winton Thomas and W. D. McHardy (Oxford: Clarendon Press, 1963), 59–71.

312 See pp. 112–13 and 141–42.

313 Cf. the even more thorough contextual blending of Deuteronomistic expansions in 1:9–12 and 2:4–5.

314 Cf. Paul Humbert, "Dieu fait sortir," *ThZ* 18 (1962): 357–61; and Joanne Wijngaards, "הוציא and העלה. A Twofold Approach to the Exodus," *VT* 15 (1965): 91–102.

exodus (1 Sam 8:8);[315] in epitomes of Israel's formative history which anticipate a subsequent detailed treatment of specific events (Ju 6:8–9; 1 Sam 12:6–8); but, most particularly, where there is also direct reference to conflict between Israel and her enemies (Dtn 20:1; 1 Sam 10:18).[316] It is in accord with these data that עלה (hipʻil) is used in v 10a; in a context where the events of the exodus and land–giving are linked, and whose purview particularly includes (v 10bβ) the military engagement already elaborated in 2:9. Thus on closer investigation, precisely of the linguistic evidence, we find no reason to suppose that v 10—with its prosaic recapitulation of Israel's early history—might have belonged to the original prophetic oracle against Israel.[317]

The second clause of the verse is even more palpably Deuteronomistic. Not only is the wording of v 10bα attested precisely in Dtn 29:4 [5] (as well as being quite close to that found in Dtn 8:2) but the very motif of the forty–year sojourn in the wilderness is unattested prior to its ample appearance in Deuteronomic–Deuteronomistic literature.[318] Hence the reference here to the forty years in the wilderness, which is without parallel in other prophetic books,[319] confirms our earlier judgment as to the secondary character of the verse. Additional confirmation is provided by the concluding phrase in v 10bβ, "to possess the land" (לרשת את [ה]ארץ), which is a typical Deuteronomic—Deuteronomistic sermonic cliche.[320] With possession of the land identified as the positive goal of the old history of salvation, along with reference to Yahweh's bringing Israel up from Egypt and his guiding them throughout forty years of wandering in the wilderness, the sombre concluding note of 2:9 has been drowned out completely by the display of divine kindness. In

effect, then, v 10 functions to underscore forcefully the "on their behalf" (מפניהם) of 2:9aα.

■ **11** Maintaining the same tone, the Deuteronomist here extends his sermon temporally beyond the giving of the land. Yahweh is pictured as recalling that he had entrusted certain of Israel's youth with special tasks, by appointing them to be prophets and Nazirites. In Deuteronomy and in the Deuteronomistic History the expression "to raise up" (קום hipʻil) also denotes the induction into office of prophets (Dtn 18:15, 18), judges (Ju 2:16, 18), deliverers (Ju 3:9, 15), priest (1 Sam 2:35), and king (1 Kgs 14:14). (As a glance at 6:14 shows, Amos himself used the same verb in quite a different sense. According to 7:15, Yahweh did not "raise up / appoint" Amos as a prophet but rather "took" him.) Biblical tradition specifically identifies as a Nazirite only Samson.[321] The Nazirite's vow of dedication to God obligated him to abstinence, especially from wine (2:12a; cf. Nu 6). The prophets referred to by our Deuteronomistic preacher were probably those comprising the chain of authorized spokesmen beginning with Moses (Dtn 18:15, 18) and extending through Elijah, Micaiah ben Imlah and others, right up to Amos himself and even beyond (cf. 2:12b with 7:16b!). Reference to the exodus tradition in association with the activity of prophets is also attested elsewhere in Deuteronomistic material.[322] Addressing Israel in the name of Yahweh, our preacher seeks the consent of his audience; the hearers can and must confirm that which Yahweh has done for them and has freely granted to them. The speech of Yahweh is concluded by the divine oracle formula, which is often likewise employed in parts of the book of Jeremiah which have undergone Deuteronomistic editing.[323]

■ **12** The events of salvation history recalled in 2:11

---

315 Cf. 1 Kgs 12:28, and Wijngaards, "הוציא," 99. Conversely one "goes down" from Palestine to Egypt: cf. the use of ירד in Is 30:2 and 31:1.

316 Humbert calls attention to the use of "to go up" (עלה qal) in referring to military expeditions (e.g., 1 Kgs 20:22 and Is 21:2): "Dieu fait sortir," ThZ 18 (1962): 360.

317 Against Humbert (ibid., 359) and Wijngaards, "הוציא," 98.

318 Dtn 1:3; 2:7; 8:4; Josh 5:6. The theme is also well attested in Priestly and later sources: cf. Ex 16:35; Nu 14:33–34; 32:13.

319 Cf. Am 5:25 and the remarks on that passage below.

320 Cf., e.g., Dtn 2:31; 9:4–5; 11:31; Josh 1:11; 18:3; Ju 2:6. Note especially Josh 24:8 and Ju 11:21, where in association with the verb "to possess" (ירשׁ), the Amorites are identified as those whose land is conquered.

321 Ju 13:5, 7; 16:17. On Samuel, cf. 1 Sam 1:11, 28; 2:20.

322 Ju 6:8–10; 2 Kgs 17:7–14; Jer 7:22–26; cf. Mi 6:4.

323 Cf., e.g., Jer 8:3; 12:17; 32:44.

become in v 12 grounds for indictment (thereby forming a transition which, after the comparable one from 2:6–8 to 9, we would not expect Amos himself to have introduced). Israel has seduced the Nazirites into breaking their vows. Affluent times could not tolerate those who, by their behavior, bore living witness to the heritage of the frugal life in the wilderness and its concomitant demand for total dedication to Yahweh. The way in which the prophets are said to have been rejected reminds one literally of the stance taken by Amaziah against Amos (7:16). The Deuteronomist presses his accusation even to this extent in order to prompt the generation of the exile to acknowledge its guilt. His indictment is thus particularly informed by the demands of Yahweh (2:11–12) as well as by the acts Yahweh has performed on Israel's behalf (2:10).

■ **13** The announcement of punishment opens with a divine self–asseveration, the emphatic pronoun "I" being a contrasting counterpart to one at the beginning of 2:9 (which, in the original oracle, immediately preceded v 13). As Yahweh had once actively sided with Israel against the strong Amorites, so now he is about to intervene against an Israel which has become an oppressor of the weak (2:6b–8).[324]

The rare verb depicting Yahweh's action against Israel (עוק hip'il) is to be understood, on the basis of the post–Biblical Hebrew noun meaning "hollow" (עוּקָה), as cognate with Arabic ʿaqqa = "to split (open)"[325] and Ugaritic ʿqq = "to rend";[326] it means "to break open," here used with reference to the ground underfoot (תחתיכם, "beneath you") and under the wheels of a heavy wagon. עגלה denotes the "cart" used by peasants to haul freight.[327] A mural from Nineveh dating to about 700 B.C. and depicting the Assyrian campaign against Lachish shows such a cart, with two spoked-

wheels, being drawn by a pair of oxen.[328] "Sheaf" (עמיר) means the harvested ears of grain which are brought from the field to the threshing floor.[329] The unusual construction rendered "full of" (המלאה לה), whose use produces a three–stress colon, is probably meant to emphasize that the cart is filled to overflowing with harvested grain. It is due to the heavy load that the cart's wheels break open the soft earth of the field, causing cracks in the ground reminiscent of those produced by an earthquake. Indeed, the point of the simile is to indicate that Yahweh will soon act against Israel by means of an earthquake. Finally, the harvest imagery itself pointedly alludes to the nature of the judgment.[330] The fourth and fifth visions of Amos similarly use the imagery of harvest (8:1–2) and earthquake (9:1–4) to portray the coming judgment.[331]

■ **14** The earthquake to be sent by Israel's God will unleash sheer panic. In times past Yahweh had miraculously thrown enemy camps into confusion;[332] now he will do the same to Israel. As in the fifth vision, where also Yahweh's weapon of war is an earthquake, here too it is announced emphatically that *no one* will be able to escape the destruction.[333] Neither swiftness (v 14aα) nor strength (v 14aβ) will be of help to the foot soldier, since every "(place of) refuge" (מנוס) is destined for destruction.

■ **15** There can be no hope for the men of the chariotry either. Amos has in mind the two–man chariot, occupied by an archer and the charioteer proper. That the archer "shall not stand" (לא יעמד) means not only that the quaking ground will make it impossible for him to aim his weapon but also that the archer himself will not survive the ordeal.[334] "He who guides the horse" (רכב הסוס) does not do so from astride the animal but from within the chariot. The interpretation "char-

324 On the formal parallelism of 2:13 and 9, the introductory use of הנה, and the possibility of reading תחתיהם for תחתיכם, see pp. 142–43.

325 Gese, "Beiträge," 421.

326 *CTA* 12 (= *UT* 75).1.27, 37; cf. Joseph Aistleitner, *Wörterbuch der Ugaritischen Sprache*, ed. Otto Eissfeldt, BVSAWL 106/3 (Berlin: Akademie-Verlag, ³1967), no. 2089.

327 Cf. 1 Sam 6:7–14; 2 Sam 6:3; and Gen 45:19–27.

328 *BRL*, 532; and Joseph Wiesner, "Wagen," *BHHW* 3, 2129.

329 Jer 9:21 [22]; Mi 4:12. Cf. Dalman, *Arbeit* 3, 52, 58.

330 Cf. Mi 4:12–13; Joel 4:13 [3:13]; and see above, pp. 80–81.

331 See p. 151.

332 1 Sam 14:15; cf. Jµ 5:4; Ps 18:8–14 [7–15].

333 On the climactic structure, see textual note "z" to 2:14.

334 See textual note "aa" to 2:15.

ioteer" is suggested by the parallelism with "he who wields the bow" = "archer," the other member of a chariot team. Furthermore, the historical evidence attests to the existence of a mounted cavalry beginning only in Persian times, the horse's military function having been restricted to the drawing of war chariots down into late Assyrian times.[335] One might expect that the charioteer would have the greatest chance to "save his own life," since the verb מלט (usually nip'al)[336] means "to escape" by fleeing swiftly from a situation threatening sure death.[337] But even this recourse is denied.

■ **16** Both the form and content of the concluding verse intensify to the utmost degree the stark image of hopeless panic. In form, the preceding pattern of symmetrical bicola here gives way to a single, long colon which makes iterative use of the roots נוס ("to flee") and אמץ ("to be firm") from 2:14a.[338] As to content, the scene now focuses upon the fate of one desperate individual, identified as "the (most) stouthearted among the warriors." "Heart" (לב) here denotes the vital center of a human being, the locus of strength and courage.[339] Yet even this most courageous and stalwart champion will be reduced to naked flight. And, in view of the utter devastation portrayed in 2:14–15, the sole survivor can flee only into nothingness. Although in his threats against foreign nations Amos always made particular reference to the national rulers, in the oracle against Israel he does not do so. On the other hand we would expect to find here a comparable reference to the fate of the rich, and it seems likely indeed that they comprise the military elite among those to be so disastrously routed. This is to happen "on that day," the day when Yahweh causes the earth to "break open" (2:13) and unleashes his awesome terror upon the hosts of Israel.[340]

Aim

So the boom gets lowered on Israel, but not on Israel alone. If we look over the composition as a whole, we note first of all how Amos assumes, as a matter of course, that Yahweh is the sole divine sovereign of all peoples. No one before Amos so clearly and unambiguously affirmed that the God of Israel also judges and punishes the Arameans, the Philistines, the Ammonites and the Moabites. There is no mention at all of other deities. The God who has entered into a special relationship with Israel is the sole God of all nations. Because Yahweh alone is the God of all, there is none who can escape his accusation and his punishment. Perhaps others would find it easier to believe in the God of the Bible were the church not so reticent about proclaiming the fact that he first calls to account those whom he has first called as his own.

All against whom the oracles are addressed are guilty of crimes against humanity. The exclusivity with which Amos determines guilt, solely on the basis of behavior manifested towards the weak and the helpless, is likewise a new feature in his prophecy. It is simply inhumane to thresh people like straw (1:3), to exchange them like trade goods (1:6), to imperil the lives of pregnant women and their unborn children (1:13), or to exploit the bones of a dead person for their material value (2:1). The last example shows clearly that such acts are not defined as criminal by Yahweh solely when they are committed against the people of God, for the abuse of an Edomite king counts no less than crimes against the inhabitants of Gilead (1:3, 13). "In the flame of his accusation shines the glow of a boundless love."[341] The cause of the helpless is a priori the cause of Yahweh. The simultaneously broad and penetrating expression of this in the oracles against the nations is precisely what makes the opening section of the total message of Amos so memorable.[342]

Although the accusation against Israel is of a kind with those leveled against the foreign nations, it is nonetheless comparatively sharper in tone, more comprehensive in scope and more elaborately specified.

---

335 Cf. Wildberger, *Jesaja*, 101ff; and Marie–Louise Henry, "Pferd," *BHHW* 3, 1439.
336 See textual note "bb" to 2:15.
337 Cf. Ju 3:29; 1 Sam 30:17; and also Georg Fohrer, "σῴζω and σωτηρία in the Old Testament," *TDNT* 7, 979.
338 See Gese, "Beiträge," 426.
339 Cf. Ps 27:14; 31:25 [24]; as well as Dtn 28:67; Is

7:2; and Ezek 21:20 [15].
340 On the concluding formula "oracle / utterance of Yahweh" (נאם יהוה), see p. 143.
341 Koehler, *Amos*, 48.
342 Cf. Karl Barth, *Church Dogmatics* 4/2, *The Doctrine Of Reconciliation*, tr. G. W. Bromily (Edinburgh: T. & T. Clark, 1958), 445–52 [*Die Kirchliche Dogmatik*, 4/2 (Zollikon–Zürich: Evangelischer Verlag,

The indictments of the other nations focus entirely on their war crimes. In the case of Israel, however, peacetime transgressions of comparable cruelty are cited, crimes committed against fellow countrymen, against the innocent (2:6b, 7a) and especially those in need of help and protection (2:6b–8). The very extent of the indictment shows that Amos considers Israel to be considerably more guilty than her foreign neighbors. Israel has no excuse; she was expected to recall that Yahweh intervenes on behalf of the weak, since precisely such an act of intervention had established her own historical existence (2:9). Israel alone was in a position to know, from the fact of Yahweh's prior intervention, that the cause of the needy is the cause of God himself. Therefore Israel is of all the most guilty.

Compassion for the oppressed is that which determines the destiny of both the people of God and of the nations in general. Against war criminals Yahweh himself will wage war. No human agent to bring about the threatened punishments is named. In the oracles against the foreign nations, fire is identified as the weapon with which Yahweh will destroy the strongholds; in the oracle against Israel, earthquake is the instrument by which Yahweh will throw Israel's heroes into panic.[343] At one time Yahweh waged holy war on Israel's behalf against her enemies (2:9). Now Israel has joined her enemies, becoming likewise a target of Yahweh's attack. The people of God has despised the privilege of compassion and has itself thus become Yahweh's enemy. "As for Amos . . . his own God, Yahweh, puts the torch to the tinder. . . . This God is ill–disposed to chat about religion with oppressors."[344]

Not a word indicates that Amos hopes for any improvement, not even on the part of Israel. Therefore the main stress in his oracles does not rest on the lists of transgressions, detailed though they are, but rather on the proclamations of impending punishment. The punishment as announced bears all the marks of being total destruction, especially so in the oracle against Israel. Amos is not preaching any edifying homilies here. His message penetrates to the eschaton, at least in the sense that it actualizes the cessation of the current course of Yahweh's historical dealings with Israel. The prophet does not project his reflections farther into the future.

The end of the history of the northern kingdom, Israel, did indeed come about not many decades after Amos had prophesied. For the Deuteronomistic redactor of his work, however, that event did not exhaust the validity of the prophetic words. As the intensified reflections upon the nature of guilt show,[345] their own historical catastrophe of the sixth century prompted the people of Judah to ponder even more deeply the reasons for the judgment of God which befell them. Today the church hears these powerful opening oracles of the book of Amos in company with the ancient people of God and in the midst of the modern world of nations. The same demand here confronts both the church and the secular world. For the sake of Jesus Christ, however, the church is more rigorously called to account if it despises weakness, violates the right of the defenseless, and forgets the fate of oppressed people. The church has no right to feel more secure about its future than do the various political powers, for if the church fails to measure its own performance by the standard of God's compassion, shown by his intervention on behalf of the oppressed, then the church has no future at all.

1955), 502–09 ("Gerichtsbotschaft des Propheten Amos")].

343 See pp. 154–55 and 171.

344 Ernst Bloch, *Das Prinzip Hoffnung* (Frankfurt am Main: Suhrkamp Verlag, 1959), 577.

345 1:9b, 11b; 2:4b, 12. See also pp. 151–52.

Election as Basis for Judgment

Bibliography

Reinhard Fey
Amos und Jesaja: Abhängigkeit und Eigenständigkeit des Jesaja, WMANT 12 (Neukirchen–Vluyn: Neukirchener Verlag, 1963), 43–45.

Rolf Knierim
Die Hauptbegriffe für Sünde im Alten Testament (Gütersloh: Gütersloher Verlagshaus [Gerd Mohn], 1965), 204–06.

Werner H. Schmidt
"Die deuteronomistische Redaktion des Amosbuches. Zu den theologischen Unterschieden zwischen dem Prophetenwort und seinem Sammler," *ZAW* 77 (1965): 168–93 (esp. 172–73).

Lawrence A. Sinclair
"The Courtroom Motif in the Book of Amos," *JBL* 85 (1966): 351–53.

3

1 Hear this word ªthat Yahweh has spokenª against you, sons of Israelᵇ [against the whole clan which I brought up out of the land of Egypt; it is this]ᶜ:

2 You only have I selected
out of all the clans of the earth.
Therefore I will requite upon you
all your transgressions.

a–a אשר דבר יהוה is taken by Max Löhr (*Untersuchungen zum Buch Amos,* BZAW 4 [Giessen, 1901]), Marti, and Morgenstern ("Amos Studies IV," 319–320) to be secondary; in this way they make a three–stress bicolon of v 1a also (as in 3:2a and 2b). But if this relative clause were omitted, "against you" (עליכם) would become syntactically cumbersome; a vocative normally follows directly upon the imperative expression, as in 4:1a (cf. also 8:4a and 3:13). In 5:1a the speaker of "this word" and the addressee are also introduced by a similar relative clause after the same exhortation to hear.

b G (οἶκος Ισραηλ ["house of Israel"]) presupposes בית ישראל (so 5:1, 3–4, 25; 6:1, 14; 7:10; 9:9), which is the more common expression in the book of Amos. However, בני ישראל is found not only in such secondary material as that of 2:11, but also in undoubtedly authentic oracles of Amos (such as 3:12; 4:5; 9:7a), where as here a number of hearers is presupposed. (See p. 164, Excursus: "*Israel*" *in the Book of Amos.*) *T* and *V* confirm *M*.

c V 1b is shown to be a gloss (1) by a premature transition from the third–person reference to Yahweh in v 1aβ to the first–person address by Yahweh in v 2; (2) by the interpretation of the עליכם ("against you") in v 1aβ and v 2b as על כל־המשפחה ("against the whole clan"); (3) by a premature anticipatory catchword reference to the כל משפחות ("all the clans") of v 2a; (4) by the linguistic similarity of the relative clause in v 1bβ to the secondary material in 2:10a; and (5) by the addition of לאמר ("it is this"), a term which does not occur in Amos in similar introductions (4:1–2; 5:1) but does appear in the secondary expansion 2:12. (לאמר otherwise occurs in the book of Amos only in 7:10 and 8:5; see p. 97; cf. Weiser, *Profetie,* 27.) The function of this gloss is the same as that of the oracle in 2:4–5, namely to hinder later Judean hearers from thinking that 3:2 was directed only against the earlier northern kingdom.

Form

Some have held 3:1–2 to be the conclusion and culmination of 1:3—2:16.[1] To be sure, 3:1–2 both mentions Israel's transgressions and makes reference to all the clans of the earth. However, a different word is here used for "sin," and furthermore Israel, guilty and facing punishment, is not simply treated as one of the several nations but rather is clearly distinguished from them. 3:1 starts with an opening formula unparalleled in chaps. 1—2. As a conclusion to 2:6–9 and 13–16, the announcement of punishment in 3:2 would especially read as a pale generalization.[2] This oracle becomes forceful in its own right only when seen as the prelude to a new set of oracles. However, it must be set apart from 3:3–8 as an independent rhetorical unit, at least because of the transitions to interrogative style (in 3:3–8) and to third–person reference to Yahweh (in 3:6, 8).

3:1b must be excised from the old oracle; it is a literary supplement of the Deuteronomistic redaction.[3] This later interpretation consciously aims at including the catastrophe of Judah in the message which had originally been delivered to the northern kingdom. It achieves this goal by preventing the "upon you" (עליכם) of both v 2b and v 1a from being interpreted too narrowly. On the other hand, no convincing reasons for assigning v 1a to a redactional stratum can be given.[4] The summons to hear must be compared not with the redactional introduction in Hos 4:1 but with the corresponding appeals in 4:1 and 5:1, which clearly are not to be set off from their succeeding verses. The expression "hear this word that Yahweh has spoken . . ." cannot be explained away as a variant of the Deuteronomistic expression "word of Yahweh, which (he spoke)." On the contrary, it must be seen as a variant of the continuation of the corresponding appeals in 4:1 and 5:1. It would be unusual to find in Amos an oracle of Yahweh employing the first person without any kind of introduction.

The proper form–critical genre of our basic summons to hear is not that of the two–part "call to receive instruction" (Lehreröffnungsruf) but that of the "call to attention" (Aufmerksamkeitsruf).[5] This is a genre which is also attested in the rhetoric of the sages.[6] The expression "hear this word" does not necessarily introduce an oracle of Yahweh, as 5:1 shows (cf. "words of Amos" in 1:1). In our present case, however, the expression used by Amos does introduce an oracle which "Yahweh has spoken."

3:2 is that oracle per se, a tightly structured oracle of judgment embodying two parts. The first part employs the perfect tense and identifies the reason for judgment; the second part, introduced by "therefore" (על־כן), employs the imperfect tense and proclaims the certitude of punishment.[7] The special feature of this oracle is the fact that Yahweh, and not those addressed in the opening summons, is the subject even in the first part. Contrary to the normal procedure, therefore, it is not an infraction of the law which is the reason for punishment, but rather it is Yahweh's own saving act which establishes the ground for punishment. 2:9 similarly mentions a saving act of Yahweh, prior to an announcement of punishment, but in this contrasting case the reference emphasizes the crimes of Israel.[8] The strict correspondence between the reason for punishment and the actual occurrence of punishment is underscored by the rigid metrical structure of the balanced bicola.

Setting

The oracle offers no clue as to when or where it may

---

1   Budde, "Amos," 75–76; most recently Maag, *Text*, 9.
2   Cf. Weiser, *Profetie*, 116–17.
3   The reasons for this assessment are listed in textual note "c" to 3:1.
4   For a contrary opinion, see Schmidt, "Redaktion," 173.
5   See Zimmerli, *Ezechiel*, 360.
6   Cf. Prv 8:32; 2 Sam 20:17; and Ju 9:7.
7   Cf. Hos 4:1–3, and see Wolff, *Hosea*, 65–66 [81–82].
8   See p. 141.

have been delivered. Precisely its nature as a comprehensive statement of principle, however, makes it understandable as the opening statement in an earlier collection of Amos' oracles, the title of which we recognized within 1:1.[9]

Interpretation

■ **1** Amos begins here, not by using the messenger formula as in 1:3—2:16,[10] but instead by speaking in the manner of a teacher of the law. To be sure, he does not proclaim his own legal wisdom, but in the first–person style of the messenger speech he announces the established verdict of his God. "Has spoken" (דִּבֶּר) is used by Amos when the act of Yahweh's speaking as such is important (3:8), in contrast to the very frequently employed "has said" (אמר) in introductory and concluding formulas.[11] A strong accent is here placed on the act of Yahweh's speaking because our passage functions to introduce a collection of oracles. This is shown by the *figura etymologica*, in which the internal object is incorporated within a relative clause.[12] Unlike 2:6–8, the prophet here directly confronts his audience with the word of Yahweh, as though Yahweh himself were delivering the oracle.

The reflective supplement in v 1b departs from this form of direct address.[13] It links together catchwords from the context being interpreted[14] with the liturgically transmitted statement of the deliverance from Egypt which the supplement in 2:10 attests in the same form.[15] The supplement thus employs the exodus tradition to interpret the original declaration, "I selected" (ידעתי 3:2a), in the sense congenial to the Deuteronomic–Deuteronomistic theology.

■ **2** This interpretive effort, however, is not in keeping with the intention of Amos, whose purpose is precisely to deny Israel the exodus tradition as a basis for claiming the security of election (9:7). How then is ידעתי to be understood? That its use is meant to establish a specific difference between Israel and the nations is unquestionably clear from the context: the verb describes Yahweh's relationship with "you only," expressly *not* "all the clans"; "out of" (מן) has here that same sense of sharply privative separation which it has elsewhere when it stands in parallelism with the negative particle.[16] The preposition designates the movement by which Israel alone was plucked out from the nations of the world. It is not to be taken in the comparative sense proposed by Vriezen,[17] an interpretation which ill accords with the use of the exclusory adverb "only" (רק), placed at the beginning of the oracle for added emphasis. Similar terminology is employed in the Deuteronomic election theology, as for example in Dtn 10:15: "Only (רק) your fathers did Yahweh love . . . and he chose (וַיִּבְחַר) their descendants . . . out of all the peoples (מִכָּל־הָעַמִּים)." Amos himself does not employ the Deuteronomic technical term for election ("to choose" [בחר]; cf. Dtn 7:7 and 14:2), but instead he uses the common verb whose semantic field encompasses both the intimate act of love between persons (Gen 4:1; 1 Kgs 1:4) and the rational comprehension of events (Hos 8:4; Prv 4:19). It is from the former meaning that this verb derives its suitability for designating election.[18] To have been elected, however, means to have been called to a task. This portentous nuance of the concept of election first appears in Amos 3:2, and hence we translate "selected."[19] Which historical tradition Amos has in mind here, with this reference to a selective election, can only be surmised on the basis of his other statements. When the exodus tradition is excluded,[20] only the tradition

9   See p. 107.
10   See pp. 135–37.
11   See pp. 135–37, 139.
12   Cf. Brockelmann, *Syntax*, par. 93e [On the *figura etymologica* = cognate accusative construction, cf. textual note "l" to 1:6, and also Gesenius–Kautzsch–Cowley, par. 117p–r; Ed.].
13   See p. 175.
14   Cf. "all the clans" (כל משפחות) in 3:2a with "upon you" (עליכם) in 3:2b and 1a.
15   See pp. 169–70.
16   Cf. Hos 6:6, and Wolff, *Hosea*, 120 [153]; and also Brockelmann, *Syntax*, par. 111c, f.
17   Theodorus Christiaan Vriezen, *Die Erwählung Israels nach dem Alten Testament*, AThANT 24 (Zürich: Zwingli–Verlag, 1953), 37: "over and above other nations."
18   Cf. Jer 1:5; Gen 18:19; and Ex 33:12, 17.
19   In 3:10 and 5:16, ידע connotes knowledge requisite for the performance of a task; in 5:12, it means the accurate perception of a given situation. Otherwise the word does not occur in Amos.
20   See above on 3:1b, and also p. 347 on 9:7.

of the giving of the land remains to be considered from among the ancient traditions of salvation history. The way in which this saving act is contrasted (2:9) with the depiction of Israel's behavior (2:6–8) indicates that it was supposed to have a normative significance for Israel. Nevertheless, the threefold occurrence in Amos of the word-pair "righteousness—justice" (צדקה— משפט 5:7, 24; 6:12) suggests that consideration should also be given to the revelation of Yahweh's will. At all events, the exclusive favor shown Israel by Yahweh, which sets it apart from all the other peoples, was meant to determine its conduct. Only thus can the statement in v 2a become the grounds for the sentence announced in v 2b. Moreover, the perfect verb (ידעתי) denotes not merely some act of the past, but one whose force effectively continues into the present. "I have lovingly chosen you from among all the clans of the earth" therefore also means: "In contrast to the other peoples of the earth, I have taken you alone into my personal confidence and I am knowledgeable concerning you," for "it is exclusively you whom I have selected for a great task, by making known to you my will."

The expression "all the clans of the earth" (כל משפחות האדמה) occurs elsewhere in the Old Testament only in Gen 12:3 and 28:14. There is no evidence that Amos was influenced by these passages. It is more likely that his cultural milieu prompted Amos to single out the clan as the sort of ethnic grouping characteristic of the population of the world. In Josh 7:14–18 the "clan" is evidently a division of the "tribe" and is composed of related "houses" (extended families).[21]

The "therefore" (על־כן) with which the second clause of v 2 opens confirms that, for Amos, election entails obligation. This is so much in keeping with his total message[22] that one must not take "therefore" to be ironic. When Israel deviates from the course to which its election has committed it, Yahweh must act accordingly. Because Yahweh has "selected" (ידע)

Israel for a special task, he must also "examine" (פקד) its performance. "Transgressions" being the object of the examinations, the basic meaning of פקד here is expanded so as to connote "to punish (on the basis of investigation), to hold responsible," in short, "to requite."[23] "All transgressions" are requited. The particular noun translated here as "transgression" (עון)[24] is a "concept of everyday language" and designates "perversity" of behavior; it focuses not so much on the attitude of deliberate malice as on the reality of the consequent act which issues in concrete results.[25] While Hosea uses the word frequently,[26] Amos employs it only here in the course of a general, comprehensive threat of punishment. This piercing address shows Amos transmitting to Israel a message from Yahweh, the judge, announcing sentence upon the guilty.

Aim

As a rule Amos speaks differently. Elsewhere specific crimes of Israel are cited as the grounds for punishment. In contrast, here is emphasized only how Yahweh has conferred distinction and dignity upon Israel before all the world through his "selecting." The position of this particular oracle at the head of a collection of oracles guards against the exegete's interpreting those subsequent to it in a narrowly anthropologizing way. It is not Israel's deeds as such that bring calamity; this is rather the result of Israel's turning away from the course prescribed by its election, a turning away that manifests itself in transgression. Thus 3:2a performs here the same function as does the recollection of the giving of the land in 2:9. Similar overtones can be heard when Yahweh says "my people" (7:8, 15; 8:2).[27]

In contrast to all the other oracles of Amos, the threat of punishment here is not concrete.[28] In this regard it finds its only parallel in the general announcement of the fourth vision: "The end has come for my people" (8:2). Equally unusual is the fact that the

---

21 Cf. Johannes Pedersen, *Israel. Its Life and Culture, I–II*, tr. Aslang Møller (London: 1926), 49–50; Noth, *World*, 63–64 [58–59]; de Vaux, *Israel*, 8; and pp. 90–91.
22 See p. 104.
23 Cf. Wolff, *Hosea*, 17–18 [19], 40 [48–49].
24 See the excursus on פֶּשַׁע ("crime") in *Amos*, pp. 152–53.
25 Knierim, *Hauptbegriffe*, 236, 238, 242.
26 See Wolff, *Hosea*, 145 [186].
27 Smend, "Nein," 409–10.
28 See pp. 102–03.

summarizing concept "all your transgressions" takes the place of a list of specific crimes. It is precisely these peculiarities, however, which enable this oracle of Amos to function so well as the introduction to a collection of oracles. "Whatever else he says is a commentary on these words."[29]

A church that rejoices in the gospel must realize how dangerous and demanding is its "privilege." "Of everyone to whom much is given, much will be required" (Lk 12:48).

---

29   Wellhausen, 75.

Compelled to Announce Disaster

Bibliography

Walter Baumgartner
"Amos 3:3–8," *ZAW* 33 (1913): 78–80.

James L. Crenshaw
"The Influence of the Wise upon Amos: The 'Doxologies of Amos' and Job 5:9–16; 9:5–10," *ZAW* 79 (1967): 42–52.

Hartmut Gese
"Kleine Beiträge zum Verständnis des Amosbuches," *VT* 12 (1962): 417–38 (esp. 424–27).

Benne Holwerda
... *Begonnen hebbende van Mozes* ... (Terneuzen: D. H. Littoij, 1953), 31–47 ("Da exegese van Amos 3:3–8").

Hubert Junker
"*Leo rugiit, quis non timebit? Deus locutus est, quis non prophetabit?* Eine textkritische und exegetische Untersuchung über Amos 3:3–8," *TrThZ* 59 (1950): 4–13.

Sigo Lehming
"Erwägungen zu Amos," *ZThK* 55 (1958): 145–69 (esp. 151–54).

Julian Morgenstern
"Amos Studies I," *HUCA* 11 (1936): 29–67 (reprinted in *idem, Amos Studies,* vol. 1 [Cincinnati, 1941], 13–51).

Henning Graf Reventlow
Das Amt des Propheten bei Amos, FRLANT 80 (Göttingen: Vandenhoeck & Ruprecht, 1962), 24–30.

Werner H. Schmidt
"Die deuteronomistische Redaktion des Amosbuches. Zu den theologischen Unterschieden zwischen dem Prophetenwort und seinem Sammler," *ZAW* 77 (1965): 168–93 (esp. 183–88).

David Winton Thomas
"Note on נוֹעָדוּ in Amos 3:3," *JTS* n.s. 7 (1956): 69–70.

3

3 Do two walk with one another
   if they have not met[a]?[b]

4 Does a lion roar in the forest
   and he has no prey?

a *G* (γνωρίσωσιν ἑαυτούς ["know one another"]) reads נוֹדְעוּ, under the influence of ידע in 3:2a. D. W. Thomas ("Note on נוֹעָדוּ in Amos 3:3," *JTS* n.s. 7 [1956]: 69–70) suggests a root-meaning "to be reconciled, to make peace," based on the Arabic cognate *wdʿ.* αʹ (συντάξωνται ["agree to come together"]) and θʹ (συνέλθωσιν ἀλλήλοις ["meet one another"]) confirm *M* as the *lectio difficilior,* as does *V* (*convenerit eis* ["they have agreed"]). יעד nipʿal usually means "to make an appointment," but later connotes "to meet (by appointment), to assemble"; see the following note.

Does a young lion raise his voice
[from his hiding place]ᶜ,
   if he did not catch anything?
5 Does a bird fall to < >ᵈ the ground
   if a wooden missileᵉ did not (hit)
   him?
Does a folding net spring up from
the ground,
   if it does not actually catch?
6 Or does one blow a trumpet in a city,ᶠ
   and people are not roused with
   fear?
Or does a calamity befall a city,
   and Yahweh has not been at work?

7 [Indeed the Lord Yahweh does not do
anything without revealing (in advance)
his plan to his servants, the prophets.]ᵍ

8 Since a lion has roared,ʰ
   who will not be afraid?

Since [the Lord]ⁱ Yahweh has spoken,ʰ
   who will not prophesy?

b Some critics doubt that v 3 belongs originally to the
unit 3:4–6 + 8 (cf. Marti; Gese, "Beiträge," 425;
Schmidt, "Redaktion," 183). In contrast to the
rhetorical questions in 3:4–6 and 8, the question in
v 3: 1) lacks a parallel; 2) does not specify two distinct subjects, its initial verb thus taking a plural
form; and 3) portrays a scene of peaceful coopera-
tion (rather than conflict). What purpose does this
supplement serve with reference to the following
series of questions? Following Marti, Gese supposes
v 3 to be a gloss on 3:2, the appointment (יעד nipʿal)
to which v 3 refers supplying the motive for the punishment announced in 3:2b. But are glosses likely
to be so subtle? V 3 could only be linked with 3:2
on Marti's assumption of catchword association
if G (נוֹדָעוּ) were original and referred to 3:2a
(יָדַעְתִּי). But is it really likely that some later reader
would have felt it necessary to clarify 3:2a by adding such a cumbersome gloss? The interrogative
style alone makes one suspect, instead, that v 3 is a
supplement to 3:4–6 + 8. The only occurrences of
the conjunction בלתי אם ("if … not") in the Old
Testament are here and in v 4 which follows (Maag,
Text, 132). יעד nipʿal is used in Ex 25:22 and 30:6,
36 to describe the meeting of God with Moses. Does
the question in v 3 allude to a comparable meeting,
preparing for the climax of the series in 3:8b? At
any rate, the secondary character of v 3 cannot be
established with certainty.

c The designation of place disturbs the line's meter,
since elsewhere in 3:4–6 the initial colon of each
question has only three stresses. It was probably
added here to create a closer parallelism with the
comparable cola in the series, all of which exhibit
such designations.

d M פח ("folding net" = T, V), not attested in G,
makes dubious sense in this context, and overbur-
dens the initial three–stress colon of the sentence
(cf. the preceding textual note). The word seems to
have entered from v 5b as a result of scribal dittography.

e Those who interpret the word מוֹקֵשׁ as "trap, snare"
(but see p. 185), must revocalize it as a participle,
e.g. מוּקָשׁ (hipʿil; so Morgenstern, "Amos Studies
I," 29) or מְיַקֵּשׁ (piʿel, "fowler, trapper").

f G⁵³⁴ exhibits πολέμῳ ("battle") rather than the
expected πόλει ("city"); this (inner–Greek) variant
interprets the situation quite correctly.

g This prose text, a dogmatic asseveration (כִּי) standing in blatant contrast to the questions which form
its context, is clearly secondary; see p. 181.

h The protasis, with its subject in initial position and
its verb in the perfect ("composite nominal clause"),
states the pre–condition for the durative response
described in the parallel apodosis by means of an
imperfect verb. The perfect designates the independent, the imperfect the dependent action;
cf. Ps 60:12 [10]; 26:1b; 148:6b; and Michel,
Tempora, 128–32.

i   אדני is superfluous, unbalancing the metrical parallelism with v 8a (Eduard Sievers and Hermann
Guthe, *Amos, metrisch bearbeitet*, Abhandlungen der
Sächsischen Gesellschaft der Wissenschaften 23/3
[Leipzig, 1907], 9; Morgenstern, "Amos Studies I,"
30); it was probably added to adjust the verse more
closely to the wording of 3:7 (Baumgärtel, "Gottesnamen," 11, 19). The text–critical evidence indicates that most of the occurrences of this word in the
book of Amos are secondary; see textual note "o"
to 1:8.

Form

3:3–8 stands out from its present context by reason
of both its dominant form (interrogative sentences)
and the theme it develops. But it is doubtful on three
counts that the section in itself can be considered a
rhetorical unit.

It can be asserted with considerable assurance that
3:7 is a later literary addition.[1] A purely declarative
sentence here appears amidst the questions. The poetic
language of strictly parallel cola is thus interrupted by
didactic prose which is reminiscent of the language of
Deuteronomistic history–writing.[2] This verse also
reveals a shift of interest regarding the nature of prophetic proclamation. The original text of Amos is
concerned with the relationship of the prophetic word
to the preceding oracle of Yahweh.[3] The Deuteronomist, on the other hand, is preoccupied with the relationship of the proclaimed word to the subsequent
deed of Yahweh. He has developed his own thesis here
on the basis of a selective reading of the earlier text,
idiosyncratically joining the "Yahweh has not been at
work" (יהוה לא עשה) of v 6b with the "who will not
prophesy" (מי לא ינבא) of v 8b,[4] and employing the
particle כי ("indeed") to effect a literary synthesis.

If it is practically certain, then, that the redaction
which has given us v 7 already presupposes a connection
between v 6 and v 8, the question still remains whether

v 8 constitutes an independent saying, or whether it
was from the outset bound up with v 6 in a single unit
of speech. To answer this question, it is first necessary
to clear up that other problem of where the unit of
speech which ends in v 6, or in v 8, has its beginning.
Does it begin in v 3 or not until v 4? In textual note
"b" to 3:3 we investigated the arguments against an
original association of v 3 with vv 4–6 and found them
less than compelling. As an isolated question, lacking
the type of parallel regularly present in the following
series, v 3 gives the impression of being a preface. The
identity of the "two" is unspecified, which is never the
case with the subjects of the subsequent questions.
Probably Amos responds here to that protest which
gave rise to the series of questions in the first place, a
protest that denied the connection between the proclamation of the prophet and the activity of Yahweh.
Only a knowledge of the words of his adversaries, not
transmitted to us, could make this opening fully understandable. However, if we are perceiving the function
of the opening question correctly, then in its enigmatic
reference to the "two" it would seem to be pointing
beyond v 6 to v 8b as its appropriate answer. In a
similar way, v 8a is reminiscent of v 4a.[5]

In spite of this, many interpreters posit separate
oracles in vv 3–6 and v 8.[6] In their view, a sufficient
oracular climax is already attained in v 6b. They note

1 Against Harper, Hugo Gressmann (*Die älteste
Geschichtsschreibung und Prophetie Israels [von Samuel
bis Amos und Hosea]*, SAT 3/1 [Göttingen, ²1921]),
Theis, Robinson, Maag (*Text*, 14), Cripps, and
others; with Marti, Duhm ("Anmerkungen," 5),
Nowack, Sellin, Weiser, Lehming ("Erwägungen"),
Gese ("Beiträge"), Schmidt ("Redaktion," 183–
88), and others.
2 Cf. the prophets as servants of Yahweh in 2 Kgs
17:13, 23; 21:10; 24:2; Jer 7:25; 25:4, etc.; "to
do [the] thing" (עשה דבר) in 2 Kgs 20:9; (17:12);
Yahweh's "council" (סוד) in Jer 23:18, 22 (cf. Prv

20:19a).
3 See pp. 186–87.
4 Weiser, *Profetie*, 128; Lehming, "Erwägungen,"
152.
5 *Ibid.*
6 Baumgartner, "Amos 3:3–8"; Gressmann, *Prophetie*,
339; Hölscher, *Profeten*, 32; Koehler, *Amos*; Schmidt,
"Redaktion," 183–84; Smend, "Nein," 412 n. 42;
and others.

that the Hebrew interrogative particle ה, which begins each bicolon of vv 3–5, is replaced in v 6 by a more intensive sign of the interrogative, namely by אם. On the other hand, in v 8 only the second colon of each line is formulated as a question, and because here the interrogative pronoun "who" (מי) is employed, a different sort of answer is expected. Furthermore, the meter of v 8 differs from that of vv 3–6. They thus claim that v 6b reflects the real issue under dispute, an issue separate from that lying behind v 8. Because the force of the analogies in vv 3–6a renders possible only the answer of "no" to the question of v 6b, this question is in effect an assertion. It as much as says, "Thus no calamity befalls the city without Yahweh being its source!"[7] Amos would then be opposing the opinion that Yahweh could do no harm to Israel, an opinion also reflected in Mi 2:6–7; 3:11; and Jer 5:12.[8]

But is the force of the question in v 6b really such as to reflect a moot issue? Does not Amos rather simply assume as a matter of course the same answer to this question as to all the others? In any case, the question of v 6b is formulated no differently than that of v 6a. Neither can one say that future threats come into the picture only in v 6, while v 5 speaks of the present and v 4 of the past;[9] each incident cited is a contemporary possibility. Finally, the relatively bland and incidental tone of v 6b makes it sound as though the decisive proclamation of Amos concerning Israel's end were open to discussion (cf. 8:2; 5:2). The expression "calamity in a city," especially when seen in conjunction with the reference to the blowing of the trumpet to sound alarm "in a city," appropriately calls to mind those less than totally catastrophic crises, such as plague, meager harvest, or hostile attack, which can issue in the proclamation of a general fast, by which the populace expresses its recognition of Yahweh as the true author of the crisis and so implores him to remove it.[10] When he exemplifies the death of Israel by depicting the fate of a city, Amos styles his proclamation along the lines of 5:1–3. Specific mention of "the land" accompanying the reference to a city is similarly attested in 3:11, in the oracle immediately following the one under discussion here.

Instead, one probably should read v 6b in association with the cases of catastrophe named in 4:6–11, or in other words not as a polemical assertion but at most as an affirmation of Yahweh's power to manipulate calamity. Seen in this regard, the initial mention of Yahweh in v 6b functions as the vitally important premise to the conclusion properly drawn in v 8b. Indeed, it might well be precisely the alteration in style which indicates that the point of this series of questions is revealed only in v 8. The placing of declarative sentences in initial position in v 8aα and 8bα, the shortening of clauses with resultant staccato effect,[11] and the transition to questions introduced by an interrogative pronoun, along with transposition of these questions into the second cola (v 8aβ and 8bβ), all show that only here does the list of recognized associations issue in the unveiling of a new insight. The change to a new syntactical structure at the end of our oracle is meant to emphasize the new thesis there advanced. In other places the preliminary pedagogical questions lead into a conclusion formulated as a declarative statement[12] or an exhortation (Job 6:22–28; 40:25–32 [41:1–8]). Am 6:12 is similar. An extrabiblical parallel to this style of writing is offered by the in part ironically quizzical, in part polemically didactic treatise of Hori from the time of the Ramessides.[13] Thus the analysis of its form justifies our regarding

7   Gressmann, *Prophetie*, 339.
8   See Schmidt, "Redaktion," 184; cf. also Am 5:14–15; 9:10.
9   Gese, "Beiträge," 426.
10   Prv 16:4; Eccl 7:14; Job 2:10; Sir 11:14; Joel 1. On this last reference, see pp. 32–35.
11   Cf. Morgenstern, "Amos Studies I," 31.
12   Is 10:8–11; 28:23–29; 40:12–17; Ezek 15:1–5; Ex 4:11–12; Job 6:5–7; 8:11–13; Sir 1:6–8.
13   For the text, see John A. Wilson, *ANET*[3], 475–79. For comment, see Hellmut Brunner, *Altägyptische*

Erziehung (Wiesbaden: O. Harrassowitz, 1957), 95–96, 170–71.

3:3–6 + 8 as a rhetorical unit.[14]

Its genre is that of a didactic disputation. The first indication of this is the fact that Yahweh is spoken of in the third person (vv 6b and 8b). Amos speaks here not as the messenger of his God, as he has done up to this point (1:3—3:2) and as he generally does subsequently, but as the defender of his office as a messenger. The salient characteristic of our genre here is the interrogative form of all the sentences. Each question is a rhetorical one and must be answered in the negative. "The 'rhetorical question' stirs up the emotions through the self–evident lack of necessity for such an interrogative formulation."[15] Thus the reader can still perceive the atmosphere of passionate controversy. This series of nine questions reveals not only the vehemence of the struggle but even more a tenacious desire to convince, an aspect best shown by the material and stylistic intensifications,[16] which progressively heighten the tension and so ultimately compel assent. The first five questions are uniformly introduced by the interrogative particle ה. No element of force or compulsion is suggested by the scene depicted in the first question (v 3). The next two questions (v 4), however, revolve around the overpowering of one animal by another, and the following two questions (v 5) have to do with a human hunter's vanquishing of animal prey. Up to this point the cause is always deduced from the effect, the rhetorical nature of the question rendering the cause indisputable. With the sixth question (v 6a) the speaker in the disputation introduces for the first time stylistic variations as well. The point of the example is now to show how compulsion takes hold of persons; the interrogative particle ה ("does . . .?") is replaced by אם ("or . . .?"); most significantly, the questioning here moves from cause to effect, a feature that can otherwise be found only in the two concluding sentences (v 8a, 8b). However, these variations do not justify the conclusion that a logical distinction between questions concerning cause and questions concerning

effect was intended. The attempt to reconstruct two distinct lexical groupings on the basis of the alternate types of questions was surely to misunderstand prophetic thinking.[17] As far as the subject matter goes, the prophet is concerned exclusively with the inseparable connection between çause and effect, between reason and result. The reversal of the direction of the question, first noticeable in v 6a, is not of logical but only of rhetorical significance. Together with the changed interrogative particle, it functions as a call to attention: here, for the first time in the series, it is people who are overwhelmed. To be sure, the seventh question (v 6b) repeats the interrogative particle אם ("or . . .?"), and people are once again the affected party. Now, however, the agent impinging on humanity is no mere human instrument, but is rather a calamitous act of Yahweh. In order to emphasize this, Amos has the reference to Yahweh fall into the second colon, thereby once again (as in vv 3–5) directing the train of thought from the event to its author. V 6 thus represents a sort of plateau in the course of the material and stylistic intensifications evident in this series of questions, in that here for the first time people are the affected party and, in the second colon, Yahweh is the initiator of the action (calamity). At the same time, v 6b is a pivotal point in the unfolding of the logic underlying these questions. The general premise which motivates the first six questions is that no event is self–explanatory (neither, then, is the phenomenon of prophetic speaking!). The seventh question renders this general premise more precise by specifying that Yahweh stands behind the phenomenon of human misery (and hence also behind announcements of calamity!). The conclusion is then explicitly drawn in the strikingly terse two–stress bicola of v 8a and 8b. (In the nature of the case at hand, it is impossible to be certain that v 8 is actually the conclusion, but our evaluation of the èvidence makes this by far the most probable assumption.) Here at last (v 8bα) the thesis is definitively stated: "Yahweh has spoken." The

---

14   The same conclusion has been reached by Marti, Sellin, Weiser, Morgenstern ("Amos Studies I"), Junker ("*Leo rugiit . . . ,*" *TrThZ* 59 [1950]: 4–13), Gese ("Beiträge"), and others.

15   Heinrich Lausberg, *Elemente der literarischen Rhetorik* (München: Heuber, ³1967), 145.

16   Cf. Gese, "Beiträge," 426.

17   Baumgartner, "Amos 3:3–8;" cf. Weiser, *Profetie*, 131; Gese, "Beiträge," 427.

concluding question (v 8bβ) then turns to the addressee with unprecedented directness: "Who can do other than become a prophet?" The parallel which precedes in v 8a is a patently obvious illustration of the fundamental principle here involved (cf. 5:18–19 and 1:2). As was shown above while dealing with the issue of the unity of this section, the final transition to the thesis is peculiar to the genre of the didactic disputation. In effect our section concludes with the following affirmation: just as no event is self–explanatory and just as even calamity comes from Yahweh, so the appearance of the messenger announcing misfortune is to be understood in the light of proclamation by Yahweh.[18]

Setting

Amos carries on a didactic struggle right to the end, hoping not only to prevail against but also to persuade his hearer. This is shown by the interrogative style which breaks through once more in the concluding thesis, in contrast to the comparable texts.[19] Amos engaged in this lively dispute while surrounded by his adversaries, who were denying that his appearance had anything to do with proclamation by Yahweh. Such a setting clearly presupposes that a certain amount of time had already elapsed since the announcement of calamity by Amos. In any case, this dispute does not belong to the beginnings of his activity. That it took place in Samaria[20] cannot be demonstrated with certainty, but in view of the subsequent oracles in 3:9—4:3 this is quite likely.

In any case, Amos wants to raise the subject of the beginning of his prophetic ministry in order to identify the grounds for his compulsion to speak. Therefore it is quite understandable why this didactic dispute was moved to the beginning of the old collection of "the words of Amos from Tekoa,"[21] immediately following the brief motto–oracle (3:1–2). After all, it has a legitimizing function similar to the call or commissioning pericopes at the head of other collections of prophetic

oracles.[22] By being drawn into the flow of the argument, the reader—just as the first hearer—is to be convinced that it was Yahweh's own speaking which irresistibly compelled Amos to issue his terrifying proclamation.

Interpretation

■ 3 V 3 belongs to the original series of questions, even though this sentence differs in tone from those that follow.[23] The reason for the nature of the opening query probably lies in the protest of the prophet's adversaries, the wording of which we do not know. At any rate, they denied that what Amos was doing corresponded with Yahweh's will for Israel. Amos opens his response with no theological statement of principle, much less with a reference to any legitimizing cultic traditions. Instead, he starts by soliciting the answer to a question about a commonplace occurrence, one with which he was especially familiar on the basis of both his trips to his sycamore plantations and also his journey from Tekoa to Bethel and from Bethel to Samaria. Two persons never walk together without first having met one another. Of course, two people may well also "make an appointment" to traverse a long distance together on trails across the steppe or on lonely paths between settlements in the sparsely settled areas of cultivated land. However, neither here nor in the subsequent questions is there any obvious allusion to an "appointment" between Yahweh and Amos. The process designated by "to meet" (יעד nipʿal) means simply an encountering, a situation calling for a mutual greeting and an exchange of questions regarding origin and destination.[24] Apparently it is only this most self–evident truth for which Amos seeks assent: two separate people cannot journey together without first having met one another. Amos responds in at most a very restrained way to the sceptical question, "What does Amos have to do with Yahweh?" Perhaps here and in what follows he is calling to mind proverbial

18   Wolff, *Amos the Prophet*, 6–16 [5–12].
19   Is 10:8–11; 28:23–29; Job 6:5–7; 8:11–13.
20   So Lehming, "Erwägungen," 164.
21   See p. 107.
22   Is 6; Jer 1; Ezek 1—3. Cf. Fey, *Amos und Jesaja*, 41.
23   See p. 181.
24   Cf. 1 Kgs 8:5; Nu 17:19 [4]; Josh 11:5. See textual notes "a" and "b" to 3:3.

expressions, such as have circulated since antiquity, in order to impress upon his hearers, "You should always ask concerning the cause!" Thus an Old Akkadian proverb says, "Copulation causes the breast to give suck."[25] In a collection of proverbs from the library of Asshurbanapal it is said ironically, "Without copulation she conceived, without eating she became plump!"[26] If Amos is being ironic, however, it is at most in the very banality of his example.

■ **4** The two following, synonymous questions also reflect the life of Amos. The livestock breeder knows no worse enemy than the lion hungry for prey. אריה is the most common word for "lion" in the Old Testament; כפיר designates the "young lion," whose ravenous appetite schools it in the techniques of catching prey (Ezek 19:3). The sheep breeder and the shepherd are quite familiar with the lion's behavior. The "roaring" and the "raising the voice" (in parallel relationship here as in 1:2) betray the fact that an animal has been carried away from the flock (cf. Hos 5:14). The lion's roar also serves to secure his prey by frightening off other creatures (v 8a). In the "forest" (יער) the prey is least likely to be snatched from the lion. The addition in v 8b[27] interprets יער as a "hiding place," by which is meant a thicket in which human beings are apt to get hopelessly entangled (2 Sam 18:8–15), rank growth and dense brush of all sorts being found there (Hos 2:14 [12]; Ezek 15:2), as well as brambles of the type which also grow on the steppe (Is 21:13). Here the lion feasts upon the "prey" (טרף) which he has snatched away from the flock (Hos 5:14) and torn apart (Hos 6:1). Even the eager young lion knows not to let out a sound before he has made his catch, in order not to frighten away the prey he is stalking or to warn the shepherds in time to take defensive action (Is 31:4).

Thus Amos can hold up before his adversaries the shepherd's old maxim: "If a lion roars, he has just made a catch." In other words, here too an incident is to be understood on the basis of a prior state of affairs. The resultant incident is always expressed by a verb in the imperfect, whereas a nominal clause (v 4aβ) or a verb in the perfect (v 4bβ, cf. v 3b) describes the antecedent cause.

■ **5** Man as well as beast is the deadly enemy of other animals. The didactic questions progress in well-ordered fashion. "To fall" (v 5a) and "to spring up" (v 5b) are artfully paralleled. Hunting is also an activity familar to the sheep breeder, he and his shepherds having more leisure time than the peasant to engage in this pursuit. Of course, the sheep breeder was no hunter of big game. Amos identifies two hunting implements by name. The first, מוקש ("wooden missile"), must be a sort of throwing stick, since it causes a bird to fall to the ground (v 5aα). There is evidence that the boomerang and the throwing stick were common hunting weapons in the ancient Near East,[28] being used primarily to catch birds though also being effective against rabbits.[29] The second, פח ("folding net"), is the snaring device[30] set up to trap either small animals or, more commonly, birds (Ps 124:7; Prv 7:23). G. R. Driver identifies the מוקש as the movable part of a trap.[31] However, even according to Driver the word designates a complete snaring device, for otherwise not only the "falling" of a bird to the ground but also the frequent parallelism of פח and מוקש would be incomprehensible.[32] The two hunting scenes serve, each in its own way, the identical purpose of impressing upon the mind the question of the causal event. In v 5a, a bird falls because it has been struck by a wooden missile. As in v 4a so also here the causal event stands in a

25   Robert H. Pfeiffer, *ANET*[3], 425 (A.K. 4347.28).
26   Robert H. Pfeiffer, *ANET*[3], 425 (A.K. 4347.27). Cf. Bruno Meissner, *Die babylonisch–assyrische Literatur* (Potsdam, 1930), 82.
27   See textual note "c" to 3:4.
28   Max von Oppenheim, *Der Tell Halaf* (Leipzig, 1931), 93–94 and pls. 9b, 17b.
29   Anton Moortgat, *Die bildende Kunst des Alten Orients und die Bergvölker* (Berlin, 1932), 44 and pl. 18. Cf. Jehuda Feliks, "Jagd," *BHHW* 2, 792; and *BRL*, 288–89.
30   *AOB*, fig. 182; and Marie–Louise Henry, "Vogelfang," *BHHW* 3, 2111.
31   Godfrey Rolles Driver, "Reflections on Recent Articles," *JBL* 73 (1954): 131–136 ("II. Hebr. *MÔQĒŠ*, 'Striker' "). Cf. Weiser.
32   Cf. Josh 23:13; Is 8:14; Ps 69:23; 140:6 [5]; 141:9. In Ps 140:6, מוקש designates something that is set up.

nominal clause (v 5aβ), while the result is described by a verb in the imperfect (v 5aα). In v 5b, the snare springs up because some animal has gotten into the net and been trapped. Once again, the result (v 5bα) is expressed by the imperfect. But this time the causal factor in the situation, namely an animal's triggering a net by getting caught in it, is also described by a verb in the imperfect (ילכוד v 5bβ), because the catching occurs simultaneously with the springing up of the snare. However, the use of the infinitive absolute (לכוד) before the verb emphasizes the catching as the causal event.[33] Those to whom the question is addressed are expected to confirm the experience of the hunter as well as that of the shepherd.

■ **6** Reference is also made to the experience of townspeople (v 6a and 6b: "in a city" [בעיר]). Assuming that Amos was speaking in Samaria, he progressively zeroes in on the world of experience of his hearers. At this point in the series of questions, humanity becomes the endangered species.[34] The causal event is the watchman's blowing of an alarm trumpet to give warning of danger (v 6aα);[35] the immediate result is the frightened arousal of the population (v 6aβ). That the verb "blow" (יתקע) is in the imperfect does not mean that there is here a transition to the future tense.[36] On the contrary, the imperfect after אם has iterative force ("whenever . . . , as often as . . ."). [37] As usual, the result ("they tremble") stands in the imperfect. In terms of subject matter as well, the analogies for the cause–effect relationship clearly move closer to their didactic goal. In Hosea, the prophet himself fulfills the role of the watchman scanning the distance and sounding alarm. [38] In Amos, the metaphor of the watchman serves to emphasize the way in which result inevitably follows cause. In the direction of its thought (from cause to effect), the question of v 6a foreshadows those of v 8. By way of contrast, v 6b asks once more concerning the cause on the basis of the resultant event, as in vv 3–5. Following the pattern familiar to us from

vv 3b and 4bβ, the causal event is stated in the perfect (v 6bβ), while the result is once again described with an imperfect (v 6bα). Although the analogy is still mainly concerned here with the connection between result and cause, nevertheless for the first time the subject matter of the question is of a theological nature. The name of Yahweh is mentioned, and there is talk of calamity (cf. 6:3; 9:4, 10). The series of questions has thus here reached a preliminary climax; already the answer is awaited with bated breath. And yet, who in Israel would think to contest the answer anticipated here? After all, there has certainly been no reference yet to the destruction of Israel; the talk has been of those periodic crises which throw a city into turmoil and motivate it to offer up prayers of lamentation before Yahweh. [39] Doubtlessly the chain of examples, reiterating the question of the interconnection of events, has reached a climax insofar as Amos alludes to commonly accepted Israelite dogma. However, he has thereby only completed preparations for reaching the goal of the dispute.

■ **8** Two novel stylistic features show that this goal is attained with v 8. First of all, the sentences no longer begin with an interrogative particle (which in every case had been followed by a verb in the imperfect); now the initial clauses are statements of fact, formulated in the perfect. Secondly, the questions concerning consequential relationship are raised in the second cola, and are formulated in a pointedly direct, personal way: "who" can avoid such a reaction? Tension is built toward the climactic question by means of an artfully contrived parallel in v 8a which takes up imagery from the beginning of the series (v 4) and relates this imagery now to humans. Thereby a concluding thematic analogy is drawn (cf. 1:2; 5:18–19), and that precisely in the style of the concluding question. Since Yahweh's speaking is thus exactly paralleled by a lion's roaring, the questions of appropriate reaction cannot receive different answers. Thus the concluding

33   On the distinction between the perfect in v 4bβ and the imperfect in v 5bβ, see Gese, "Beiträge," 426.
34   On the intensification, see pp. 183–84.
35   See Wolff, *Hosea*, 112 [143], on Hos 5:8, and p. 43, on Joel 2:1.
36   Against Gese, "Beiträge," 426.
37   Cf. Brockelmann, *Syntax*, pars. 164b and 169c.

38   Hos 8:1; cf. 5:8. Cf. also Jer 6:17; Ezek 3:17; and Hab 2:1.
39   See p. 182.

sentence of the disputation has acquired absolutely convincing force.[40] The adversaries of the prophet have to take note of the undeniable fact that Yahweh has spoken to Amos. Apart from 3:1, the verb "has spoken" (דִּבֶּר) is attested only here as referring to Yahweh's speaking. In contrast to the verb "has said" (אמר), which introduces direct speeches, our verb here emphasizes the act of speaking as such (cf. "who testifies [= speaks] fully" [דֹּבֵר תָּמִים] in 5:10), the transmitting of a "word" (דָּבָר). The perfect tense does not restrict the action of the verb solely to the past here, any more than it does in vv 3b, 4b, 6b and 8a. Consequently, it is not permissible to limit the scope of the reference in v 8b only to the prophet's call (cf. 7:15). The range is broad enough to include all new interventions by Yahweh through his word, the ever–unavoidable result of which is the act of proclamation, this being a reflex action much like the startled arousal when a lion roars. "To prophesy, proclaim" (נבא nip'al) is the expression used by Amos to describe this response. Both here and in 7:15 Amos uses this word as a matter of course to describe his proclamation. It suggests the authority of the one who must speak out in no uncertain terms against the expectations of the people. He must do this just as surely as Yahweh placed his awesome demand upon him, quite apart from any desire of his own.

■ **7** The Deuteronomistic assertion,[41] only loosely connected with the prophetic disputation, expounds upon the recognition of the tie between the events of history and the previously proclaimed word of Yahweh. The view that Yahweh does nothing without prior prophetic announcement can scarcely be attributed to Amos.[42] Certainly he shares the general perspective of Israel that Yahweh initiates calamity (v 6b), but what he must impress upon the people is precisely that Yahweh does speak and so compel a prophet to proclaim (v 8), and that he does this as an act of his free and uncoerced will. The Deuteronomistic school, on the other hand, explored the whole history of Israel for the interlocking of prophetic word and historical event.[43] It is in accord with the theology of this school that our interpreter wishes to explain the disputation of Amos. Here דבר means "thing, event, a certain matter."[44] Not a thing is carried out by Yahweh unless he reveals his plan (in advance!). The expression "to reveal a plan" (גלה סוד) is otherwise at home in proverbial wisdom. In that context it describes the activity of undisciplined gossipers, activity objectionable to the human community, and could even be translated, "to tattle a secret" (cf. Prv 11:13; 20:19; 25:9). However, one cannot interpret this expression in Amos by reference to its wisdom background,[45] even though its meaning there likewise derives from the original conception of the סוד, the "circle" in which people consult with one another in a spirit of intimacy and trust.[46] The interpretation of our passage must rest on the recognition that it was also possible to speak of the "council of Yahweh" (סוד יהוה Jer 23:18, 22).[47] In Jer 23:18 and 22 the fact that a prophet has "stood" (עמד) in the intimate circle around Yahweh has become the criterion of true prophecy. Amos' commentator no

---

40 On the syntax, see textual note "h" to 3:8.
41 See p. 181.
42 Fey, *Amos und Jesaja*, 42.
43 Cf. Gerhard von Rad, "History in *I* and *II Kings*" in *The Problem of the Hexateuch and Other Essays*, tr. E. W. Trueman Dicken (New York: McGraw–Hill, 1966), 208–11 [*Gesammelte Studien zum Alten Testament*, ThB 8 (München: Chr. Kaiser, 1958), 193–96]; and Wolff, "Kerygma," 83–86 [171–74 (= *Gesammelte Studien*, 308–11)].
44 Cf. Gen 24:66; Ju 6:29; and also James Barr, *The Semantics of Biblical Language* (London: Oxford University Press, 1961), 129–40.
45 Against Samuel Terrien, "Amos and Wisdom" in *Israel's Prophetic Heritage: Essays in honor of James Muilenburg*, ed. Bernhard W. Anderson and Walter

Harrelson (New York: Harper & Brothers, 1962), 112.
46 Cf. Gen 49:6; Ps 55:15 [14]; Jer 6:11; Ezek 13:9. See also Ludwig Koehler, *Hebrew Man*, tr. Peter R. Ackroyd (London: SCM, 1956), 102–04 [*Der hebräische Mensch* (Tübingen: J. C. B. Mohr [Paul Siebeck], 1953), 89–91]; and Zimmerli, *Ezechiel*, 292–93.
47 Cf. Job 15:8. Although the word itself is lacking, the same concept is found in 1 Kgs 22:19ff; Job 1:6ff.

longer thinks of the circle around Yahweh, however, but rather of that which Yahweh has proclaimed in it, namely his plan. That is shown most clearly by the verb here employed: Yahweh "uncovers, discloses" (גלה) his decision. He does not want it to remain a secret; he himself "lays it open."[48] He establishes intimate communication with his people "through his servants, the prophets."[49] In connection with the designation of the prophet as "servant" (עבד), we must remember that high–ranking royal courtiers were also called "servants."[50]

Aim

These were extremely provocative sayings that the leading circles of Israel and of the royal residence, Samaria, had to endure. Amos' words not only attack pride and self–reliance, but they also shatter every hope. Precisely because of the severity of his message, the prophet is concerned that he be understood. Using the thought–forms and the pedagogic techniques of his day, his artful and clever rhetoric becoming progressively more intense, he struggles to gain recognition for the necessity of his unbelievably frightening proclamation. By means of rhetorical questions, he reminds his hearers of the incontestable laws of world order. By citing an array of examples from the life of travelers, beasts of prey, hunters and townspeople, he points out that one must probe back into the causal factors, especially in the case of dreadful events. A preliminary climax demands acceptance of the insight that calamity is to be traced back to Yahweh (v 6b). Assent to this demand makes it impossible for the hearer to deny the ultimate assertion, namely that also the prophetic proclamation of Amos can be understood only by reference to Yahweh having spoken (v 8b). To be sure, this conclusion is not theoretically demanded. Amos sets forth in thesis–form the event which he has experienced and to which he bears witness: "Yahweh has spoken." The irresistible word permits no silence. Any other person in Israel who might have experienced that which befell the sheep breeder from Tekoa would likewise have had to appear on the scene with this message. Yahweh has spoken—that is the only legitimation of Amos. With his questions about cause and effect, Amos seeks to awaken in his hearers an understanding of the inevitable consequence of Yahweh's forceful intervention and an appreciation for the correlative necessity of his own shattering proclamation.

Thus Amos is one of the first of those biblical witnesses who attest to that inescapable constraint which compelled them to minister as messengers. Suffering under such constraint, Jeremiah will raise bitter accusation against his God (Jer 20:7–9). Paul sets forth to the congregation the fact that it was irrefutable constraint, and not any form of self–willed decision, that led him to the preaching of the gospel (1 Cor 9:16–17). The voice of God comes to persons in the arena of human history. Whoever does not respond directly to this voice, but rather interprets it anthropologically as stemming from human will, must of necessity misunderstand it (cf. 7:10–17!). The Deuteronomistic interpreter in v 7, in all reticence, allows us to sense the compassion underlying the fact that God entrusts to human beings the mystery of his will.

---

48 Cf. from this vantage point, in retrospect, the parallels to our expression in Prv 11:13; 20:19; 25:9; and see Ernst Jenni, *Das hebräische Pi'el* (Zürich: EVZ–Verlag, 1968), 202–03.

49 On the Dtr. usage, see p. 181 n. 2.
50 Walther Zimmerli, *TDNT* 5, 664–65.

Terror in Samaria

Bibliography

Albrecht Alt
"Der Stadtstaat Samaria" in *Kleine Schriften* 3, 258–302.

Frank Crüsemann
Studien zur Formgeschichte von Hymnus und Danklied in Israel, WMANT 32 (Neukirchen–Vluyn: Neukirchener Verlag, 1969), 50–55 ("Exkurs: Die Heroldsinstruktion").

Herbert Donner
"Die soziale Botschaft der Propheten im Lichte der Gesellschaftsordnung in Israel," *OrAnt* 2 (1963): 229–45.

H. S. Pelser
"Amos 3:11—A Communication" in *Studies in the Books of Hosea and Amos* (*Die Ou Testamentiese Werkgemeenskap in Suid–Afrika, 7th and 8th Congresses [1964–65]*) (Potchefstroom: Rege–Pers Beperk, 1965), 153–56.

Isac Leo Seeligmann
"Zur Terminologie für das Gerichtsverfahren im Wortschatz des biblischen Hebräisch" in *Hebräische Wortforschung: Festschrift zum 80. Geburtstag von Walter Baumgartner*, ed. Benedikt Hartmann *et al.*, SVT 16 (Leiden: E. J. Brill, 1967), 251–78.

Samuel Terrien
"Amos and Wisdom" in *Israel's Prophetic Heritage: Essays in honor of James Muilenburg*, ed. Bernhard W. Anderson and Walter Harrelson (New York: Harper & Brothers, 1962), 108–15.

Hans Walter Wolff
Amos the Prophet: The Man and His Background, tr. Foster R. McCurley (Philadelphia: Fortress, 1973), 56–59 [38–40].

3

9   **Proclaim it over the strongholds[a] of Ashdod,[b]**
     over the strongholds[c] in the land of Egypt!

a   *G* (χώραις ["lands"]) seems to have read both here and in 3:10, 11 and in 6:8 the more familiar noun ארצות instead of ארמנות; see textual note "c" below.

b   *G* (ἐν Ἀσσυρίοις ["in Assyria"]) presupposes בְּאַשּׁוּר, parallel to בארץ מצרים ("in the land of Egypt"). The language of Hosea (7:11; 9:3; 11:5 [*G*], 11; 12:2; see Wolff, *Hosea*, 145–46 [187]) may have exerted an influence here. Amos himself never mentions Assyria, but he does refer to Ashdod in 1:8. Ashdod in parallelism with Egypt is scarcely explainable as a secondary reading. *M* is supported both by the rest of the Greek translations (ἐν ἀζώτῳ) and by *T* and *V*.

c   *G* (ἐπὶ τὰς χώρας ["over the lands"]) again presupposes אֲרָצֹת. Consequently, and understandably, nothing in *G* corresponds to the בארץ which follows

Say: Assemble yourselves upon
<Mount>[d] Samaria!
  See the boundless terror[e] in her
  midst
    and the oppressed[f] within her![g]
10 They do not know how to do what is
right, [utterance of Yahweh],[h]
  those who store up violence
  and devastation in their strongholds.[i]

11 Therefore thus [the Lord][j] Yahweh has
said:
  An adversary[k] <shall surround>[l] the
  land;
  he will tear[m] down your might from
  you,
    and your strongholds[n] will be
    plundered.

in *M*. If v 9aβ originally specified only one locale before naming Egypt, it is more probable that the expression בארץ (familiar in other contexts as well; cf. 9:7; [2:10; 3:1]) was used than the phrase על־ארמנות, which repeats an element of v 9aα. In the light of 3:10b and 11b, however, it may be that a repetition in v 9aα and 9aβ of the catchword ארמנות was originally intended.

d   *G* (ἐπὶ τὸ ὄρος) presupposes the singular, הַר, and thus corresponds to the usage of Amos in 4:1 and 6:1. The plural, otherwise attested only in Jer 31:5, refers to the mountains of the whole district, the later Assyrian province of Samaria. *M* (= *T* and *V*) thinks of the mountains immediately surrounding the city of Samaria, because it was a common notion that an assembly of peoples would require extensive space. Indeed, the mountains forming the semicircle just to the east of Samaria are higher than the hill upon which the city is located (the highest elevation in the city being 463 meters), but the actual peaks of these mountains (to the south 523 meters, to the east 676 meters, to the north-northeast 689 meters, to the north-northwest 585 meters) lie four or more kilometers from the city. Hence, they are too distant to provide a vantage point from which to observe the oppression of people in the city—the real concern of Amos.

e   *G* (θαυμαστά) reads "something marvelous," σ' (ἀχορτασίας) "famines," *V* (*insanias*) "madnesses"; on the meaning of the Hebrew term, see p. 193.

f   The plural (עֲשׁוּקִים) can designate either the oppressed persons or the oppression as such, as Eccl 4:1 well illustrates. According to the sequence observed there (Eccl 4:1b!), and in keeping with the tendency of Amos (cf. 4:1 הָעֲשֻׁקוֹת), one should here probably interpret the word as referring to the victims of the turmoil (against Gesenius–Buhl, 625; and Koehler–Baumgartner, 743). Admittedly the parallel מהומת ("terror") speaks in favor of reading עֲשׁוּקִים as an abstract plural.

g   Literally "in her midst"; בקרב in Amos means, as a rule, "in the midst of" assemblies of people (5:17; 7:8, 10; 2:3).

h   The phrase must be considered secondary, since the actual oracle of Yahweh, introduced with the messenger formula, does not begin until 3:11 (Sellin; Maag, *Text*, 15). *G* (λέγει κύριος) already presupposes this addition; see p. 143.

i   On *G* (ἐν ταῖς χώραις αὐτῶν ["in their lands"]), see textual note "a" above.

j   Missing in *S* and the Sahidic text, and not customary in the messenger formula as used in Amos; see also textual note "o" to 1:8.

k   *G* and α' (τύρος) vocalize incorrectly צֹר (as in 1:10). *T* (עקה), σ' (πολιορκία), and θ' (*fortitudo*) probably presuppose the noun צַר ("narrowness") in the sense of "distress, siege." According to the context (see textual note "l" below), *M* has apparently also understood the noun in this sense. *V* (*tribulator* ["be in

190

tribulation"]) translates the same word as a qal perfect of צרר = "to be oppressed." The context as a whole, however, and especially v 11b, urges one to interpret this noun as referring to the person of the oppressor.

l   *M* reads the noun "circumference," in the construct state, and takes it to be parallel to צַר ("distress"), probably in the sense of "encirclement." In that case, however, a predicate is missing in v 11aβ, as is also true in the proposal of Robinson, H. S. Pelser ("Amos 3:11—A Communication" in *Studies in the Books of Hosea and Amos* [*Die Ou Testamentiese Werkgemeenskap in Suid–Afrika, 7th and 8th Congresses (1964–65)*] [Potchefstroom: Rege–Pers Beperk, 1965], 153–56) and others, to read מְסָבִיב (cf. *G* καὶ κυκλόθεν). *T* (תקפה) and *V* (*circuietur* ["be encompassed"]) suggest that the original form was יְסוֹבֵב (Wellhausen).

m   Literally "makes to step down"; *T* (ויבטל) and *V* (*detrahetur* ["be taken away"]) perhaps presuppose הוּרַד, parallel to the passive form ונבזו. *G* (κατάξει) confirms *M*.

n   See textual note "a" above.

Form

Stylistic and thematic features set this oracle off as a unit distinct both from the preceding questions (3:8) and from the following section, which is introduced by a new messenger formula (3:12). Its inner structure also shows it to be a rhetorical composition complete in itself.

Seen in a form–critical perspective, we are dealing here with a development, peculiar to Amos, of the genre of the prophetic judgment speech.[1] Its beginning is peculiar, since Amos appears not as a messenger but as one who himself sends messengers. Thus his role here is that of someone in a high position of authority. He employs in his address the distinctive feature of "instruction to heralds" (a genre whose life–setting was the occasion when emissaries were commissioned),[2] i.e., a series of imperatives assigning the messengers their tasks. The imperatives "proclaim!" (השמיעו) and "say!" (אמרו) belong quite regularly to the thematic content of such directives.[3] The use of the preposition "over" (על) in identifying the addressee in this genre is elsewhere attested only in Jer 4:16. The subsequent content of the message is also made up of commands in Joel 4:9 [3:9] and Jer 5:20 and 4:5, the latter citation resembling our Amos passage in likewise containing an exhortation to assemble together ("assemble yourselves" [האספו]). The sole function of the exhortation in Amos is to elicit an eyewitness report concerning the conditions in Samaria ("see!" [וראו] v 9bβ). The nature of the exhortation clarifies the function of the instruction to heralds within the whole of the oracle: the guilt of Samaria is to be substantiated (vv 9bβ–10) by independent and competent observers. The content of the instruction to the heralds, namely the directive to summon witnesses, thus gives to the first element of the prophetic judgment speech, the demonstration of guilt, its peculiar stamp here in Amos. The second element of the prophetic judgment speech, the announcement of

1   See Wolff, *Hosea*, 222 [288].
2   Cf. Crüsemann, *Studien*, 50–55.
3   The two occur together in Jer 4:5; 31:7; 46:14; 50:2; and Is 48:20. "Proclaim!" (השמיעו) also occurs in Jer 4:16 and 5:20; an imperative form of אמר ("to say") is found in Is 40:9 and 62:11.

punishment, is introduced by "therefore" (לכן v 11), as is frequently the case in Amos (5:11, 16; 6:7; 7:17) and elsewhere.[4] The messenger formula is characteristically not used until we come to this second element, which is thereby introduced as Yahweh's word (cf. also 5:16; 7:17). To announce the divine judgment is a task that has been imposed upon the prophet by Yahweh.[5] To demonstrate the justice of the punishment is a responsibility which the prophet himself properly assumes. Amos carries out this responsibility in a way that is bound to attract attention, in that the reasons he advances are recognizably valid on an international scale.[6]

The oracle is poetic in structure, though not rigidly so. The purest poetry is found in the announcement of punishment following upon the messenger formula in v 11, with three parallel cola. The first two of them are doubtlessly to be read as having three stresses (they depict the action of the enemy), the third perhaps with two stresses (it describes the mournful consequences). Amos likes to conclude with a staccato effect. The instruction to heralds, in any case, proceeds with considerably greater breadth. The commission begins in v 9a ("Proclaim ...!") with two serenely parallel three–stress cola; the more precise instruction in v 9b should probably be read as an initial four–stress bicolon ("and say ... and see ..."), with an additional line of two stresses standing parallel to the second colon, so that altogether the instruction to heralds is formed by a combination of a bicolon and a tricolon. The summarizing judgment in v 10 is perhaps meant to be read as a four–stress bicolon. On the whole, therefore, we note free rhythms. The prophet indeed wishes to express his concern forcefully, but he aims at completeness as well.

Setting

One cannot imagine any more fitting place for the proclamation of this oracle than Samaria, the capital of Israel (cf. v 9bα). The prophet has in mind here those circles responsible for the conditions in that city. The literary genre of the instruction to heralds presupposes that the primary addressees are those prominent personages who alone are of importance in matters of diplomatic exchange.

In its literary setting this oracle, following upon the inserted legitimation dispute (3:3–6 + 8), provides the first commentary on the statement of principle contained in the oracle at the head of "the words of Amos from Tekoa" (3:1–2).[7] It spells out concretely which crimes Yahweh will punish and how he will do it.

Interpretation

■ 9 An amazing frankness and an impregnable self–confidence is displayed by the sheep breeder from Tekoa when he exhorts leading citizens of Samaria, not without irony, to dispatch delegations to Ashdod and Egypt. Such boldness comes to one who has been overpowered by Yahweh's speaking (3:8). Even at that, however, he is ready to submit his judgment to international examination. Owners of foreign "strongholds" are summoned because the "strongholds" of Samaria are to be evaluated (3:10b).[8] In case one might question the evaluative competence of Amos himself, experts with respect to a highly developed style of living are to be brought in. To credit non–Israelites with a sense of justice valid in the eyes of Yahweh attests to the "wisdom" of Amos and, at the same time, to his freedom (qualities presupposed also by his oracles against foreign nations in 1:3—2:3).

He has witnesses called from Ashdod and Egypt. The textual variant here, which reads Assyria in place of Ashdod, has long found supporters who argue that it forms a better parallel to Egypt.[10] However, Assyria had not yet come within Amos' political horizon,[11] whereas Philistine cities had occupied his attention elsewhere as well.[12] Perhaps the strongholds of Ashdod had impressed him during the course of his own wan-

---

4   See Wolff, *Hosea*, 222 [288].

5   On the secondary character of "utterance of Yahweh" (נאם יהוה) in 3:10, see textual note "h."

6   On placing the accusation first, cf. Hans Walter Wolff, "Die Begründungen der prophetischen Heils– and Unheilssprüche," *ZAW* 52 (1934): 1–7 (= idem, *Gesammelte Studien*, 9–16).

7   See p. 175.

8   On the meaning of ארמנות, see p. 155.

9   See p. 172.

10 See textual note "b" to 3:9.

11 Cf. Martin Noth, "Der historische Hintergrund der Inschriften von sefire," *ZDPV* 77 (1961): 172 (= idem, *Aufsätze* 2, 210); and pp. 89, 149–51.

12 See p. 158, on 1:8, and also the discussion there of the location of Ashdod.

derings.[13] In any case, these strongholds must have been as well known to him and his hearers as was the architecture and the wealth of Egypt. The ivory carvings of Samaria exhibit a style largely patterned after that of Egypt, as for example the Horus–child on a lotus flower, a winged sphinx, and the like.[14] Perhaps the paralleling of Ashdod with Egypt implies a gradation such as Amos likes to use in the progression of his oratory.

Assembled upon the mountain,[15] the witnesses will have a chance to see in the capital city scenes such as those of 4:1 and 6:1, 3–6, scenes which are described initially as "boundless terror." מהומת ("terror") is usually associated with a form of "much" (רב, Ezek 22:5; Zech 14:13; 2 Chr 15:5) or of "great" (גָּדוֹל, Dtn 7:23; 1 Sam 5:9; 14:20). As a rule it designates the destructive confusion which Yahweh himself brings upon an army in war,[16] confusion resulting in a carnage of self–destruction (Dtn 7:23). Thus 1 Sam 5:11 can speak of a "deathly panic" (מְהוּמַת־מָוֶת); it is the extreme counterpart to the condition of "peace" (שָׁלוֹם) (2 Chr 15:5). Therefore one will have to take this word as referring here to modes of behavior which endanger life, even though Amos is envisioning no activities outside the realm of human interaction. A similar restriction to the connotation of this word is elsewhere attested only in Ezek 22:5 and Prv 15:16. The comparative didactic saying of the latter citation, especially, corresponds to the message of Amos: "Better is a little with the fear of Yahweh than great 'treasure' (אוֹצָר) and 'turmoil' (מְהוּמָה) with it." For in Amos also the "terror" (מהומת) means the acts of those who "store up" supplies (האוצרים v 10b). To capture something of the basically martial and homicidal tenor of מהומה, the translation "terror" is appropriate even when the word

designates social intercourse. The plural form is to be understood as an abstract plural, signifying an intensification.[17] Perhaps the following "oppressed" (עשוקים) is also to be interpreted as an abstract plural; as such the word occurs otherwise only in wisdom literature (Job 25:9; Eccl 4:1).[18] But it would be strange if Amos were not intending here to mention, as in numerous related accusations, the personal victims of the terrorizing activity.[19]

■ **10** Seeing, as one does, the association between terrorizing social behavior and the reprehensible amassing of private fortunes (vv 9b–10b), as attested also in the proverbial wisdom material (Prv 15:16), one is not surprised to find Amos designating the positive behavior which is lacking, not with a term drawn from Israel's legal traditions, but with one likewise known from the realm of wisdom. "Right" (נכחה) means that which is "straight" in the abstract sense of being upright, honest or just.[20] That the word appears in the postexilic texts (Is 26:10; 57:2 and 59:14)[21] does not dispute the fact that it was originally current in the sapiential instruction, in legal matters within the Israelite clans, and then also at the Jerusalem court. This right, in which Israel has been instructed, is something that the leaders of Samaria do not know how to practice.

They are the rich, for they are described as "those who store up" (אוצרים)—i.e., who amass supplies. With acid criticism Amos assumes the hoarded treasures to be "violence and devastation" (חמס ושד). This pair of words is found frequently.[22] In Ezek 45:9 it stands in contrasting relationship to the word pair "justice and righteousness" (משפט וצדקה), a pair that is highly important to Amos also (5:7, 24; 6:12). It is still possible to determine the original meaning of the two words, and therefore to grasp their sense in the com-

---

13 See. pp. 90–91.
14 See André Parrot, *Samaria: The Capital of the Kingdom of Israel*, tr. S. H. Hooke; Studies in Biblical Archeology 7 (London: SCM, 1958) 63–72, and pls. 2–6.
15 On the singular reading, see textual note "d" to 3:9.
16 1 Sam 5:9; 14:20; Is 22:5; Zech 14:13; 2 Chr 15:5; Dtn 28:20.
17 Gesenius–Kautzsch–Cowley, par. 124e.
18 See textual note "f" to 3:9.
19 On the qal passive participle of עשק ("to oppress"), cf. the active participle in 4:1, and further, on the

subject matter, 2:6–8 and 5:11–12.
20 Cf. Prv 8:9; 24:26; Sir 11:21; 2 Sam 15:3; and also Is 30:10. Cf. also Terrien, "Amos and Wisdom," 112–13; and Wolff, *Amos the Prophet*, 56–59 [38–40].
21 Cf. Crenshaw, "Influence," 46.
22 Jer 6:7; 20:8; Is 60:18; Hab 1:3; 2:17.

bined usage.[23] "Violence" (חמס) designates a mortal attack; he whose person is so attacked utters our word as a cry of distress.[24] Frequently also "violence" stands in parallelism with "blood" (דמ[ים] singular or plural).[25] Just like blood (Is 1:15), violence can stick to someone's hands (Job 16:17). Considering all this, "violence" primarily means (attempted) murder, or at least assault against life and limb. On the other hand, "devastation" (שׁד) seems to signify more the damaging of material goods. The root appears in parallelism with "to steal" in Ob 5.[26] Paired with "violence" (חמס), therefore, שׁד probably designates "crimes perpetrated against goods and property."[27] Thus the word pair combines acts of violence against persons and against property and ultimately stands, quite simply, for "murder and robbery." Those are the treasures that have been accumulated in the strongholds of Samaria. In an ironically intensified accusation, the prophet substitutes the underlying harassment and exploitation of the people for its profitable result, which is represented by the furnishings in the homes of the ruling class (cf. 3:12b, 15; 5:11; 6:4–6). They have imported murder and robbery right into their homes, in the form of their luxurious furnishings. The activity denounced by Amos probably reflects the manner and way in which Canaanite culture had developed its methods of ruling, conducting business and administering the law in the capital city of Israel. The manipulations of Canaanite officialdom will have had a determining influence upon the authoritative Israelite circles. Thus the capital was the center and source of the ever–spreading social abuses.[28]

■ **11** This is precisely why the country will go to ruin. The divine word which announces the punishment repeats literally, at the end, the catchword concerning the "strongholds" which stood similarly at the conclusion of the accusation in v 10b, and which is also found in the opening where the witnesses from abroad are summoned (v 9a). The houses of the robbers will themselves be robbed; the scene of guilt becomes the place of punishment. However, all that is only the sharply personalized consequence, for the hearers, of the comprehensive catastrophe which terrorizing activity draws in its wake. "An adversary ⟨shall surround⟩ the land."[29] An invasion that will affect the whole country is announced; this is more than "a calamity in the city" (v 6b). The enemy strips the state of its might—i.e., of its ability to defend itself and, therefore, to exist. It is not said just who the adversary will be, though it will be a superior military power. Nonetheless it is Yahweh whose word calls forth such destruction.

Aim

The historical power, whose destructive advance is announced by Yahweh's word, remains unidentified. But the results are clearly specified: conquest of the land, destruction of political independence and concomitant plundering of the houses of those who themselves had become robbers. The announcement of judgment briefly and tersely formulates the single harsh message which Amos was compelled to pro-

23 Cf. Seeligmann, "Gerichtsverfahren," 257–59; and Rolf Knierim, *Studien zur israelitischen Rechts– und Kulturgeschichte I: ḥṭʾ und ḥms. Zwei Begriffe für Sünde in Israel und ihr Sitz im Leben*, Unpub. Diss. (Heidelberg, 1957), 125–46.

24 Job 19:7; Hab 1:2; Jer 20:8. Cf. von Rad, *Theology* 1, 157 [170]; and Hans Jochen Boecker, *Redeformen des Rechtslebens im Alten Testament*, WMANT 14 (Neukirchen–Vluyn: Neukirchener Verlag, 1964), 60–61.

25 Hab 2:8, 17; Jer 51:35; Ezek 7:23; 9:9.

26 Cf. Mi 2:4 and the repeated use of שׁד to describe the despoiling and devastation of the land in Hosea (9:6; 10:2, 14). See also Wolff, *Hosea*, 187 [243].

27 Seeligmann, "Gerichtsverfahren," 257.

28 Cf. Alt, "Samaria," 298–99; and Donner, "Botschaft," 235–36.

29 See textual note "l" to 3:11.

claim—the end of Israel's existence. The introduction to this message, which gives the reasons for the announcement of punishment, has been worked out much more elaborately by the prophet. One senses in it the intensity with which he struggles to have the righteousness of his God acknowledged. An unusual feature is the marshaling of Philistine and Egyptian witnesses. In this way Amos hopes to counter the suspicion that his strictures against the wealthy leaders of Israel are nothing more than a subjective judgment. Terror, suppression and exploitation of human beings are the negation of what is correct, a negation by which God's people robs itself of its own future.

"Rescue" as Proof of Death

Bibliography

Hartmut Gese
"Kleine Beiträge zum Verständnis des Amos-buches," *VT* 12 (1962): 417–38 (esp. 427–32).

Henry R. Moeller
"Ambiguity at Amos 3:12," *The Bible Translator* 15 (1964): 31–34.

Isaac Rabinowitz
"The Crux at Amos 3:12," *VT* 11 (1961): 228–31.

3

12   Thus Yahweh has said:

Just as the shepherd rescues from
the mouth of the lion
two splint-bones
or a tip of an ear,
so will the sons of Israel be rescued,
who sit in Samaria
ᵃat the footboard of the couchᵃ
and at the ⟨headboard⟩ᵇ of the
bed.ᶜ

a–a *G* (κατέναντι φυλῆς) erroneously reads the familiar words לְקִרְאַת מֹשֶׁה = "over against the tribe (people)"; α' (ἐν κλίματι κλίνης) and σ' (ἐκ κλίματος κλίνη) confirm *M*.

b With Gese ("Beiträge," 427–32) I read בְּאָמְשָׁת. Gese has compared the ancient versions thoroughly; on Akkadian *amartu*, which is also attested in New and Late Babylonian in the form *amaštu*, cf. *AHW* 1, 40b; on the transition from *rt* to *št*, which is not without its difficulties for New Assyrian, see Wolfram von Soden, *Grundriss der akkadischen Grammatik*, AnOr 33 (Roma: Pontificium Institutum Biblicum, 1952) par. 35c; and R. Borger, "Die Aussprache des Gottesnamens Ninurta," *Orientalia* N.S. 30 (1961): 203. G. R. Driver ("Difficult Words in the Hebrew Prophets" in *Studies in Old Testament Prophecy Presented to Professor Theodore H. Robinson*, ed. H. H. Rowley [New York: Charles Scribner's Sons, 1950], 69) proposed וּבְמִקְרַשׁ ("on the edge [of the bed]"). However, that word is neither attested, nor does it form—in contrast to Gese's proposal—a counterpart to פאה. *M* (וּבִדְמֶשֶׁק) is unintelligible (the fabric "damask"? cf. Henry R. Moeller, "Ambiguity at Amos 3:12," *The Bible Translator* 15 [1964]: 31–34); it was early already regarded as a parallel to בשמרון, and it was misread as וּבְדַמֶּשֶׁק: *G* (ἐν Δαμασκῷ), and in the same way by *S*, α', σ', θ', *T*, and *V*, an interpretation easily arrived at on the basis of 1:3 and 5 (cf. 5:27). If one wants to translate "Damascus–bed," one has to change the order of words, as Maag (*Text*, 17) does: וּבְעֶרֶשׂ דַּמֶּשֶׂק. But the parallel expression בפאת מטה is a clear indication against this. Isaac Rabinowitz ("The Crux at Amos 3:12," *VT* 11 [1961]: 228–31) proposed to read וּבַד מֵשׁק ("a part of the foot"), and takes ב in בפאת מטה as ב-*essentiae*: he renders 3:12b as follows: "So shall the Israelites who dwell in Samaria be 'reserved'—in the form of a corner of a couch, and of a piece out of the leg of a bed." But שׁק ("thigh, shank") is never used for a foot (of a bed), and after the simile in v 12a such a new pictorial expression is neither to be expected nor is it clearly understandable.

G (ἱερεῖς ["priests"]) either presupposes a different text, or we are dealing with an inner-Greek scribal error, based on a misreading of the initially transcribed (the meaning of the Hebrew term not being understood) vocable עֶרֶשׂ = ἔρες; in 6:4 G renders עֶרֶשׂ by στρωμνή ("couches"). It has probably read the word as a vocative belonging to v 13 (see Edwin Hatch and Henry A. Redpath, *A Concordance to the Septuagint*, vol 1 [A–I], [Graz: Akademische Druck– u. Verlagsanstalt, 1954 = 1897], 682a).

Form

The messenger formula opens a new oracle. A direct connection with the announcement of punishment in 3:11 is not evidenced by the style, nor does the subject matter readily suggest such a connection either. The ending is controversial. Many would like to see the oracle as concluding with the short sentence, ". . . so will the sons of Israel be rescued." The continuation, starting with the participle "who sit" (הַיֹּשְׁבִים), is then said to belong to 3:13–15.[1] These exegetes sense the lack both of a closer determination of the addressees of 3:13 and of a motivation for the announcement of judgment in 3:14–15. Thereby a problem is defined which does demand a solution. However, one can hardly solve it by separating the end of v 12 (bα²β) from what goes before, because then almost the same problem would emerge for the rest of v 12 (a, bα¹)—it would lack an accusation, an element which could otherwise be recognized in the concluding participial clause standing in apposition to "sons of Israel" (בְּנֵי־יִשְׂרָאֵל). In addition, it is quite uncertain whether such isolated participles ever stood in initial position within rhetorical discourse in Amos oracles; at least in 2:7; 3:10b and 5:12b, they likewise appear only towards the end of the accusation. The participle follows upon an imperative in 4:1. If one were to read the participial element of 3:12 as belonging with the oracle in 3:13–15, one would then have the peculiar situation of a participle preceding an imperative at the opening of an oracle. Only 5:7 and 6:13 could be cited as additional examples of oracles opened by participles, but both of these are uncertain on text–critical grounds. Hence it seems to me that, on the whole, the preponderance of the evidence is in favor of accepting the whole of 3:12 as a rhetorical unit.[2]

The oracle which we have thus defined presents us with a symmetrically structured simile. The "so" (כֵּן) clause is then comparable in length to the "as" (כַּאֲשֶׁר) clause; the application corresponds neatly with the comparison, as one would already expect on the basis of the resumption of the verb "snatches" (יַצִּיל) in "will be snatched away" (יִנָּצְלוּ). Also in terms of rhythm the comparison–clause and the application–clause run parallel; each is composed of two–stress bicola,[3] if one grants that "as" and "so" can be taken as extra–metrical (unstressed). The messenger speech here corresponds to 3:11 in the fact that in neither is the divine first person used, in notable contrast to the oracles in 1:3–2:16 and 3:1–2. Were it not for the messenger formula, one would most readily consider 3:12, on the basis of its ironic comparison, to be a disputation speech.

Setting

The genre of the disputation speech is suggested by the way in which the key word "to rescue" (v 12aα, 12bα) is introduced. Here it seems as though Amos is taking up a catchword of his antagonistic hearers, people who opposed his announcement of judgment by reminding the prophet of the confession that Yahweh is the savior of Israel. Thus the oracle is most readily imaginable in the context of an appearance by the prophet in Samaria (v 12bα). It is therefore hardly a matter of chance that our oracle found its literary place among announcements of judgment that were no doubt also proclaimed in the capital of the country (3:9–11; 4:1–3).[4]

Interpretation

At first glance, Amos seems to agree that there will be a deliverance to which Israel can look forward in spite of

---

1 Gressmann (*Prophetie*), Weiser, Nötscher, Maag (*Text*, 17), Amsler, and others.
2 So also Deden, Fosbroke, Gese ("Beiträge"), and others; for related discussion, see pp. 93, 96, and 99.
3 See Gese, "Beiträge," 428–29.
4 On 3:13–15, see p. 200.

his prophetic message. Just how that deliverance might look, however, is illustrated by an example drawn from his professional experience. This example presupposes a specific statute drawn from the laws governing shepherds (cf. Ex 22:9–12 [10–13]). Whoever allows an animal entrusted to his care to be stolen must make restitution for it to its owner. But if the animal was torn by a beast of prey, this obligation of restitution is nullified, as long as the shepherd can substantiate his claim by offering "evidence" (עֵד Ex 22:12 [13]; cf. Gen 31:39). Two thin splint–bones or merely the tip of an ear would constitute admissible pieces of evidence. Those little bits of "rescued" evidence are, therefore, nothing other than proof that total loss was unavoidable. Thus the verbatim resumption of the catchword "rescue" is to be interpreted sarcastically: Israel will actually be torn to pieces and devoured by an irresistible predator. The content of this new messenger speech confirms, under the form of a disputation, the announcement of punishment which precedes in 3:11.

Again reflecting the situation in 3:9–11, the oracle of v 12 is likewise directed against the inhabitants of "Samaria" (בשמרון). The allusion to their luxurious and dissolute style of life hints at the reason for their destruction. In the light of 6:4a, "to sit" (ישׁב) must here mean a lazy lounging around and sensuous carousing. The nouns מטה and ערש are also used in parallelism in 6:4. A מטה is a cot or "couch" upon which one "stretches out" (נטה).[5] ערש corresponds to the common Semitic collective term for "bed";[6] its root has the basic meaning "to lie, rest."[7]

The Assyrian bed had "two walls," namely a headboard and a footboard.[8] The appropriate Akkadian designations, amar/štu—pūtu, correspond to the Hebrew word pair ʾāméšet—pēʾāh.[9] פאה, then, designates the footboard, while אמשת must be interpreted as the part built up for the head. A particularly well–executed example of this part, formed by a beam curved upward in a semicircle and upholstered with cushions, is offered by the seventh–century bas–relief depicting Asshurbanapal reclining on his divan.[10] A corresponding part can also be recognized on simple beds.[11] It is possible that the simile employed by Amos was particularly effective for his addressees because the furniture upon which they reclined was likely built in corresponding style. The headboard may have been shaped to depict a demon, the feet being carved to represent lion's feet.[12] Beds were also decorated by reliefs carved in ivory (cf. 6:4aα),[13] but Amos does not allude to such decorations here.

Aim

At any rate, the point of the simile is clear. Yahweh wrenches away from the self–assured that in which they uncritically place their trust. Only the memory of a comfortable life is "rescued." Fragments of past splendor will be able to do no more than certify the downfall of the glory of Israel (cf. 3:15). Thus Amos brings to a state of startled awareness particularly those among God's people who have so far enjoyed their rest undisturbed and have not recognized that their lives are endangered.

---

5 Cf. Ugaritic mṭṭ (CTA 14 [= UT Krt].30); and 2 Sam 3:31 (the "bier").

6 Cf. Akkadian eršu (AHW 1, 246b) and Ugaritic ʿrš (Gordon, UT, 461–62, no. 1927).

7 Armas Salonen, Die Möbel des alten Mesopotamien nach sumerisch–akkadischen Quellen, AASF B/127 (Helsinki: Suomalainen Tiedeakatemia, 1963), 110.

8 Salonen, Möbel, 148–51.

9 Cf. Karlheinz Deller, review of Armas Salonen's Die Möbel des alten Mesopotamien, Orientalia N.s. 33 (1964): 102, who accepts the proposal of Gese, "Beiträge," 428–31; see textual note "b" to 3:12.

10 AOB, fig. 149; ANEP, fig. 451.

11 AOB, fig. 387; ANEP, figs. 658, 660.

12 See Gese, "Beiträge," 431.

13 See also the comments on 3:15, p. 202. An example is given by Salonen, Möbel, pl. XLIV, from the latter half of the eighth century.

The Destruction of Buildings

Bibliography

H. Keith Beebe
"Ancient Palestinian Dwellings," *BA* 31 (1968): 38–58.

Herbert Donner
"Die soziale Botschaft der Propheten im Lichte der Gesellschaftsordnung in Israel," *OrAnt* 2 (1963): 229–45.

George S. Glanzman
"Two Notes: Am 3:15 and Os 11:8–9," *CBQ* 23 (1961): 227–33.

3

13 Hear and attest against Jacob's house
   [utterance of the Lord Yahweh, the God of the Hosts][a]:

14 Indeed, on the day when I requite Israel's crimes upon it,
   [thus will I requite the altars of Bethel][b]
the horns of the altar shall be hewn off and shall drop to the ground.

15 I will wreck the winter house with the summer house.
   The houses of ivory shall disappear.
   The numerous[c] structures shall fall[d]

   —oracle of Yahweh.

a   The pleonastic style is more in keeping with the hand responsible for the glosses than with Amos. This gloss anticipates the divine oracle formula in v 15bβ, in order to identify immediately the speaker in vv 14–15. See the excursus on p. 143 and textual note "c" to 6:14.

b   In a characteristically interpretive manner, catchwords are taken up from the immediate context (פקד "to requite" v 14a; מזבח "altar" v 14bβ) and referred to Bethel (cf. 4:4), whereas the broader context makes one think of Samaria (3:9; cf. 3:12). *V* (*super eum visitabo, et super altaria Bethel* ["I will visit upon him, and upon the altar of Bethel"]) attempts to smooth out this difficulty by drawing the עליו ("upon it") into conjunction with the ופקדתי ("thus will I requite") of the following clause, and by inserting a copula before על־מזבחות בית־אל ("upon the altars of Bethel"). However, such a move ignores both Hebrew syntax and the Masoretic division of the clauses.

c   Since Marti, many have read הָבְנִים = "(buildings of) ebony"; so recently Robinson, Maag (*Text*, 17), and Osty. Donner ("Botschaft," 237) proposes בְּרֹמִים = "curtains woven in many colors" (cf. Zimmerli, *Ezechiel*, textual note 27:24c). But (1) these words are otherwise attested only in Ezek 27:15 (הבנים) and Ezek 27:24 (ברמים); (2) the word רבים ("many, great") is frequent in Amos (3:9; 5:12; cf. 6:2; 7:4; 8:3); (3) רבים is supported by *G* (ἕτεροι πολλοί ["many other"]), *T* (סגיאין ["numerous"]) and *V* (*multae* ["many"]). In keeping with these ancient translations, one should not translate "the great houses" (as do Deden, Cripps and others), since that expression would be much too "pale" (Marti: "matt") beside the winter, summer, and ivory houses. The intent of the concluding sentence is not to elaborate but to summarize.

d   Literally "come to an end." *G* (καὶ προστεθήσονται ["are added onto"]) presupposes the root יסף instead of the root סוף, perhaps in the form וְנוֹסְפוּ.

Form

The new oracle opens with the double imperative to hear and to witness. We have shown how it is unlikely that those addressed here are the same Israelites who are characterized more precisely in participial style in 3:12b.[1] However, we had to leave open the question of how to explain the unusual absence here of any demonstration of guilt. The same element is occasionally lacking elsewhere as well (5:1–3). In 3:13–15, however, the problem of the identity of the addressee is linked to this question. Those who are summoned to hear are to function as witnesses (והעידו v 13); they are to "note well" the way in which Yahweh punishes Israel's crimes (vv 14–15). Perhaps, then, non–Israelites are addressed. Could they be the same as those who were to be fetched by the heralds in 3:9? It is more likely that other foreigners, who are already present in Samaria, are addressed. Those in 3:9 were to become witnesses of Israel's guilt (3:9b–10); towards that end, they were to "see" for themselves (וראו 3:9b). Now witnesses of Yahweh's punishment are to be summoned; they can become such witnesses only if they first "hear" Yahweh's announcement of punishment (שמעו v 13a). In this oracle, therefore, witnesses of the punishment are added to the witnesses of the guilt. They are prepared for their task in that, in the divine speech itself, the expected proceedings are proclaimed to them in advance as being in fact acts of Yahweh (vv 14–15). If only the subsequent oracle (and not also that which is therein announced) is to be certified, then it is possible that some Israelite hearers are also being addressed. In any case, the oracle we have before us belongs to the genre of the "installation of witnesses" (*Zeugenbestallung*).[2]

Setting

It is true that, unlike in 3:9 and 12, Samaria is not named here. Nevertheless this oracle was probably also proclaimed in the capital city, since it is there that the splendid buildings and the owners of summer and winter houses (v 15) are most likely to be found. That it is impending destruction which this rare form of oracle prepares the witnesses to observe makes even more probable a close spatial as well as temporal connection with the two preceding oracles (3:9–11, 12). This explains the absence of the demonstration of guilt—it was already given in 3:9b–10. The punishment depicted here, namely the destruction of the buildings, corresponds to the guilt which was demonstrated above in conjunction with the "strongholds." And yet, one should not read vv 13–15 as a direct continuation of 3:9–11. Not only does the messenger speech in 3:11 conclude a well–rounded oracle,[3] but it is highly probable that 3:12 also belongs to the presuppositions of our new oracle. In the oracle of comparison in 3:12, the admissible type of evidence is identified under the form of a simile (cf. the עֵד ["evidence"] of Ex 22:12 [13] with the imagery of 3:12a). Now in our present oracle the actual pieces of evidence for the destruction of Israel are identified for the witnesses (העידו v 13aα)—the wreckage of the buildings. In terms of content, therefore, vv 13–15 should probably be seen as a continuation of both 3:9–11 and of 3:12. Nonetheless, vv 13–15 most likely form an independent rhetorical unit. It was probably delivered in response to a further question, based on the simile in 3:12a, regarding the nature of the items of evidence for the coming catastrophe of Israel. Thus as a composite literary unit 3:9–15 may best be explained as a précis of the prophet's actual words, comparable to that in Hos 4:4–19.[4]

Interpretation

■13 Those people summoned to hear are to be equipped for their task as witnesses. עוד in the hip'il can mean "to install as a witness" (cf. Is 8:2; Jer 32:10, 25, 44). The preposition ב then introduces the one against whom the witness is to appear (Dtn 4:26). However,

---

1   See p. 197.
2   Cf. Dtn 4:26; Is 8:2; and Jer 32:10.
3   See p. 194.
4   See Wolff, *Hosea*, 75–76 [93]. [I.e., like Hos 4:4–19, Am 3:9–15 offers a sort of outline sketch or scenario (*Auftrittsskizze*) of the prophet's utterances delivered on a particular occasion, jotted down—by the prophet or a disciple?—soon after the actual rhetorical confrontation, but not recording the rejoinders, questions and counter–arguments of the prophet's audience; Ed.]

these citations always show the witnesses named as standing in the accusative case. Where the accusative case does not appear, but where the preposition ב identifies the recipients of the action of the verb, עוד in the hip'il, when followed by admonitions, means "to admonish," and when followed by announcements of impending events, which those summoned are to witness, it means "attest." [5] It is against "Jacob's house" that the hearers are to prepare themselves to give testimony. This designation for Israel is found elsewhere in Amos only in the secondary passage 9:8b;[6] it seems to function as a special reminder of election.[7]

■ **14** "Indeed" (כי) introduces those facts to which the witnesses are to bear testimony.[8] First of all, the date of the impending events is given: they will occur at the time when Yahweh punishes the crimes of Israel.[9]

The first evidence for the total judgment will be that the horns of the altar get hewn off. In a situation of blood vengeance and punitive pursuit, a fugitive could grasp and hold on to these horns. Because the altar also functions as a place of asylum, the fugitive was thereby safe from his pursuers (1 Kgs 1:50; 2:28; Ex 21:13–14). But already the ancient covenant law had decreed that the murderer was to be torn away from the horns of the altar by force (Ex 21:14). Now all Israel has become guilty of such grave crimes that Yahweh himself destroys the place of refuge. If the contemporaries of Amos already looked upon the altar as a place of expiation and atonement (Ezek 43:20),[10] then Israel is to be deprived also of this means of deliverance. The horns of the altar, which have been hewn off and have fallen to the ground, provide the witnesses with their first pieces of evidence for the total judgment, just as the tip of an ear serves for the shepherd as proof of the lost animal.[11]

■ **15** The divine first–person speech at the opening of v 15 once again expresses the fact that it is Yahweh himself who, in punishing (v 14a), brings about the destruction.[12] נכה hip'il means the destructive wrecking of buildings which leaves nothing but broken pieces (cf. 6:11!). Are the summer house and the winter house different buildings, or are they two dwellings within the same structure? Certainly there were two–story houses, with a heatable lower story and a cooler upper story. We hear, for example, of the cool upper chamber of Eglon in Ju 3:20, and of the heated "winter house" (בית־החרף) in the palace precinct of Jerusalem in Jer 36:22. But it is not certain here in Amos whether "house" (בית) merely means a room within a larger building.[13] In any case, the only ancient Near Eastern text known so far, besides our Amos passage, which mentions summer house and winter house side by side, clearly refers to two different buildings. In his building inscription from the latter half of the eighth century B.C., king Barrākib of Sam'al stresses that his fathers did not have a good house, because the one they used had to serve both as בית שתוא ("the winter house") and בית כיצא ("the summer house").[14] The building to which this dedicatory inscription refers ". . . was apparently meant to remedy the drawback that the kings of Sam'al had only one palace to serve as both their summer and winter quarters."[15] According to this, then, the designations "winter house" and "summer house" meant houses differently situated, erected for appropriate seasonal use. Already in the ninth century king Ahab of Israel owned one palace in the warmer plain in Jezreel (1 Kgs 21:1) and another on Mount Samaria (1 Kgs 21:18). Even when considered by itself, our clause in Amos suggests this meaning. Surely v 15a does not want to say that (only) the winter

---

5   Cf. Dtn 8:19; Jer 6:10; and Zech 3:6. Cf. also Odil Hannes Steck, *Israel und das gewaltsame Geschick der Propheten*, WMANT 23 (Neukirchen–Vluyn: Neukirchener Verlag, 1967), 69–70.

6   But cf. "Jacob" in 6:8; 7:2, 5; 8:7; and see also the comments below, on 7:2!

7   Cf. Is 18:17; Mi 2:7; and Ob 17–18. On 3:13b, see textual note "a."

8   Cf. the use of כי after עוד hip'il with ב in Dtn 4:26; 8:19; and 31:28–29. See also Wolff, *Hosea*, 90–91 [114], 135 [177] on Hos 4:16 and 8:7.

9   On פקד ("to requite"), see p. 177, on 3:2; on פשע

("crime"), see p. 152–53. On 3:14bα as a later addition from the time of Josiah, see p. 111 and textual note "b" to 3:14.

10   See Zimmerli, *Ezechiel*, 1102.

11   See p. 198.

12   See pp. 102–03.

13   Thus Dalman, *Arbeit* 1/2, 473; and *Arbeit* 7, 79; so also Koehler–Baumgartner, 122 (בית 1c).

14   *KAI* 216.18–19.

15   Donner–Röllig, *KAI* 2, 234.

house "above" (על v 15aβ) the summer house would be wrecked. Quite apart from the fact that, in two–story houses, the airy summer dwelling is the upper one (cf. Ju 3:20), the context obviously stresses the fact of total destruction. Thus the preposition here does not designate a difference in level but rather denotes an addition; it means not "above" but "together with." It is likely that, besides the king, "newly rich members of the civil service,"[16] as well as the upper class in general, also availed themselves of the luxury of two dwellings.[17] A more exact knowledge of the summer and winter houses is not yet available.[18]

The "houses of ivory" must mean luxury villas with interior furnishings of ivory (cf. 6:4). In the days of Amos, such ivory carvings were probably not limited to the royal palace (cf. 1 Kgs 22:39; Ps 45:9 [8]), even though the excavations of the palace area have understandably produced the bulk of ivory finds from Samaria.[19] The villas were distinguished by reliefs carved into ivory plates, decorating the furniture. The reference to "numerous structures" reminds one of the fact that the lively building activity, which had flourished in northern Israel during the reign of Ahab, experi-

enced a last revival under Jeroboam II (cf. 5:11; 6:11). The same expression ("numerous structures" [בתים רבים]) occurs in Is 5:9, in a context (cf. Is 5:8) which recalls the amassing of real estate and land holdings in the hands of a small upper class, a phenomenon which thus dissolved the ancient Israelite system of property laws.[20] Such activity is consigned to destruction ("shall disappear" [ואבדו]) and ruin ("shall fall" [וספו]).

Aim

Through the proclamation of his prophet, Yahweh appoints for himself witnesses who will attest to the fact that he himself executes punishment upon his chosen people. Because of its crimes, Israel is to be deprived of all its foci of security and well–being, be they sacred (v 14) or profane (v 15). So convinced were people that this oracle of Amos was fulfilled when the altar of Bethel was destroyed in the time of Josiah (cf. 2 Kgs 23:15, 17) that they thought they could interpret our oracle on the basis of this event (v 14bα).

16   Donner, "Botschaft," 237.
17   Cf. Alt, "Samaria," 272.
18   Cf. H. Keith Beebe, "Ancient Palestinian Dwellings," *BA* 31 (1968): 57.
19   Cf. J. W. Crowfoot and Grace M. Crowfoot, *Early Ivories from Samaria*, Samaria–Sebaste 2 (London,

1938); André Parrot, *Samaria: The Capital of the Kingdom of Israel*, tr. S. H. Hooke; Studies in Biblical Archeology 7 (London: SCM, 1958), 53–71; and Noth, *World*, 161–62 [148].
20   Cf. the example set by the king in 1 Kgs 21; and also de Vaux, *Israel*, 166–67.

Against the Women of Samaria

Bibliography

J. J. Glück
"The Verb *PRṢ* in the Bible and in the Qumran Literature," *RQ* 5 (1964–65): 123–27.

Siegfried J. Schwantes
"Note on Amos 4:2b," *ZAW* 79 (1967): 82–83.

Salomon Speier
"Bermerkungen zu Amos," *VT* 3 (1953): 305–10 (esp. 306–07).

Eugenio Zolli
"Amos 4:2b," *Antonianum* 30 (1955): 188–89.

4

1 Hear[a] this word
  cows of Bashan
    who (feed) on Mount Samaria!
  who oppress the poor,
    harass the needy,
  who say to their[b] lords:
    "Fetch,[c] that we may imbibe!"

2 [The Lord][d] Yahweh has sworn by his holiness:

  Indeed[e] (it shall be) so!
  Days are coming upon you:[f]
    when you[f] shall be hauled away[g]
    with ropes[h]

a See textual note "f" to Joel 2:22.

b The deviation here from the form of direct address is acceptable within the series of appositional participles; the third plural suffix is presupposed in both *G* (τοῖς κυρίοις αὐτῶν) and *T* (לרבונהן); see also 5:12a–b! *V* (*dominis vestris*) presupposes לאדניכן ("to your lords"). On the use of the masculine plural suffix, see textual note "f" below.

c *G* (ἐπίδοτε), *S*, and *V* (*afferte*) read the plural, bringing the form into agreement with the plurality of those being addressed. The singular form in *M* has a distributive sense.

d Absent from *G* and *S*; see textual note "j" to 3:11.

e נשבע . . . כי is a normal construction, as the following occurrences indicate: Gen 22:16; Is 45:23; Jer 22:5; 49:13; 1 Kgs 1:13, 17, 30. כי is used emphatically (Joüon, par. 165b).

f It is impossible to decide with certainty whether feminine suffixes (כֶ‍ן‍) were originally present here as in v 2bβ (אחריתכן). The substitution of a masculine form for the second person feminine plural can be seen already in the introductory imperative (v 1); see textual note "f" to Joel 2:22.

g The third person singular of the perfect, here pi'el, may be used to express an indefinite subject (Brockelmann, *Syntax*, par. 36d). But a passive (nip'al) reading of the verb is more likely, even though the logical subject stands in the accusative and in spite of lack of congruency (singular verb and plural subject); cf. Gen 27:42 (Brockelmann, *Syntax*, par. 35d). *G* (λήμψονται ὑμᾶς ["they shall take you"]), *V* (*levabunt vos* ["they shall lift you up"]), *T* (ויטלון יתכון ["and they shall carry you off"], similarly *S*) read the pi'el here.

h *G* interprets ἐν ὅπλοις ("with weapons"), and similarly *V* (*in contis* ["on pikes"]) and *T* (על תריסיהן ["upon their shields"]); they read here the same word as in Ps 5:13 [12] and 91:4. α' (θυρεοῖς ["with shields"]) corresponds closely to the versions but shows at the same time their readings are inappropriate here. All these translations presuppose צִנָּה

and your remnant[j] (prodded) with harpoons,[j]

through the breaches[k] you shall depart,[l]

every woman straight ahead.[m]

You ⟨shall be cast off⟩[n]

⟨toward Hermon⟩[o]

—oracle of Yahweh.

i   plural = "(large) shield, weapon." On the basis of the parallel noun (סירות) it is more likely that we have here an irregular plural of צֵ ; for an explanation of the Hebrew word, see pp. 206–07.

i   To assign אחרית the unusual meaning "back (side)" (Duhm, "Anmerkungen," 6; Nowack; Procksch, *BH³*, n. "c" to Am 4:2: אַחֲרִיכֶן) not only assumes a change of אתכם ("you" v 2bα) into אַפְּכֶן ("your nose") but also runs counter to the usage of the word elsewhere in Amos (cf. 8:10; 9:1), where it occurs in the stylistic form of the "unreal *synchoresis*" (see Gese, "Beiträge," 436–37).

j   *G* translates v 2bβ καὶ τοὺς μεθ' ὑμῶν εἰς λέβητας ὑποκαιομένους ἐμβαλοῦσιν ἔμπυροι λοιμοί ("and fiery destroyers shall throw those with you into seething caldrons"), i.e., it understands סירות as "caldrons" (Jer 1:13). Instead of דוגה, *G* perhaps read דַּלְּקָה ("to set fire to"; so also *V: in ollis ferventibus* ["in boiling pots"]), and the first word of v 3 (probably read וּפְרָצִים; cf. Ezek 18:10) was brought into v 2 as the subject ("fiery destroyers" = "feverish pestilences"?).

k   On the accusative as a case expressing direction ("through the breaches"), see Brockelmann, *Syntax*, par. 89 and cf. Gen 9:10 and 44:4. Marti's proposal to read וַעֲרֻמִּים ("and naked") has no recourse to *G*, since the latter has already drawn ופרצים into v 2 (see textual note "j" above) and since its attestation of γυμναί ("naked") is an inner-Greek corruption of γυνή ("woman"; thus *G*^Qms and also α' and θ'); furthermore, one would expect the feminine plural. *V* (*et per aperturas* ["and through breaches"]) supports *M*.

l   *G* (ἐξενεχθήσεσθε ["you shall be brought forth"]) perhaps vocalizes תֵּצֶנָה; cf. Weiser, *Profetie*, 157.

m   Literally "(straight) in front of her"; on this see p. 207.

n   *G* (ἀπορριφήσεσθε ["you shall be cast forth"]) presupposes וְהָשְׁלַכְתֶּנָה (hop'al); *M* (hip'il) may be connected with the misunderstanding of the following word.

o   *G* (εἰς τὸ ὄρος τὸ Ρεμμαν ["on the mountain Remman"]; cf. the variants in Ziegler, *Duodecim prophetae*, 188) reads הָהָר הָרִמּוֹן (with dittography). The Hexaplaric recension and the Catena group, as well as α' (Eusebius, *Onomasticon*), read ἔρμωνα; *V Armon*; *T* חורמיני = σ' ἀρμενίαν (Armenia?). Therefore one should probably read here חֲרְמוֹנָה (cf. Albin van Hoonacker, *Les douze petits Prophètes*, ÉtB [Paris, 1908], 234: חֶרְמוֹן; and Sellin). Whether *M* has the "place of banishment" ("Bannort"; so rendered by Buber, *Kündung*, 639) in mind is a completely open question.

Form

The call to attention,[1] together with the invocation of a precisely specified audience, opens a new judgment speech. The demonstration of guilt is directly joined to the invocation, which is itself formulated as an expression of abuse, developed by means of three appositional participles that culminate in a quotation. The announcement of punishment, which is the essential element of the proclamation, is linked to the foregoing, not by means of a messenger formula (cf. 3:11; 5:3, 16; 7:17), but by an oath formula. This formula for introducing an oath is also found in 6:8 and 8:7; otherwise it is foreign to older prophecy. In Deuteronomic literature the divine oath often confirms the promise of the land.[2] In all likelihood the association of the promise of the land with the divine oath formula is younger than Amos. In any case, he employs the formula to introduce an oath whose threatening content is the direct opposite of the promises to the fathers, an oath announcing that expulsion from the land is the irrevocable will of God. In later prophecy the same formula introduces threats against foreign nations.[3] The oath threatening punishment in our oracle retains the second person plural address of the accusatory invocation. The oracle formula[4] concludes this particularly penetrating variation on a judgment speech.[5] The following verses advance neither the form nor the content of our oracle.

Once again a loose prosodic structure is exhibited by the oracle. If one disregards the opening phrases in v 1aα[1] and v 2a, as well as "oracle of Yahweh" (נאם־ יהוה) at the end of v 3, the accusatory invocation in v 1 can be read as a four–stress tricolon (4 // 4 // 4), or else (in view of the clear parallelism within the second four–stress colon) as three intensive two–stress bicola (2//2:2//2:2//2). The threat of judgment should probably be understood as comprising a three–stress bicolon in v 2b and two two–stress bicola in v 3 (assuming that each of the two words in v 3bα is to be read as having two stresses). The net result is once again a staccato effect at the end of the unit.

Setting

This oracle is addressed to a segment of the inhabitants of Samaria (v 1a) and was therefore clearly proclaimed by Amos in the capital city of the state of Israel. Where in that context could he address such an elegant lot of tyrannical and drink–happy ladies? Did he speak in the gate at the eastern edge of the city? Or did he make his way into the extensive palace precincts? This oracle is a continuation of the oracular series in 3:9–15, the setting of which is undoubtedly Samaria. The call to attention, moreover, reminds one of 3:1. At least in the earliest literary collection, this oracle was an integral part of the complex now forming chap. 3.

Interpretation

■ 1 The subsequent, more exact identifications make it quite clear that by "cows of Bashan on Mount Samaria" is meant women of the elite social stratum of the capital city. They are the wives of the court officials,[6] of the wealthy proprietors of large estates (cf. 5:11–12) and of the merchants (cf. 8:4–6). It is quite uncertain whether the metaphorical designation "cows of Bashan" is meant chiefly to have "a catchy effect on its hearers,"[7] such as the effect intended by the resumption of the catchword "to rescue" in 3:12 or the repetition of cultic forms of speech and confession in 3:2a; 4:4, and 5:4, so that those addressed would feel themselves recognized as "full–blooded nobility."[8] Equally uncertain is the opinion that Amos speaks here in the professional jargon of the cattle breeder. In any case, the appositions quickly show that it is a shocking term of abuse which is here hurled at the cultivated ladies. "Bashan" carries the basic meaning of "fertile stoneless plain,"[9] and it here refers to that plain in Transjordan situated on both sides of the middle and upper Yarmuk, at an altitude of 500–600 meters, which is famous as lush pasture country (Mi 7:14; Jer 50:19; Dtn 32:14). Its cattle are expressly called "fatlings" (Ezek 39:18).[10] According to Ps 22:13 [12] ("Many bulls encompass me, strong bulls of Bashan surround me"), cows of Bashan were especially demanding of their herdsmen. Perhaps Am 4:1 contains an allusion to the fact that

---

1   See p. 175, on 3:1.
2   Dtn 6:10, 18, 23; etc. Cf. the earlier occurrences in Gen 24:7; 50:24; Ex 13:5; etc.
3   Is 14:24; Jer 49:13; 51:14; etc. Cf. Friedrich Horst, "Der Eid im Alten Testament," *EvTh* 17 (1957): 370–73 (= *idem, Gottes Recht*, 298–301); and Wildberger, *Jesaja*, 184.
4   See pp. 92, 143.
5   Cf. 3:9–11, and above pp. 191–92.
6   See p. 192, on 3:9.
7   Weiser, *Prophetie*, 156.
8   Cf. σ': βόες εὔτροφοι ("well–fed cattle")!
9   Koehler–Baumgartner, 158; and cf. the literature there cited.
10 Cf. Hans Jochen Boecker, "Basan," *BHHW* 1, 203; and Wildberger, *Jesaja*, 109.

"they demanded of their herdsmen that they bring them their drinking water."[11] On the basis of modern Arabic usage, Salomon Speier suspects the expression here is a double–entendre for a "voluptuously endowed maiden."[12] What follows, however, shows that for Amos the point of the simile is not fullness of bodily features, but abusive social attitudes and behavior.[13] In 2:6–7 and 3:9–10[14] (together with 5:12 and 8:4–6) we have practical illustrations of how the abuses were perpetrated—through oppression and extortion (עשׁק ["to oppress"]), through striking and beating (רצץ ["to harass"]). These two verbs for oppression are also used in parallelism in Hos 5:11; 1 Sam 12:3–4; and Dtn 28:33. The combination of "to oppress" (עשׁק) and "poor" (דל), with "needy" (אביון) used as a parallel to the latter, is found in Prv 14:31 (cf. Prv 22:16; 28:3), while a contrasting portrait of the compassionate woman appears in Prv 31:20. Dissolute living is especially reproved in Proverbs,[15] and Amos' accusation here culminates in a comparable fashion. As proof that the women of Samaria are self–indulgent, he quotes the demand they make on their husbands to supply them with intoxicating drink. The husband is usually called "master" (בעל);[16] "lord" (אדון) is used unequivocally in this sense only in Gen 18:12 (cf. Ju 19:26; Ps 45:12 [11]), and thus it is at least possible that we are dealing here with concubines. The wives of the elite (and their concubines?) confront not only their slaves but also their "lords" with demands.[17] Under the prophetic accusation women achieve fully independent responsibility.

■ **2** So the women too must receive their punishment. The threat is introduced as an oath of Yahweh,[18] which he swears "by his holiness." This expression has no parallel elsewhere in Amos (cf. 6:8; 8:7), and in the rest of the Old Testament only Ps 89:36 [35] offers an equivalent, where the context indicates its special meaning: the oath of Yahweh, sworn by his holiness, is both immutable (v 35 [34]) and free of any deception (v 36b [35b]), excluding the possibility of breach of treaty or faith (vv 34–35 [33–34]).[19] Holiness is the absolutely supreme divinity of God himself, which stands opposed to all human unfaithfulness and frailty (cf. Nu 23:19). When the oath formula replaces the messenger formula,[20] the irrevocable nature of that which is proclaimed is set forth in the strongest terms.[21]

The reference to "days [that] are coming" focuses attention upon events of a new era, events which will completely transform the present.[22] The detailed portrayal of the things to come, which follows this, begins, as is usual, with a perfect consecutive construction.[23] Deportation is announced. In 2 Kgs 20:17 נשׂא nip'al refers to the carrying away into exile of material valuables. For נשׂא pi'el, 1 Kgs 9:11 offers a formulation with the same prepositions that are found here in Amos: "Hiram 'supplied' (נִשָּׂא אֶת) Solomon 'with' (בּ) cedar timber." Since the context of our verse clearly presupposes deportation, the passive (nip'al) interpretation is here the more likely.[24] צנות should refer to the instruments used in the deportation, though the precise meaning of the word is still uncertain.[25] "Hooks" would more likely be employed to carry off

---

11　Dalman, *Arbeit* 6, 176.
12　"Bemerkungen," 306–07.
13　On the designation of the "poor" and "needy," see pp. 165–66, on 2:6–7.
14　See pp. 193–94.
15　See Prv 20:1; 21:17; 23:29–35; 31:4–7.
16　See, e.g., Ex 21:22; 2 Sam 11:26; and Prv 12:4.
17　Cf. the behavior of Jezebel towards Ahab in 1 Kgs 21:5–15.
18　See p. 205.
19　Cf. Klopfenstein, *Lüge*, 12, 40.
20　See pp. 135–37.
21　On כי as the initial element of a divine oath, see textual note "e" to 4:2; on הנה, see p. 142.
22　Cf. 1 Sam 2:31 and 2 Kgs 20:17. The formula is used frequently in the book of Jeremiah, e.g., 7:32;

9:24 [25]; 16:14. Cf. also von Rad, *TDNT* 2, 946–47.
23　See Gesenius–Kautzsch–Cowley, par. 112x; cf. Am 8:11; 9:13; 1 Sam 2:31; Jer 9:24 [25]; etc.
24　See textual note "g" to 4:2.
25　Cf. Koehler–Baumgartner, 308.

dead cattle than to lead away livestock; hence an interpretation "ropes" seems a better possibility, in light of Akkadian *ṣerretu* > *ṣinnitu*.[26] No "remnant"[27] will remain, and those who, perhaps stubbornly, refuse to be led away with ropes will have other instruments used on them. סירות דוגה means some sort of fishing gear, though hardly angling hooks. Instead, some kind of harpoon is envisioned,[28] which may have been considered a cattle prod peculiar enough to be suited to this unusual and violent deportation.

■ **3** V 3a stresses again that this deportation will be total and will proceed without delay. "Breaches" (פרצים) are the gaps in the walls (cf. 9:11; 1 Kgs 11:27; Neh 6:1) left behind by the enemy conquest.[29] The thoroughness of the destruction will make it unnecessary to exit through a city gate; each individual woman will be driven out of the city "straight ahead" through the breaches. "Every woman straight ahead" (אשה נגדה) corresponds exactly to the expression "every man straight ahead" (אִישׁ גֶּנְדּוֹ) in Josh 6:5, 20 (see Jer 31:39!). Just as in that story, after the collapse of the city walls of Jericho every Israelite could enter "straight ahead," directly into the city, so now every woman of Samaria must leave by the shortest and fastest route. "To be cast toward"[30] depicts what is done with corpses[31] or organisms that are totally despised (Ezek 16:5); in Jer 22:28 the word is used with reference to the deportation of Jehoiachin. The direction of the deportation is stated in general terms only: "toward Hermon."[32] From many sites of higher elevation in the state of Israel, one can see that southern part of the Antilebanon (which lies some 120–150 kilometers north north–east of Samaria) with its peaks in excess of 2800 meters. This high mountain range is, in places, perpetually snow–covered and is accordingly called today *Jebel 'et–Telj* ("Snow–Mountain"). It lies in the general direction of Damascus (cf. 5:27), the capital city of the Aramean kingdom, the old archenemy of Israel.[33] However, neither here nor elsewhere in the transmitted oracles does Amos mention by name (cf. 3:11; 6:14) the enemy power which Yahweh will use to accomplish his purposes.

Aim

The oracle is a further exposition of the basic conviction of Amos that the impending punishment of all transgressions (3:2b) will mean the total end of Israel (8:2). It will mean not only the end of the nation's power (3:11) and splendor (3:15), but also of its people. From among the careless, pleasure–seeking population of Samaria as a whole (whose masculine element is primarily in view in 3:12 and 6:1–7), the feminine segment of the capital's elite social class is here singled out for accusation and threat. The women, no less than the men, are held accountable for their attitudes and actions towards the poor. Women are here explicitly placed under the judgment of Yahweh; their responsibility for the future of Israel is thus taken in deadly earnest, which reflects an attitude by no means commonplace in the world of the ancient Near East. A similar accusation, though one differently motivated, is to be found only in Isaiah (3:16–24).[34] For the first time, total deportation figures as the punishment (cf. 7:11, 17; 6:7; 5:5, 27). The provocative comparison with indulgent, fatted cattle is sustained, in an unusual way, from the accusation right through to the details of the sentencing. It would be surprising indeed if such shocking oracles did not already provide a legal suit for breach of public peace and insurrection in Samaria (cf. 7:10–11). Perhaps report of such a reaction has merely not been transmitted to us. Amos may well have been coerced into moving on from Samaria to Bethel.

---

26 Cf. *CAD* 16, 201; and especially *Enūma eliš* 1.72, on which see Siegfried J. Schwantes, "Note on Amos 4:2b," *ZAW* 79 (1967): 82–83. G. R. Driver ("Babylonian and Hebrew Notes," *WO* 2 [1954]: 20–21) follows *G* in reading here "shields," but such would be a highly unlikely means for transporting cattle. See textual note "h" to 4:2.

27 Cf. 9:1; 8:10; 1:8; and Gese, "Beiträge," 436–37.

28 Cf. Dalman, *Arbeit* 6, 360.

29 On that subject, see 3:11bα!

30 See textual note "n" to 4:3.

31 Am 8:3; 1 Kgs 13:24–25; Jer 14:16, etc.

32 See textual note "o" to 4:3.

33 See p. 153.

34 Cf. Wildberger, *Jesaja*, 145.

On the broader issue, see 2:13–16 and 3:12.

A Reproach of the Cult Pilgrims and Its Later Interpretation

Bibliography

Joachim Begrich
"Die priesterliche Tora" in *Werden und Wesen des Alten Testaments*, ed. Paul Volz, Friedrich Stummer, and Johannes Hempel; BZAW 66 (Berlin, 1936), 63–88 (reprinted in *idem, Gesammelte Studien*, 232–60).

G. Johannes Botterweck
"Zur Authentizität des Buches Amos," *BZ* N.F. 2 (1958): 176–89 (esp. 182–86).

Walter Brueggemann
"Amos 4:4–13 and Israel's Covenant Worship," *VT* 15 (1965): 1–15.

James L. Crenshaw
"Amos and the Theophanic Tradition," *ZAW* 80 (1968): 203–15.

Frank Crüsemann
Studien zur Formgeschichte von Hymnus und Danklied in Israel, WMANT 32 (Neukirchen–Vluyn: Neukirchener Verlag, 1969), 97–106 ("Die Amos–Doxologien").

Reinhard Fey
Amos und Jesaja: Abhängigkeit und Eigenständigkeit des Jesaja, WMANT 12 (Neukirchen–Vluyn: Neukirchener Verlag, 1963), 88–96.

Kurt Galling
"Bethel und Gilgal," *ZDPV* 66 (1943): 140–55; 67 (1944–45): 21–43.

Theodor H. Gaster
"An Ancient Hymn in the Prophecies of Amos," *Journal of the Manchester Egyptian and Oriental Society* 19 (1935): 23–26.

Friedrich Horst
"Die Doxologien im Amosbuch," *ZAW* 47 (1929): 45–54 (reprinted in *idem, Gottes Recht*, 155–66).

Henning Graf Reventlow
Das Amt des Propheten bei Amos, FRLANT 80 (Göttingen: Vandenhoeck & Ruprecht, 1962), 75–90.

René Vuilleumier–Bessard
La tradition cultuelle d'Israël dans la prophétie d'Amos et d'Osée, CTh 45 (Neuchâtel and Paris: Delachaux & Niestlé, 1960), 88–90.

John D. W. Watts
Vision and Prophecy in Amos (Grand Rapids: Eerdmans, 1958), 51–67.

4

4   Enter into Bethel and transgress,
       into Gilgal, ᵃtransgress even more!ᵃ
   Bring your sacrifices in the morning,
       your tithes on the third day!

a–a   See Gesenius-Kautzsch-Cowley, par. 114n. Since Samuel Oettli (*Amos und Hosea. Zwei Zeugen gegen die Anwendung der Evolutionstheorie auf die Religion Israels*, BFChrTh 5/4 [Gütersloh, 1901], 69) וְהַרְבּוּ has often been proposed. This cannot be supported by *G* (καὶ εἰς Γαλγαλα ἐπληθύνατε τοῦ ἀσεβῆσαι ["and in Gilgal you increased in sinning"]), or by *T* (בגלגלא אסגיאו ["in Gilgal they increased"]); at best, it

5 Kindle[b] a thanksgiving sacrifice
from that which is leavened,
  and proclaim freewill offerings,[c]
    loud–and–clear![d]
For so you love (to do), sons of Israel!

      —oracle of [the Lord][e] Yah-
      weh.

6 [Even though I gave you[f]
shining[g] teeth in all your cities,
and lack of bread in all your settlements,
(still) you did not return to me
        —utterance of Yahweh.

7 {Even though I}[h] withheld the rain
from you
while there were still three months
to the harvest—
  I would send rain upon one city,
  but upon another city I would send
  no rain.
  One field would receive rain,
  while a field upon which [it did
  not rain][i] would become parched.

finds support in *V* (*ad Galgalam, et multiplicate prae-varicationem* ["to Gilgal, and multiply transgres-sions"]). "Moreover, the harsh stylistic forms (asyn-deton in vv 4αβ, 5αβ; the infinitive instead of the softer imperative v 5αα) effectively undergird the harshness of the words themselves" (Weiser, *Profetie*, 162). On the meaning of פשע, see Knierim, *Haupt-begriffe*, 178.

b   The infinitive absolute amidst imperative forms, and itself functioning as an imperative, is not impossible; see Gesenius–Kautzsch–Cowley, par. 113z; Joüon, par. 123x; and Is 37:30b (Ketib). Since Henricus Oort ("De profeet Amos," *Theologisch Tijdschrift* 14 [1880], 144), this form is usually adjusted to the con-text (וְקַטְּרוּ = *V et sacrificate* ["and sacrifice"]). *G* (καὶ ἀνέγνωσαν ἔξω νόμον ["and they proclaimed law without"]) reads a completely different text (וְקָרְאוּ מֵחוּץ תּוֹרָה). α′ (εὐχαριστίαν ["thank–offer-ing"]) confirms *M*.

c   *S* (ונדורו נדרא) supposes "vows" (due to a misread-ing of the ב in נדבות as ר), and it therefore reads וּשְׁלֵמוּ = "and fulfills" (the vows), instead of the השמיעו which follows in *M*.

d   See textual note "c" above. *M* reads literally "Make proclamation!" (second person plural), but means, functioning in asyndetic attachment, "publicly!" *G* (ἀπαγγείλατε ["proclaim!"]) joins this imperative to the following line, which accordingly is changed from second–person plural direct address to a third–person plural form (ὅτι ταῦτα ἠγάπησαν οἱ υἱοὶ Ισραηλ ["that the children of Israel loved these things"]).

e   See textual note "i" to 3:8.

f   *G* (καὶ ἐγὼ δώσω ["and I will give"]) in using the future tense interprets this new oracle as a threat of punishment, attached to v 5. *V* (*dedi* ["I gave"]) follows *M*.

g   *M* reads literally "cleanness of teeth," meaning "nothing to eat" (Koehler–Baumgartner, 632–33). *G* (γομφιασμὸν ὀδόντων) thinks of toothaches and—like *T* (אקהיות), *S* (קהיות), and *V* (*stuporem*)—prob-ably read קהיון, which was interpreted as "dullness" of the teeth, in accord with קָהָה (Jer 31:29–30; Ezek 18:2). σ′ and θ′ (καθαρισμόν) support *M*.

h   וגם אנכי is probably a later addition. While אנכי was certainly used by Amos himself (see p. 213 n. 10), it seems strange alongside אני in v 6. Moreover, all the following strophes begin directly with a verb in the perfect (cf. vv 9, 10, 11).

i–i   *G* (βρέξω) and *V* (*plui*) presuppose אַמְטִיר, ("I will send rain"), corresponding to v 7αβ. A nipʿal read-ing תָּמָּטֵר (so H. Graetz, *Emendationes in plerosque Sacrae Scripturae Veteris Testamenti libros*, fasc. 2; ed. G. Bacher [Breslau, 1893], *ad loc.*; followed by Buber, *Kündung*, 639) is ruled out by the following עליה ("upon it"). The text transmitted by *M* must be understood as a neutral feminine, as in the cases of תַּשְׁלֵג ("it snows") in Ps 68:15 [14] and נִשְׂעָרָה ("it storms") in Ps 50:3. See Brockelmann, *Syntax*, par. 35a, and Joüon, par. 152e.

8

And two or three cities would
stagger[j] to another to drink water,
but they would not be sated—
(still) you did not[k] return to me
—utterance of Yahweh.

9

[I smote you with blight and mildew.]
<I scorched>[m] your gardens and your
vineyards.
The locust devoured your fig trees
and your olive trees.
(Still) you did not[n] return to me.
—utterance of Yahweh.

10

I sent against you plague[o] after the
manner[p] of Egypt.
I slew with the sword your youths,
together with your well-trapped[q]
horses.
I made the stench[r] of your camp rise up,
even[s] into your own nostrils.
(Still) you did not[t] return to me
—utterance of Yahweh.

11

I overthrew you, as God overthrew
Sodom and Gomorrah.
Then you were like a brand plucked
from the burning.
(Still) you did not[u] return to me
—utterance of Yahweh.

12

Therefore thus I am about to do to you,
Israel!
Precisely because this (is what) I am
about to do to you,
prepare[v] to meet[w] your God, Israel!

j *G* (καὶ συναθροισθήσονται ["and they shall be gathered together"]) and *S* seem to have read וְנֹעֲדוּ, as
in Nu 16:11; cf. Harper.

k *G* (καὶ οὐδ' ὧς . . . ["and not even in this way . . ."])
employs here (and also in vv 9, 10, 11) a more intense expression than that in v 6 (καὶ οὐκ ["and
not"]).

l–l *G* (ἐπάταξα ὑμᾶς ἐν πυρώσει καὶ ἐν ἰκτέρῳ ["I smote
you with fever and jaundice"]) here found references to human illnesses. Corresponding to Hag
2:17, where the same initial four words as here are
followed by וּבַבָּרָד ("and with hail"), *S* adds
ובברדא to its translation.

m *G* (ἐπληθύνατε) reflects הַרְבֵּיתֶם, which thus creates
a clause antithetically related to what follows: "You
increased . . ., but . . . the locust devours"; cf. the
similar construction in 5:11aβb. *T* (סגיות), σ' and
θ' (τὸ πλῆθος),.and *V* (multitudinem) already presuppose the reading of *M* (the hipʿil infinitive construct
of רבה) (or רְבָבוֹת?). The structure of the other
strophes makes it likely that an original verbal form
הֶחֱרַבְתִּי (Wellhausen) was copied incorrectly.

n See textual note "k" above.

o *G* (θάνατον ["death"]) interprets the word here just
as it does in Ex 5:3; 9:3, 15; Lev 26:25; Nu 14:12;
Dtn 28:21; etc. α' (λοιμόν ["plague"]) understands
M correctly (cf. Ziegler, *Duodecim prophetae*, 109).

p Otto Procksch (*Die kleinen prophetischen Schriften vor
dem Exil* [Calw and Stuttgart, 1910], and *BH*[3], n.
"a" to Am 4:10) and Morgenstern ("Amos Studies
IV," 318) propose כְּדֶבֶר ("like [the] plague") in
place of *M*'s בדרך. Fey (*Amos und Jesaja*, 92) supports this emendation by pointing to v 11a as an
analogous construction, which is not at all compelling however. כְּדֶרֶךְ should probably be read
here, analogous to Gen 19:31: כְּדֶרֶךְ כָּל־הָאָרֶץ
("according to the manner of all the earth"; cf. Gen
31:35 and Jer 10:2). *G* (ἐν ὁδῷ ["in (the) way"])
already presupposes בדרך.

q Since Zeijdner (1886) many critics have read צְבִי
("ornament"); see Maag, *Text*, 22. Considering the
sense, it is unlikely that the reference was originally
to "horses captured in war," as *M* now reads.

r *G* (ἐν πυρί ["in fire"]) reads the more common בְּאֵשׁ
instead of בְּאֹשׁ ("stench").

s On the *waw explicativum*, see Gesenius–Kautzsch–
Cowley, par. 154a (n. 1b).

t See textual note "k" above.

u See textual note "k" above.

v The form הִכּוֹן occurs elsewhere only in Ezek 38:7,
in the context of a summons to battle.

w *G* (τοῦ ἐπικαλεῖσθαι ["to call upon"] = *S*) read perhaps (?) לִקְרֹאת (אֶת) and thought of the meeting as
an invocation. But the infinitive form לקראת is
never derived from the root קרא I ("to call, summon"). *V* (in occursum), α' (κατέναντι), σ' and ε'
(praeparare ut adverseris deo tuo), and θ' (εἰς ἀπάντησιν)
support *M*.

13   For (it is) so!

ˣHe who forms mountainsˣ and
creates breath,
who declares to mankind what is
his plan,ʸ
who makes dawn (into)ᶻ misty–
darkness,ᵃᵃ
who treads upon the heights of the
earth:
Yahweh {God of Hosts}ᵇᵇ is his
name!]

x–x G (ἐγὼ στερεῶν βροντὴν ["I (it is) who makes the thunder strong"]) initially continues the first person style of the preceding speech and presupposes רַעַם ("thunder") as a parallel to רוח ("wind, breath"), but the reading is supported by none of the other ancient translations.

y The noun here is derived from the root שׂיח "to occupy oneself with something." G (τὸν χριστὸν αὐτοῦ ["his anointed one, messiah"]) reads the more familiar מְשִׁיחוֹ. α′ (τίς ὁμιλία αὐτοῦ ["what his instruction (is)"]), σ′ (τὸ φώνημα αὐτοῦ ["his utterance"]), θ′ (τὸν λόγον αὐτοῦ ["his word"]), and V (eloquium suum ["his expressed (plan)"]) confirm and interpret M. T (מא עובדוהי ["what (is) his work"]) could have read מַעֲשֵׂהוּ, as Ehrlich (Randglossen 5, 239) also conjectures.

z G (ὄρθρον καὶ ὁμίχλην ["dawn and mist"]) presupposes וְעֵיפָה, as do some manuscripts of M. In view of 5:8aα¹, we might well suppose that G reflects the more original text. 5:8aα²–β, however, argues for M; cf. Joüon, par. 125w. M is already presupposed by V, which renders faciens matutinam nebulam ("making [the] morning mist"); G also understood עיפה to mean "mist, fog." Akkadian upū = "clouds."

aa σ′ (ἑσπέραν ["evening"]) reinforces the antithesis.

bb The parallel strophes attest to the originality of the shorter form (cf. 5:8; 9:6); on the expansion, see textual note "a" to 3:13, and textual note "c" to 6:14.

Form

Although at first glance the elements combined in 4:4–13 seem to lack any coherence, it is nonetheless clear that they are closely interlocked in the received literary tradition. To begin to discern this, one need only compare the initial phrases in vv 6, 12a, 12b, and 13. After 4:4 the beginning of a new formal and thematic unit is not clearly evident until we reach 5:1. Thus it is understandable that new attempts have recently been made to see the whole section as a unified speech,[1] after it had become customary to divide it into at least three independent units (vv 4–5, 6–12, 13)[2]—a procedure in which the assignment of the sentences in v 12 created special difficulties. So we must raise anew the question of the relationship of the trans-

mitted literary complex to the oral proclamation of the prophet.

4:4–5   First, vv 4–5 stand out clearly from that which follows. Both the concluding oracle formula in v 5b,[3] as well as the end of sharply defined prosody and the change of theme, mark a major literary break.

From the form–critical perspective, the oracle must be understood as a "parody of a priestly torah."[4] We have to assume that the formal elements of the priestly torah were, first of all, cultic instructions addressed in the imperative plural and, secondly, an evaluative concluding statement which could be introduced by כי ("for, because").[5] Amos parodies this solemn form in a twofold way. At the very outset, in v 4a, he refers twice to criminal activity as the goal of the instruction,

---

1   Brueggemann, "Amos 4:4–13"; see earlier Wellhausen, Harper, and Cripps.
2   Cf. Weiser; Maag, Text, 20–24; and Amsler.
3   See p. 143.
4   Begrich, "Tora," 77 (= idem, Gesammelte Studien, 247–48).
5   Cf. Lev 7:22–25; 19:5–8; and Dtn 14:4–8, 21.

while the priestly torah promised life as its goal [6] Secondly, the conclusion in v 5b grounds the ritual instruction not in the will of Yahweh but ironically in the (arbitrary) self-love of those addressed. In such a way, then, this oracle parodies the goal and the foundation of priestly cultic instructions. The form is hence turned into a reproach, one which no doubt originated with Amos. The instructions are issued in three regular three-stress bicola, the second member of each bicolon intensifying its preceding parallel (as is especially evident in v 4a and v 5a). The sentence pronounced at the end (excluding the oracle formula), with its two-stress bicolon, creates the familiar staccato effect.

4:6-11 When set alongside the highly polished oracle of vv 4-5, how is the continuation to be evaluated? On the whole, a uniform sentence structure is sustained throughout vv 6-11. The oracle formula at the end of vv 6, 8, 9, 10 and 11 initially divides the material into five sections. That this arrangement is appropriate to the content is shown by the sentence which precedes the oracle formula in each case: "(Still) you did not return to me." The sections always begin with a verb in the first-person singular perfect, introducing a report of God's punitive acts that were meant to effect a return.[7] The first-person speech of Yahweh (with the exception of "God" [אלהים] in v 11a) and the form of direct address (second person plural) are maintained. The uniform shape of the accusation of continued unwillingness to repent, together with the five-part structure (reminiscent of the cycles of the oracles against the nations and the visions), has made it seem indisputable that this pericope derives in the main from Amos himself.

Yet this assumption needs to be reexamined, initially for stylistic reasons. Those who want to attribute the text to Amos must delete numerous clauses and expressions, but since the criteria for doing so are unclear the various proposals have differed widely.[8] It is the

exception in this section to find even an approximately regular parallelism (vv 6a, 7aβ, 9a). Otherwise one can recognize in the prosodic structure at best only loose parallels, which can hardly be improved by arbitrary deletions (vv 7b, 10a, 10bα). One even finds purely prose sentences (vv 8, 11). In the extant text, then, the sentence structures vary between poetic and prose types, with the latter sort increasing in frequency towards the end of our pericope. If one starts out from the fivefold occurrence of the refrain and tries thereby to identify "strophes" one encounters, in addition to the lack of prosodic uniformity, a great variation in length. For example, the first speech unit (v 6) comprises ten, the second (vv 7-8) thirty-seven words (disregarding connectives and concluding expressions). As a rule, only one plague at a time is treated, more or less extensively (hunger in v 6, drought in v 7, harvest damages in v 9, "overthrow" in v 11), but in v 10 at least two (plague and sword) are handled. Ludwig Koehler has described this pericope as a "truncated torso" and "a fragment with elaborations."[9] If one compares these five units of speech with the five strophes of the cycle of oracles against the nations and even with the cycle of visions, it is immediately evident that the strophic structure of the cycles exhibit a much stricter regularity. One notes in the cycles a much tighter thematic development, which involves a steadily increasing intensity, and finally that those expansions which are present in the text are easily detachable and self-contained supplementations, rather than being barely recognizable insertions. Above all, every strophe in these two cycles is dominated by the element of the announcement of punishment. Here, however, we find within the five uniformly concluded units of speech only accusations. Thus the style in vv 6-11 deviates in many respects from that of comparable oracles of Amos, even with their secondary reworking, and no attempt at reducing the length of the oracles in vv 6-11 can erase this well-founded impression. Moreover, the linking of our

---

6   Cf. Am 5:4b; Lev 18:5a; and Ezek 33:13-16. On the latter text, see Walther Zimmerli, "'Leben' und 'Tod' im Buche des Propheten Ezechiel," *ThZ* 13 (1957): 494-508 (reprinted in *idem, Gottes Offenbarung*, 178-91).

7   On the interlinking in v 6α and v 7aα, see below, and textual note "h" to 4:7.

8   Cf. Weiser, *Profetie*, 165-74; Morgenstern "Amos

Studies IV," 318; and Reventlow, *Amt*, 85-86.

9   Koehler, *Amos*, 17.

pericope with the preceding reproach in 4:4–5 by means of "even though I" (וגם־אני v 6a) is striking, because both the particle וגם as a device for connecting oracles (quite different in 7:6!) and the first–person pronoun in the form אני[10] are otherwise foreign to the book of Amos. Outside of Amos וגם־אני is often used in prophetic oracles to attach to an element of accusation the corresponding threat of appropriate punishment.[11] In contrast, here וגם introduces reminiscences of events which occurred well before the contemporary accusation, and thus we must understand it to be a secondary linking device, as it frequently is elsewhere.[12] We never find authentic oracles of Amos joined in this fashion.[13] What, then, is the derivation of our stylistically un-usual pericope?

Let us turn first to an investigation of its linguistic features. A comparison of our text with enumerations of plagues in ancient Near Eastern[14] and other Old Testament texts (for example Ex 7—12) brings to light especially close points of contact between Am 4:6–11 and the announcements of reward and punishment at the end of the Holiness Code in Lev 26.[15] Likewise in this chapter, as in the whole of the Holiness Code (in contrast to Amos and to the language of Deuteronomy), the form אני ("I") with reference to Yahweh is cur-rent.[16] Above all, however, all the plagues which Am 4:6–11 enumerates are referred to here in substance, with even the same terminology being employed to a large extent. A similar situation obtains with reference to both the curses of Dtn 28 and the royal intercessory prayer of Solomon in 1 Kgs 8:33–37.

Am 4		Lev 26		Dtn 28		1 Kgs 8	
6	נתתי	4, 6, 11, 17, 19					
		30–31	וְנָתַתִּי				
	Hunger	26, 29		48, 53ff		37	
	חסר לחם	26	לֶחֶם	48, 57	חֹסֶר כֹּל		
7–8	*Drought*	19		23–24		35	
7	הגשם	4	גֻּשְׁמֵיכֶם				
	והמטרתי			24	...אֶת־מְטַר...	35	מָטָר
8	ולא ישבעו	26	וְלֹא תִשְׂבָּעוּ				
9	הכיתי אתכם	24	וְהִכֵּיתִי אֶתְכֶם				
	Crop Failure	20		22, 38		37	
	בשדפון ובירקון			22	וּבַשִּׁדָּפוֹן וּבַיֵּרָקוֹן	37	שִׁדָּפוֹן יֵרָקוֹן
	וכרמיכם			30	כְּרָמִים 39 כֶּרֶם	37	
	וזיתיכם			40	זֵיתִים		
	Locusts			38		37	
10	*Pestilence*	16, 25		21, 27, 35		37	
	שלחתי בכל דבר	25	וְשִׁלַּחְתִּי דֶבֶר	21	הַדֶּבֶר	37	דֶּבֶר
	בדרך מצרים			27	בְּשִׁחִיו מִצְרַיִם		
	Sword	25, 33, 36–37		22		33	
	בחרב	25, 33, 36–37	חֶרֶב	22	וּבַחֶרֶב	33	
11	"*Overthrow*"	30–33					

10 Elsewhere אנכי is always used: 2:13; 5:1; 6:8; 7:14; 9:9.

11 So Mi 6:13; Jer 13:26; Ezek 16:43; 20:25; and Mal 2:9.

12 Cf. Joel 4:4 [3:4] (see above, p. 74); Is 28:7; 31:2; Jer 5:18; 26:20; etc. On the use of גם as a device for introducing Judaic glosses in the book of Hosea, see Wolff, *Hosea*, on 4:5; 5:5; and 6:11.

13 Usually in Amos oracles are simply juxtaposed; in 5:4, and apparently also in 5:12, כִּי functions as a literary link, while לָכֵן is similarly used in 5:11 (cf. 5:13).

14 For example, *KAI* 222 A.14ff; cf. also F. Charles Fensham, "Common Trends in Curses of the Near Eastern Treaties and *kudurru* Inscriptions compared with Maledictions of Amos and Isaiah," *ZAW* 75 (1963): 168.

15 Cf. Reventlow, *Amt*, 83–90; and Brueggemann, "Amos 4:4–13," 7–8.

16 Cf. Lev 26:16, 24 (גם־אני), 28, 32, 41, 44; and, for a complete listing of occurrences in the Pentateuch, Solomon Mandelkern, *Veteris Testamenti Concordantiae Hebraicae atque Chaldaicae* (Tel–Aviv: Schocken, ⁴1962), 1254.

The expression "as God overthrew Sodom and Gomorrah" (כמהפכת אלהים את־סדם ואת־עמרה v 11) occurs verbatim in Is 13:19b and Jer 50:40 (analogously applied to Babylon) and nearly verbatim in Jer 49:18 (analogously applied to Edom) and Dtn 29:22 [23] (analogously applied to Israel), but it is not found at all in Lev 26, Dtn 28 or 1 Kgs 8. Is one to understand this on the basis of the specific historical setting of our pericope? In addition to this correspondence in details, Am 4:6–11 is related to Lev 26 in several other ways. The classical triad of plagues—hunger, sword, pestilence[17]—is developed extensively in both and expanded in several layers. The style in each case can be characterized as rhythmic prose.[18] The use of the first–person divine speech and direct address in the plural further associates Lev 26 with Am 4:6–11. The difference consists in the fact that everything which in Lev 26 is conditionally threatened in the event of disobedience is stated in Am 4:6–11 as God's accomplished act. That a transposition in perspective from future to past has taken place can be further recognized by the fact that although the opening verbs of the five units of speech consistently exhibit the perfect tense, in the continuation of the speeches the older form of the threat has in several instances still been preserved (so vv 7aβ, 7b, 8, 9aα).[19] Such an inconsistency in the use of verb forms can hardly be expected of Amos.

On the basis of our observations thus far—regarding the style of 4:6–11, its connection with 4:4–5, and its language—there is no reason to suppose that Amos stands "in the succession of a well defined office,"[20] or that he was celebrating the liturgy of a covenant renewal.[21] One must rather conclude that Am 4:6–11 stands in proximity to the Holiness Code, which probably came into being in the latest period of the pre-exilic cultus.[22] Lev 26 "presumably developed from a part of the agenda for the great autumn festival."[23] Dtn 28, with its curses and, especially, with its references to Yahweh in the third person, is more distantly related.

Following loosely upon the genuine oracle of Amos in 4:4–5, vv 6–11 emphasize the manifold prior punitive acts of Yahweh, thus serving to expose as Israel's great guilt its stubborn refusal to repent. But such a proclamation is in two respects foreign to Amos' own. When the prophet elsewhere measures Israel against the acts of God, he does so by confronting it with divine acts of deliverance (2:9; 3:2). Secondly, Israel's guilt is never elsewhere characterized by Amos as obduracy regarding Yahweh's prior threats; its culpability is rather always defined as transgression against fellow human beings. Nonetheless, it is also the case that the plagues of Yahweh are enumerated here under a different viewpoint than they are in the threats of punishment in Lev 26 (where their goal is chastisement leading to obedience, cf. vv 18, 23, 28) and in the curses of Dtn 28. With each plague, according to Am 4:6–11, Yahweh anticipated repentance. This combination of the plague series with the theme of "return" is otherwise found only in a particular stratum of 1 Kgs 8 (a stratum which does not correspond to the final Deuteronomistic stratum),[24] namely in 1 Kgs 8:33 and 35.[25] 1 Kgs 8 connects these themes within an intercessory prayer, while Am 4:6–11 does so within an accusation. In short, we find that a five–part homily has been attached to the old reproach of Amos in 4:4–5. This homily interpreted the punishments threatened in cultic curse formularies (punishments like those of 1 Kgs 8:33–37) as admonitions to return, to which Israel had, however, thus far responded only with contumaciousness. The question of the setting in which such an accusation was made becomes more urgent.

4:12 Once having recognized the great distance between the accusation in 4:6–11 and any genuine oracles of Amos, the reader is no longer very surprised at v 12, even though this verse is indeed strange in light of the message of Amos. Amos employs לכן ("there-

17   Jer 14:12; 21:7, 9, etc.; Ezek 6:11–12; 12:16. Cf. Elliger, *Leviticus*, 367–69.
18   *Ibid.* 367, 369.
19   Cf. Reventlow, *Amt*, 87.
20   *Ibid.*, 90.
21   Brueggemann, "Amos 4:4–13," 13.
22   Martin Noth, *Leviticus: A Commentary*, tr. J. E. Anderson, OTL (Philadelphia: Westminster, 1965),

126–27 [*Das dritte Buch Mose: Leviticus*, ATD 6 (Göttingen: Vandenhoeck & Ruprecht, 1962), 109–10].
23   Elliger, *Leviticus*, 371.
24   Cf. Noth, *Könige*, 188–89.
25   See chart, p. 213.

fore'') following accusations to attach either "thus Yahweh has said" (כה אמר יהוה 3:11; 5:16; 7:17) or a description of an event in which those being threatened are the subject (5:11; 6:7). In each case the punishment announced is quite concrete. Here, on the other hand, while "thus" (כה) in v 12a indeed refers to a specific action of Yahweh, the precise nature of this action is left unexplained. Instead, v 12b apparently refers back by means of "this" (זאת) to the very same action of Yahweh, using this action as a ground (עקב כי ["precisely because"]) for summoning Israel to meet its God. Twice "Israel" is here solemnly addressed (at the end of v 12a and of v 12b), which is a form of invocation otherwise unattested in Amos[26] but characteristic of liturgical addresses. This fact serves to remove the widespread regret that we have preserved for us in v 12a merely a truncated announcement of punishment by Amos. Instead of postulating vague expansions, we should rather ask what concrete event it is to which we are referred by "thus" (כה) and "this" (זאת), and what historical connection we ought to see between v 12a and 4:6–11 on the one hand, and v 12b and 4:13 on the other. In any case v 12, with its insistent reference to a process which was apparently evident to the initial hearers, and therefore needed no explanation, functions now as a highly peculiar transitional device between 4:6–11 and 13.

4:13 The use of כי ("for") in v 13a as a linking device itself shows that the exhortation to meet God (4:12b) is to be explicated by v 13, and that v 13 indeed informs us of the manner in which this meeting is to be realized. What follows is the special form of a hymn in the participial style, closing with the confession of the name of Yahweh. What kind of a meeting with Yahweh does it intimate, to judge by its veiled pointer to Yahweh's action?

No other text links together an enumeration of chastising plagues, the theme of return, and the praise of Yahweh's name in the same way as 1 Kgs 8:33–37.

According to vv 33 and 35 ("and acknowledge your name" [וְהוֹדוּ אֶת־שְׁמֶךָ]), it is precisely in the confession of Yahweh's name that the contrite "return" finds its consummation.[27] 1 Kgs 8:33–37 shows, furthermore, that the linking together of enumeration of plagues, expectation of repentance, and praise, as found in Am 4:6–13, forms a judgment–doxology acknowledging the just nature of divine punishment.[28]

The Hymnic Passages in the Book of Amos

Am 4:13; 5:8–9; and 9:5–6 must be assessed together, this being demanded in equal measure by their formal congruity, their thematic interrelatedness and the contexts in which they are found in the book of Amos.

Three formal characteristics of these passages especially stand out: the use of participles at the beginning of each colon or bicolon; the closure of several cola with "Yahweh [God of Hosts] is his name" (יהוה [אלהי־צבאות] שמו 4:13; 5:8; 9:6); and the, on the whole, unusual regularity of balanced three–stress bicola. Nevertheless, the question must be asked whether we have before us three different hymns[29] or possibly two,[30] or three[31] or even four[32] strophes of a single hymn. A number of factors favor the view that different hymns are here represented. The number of cola preceding the refrain varies in the extant text between four (4:13) and nine (9:5–6). The participles are indefinite in 4:13 and 5:8a but are always definite thereafter. Each colon in 4:13 and 5:8a begins with a participle, after which participial and finite verb forms alternate. Finally, it is uncertain whether 4:13aα (without כי הנה) is to be read as a three–stress bicolon. Even if one reads the colon with three stresses, it represents with its two participles a deviation from all the other cola. On the other hand, both the otherwise shared formal characteristics and also the meshing of themes force one to think here of a single hymn of several strophes. This view becomes especially compelling in the one case where a whole segment is repeated verbatim (5:8b = 9:6b).

Or was one of these segments added secondarily? Perhaps this question is to be answered in the affirmative, since 9:5b also has a verbal parallel in 8:8b.

---

26 Cf. בני ישראל ("sons of Israel") in 4:5b and see also the excursus on p. 164.

27 Cf. the pertinent points already raised by Horst ("Doxologien," 50–53 [= idem, Gottes Recht, 162–66]) on the subject of the hymns in the book of Amos, which he has explained (with reference to Josh 7:19) as exhomologesis from the administration of sacral law, functioning simultaneously as con-

fession and as doxology.

28 Cf. von Rad, Theology 1, 370–83 [368–80]; and Crenshaw, "Theophanic Tradition," 211–12.

29 So Weiser and Cripps.

30 So Horst ("Doxologien").

31 So Watts (Vision).

32 So Maag (Text) and Gaster ("Hymn").

Indeed, in the case of 9:5b a subsequent addition is highly probable. In the first place, this bicolon is the only one in the hymnic material which does not contain a participle in either of its two cola. Secondly, 9:5b is easily understood as a later addition from the fact that 9:5aβ had already reminded the copyist of the colon in 8:8aβ and thereby had prepared him to find the continuation in 8:8b to be appropriate in the latter context as well. That there was a later filling out is probable in the case of 5:9 also, for this verse stands strangely isolated after the closing statement "Yahweh is his name" (יהוה שמו) in 5:8. Thematically as well, 5:9 shows no real connection with the other hymnic pieces. Furthermore, the text here has been more poorly transmitted than is the case elsewhere within this material. Since a tendency toward secondary expansion of these texts is thus evident in perhaps three places, the question arises as to whether the first colon of 5:8 (being the only remaining, isolated three–stress colon in the hymnic material) should be supplied with a parallel member, i.e., reconstructing a colon supposedly lost in transmission. On the basis of Job 38:32, Theodor H. Gaster proposed the restoration of וּמוֹצִיא מַזָּרוֹת בְּעִתּוֹ ("And [can you] lead forth Mazzarot in its season?").[33] Because of the close relationship of the book of Amos to Job 5:9–16 and 9:5–10,[34] Frank Crüsemann's restoration on the basis of Job 9:9 is more convincing: "and the lion [so Crüsemann] and the chambers of the South" (וְעָשׁ וְחַדְרֵי תֵּמָן).[35] Yet the possibility must be left open that 5:8aα¹ is secondary too. The grounds for such a supposition include the fact that the three words transmitted in Am 5:8aα¹ serve in Job 9:9 to continue the second colon of Job 9:8 ("and who treads upon the heights of Sea" (וְדוֹרֵךְ עַל־בָּמֳתֵי יָם), a colon that is strongly reminiscent of Am 4:13bβ. Further, "he who made" (עשה) at the beginning of 5:8 would be the only repetition of a participle (cf. 4:13aβ) in all the strophes. Adding 5:8aα would have necessitated inserting the conjunction ו ("and") before the following "he who turns" (הפך) with perhaps a concomitant displacement of an original definite article. In this particular case, however, certainty is even less assured than in the cases of possible expansion treated previously. Thus all attempts at reconstruction must be viewed with the greatest reserve.[36]

Having strongly sounded this note of caution, it may nevertheless be possible to recognize in 4:13 the pattern for three regularly structured strophes. In so doing, the two introductory words כי הנה ("For [it is] so!") must be set aside as a secondary insertion into the old hymnic text. In the closing sentence, "God of Hosts" (אלהי־צבאות), must likewise be regarded as a secondary expansion.[37] This leaves us with two prosodic units (each a bicolon) consisting of participial clauses, with "Yahweh is his name" as a conclusion. 5:8, as the second strophe, would also consist of two three–stress bicola if we consider the first isolated three–stress colon and 5:9 to be later additions. Finally, 9:5–6 also exhibits the same strophic structure of two three–stress bicola, supposing not only the first three words in 9:5 (corresponding to the expansion in 4:13b) but also 9:5b (from 8:8b) and 9:6b (from 5:8b) to be secondary. The results give us the following reconstruction:

ומגיד לאדם מה שחו   יוצר הרים וברא רוח
ודרך על במתי ארץ   עשה שחר עיפה
יהוה שמו

ויום לילה החשיך   ההפך לבקר צלמות
וישפכם על־פני הארץ   הקורא למי־הים
יהוה שמו

ואבלו כל־יושבי בה   הנוגע בארץ ותמוג
ואגדתו על־ארץ יסדה   הבונה בשמים מעלותיו
יהוה שמו

The fact that the final colon of each strophe preceding the refrain makes a statement concerning the "earth" might be taken as an additional argument that we are dealing here with an originally symmetrically structured hymn of three strophes. Yet the irregularities mentioned above remind us of the uncertainty of any such attempt at reconstructing a unified hymn. In the case of each passage we must reckon with the possibility that at least some of the expansion which we now find may have occurred as the hymnic matter was incorporated into the book of Amos. The type of participial hymn here attested, with "Yahweh is his name" (יהוה שמו) employed as a refrain concluding each strophe, is not represented in the Psalter. Yet Crüsemann has identified this structure as one basic form of the hymn in Israel.[38] Besides the three instances in Amos, it is reflected in the material preserved in both Deutero–Isaiah and Jeremiah.[39] Especially with reference to Deutero–Isaiah it can be

---

33 Gaster, "Hymn," 24.
34 See also Crenshaw, "Theophanic Tradition," 211.
35 *Studien*, 100.
36 Cf. G. Johannes Botterweck, "Zur Authentizität des Buches Amos," *BZ* N.F. 2 (1958): 182–86; and especially Crüsemann, *Studien*, 99–100.
37 Cf. 3:13; 5:14, 15, 16, 27; 6:8, 14, and especially the short version of the closing sentence in 5:8 and 9:6.
38 *Studien*, 83–154.
39 See Is 47:4; 51:15; 54:4–5; and Jer 10:12–16 = 51:15–19; 31:35; 32:18; 33:2; 50:34.

shown that participial cola (Is 40:22–23, 26–29; 42:5; 45:7, 18) are informed by a special hymnic tradition which celebrated the general activity of God in the world of nature and humanity (cf. Job 5:9–16; 9:5–10). Yahweh's special acts in the salvation history of Israel, on the other hand, were sung in hymns characterized by the presence of verbs in the imperative.[40] The themes as well as the form of the participial hymn find close analogies in the world surrounding Israel.[41] With the conclusion "Yahweh is his name," the God of Israel is confessed as the true author of those deeds elsewhere attributed to other gods. Thus it is easy to see that this type of hymn grew out of Israel's conflict with its cultural environment, a conflict which was already taking place in preexilic times. But how is the occurrence of this hymnic type in the book of Amos to be explained?

Setting

4:4–5 Only the reproach (vv 4–5) can be attributed with certainty to Amos. It is impossible to determine whether it was proclaimed in Bethel, in Gilgal, or—as the oracles immediately preceding it—in Samaria. Just as in the cases of the preceding oracles, this parody is incorporated into "the words of Amos from Tekoa" without any linking formula.

4:6–13 As far as the verses following the reproach are concerned, however, we are warned already by the nature of the transitional material in v 6 against regarding Amos as the author. Further arguments against Amos' authorship of vv 6–13 include the various stylistic peculiarities, the veiled reference in v 12 to a definite but unspecified happening, and the joining of the accusation (vv 6–11) with the hymn (v 13) which also occurs here. The tight stylistic interlocking of vv 6–11, 12a, 12b, and 13, and the way in which the content of the accusation of an unrepentant attitude is intertwined with present historical events of judgment and with a hymnic acknowledgement of Yahweh (cf. 1 Kgs 8:33ff) remind one of a liturgical act.[42] Yet one should neither speak here of covenant renewal,[43] nor label Amos the liturgist of such an act.[44] We have al-

ready seen how both language and theme argue otherwise. However, the style and concerns of this extensive supplement are also clearly distinguishable from those of the Deuteronomistic redactors, and especially from those of the postexilic eschatologists of salvation.[45]

In our search for the setting and function of this liturgy we will have to start from the fact that "thus" (כה) in v 12a (cf. "this" [זאת] in v 12b) is used to point to something which is visible to the audience (cf. Gen 15:5b), to some tangibly represented event (1 Sam 11:7), a happening to which the speaker can refer with a gesture of his hand (Ex 5:15). Do we know of any historical event subsequent to Amos which posterity could associate with the ancient prophetic word? The timing of this event would have to be such as to render intelligible both the language and the themes of this section. It should furthermore clarify why it is precisely in 5:8–9 and 9:5–6 that we find hymnic pieces of the same kind as in 4:13. Now, Ernst Sellin has already pointed out that the redactor of the hymns adjoins his material to those passages which proclaim the destruction of the sanctuary of Bethel.[46] This observation suits 4:13 (which follows at some interval the actual reproach against the pilgrims to Bethel in 4:4–5) only when one also takes vv 6–12 into consideration. It suits 5:8–9 if one shifts 5:7 to precede 5:10 and recognizes 5:6 as a later interpretation of 5:4–5; it suits 9:5–6 if one recognizes that the redactor as a matter of course locates the altar of 9:1 in Bethel, just as the glossator of 3:14bα does with the altar of 3:14bβ. What event would better account for someone after Amos having supplemented these oracles against (the altar and) Bethel than the destruction of the altar of Bethel by Josiah, which is reported in 2 Kgs 23:15–20? This is all the more likely since the report in 2 Kgs understands this cultic–political measure of Josiah as being the fulfillment of the word of Yahweh which a man from Judah had proclaimed (vv 16–17).[47]

Indeed, many elements of vv 6–13 become intelligible

40 Crüsemann, *Studien*, 86–95.
41 Cf. the parallels cited, *ibid.*, 136–50; and see pp. 223–24, and the comments on 5:8 and 9:5–6.
42 On "to turn, return" (שׁוב), see p. 220, on 4:6.
43 Brueggemann, "Amos 4:4–13," 13.
44 Reventlow, *Amt*, 90.
45 See pp. 112–13.
46 Sellin, 193.
47 For an evaluation of 1 Kgs 13 in light of 2 Kgs 23:16–18, cf. Noth, *Könige*, 293–94 with Otto Eissfeldt, "Amos und Jona in volkstümlicher Überlieferung" in *Kleine Schriften*, vol. 4, ed. Rudolf Sellheim and Fritz Maas (Tübingen: J. C. B. Mohr [Paul Siebeck], 1968), 138–39.

from the perspective that here are preserved the words of a liturgist who appeared on the scene in Bethel, inspired by Josiah's deed. Then the veiled "thus" (כה) and "this" (זאת) in v 12 become clear. Then the closeness to Lev 26 and 1 Kgs 8:33–37 also becomes understandable. Unlike the material in 2:4–5, however, one should not term this section Deuteronomistic.[48] The hymn points to a (proto–Deuteronomic) time of struggle with the gods of the surrounding world,[49] a struggle that was of particular and acute relevance for the sanctuary of Bethel after the Assyrian conquest of Samaria. This was the time in which the historical–theological interpretation of the catastrophe that befell the northern kingdom was beginning to take shape, wherein the national collapse was traced back to the lack of Israel's willingness to repent of its transgressions (2 Kgs 17:13–14). But the liturgist does not yet put the prophetic word to use directly as a call to repentance. Working independently, though relying upon existing lists, he instead tries to motivate repentance by enumerating Yahweh's acts of judgment (cf. Lev 26:18, 23–24, 27–28; 1 Kgs 8:33–37). After listing the traditional topics (vv 6–10)—which also appear in Lev 26, 1 Kgs 8, and Dtn 28—he makes an especially climactic reference to that overthrow reminiscent of the one of Sodom and Gomorrah, a paradigmatic event of punitive destruction applied analogously in the same wording to the prophesied demise of Babylon in Is 13:19 and Jer 50:40, which here in v 11 is probably meant to designate the overall political catastrophe which befell the northern kingdom.[50] Those who still remained in Bethel to be addressed at the time of our preacher, in the days of Josiah, could indeed be called only "a brand plucked from the burning." This remnant, after its long period of unreadiness

to repent, is summoned now to acknowledge Josiah's destruction of the altar at Bethel as being Yahweh's act of judgment and so, by responding in the words of the hymn, to give glory to God. The hymn as "todah" (תּוֹדָה) is at once a confession of guilt and a rendering of praise, an appropriate ". . . response to an experienced demonstration of God's power."[51]

As a means of controlling our process of dating here, it is advisable to take a comparative glance at the most closely related strophic poem stemming from the century in which Amos was active, namely Is 9:7–20 [8–21] and 5:25–29. How much farther it is from liturgical language! How much more concretely it refers to political afflictions! How much more regular it is in its metrical and strophic structure![52]

The redactor who inserted into the traditions of Amos this homily and introduction to a judgment-doxology saw in Josiah's action against Bethel a confirmation of the words of the prophet against the northern kingdom.

Interpretation

■ 4 Amos' initial words here—"Enter into Bethel!" (בֹּאוּ בֵית־אֵל)—could correspond to an official priestly instruction. The verb (בוא) refers to the entrance of the pilgrims into the sanctuary.[53] In a summons immediately following the call to enter, the Psalms may designate the praising of Yahweh to be the goal of the entering (Ps 95:6; 100:4), while the priestly torah promises life to those entering the sanctuary.[54] Parodying the torah form,[55] Amos adds in a second imperative the exhortation to "transgress," an exhortation which is immediately repeated in intensified form: "transgress even more." Keeping in view that a sharp contrast with the original purpose of participation in the cultus is

---

48 Cf. Koehler, *Amos*, 53.
49 See p. 217.
50 See pp. 221–22, on 4:11.
51 Günther Bornkamm, "Lobpreis, Bekenntnis und Opfer: Eine alttestamentliche Studie" in *Geschichte und Glaube*, vol. 1 (Gesammelte Aufsätze 3), (München: Chr. Kaiser, 1968), 126.
52 Cf. Wildberger, *Jesaja*, 208–10.
53 Cf. Am 5:5; Ps 95:6; 100:2; Hos 4:15; Is 1:12; Joel 1:13; Ps 100:4 (through the gates); Ps 96:8 (into the outer courts); cf. further Ex 34:34 and see also Kraus, *Psalmen*, 661, 687.
54 See pp. 211–12.
55 See p. 212.

here intended, פשע then has the connotation "to break with (Yahweh)."[56] The pilgrimage becomes a rebellion against Yahweh, as far as Amos is concerned. Only here does Amos use פשע in its verbal form; everywhere else he uses it in its substantival form[57] and designates thereby crimes against human community. This customary usage is also the basis upon which one is here to interpret the sense of the breaking with Yahweh (cf. 5:4–5 with 5:14–15). Amos names as sanctuaries Bethel and Gilgal. Bethel is situated approximately forty kilometers south of Samaria and eighteen kilometers north of Jerusalem. The old sanctuary lay east of the town at *Burj Beitîn*.[58] Gilgal is to be sought some thirty kilometers east–southeast of Bethel, in the rift valley of the Jordan, very probably at *Hirbet 'el–Mefjer*, two kilometers north of *'Erîḥa*.[59] While Bethel had been selected as chief sanctuary of the northern kingdom by Jeroboam I (1 Kgs 12:29),[60] Gilgal had functioned as central sanctuary at the time of the initial occupation of the land.[61]

Amos goes on to explain the criminal activity by reference to the sacrificial practices. What he has in mind here is probably the substitution of cultic offerings for justice towards the oppressed (cf. 5:21–24 and the oracles immediately preceding ours in 3:9—4:3!). "To bring" (בוא hip'il) designates "the process of sacrificing as a whole."[62] It is not certain whether לבקר ("in the morning") is to be read in a distributive sense,[63] for such a meaning is usually expressed by the plural form לבקרים ("every morning").[64] The reference to a specifically fixed day in the following colon

suggests rather that it is the morning after the arrival at the place of pilgrimage which is intended here.[65] Hosea also attests to the slaughtering of animals as being the basic type of sacrifice at that time (Hos 3:4; 8:13; 12:12 [11]). Such sacrifices are particularly favored because they culminate in a banquet at which the meat is consumed (cf. Hos 4:13; 8:13).[66] Tithes are to be brought "on the third day," which probably means the day following that of the morning after the arrival. One can hardly determine whether the third day had any special significance in the cultus of the eighth century.[67] The Elohist traces the practice of tithing at Bethel as far back as Jacob (Gen 28:22). Deuteronomy names grain, wine and oil as harvested produce which is to be tithed (12:17; 14:23). The older legal statute in Dtn 14:22 refers only to the produce of the seeded field. It is not impossible that the yield from the flock was also tithed in older times, as it was under the so–called "right of the king" (1 Sam 8:15, 17). According to Deuteronomy, the tithes offered at the sanctuary were to be used for a festive communal banquet (Dtn 12:6–7, 11–12, 17–18; 14:23, 26); the priests were probably able to claim as their share only a part of it.[68] Amos says "*your* sacrifices" and "*your* tithes" because, in his judgment, such things are not the real concern of Yahweh.

■ 5 Hosea also mentions burnt offerings (קטר "to burn, kindle") in parallelism with slaughtered sacrifices (Hos 4:13; 11:2),[69] perhaps considering the fat of the slaughtered animal as the material which was burned (cf. 1 Sam 2:13–16).[70] When Amos mentions burnt

---

56 Cf. Is 1:28; 1 Kgs 12:19 and 2 Kgs 8:22 (referring to political revolts); see further Knierim, *Hauptbegriffe*, 150, 178.

57 See the excursus on pp. 152–53.

58 Cf. Wolff, *Hosea*, 90 [113], 112–13 [143]; and Noth, *Könige*, 283.

59 Cf. Klaus Dietrich Schunck, *Benjamin*, BZAW 86 (Berlin: A. Töpelmann, 1963), 39–48; and Wolff, *Hosea*, 89–90 [113].

60 See comments on 7:13.

61 Klaus Dietrich Schunck, *Benjamin*, BZAW 86 (Berlin: A. Töpelmann, 1963), 44; and Hans–Joachim Kraus, "Gilgal: Eine Beitrag zur Kultgeschichte Israels," *VT* 1 (1951): 181–99.

62 Rolf Rendtorff, *Studien zur Geschichte des Opfers im alten Israel*, WMANT 24 (Neukirchen–Vluyn: Neukirchener Verlag, 1967), 148.

63 So Cripps, and Robinson, on this passage; and Delekat, "Wörterbuch," 8: "day by day anew."

64 See Is 33:2; Ps 73:14; 101:8; and Lam 3:23.

65 Weiser, *Profetie*, 162.

66 Cf. Rendtorff, *Studien*, 144–45.

67 Cf. Christoph Barth, "Theophanie, Bundschließung und neuer Anfang am dritten Tage," *EvTh* 28 (1968): 521–33 (esp. 531).

68 Cf. Friedrich Horst, *Das Privilegrecht Jahwes: Religionsgeschichtliche Untersuchungen zum Deuteronomium*, FRLANT 45 (Göttingen: 1930), 122 (= idem, *Gottes Recht*, 153); and Werner H. Schmidt, "Zehnten," *RGG*³, 6, 1878.

69 Cf. Wolff, *Hosea*, 40 [48], 86 [107].

70 See Rendtorff, *Studien*, 147–48.

offerings, however, he refers explicitly to offerings "from that which is leavened" (cf. Ex 23:18). "From" (מן) is used here not with a privative sense[71] but with a partitive sense.[72] Rings of bread from leavened dough are identified as thanksgiving offerings in Lev 7:13. Does the sacrificer partake of this type of offering, getting physical enjoyment from it? In any case the sacrificer's reputation is enhanced by his contributions of both "thanksgiving" and "freewill" offerings; hence they are proclaimed "loud–and–clear."

The terse, concluding causal clause uses the formula of self–will to focus the judgment already announced in v 4a by the use of the verb פשע ("to transgress") and developed in v 4b using suffixed nouns ("your sacrifices . . . your tithes"). The sacrificial offerings increase the enjoyment and enhance the reputations of the sacrificers. The causal clause thereby merely explains why the hearers indeed act as they do. Amos does not turn against the cultus but against the participants in it.

■ 6 A redactor has joined[73] to the foregoing an accusation probably made in Yahweh's name by a preacher on the occasion of the destruction of the sanctuary of Bethel by king Josiah.[74] While Amos is always concerned with Israel's present culpability, which stands in contradiction to Yahweh's saving acts (e.g., 2:6–9; 3:2),[75] the accusation in vv 6–7 presents from a historical–theological perspective, as a progressive accumulation of guilt, a series of past wrong responses to Yahweh's acts of chastisement. Drawing freely upon traditional enumerations of plagues,[76] God first reminds the audience of famines which he had sent upon all localities. An unusual euphemistic expression, "shining teeth," is followed by an unambiguous interpretation: "lack of bread." The aim of this plague, as of all the following ones, was to bring about a return

to Yahweh. As far as we know, Hosea (2:9 [7]; 3:4–5; 14:2 [1]) and Isaiah (9:12 [13]; 30:15) were the first to recognize that the purpose of judgment was to promote such a "return"; the Deuteronomist elevated the concept to the status of an admonition.[77] Our preacher stands in this succession; he connects "to return" (שוב) with "unto" (עד) in a way found otherwise only in Hos 14:2 [1]; Is 9:12 [13]; (19:22); and Dtn 4:30; 30:2. From Hosea (14:2 [1]; cf. 2:9 [7]; 3:4–5) to the Deuteronomist (Dtn 4:30 [cf. 4:28–29]; 1 Sam 7:3; 2 Kgs 23:25), "to return unto" (שוב עד) means primarily the return from foreign deities to Yahweh. This theme is unknown to Amos, but in Josiah's days it had become a burning concern, especially, it would appear, at the sanctuary of Bethel (2 Kgs 23:15–20).[78]

The oracle formula concludes this and every following section (vv 8, 9, 10, 11). Amos concluded strophic structures with אמר יהוה ("Yahweh has said" 1:5, 8, 15; 2:3; 7:3, 6); he used נאם־יהוה ("oracle of Yahweh") only to conclude individual oracles (3:15; 4:3, 5; 9:7) or a larger composition (2:16). The frequency of the formula's occurrence here corresponds to its popular usage in later times.[79] The preacher from the time of Josiah may well have selected this formula in view of its appearance in 4:5.

■ 7–8 As the second element of the accusation, the punishment of drought is described in unusual breadth. It is possible that large parts of this piece were added later, along with the new transitional device.[80] However, every attempted excision remains quite hypothetical. The absence of "rain" (גשם)[81] in spring (March/April) creates particularly difficult circumstances, because a drought during the three months prior to the "harvest" (קציר) is simply too long, inhibiting especially the proper ripening of barley and wheat which are usually

---

71 I.e., to denote "without leaven," excluding the use of leavening products in the offering, as is supposed by Robinson. [Cf. the NEB rendering of Am 4:5; Ed.]

72 Brockelmann, *Syntax*, par. 111a; cf. Hans Jürgen Hermisson, *Sprache und Ritus im altisraelitischen Kult*, WMANT 19 (Neukirchen–Vluyn: Neukirchener Verlag, 1965), 33.

73 On the linking formula, וגם־אני, see p. 213.

74 See pp. 217–18.

75 See pp. 104, 150.

76 See pp. 213–14.

77 Wolff, "Kerygma," 90–97 [178–83 (= *Gesammelte Studien*, 315–21)].

78 See pp. 217–18.

79 See the excursus on p. 143.

80 See textual note "h" to 4:7.

81 See p. 64.

harvested in May / June.[82] It is an additional hardship that the land receives rain only here and there. Many cities remain in the drought–zone (v 8aβ). Thus it happens that individual cities have to share their supply of drinking water with two or three others, and no one receives a really sufficient amount (v 8aα). Obviously v 7aβ and v 8 belong together. V 7b intrudes and draws into view the arable land as also being affected by the localized rainfall, but it does not go on to detail the particular hardships that result from this. Here the suspicion of a later supplement is particularly difficult to quell. Likewise times of drought do not prompt repentance.

■ 9 The third section starts out by referring to grain damage. "Blight" (שדפון) is always associated with "mildew" (ירקון).[83] "Blight" is caused by the hot east wind, when it "dries up" (cf. שדף Gen 41:6) the grain prematurely, even scorches it, so that it turns brown.[84] (G translates שדפון in Dtn 28:22 and 2 Chr 6:28 as ἀνεμοφθορία ["wind damage, wind breakage"], so it knows of the connection between grain damage and the east wind.) "Mildew" (ירקון; in Jer 30:6 referring to "paleness" of the face) means here—as always elsewhere when used in association with "blight" (שדפון)— the "turning pale of the tips of the green grain due to the build–up of [parasitic] worms."[85] G understood our passage to be referring to human illness.[86] The old text mentions additional harvest losses besides the damage to the grain. The produce of the "gardens" could include not only vegetables (Dtn 11:10; 1 Kgs 21:2) but also fruit of trees (Gen 2:9–10). This produce along with the grape–clusters in the vineyards was "scorched" (?),[87] assuming the vines had not already fallen prey (according to the Masoretic accents) to the locust, as happens as well with the fig trees and the olive trees.[88] Neither do these harvest damages call forth repentance.

■ 10 The fourth section names "plague" (דבר) as the next chastisement, defining it more closely as "after the manner of Egypt." This is a reminder of the epidemic which, according to Ex 9:3–7 (J), fell upon all the livestock of Egypt: horses, donkeys, camels, cattle, and beasts of the flock. However, the word "plague" also appropriately denotes pestilence that afflicts humanity.[89] It always refers to a lethal epidemic,[90] and hence it often stands, as here, in parallelism with "sword."[91] Here it is particularly the youth who are affected, בחורים referring to the full–grown, strong young men who comprise the elite of the combat troops.[92] The "horses" were decisive for the fighting strength of the chariot corps.[93] "Camp" (מחנה singular) encompasses, in its meaning of "military camp," the whole army (Dtn 23:10 [9]; Ju 7:9–12), and it is that which was abandoned to destruction and whose stench of decay was brought into the nostrils of the people.[94] Even such military defeats did not result in a return to Yahweh.

■ 11 Already in v 10 the preacher has moved from the realm of natural catastrophe to interventions of Yahweh in political history. Now at the end he intensifies the list of plagues (which up to this point have been drawn almost entirely from the frequently attested lists of punishments)[95] in a quite unusual fashion. Was it not his intention here to remind the audience of the final destruction of the northern kingdom as an independent political entity by the Assyrians in 721? The familiar expression "as God overthrew Sodom and Gomorrah" is used always to denote the total destruction of political entities.[96] The preacher of Josiah's time looks back upon the destruction of the northern kingdom, and it

82 Dalman, *Arbeit* 3, 4–6.
83 See 1 Kgs 8:37 = 2 Chr 6:28; Dtn 28:22; and Hag 2:17.
84 Dalman, *Arbeit* 2, 333–34: "Brown–rust" (*Braun-rost*).
85 Dalman, *Arbeit* 1/2, 326.
86 See textual note "l" to 4:9.
87 See textual note "m" to 4:9.
88 On the locust plague, see the excursus on pp. 27–28, and Joel 1:6–7, according to which the locusts peel the bark from the vines and fig trees.
89 Ezek 14:19; Ex 9:15 (J); cf. Ex 9:9–10 (P) and

Dtn 28:27.
90 Ex 9:6; Jer 14:12; Ezek 14:19.
91 E.g., Lev 26:25; Ex 5:3; Ezek 5:17; 14:12; Jer 21:7, 9, etc.
92 1 Sam 9:2; Is 9:16 [17]; and cf. Wildberger, *Jesaja*, 218.
93 See pp. 171–72, on 2:15.
94 Cf. Joel 2:11 and p. 62.
95 See pp. 213–14.
96 With reference to Babylon in Is 13:19 and Jer 50:40; to Edom in Jer 49:18; and to Israel in Dtn 29:22 [23].

is quite understandable that he can compare those addressed in Bethel to a brand plucked from the fire. This fifth section would be especially difficult to explain as coming from the mouth of Amos. Where does he elsewhere speak of "God" (אלהים)? The whole expression "as God overthrew Sodom and Gomorrah" is attested much later as a widely used formula. Were we to suppose that הפך here might refer to the earthquake announced by Amos (2:13; [8:8]; 9:1), it would be necessary to consider that the word is indeed used in the Sodom–tradition (Gen 19:21, 25, 29) but not in connection with an earthquake. Furthermore, the proclamation of Amos must be dated "two years *before* the earthquake" (1:1b), and hence a recollection of that event here by the prophet himself is quite unlikely.[97] The accusations in 4:6–11, therefore, were apparently leveled by someone who deplored the lack of willingness to repent on the part of those who, even after the Assyrian conquest of the region, continued to venerate foreign gods (cf. 2 Kgs 17:13–33, esp. v 28).

■ **12–13** "Therefore"—because all the chastisements of Yahweh could not move the remaining adherents of the sanctuary of Bethel to return to Yahweh—the preacher now points his finger ("thus" כה) at this sanctuary destroyed by Josiah as though it were Yahweh's act.[98] So interpreted with direct reference to the contemporary measure of Josiah, this formulation—quite unparalleled in Amos' own linguistic usage, where "therefore" is usually followed by a specific threat[99]—becomes intelligible. The imperfect forms (אעשה) serve here to express concrete, present–future action.[100] Thus all forced interpretations and explanations of the sentence become superfluous. It is not true that the more detailed circumstances remain ". . . intentionally in the dark, since the unknown is often more uncanny

and terrifying than the familiar."[101] Where did Amos ever leave the coming judgment in the dark? It would be arbitrary to transpose another of Amos' threats to this place,[102] or to assume that an especially horrible threat has been deleted here.[103] Why were there no deletions in 2:13–16; 4:1–3; 5:1–2 and many similar oracles? All such surmises are misleading for the simple reason that v 12a never did introduce a more specific sentence of judgment.

If our supposition is correct, namely that the clause in v 12a actually interprets Josiah's action at Bethel as God's righteous judgment, then the transition in v 12b likewise becomes intelligible without requiring any forced explanation. Then this action becomes the concrete reason for exhorting the assembled congregation of Israel to meet its God. The imperative "prepare!" (הכון) is attested only one other time, in Ezek 38:7, where Gog is exhorted to place itself at Yahewh's disposal.[104] The Sinai–pericope employs the same root in a participial combination,[105] expressing thereby the readiness of Israel, or respectively of Moses, to meet God. In the same context the actual encounter is expressed in the words "to meet God" (לִקְרַאת הָאֱלֹהִים Ex 19:17 [E]).[106] Given the ways in which traditional forms of speech are incorporated, the "your God" (אלהיך) within the context of the first–person divine speech in the liturgical direct address may no more be considered a break in style than the "your God" in the formula "I am Yahweh, your God" (cf. also Lev 26:44, etc.). However, the use of the word "God" (אלהים), with or without a suffix (cf. 4:11), is foreign to Amos.[107]

Thus it is most likely that we have here a liturgical directive, spoken at the destroyed altar of Bethel, which calls upon those assembled there to give themselves over to Yahweh, "just as Achan was set directly under the

---

97 Cf. Budde, "Amos," 50; and Weiser, *Profetie*, 171.
98 Cf. 2 Kgs 23:15–17; and see above, p. 217.
99 See pp. 214–15.
100 See Brockelmann, *Syntax*, pars. 42–43.
101 Robinson, 87.
102 Sellin (220) suggests transposing 3:14–15, which necessitates still further conjectures.
103 So Gressmann, *Prophetie*, 344: "A pen refused to copy it!"
104 On the text, see Zimmerli, *Ezechiel*, 926.
105 Ex 19:11, וְהָיוּ נְכֹנִים; Ex 19:15, הֱיוּ נְכֹנִים; Ex 34:2, וְהְיֵה נָכוֹן ("be ready").
106 Cf. Horst, "Doxologien," 53 (= *idem*, *Gottes Recht*, 165); and Brueggemann, "Amos 4:4–13," 2–4. Cf. also with לקראת here, the use of קרי in Lev 26:21, 23–24, 27–28, 40–41.
107 On its occurrence in 2:8, see textual note "r" to that verse. Cf. the use of "Yahweh" within divine speech in Hos 1:2, etc.; on which see Wolff, *Hosea*, 16 [16–17].

gaze of the judging God through the process of the divine ordeal."[108] Even more direct illumination on our context comes from the advice which Eliphaz, who thinks that Job has been justly punished, gives to his tormented friend (Job 5:8): "I would seek God." Following this advice (Job 5:9–16) are hymnic statements in the participial style, which by reason of both form and content have already reminded us of the hymn which follows in the book of Amos.[109] By reciting this hymn, the chastised community in Bethel is to follow sacral procedure and give glory to Yahweh.[110] כי הנה ("for [it is] so") focuses direct attention upon the doxology which is to be intoned.[111] First the mighty creator is praised, who "forms mountains" in a way that mortals can shape only clay figures. The verb "to form" (יצר) refers to that plastic shaping by which the artist crafts his work (cf. Jer 18:3–6).[112] Only in Deutero–Isaiah (Is 43:1, 7; 45:7, 18) does "to form" (יצר) stand in parallelism with "to create" (ברא), the word which the Priestly Work (Gen 1:1, 21, 27, etc.) has substituted for the use of יצר in the Yahwistic creation account as the designation for the creative activity of God (Gen 2:7–8, 19).[113] However, no theological differentiation between the two verbs is intended either here or in the cited passages in Deutero–Isaiah. Both our passage and Ezek 28:13 and 15 support the supposition that "to create" (ברא) belongs to preexilic, Canaanite cultic language.[114] What does רוח (here translated "breath") mean? In view of the parallelism with the preceding "mountains" (הרים), one first thinks of wind; alongside a visible witness to God's might stands an invisible one. Even the wind, to which mythology ascribes a creative power, is a mere creature in the biblical perspective.[115] It is true that G does not translate ἄνεμος ("wind") but πνεῦμα ("spirit") here, thinking of the human spirit and so forming a smooth transition to the following colon. While humanity is frequently the recipient of the action designated by the verb "to create" (ברא),[116] nonetheless other objects result from this particular type of activity as well.[117] Furthermore, in those passages where ברא and יצר stand in parallelism they describe the creation not only of human beings (Is 43:1, 7) but of other things as well (darkness, woe [Is 45:7]; heaven, earth [Is 45:18]). In Is 45:12, the "making" (עשה) of the earth is followed by the "creating" (ברא) of humanity. רוח never occurs elsewhere as the immediate object of ברא, though it does stand within its wider semantic field in Ps 51:12 [10], where it refers to the human spirit. And in Is 42:5, following the statement about the creation of the earth, there is reference to the gift of the breath of life and of רוח to the earth's inhabitants. It is probably advisable to keep in mind the polarity of meaning in the Hebrew word רוח ("wind—spirit"), particularly here at the point of transition between the first and the third participial cola of our hymn. Our translation "breath" is intended to be a reminder of this polarity.[118]

The next statement leads us unequivocally to mankind. God is praised because he establishes contact with humanity in his word. The pronominal suffix in שחו ("his plan") is problematic. Does God make known his own planning, or that of mankind? The latter possi-

---

108 Horst, "Doxologien," 53 (= idem, Gottes Recht, 165), with reference to Josh 7:19.

109 See p. 216.

110 Cf. Horst, Hiob, 64, 82–83.

111 On the style and context of the doxology, see the excursus on pp. 215–17.

112 Cf. also Paul Humbert, "Emploi et portée bibliques du verbe yāṣar et de ses dérivés substantifs" in Von Ugarit nach Qumran: Beiträge zur Alttestamentlichen und Altorientalischen Forschung, ed. Johannes Hempel and Leonard Rost, BZAW 77 (Berlin: A. Töpelmann, 1958), 82–88.

113 Cf. Claus Westermann, Genesis, BK 1/1 (Neukirchen–Vluyn: Neukirchener Verlag, 1974), 136–38; and Werner H. Schmidt, Die Schöpfungsgeschichte der Priesterschrift, WMANT 17 (Neukirchen–Vluyn: Neukirchener Verlag, ²1967), 164–67, 200.

114 Cf. Humbert, "Emploi et portée du verbe bārā (créer) dans l'Ancien Testament," ThZ 3 (1947): 401–22 (reprinted in idem, Opuscules d'un Hébraïsant [Neuchâtel: Secrétariat de l'Université, 1958], 146–165); and Zimmerli, Ezechiel, 682.

115 Cf. Kurt Galling, "Der Charakter der Chaosschilderung in Gen 1:2," ZThK 47 (1950): 154; and Westermann, Genesis, 149–50.

116 This is always the case where ברא is used in Ezekiel (21:35 [30]; 28:13, 15) and predominantly so in the Priestly Work (Gen 1:27; 5:1–2; 6:7), but it holds true only in the smaller number of the attestations of the verb in Deutero–Isaiah (Is 43:1, 7, 15; 45:12; 54:16).

117 Cf. Gen 1:1, 21; 2:3; Is 40:26, 28; 41:20; 42:5; 45:7–8, 18.

118 Cf. Daniel Lys, 'Rûach'. Le souffle dans l'Ancien Testa-

bility might be argued by reference to the similar participial statements in Jer 11:20 ("who tests the kidneys [= mind] and the heart") and Ps 94:11 ("who knows the plans of mankind").[119] But both the *hapax legomenon* "plan" (שֵׂחַ) and also the participle "who declares" (מַגִּיד) cause one rather to think of God's plan.[120] In this way Am 3:7 also forms a closer parallel in terms of subject matter. The creator enters into verbal communication with humanity. Here one notes for the first time a reference in the hymn to the preceding homily. This reference becomes even clearer in what follows, especially if one reads with *M*, "who makes dawn into darkness." The audience present could interpret this as a reference to the work of judgment. The final statement, "who treads upon the heights of the earth," could be referred directly to the high place of Bethel. This expression, widely attested with only minor variations,[121] could well derive from Canaanite tradition.[122] In contrast to Hadad, Ba'l Šāmêm takes possession of all high places of the land.[123] However, this expression along with all the others has been wrested from the foreign deity and now motivates the praise of Yahweh. Yahweh is the name to which alone these glorious deeds are to be ascribed. Thus this hymn, which bears the marks of the struggle against syncretism, is especially suited to bring about the final return to Yahweh, a return prompted by the judgment upon Bethel and made manifest by acceptance of this judgment and by confession of loyalty to the divine judge.

Aim

If we look back on 4:4–13, we see before us a segment of the history of biblical proclamation stretching at least 130 years. Amos has in view in vv 4–5, when the northern kingdom was still flourishing, the most zealous enthusiasm for pilgrimages and for the sacrificial services at the sanctuaries of Bethel and Gilgal. From under the cloak of priestly instruction he thrusts forth the naked, accusing fist of prophetic judgment: by pious busywork you are breaking with Yahweh and carrying on what you yourselves love! It is not against the cult–places, the cultic objects, or the customs of the cult that the prophet takes his stand, but against the people who make use of them. In the way it exposed underlying realities, this prophetic reproach drove following generations to raise questions. What is the impetus behind acts of worship? What influence do they exert on everyday life? Amos regarded such acts as being primarily a breaking away from Yahweh, because the performance of them did not prevent the continuation of crimes against oppressed fellow human beings.[124] If our interpretation holds, namely that 4:6–13 derives from the time of Josiah, then a speaker from one of the following generations, near the end of the time of Assyrian hegemony, understood Amos anew in the face of the destruction of the sanctuary of Bethel. During the preceding hundred years, that cult–place had belonged to the Assyrian province of Samaria. It had probably opened its doors not only to the gods of Canaan, as in the time of Hosea,[125] but beyond that to the gods of the empire of Assyria. The preacher recognizes in Josiah's harsh measure against the altar of Bethel an act of his God (v 12), the act culminating a long series of chastisements by means of natural and historical catastrophes (vv 6–11). It was the aim of this preacher finally to bring about a proper understanding of Amos' accusation. However, this preacher of repentance saw the nature of guilt as lying not so much in the lack of justice towards impoverished social classes as in

---

ment. *Enquête anthropologique à travers l'histoire théologique d'Israel*, EHPR 56 (Paris: Universitaires de France, 1962), 66.

119 On שִׂיחה in Job 15:4, see Horst, *Hiob*, 222.

120 Thus also the ancient translations throughout; see textual note "y" to 4:13.

121 Cf. Mi 1:3; Job 9:8, speaking of the waves (= heights) of the sea; Is 14:14, speaking of 'Elyôn enthroned upon the heights of the clouds.

122 On "height, high place" (בָּמָה), see Wolff, *Hosea*, 176 [229].

123 Cf. R. Hillmann, *Wasser und Berg*, Unpub. Diss.

(Halle, 1965), 195.

124 See p. 219.

125 Cf. Hos 4:15; 10:5; and also Wolff, *Hosea*, 175 [227–28].

the turning towards alien deities.[126] The return to Yahweh, heretofore neglected, is now finally to become a reality through repentant confession to and fervent praise of him (v 13). Amos saw in his own day a flourishing life of worship, but this worship served the interests of power and of pleasure at the expense of the oppressed. In contrast, the later speaker directs his words against a cultic community which had enthroned, in the place of Yahweh, fertility gods for the sake of economic productivity and state–deities as a way of currying favor with the politically dominant power.

Proper worship is threatened in different ways at different times. Amos formulated in an ironic fashion the basic question for times of prosperity. What sort of love moves you—love of self or love for the God of Israel? The later voice, under the impact of God's judgments, phrases the question anew. To whom will you resolutely direct your praise? The redacted combination challenges each generation of readers to examine the false elements in its own worship.

---

126   See p. 200.

Funerary Lamentation over Israel

Bibliography

Samuel Amsler
"Amos, prophète de la onzième heure," *ThZ* 21 (1965): 318–28.

Richard J. Clifford
"The Use of *Hôy* in the Prophets," *CBQ* 28 (1966): 458–64.

James L. Crenshaw
"The Influence of the Wise upon Amos: The 'Doxologies of Amos' and Job 5:9–16; 9:5–10," *ZAW* 79 (1967): 42–52.

Frank Crüsemann
Studien zur Formgeschichte von Hymnus und Danklied in Israel, WMANT 32 (Neukirchen–Vluyn: Neukirchener Verlag, 1969).

Godfrey Rolles Driver
"Two Astronomical Passages in the Old Testament," *JTS* n.s. 4 (1953): 208–12.

Georg Fohrer
"Prophetie und Magie," *ZAW* 78 (1966): 25–47 (esp. 37–38) (reprinted in *idem, Studien*, 242–64 [254–55]).

Erhard Gerstenberger
"The Woe–Oracles of the Prophets," *JBL* 81 (1962): 249–63.

Hartmut Gese
"Kleine Beiträge zum Verständnis des Amosbuches," *VT* 12 (1962): 432–36 ("אִכָּר 'Ackerknecht' und Am 5:7–17").

J. J. Glück
"Three Notes on the Book of Amos" in *Studies on the Books of Hosea and Amos* (*Die Ou Testamentiese Werkgemeenskap in Suid–Afrika, 7th and 8th Congresses* [*1964–65*]) (Potchefstroom: Rege–Pers Beperk, 1965), 115–21.

Hans Gottlieb
"Amos und Jerusalem," *VT* 17 (1967): 451–54.

Hans Jürgen Hermisson
Studien zur israelitischen Spruchweisheit, WMANT 28 (Neukirchen–Vluyn: Neukirchener Verlag, 1968), 88–89.

Franz Hesse
"Amos 5:4–6, 14f," *ZAW* 68 (1956): 1–17.

Friedrich Horst
"Die Kennzeichen der hebräischen Poesie," *ThR* 21 (1953): 97–121.

Hedwig Jahnow
Das hebräische Leichenlied im Rahmen der Völkerdichtung, BZAW 36 (Giessen, 1923).

Karl Wilhelm Neubauer
"Erwägungen zu Amos 5:4–15," *ZAW* 78 (1966): 292–316.

Horst Dietrich Preuss
Jahweglaube und Zukunftserwartung, BWANT 87 (Stuttgart: W. Kohlhammer, 1968), 158–61, 181–82.

Salomon Speier
"Bemerkungen zu Amos," *VT* 3 (1953): 305–10.

Gunther Wanke
"אוֹי und הוֹי," *ZAW* 78 (1966): 215–18.

John D. W. Watts
"Note on the Text of Amos 5:7," *VT* 4 (1954): 215–16.

Idem
Vision and Prophecy in Amos (Grand Rapids: Eerdmans, 1958), 54–57.

Claus Westermann
Basic Forms of Prophetic Speech, tr. Hugh Clayton White (Philadelphia: Westminster, 1967), 189–98 [137–42].

Hans Wildberger
Jesaja, BK 10/1 (Neukirchen–Vluyn: Neukirchener Verlag, 1972), 175–202 ("Weherufe über Rücksichtslosigkeit und Leichtsinn").

James G. Williams
"The Alas-Oracles of the Eighth Century Prophets," *HUCA* 38 (1967): 75–91.

Hans Walter Wolff
Amos the Prophet: The Man and His Background, tr. Foster R. McCurley (Philadelphia: Fortress, 1973), 17–34 [12–23], 59–67 [40–46].

5

1 Hear this word[a] which I raise over you[b] (as) a lamentation, house of Israel:[c]

2 She has fallen, no more to rise, virgin Israel;[d]
she lies stretched out on her own soil,
[e]with no one to raise her up.[e]

3 For thus [the Lord][f] Yahweh has said <concerning the house of Israel>:[g]
The city that[h] went forth a thousand, will get back a hundred;
and (the one which)[i] went forth a hundred,
will get back ten < >.[g]

a *G* (τὸν λόγον κυρίου ["the word of the Lord"]) takes the first opportunity to make clear that Amos is proclaiming Yahweh's word. The ancient text, however, clearly sets off the old message of Amos from the oracle of Yahweh, which is not introduced until v 3. Cf. already *M* in 3:10 (see textual note "h" to 3:10).

b Collective בית ישראל ("house of Israel") is treated as a plural also in the context of 5:4, 25; 6:14.

c *G* (οἶκος Ισραηλ) and *V* (*Domus Israhel*) connect "house of Israel" to the following sentence as its subject. In keeping with that, *V* assigns *virgo Israhel* in v 2 to the next clause. The attachment of the vocative to the similarly constructed exhortations to hear in 3:1a and 4:1a argues against these readings.

d See above, textual note "c." *T* (בנתא חדא כנשתא דישראל) circumspectly renders "one of the daughters from the congregation of Israel" and thereby restricts the scope of the word of judgment.

e–e The participial description of the situation literally reads "There is no one who causes her to rise."

f See textual note "o" to 1:8. The messenger formula in the book of Amos regularly uses only יהוה.

g The parallel in v 4 (cf. v 1) argues for shifting לבית ישראל from the end of the verse, where it makes little sense, to this position. Perhaps the phrase should be deleted altogether and explained as a copyist's error.

h *G* interprets idiomatically (ἐξ ἧς ["out of which"]), as do *T*, *S*, and *V*.

i There is no textual basis for supplying וְהָעִיר ("and the city") at the beginning of v 3b (so Gressmann,

4 Indeed, thus Yahweh has said concerning the house of Israel:
  Seek me! Then[j] you shall live.
5   Do not seek Bethel!
    Do not enter into Gilgal!
    >Do not cross over to Beer-
    sheba[k]!<[l]
  For Gilgal will surely depart[m] into
  exile,
    and Bethel will become[m] adversity.[n]

6 [Seek Yahweh! Then you shall live.
Lest the house of Joseph ignite[o] like
fire and devour, and there be none to
quench [p]concerning Bethel.[p]]

Prophetie; Maag, *Text*, 26), and such an addition
cannot be defended on metrical grounds alone.

j The sense of the second imperative is nearly that of
a telic clause (see Joüon, pars. 116–17, 168a), but it
is not, as in v 14, so designated by למען ("that . . .");
see Hesse, "Amos 5," 4–5, n. 22. The first imperative acquires the sense of a condition (Gesenius–
Kautzsch–Cowley, pars. 110–11; cf. Klaus Beyer,
Semitische Syntax im Neuen Testament, vol. 1 [Göt-
tingen: Vandenhoeck & Ruprecht, ²1968], 243).

k G (τὸ φρέαρ τοῦ ὅρκου) does not render the proper
name, in contrast to 8:14, but interprets "the well of
the oath," as in Gen 21:14, 31 and generally.

l Since the line has no counterpart in v 5b, it should
probably be considered a later addition; see already
August von Gall, *Altisraelitische Kultstätten*, BZAW 3
(Giessen, 1898), 50. Morgenstern speaks of a Judean
gloss ("Amos Studies IV," 319); see pp. 109–10.

m Contrary to usual practice, the city names are here
treated as masculine; the reference is more to the
inhabitants of the cities than to the cities as separate
entities (cf. Mi 5:1). Joüon (par. 134g) explains this
situation only for city names formed with בית.

n G (ὡς οὐχ ὑπάρχουσα ["like that which is not."])
reads אַיִן or interprets M's אָוֶן as meaning "non-
existent."

o G (ἀναλάμψῃ ["flame up"]) probably interpreted
צלח contextually; cf. the use of צלח to denote the
becoming effective of the רוּחַ in Ju 14:6, 19; etc.
The conjecture יְשַׁלַּח ("[lest] he cast") (Maag, *Text*,
26) leads to the changing of the following word into
בָּאֵשׁ (so already Sellin, 227) and cannot appeal to
the similar expression in 1:4, 7, etc., for support.
Hesse ("Amos 5," 6 n. 28) wants to read תצלח אש.
The textual evidence unanimously supports M; cf.
the similar construction in Jer 4:4b and 21:12b.

p–p G (τῷ οἴκῳ Ισραηλ ["for the house of Israel"]) gener-
alizes M, the text of which is also presupposed by T,
α′, σ′, θ′, and V. The פ-clause ("lest . . .") with its
threefold change of subject appears tortured in any
case; אכל ("devour") and כבה pi'el ("quench")
are otherwise always construed with an accusative.
לבית-אל states the actual goal of the clause, the
preposition ל "denoting the special relation" [here,
between "Bethel" and the burning] (Koehler–
Baumgartner, 465 no. 19; cf. Brockelmann, *Syntax*,
par. 107i) and indicating that v 6b is an interpretation of v 5. It must therefore in no case be deleted
(so Robinson; Maag, *Text*, 26–27; Hesse, "Amos
5"; and others) or changed, with G, to לבית ישראל
(so Nowack; Gressmann, *Prophetie*; and others).

q Following George Adam Smith (*The Book of the
Twelve Prophets*, vol. 1 ["Amos, Hosea, and Micah"], The Expositor's Bible [London, 1896]) a הוי
("woe"), as in 5:18 and 6:1, has customarily been
reconstructued at the beginning of this verse; the
particle could easily have been lost by haplography.
See textual note "r," and the excursus on pp. 242–
45.

7   ⟨Woe⟩^q (to those) who turn justice into
wormwood^r
    and cast righteousness to the
    ground.^s

8   [{He who made the Pleiades and
Orion}^t]
    who turns deep–darkness into dawn,
      who darkens day into night,
    who summons the waters of the sea
      and pours them out upon the face
      of the earth:
    Yahweh { }^u is his name.

r   Following *G* (εἰς ὕψος ["on high"]), Budde ("Amos 5," 108–09) and Maag (*Text*, 30) read לְמַעְלָה. It is true that the expression הפך למעלה is attested in Ju 7:13 with the meaning "to turn upside down," but that is unlikely here on the basis of both the sense (Maag: "to set [justice] on its head") and the parallel represented by 6:12b.

s   *G* (κύριος ὁ ποιῶν εἰς ὕψος κρίμα καὶ δικαιοσύνην εἰς γῆν ἔθηκε ["The Lord (it is) who renders judgment on high and justice on earth he has established"]) read the first two words of v 7, and consequently also the last one, differently than *M*. Instead of ההפכים ללענה ("those who turn [justice] into wormwood") *G* perhaps presupposes יהוה פָּכֶּה מִלְמַעְלָה, and at the end of the verse the corresponding singular form הִנִּיחַ. (So Watts, "Amos 5:7," 215–16. However, instead of פָּכֶּה [?] as the *Vorlage* of ποιῶν, we would rather expect—on the basis of *G*'s translation practice elsewhere in the book of Amos—either עָשָׂה or פָּעַל, the latter conforming more closely to the epigraphic picture [see below]). *G* thereby sought to harmonize the text stylistically with the two following hymnic verses, but did not bring them into thematic congruity (see above p. 216). (Watts ["Amos 5:7," 215–16] renders his reconstructed text: "It is Yahweh who pours out justice from above and who grants righteousness to the earth.") On the other hand, there are several arguments in favour of *M* as the original text. 1) In the book of Amos the hymnic inclusions do not begin with יהוה; the refrain יהוה שְׁמוֹ at the end actually excludes this beginning (see p. 215). 2) The content of the *M*–text corresponds to the language of Amos elsewhere (6:12; cf. 5:24), and the context here much rather leads one to expect a statement about human beings than about Yahweh. 3) Without v 7, v 10 remains a fragment; v 10 actually requires v 7 as its opening, though with a conjectured הוֹי ("woe!"). Now, we may suppose that *G*'s translation effort was made possible by a badly damaged *Vorlage* at the beginning of v 7. The number of damaged letters was apparently such that, if for no other reason, it seems probable that a הוֹי had originally preceded the text as we have it now in *M*. What *G* read as יהוה פכה (פעל) מ", probably read in its uncorrupted form הוי ההפכים.

t   This isolated three–stress colon is apparently either secondary or we must suppose that an originally parallel colon has been lost; see p. 216. *G* (ποιῶν πάντα καὶ μετασκευάζων ["He who makes and transforms everything"]) found no reference to the constellations here, unlike its reading of Job 9:9 and 38:31; instead it summarizes the sense of what follows.

u   *G* (ὁ θεὸς ὁ παντοκράτωρ) presupposes an additional אלהי צבאות ("God of Hosts"), as in the *M* text of 4:13.

v   *G* (ὁ διαιρῶν ["he who distributes"]) perhaps read הַמַּבְדִּיל in the sense of "set apart, appoint to"

9   {<He who appoints>ᵛ devastation
upon (the) strong,
      and devastationʷ will comeˣ upon
      (the) fortified city.}ʸ]

10   In the gate they hate one who reproves,
      and abhor ᶻone who testifies fully.ᶻ

11   Therefore:
Because you extort rentᵃᵃ from (the)
poor
      and take grain—tax from him:
You have built houses of hewn stone,
      but you will not dwell in them.
You have planted splendid vineyards,
      but you will not drink their wine.

12   Indeedᵇᵇ I know (how) numerous are
your crimes,
      and (how) ᶜᶜformidable are your
      wrongdoings;ᶜᶜ
persecutors of (the) innocent,
      who accept bribes,
         and turn aside (the) needy in the
         gate.ᵈᵈ

(cf. 1 Chr 25:1 and 2 Chr 25:10). *M* ("the one who makes glad"; cf. Ps 39:14 [13]; Job 9:27; 10:20) would have to be interpreted in this context as "he who makes to shine forth" [cf. RSV]. Following Oort ("Amos," 118) and Sellin, Maag (*Text*, 25) proposes a reconstruction along the lines of *G*:

הַמַּפְלִיג שֶׁבֶר עַל־עֹז   "He who makes destruction break in upon
stronghold(s)

וְשֹׁד עַל־מִבְצָר יָבִיא   and brings devastation
upon fortress(es)."

w   The repetition of שֹׁד violates the law of variation within *parallelismus membrorum* which is otherwise sustained throughout the hymnic pieces (4:13; 5:8; 9:5–6), except in 9:5aα²β, a bicolon which was probably added later, just as 5:9 was (cf. 8:8a, and p. 216).

x   In such a stylistically tortured supplement as this one, it must remain quite uncertain whether יָבִיא ("he brings") is to be read here, following *G* (ἐπ-άγων).

y   After the conclusion of the strophe in v 8b, this verse gives the impression of being a later addition; see p. 216. Maag (*Text*, 25) calls it a "hymnic splinter."

z–z דבר תמים could also mean "spokesman of (the) innocent," but it probably designates here the one "who testifies fully"; see p. 246.

aa   According to Harry Torczyner ("Presidential Address," *JPOS* 16 (1936): 6–7) בשס is to be understood on the basis of Akkadian *šabāšu* = "to levy taxes." The unusual (poʿel) form makes one think here of an infinitive construct with suffix. Perhaps an original qal infinitive construct with suffix (שָׁבְסְכֶם or שׁוֹבְסְכֶם [Torczyner (*ibid.*, 7) proposed בְּשָׁסְכֶם or בְּשׁוֹסְכֶם as the original reading; in a private communication Klaus Beyer has suggested שׁוּבְסְכֶם]) was revocalized after the first two consonants of the form had been transposed. Since Wellhausen, the tendency here has been to read בּוּסְכֶם ("your trampling" [cf. RSV, etc.]). *G* (κατεκονδυλίζετε ["you struck with your knuckles"]) thinks of blows with the fist or boxing of the ears, and seems to presuppose an imperfect second person plural in close parallelism to תקחו (ἐδέξασθε "you took").

bb כי opening an oracle is found in 3:14; 4:2aβ; 6:14a. In 3:7 and 5:4 it serves as a literary connective device; see p. 233.

cc– Since Wellhausen, the masculine form עצמים ("for-
cc midable") has often prompted the reading of the corresponding masculine form חֲטָאֵיכֶם ("your wrongdoings"; cf. Is 1:18). However, the influence of the masculine forms in the parallel colon (v 12aα) may have led to the incongruity of gender in *M* of v 12aβ, the feminine having been original here, as *G* presupposes (καὶ ἰσχυραὶ αἱ ἁμαρτίαι ὑμῶν).

dd On the transition of the form of direct address in v 12a to the third person after the participles, cf. 4:1 and textual note "b" thereto.

13   >Therefore the one who is prudent in that time keeps silent, for it is an evil time.

14   Seek good, and not evil, that you may stay alive and (that) it may be so— "Yahweh [God of Hosts]ee is with you!"—just as you say.

15   ffHate evil, and love good!ff
        Establish justice in the gate!
        Perhapsff Yahweh [God of Hosts]gg may be gracious to the remnant of Joseph.<

16   Therefore thus Yahweh [God of Hosts, the Lord]hh has said:

        In all squares, lamentation!
            In all streets they shout: "Alas! Alas!"
        They call the farmhand to mourning,
            <and to lamentation>ii those
            who are skilled in wailing.
17   In all vineyards (one hears) lamentation.
        For I will pass through your midst

        —Yahweh has said.

ee   אלהי צבאות is probably a later addition, as in 4:13; see textual note "bb" to that verse.

ff–   G (μεμισήκαμεν τὰ πονηρὰ καὶ ἠγαπήκαμεν τὰ καλά)
ff   presents the verbs in the first person plural and the objects in the plural, as if we were dealing here with a confession that would explain the compassion of Yahweh. Consequently, v 12b is introduced with ὅπως (ἐλεήσῃ) ("in order that [he might have mercy]") instead of אולי ("perhaps").

gg   See textual note "ee" above.

hh   G (ὁ θεὸς ὁ παντοκράτωρ) does not reflect אדני ("the Lord"), and hence it represents an intermediary stage between the style of Amos, which was probably quite terse, and the liturgical breadth of the final redaction (see textual notes "f" and "ee" above).

ii   G (καὶ κοπετὸν καὶ εἰς εἰδότας θρῆνον ["and lamentation and to those knowing how to wail"]) already presupposes M. One must probably accept וְאֶל־מִסְפֵּד ("and to lamentation") as original, in keeping with the preceding parallel colon in v 16b (Wellhausen). The transposition of אֶל is to be explained as a copyist's error.

Form

In 5:1–17 the most varied oracles are placed together. Only five of them can be assigned with reasonable certainty to the early collection of "the words of Amos from Tekoa"[1] (vv 1–3, 4–5, 7 + 10, 11, 12 + 16–17). The remaining material quite probably belongs to various layers of interpretation (6 + 8 + 9, 13, 14–15). Thus the two elements already observed in chaps. 3 and 4, namely a basic collection and later additions, are here continued. Initially the only reason for treating these oracles in common is methodological. From v 1 through v 17 the utterances are so curiously linked with one another on the one hand, and so difficult to understand in their mutuality on the other, that questions concerning the original rhetorical units, their form and their literary–historical development into the shape of the text as we have it are best discussed jointly. By doing so it becomes evident that utterances appropriate to a funerary lament (vv 1–2, vv 16–17) bracket the intervening words.

5:1–3 Just as in 3:1 and 4:1, the initial oracle here opens with the call to attention (v 1), which indicates that it too belongs to the same larger collection of oracles. However, the oracle which directly follows contains no reference whatsoever to Israel's guilt. Rather, it is a fictitious funerary lament, singing in traditional mourning rhythms of the recently transpired death of the "virgin Israel" who, according to the introductory statement, is a personification referring to the "house of Israel" assembled around and listening to Amos. כי ("for") along with the messenger formula then links to this an oracle of Yahweh announcing the decimation of the army which marches out from a city. Do the funerary lament of Amos and the following oracle of Yahweh belong together? That cannot be taken for granted. The former refers to all Israel, the latter only to a city. Moreover, כי is used elsewhere (5:4) to link, at the stage of literary compilation, originally independent rhetorical units. But the arguments supporting the unity of vv 1–3 are stronger. The meter of the funerary lament, begun in v 2, continues through v 3αβ; the theme of v 2—national death personified—illustrates v 3; above all, we know of no announcement of judgment by the prophet, least of all one so comprehensive, that has remained without a legitimizing oracle of Yahweh. Thus one

1   See p. 107.

probably has to take the statement concerning "the city" as exemplary of all Israel. To designate a generic concept as a collective singular, i.e., ". . . to denote the *sum total* of individuals belonging to the class . . . ,"[2] the Hebrew language adds to that generic term the definite article. In effect, then, "the city" means here "each city." The introductory "for" (כי) thus announces the explication of, and at the same time the authorization for, the funerary lament. It is unusual for Amos to have preceding a judgment speech, not an accusation upon which the punishment is based (cf. 3:2, 9–11; 4:1–3; 5:12 + 16–17; and 7:16–17), but rather a song, fictitious in content, which concretizes and actualizes the impending calamity itself.

5:4–5 The clause in v 4a employs precisely the same wording that we found in v 3aα to attach the next oracle. The new exhortation which follows immediately refers to life and is thus antithetically related to the funerary lament. Although כי can certainly open independent oracles,[3] nonetheless its use here probably belongs only to the stage of literary combination. In the first place, neither in general nor here specifically (as a double motivation for the funerary lament in 5:2) would one expect two distinct sayings of Yahweh, each introduced by the messenger formula, in immediate succession within the same oracular framework. Furthermore, the theme moves from the battlefield and death in battle (v 3) to sanctuaries and exile (v 5). Finally, the sequence of admonition (v 4b), warning (v 5a) and motivation (v 5b) shows that the oracle has a wholeness of its own. Seen in form–critical perspective, this is an original composition. It is true that elements of the priestly torah flow in, insofar as the admonition (v 4) issues in the promise of life, and insofar as negative instructions for pilgrimage can be seen behind the warning (v 5a).[4] Yet the antithetic parallelism of the imperative (v 4b) and vetitive (v 5a) shows a structural element that typically belongs to wisdom. The promise of life is also especially close to

sapiential admonition.[5] However, totally new in this word of admonition, or warning, is the fact that the element of motivation is a future event. Neither the ancient will of God (as in the priestly torah), nor the demonstration of the consequences (as in the sapiential word of admonition) confirm the instruction, but rather the impending act of God announced by the prophet. With the recognition of this new element, we encounter here for the first time the form–critical genre of the prophetic admonition.

5:6, 8–9 V 6 first of all transposes the admonition in 5:4b from the first person of divine speech into the third person. In the place of the antithetic vetitive and of the reference to an impending event of judgment, functioning as an element of motivation, there appears here a פן–clause ("lest . . .") which makes the punishment conditional and thus transforms the admonition into an ultimatum–like warning. In form–critical terms, this genre is to be explained as stemming from the phenomenon of the arbitration proposal.[6] Moreover, not only is the punishment in this פן–clause of a different sort than in 5:5b, but the style here has become prosaic, indeed quite laborious.[7] Finally, there is reference to Bethel but not to Gilgal. These differences in form and content lead one to suspect a later addition here, one which attaches itself to the message of Amos concerning Bethel and Gilgal in 5:4–5 in a way similar to the attachment of 4:6–12 to 4:4–5. The cumbersome sentence structure reminds one especially of 4:12. Added to this is the fact that here also a hymnic fragment (5:8 [–9])[8] follows in closest proximity. Thus the complex of 5:4–5, 6 and 8 [–9] appears to be an abbreviated analogy to 4:4–5, 6–12 and 13. In terms of our analogue, it is the middle part which has here been abbreviated; to the old oracle of Amos is now attached an ultimatum–like warning (5:6) which, as a transition to the hymn (5:8 [–9], performs the same function of summoning the hearer to recite the judgment–doxology as does 4:12bβ.[9]

2   Gesenius–Kautzsch–Cowley, par. 126m; cf. Brockelmann, *Syntax*, par. 21cβ.

3   See 5:12, together with textual note "bb."

4   See pp. 211–12, on 4:4–5.

5   Cf. Prv 4:4–6; 9:6–8; 19:18; 20:13, 20, 22; 24:21; 30:7–8; and also Wolff, *Amos the Prophet*, 44–53 [30–36].

6   Cf. Wolff, *Hosea*, xxiv [xv] and 31–34 [37–39] on

Hos 2:4–5.

7   See textual note "p–p" to 5:7.

8   On the problem of the secondary expansion of the fragment, see p. 216.

9   Cf. "to seek" (דרש) in the directive to doxological confession of guilt in Job 5:8; on that, see further Horst, *Hiob*, 64, 82; see also above, pp. 222–23.

5:7, 10 This connection ought to be so clear that the interpolation of v 7 in the transmitted text must be traced back to a copyist's error. Initially, 5:6 + 8 [–9] was an addition placed in the margin, from whence it could very easily have been inserted into the body of the text at different places during the course of the next copying. The theme makes it clear that v 7 and v 10 belong together. We are probably here dealing with a woe–oracle,[10] which even in the limited extent represented here can certainly be an independent rhetorical unit.[11]

5:11 Up until now many interpreters have wanted to regard v 11 as the immediate continuation of 5:7 + 10.[12] At first glance that is justified, since in the old oracles of Amos "therefore" (לכן) frequently connects an announcement of punishment to a preceding statement of the grounds for punishment (cf. 3:11; 5:16; 6:7; and 7:17). Yet those scholars who want to separate v 11 from at least v 10 surely have the better arguments on their side.[13] 1) The combination "therefore: because" (לכן יען) is unique. "Therefore" (לכן) occurs over 200 times in the Old Testament, and "because" (יען) approximately 100 times, but nowhere else can their immediate juxtaposition be found. It is frequently the case, however, that an oracle exhibits יען introducing a motivation clause and then has a following result clause introduced by לכן.[14] Thus word–statistics alone make it improbable that the combination לכן יען functioned at the oral stage to connect v 10 and v 11. 2) V 7 and v 10 level an accusation in the third person; in v 11 the second person is used. 3) The theme of vv 7 + 10 is not the same as that of v 11. The oracle in vv 7 + 10 charges breach of justice in the gate; v 11 is a judgment on demanding taxes from the poor. 4) V 11, beginning with "because" (יען), is in itself a completely rounded unit. It is a judgment speech (cf. 3:2, 9–11; 4:1–3; 5:12 + 16–17) complete with establishment of evidence (v 11aα) and determination of consequences (v 11aβ–b), both parts having the form

of direct address as in 3:2 and 4:1–3. The conclusion from all this is that "therefore" (לכן) must here be regarded as a literary device connecting the independent oracles of vv 7 + 10 and v 11 (beginning with "because" [יען]). The closely following oracle in 5:13 offers a prime example of the fact that "therefore" (לכן) serves elsewhere as well as a purely literary connective device.

5:12, 16–17 But first the כי ("indeed") of v 12 leads into a new judgment speech.[15] One cannot be certain whether the particle כי was already included at the stage of oral delivery (cf. 3:14; 4:2a and 6:14, where in each case this particle stands at the beginning of divine speech announcing punishment) or—somewhat more likely in this case—whether it was added at the literary stage of development, as in (3:7 and) 5:4. In any case, a determination of guilt is introduced in v 12 in the form of direct address. Here one is probably to see the first element of a judgment speech which concludes with the announcement of punishment in vv 16–17, where the opening "therefore" (לכן) comples one to ask concerning a preceding grounds for punishment.[16] Among the preceding verses, the requisite grounds are to be found only in v 12. Since the announcement of punishment is explicitly introduced as a word of Yahweh, the first–person pronoun of v 12 indicates that in this part of the oracle Amos himself is speaking, just as he does in 3:9–10; 4:1; and 5:1–2.

5:13 In the present text, however, there follows immediately upon 5:12 yet another לכן–clause ("therefore . . ." v 13), one which does not see in v 12 a reason for Yahweh's intervention (5:16–17) but which rather draws from v 12 a consequence for human behavior. That it does not derive from Amos, nor even from the first collection of "the words of Amos from Tekoa," follows from the fact that Amos was not permitted to belong to the prudent keepers of silence (cf. 3:8), and that the verse, together with vv 14–15, interrupts the connection of 5:12 + 16–17.

---

10 On the text, see textual note "q" to 5:7.
11 See the excursus on pp. 242–45.
12 Sellin, Maag (*Text*, 30), Amsler, and others.
13 Weiser, Robinson, Neubauer ("Erwägungen," 313).
14 Cf. 2 Kgs 1:16; Is 29:13–14; 30:12–13; Jer 23:38aβb, 39; and Ezek 13:22–23. Cf. also Zimmerli, *Ezechiel*, 58*.
15 See textual note "bb" to 5:12.
16 Cf. the similar function of "therefore" (לכן) in 3:11; 6:7; 7:17 and the contrasting usage of the "therefore: because" (לכן יען) in 5:11 (on which, see above).

5:14–15 It is indeed the case that the majority of scholars are inclined to regard vv 14–15 as an authentic oracle of Amos,[17] only a few having expressed serious reservations.[18] In support of these few, one should pause to consider several important factors. Vv 14–15 join the undoubtedly secondary v 13 in splitting the unit composed of 5:12 + 16–17. Upon close inspection, vv 14–15 prove to be an interpretation of 5:4b (cf. v 14a), one constructed with the help of 5:7 + 10–12 (cf. v 15a with 5:7a, 10a, 12b). This interpretation employs a discursive style (v 14b) which accommodates the hopes of the audience in a way otherwise unknown in Amos, as it substitutes for the devastating punishments announced in 5:2–3, 5b, and 16–17, a note—likewise unattested elsewhere in Amos—that "perhaps" God will deal compassionately with a remnant (v 15b). Furthermore, there are small but telling differences in language. A telic clause, "that you may stay alive" (למען תחיו), takes the place of the second imperative in the admonition at 5:4b ("then you shall live" [וחיו]); "Israel" (5:4a; cf. 5:1–2) is here called "Joseph" (v 15b), a designation elsewhere employed in the book of Amos only in the likewise supplementary sentence in 6:6b.[19]

Prosody in Am 5:1–17

Before we pursue the question of the setting of these various later interpretations, we should state that all of them can also be distinguished from the authentic oracles of Amos by their prosaic style (cf. vv 6, 13). Vv 14–15 show only feeble attempts at elevated language, in the antitheses of v 14a and v 15a; the hymnic fragment in vv 8 [–9], which goes with v 6, understandably forms an exception here. But it is only the older prophetic utterances which exhibit clear *parallelismus membrorum* throughout. The funerary lament (v 2) places two five–stress prosodic units, typical of this genre (cf. Lam), into parallelism.[20] Each five–stress unit consists of two cola of unequal length. It is the second and shorter colon, with its premature breaking off, which gives rise to the "limping rhythms" that serve to awaken a "mood of despair."[21] The messenger speech (v 3) presents two strictly parallel bicola, of which the first continues the rhythm of the funerary lament (3//2), so that a kind of staccato effect is created at the end, as is often the case in Amos' utterances. The next messenger speech (vv 4b–5) places a short up–beat line (v 4b) into antithetic parallelism with an initial three–stress bicolon (v 5aα–β), whose two cola are synonymously parallel, as are those of the second and concluding three–stress bicolon (v 5b). Within the whole oracle, v 5b forms a synthetic parallel to v 5aα. The fact that the cola stand in chiastic relationship to each other (Bethel–Gilgal // Gilgal–Bethel), as well as the alliteration in v 5b, testify to especially artistic workmanship. The woe–oracle (vv 7 + 10)[22] consists of two clear three–stress bicola, the bicola being synonymously parallel with each other (3//3 :: 3//3). The same metrical structure of three–stress bicola predominates throughout the two judgment speeches. V 11 comprises three three–stress bicola, the first of which exhibits internal synonymous parallelism, while the other two stand in synonymous parallelism with each other. In vv 12 + 16–17 the form of three–stress bicola (vv 12a, 16aβb) with internal synonymous parallelism is exhibited for the most part, though by means of small variations a climactic effect is created in the closing cola of both the accusation

---

17 Duhm ("Anmerkungen," 8–9), Marti, Maag (*Text*, 31–32), Hesse ("Amos 5," 11–13), Neubauer ("Erwägungen," 296ff), and others.

18 So, e.g., Weiser, *Profetie*, 185–89.

19 See pp. 109–10. The expression "house of Joseph" is found in 5:6, but in terms of both style and content this expression is a completely different sort of interpretation of 5:4.

20 Cf. Karl Budde, "Das hebräische Klagelied," *ZAW* 2 (1882): 1–52; and Joachim Begrich, "Der Satzstil im Fünfer," *Zeitschrift für Semitistik und verwandte Gebiete* 9 (1933–34): 169–209 (esp. 185) (reprinted in *idem, Gesammelte Studien*, 132–67 [147]); and Zimmerli, *Ezechiel*, 420. Cf. also the different view of Friedrich Horst, "Die Kennzeichen der hebräischen Poesie," *ThR* 21 (1953): 118. According to more recent investigations, the "accentuating system" of describing Hebrew prosody appears to merit preference over the "alternating system," at least when dealing with poetic literature from the period of the Israelite monarchy. So Stanislav Segert, "Problems of Hebrew Prosody" in *Congress Volume, Oxford, 1959*, SVT 7 (Leiden: E. J. Brill, 1960), 283–91; cf. David Noel Freedman, "Archaic Forms in Early Hebrew Poetry," *ZAW* 72 (1960): 101–07.

21 Jahnow, *Leichenlied*, 90–92.

22 See p. 233.

and the announcement of punishment. Thus v 12b replaces the three–stress bicolon pattern with a seven–stress unit in which an initial two–stress bicolon is followed by a parallel three–stress colon (2//2//3) which effectively closes the accusation. The synthetic parallelism of v 17 concludes the announcement of punishment in a way that also attacts attention. Particularly noticeable is the final colon, introduced by כי ("for"), even though this colon is probably to be read as having not two but rather three stresses (similar to the colon at the beginning of the oracle in v 12aβ). The introductory and concluding structural formulas, as well as the literary linking particles, are extrametrical.

Setting

We cannot determine with certainty where any of the oracles of Amos in this section was originally spoken. At no place within 5:1–17 is an addressee designated as precisely as in 3:9–4:3; both accusations and threats always reach far beyond any one individual locality. The first oracle (vv 1–3) summarizes like no other the fate of the whole state of Israel. The last oracle of our section sums up in its accusation (v 12) the crimes named earlier in vv 7 + 10 and v 11, and in its announcement of punishment it underscores the sweeping scope of Israel's fatal destiny (cf. the three-fold repetition of "all" [כל] in vv 16–17). The unified theme of the funerary lament brackets all the oracles (vv 1–2 and vv 16–17), and individual oracles appear in several instances to have been combined by literary means (vv 4, 11, 12). One thus gets the impression that even in the judgment of the initial transcribers only one and the same setting is to be considered for all the oracles, be that setting Bethel or Samaria. Then we would have before us again a kind of précis or scenario in connection with which one ought to suppose that there were (unrecorded) rejoinders by the audience between the delivery of the individual oracles.[23]

The first supplement (5:6, 8 [–9]) may well have been spoken at Bethel in connection with the destruction of the shrine by Josiah.[24] The reasons for this are the formal analogy to 4:6–13 (discussed above) and the selective interpretation of 5:4–5 by focusing attention solely on Bethel (5:6b). Perhaps the liturgist first read aloud appropriate oracles of Amos, such as 4:4–5, along with the announcement here in 5:4–5 that "Bethel will become adversity" (cf. 2 Kgs 23:17). On the other hand, he may have taken elements of a proclamation, loosely dependent upon Amos, and inserted them into "the words of Amos from Tekoa" at precisely these suitable places.

The later addition in 5:14–15 is distinguished in form and content from both 5:6 and from the Deuteronomistic additions. Though it clearly stands out from Amos' own oracles,[25] it nonetheless also clearly bears a close relationship to the proclamation of the prophet. It interprets, as it were, 5:4b (cf. v 14a) with the help of 5:10 and 12. Since other texts (especially 7:10–17)[26] compel us to postulate the activity of one or more disciples of Amos, this text is also most probably to be traced back to such circles. These circles of disciples, continuing to discuss (5:14b) the message of their master in the immediately ensuing decades, carried on that message and developed it to the point where there was hope for a "remnant." By the time of these disciples, the boundaries which the northern kingdom had known under Jeroboam II seem already to have been reduced considerably.[27] If these disciples of Amos were at home in the same Judean circles as their master, then 5:13 is most likely also to be ascribed to their supplementation of "the words of Amos from Tekoa."

Interpretation

■1 The opening call to attention, composed of a single structural element, issues a summons to hear, at least initially, not the word of Yahweh (as in 3:1) but rather words of the prophetic speaker himself (as in 4:1). The summons to heed a human speaker is likewise characteristic of both the sapiential call to attention and wisdom's two–part summons introducing instruction.[28] Such a "hear!" as in 5:1 also introduces the lament in Lam 1:18. That the funerary lament is opened with the call to attention is especially understandable if indeed the initial function of such a call was to announce a recently

---

23 See p. 200 and n. 4.
24 See pp. 217–18.
25 See p. 234.

26 See pp. 108–10.
27 See p. 110.
28 Cf. Prv 5:7; 7:24; 8:32–33; Job 34:2, 10. See further Wolff, *Hosea*, 97 [122–23].

transpired death.[29] Amos announces a death whose occurrence was still completely unknown to all his hearers. For the purpose of initiating the funerary lament, Amos employs an expression later attested also in Jeremiah and particularly in Ezekiel, namely "to raise a lament over [someone]" (נשׂא קינה על־).[30] Unique is the fact that the hearers themselves ("over you" [עליכם]) are addressed as the corpses over whom lamentation is raised. The hearers are addressed as the "house of Israel," or in other words as being equivalent to the whole state of the northern kingdom.[31] Only the funerary laments in Ezekiel over foreign nations like Tyre (26:17; 27:32) and Egypt (32:2) are comparable to this. It is not strange that Amos, as a man, should intone a funerary lament; also in 5:16 men are introduced as singers of lamentation. In 2 Sam 3:31 David orders Joab and all the people to make lamentation; he himself intones the "lament" (קינה) ("and the king lamented" [וַיְקֹנֵן] 2 Sam 3:33). Likewise in 2 Chr 35:25 male as well as female singers perform the funerary lamentation of Jeremiah over Josiah. Only later do women come to occupy the central role in general funerary lamentation.[32]

■2 There is thus nothing unusual about the lament of Amos in the fact that it is voiced by a male. Even less unusual is its form, which corresponds closely both in rhythm[33] and in thematic content to a customary type. David, too, laments for Saul and Jonathan because they have "fallen." "How are the mighty *fallen* (נָפְלוּ)!" is in fact the *cantus firmus* of this type of funerary lament (2 Sam 1:19, 25, 27). Abner is lamented in a similar way: "as one falls before the wicked, you have fallen" (2 Sam 3:34). It is always death by the sword which is in mind, as Lam 2:21 explicitly and mournfully attests concerning the youth of Jerusalem: "they

have fallen by the sword" (נָפְלוּ בֶחָרֶב) (cf. Jer 9:21) [22]. The youth referred to include both "maidens" (בְּתוּלוֹת) and "young men" (בַּחוּרִים). Amos takes up not only the catchword "fallen" but also its usage in the perfect tense. Does one catch the prophet's intent if one speaks of a fictitious funerary lament? Does he not fully intend, with the image of the fallen virgin, to portray the demise of Israel as an accomplished fact in the eyes of God and therefore as a present reality already to be lamented (cf. 8:2)? She who has fallen will rise no more; her collapse is final, because it is fatal. Only the identification of the deceased, the "virgin Israel," falls outside the scope of the usual funerary laments. In Amos the "lament" (קינה) is applied for the first time to a collective entity, in this case to the state of Israel. Elsewhere this genre is always applied to individuals, until Ezekiel uses it in the same way as Amos to refer to Tyre (26:17; 27:2, 32; 28:12).[34] Isaiah, in 1:21–22, laments not the death but rather the unfaithfulness of Jerusalem.[35] The mourning is especially painful because it is for an Israel who was still a "virgin."[36] The term "virgin" connotes both youthfulness and virginity at the same time (cf. the mourning for Jephthah's daughter in Ju 11:39–40). The Israel of Amos' day feels herself to be in the full flush of youthful vigor,[37] but her fate is sealed and she is to come to an untimely end. Israel falls "on her own soil." The notion of an enemy incursion into Israelite political territory is here presupposed (cf. 3:11; 4:3; and 6:14). "To lie stretched out" (נטשׁ nip'al) signifies that the corpse lies there unattended and ignored, "abandoned" (by God).[38] As in the first bicolon ("no more to rise" [לא תוסיף קום]), so also at the end of the song is it expressed—this time in terse participial form—that any help is excluded ("with no one to raise her up" אין מקימה).

29 Jahnow, *Leichenlied*, 101.

30 Cf. Jer 7:29; 9:9 [10]; and Ezek 19:1; 26:17; 27:2, 32; 28:12; 32:2.

31 See p. 164.

32 Apart from the special case of the mourning of the daughters of Israel for Jephthah's daughter in Ju 11:40, specific reference to women as mourners does not occur until such a late text as Jer 9:16–21 [17–22]; cf. Lk 23:27. Cf. Gustav Stählin, "Θρηνέω, Θρῆνος," *TDNT* 3, 150–52.

33 See p. 234.

34 But cf. also Na 2:12–13 [11–12]; 3:7; Zeph 2:15b; Mi 1:8ff, 16; and Jer 9:16–21 [17–22]; 48:17; 49:3 (suggested by Jörg Jeremias).

35 Fey, *Amos und Jesaja*, 65.

36 On בתולה see pp. 30–31, and also Lam 2:21 (in Joel 1:8 the "virgin" is the one who laments, not the one who is lamented).

37 See pp. 89–90.

38 נטשׁ qal ("forsake, abandon") often refers to God's forsaking his people; cf. Ju 6:13; 1 Sam 12:22; 1 Kgs 8:57; 2 Kgs 21:14; and Is 2:6. See further Wildberger, *Jesaja*, 97–98.

The funerary lament in Jer 9:20–21 [21–22] concludes in a similar way with the image of cut sheaves that no one gathers up ("and none shall gather [them]" [וְאֵין מְאַסֵּף]). "To raise up" (קום hip'il) designates, as in Hos 6:2, the act of helping up someone seriously wounded, or in other words helping to restore the person to life. Here one sees the particular pain inherent in this lament. Vigorous and as yet unfulfilled life has been given over to death, without there being anyone who could help. While the funerary "lament" (קינה) elsewhere may depict in sweeping and lyric tones the happenings, the effects, the contrast of once and now, and other motifs,[39] Amos hardly embellishes at all. He simply offers a brief, bitter report of the death, a report which emphasizes repeatedly the finality of that death.

■ 3 The immediately following oracle of Yahweh, which is explicitly identified by its introductory כי ("for") as supplying the underlying reason for the lament, relates the allusions in v 2 to a military debacle ("to fall" [נפל]) on native soil ("on her own soil" [עַל־אַדְמָתָהּ]).[40] A city may be the gathering place as well as the place of residence of a "clan" (מִשְׁפָּחָה), which latter may be understood as referring to a community settled in a given area (cf. 1 Sam 20:6, 29; Mi 5:1 [2]). Now, as its contingent of the military levy of the tribe (Josh 7:16–18), a clan provides a detachment of a "thousand"[41] which is further divided into companies of "hundreds."[42] "To go forth" (יצא) designates the marching out of the troops to battle.[43] Half of an army may be lost without the battle's having become hopeless, as long as the king is still safe (2 Sam 18:3). But a decimation like the one here announced means "a bloodletting of the people of such proportions that a recuperation is impossible."[44] It is true that interpreters still want to see in this oracle reference to a saved remnant,[45] but Amos' own interpretation of this oracle, found in the immediately preceding funerary lament, shows that there is as little thought of a remnant here in 5:3 as there is in 3:12. If in Israel's cities only a hundred men out of a thousand, or ten out of a hundred return from the war, then the death sentence has been pronounced over the state of Israel.

■ 4 How is it to be explained that, to the words proclaiming Yahweh's immutable decision concerning the thorough decimation of Israel, there is attached an exhortation holding open the prospect of life? Such a speech of admonition is quite unique among the oracles of Amos. The attached promise of life actually stands in contradiction to that which precedes, as well as to the total message of the prophet. Only the later interpretations of v 4, in 5:6 and 14–15, say anything similar. Nonetheless, there is no reason to deny that vv 4–5, as well as 5:6 and 14–15, stem from Amos himself.

First we must consider three explanations of v 4 that have already been proposed. Weiser[46] hears in 5:4 a tone of irony similar to, though more subdued than that in 4:4–5. He feels that Amos here makes effective use of paradox; the positive demand in v 4b stands "completely in the shadow of the following words against Bethel and Gilgal."[47] It is obvious that the two words of exhortation and of promise in v 4b are completely overshadowed by the artfully constructed utterance in 5:5. Yet Würthwein[48] and Hesse[49] have already rejected the conjecture of an ironic paradox. This oracle does not at all show the features characteristic of oracles such as 3:12 or 4:4–5. Thus Hesse reaches a different conclusion: "Here for once the prophet's otherwise so rigid proclamation, which in all its basic aspects conforms to God's commission, is noticeably unsettled

39 Cf. 2 Sam 1:19–27; Jer 9:16–21 [17–22]; Ezek 19; 26:17–18; 27:3–10, 26, 28–32, 34–35.

40 On the connection of 5:2 and 3, see also pp. 231–32. where an exemplary (generic) meaning for the reference in v 3 to "the city" is argued.

41 Cf. 1 Sam 10:19 ("thousand" [אלף]) with 1 Sam 10:21 ("clan" [משפחה]). See also Gerhard von Rad, *Der Heilige Krieg im alten Israel* (Göttingen: Vandenhoeck & Ruprecht, ³1958), 26–27; and de Vaux, *Israel*, 216.

42 Ju 7:16; 1 Sam 22:7; 2 Sam 18:1, 4.

43 E.g., 2 Sam 18:2–4, 6; 2 Kgs 5:2; Is 37:9.

44 Weiser, *Profetie*, 180.

45 Horst Dietrich Preuss, *Jahweglaube und Zukunftserwartung*, BWANT 87 (Stuttgart: W. Kohlhammer, 1968), 159–81.

46 Weiser, *Profetie*, 190–92.

47 *Ibid.*, 191.

48 "Amos-Studien," 38.

49 "Amos 5," 7–10.

by another word of Yahweh which comes upon the prophet, a word so strange as to seem an intrusion from another world. . . . Here it becomes evident . . . that this God has the freedom to break into the prophet's conceptual world, into his 'views on divine and worldly reality,' and to overturn all his established notions."[50] This indication of how the prophet is left completely to the freedom of his God is noteworthy. However, it is precisely in the continuation of v 4, in the nonetheless still dominant v 5, that we see the basic proclamation of Amos being firmly maintained. V 4b is almost lost in the shadow cast by v 5 and by the overall proclamation of Amos in general. A third attempt at explanation remains to be considered. Albrecht Alt is probably justified in distinguishing between the attitude of the upper class in the capital city and that of the great masses of the rural population regarding Yahweh's desire for justice.[51] He reckons with the possibility that Amos spoke differently to the rural populace then he did to those in the leading circles; he understands the prophet's word from that vantage point. "Where he speaks to the masses he can therefore at times depart from reproaching and threatening and move into exhortation, apparently with the—admittedly hesitant—expectation that it . . . might still fall on fertile soil."[52] From this perspective the connection with v 5 also becomes intelligible. Amos would then be attempting to separate the "great masses of the rural population" from the official circles of the cultic and political leadership, something which was also done in a similar way in Hosea (2:4ff).[53] However, the attempt to read Amos in this way falls apart for two reasons. First of all, we can find a distinction of this kind nowhere else in his words; on the contrary, judgment is unreservedly (2:14–16; 9:1–4) announced not only upon the leaders but upon all Israel (3:2; 5:21–27; 7:11, 17). Even more significantly, our oracle here is directed to the very same audience which received the immediately preceding announcement of death (cf. "concerning the house of Israel" [לבית ישראל] in v 4a with the same designation in 5:1 and 3!).

One will have to reckon with the fact that the terse prelude (v 4) to the main oracle (v 5) repeats a slogan which had been held up to the prophet by his hearers after his announcement of death in vv 2–3. This slogan referred to the pilgrimage sites[54] and recalled Yahweh's promise of life, a promise grounded in the cultic tradition. If Amos really began his reply as an exhortation with a promise, then one can indeed suspect in this oracle the influence of priestly–cultic speech.[55] However, the exhortation to seek Yahweh, in the form of an imperative of דרש ("to seek"), nowhere in the Old Testament refers to calling upon Yahweh in a sanctuary; it usually means inquiring of a prophet or of Yahweh through a prophet.[56] Given this fact, the meaning here is that Amos summons his audience to ask after the word of Yahweh as it is mediated through himself as a prophet. "Against the turning to Yahweh at a cultic place Amos juxtaposes the turning to Yahweh which is possible *only* through a prophet."[57] (To think of Jerusalem as that which is to be sought would completely miss the point and can find no support in the book of Amos.[58])

"Then you shall live" (וחיו) states the result of such a seeking.[59] As the second of two consecutive imperatives "then you shall live" occurs altogether eight times in the Old Testament. In no place does this formulation belong to cultic language, with the possible exception of the later addition in Ezek 18:32b.[60] Rather than to those who seek, life is elsewhere prof-

50 *Ibid.*, 9.
51 Alt, "Die Heimat des Deteronomiums" in *Kleine Schriften* 2, 269.
52 *Ibid.*
53 Cf. Wolff, *Hosea*, 33–34 [39–40]; also xxiii [xiv] on the necessity of distinguishing various circles of addressees in Hosea.
54 See pp. 211–12, on 4:4.
55 Cf. Zimmerli, *Ezechiel*, 339–40, 415.
56 1 Kgs 22:5 = 2 Chr 18:4; 2 Kgs 22:13 = 2 Chr 34:21; Jer 21:2. See further Claus Westermann, "Die Begriffe für Fragen und Suchen im Alten Testament," *KuD* 6 (1960): 2–30; and Wolff, *Hosea*, 186 [241–42].
57 Westermann, "Fragen," 22.
58 This is rightly emphasized by Hans Gottlieb, "Amos und Jerusalem," *VT* 17 (1967): 453, against Kapelrud, *Central Ideas*, 57. On Am 1:2, see pp. 121–22.
59 On the syntax, see textual note "j" to 5:4.
60 Cf. Zimmerli, *Ezechiel*, 415.

fered to those who follow a prudent (Gen 42:18), wise (Prv 9:6), or even a concrete counsel (2 Kgs 18:32; Jer 27:12, 17). Especially the last–mentioned passages offer parallels to Amos' initial response to the reaction of his audience following his death–threat against the state.

Thus the promissory appeal of v 4b must be understood as making the survival of the audience conditional. Yahweh answers them, "If you listen to my word, which my messenger proclaims to you, then you will stay alive." This exhortation is not tinged by any irony;[61] Yahweh's freedom to stand by his life–giving word, even in the hour of death, asserts itself.[62] However, as a response to a retort contradicting the prophet, this exhortation hardly reckons on prompting obedient response. At the most, it intends to recall a venerable but long since disregarded word of Yahweh. It sounds impressive, but is it still in effect? In any case it must promptly yield to the more extensive word of admonition and threat (v 5), which obviously conveys the real message to be impressed on the hearers.[63]

■ **5** The prohibitives in v 5a stand in antithesis to the imperatives in v 4b; a distinction between אַל ("not") with the jussive as a vetitive and לֹא ("not") with the jussive as a prohibitive[64] would allow one to recognize an artful intensification in v 5a. The warning against seeking Bethel antithetically reiterates the "seek" (דרש) of v 4b; the sanctuary competes with the prophetic word of God.[65]

The later addition[66] of Beer–sheba is perhaps to be ascribed to disciples of Amos in Judah,[67] who may well have discussed the words of Amos with pilgrims to Beer–sheba from the northern kingdom. The route of Elijah's flight (1 Kgs 19:3–4) and the activity of the sons of Samuel (1 Sam 8:2) both constitute evidence that ancient pilgrimage connections with Beer–sheba were cultivated in the northern kingdom.[68] From a starting point in the mountains of Ephraim, one reached this border sanctuary in the far south of Judah by a circuitous route that avoided the Judahite cultic center of Jerusalem. It is possible that ties with the Edomites were cultivated here, reflecting the notion of Esau's having been a related tribal patriarch (cf. "Isaac" in 7:9, 16).[69] The following generations are also to know that there is no way to avoid the prophetic accusation.

While the later addition concerning Beer–sheba remains without a corresponding threat, Gilgal is threatened with exile, just as are the leading circles in Samaria (4:2–3; 6:7), the participants in the cultus (5:21–23, 27), and indeed the whole people (7:11, 17). Here the mention of Gilgal obviously refers to those who assemble there. The alliteration[70] and the chiastic arrangement of the parallel bicola (v 5aα//aβ : : bα//bβ) show a consciously artistic shaping[71] and thereby attest to the prophetic intention of making precisely this part of the oracle (in contrast to the mere prelude in v 4b) impressively memorable. Just as Gilgal, a monument to the occupation of the land (Josh 4:20ff), shall become a memorial of the expulsion from the land, so Bethel, the house of God (Gen 28:16 [J], 17 [E]), shall fall prey to a shameful destruction. The word which we have translated as "adversity" (אָוֶן) connotes at once disaster,

---

61 *Contra* Weiser, *Profetie,* 190–92.

62 So Hesse, "Amos 5," 9.

63 Cf. the functional alteration of the admonition speech into a demonstration of guilt in 5:23–24; see pp. 260–61.

64 So Wolfgang Richter, *Recht und Ethos: Versuch einer Ortung des weisheitlichen Mahnspruchs,* StANT 15 (München: Kösel–Verlag, 1966), 71–78 and n. 88, following Wolfram von Soden, *Grundriss der Akkadischen Grammatik,* AnOr 33 (Roma: Pontificium Institutum Biblicum, 1952), pars. 81h, i.

65 On Bethel, Gilgal, and בוא ("to enter") as a technical term in the context of pilgrimages, see pp. 218–19, on 4:4.

66 On the secondary character of the warnings against Beer–sheba, see textual note "l" to 5:5.

67 See pp. 109–10.

68 Cf. Walther Zimmerli, *Geschichte und Tradition von Beerseba im Alten Testament* (Göttingen, 1932), 4–7.

69 Cf. Kurt Galling, "Das Gemeindegesetz in Deuteronomium 23" in *Festschrift für Alfred Bertholet,* ed. Walther Baumgartner, *et al.* (Tübingen: J. C. B. Mohr [Paul Siebeck], 1950), 182–83; Albrecht Alt, "The God of the Fathers" in *Essays on Old Testament History and Religion,* tr. R. A. Wilson (Garden City, New York: Doubleday Anchor Books, 1968), 67–68 ["Der Gott der Väter" in *Kleine Schriften* 1, 53]; and Kraus, *Worship,* 172–73 [201–02].

70 A fourfold repetition of the consonants *g* and *l*. [In transliteration the Hebrew reads: *kî gilgāl gālōh yigleh*; Trans.]

71 See p. 234.

injustice, and nothingness.[72] That this oracle of Amos, and especially its latter part, was indeed etched indelibly upon the memory is attested by Hosea. In referring to Bethel as "Beth–aven" (בֵּית־אָוֶן Hos 4:15; 5:8),[73] he seems to have renamed that venerable sanctuary precisely in accord with this oracle of Amos. Wellhausen's free rendering excellently captures both the poetic power and the harshness of the content: "Gilgal will go to the gallows, and Bethel will become pandemonium."[74] Any chance that the old promissory exhortation, which Amos perhaps took up by way of disputation, might still find a hearing and indeed avert the fate of Israel, vanished completely before the certainty of the annihilating onslaught.

Thus the impression remains, as one looks back from v 5 to v 4b, that while Amos did not impugn the old word of promise, he certainly did deny the expectation that Israel's death could still be averted. Despite the uniqueness of his exhortation, his admonition remains dominant, and everything is finally overshadowed by the announcement of judgment, which is unequivocally the last word here.

■ **6** Increasingly, interpreters[75] are coming to see that v 6, with its transposition of divine speech into prophetic speech and its alteration of the uncompromising sentence of judgment into a forewarning, represents an "exegesis" or "interpretation" of 5:4–5. But one must conclude from the language[76] and the style[77] that this verse does not derive from the prophet himself. Its similarity to 4:6–13, the restriction of its warning to Bethel, and its association with the hymn in 5:8–9,[78] all lead to the supposition that we have here an interpretation of the preceding oracle of Amos (5:4–5) which dates from the time of the Josianic destruction of the sanctuary at Bethel. Thus old doubts concerning its authenticity are confirmed.[79] It is therefore no longer necessary, following Sellin, to look for some reference to Gilgal alongside Bethel here. This verse issues a warning to the inhabitants of the former north-ern kingdom, so that there might not break out an all–consuming, unquenchable fire "concerning Bethel" (לְבֵית־אֵל).[80] Amos' old image of judgment, namely that of the devouring fire (1:4, 7; 2:2), is taken up in an awkwardly constructed sentence. Perhaps the interpreter also has in mind that, in the second vision (7:4–6), the threat of judgment with fire is likewise rescinded. By submitting anew to the word of Yahweh (v 6a) and to his punishment as manifest in the destruction of Bethel by Josiah (2 Kgs 23:15–18), this generation might also be spared. This is the only place where those affected are called "house of Joseph." This expression refers to the tribes of central Palestine (Ephraim and Manasseh), and by extension to the northern kingdom as a whole,[81] especially when it stands in juxtaposition to Judah (Ezek 37:16, 19). After the end of the state of Israel and the adoption of the name Israel to refer to the legitimate people of God, the designation "house of Joseph" for the Israelite inhabitants of the Assyrian province of Samaria (who thought of themselves as belonging to the sanctuary of Bethel) becomes especially understandable. The judgment upon Bethel (4:12; cf. 2 Kgs 23:15–18) had been brought about by the lack of readiness to repent on the part of those who had fallen away from Yahweh (4:6–11). However, the word of Amos newly appropriated (v 6a, based on 5:4b) can nonetheless show the population—that which remained after the judgment which fell in the year 721 (5:5b)—how to avoid becoming the victims of yet another fiery judgment (v 6b).

■ **8** By reciting the hymn, the people around Bethel give testimony to their renewed quest of and search for Yahweh.[82] 5:8 goes with 5:6, just as 4:13 goes with 4:6–11 and 9:5–6 goes with 9:1–4, provided that correspondingly similar points of reference are to be assumed for the similar hymnic fragments in the book of Amos. This is the case only with reference to oracles directed against the altar of Bethel;[83] the motif of the earthquake[84] does not provide such a common point

72   Cf. Koehler–Baumgartner (³1967), 21–22.

73   Cf. Wolff, *Hosea*, 90 [113].

74   Wellhausen, 8: "Gilgal wird zum Galgen gehn und Bethel wird des Teufels werden."

75   Hesse, "Amos 5," 6; Neubauer, "Erwägungen," 315–16.

76   See textual notes "o" and "p–p" to 5:6.

77   See p. 232.

78   See pp. 111 and 232.

79   The attribution of the verse to Amos was already questioned by Oort, "Amos;" cf. Harper, 121.

80   See textual note "p–p" to 5:6.

81   2 Sam 19:21 [20] can designate the Benjaminite Shimei as a representative of the "house of Joseph."

82   See p. 232 n. 9 on the use of דרש ("to seek") to introduce the judgment doxology, in accordance

of reference, since it appears neither in 4:13 nor in 5:8–9, playing a role in the context of the oracles of Amos only in 9:1–4 + 5–6. It remains uncertain whether the inclusion of v 8 (the hymn may initially have been added in the margin or at the end of the column) after v 7, rather than after v 6, is to be explained on the basis of a "catchword association" ("those who turn—who turns" [ההפכים—והפך]).[85] If this were the case, however, then it would be unlikely that the first three Hebrew words of v 8 already belonged to the hymn when it was transcribed into the text.[86] The praise of the creator of the constellations stands in isolation. כימה, which on the basis of its etymology means "herd" or "heap,"[87] designates as a "heap of stars" the "constellation of seven," the Pleiades.[88] כסיל, literally the "brash one," is translated correctly by *V*, both here and at Job 38:31, as "Orion."[89] These two constellations appear as a pair also in Job 9:9 and 38:31; it is questionable whether their juxtaposition is intended as an allusion to the alternation of seasons (Orion being associated with summer and the Pleiades with winter[90]).

The isolated three-stress colon is followed by a pair of three–stress bicola exhibiting synonymous parallelism, which may well have alone comprised the original text of the hymn at this point.[91] The two bicola praise the one who causes the great transformations to take place, the first bicolon paralleling the changes of "deep–darkness"[92] into dawn and of day into night. The second bicolon lauds the one "who summons the waters of the sea," which in effect may well mean "he gathers

them,"[93] and who then, antithetically, pours them back upon the earth. The worship of the one who works these great cosmic transformations,[94] when applied to Yahweh, must have been well–suited to Israel as it confessed the justice of his past acts of judgment (for example, as here, the destruction of the sanctuary of Bethel) and praised his future work of preservation (cf. 5:6).

■ **9** It is true that the hymnic style is still recognizable in the following verse. But its text is so badly damaged and difficult to interpret[95] that v 9 can be regarded for this reason alone as a later addition which subsequent copyists found difficult to decipher. But above all, the verse departs from the theme of the rest of the hymnic segments, which are concerned predominantly with the cosmic governance of God, and only once with his general activity in regard to humanity (4:13aβ, and then how differently from 5:9!).[96] In those places where the text is reasonably certain, there is reference to "fortified city," "strong" and "devastation."[97] Thus it seems that a bicolon concerning Yahweh's judgment was added to the older hymn, praising his powerful and warlike intervention (cf. 5:3) against the violent (5:7, 10–12).

■ **7** Just as 5:2–3 and 4–5 revolve around Israel's fatal destiny, so also the introductory element of 5:7 probably repeats the chief word of the funerary lament, assuming that "woe, alas" (הוֹי) originally opened this oracle.[98] But this raises questions that demand a general investigation of the "woe–cries" (*Weherufe*).

with Job 5:8.

83 Sellin; see above pp. 217–18.

84 So Weiser, *Profetie*, 202.

85 So Weiser, *Profetie*, 202; and Gese, "Beiträge," 434.

86 There are other arguments as well in support of this observation regarding 5:8; see p. 216.

87 Koehler–Baumgartner, 434. *G* translates πάντα ("[who makes] everything")!

88 This is how *G* interprets *M* at Job 38:31; *V* in Am 5:8 reads *Arcturus* (as *G* reads *M* at Job 9:9), meaning the "Bear Hunter," i.e., the star which follows the Great Bear.

89 *G* renders כסיל in Job 9:9 as Ἕσπερος; ("Evening Star").

90 Thus Georg Fohrer, *Das Buch Hiob*, KAT 16 (Gütersloh: Gütersloher Verlagshaus Gerd Mohn, 1963), 216.

91 See p. 216.

92 "Deep–darkness" (צַלְמָוֶת) must have struck the ancient Hebrew ear as "shadow of death."

93 Thus Speier, "Bemerkungen," 307. Would the reference in this colon be to the formation of clouds, to drought, or to the recession of flood waters?

94 Cf. *G*'s rendering of 5:8aα (textual note "t") and also textual note "v" to 5:9!

95 See textual notes "v" through "y" to 5:9.

96 See also pp. 216–17.

97 Cf. the contiguous occurrence of מבצר and ושד in Hos 10:14: ". . . all your fortresses shall be destroyed."

98 See textual note "q" to 5:7.

Form–Criticism of the "Woe–Cries"

This topic has been the subject of lively recent discussion.[99] With regard to Amos, we have to inquire concerning the provenance of the combination of the cry "woe!" (הוֹי) with participles in the plural or with substantives descriptive of a deplorable manner of behavior (5:18; 6:1; 5:7 cj.). There are currently three contested answers to this question of provenance.

a) The prophetic woe–cries are transformations of cultic curses of the sort found in the curse–dodecalogue of Dtn 27:15–26. This thesis was suggested by Mowinckel[100] and has been worked out by Westermann.[101]

b) The woe–cries have been freely fashioned by the prophets, who took up הוֹי from the funerary lament. Hempel already regarded the woe–cry as one of those forms of prophetic speech which "express . . . the prophet's personal empathy."[102] Wanke[103] proposed the actual thesis on the basis of more precise observations, and Clifford[104] worked it out independently of Wanke.

c) The basic form of the woe–cry, with participles in the plural or with substantives descriptive of a deplorable manner of behavior, must be sought in pedagogical clan wisdom.[105]

The following assured results can be drawn from the investigations under consideration:

1. The series of curses ("cursed . . ." [. . . אָרוּר]) in Dtn 27:15–26 exhibits a structure similar to that of the woe–cries attested in Amos.

2. A clear distinction can be recognized between הוֹי ("woe, alas") utterances and אוֹי ("woe, ah") utterances: אוֹי occurs twenty–three times and is combined with the preposition ל twenty times (e.g., Hos 7:13; 9:12; Is 3:9). Characteristic are the combinations "Woe unto me!" (אוֹי לִי Is 6:5; Jer 4:31;

10:19) and "Woe unto us!" (אוֹי לָנוּ 1 Sam 4:7–8; Jer 4:13; 6:4), which can be designated the "cry of anxiety." If the ל is combined with a second or third–person pronominal suffix, "the cry acquires a threatening overtone."[106]

3. On the other hand, הוֹי is initially a pure interjection,[107] and for that reason alone it must be considered in conjunction with the isolated cry of funerary lamentation ("Alas! alas!" [הוֹ־הוֹ 5:16]). הוֹי occurs a total of fifty–one times, but in combination with a preposition ("to, over, unto" [לְ, אֶל, עַל]) only four times. Of the forty–seven remaining instances, six belong (as in the case of 5:16) directly to funerary lamentation (1 Kgs 13:30; Jer 22:18 [four times] and 34:5); four further instances show that in later times the word deteriorated to a general exhortation ("Ho!" "Up!" Is 55:1; Zech 2:10 [6] [twice], 11 [7]). In the great majority of the remaining passages, הוֹי is followed by a participle, (twenty–three times); otherwise it is usually followed by a noun which, like the participle, characterizes the behavior of the one to whom this catchword of funerary lamentation is applied. Occasionally our interjection is followed by a name.[108]

On the basis of these inquiries, one can maintain that there is a clear syntactic difference between "woe unto" (אוֹי לְ־) and "woe, alas" (הוֹי) continued by a nominative but without intervening preposition; the two expressions are recognizable, in terms of their respective primary meanings, as on the one hand a cry of anxiety ("woe unto me/us" [אוֹי לִי / לָנוּ]), and on the other hand as a cry of funerary lamentation ("Alas my brother/sister" [הוֹי אָחִי / אָחוֹת]).

Turning to a consideration of the still unresolved problems, it seems to me that the question of the relationship between the woe–sayings and the series of curses is relatively easy to answer. Several arguments

---

99   Of the literature cited on pp. 226–27, the following studies (listed in order of first publication) should be singled out here: Westermann, *Basic Forms* 189–98 [137–42] (1967 [1960, ²1964]); Gerstenberger, "Woe–Oracles," 249–63 (1962); Wolff, *Amos the Prophet*, 17–34 [12–23] (1973 [1964]); Fohrer, "Prophetie," 25–47 (1966); Wanke, "אוֹי," 215–18 (1966); Clifford, "*Hôy*," 458–64 (1966); Williams, "Alas–Oracles," 75–91 (1967); Crenshaw, "Influence," 42–52 (1967); Wildberger, *Jesaja*, 175–202 (1968); Hermisson, *Spruchweisheit*, 88–89 (1968).

100   Sigmund Mowinckel, *Psalmenstudien V: Segen und Fluch in Israels Kult und Psalmendichtung*, Videnaskapsselskapets Skrifter, II. Hist.–Filos. Klasse, 1923/3 (Kristiania, 1924), 119. [Cf. *idem, The Psalms in Israel's Worship*, vol. 2, tr. D. R. Ap–Thomas (New York and Nashville: Abingdon, 1962), 50.]

101   *Basic Forms*, 190–98 [137ff].

102   Johannes Hempel, *Die althebräische Literatur und ihr hellenistisch–jüdisches Nachleben* (Wildpark–Potsdam, 1930), 66.

103   "אוֹי," 218.

104   "*Hôy*," 458–64.

105   Gerstenberger, "Woe–Oracles"; Wolff, *Amos the Prophet*, 17ff [12ff]; Williams, "Alas–Oracles," 84–85.

106   Wanke, "אוֹי," 217.

107   Williams, "Alas–Oracles," 82, 86, 89.

108   The stafistics offered above reveal considerable variations in places. Christof Hardmeier has re–examined them and has presented the following results for the total of fifty–one הוֹי passages:
a) 6x funerary lamentation: 1 Kgs 13:30; Jer 22:18 (4x); 34:5.

speak for the independence of the woe–cries. They are widely attested in the older prophecy, exhibiting a constant basic form with a variety of nuances. In contrast, the related form of the curse here under consideration, "cursed be he who . . ." (אָרוּר plus participle), is to be found only in the curse–dodecalogue of Dtn 27. If this particular form were characteristic of the curses, one would expect to find it more widely attested. Above all, the complete absence of curses in the older prophecy, in contrast to the presence there of numerous woe–cries, is hardly an intelligible phenomenon if we suppose the prophets to have developed their woe–cries merely by altering the form of curse–utterances. Finally, the series of curses is constructed throughout of single participial clauses, with the participles in the singular; conversely, the woe–cries regularly exhibit a combination of plural participles and finite verb forms (Hardmeier). Consequently, the more recent studies have generally ceased to deny the independence of the woe–cries.[109]

More difficult to resolve remains the question of whether the prophets adopted the cry of funerary lamentation when they first came to shape their woe–oracles, or whether instead the basic form of the woe–oracle, attested for the first time in Amos, already existed in the milieu of pedagogical clan wisdom. The main objection against the latter postulate is that there is no literary evidence for such a form in clan wisdom. Nevertheless, I am of the opinion that the basic form was available to Amos.

1. Although it is probable that the "alas! alas!" (הוֹ־הוֹ) cry of the skilled mourners, which Amos cites

in 5:16, is very closely related to the cry of "woe!" (הוֹי), it is nonetheless significant that Amos does not open his woe–oracle with this cry of הוֹ which he knew from the practice of funerary lamentation. This can adequately be explained only on the grounds that the form underlying the oracle with הוֹי had already been coined.

2. However, this הוֹי participle is also attested elsewhere in cries of funerary lamentation: the expressions "Alas my brother" (הוֹי אָחִי 1 Kgs 13:30; Jer 22:18a), "Alas (my) sister" (הוֹי אָחוֹת Jer 22:18a), "Alas (my) lord" (הוֹי אָדוֹן Jer 22:18b; 34:5), viewed in conjunction with the use of הוֹ in 5:16, show that the cry was at home in the extended family, in the settlement–community of the clan. If one is to assume the existence of a basic form of the woe–oracles before Amos, then it is to be found precisely in this realm of the clan. The distance between those who performed funerary lamentation (cf. "those who are skilled in wailing" [יוֹדְעֵי נֶהִי] in 5:16) and those who intoned artistic funerary lament songs (as does Amos himself in 5:2) could not have been very great. In Jer 9:16 [17] the mourning women are called at the same time the "wise women."

3. Within the prophecy of the eighth century, the same formal type of woe–oracle attested in Amos is also found in Isaiah (5:8–24; 10:1–4; 28:1ff; 29:1ff, 15; 30:1ff; 31:1ff) and Micah (2:1ff). Isaiah, while preserving the same basic form, shows on the one hand a special closeness to uniquely sapiential themes (5:20–21), and on the other hand extensive variations on that basic form. Considering the passage in Micah

---

b) 8x independent interjection:
  4x "Woe!" Is 1:24; 17:12; Jer 30:7; 47:6;
  4x "Ho!" "Up!" Is 55:1; Zech 2:10 [6] (2x), 11 [7].
c) 2x with names, without preposition: Is 10:5 (Assyria); Is 29:1 (Ariel).
d) 4x with preposition:
  "against" (עַל) Jer 50:27 (+suffix); Ezek 13:3 (+noun);
  "unto" (אֶל) Jer 48:1 (+name);
  "to" (לְ) Ezek 13:18 (+participle).
e) 3x with adjective: Is 5:21, 22; Am 6:1.
f) 5x with substantive: Is 1:4; 18:1; 28:1; 30:1; Nah 3:1.
g) 4x with a substantivized participle: Jer 23:1; Ezek 34:2; Zeph 2:5; Zech 11:17.
h) 19x with participle: Is 5:8, 11, 18, 20; 10:1; 29:15; 31:1; 45:9, 10; Jer 22:13; Am 5:18; Mi 2:1; Hab 2:6, 9, 12, 15, 19; Zeph 3:1.
  In the older texts the participles are almost always plural (12x: Is 5:8, 11, 18, 20; 10:1; 29:15; 31:1; Am 5:18; Mi 2:1; Jer 23:1; Ezek 34:2; Zeph

2:5); in the younger ones they are usually singular (11x: Is 33:1; 45:9, 10; Jer 22:13; Hab 2:6, 9, 12, 15, 19; Zeph 3:1; Zech 11:17).

Only the Masoretic text forms have been considered, and none of the conjectures (on Am 5:7, see textual note "g"; on 6:13, see textual note "a"). Also, these statistics refer only to the words immediately subsequent to הוֹי; they do not include, for example, the participles which frequently occur in the continuation of the oracle (cf. Am 6:1 + 3–6).

109 So Wanke, "אוֹי"; Clifford, "Hôy"; and Williams, "Alas–Oracles."

as well, it is highly unlikely that both of these eighth century prophets were directly dependent upon Amos; it is more probable that there was a common form available to all three, a form that was cultivated in certain circles of Israel.[110] This in no way excludes the possibility that the traditions of Amos, transmitted by the school of Amos' disciples, exerted a formative influence in certain areas.

4. In the case of Isaiah it can be seen that alongside the woe–cries there can appear an אוֹי–saying, clearly distinguishable in terms of its origin. Such a saying is also to be found in Eccl 10:16 (following the customary textual emendation), and it is presupposed in Prv 23:29–30. The interchange between the different expressions "woe–sorrow" (אוֹי—אֲבוֹי) in this last reference, in conjunction with the participial formulations familiar from the woe–cries, shows that there were sapiential circles in Israel in which the old distinctions between הוֹי and אוֹי, as well as the dialectal differences between "woe" (הוֹי) and "alas!" (הוֹ), had become fuzzy.[111] In view of such possible transformations, one learns also to keep an eye open for related themes, especially since no one denies that at least the here–cited אוֹי–sayings belong to the larger stock of wisdom sayings.[112]

5. If it is methodologically correct, on the basis of several passages exhibiting a fluent form–critical transition between הוֹי–sayings and אוֹי–sayings, to draw also the latter into our considerations, then we find ourselves with a relatively small set of themes which indicate very strongly the wisdom origin of the prophetic woe–oracle. There are certain basic pedagogical, legal and socio–ethical questions which must be clarified within the context of human life in community. The set of themes encompassed by these questions clearly ties the prophetic woe–oracles together and further indicates their association with wisdom material. "Justice" (מֹשׁפֹט) and "righteous(ness)" (צֹדֹק[ה]) are the theme not only of Am 5:7 but also of the woe–oracle in Jer 22:13 (cf. v 18!). These concepts also stand behind Is 5:20 and 23–24 (cf. v 7), where the element of the comparison with bitterness

reminds one especially vividly of Am 5:7a (cf. Prv 5:4). The concomitant craving for pleasure and greed for power ties Am 6:1 + 3–6 thematically not only to Is 5:8, 11, 22 and Mi 2:1–2 but also to Prv 23:29–35 and Eccl 10:16. The arrogance of the leaders appears in Am 6:1 as in Is 5:19 and 21. One consistently observes an underlying relationship in basic form while the nature of the actual expression varies. Such similarity becomes understandable if there was a wisdom ethos, familiar to Amos, which treated such themes in this basic form.[113]

6. The likelihood that Amos was not the first to coin woe–sayings is considerable, since it is demonstrable and uncontested that he took up other wisdom forms elsewhere. Besides the didactic questions,[114] we must recall in this connection especially the graded numerical sayings, which he presupposes to be well known.[115] The recollection of these sayings also disarms the objection that woe–cries, in the oracular form in which they first appear in Amos and then soon afterwards in Isaiah and Micah, are not elsewhere literarily attested. Numerical sayings of the three–four sequence, reminiscent of Am 1:3—2:6, are elsewhere attested with regard to their form; with regard to their content, however, they are without literary parallels. Here is another case in which we are dealing with a stock of aphoristic material which, like the woe–cries, was transmitted solely by oral means (unlike the practice in the schools of the royal court). It was in these clan circles that Amos was nurtured. The same situation applies with regard to funerary laments of the sort we encounter in 5:2; this became literature only with Amos, but the genre itself was certainly not invented by him. Numerical sayings, woe–oracles and funerary laments are all strongly inclined to take over pre–shaped elements of oral clan wisdom; after all, the younger generation of the extended family needed instruction. Why should it be more probable that Amos adopted "sophisticated wisdom," perhaps at the school of higher learning in Jerusalem?[116] Why should not Judean country towns like Tekoa, with their "circle" (סוֹד) of elders, have

---

110 Wolff, *Amos the Prophet*, 77–85 [53–58].

111 Cf. Fohrer, "Prophetie," 38; Williams, "Alas–Oracles," 82.

112 Cf. Wildberger, *Jesaja*, 126–27; William L. Holladay, "Isa. 3:10–11: An Archaic Wisdom Passage," *VT* 18 (1968): 481–87. For the parallel offered by the "happy / blessed" (אֹשֹׁרֹי) sayings, I merely refer briefly here to Wildberger, *Jesaja*, 126–27; and Wolff, *Amos the Prophet*, 25–29 [18–21]; and for the comparable Egyptian material to Christa Bauer–Kayatz, *Studien zu Proverbien 1–9*, WMANT 22 (Neukirchen–Vluyn: Neukirchener Verlag, 1966), 51–52.

113 See the discussion of the key words below.

114 See p. 93–94.

115 See p. 96.

116 Cf. Hermisson, *Spruchweisheit*, 91–92.

been places where ancient Israelite clan wisdom was cultivated?[117] Why should such clan wisdom not have been taken up also in the "schools" accessible to Micah and Isaiah?

7. It is the dynamics of oral tradition, in the last analysis, which explains the variants in the basic form of the woe–cry. The pedagogic woe–sayings, whose existence within oral clan wisdom must be postulated, contained no elaborated element of threat. The function of these sayings was, of course, to issue a warning against the way which led to death. This function explains why 5:7 + 10 represents a closed oracular unit, without a concluding element of threat.[118] The prophet was free to expand the basic form of the woe–cry through addition of an announcement of judgment (cf. 6:7 following 6:1 + 3–6), an element not customary in the earlier wisdom form (cf. also Is 5:21–22). One must certainly stress the fact that, because of its context, the הוי of Amos resonates much more strongly with the unnerving tone of the cry of funerary lamentation than is the case in our postulated pedagogic wisdom sayings.[119]

Those who violated "justice" (משפט) and "righteousness" (צדקה) have led Israel on the road to death. This word pair is of central importance in Amos. It recurs in parallel statements in 5:24 and 6:12, and "justice" (משפט) appears alone in the later interpretation at 5:15.[120] It may be surprising that this word pair is completely unknown in Israel's ancient legal collections in the Pentateuch. We do meet it in similarly parallel statements, however, in old sapiential material. For example, "Better is a little with 'righteousness' (צדקה) than great revenues without 'justice' (משפט)" (Prv 16:8), or "To do 'righteousness' (צדקה) and 'justice' (משפט) is more acceptable to Yahweh than sacrifice" (Prv 21:3). Wisdom even says of herself, "I walk in the way of 'righteousness' (צדקה), in the paths of 'justice' (משפט)" (Prv 8:20). It is therefore not surprising that later the whole of wisdom can be summed up by this word pair (Prv 1:3; 2:9; cf. Gen 18:19). The motive force behind Israel's proverbial

wisdom is thus that the people should not lack "justice" and "righteousness." The next datable occurrence of this word pair, after Amos, is in Isaiah, who accuses Israel of having squandered and spoiled this double gift (1:21; 5:7; 28:17). From their ancient Israelite starting point in the knowledge cultivated by the clans, "justice" and "righteousness" must have spread into the wisdom circles of the royal court, functioning in the place of the Egyptian *maat* as the real foundation of the royal throne and as the measuring standard of the kingdom.[121] It is noteworthy that, in the comparison of Jehoiakim with his father, Josiah, "justice" and "righteousness" are explicitly exercised for the benefit of the poor and the oppressed (Jer 22:16–17); it is for the sake of those in need that these qualities are granted to the king. The same point is made in the royal Psalm 72 (vv 1–4, 12–14!). The course of tradition as here sketched should be enough to make it clear that Amos stood very near the sources of the history of our word pair in Israel. For Amos the exercising of "justice" —i.e., the proper functioning of judicial procedures— takes place "in the gate" (בשער 5:10, cf. 5:15). He does not yet speak, as does Hosea shortly after him (5:1), of functions which the royal court and the priests were to perform in the administration of law.[122] Thus by "justice" (משפט) Amos means that order which establishes and preserves peace under the law; this order is realized in practice through the legal decisions made in the gate, where matters of local jurisdiction were settled. "Righteousness" (צדקה) designates behavior which is in keeping with this order, e.g., the willingness of one who himself is legally "in the right" (צדיק) to stand up in defense of another who is צדיק, who has been unjustly accused (cf. 2:6 and 5:12).[123]

Amos bemoans those who "turn into" (הפך ל) its opposite the order of law, using here the same verbal expression found in 5:8; 6:12; 8:10 and elsewhere in the Old Testament. Thus "justice" becomes "wormwood" (*Artemisia absinthium*). This little bush–like

---

117 Wolff, *Amos the Prophet*, 77–78 [53–54].
118 On "therefore" (לכן) in 5:11, see p. 233.
119 Cf. Williams, "Alas–Oracles," 85–86.
120 See p. 234.
121 Cf. Hans Walter Wolff, *Frieden ohne Ende: Jesaja 7, 1–17 und 9, 1–6 ausgelegt*, BSt 35 (Neukirchen–Vluyn: Neukirchener Verlag, 1962), 72, where additional literature is cited. Here only the following

texts need be noted: 2 Sam 8:15; Is 9:6 [7]; Ps 72:1–2; and Jer 22:15 in a woe–cry!
122 See Wolff, *Hosea*, 97–98 [125–26].
123 Cf. Alfred Jepsen, "צדק und צדקה im Alten Testament" in *Gottes Wort und Gottes Land: Festschrift H. W. Hertzberg*, ed. Henning Graf Reventlow (Göttingen: Vandenhoeck & Ruprecht, 1965), 78–89; and Hans Heinrich Schmid, *Gerechtigkeit als Weltordnung*:

plant, which can reach a height of 1.2 meters and has finely pinnate leaves, thrives in the area stretching from Spain across north Africa and as far as Iran. In early winter it blossoms and bears fruit. In Palestine it grows primarily in the Negeb, in the Wilderness of Judah, and in the Transjordan region.[124] Though known for its very sharply bitter pulp (cf. Prv 5:4), it is not poisonous. But because it is associated with a repulsive taste, it usually appears in parallelism with "poison" (רֹאשׁ 6:12; Dtn 29:17 [18]; Jer 23:15; Lam 3:19). The word serves to describe the fate of the godless (Dtn 29:17 [18]), of the one driven into exile (Jer 9:14–15 [15–16]), and of one in the misery of dying (Lam 3:19). The legal order was supposed to be the medicinal herb which Yahweh had granted for the purpose of restoring those wronged and freeing those oppressed. Proverbial wisdom had it that "justice" also comes from Yahweh (Prv 29:26; cf. 16:33). Insofar as men call the good evil and the evil good, however, they transform the "sweet" into the "bitter."[125] The parallel colon, employing a new metaphor, says of "righteousness" that it is "cast to the ground" (הניח לארץ; cf. Is 28:2, where the same expression is used to refer to the destructive effect of flood waters). By means of these images, what is happening to the innocent and to those who stand up for them becomes obvious.

■ **10** The righteous encounter—now the imagery of 5:7 is left behind—hatred and aversion. "To hate" (שׂנא) never occurs in the Pentateuchal texts which regulate behavior appropriate to litigation. The older proverbial wisdom, on the other hand, speaks frequently of hatred as a response to honest speech. "He who hates 'reproof' (תּוֹכַחַת) is stupid" (Prv 12:1) or "will die" (Prv 15:10). "Reproof" (תּוֹכַחַת) is what is spoken by "one who reproves" (מוכיח). "A righteous man hates 'the lying word' (דְּבַד־שֶׁקֶר)" (Prv 13:5). "Bloodthirsty men hate one who is 'blameless' (תָּם)" (Prv 29:10; cf. Prv 26:28). Amos reflects this realm of language when he speaks of those who abhor "one who testifies fully" (דבר תמים). He has in mind hatred "in the gate," in the clan's place of judgment. Proverbial wisdom also knows of injustice in the gate (Prv 22:22). The specific reference is to the space in front of the inner side of the gate, together with the side rooms of the gate's passageway with its niches, which were partially lined with benches.[126] There the plaintiff, the accused, and the witnesses assembled before the elders (Dtn 21:19; 25:7; Ruth 4:11), among whom was the "one who reproves" (מוכיח).[127] Specifically, he was the one in the circle of the elders who determined which party was in the right.[128] While the "one who reproves" wielded the authority of decision—even though it must not be assumed that he held an ongoing office in the circle of elders—the "one who testifies fully" (דבר תמים) must be sought in the circle of the witnesses. On the basis of Prv 29:10, one could think that this expression refers to a "spokesman for the blameless." However, it is much more likely that the word תמים identifies a quality of the speaker; he is a "truthful" speaker and as such hates the "lying word" (דְּבַר־שֶׁקֶר Prv 13:5). Therefore "one who testifies fully" (דבר תמים) can elsewhere stand in parallelism to "one who walks in integrity" (הוֹלֵךְ תָּמִים Prv 28:18; Ps 15:2). Thus the particular choice of words in this woe–oracle of Amos shows it to have been shaped by an ethos which must have been known to Amos on the basis of his own participation within the circle of the clan elders. The woe–oracle remains without an elaborated announcement of judgment.

Hintergrund und Geschichte des alttestamentlichen Gerechtigkeitsbegriffes, BHTh 40 (Tübingen: J. C. B. Mohr [Paul Siebeck], 1968), 111–13, and 1–2 (where voluminous literature is listed). On the meaning of νόμος and δίκη in the Greek Polis after Hesiod (c. 700) and Solon (c. 650), cf. Rudolf Bultmann, *Primitive Christianity in its Contemporary Setting*, tr. R. H. Fuller (New York: Meridian Books, 1956), 105 [*Das Urchristentum im Rahmen des antiken Religionen* (Zürich: Artemis–Verlag, 1949), 117–18].

124 Cf. M. Zohary, *Plant Life of Palestine*, Chronica Botanica, New Series of Plant Science Books 33 (New York: Ronald Press Co., 1962), 134; and Carl Heinz Peisker, "Wermut," *BHHW* 3, 2167.

125 See the corresponding woe–oracle of Isaiah in 5:20–23; and on the context of these passages, Wildberger, *Jesaja*, 195–96.

126 Cf. Noth, *World*, 151–52 [138]; Lienhard Delekat, "Tor, Tür," *BHHW* 3, 2009–10; de Vaux, *Israel*, 152–55.

127 On יכח hip'il ("to reprove"), see Wolff, *Hosea*, 76 [94].

128 Cf. Prv 24:25 with vv 23–24; cf. also Prv 28:23; 25:12; Is 29:21; and Hans Jochen Boecker, *Rede-*

■ **11** Probably only subsequently attached to the foregoing, by means of a "therefore" (לָכֵן),[129] v 11 is an independent and differently motivated threat of punishment. Furthermore, this oracle moves into direct address. Now it is the greedy urge to multiply possessions at the expense of the poor which leads to the accusation. The second colon certainly refers to tribute exacted in "grain." In contrast to the more common דָּגָן, the word בַּר designates that "grain" which becomes a trade commodity (as 8:5–6 well illustrates).[130] The corresponding element in the first colon is uncertain, but the parallelism certainly suggests the conjecture "to extort rent."[131] In invoices from the temple archive in Nippur from Cassite times there appears the expression *šabāšu šibša ina eqli* ("to receive rent from a field").[132] Ex 22:24 [25] forbids the taking of interest on money lent to a "poor man" (עָנִי; cf. Lev 25:37; Dtn 23:20 [19]). Proverbial wisdom has even more to say on this subject, and here too Amos stands closer to the sapiential than to the legal realm. Prv 28:8 ("He who increases his wealth by interest and usury gathers it for him who is kind to the poor") speaks not only in general terms of property and raising of prices but also refers to the poor as דַּלִּים, just as does Amos. The word דלים in this particular context is unknown to the collections of cultic law. Ex 23:3 and Lev 19:15 use it, but the reference is solely to instructions for judicial proceedings. The cultic law also restricts its reference to money alone when the subject of interest arises. Furthermore, unlike proverbial wisdom it is unfamiliar with the word which designates grain in its

capacity as a trade commodity (בר Prv 11:26; 14:4).

It is at the expense of their impoverished tenants that the ones here addressed have been able to afford expensive buildings of smoothly hewn stone instead of the clay brick houses that crumble easily (cf. Is 9:9 [10]).[133] This method of building with stone, perhaps learned from the Phoenicians, was used for the first time in Israel when Solomon built the Temple and the palace in Jerusalem.[134] "Splendid" (חמר) vineyards have also been planted; their desirable location and their exemplary layout are what render them particularly valuable (cf. Is 5:1–2). The building of a house and the planting of a vineyard are uniquely the undertakings which establish for a man a free and independent life, but the leading class of Amos' contemporaries are carrying out these ventures in a pretentious manner previously unknown. However, this class will not get to enjoy its magnificent embellishments. The form of the threat reminds one of curses in the Sefîre texts leveled against those guilty of breach of treaty: ". . . Seven mares shall suckle a colt, and it shall not be s[ated. Seven] cows shall suckle a calf, and it shall not be sated. Seven ewes shall suckle a lamb, and [it shall not be s]ated. His seven *daughters* shall go *in search of* food, and they shall not *arouse concern*."[135] The same form of speech, which states an activity in the first clause and in the subsequent clause identifies it as futile, is well attested in the Old Testament;[136] in Dtn 28:30aβb even the content is similar. Nowhere else is there found in Amos this form of threat, namely of the futility of high human achievement and of the

---

formen des Rechtslebens im Alten Testament, WMANT 14 (Neukirchen–Vluyn: Neukirchener Verlag, 1964), 45–47. Cf. further Seeligmann, "Gerichtsverfahren," 266ff. On the connection of this office with the "school of wisdom," see Richter, *Recht*, 166–86.

129 See p. 233.

130 Cf. also Gen 42:3, 25–26; Prv 11:26; etc. Cf. also Dalman, *Arbeit* 3, 161. It is also noteworthy that Akkadian *bāru* III means "tax, tribute" (*AHW* 1, 108) and thus corresponds precisely to מַשְׂאֵת ("levy, tribute").

131 See textual note "aa" to 5:11.

132 Cf. Harry Torczyner (Tur–Sinai), *Altbabylonische Tempelrechnungen*, Denkschriften d. kais. Akad. d. Wiss. in Wien 55 (Vienna, 1913), 130, citing numerous instances of *šibšu* = "rent, tribute."

133 Cf. Noth, *World*, 153–54 [139–40] and 149 [137] figs. D 1–2; and Rolf Knierim, "Haus," *BHHW* 2, 657–60.

134 1 Kgs 5:31 [17]; 6:36; 7:9, 11, 12. See Noth, *Könige*, 139; and also Albrecht Alt, "Archäologische Fragen zur Baugeschichte von Jerusalem und Samaria in der israelitischen Königszeit" in *Kleine Schiften* 3, 311–19.

135 Franz Rosenthal, *ANET*[3], 659b. Text: *KAI* 222A.22–24. Cf. the Annals of Ashurbanipal 9: A. Leo Oppenheim, *ANET*[3], 300a.

136 Hos 4:10; Mi 6:14–15; Lev 26:26b; Dtn 28:30, 38–41. On the curse of futility or uselessness, cf. Delbert R. Hillers, *Treaty–Curses and the Old Testament Prophets*, Biblica et Orientalia 16 (Rome: Pontifical Biblical Institute, 1964), 28–29.

unattainability of pursued goals.[137]

■ 12 With v 12 the element of accusation in a new oracle begins.[138] It indeed seems more likely that the one speaking here is Amos rather than Yahweh, especially since it is not until 5:16–17, which in all probability is the original continuation of this verse,[139] that we meet an introductory messenger formula, which identifies a speech as an oracle of Yahweh. Elsewhere as well the accusation as an utterance of the prophet may precede the oracle of Yahweh (3:9–10; 4:1; 7:16). Amos has already introduced himself as the speaker in 5:1. Just as in the preceding v 11, but differently from the woe–oracle in 5:7 + 10, the accused are addressed directly. That woe–oracle may have provoked a passionate defence, against which Amos now cites further examples of the sort of injustice identified in v 11. First of all, however, Amos affirms in a summary statement that he has indeed learned of ("I know" [ידעתי]) "numerous crimes and formidable wrong-doings."[140] Apparently here too the oracle is directed against personal malfeasance (cf. v 12b). The word חטאת ("sin, wrongdoing"), which is very common throughout the rest of the Old Testament but appears only rarely in Amos, is generally applied without precise distinction to misdeeds of a legal, socio–ethical or cultic sort, but here it merely adds emphasis to the particular crimes in the gate (v 12b) which comprise the specifics of the accusation. The parallel "numerous—formidable" (עצמים—רבים) occurs frequently,[141] but nations constitute the usual point of reference. This summarizing statement (v 12a) gives added weight to the newly reopened accusation. The following three individual examples, two formed by participial expressions and one using a finite verb, detail the accusation. 1) The accused persecute the "innocent" (צדיק), who here—as in 2:6—is one practicing "righteousness" (צדקה 5:7), conducting himself in a humane fashion, and who is therefore able to stand blameless before a court of law. Such innocent people are treated with hostility; "to constrict, press hard" (צרר) describes the activity of the "persecutor" or "oppressor" (צר; cf. 3:11, referring to the military adversary who surrounds his enemy). 2) The next statement becomes more concrete, accusing of accepting bribes those whose task it is to determine which party is in the right. This is an illustration of the general reproach in v 7 ("cast righteousness to the ground"). In Is 1:23 and the woe–oracle of Is 5:23, Isaiah uses terminology different from that of Amos. Isaiah calls the bribe שֹׁחַד ("gift"), whereas Amos calls it כֹּפֶר (literally "that which is to cover up something," hence perhaps "hush–money"). The two terms are combined in the same saying in Prv 6:35. This second elaboration is closely related to the first. Bribery leads to declaring the innocent guilty and the guilty innocent. The sapiential teachings concerning administration of justice fiercely combat bribery (Is 5:23; Prv 17:15). The great Hymn to Shamash offers an extra–biblical parallel:[142]

> The unrighteous judge
>   thou dost make to see imprisonment.
> The receiver of a bribe who perverts (justice)
>   thou dost make to bear punishment.
> He who does not accept a bribe
>   (but) intercedes for the weak,
> Is well–pleasing to Shamash
>   (and) enriches (his) life.
> . . . .
> He who invests money
>   at an exorbitant rate of reckoning—
>   what does he gain?

3) The final verbal clause wraps up the detailing of the accusation with a reference to the most cherished concern of the prophet, namely the "needy" (אביונים).[143] As the oppressed innocents, the "poor" become the truly "righteous" in Israel.[144] The expression "in the gate" (בשער) shows that in the whole of v 12 it is the local judiciary proceeding which is in view, as in 5:7 + 10.[145] "To turn aside" (נטה hip'il) usually has

137   Cf. the woe–oracle in Is 5:8–10 for a conceptual parallel.

138   On כי ("indeed") as well as on the connection between 5:12 and 16–17, see p. 233.

139   See p. 233.

140   On פשע, see pp. 152–53.

141   Cf. Is 8:7; Mi 4:3; Is 53:12; Zech 8:22; Dtn 7:1; Ps 135:10; Prv 7:26.

142   2.41–47: Ferris J. Stephens, *ANET*³, 388; also translated in Adam Falkenstein and Wolfram von Soden, *Sumerische und Akkadische Hymnen und Gebete*, Bibliothek der Alten Welt. Reihe Der Alte Orient (Zürich: Artemis Verlag, 1953), 243–44.

143   On this concept, see p. 165.

144   Cf. Arvid S. Kapelrud, "New Ideas in Amos" in *Volume du Congrès, Genève, 1965*, SVT 15 (Leiden:

as its direct object "justice" (מֹשֶפָּט).[146] In his abbreviated form of the usual expression, however, Amos sees immediately that it is the poor themselves who are laid low, who are denied access to their rights. Thus the woe–oracle against those who practice injustice (5:7 + 10) is here, as in 5:11aα, illustrated in the final analysis by reference to those victimized by that injustice.

■ **16, 17** The judgment announced because of the perversions of justice (5:12) calls to mind the original "woe" of funerary lamentation which stands behind the "woe" of the woe–oracle (5:7 cj.).[147] "Lamentation" (מֹסְפֵּד, three times in vv 16–17!) and "mourning" (אֵבֶל) are cited as the technical terms for the cries of funerary lamentation and the accompanying ritual.[148] The frequency of this terminology already suggests that which is then made clear by the descriptions of locale, namely how widespread the funerary lamentation is to be. It will not only be intoned in all the open "squares" (רְחֹבוֹת designates the more spacious areas where people can assemble, such as before the gate, at the sanctuary, or upon the local threshing floor), but it will also penetrate into the narrow "streets" (חוּצוֹת) between the houses of the city. It will even be carried from the settlements out into the vineyards, which otherwise provide the setting for pleasant anticipation and unrestrained joy (cf. 5:11b). Gese's proposal[149] to read "and among all vinedressers" (וּבְכָל-כֹּרְמִים) in place of M's "and in all vineyards" (וּבְכָל-כְּרָמִים) is unlikely in view of the fact that both the parallel expressions in v 16αβ–γ ("in all squares" [וּבְכָל-רְחֹבוֹת] and "in all streets" [בְּכָל-חוּצוֹת]) are designations of place. On the other hand, Gese's philological explanation[150] of אִכָּר ("farmhand") as referring to the landless agricultural laborer is of conceptual significance insofar as it helps

to illustrate the fact that the exploited and the victimized (5:11a, 12b) are even further called upon to perform the service of funerary lamentation for their oppressors. "Those who are skilled in wailing" (יוֹדְעֵי נֶהִי) cannot alone fulfill their duties in the face of the vast number who have died. The Hebrew idiom here suggests that there must have been a whole guild of funerary singers[151] in which the personnel received special training. In Jer 9:16 [17] the mourning women are at the same time called "wise, skillful women" (חֲכָמוֹת). Those "skilled in wailing" surely did not only shout forth "Alas! Alas!" (הוֹ-הוֹ) in endless repetition. (Perhaps "wailing" [נֶהִי] is etymologically related to "alas" [הוֹ].[152]) They must also have mastered in some degree the poet's art, at least as appropriate to the forms of public proclamation and of lamentation in the case of death (cf. 5:1–2). Furthermore, they must also have been knowledgeable concerning the comprehensive ceremonial requirements of fasting: rending of clothes, wearing of "sackcloth," shearing the hair, sprinkling dust on the head, and much else besides (cf. 8:10).[153] Thus the oracle of Yahweh mediated through Amos envisions Israelite city and countryside submerged in a single swell of funerary lamentation.

At the very end of the oracle there is a brief, terse underscoring of who actually stands behind this nationwide loss of life. Yahweh himself says, "For I will pass through your midst." It is like an echo of the third and fourth visions (7:8; 8:2); Yahweh no longer "passes by" (עָבַר ל), sparing his people (cf. 9:4). No punitive acts by Yahweh of any kind are specified,[154] but neither is it merely Yahweh's absence that constitutes his punishment upon Israel. His active presence alone, his personal intervention, will effect Israel's death.[155]

■ **13** V 13 makes much less sense as the original con-

E. J. Brill, 1966), 193–206.

145 See pp. 245–46.

146 Prv 17:23 (in connection with a reference to a bribe!); Ex 23:6; Dtn 16:19; 1 Sam 8:3, etc. Cf. Richter, *Recht*, 156; and above p. 166 on 2:7aβ.

147 On "Alas! alas!" (הוֹ-הוֹ) in relation to "woe" (הוֹי), see pp. 243–44.

148 See pp. 32–33 on Joel 1:11–14, and pp. 235–37, on Am 5:1–2.

149 "Beiträge," 434.

150 *Ibid.*, 432–33.

151 Jahnow, *Leichenlied*, 2, 58.

152 *Ibid.*, 91. Cf. Koehler–Baumgartner, 599.

153 Cf. Kutsch, "Trauerbräuche," 25–42; and also Gustav Stählin, *TDNT* 3, 150, with reference to the θρήνων ἔξαρχοι ("precentors of funeral dirges") of Homer and the "paid θρήνων σοφισταί ["masters of funeral dirges"] of the Greeks."

154 See pp. 102–03.

155 On the expression "to pass through" (עָבַר ב), cf. especially Ex 12:12; Na 2:1 [1:15]; and also Crenshaw, "Theophanic Tradition," 206–07.

tinuation of 5:12 than does 5:16–17. When would Amos have allowed an accusation like that of 5:12 to dissipate into such a reflection? Would he have here expressed his own wisdom, which he then had to contravene on Yahweh's command?[156] As a later addition to the coherent oracle in 5:12 + 16–17, however, this statement becomes intelligible. The person of insight will keep silent, not with respect to the injustice in the gate (5:12) but rather with respect to the judgment which Yahweh sends against the land (5:16–17). That is the "evil time" (cf. Mi 2:3bβ). The explanation that silence has been called for would be understandable on the part of a disciple of Amos, because he probably sees the judgment formerly proclaimed upon the northern kingdom as already drawing near.[157] He reminds the person of understanding that resistance to the old prophetic word (cf. 7:10–11) has now finally lost every justification. The fact that v 13, together with 5:14–15, breaks the old connection of 5:12 and 16 argues in favor of that interpretation of v 13 which sees it as having arisen in the course of the discussion concerning the transmitted message of Amos, and that especially in the time when Assyria was threatening the security of the northern kingdom.

■ **14** Vv 14–15 lead us right into this discussion. These verses have rightly been regarded as an interpretation of 5:4–5.[158] In the light of their variations, however, these interpretive verses are more readily explainable as having come from a disciple of Amos[159] than as having issued from the prophet's own mouth. The antithetic parallelism of admonition and warning, with an ensuing purpose clause, is a construction of purely sapiential character,[160] here functioning as an imitation and interpretation of 5:4–5. The "seek me" (Yahweh) of 5:4 is here read to mean "seek good"; the "do not seek Bethel . . . Gilgal" of 5:5 here becomes ". . . not evil." "And not evil" (וְלֹא־רָע) is an abbreviated vetitive, to which one must mentally supply the imperative "seek!" (דִּרְשׁוּ) from the immediately pre-

ceding element.[161] Apart from the antithesis constitutive of the form, the only other significant borrowing from the old prophetic oracle is the use of the imperative "seek!" (דִּרְשׁוּ). The particular juxtaposition "seek good" (דִּרְשׁוּ טוֹב) is elsewhere attested only in Est 10:3. However, a similar formulation is found in Prv 11:27: "He who pursues good (שֹׁחֵר טוֹב) gains favor, but he who seeks evil (וְדֹרֵשׁ רָעָה), it will find him." דרש here means "to be intent upon, to be concerned for."[162] For the wise man, ability to discern between good and evil is that which is really worth striving for (1 Kgs 3:9). V 15a further defines this ability as the capacity to make the right judicial decision ("justice" [מִשְׁפָּט]), and in so doing it stands both in succession to Amos (5:7, 10, 12) and within the traditions of wisdom (1 Kgs 3:11).[163] "This is not the language of a man who wants to regulate life by law."[164]

The assurance of life in 5:4b is likewise more closely defined. For one thing, the conjunction "that" (לְמַעַן), more than the juxtaposition of the two imperatives in 5:4b, emphasizes "life" as the goal, now being more intensely pursued because it has in the meantime obviously become more endangered. Above all, however, that assurance is elaborated upon by the final clause of v 14, which picks up a discussion: "and (that) it may be so—Yahweh is with you!—just as you say." "Yahweh is with you," an ancient word of assurance within the context of holy war,[165] was probably used during the Assyrian crisis as a slogan against those who reminded their hearers of the old threat of Amos. If the later additions derive from discussions with pilgrims to Beer–sheba from the northern kingdom,[166] then these pilgrims may also have affirmed as their special creed the promise of loyalty to Isaac (cf. Gen 46:4a; 26:3).[167] No matter how the security of his antagonists may have been defended, however, the disciple of Amos puts them under the obligation to seek good. V 14a and v 14b doubtlessly stand "in a conditional relationship to each other," even though כן ("so") must be under-

---

156 So Amsler, 211.
157 On the question of the dating of the old school of Amos, see p. 110.
158 So Hesse, "Amos 5," 1–17.
159 See p. 234.
160 Cf. Prv 24:21–22 and 25:9–10. On the use of לְמַעַן ("in order that") cf., e.g., Prv 19:20 and Ex 20:12.
161 Gesenius–Kautzsch–Cowley, par. 152g.

162 Cf. p. 238, on 5:4; and Westermann, "Fragen," 15.
163 Cf. Noth, Könige, 51.
164 von Rad, Theology 2, 186 [193].
165 Dtn 20:4; Mi 3:11; Is 7:14; 8:10; Ps 46:8 [7], 12 [11].
166 See p. 239, on 5:5aβ.
167 On the promise, see Horst Dietrich Preuss, ". . . ich will mit dir sein!" ZAW 80 (1968): 153.

stood with reference to the final clause (כאשר "just as . . ."; cf. 3:12).[168]

■ **15** The popular cultic slogan about life is once more confronted with its unalterable and now doubly clarified condition. "Seek!" (v 14a)—the decisive act—is now defined as hate and love in relation to evil and good. The chiastic arrangement "good—evil" (v 14a) and "evil—good" (v 15a) indicates that now, in v 15, the emphasis shifts to a renunciation of that sort of life also rejected by Amos. To do good, for its part, is explained as to "establish justice in the gate." Thus 5:4–5 is interpreted with the help of 5:7, 10, and 12. "To establish" (יצג hip'il) generally designates the setting up of objects;[169] here it means "to render effective."[170]

V 14 made conditional the religiously based sense of security with regard to the political future; v 15 goes on to place Yahweh's turning away from executing the full judgment threatened by the prophet, even in the case of improved behavior, under a "perhaps." A prophet's disciple, one schooled in the wisdom traditions, could speak in such a reticent, almost skeptical manner.[171] However, no prophet like an Amos could speak in this way. What Yahweh may "perhaps" do is "be gracious" (חנן). In its original meaning, this word expresses the obligation of a master to treat his servant benevolently and in accord with a sense of confraternity. The word presupposes magnanimity on the part of the superior, and loyalty on the part of the inferior; the semantic range of this word does not really embrace forgiveness and guilt.[172] The word is used with reference to Yahweh very often in the cultic cry of the psalms: "Be gracious to me!" (חָנֵּנִי) or "Be gracious to us!" (חָנֵּנוּ).[173] Thus here also the interpreter is probably responding to statements of the participants in the dispute. If all one can hope for is

that Yahweh may be gracious to a "remnant of Joseph," then apparently irrevocable losses are already presupposed. Such losses did occur under Tiglath–pileser III in 733, when the regions of Dor, Megiddo and Gilead were annexed as Assyrian provinces.[174] Amos himself never refers to the northern kingdom as "Joseph."[175]

Aim

A stench of death permeates all the original oracles of Amos in this section. The funerary lament, which the prophet himself intones at the beginning (v 2) over an Israel doomed to an untimely death, reverberates polyphonically at the end (vv 16–17) across city and countryside. In between there stand images of an army bled white (v 3) and of devasted houses and vineyards (v 11). The reason for it all is seen in Israel's behavior, which stands under the old woe–cry of funerary lamentation (vv 7 + 10) and which consists of manipulating the rights of the innocent and practicing extortion upon the dispossessed (vv 11, 12). Neither Bethel nor Gilgal, which is to say no pilgrimage to the old sites memorializing the promises to the fathers and the giving of the land, can save those who have perverted, to the detriment of the poor, the beneficial ordering of Israelite clan life (v 5).

Like a faint reminiscence of something nearly forgotten or otherwise hard to place, there glimmer from out of the dark shadows of death the words "Seek me! Then you shall live!" (v 4b). No sooner are these words spoken by Amos than they are again swallowed up by dark threats (v 5b).[176] Amos is the prophet, not of the eleventh, but of the twelfth hour.[177] For the state of the northern kingdom as a whole, there appears to be no way at all to avoid the fate of death. "Through death alone wends the way." However, Amos identifies

168 *Contra* Neubauer, "Erwägungen," 305–06.
169 Gen 30:38; Ju 8:27; 1 Sam 5:2; 2 Sam 6:17.
170 On "gate," see p. 246.
171 Cf. Joel 2:14; Jon 3:9; Zeph 2:3; and also above, p. 50.
172 Cf. Karl Wilhelm Neubauer, *Der Stamm* chnn *im Sprachgebrauch des Alten Testaments*, Unpub. Diss. (Berlin, 1964), 55, 110.
173 For the former (which occurs altogether eighteen times) see, e.g., Ps 4:2 [!]; 6:3 [2]; and 9:14 [13]; for the latter, Ps 123:3.
174 Wolff, *Hosea*, 111 [140].

175 Note the different use of terminology in the later interpretation of 5:6 ("house of Joseph"), on the meaning of which see above p. 240. On 6:6b, see below.
176 See pp. 239–40.
177 Cf. Amsler, "Amos," 318–28.

as the death–dealing blow only Yahweh's own intervention (v 17b).

The words in vv 13–15, which interrupt the older course of the material, show that the old prophetic word remained alive in the memory of Isarel down to the beginnings of its fulfillment under Tiglath–pileser III. To those who still lived in the conflict between the prophetic message of death and the old traditons of Yahweh's support and favor, the exhortation merely hinted at by a single word in Amos (v 4b) is now broadly developed as perhaps a possible help toward deliverance. The serious call to decide for the good, by which is meant a prudent restoration of the legal order for the poor, is unambiguous in its formulation. The bolstering of the religiously grounded confidence, on the other hand, is formulated in a strikingly reserved way (vv 14–15). Nonetheless, it is in keeping with the thought of these disciples of the prophet to say "As long as something is given up, so long is humanity not given up hopelessly." [178] Do these same disciples want to assert that the precondition for ultimate hope is the silent acceptance of the intermediate "evil time" (v 13)?

We go on to see how, a century later, the prophetic word continued to play a shaping role on the future. This new sermon in v 6,[179] clearly distinguishable from the work of Amos and his immediate disciples, takes vv 4–5 as its starting point, just as do vv 14–15. If it is correct that v 6 comes from the days of Josiah and his expedition against the sanctuary of Bethel,[180] then the old oracle becomes here, in the face of an accomplished act of divine judgment, an admonition to return and repent; the ultimatum–like warning summons the hearer to render praise to the judge (v 8).

It is remarkable that, of the old oracles of Amos which brought a sweeping message of death for the northern kingdom, only the word "Seek me, then you shall live!" has led to an ongoing proclamation in new situations, an utterance which stood completely in the background for the prophet. What would be more natural than to tie into this same line of development, under the authority of the New Testament message? But should a Christian proclamation be allowed to put more distance between itself and the terror of the prophetic threat of judgment than does the interpretation in vv 13–15 and vv 6 + 8–9? Neither the meaning of Jesus' death on the cross nor the present state of guilt allows that. It would be better to ask whether the funerary lament of Amos ought not to be intoned over whole zones of traditional Christendom, just as it was formerly recited over the northern kingdom. The reasons which prompted Amos to take up funerary lamentation over Israel could help to uncover the corresponding grounds for lamentation presented in the Gospel itself.

---

178 Søren Kierkegaard, *Das Evangelium der Leiden*, tr. Hayo Gerdes; Gesammelte Werke 18 (Düsseldorf: Diederichs, 1953–66), 291.
179 See p. 232.
180 See p. 240.

The Inescapable Grip of Yahweh

Bibliography

Ronald E. Clements
Prophecy and Covenant, SBT 43 (London: SCM, 1965), 107–10.

Siegfried Herrmann
Die prophetischen Heilserwartungen im Alten Testament: Ursprung und Gestaltwandel, BWANT 85 (Stuttgart: W. Kohlhammer, 1965), 120–22.

Gerhard von Rad
Old Testament Theology, vol. 2, tr. D. M. G. Stalker (New York and Evanston: Harper & Row, 1965), 115–20 [129–33].

Klaus Dietrich Schunck
"Strukturlinien in der Entwicklung der Vorstellung vom 'Tag Jahwes'," *VT* 14 (1964): 319–30.

Meir Weiss
"The Origin of the 'Day of the Lord'—Reconsidered," *HUCA* 37 (1966): 29–72.

Hans Wildberger
Jesaja, BK 10/1 (Neukirchen–Vluyn: Neukirchener Verlag, 1972), 91–115 (esp. 91, 105–6).

Walther Zimmerli
Ezechiel, BK 13/1 (Neukirchen–Vluyn: Neukirchener Verlag, 1969), 158–86 (esp. 166–68).

See above pp. 33–34, *Excursus: The "Day of Yahweh."*

5

18   Woe (to those) who desire the Day of Yahweh!

What will the Day of Yahweh really[a] (mean) for you?
   [It (means) darkness, and not light.][b]

19   Just as though someone were fleeing from a lion,
   and a bear confronts him;
when he (finally) reaches home[c]
   and leans his hand against the wall,
   then a serpent bites him—

20   will not the Day of Yahweh (likewise mean) darkness and not light?
   Yes, gloom[d] and no brightness (will there be) to it![e]

a   *V* (*ad quid eam vobis* ["to what (purpose) is this to you?"]), just as *G* (αὔτη), does not understand זֶה as an intensification (i.e., "really") of the interrogative למה (as would be correct according to Gen 18:13; 1 Sam 17:28; 2 Sam 12:23, and Gesenius–Kautzsch–Cowley, par. 136c) but as a demonstrative pronoun. In keeping with that, *V* assigns the second occurrence of יום יהוה ("Day of Yahweh") to v 18bβ.

b   Here a judgment regarding the nature of the Day of Yahweh anticipates the rhetorical question of 5:20a. In view of the tenor of the oracle as a whole (see pp. 256–57), this premature denouement is probably secondary (so already Löhr, *Amos*, 19; Duhm, "Anmerkungen," 10; Procksch; Sellin; cf. Weiser, *Profetie*, 213). 5:19 does not explain a prior reference to חֹשֶׁךְ ("darkness"), but rather leads up to such a reference in v 20.

c   *G* (εἰς τὸν οἶκον αὐτοῦ ["into his house"]) interprets הבית as though it were בֵּיתוֹ ("his house").

d   Ehrlich, *Randglossen* 5, 241, proposed the vocalization וְאֹפֶל for reasons of rhythm. אָפֵל is otherwise unattested; read as an adjective (Gesenius–Buhl, 59; Koehler–Baumgartner [³1967], 76), it is unlikely alongside the three parallel nouns. *G* (γνόφος) and *V* (*caligo*) understood אפל to be a noun, "darkness."

e   *G* rightly refused to make v 20b dependent on the

interrogative particle in v 20a, translating here an independent sentence ($\kappa\alpha\grave{\iota}$ $\gamma\nu\acute{o}\phi$os $o\mathring{v}\kappa$ $\mathring{\epsilon}\chi\omega\nu$ $\phi\acute{\epsilon}\gamma\gamma$os $\alpha\mathring{v}\tau\widehat{\eta}$ ["and darkness (it is), not having light to it"]). In spite of the conjunction ו in וְאֹפֶל, which will here have to be understood as an explicative, the concluding לוֹ ("to it") indicates clearly enough that we are dealing with an independent nominal sentence.

Form

Although the traditional basic form of the woe–cry, הוֹי followed by plural participle,[1] dominates the opening of the oracle, this form is broken and expanded in three ways. It is broken initially already in v 18b, with the transition to the form of direct address (second–person plural), since use of the third–person plural was a part of the original, didactic tone of the sapiential woe–saying.[2] We see that prophets like Amos only rarely take up traditional genres without reshaping and expanding them.[3] (In a similar way 6:3b moves over into direct address within a woe–oracle.) It is broken secondly in that the interrogative format of v 18b, which intensifies the obtrusive character of the oracle, goes beyond the definitive elements of the genre of the woe–oracle. The interrogative format is repeated in v 20a.[4] While the first question (v 18b) has a provocative, inquisitorial tone, the second (v 20a) is marked by its aim of provoking assent; it is in effect a reformulation of the כֵּן–clause of a two–part speech of comparison (cf. "just as ... so" [כַּאֲשֶׁר ... כֵּן] of 3:12) or of the concluding part to a simile (cf. 2:13). Thirdly, here the simile itself (v 19) introduces the most comprehensive new element into the total oracle, "the story of an unlucky fellow who escapes from two dangers, only to succumb to a third."[5] Here events of greatest import and interest are compressed to the limit;

an individual figure represents all Israel (cf. 3:12 and 5:2). Thus the oracle is a brilliant example of the creative power of the prophet. Into the structural genre of the woe–oracle is inserted, as a component genre, didactic questions in the form of direct address, and into the latter is further incorporated a brief tale functioning as a simile. If our syntactical characterization of v 20b is correct,[6] then at the conclusion of his oracle Amos hurls in the face of his audience, compressed into the briefest possible thesis, his own answer to the questions he had just posed.[7]

Setting

The oracle constitutes an independent rhetorical unit; no linkage with the contiguous oracles is apparent. The fate of Israel is compared to a death under circumstances quite different from those in 5:1–17 (cf. vv 2, and 16–17). In terms of its content, the oracle is well–adapted literarily to the material which precedes it. That this oracle was a further word arising within the context of the same public appearance of Amos which ultimately stands behind 5:1–17 is something which can be neither confirmed nor repudiated; it must remain in the realm of possibility. Someone could have countered the prophet's threat of death with a reference to an expected Day of Yahweh, one which would correspond to the great days of the past when

1   See pp. 242–45.
2   E.g., Am 5:7, 10; 6:1, 4–6; Is 5:8ff; and Mi 2:1.
3   Cf. Gerstenberger, "Woe–Oracles," 249–63, esp. 253–54.
4   See pp. 181–83 on 3:3–8; and p. 284 on 6:12; and p. 345 on 9:7.
5   Walter Baumgartner, *RGG*[3] 4, 586–87. Baumgartner assigns this episode to the category of the "fairy tale" (*Märchen*).
6   See textual note "e" to 5:20.
7   On the combination of "structural genres" (*Rahmengattungen*) and "component genres" (*Gliedgattungen*),
    cf. Klaus Koch, *The Growth of the Biblical Tradition: The Form–Critical Method*, tr. S. M. Cupitt (New York: Charles Scribner's Sons, 1969), 23–25 [*Was ist Formgeschichte?* Neukirchen–Vluyn: Neukirchener Verlag, [2]1967), 29–31].

Yahweh intervened on behalf of his people.[8] Here, too, it cannot be determined whether Amos delivered the oracle in Samaria or in Bethel.

Interpretation

■ **18** The "woe" depicts as being embarked on a perilous byway those who as eagerly wish for the Day of Yahweh to come as hungry persons crave food (Nu 11:34), thirsty ones water (2 Sam 23:15) and greedy ones delicacies (Prv 23:3, 6). In all these cases we find the verb "to desire" (אוה hitpaʿel) being used. Desire is a chief subject of wisdom education, for it is a characteristic of the lazy person (Prv 13:4; 21:25), of the wicked (Prv 11:23; 21:26) and of everyone who lacks discipline (Prv 23:3, 6; cf. 24:1). Therefore it is quite possible that covetousness, just as the violation of law and order (5:7), may have been among the themes treated by the pedagogical woe–sayings already known to Amos through oral tradition. However, to subsume the yearning for the Day of Yahweh under the catchword of funerary lamentation was certainly a creative step first taken by our prophet.

The expression "Day of Yahweh" finds its earliest literary attestation in Amos, but one should probably not regard it as a term newly coined by him. Meir Weiss considers it likely that Amos' audience had not previously encountered this expression, hearing it for the first time as it issued from the prophet's mouth.[9] The Israelite understood by "day" not primarily a calendrically fixed span of time; rather, a "day" was defined in terms of the events, interruptions and outcomes which occurred within that span of time.[10] Therefore one could see in the expression "Day of Yahweh" a completely neutral reference to a general course of events determined by Yahweh. However, the context of our text ultimately prohibits such an interpretation. Amos evidently grapples with this expression, whose threefold repetition (5:18a, 18b, 20) clearly shows it to be the point of contention in this oracle. Not only is the Day of

Yahweh—under precisely this catchword—obviously anticipated with eagerness by the people, but furthermore it is directly with reference to their understanding of this slogan that the hearers are queried (v 18b). Now, Gerhard von Rad has rightly warned against overestimating the value of v 18 as a proof–text regarding the notions which the contemporaries of Amos associated with the Day of Yahweh.[11] Initially all this text reveals is that Israel saw in the Day of Yahweh reference to some event eagerly to be anticipated (v 18a). To go beyond this, one will have to adduce later texts that deal with the Day of Yahweh.[12]

There is increasing confirmation for von Rad's proposal that the concept is best understood on the basis of the traditions of holy war and, hence, that it originally referred to a day of Yahweh's setting out against the enemies of Israel, such as happened, for example, on "the day of Midian" (Is 9:3 [4]; cf. Ju 7).[13] Against Amos, Israel could invoke many a great day when Yahweh had given historical proof of his readiness to save his people. The ancient destruction of the Amorites, cited by Amos himself (2:9), could just as well have fallen under this catchword as the most recent military successes, assuming such victories were theologically interpreted (cf. 6:13). Could one not counter the prophetic threat of a final defeat of Israel (5:3! cf. 5:2, 26–27) by claiming that Yahweh would show himself to be just as much a deliverer in the case of a new threat as he had been in former times? Could one not, in defiance of Amos, openly express a yearning for such a day? However, the prophet immediately questions whether that day would indeed be a happy one. The idiom למה ל inquires after the meaning, the usefulness or the disadvantage, of something for someone.[14]

■ **19** Now one should note both the fact that, and how, Amos himself draws attention to our slogan and uses a simile to lead up to the answer to his own question. The simile is a brief tale about someone trying to flee.

---

8 See p. 256.

9 "The Origin of the 'Day of Yahweh'—Reconsidered," *HUCA* 37 (1966): 46.

10 Cf. Johannes Pedersen, *Israel. Its Life and Culture, I–II*, tr. Aslang Møller (London, 1926), 120; and Herrmann, *Heilserwartungen*, 121.

11 *Theology* 2, 119 [133].

12 See pp. 33–34.

13 For a confirmation, and a refutation of older attempts at interpretation, see Klaus Dietrich Schunck, "Strukturlinien in der Entwicklung der Vorstellung vom 'Tag Yahwehs,'" *VT* 14 (1964): 319–30; cf. further Herrmann, *Heilserwartungen*, 122–23.

14 Cf. Job 30:2: "What could I gain (לָמָּה לִּי) from the strength of their hands?" On זֶה as an intensifying particle, see textual note "a" to 5:18.

The chain of consecutive perfects and the single reference to "someone" (אִישׁ, literally "a man") speak unequivocally in favor of there being here one single story.[15] This little story tells of someone who, in having to flee from a lion, suddenly finds himself confronted by a bear, an animal at least as dangerous as a lion.[16] However, the one pursued is able to escape this threat to his life as well, even managing to flee into a house. There he leans his hand against the wall, as much from exhaustion as from relief, only to have an unnoticed snake bite him. The story obviously implies that the outcome was fatal. Indeed, in the Old Testament the serpent is the deadly enemy of man.[17] The subject matter here is fully in keeping with the realm of a sheep breeder's experience, just as was the case with the didactic questions in 3:3–6+8 and the simile in 3:12. Nothing compels us to see a "fairy tale" being transmitted here.[18] On the contrary, it is more in keeping with the manner and the style of the prophet to suppose that he composed on his own a story relating to the issue of the Day of Yahweh. Given the precision of the other statements of Amos, can it really be that this tale intends to say nothing more than that the Day of Yahweh, as a gloomy day of judgment, is inescapable? Is it not almost unnecessary to assume that the story seeks directly to confront the fact that the hearers desire the Day of Yahweh because they know it to be a day of victory? In any case, this dramatic sketch says that the man in question, who twice escaped from the danger to his life, went on to be fatally bitten precisely at the moment when he felt secure. Surely every clause here hits home with greatest precision when one assumes that the audience, due to earlier Days of Yahweh that brought deliverance from foes of superior might, fears in this case no coming war threatened by Amos (2:14–16; 3:11; 5:3). Such a reconstruction enables our text, with its pedagogical wisdom tale whose scenes unfold so eloquently, to give more support to von Rad's interpretation of the Day of Yahweh through reference to holy war—and, to be sure, to this interpretation only—than has been assumed so far. It makes understandable at the same time the reversal in the meaning of the Day of Yahweh which came about with Amos. Israel had repeatedly been able to escape from its foes and experience deliverance; therefore the Day of Yahweh had come to mean for it a time for rejoicing and gathering of spoils. But none of this excludes the fact that now the Day of Yahweh will bring death to Israel. If we are interpreting this story correctly, then this would not be the first time that the prophet represents Israel's changing fate under the guise of a single individual (cf. 3:12; 5:2). Not only is the possibility not to be excluded, but on the contrary it repeatedly comes to the fore, that Amos' similes are to be interpreted almost allegorically. For example, in 5:2 it was not only the death that was the point of the comparison; alongside this the elements of "virgin" and "own soil" had interpretive significance as well.[19] Certainty of interpretation can probably not be reached here. Yet surely the polished short story speaks not only of the death of him who feels secure but also relates a preceding history of repeated deliverance. Perhaps it is in this allegorical manner that Amos links in his ironical way (cf. 3:12!) the catchword of certainty of salvation with his new interpretation directed toward the coming day of judgment.

■ **20** The rhetorical question (v 20a) expects the respondent to agree that only the understanding of the Day of Yahweh as a day of calamity has continued validity. Darkness and gloom are code words for fatal devastation; they belong to the traditional material of holy war and, from the time of Amos on, remain part of the concept of the Day of Yahweh.[20] Amos himself may have derived the practice of using a sharp antithesis, and thereby the contrast between darkness and light, from the wisdom tradition (cf. Is 2:20). On the other hand, at least the term "gleam, brightness" (נֹגַהּ)

---

15 So Joüon, par. 119q; rather than two brief stories as Brockelmann (*Syntax*, par. 41k) supposes: someone fleeing from a lion is stopped short by a bear; someone (else) seeking refuge in a house is bitten by a serpent.

16 Perhaps there is even a slight element of intensification here; cf. Hos 13:7–8.

17 Gen 3:15; Nu 21:6; Jer 8:17. Cf. Oskar Grether

and Johannes Fichtner, *TDNT* 5, 572–73. Cf. further, Is 14:29 and Prv 23:32, and Wolff, *Amos the Prophet*, 15–16 [11].

18 Against Walter Baumgartner, *RGG*³ 4, 586–87; see p. 254.

19 Cf. also p. 200, on 3:14–15 as an interpretation of 3:12.

20 Cf. Zeph 1:15; Is 13:10; and Joel 2:2; 3:4 [2:31];

seems to be rooted especially strongly in those texts which sing about Yahweh's epiphany to effect deliverance from enemies.[21] It is precisely such illustrious deliverance that is definitively rejected in the end. Thus is our multi-faceted, form-critically artistic oracle thematically shaped to perfection throughout.

Aim

This woe-oracle, with its provocative questions and dramatic simile-narrative, seeks by unusual and varied means to draw the audience out of the confines of its self-security. It casts disillusionment upon any care-free attitude. Israel believes, perhaps due to earlier experiences of deliverance, that it has escaped from danger once and for all; but precisely this conscious-ness of deliverance will finally doom Israel to death's darkness.

The oracle can be called eschatological only in the precise sense that it testifies, in the face of renewed assurances of security, that the end of the state of Israel is totally inescapable. Luther already denied its application to the "Last Day," observing that Amos speaks "not about the last judgment" (*Non de extremo iudicio*) but about the time of judgment and the devastation at the hands of the Assyrians.[22] And the oracle continues to attack any attitude of self-assurance which the wandering people of God might ground upon their history of salvation.

---

see also pp. 44, 68.

21 Is 9:1 [2]; Ps 18:13 [12], 29 [28]; Hab 3:4, 11; Is 13:10. Cf. Frank Schnutenhaus, "Das Kommen und Erscheinen Gottes im Alten Testament," *ZAW* 76 (1964): 1-22 (esp. 9-10).

22 As cited in Krause, *Studien*, 319.

The Rejection of Worship

Bibliography

Seth Erlandsson
"Amos 5:25–27, ett crux interpretum," *SEÅ* 33 (1968): 76–82.

Stanley Gevirtz
"A New Look at an Old Crux: Amos 5:26," *JBL* 87 (1968): 267–76.

Richard Hentschke
Die Stellung der vorexilischen Schriftpropheten zum Kultus, BZAW 75 (Berlin: A. Töpelmann, 1957), 24–26.

Hans Wilhelm Hertzberg
"Die prophetische Kritik am Kult," *ThLZ* 75 (1950): 219–26 (reprinted in *idem, Beiträge zur Traditionsgeschichte und Theologie des Alten Testaments* [Göttingen: Vandenhoeck & Ruprecht, 1962], 81–90).

J. Philip Hyatt
The Prophetic Criticism of Israelite Worship (Cincinnati: Hebrew Union College Press, 1963).

Idem
"The Translation and Meaning of Am 5:23–24," *ZAW* 68 (1956): 17–24.

Hubert Junker
"Amos und die 'opferlose Mosezeit'," *ThG* 27 (1935): 686–95.

Werner H. Schmidt
"Die deuteronomistische Redaktion des Amosbuches. Zu den theologischen Unterschieden zwischen dem Prophetenwort und seinem Sammler," *ZAW* 77 (1965): 168–93 (esp. 188–91).

Masao Sekine
"Das Problem der Kultpolemik bei den Propheten," *EvTh* 28 (1968): 605–09.

Ephraim Avigdor Speiser
"Note on Amos 5:26," *BASOR* 108 (1947): 5–6.

Ernst Würthwein
"Amos 5:21–27," *ThLZ* 72 (1947): 143–52.

Idem
"Kultpolemik oder Kultbescheid?" in *Tradition und Situation: Studien zur alttestamentlichen Prophetie, Festschrift für A. Weiser*, ed. Ernst Würthwein and Otto Kaiser (Göttingen: Vandenhoeck & Ruprecht, 1963), 115–31.

5

21 I hate, [a]I reject[b] your feasts.
    I will not savor your assemblies.
22   [Unless you offer me burnt–offerings.][c]
I will not accept your offerings.
    I will not look upon the banquet–offering of your fatted cattle.

a   Verbs describing a unified action are often juxtaposed asyndetically; cf. Hos 9:9 הֶעְמִיקוּ שִׁחֵתוּ ["They made deep, they corrupted" = "they deeply corrupted"]); Zeph 3:7 הִשְׁכִּימוּ הִשְׁחִיתוּ ["they arose early, they made corrupt" = "they hastened to make corrupt"]); and Brockelmann, *Syntax*, par. 133b.

b   Especially with verbs expressing a mental or a spir-

23 Remove[d] from me the noise of your songs!
I will not listen to the melody of your lute.

24 But let justice cascade[e] like water, righteousness like a perennial stream.

ᵗual state, the perfect has the quality of a present statement; cf. Ps 103:13 (רָחַם ["has compassion"]); Jer 2:2 (זָכַרְתִּי ["I remember"]); and Joüon, par. 112a; Brockelmann, *Syntax*, par. 41c.

c This colon disturbs the strict parallelism of members in 5:21–24; it also breaks the pattern through its change of subject (second–person plural instead of first–person singular as in vv 21, 22aβ) and the absence of a pronominal suffix on עלות ("burnt–offerings"). Even if one assumes the loss of a colon after v 22a (Würthwein, "Kultbescheid," 117), one still cannot restore a parallelism suitable to the context; cf. the proposal of Morgenstern ("Amos Studies IV," 302, 319) to insert לא אקחינה מידיכם ("I will not accept them from your hands"). If one were to take v 22aα as protasis to v 22aβ–b ("Even if you . . ., I will not . . ."), then עלות would have to be understood as designating the general category to which מנחות and שלם belonged, but this is hardly an acceptable interpretation (see p. 263). In addition, כי אם ("unless, except") when following negative sentences has a concessive function (cf. Am 3:7; 8:11; Gen 32:27 [26]; 1 Kgs 17:1; Ezek 33:11; and Brockelmann, *Syntax*, par. 168; Gesenius–Kautzsch–Cowley, par. 163c). Such a concession, however, can only have reflected the interest of a later glossator; the expression העלה עלות ("to offer up burnt–offerings") is very frequent in the Chronicler's history (1 Chr 16:2, 40; 21:24, 26; 23:31; 29:21; 2 Chr 1:6; 8:12; 23:18; 24:14; 29:7, 27; 35:14, 16; Ezr 3:3, 6). *G* did not recognize this exceptive clause (see Gesenius–Kautzsch–Cowley, par. 163c) but instead fused it with the following sentence: διότι ἐὰν ἐνέγκητέ μοι ὁλοκαυτώματα καὶ θυσίας ὑμῶν, οὐ προσδέξομαι ("Wherefore if you bring me your whole burnt–offerings and your sacrifices, I will not accept [them]").

d After the plural forms in vv 21–22, the singular imperative and the singular suffixes seem strange. Was הסר ("withhold"), like קַטֵּר ("kindle") in 4:5, meant originally to be read as an infinitive absolute and connected with objects having plural suffixes שִׁירֵיכֶם ["your songs"] and נִבְלֵיכֶם ["your harps"] according to Würthwein, "Kultbescheid," 117), which after a later misunderstanding of the syntax were changed to second–person singular pronominal suffixes? But it is most uncertain that copyists would proceed in such a manner. The ancient versions confirm *M*. Perhaps the transition to the singular along with the transition to an imperative construction is to be explained on the basis of the dependence of the new formal element upon another genre (see p. 263).

e גלל (nip'al jussive) means literally "to roll along, tumble."

f–f The purely prose style and the transition to specialized theological questions concerning history and the cultus betray here the hand of a glossator. V 24 already made a transition from the rejection of

25	f[Did you bring to me sacrifices and meal–offering(s) for forty years in the wilderness, house of Israel?]g
26	And did you (then) carry about Sakkûth {your king}j and Kêwān,i your images {the star of your gods,}j which you made for yourselves?]f
27	Hence I will send you into exile, beyond Damascus

—Yahweh has said
[God of Hosts is his name].k

the cultus to a contrasting positive statement, and so vv 25–26 appear to be a later supplement to vv 21–23. Furthermore, the occurrence of the term מנחה in the singular (v 25) next to the plural מנחתיכם ("your offerings" v 22) attracts attention. The position of this sentence clearly shows that it is the legitimacy of sacrifices *per se* which is here being questioned (Marti), and not whether they should be made to Yahweh or to other gods (Hans Wilhelm Hertzberg, "Die prophetische Kritik am Kult," *ThLZ* 75 [1950]: 219–26). Nothing precludes seeing in v 26 the continuation of the question of v 25 (so Hermann Guthe, "Der Prophet Amos" in *Die Heilige Schrift des Alten Testaments*, vol. 2, ed. E. Kautzsch and A. Bertholet [Tübingen, ⁴1923], 40; Marti; Sellin; Maag, *Text*, 35; Würthwein, "Kultbescheid," 117; and Amsler; differently Nowack; Robinson; and Weiser, *Profetie*, 222–25).

g   Gᴼ and others add λέγει κύριος ("says [the] Lord") and so continue the practice of adding a נאם יהוה (see p. 143). On the peculiar variants of the Alexandrine text, cf. Ziegler, *Duodecim prophetae*, 40–43.

h   G (τὴν σκηνὴν τοῦ Μολοχ ["the tent of Moloch"]) read סֻכַּת ("hut, tent, booth"). On the basis of the corresponding name of the corresponding Akkadian deity, one should vocalize סַכּוּת; the Masoretic vocalization סִכּוּת probably intends to remind the reader of שִׁקּוּץ ("detested thing").

i   Ραιφαν in *G* is generally regarded as an inner–Greek disfiguration of Καιφαν; the reading כִּיָן corresponds to *S* (*ke'wān*) and Akkadian *kayyamānu* = "Saturn" (*AHW* 1, 420) [*kaywan > kêwān*; Ed.]. On the present *M* vocalization (כִּיּוּן), see textual note "h" above; cf. also Eberhard Schrader, *Die Keilinschriften und das Alte Testament* (Berlin, ³1903), 408–10.

j   The appositions strike one as being subsequently inserted explanations. *G* (τοῦ Μολοχ καὶ τὸ ἄστρον τοῦ θεοῦ ὑμῶν ["of Moloch and the star of your god"]) still reflects the two additions side by side and reads the relative clause as modifying צלמיכם (τοὺς τύπους αὐτῶν, οὓς ἐποιήσατε ἑαυτοῖς ["their images, which you made for yourselves"]).

k   The short form of the closing messenger formula (attested in 1:5, 8 [cj.], 15; 2:3; 5:17) is here expanded in accord with the final form in 4:13b.

Form

5:21–27 is stylistically differentiated from the preceding unit (5:18–20) by the shift to first–person divine speech which is maintained throughout. Until we reach the next woe–cry in 6:1 there is nothing to indicate the beginning of a new, independent rhetorical unit. However, 5:25–26 proves to be a later addition (as is 5:22aα).[1] To the observations cited in textual note "f–f" must be added that the subject of the statement here (as in v 22aα) is not Yahweh, as both before and after,

but Israel, addressed in the second–person plural. Although the form of direct address is thus maintained in vv 25–26, its character is different. Between the sentences formulated in the indicative (vv 21–22, 27) and the imperative (vv 23–24 in the singular!) is juxtaposed a double question reminiscent of the parenetic style of 2:10–12 (v 11b!). The mention of the forty years in the wilderness also connects 5:25–26 with the latter text (2:10bα). Thus the old oracle probably consisted only of 5:21, 22aβb, 23–24, and 27. The following stand out clearly on syntactical grounds as constitutive elements: (a) vv 21, 22aβb, (b) vv 23–24, (c) v 27.

The "I" of Yahweh can be recognized already in the first element (a). It is true that the prophetic "I" may also appear at the beginning of oracles concerned with demonstrating the guilt of Israel (5:12).[2] In such cases, however, Yahweh's announcement of punishment is explicitly set off from what precedes,[3] while here the announcement of punishment (5:27) is attached to the preceding material by means of a perfect consecutive form, just as in the oracles against foreign nations (1:3–8; 1:13—2:3) where also divine first–person speech is maintained throughout. Thus 5:21–27 shows in all its elements the basic form of the messenger speech; the use of the concluding messenger formula is consonant with this.[4] To be sure, an intro–ductory "Thus Yahweh has said" (כֹּה אָמַר יהוה) is absent. But even if one suspected that such a formula, originally standing before the announcement of punishment in v 27, had been lost when vv 25–26 were incorporated, it would still be necessary on form–critical grounds to understand the "I" in vv 21–23 as referring to Yahweh. 5:21–22 must be recognized as belonging to the genre of the cultic decision or response,[5] comparable to an "assurance oracle answering a plea," such as must be presupposed to have intervened in certain psalms between the element of complaint and the hymn of thanksgiving.[6] A negative cultic decision is attested several times in prophecy.[7] In all such cases it is Yahweh himself who speaks.[8] One can assume that, within the context of a ritual of lamentation, a cultic spokesman gave voice to Yahweh's word. The most important verbal terms in vv 21–22 also point to the genre of cultic decision.[9] Thus in the first part of our oracle, as in 4:4–5, Amos uses a form of cultic speech. Here, however, the form is not that of the priest whose instructions precede cultic activity,[10] but rather that appropriate to one who, functioning in the midst of the activity of worship, proclaims the decision of Yahweh in the form of a declaration.[11] The genre of the cultic decision must therefore be seen as standing behind the first formal element of our oracle. Our detailed observations will show that Amos elaborates this genre freely and that he incorporates it into his oracle only as a component genre.

(b) The second formal element (5:23–24) derives from a different realm. It supplements the cultic decision, which still reverberates in v 23b, with an instruction (vv 23a, 24). The sequential arrangement of an imperative in v 23a and a description of its consequences in v 24 (the content of which identifies the positive expectation over against the prohibited behavior), together with the theme of v 23, reminds one quite forcefully of 4:4–5 (cf. 5:4b) and makes Begrich's comparison with priestly torah understandable.[12] Yet we have here a severe injunction whose antithesis of cultus and justice and whose focus in v 24 reminds one even more strongly of sapiential admonition. Perhaps the dependence on a different genre explains the transition to the second–person singular. However, the sapiential admonition is now transposed into the basic form of messenger speech and linked up with the element of the negative cultic decision. The formal elements joined together in vv 21–24, namely those of the cultic decision and the pedagogic admonition (just as in Is 1:11–15 + 16–17), are here used by Amos in their combined form in the place of the accusation in the normal prophetic judgment speech. The admonition,

1   See textual note "c" to 5:22.
2   See p. 248.
3   As in the relationship between 5:12 and the oracle in 5:16–17; see also 3:11; 4:2; and 5:3.
4   See p. 139.
5   Cf. Würthwein, "Kultbescheid."
6   Cf. Ps 28:1–2 with v 6; and Hos 6:1–3 with vv 4–11a; on the latter, see Wolff, *Hosea*, 119 [151].
7   Is 1:10–17; Jer 6:19–21; Mal 1:10.
8   Cf. also Ps 35:3: "Say to my soul, 'I am your deliverance!'"
9   See the discussion of the individual words below.
10 Against Begrich, "Tora," 73 (= *idem, Gesammelte Studien*, 243), who designates our unit as a priestly torah.
11 So Würthwein, "Kultbescheid."
12 See n. 10 above.

since it is not heeded, also serves to demonstrate guilt; it holds up before Israel, as it were, a mirror in which it is expected to recognize itself (cf. 5:4b).

(c) Only by such an interpretation does the immediate attachment of the third formal element, the announcement of punishment, become understandable. It is this attachment which reveals the whole oracle to be a new, peculiar alteration of the basic genre of the prophetic judgment speech.[13] In our resulting composite genre, the aim of exposing guilt has led to the exceptional insertion, as constituent genres, of an imitation of a cultic decision and of an admonition before the concluding announcement of calamity.

> The differing elements of the constitutive genres also explain slight deviations in the rhythm. While one can recognize almost completely uniform three–stress bicola in vv 21, 22aβb (must v 22b be read with four stresses?), v 23 is comprised of a four–stress bicolon, to which is attached in v 24 another three–stress bicolon. After the prose insertion (vv 25–26), v 27 concludes with a two–stress bicolon, which creates a staccato effect intensifying the announcement of punishment.

Setting
Theme as well as the formal element of the cultic decision suggest that this oracle was more probably proclaimed at the state sanctuary in Bethel than anywhere else. 7:11b presupposes that a threat of exile was proclaimed by the prophet at Bethel. The abruptness with which the divine first–person address begins is striking; elsewhere we find an introductory "Thus Yahweh has said" (כֹּה אָמַר יהוה),[14] or a "Hear this word . . . !"[15] If the textual tradition corresponds to the oral proclamation, one must probably imagine that Amos interrupted the discourse of a cultic spokesman at the sanctuary. This might also account for the asyndetic juxtaposition of the first two verbs, apparently spoken with excitement: "I hate, I reject . . . ."

The supplement in 5:25–26 is probably to be traced to the Deuteronomistic redaction.[16] Then the relationships to 2:10bα–11b[17] become understandable, as does the criticism from the standpoint of salvation history of the execution of certain Yahwistic rituals[18] and of the cult of foreign deities.

Interpretation
■ **21** Nowhere but here do we find immediately juxtaposed these harshest of renunciatory statements, "I hate, I reject."[19] Expressions of trust in the Psalter contain the confession that Yahweh "hates" evildoers (Ps 5:6 [5]), those who love violence (Ps 11:5), and those who venerate vain idols (Ps 31:7 [6] cj.). However, that such a confession might ultimately go back to corresponding cultic decisions is not attested for us. In Amos "to hate" (שׂנא) is otherwise found only in (5:10, 15), where the reference is to human hatred, and in 6:8 where, as here, the reference is to Yahweh's hatred. The rejection (מאס ["to reject"]) of Israel by Yahweh is spoken of in Ps 78:59 and 67; the rejection of apostates is the theme in Ps 53:6 [5]. As a rule, such divine rejection is the reaction of Yahweh to having been rejected by men (1 Sam 15:23; Hos 4:6). The prophetic language of rejection continues to exert influence in the Deuteronomistic History.[20] Here in Amos, as in Is 1:14, it is the "feasts" which are the object of rejection.

There follows directly upon this fundamental statement, which passionately rejects the cultic festivities, a clarification of the divine attitude as well as of the festal activities in question. Yahweh's "savoring" pertains originally to sacrificial gifts.[21] Amos makes the object of the savoring the festal "assembly,"[22] in this way generalizing concepts which had a technical significance within the sacrificial cultus. Both Yahweh's attitude, as revealed in the initial bicolon, and the things which he rejects lend to this "cultic decision" a severity and breadth quite unparalleled in earlier literature.[23]

---

13 Cf. 3:1–2, 9–11; 4:1–3; 5:11, 12 + 16–17; 7:16–17.
14 See pp. 135–36.
15 See p. 176 on 3:1.
16 So Schmidt, "Redaktion," 188–91.
17 See p. 260.
18 Wolff, "Kerygma," 98–99 [183–84 (= *Gesammelte Studien*, 321–22)].
19 They occur together elsewhere, but in less proximate

juxtaposition, only in Hos 9:15, 17, and Ps 36:3 [2], 5 [4].
20 2 Kgs 17:20; 23:27; cf. Jer 7:29.
21 Gen 8:21; Lev 26:31; and 1 Sam 26:19, where the savoring of the "offering" (מִנְחָה, cf. Am 5:22aβ) is connected with a reference to the propitiatory function of the sacrifice. Cf. Rendtorff, *Studien*, 253.
22 Both here and in Is 1:13, עצרה unquestionably has

■ **22** (On v 22aα see textual note "c.") The term מִנְחָה is used by Amos as a collective concept designating all the different sorts of sacrifices which may be presented.[24] That fact is underscored by Amos' use of the plural, which is otherwise very rare with this word.[25] Thus it is to all sacrifices that Yahweh refers when he says, "I will not accept them." In contrast to the more specialized terms "to savor" (v 21b), "to look upon" (v 22b), and "to listen to" (v 23b), the verb "to accept" (רצה) is the most frequently employed and most comprehensive word for expressing the approbatory and, especially, the official acceptance of sacrifices. When a sacrifice does not correspond to the ritual prescriptions, priestly torah determines that "it will not be accepted" (לֹא יֵרָצֶה).[26] In the case of actual performance of sacrifice, then, the cultic spokesman would accordingly declare in Yahweh's name either "I will accept" (ארצה) or "I will not accept" (לֹא ארצה).[27] Speaking as the messenger of Yahweh, Amos proclaims to his audience the sweeping rejection of all their cultic offerings. "Banquet–offering" (שֶׁלֶם) occurs in the singular only here; with this word Amos draws attention to that type of sacrifice which is elsewhere always referred to in the plural as "(sacrifice of) banquet–offerings" (זֶבַח שְׁלָמִים]). The traditional translation for this term is "peace–offering." However, the word is probably not to be interpreted etymologically by reference to the related noun "peace" (שָׁלוֹם), meaning thereby something like "salutory–offering." Rather, the term is to be clarified on the basis of the verb "to complete" (שלם pi'el) and means approximately "concluding–sacrifice," reflecting the fact that the cultic celebration is concluded by a great sacrificial banquet.[28] That "fatted cattle" were needed for this is probably mentioned by Amos less because of the fat

presented to Yahweh (Is 1:11) than because of the meat consumed by the festal congregation (cf. 6:4b). In any case, Yahweh's attitude in this particular instance is not described by a technical term from the sacrificial *tôrôt*. "To look upon" (נבט hip'il) is not elsewhere found in the context of the presentation of sacrifices;[29] the word customarily designates watching and paying attention to people (Ps 13:4 [3]; 33:13; 80:15 [14]).

■ **23** The worship celebration resembles the banquet described in 6:4–5 in combining with the partaking of meat both singing and the playing of the lute. Singing is not rejected by means of the renunciatory cultic decision; instead, an injunction demands its immediate removal. While up to this point Yahweh has only closed himself off to the cultic acts, now he actually drives the festal assembly from his presence. The sound of the songs is referred to as "noise" (הָמוֹן), a word also used to describe the din of battle.[30] Here the reference is most likely to the sheer, ecstatic tumult of the singers at the harvest festivals.[31] The transition to the imperative, and to direct address in the singular, could indicate that with this new form of speech Amos has turned to a new addressee.[32] Does he demand of the priest in charge (cf. 7:10–17) that he put an end to the bellowing, or is his injunction directed toward another important individual?[33] Or is the cultic community as a whole addressed in the singular, as in Dtn 6:4?

Further substantiation for the injunction is provided by another sentence formulated as a cultic decision (v 23b). Grammatically, it refers only to the instruments that accompany the singing; conceptually, it pertains equally to the singing and the instrumental accompaniment, as does the preceding command to remove the uproar. "To play" (זמר pi'el) designates the playing of a musical instrument, here the lute. The

---

the meaning "assembly," unlike its connotation in Joel 1:14 and elsewhere; see p. 33.

23 See p. 261.

24 The same is true of Isaiah; cf. 1:13, and Wildberger, *Jesaja*, 38, 41; cf. further Gen 4:3–5, and Richard Hentschke, *RGG*³ 4, 1645.

25 Rendtorff, *Studien*, 58; cf. 197–98.

26 Lev 19:7 (cf. vv 5–6); 7:18; 22:23, 27.

27 Ezek 20:41; Mal 1:10; cf. Ps 51:18 [16]; Jer 14:12; 2 Sam 24:23. See also Würthwein, "Kultbescheid," 122–23; and Rendtorff, *Studien*, 253–58.

28 Cf. Koehler–Baumgartner, 980; Rendtorff, *Studien*,

132–33; and above p. 219, on 4:4.

29 Ernst Würthwein, ("Amos 5:21–27," *ThLZ* 72 [1947]: 147) can refer only to Lam 4:16.

30 Cf. 1 Kgs 20:13, and also above p. 81 on Joel 4:14 [3:14].

31 Cf. Am 8:10; Hos 9:1, and Wolff, *Hosea*, 153 [197]. Cf. also Hentschke, *Stellung*, 77–78.

32 See pp. 261–62.

33 Cf. Ps 144:9, where in the context of a royal vow there also appears in parallelism the expressions "song" (שִׁיר) and "play on a harp" (זַמֵּר בְּנֵבֶל); see further Kraus, *Psalmen*, 942, 944.

נֶבֶל is a stringed instrument, apparently with an angular yoke and a bulging (נֶבֶל also means "jug") resonance chamber.[34] G gives the pale translation ὄργανον "[musical] instrument"); V more precisely translates lyra (in 6:5, psalterium). Following V, and drawing upon the archaeological findings, the translation "lyre" or "lute" commends itself. It is the oldest and most important stringed instrument in Israel,[35] which could have as many as ten strings.[36] Having already shut his nostrils (v 21b) and closed his eyes (v 22b), Yahweh now also stops up his ears. Unlike Is 1:15 and Jer 14:12, the reference here is not to a prayer of complaint. The "song" (שִׁיר), which in 8:10 appears as the opposite of the "lament" (קִינָה), and the playing of the lute are forms of rendering cultic praise.[37] Thus one should not suppose that the verb שָׁמַע is used here with the specialized meaning "to hear [with favor], to grant" which it has, for example, in Ps 6:9–10 [8–9] and 28:2, 6.[38] Instead, just as is the case with "look upon" (נבט hip'il) in v 22b, the verb here has its ordinary sense: Yahweh simply does not want to "hear" the festal music.

■ 24 Rather than the noise of cultic praise, something altogether different was to be heard and, consequently, practiced in the assembly of Israel: "justice" and "righteousness" (משפט and צדקה).[39] The jussive form יגל ("let cascade") is attached to the preceding verse by means of a waw-copulativum. V 24 has been regarded as the beginning of the judgment threat,[40] but such an element should rather have been introduced by means of a perfect consecutive form (5:27; cf. 1:4).[41] Also, if v 24 begins the threat of judgment, then "justice"

and "righteousness" would have to be interpreted as referring to acts of Yahweh, which is never the case with these words elsewhere in Amos (cf. 5:7, 6:12). Finally, in Is 1:13–17 there is a thematically comparable transition from the cultic sphere to the legal ("justice" [משפט] in Is 1:17). If the jussive interpretation of the sentence can be considered assured,[42] then the adversative structure used by Amos in vv 23–24 recalls the sapiential juxtaposition of sacrifice and prayer with "justice and righteousness."[43] According to Amos, justice and righteousness are supposed to roll along "like water," indeed like a river that never dries up. The adjective איתן carries the basic meaning of "flowing voluminously" and thus serves to distinguish the "stream [–bed]" (נחל) which carries water throughout the year, even in the dry months, from the winter brooks that dry up easily.[44] That which Israel has perverted into wormwood and poison (5:7; 6:12) was meant to effect blessing and prosperity among the people, just as the streams and rivers of a land bring the gift of fertility and life.[45] If v 23 has a responsible individual in view, then in v 24 that person is addressed quite precisely with regard to what his proper duties should be.[46]

■ 25 Recalling the history of salvation, the Deuteronomistic redactor confronts his generation with a fundamental question regarding the cult. The notion that sacrifices were not offered at any early period in Israel's history is otherwise found only in the Deuteronomistic editing of the book of Jeremiah (7:21–23). In using the word "sacrifices" (זבחים),[47] the redactor

---

34   BRL 391; Gerhard Wallis, "Harfe," BHHW 2, 647–48, and idem, "Musik, Musikinstrumente," BHHW 2, 1259–60, fig. 2.; Gordon Loud, The Megiddo Ivories (Chicago, 1939), pl. 4; ANEP, figs. 193, 199, 202, 208.

35   Cf. Carl Hermann Kraeling, "Music in the Bible" in Ancient and Oriental Music, ed. Egon Wellesz; Oxford History of Music, vol. 1 (London: Oxford University Press, 1957), 283–312 (esp. 296).

36   Ps 33:2; 144:9. Cf. the representation of a lute with ten strings from Asshur, ibid., pl. VIIIa. Cf. further, AOB, fig. 151 (prisoners making music, perhaps Judeans from Lachish; Nineveh c. 700); and ANEP, fig. 200 (Carchemish, ninth–eighth century; a lute player on the left).

37   Ps 33:2–3; 57:8–9 [7–8]; 71:22; 98:1; 108:2–3 [1–2]; 144:9; 150:3.

38   Cf. Würthwein, "Kultbescheid," 126.

39   For discussions of the words, see p. 245, on 5:7.

40   So Keil, Sellin, and Weiser.

41   See also p. 261.

42   Cf. Hentschke, Stellung, 78–81.

43   Cf. Is 1:11–17 (and Wildberger, Jesaja, 35–36); and also Prv 15:8; 21:3, 27; and the Egyptian Instruction for King Meri–ka–re, 129: "More acceptable is the character of one upright of heart than the ox of the evildoer" (John A. Wilson, ANET³, 417b). Cf. further Hos 6:5b–6.

44   Cf. Armin W. Schwarzenbach, Die geographische Terminologie im Hebräischen des Alten Testaments (Leiden: E. J. Brill, 1954), 30–32.

45   Dtn 8:7; 1 Kgs 17:4, 6; Is 35:6.

46   Cf. Hos 4:4–6, and Wolff, Hosea, 79–80 [97–98].

47   See p. 219, on 4:4.

first of all supplies a term which was lacking in the text of Amos as transmitted to him. מנחה ("meal–offering"), which appears here—in contrast to 5:22—in the customary singular form, no longer serves as the collective designation for sacrifices;[48] instead it carries the meaning, attested in 2 Kgs 16:15 and generally in times subsequent to that, of a separate vegetable offering.[49] It is only in the language of the sixth century that the "slaughtered sacrifice" and the "vegetable offering" together come to designate the totality of all cultic offerings. The recollection of the "wilderness" as such (not yet in Jer 7:22!) probably evoked the thought that material for vegetable offerings (flour, oil, incense), to say nothing of animal sacrifices, was simply not available there. Above all, however, our theologian is dominated by the idea of Hosea and Jeremiah that the time in the wilderness was the time of absolute faithfulness.[50] Already in 2:10 he introduced this as the period of the "forty years."[51] From his viewpoint, "forty years" means the span of time ". . . during which, as a rule, the total number of the adult men actively involved in the affairs of life undergoes a complete change,"[52] i.e., the period required for a whole generation to die out. Here a tradition lives on according to which the first generation of Israel abided only under God's law, free from the demand to sacrifice.[53]

■ **26** If even the sacrifices were absent, then how much more was this true of foreign deities! Since the subject and the tense of v 26 correspond to those of the question in v 25, it seems most reasonable to assume v 26 to be

a continuation of the question.[54] Whoever would draw v 26 into conjunction with v 27 as a threat must revocalize the verb,[55] and must either place v 25 before v 24, as does Weiser (which renders problematic the resulting connection of v 24 with v 26, since the tenses differ and the meaning of "justice" [משפט] and "righteousness" [צדקה] becomes confused),[56] or must put v 26 after v 27 (since in the announcement of punishment the depiction of Yahweh's intervention always precedes the description of the consequences of such intervention on those affected).[57]

Presupposed as the recipients of the action of the verb "carried" (נשא) are images of deities fixed atop standards.[58] Such standards are known from Mesopotamia. Besides the bull–standard from Mari,[59] we would direct attention here especially to a brick orthostat from late eighth–century Assyria, upon which a multi–colored enamel mosaic depicts a supplicant with a standard, standing before a god.[60] At the tip of the supplicant's standard is attached the eight–pointed star which can be seen (in larger form) above the head of the deity. Most likely the Deuteronomist designates as Sakkût and Kêwān[61] those astral deities who probably found acceptance among the inhabitants of the northern kingdom in conjunction with the Assyrian occupation and resettlement (cf. 2 Kgs 17:29–31), and who had also become known in Jerusalem. The foreign deities are rejected merely on the grounds that they are made by human hands. "To make (for oneself)" ([ל] עשה), with idols as the object, is an expression used by the Deuteronomist in dependence on Hosea.[62] The term

48 See p. 263.
49 Rendtorff, *Studien*, 197.
50 Hos 9:10; Jer 2:2. Cf. Wolff, *Hosea*, 163 [212–13].
51 See p. 170.
52 Martin Noth, *Überlieferungsgeschichtliche Studien*, (Tübingen: M. Niemeyer, [3]1967), 21.
53 Cf. Kraus, *Worship*, 112–13 [134–35].
54 So, after thorough consideration, both Marti (196–97) and Sellin (236–39). See textual note "f–f" to 5:26–27.
55 וְנִשָׂאתֶם > וּנְשָׂאתֶם ("and you will be carried"). Cf. 4:2b and Hentschke, *Stellung*, 87.
56 *Profetie*, 221–25. On the meaning of "justice" and "righteousness" in this connection, see p. 264.
57 Cf. 2:13–16, and Westermann, *Basic Forms*, 149–63 [107ff.].
58 Cf. Otto Eissfeldt, "Lade und Stierbild," *ZAW* 58

(1940–41): 190–215 (reprinted in *idem*, *Kleine Schriften* 3, 282–305).
59 *ANEP*, fig. 305; see also figs. 104, 625, 684.
60 *ANEP*, fig. 535.
61 See textual notes "h" and "i" to 5:25.
62 Cf. 1 Kgs 14:9 and 2 Kgs 17:29–31; with Hos 8:4, 6; and 13:2.

'images'' (צלמים), unusual in the texts which prohibit the manufacture of plastic representations, appears in 1 Sam 6:5 and 2 Kgs 11:18; the expression "to make images" (עשה צלמים) is found in Ezek 7:20 and 16:17.[63] Whoever wants to interpret this text as an authentic oracle of Amos is forced to make radical textual changes—and still without being able to clarify its sense for the time of Jeroboam II or to harmonize it with the proclamation of the prophet as otherwise known.[64] Even then the Masoretic vocalization of סכות (sikkût) and כיון (kiyyûn) as the names for the idols[65] remains mysterious, as does the explanatory addition ''star.''

■ 27 Amos' announcement of punishment upon those who "despise God's commandments and at the same time deceive themselves by presuming to maintain through the cultus a stable relationship with God"[66] corresponds to the threat against Gilgal which, extended to all Israel, is explicitly repeated before Amaziah at Bethel (7:17; cf. 7:11), namely deportation. In this connection Yahweh introduces himself as the commander–in–chief who decrees the deportation into exile (cf. 1:4, 7–8, 14; 2:2–3; 3:15; and 6:14). 1:5 suffices to show that Amos knew of forced resettlement on a large scale.[67] The destination envisioned for the removal into exile remains just as vague here as it was in 4:3.[68] The parallel uses of מהלאה (''beyond'')[69] in Gen 35:21 and Jer 22:19 indicate that no great distance from the place designated is intended; the expression merely emphasizes that the goal lies ''outside of,'' and in that sense ''beyond'' the place in question—in other words, in its hinterland. Thus ''beyond Damascus'' does not at all ''. . . show clearly that Amos has the Assyrians in mind.''[70] Apart from the fact that Amos otherwise never mentions Assyria,[71] we must recall that he recognizes the vast extent of the Aramean kingdom (1:5).[72] Damascus was the metropolis of Israel's ancient and also contemporary archenemy.[73] The city would no doubt have been known to those hearing the prophet as the place from which major highways lead out not only through the desert, via Tadmor–Palmyra, to the middle Euphrates, but also westward or eastward past the Lebanon to northern Syria.[74] But the audience finds out no more than that the place of exile is situated in the hinterland of Damascus.

Am 5:26–27 in the Damascus Document (the Zadokite Document)

In the Damascus Document (CD 7.13–19), the congregation of Qumran–Damascus interpreted Am 5:27, together with v 26, as a justification for those who had separated themselves from the priesthood in Jerusalem and had constituted the ''congregation of the new covenant in the land of Damascus'' (cf. CD 6.5, 19; 8.21). The interpretation begins (7.13b–15a):
. . . all who turned back were given over to the sword, while those who stood firm escaped to the land of the north, just as he had said: "I will send into exile Sakkût [סכות], your king, and Kêwăn, your images, beyond the tents of [מאהלי] Damascus."
Here, then, Am 5:27 (with the minor misreading of מהלאה, ''beyond,'' as ''beyond the tents of'') and 5:26 are combined to form a citation which is inter-

63 Cf. Schmidt, "Redaktion," 190.
64 Cf. the attempts to restore an original text in the following: Sellin; Weiser; Maag, *Text*, 34–35; Hentschke, *Stellung*, 24–26, 87; Amsler; and Stanley Gevirtz, "A New Look at an Old Crux: Amos 5:26," *JBL* 87 (1968): 267–76.
65 Vocalized in analogy with שִׁקּוּץ (šiqqûs "detestable thing"); cf. גִּלּוּלִים (gillûlîm "idols"). Cf. Dtn 29:16 [17]; and Zimmerli, *Ezechiel*, 150; and Marti, 197.
66 Gerhard von Rad, "Literarkritische und überlieferungsgeschichtliche Forschung im Alten Testament," *Verkündigung und Forschung (1947–48)* 3 (1950): 184.
67 See p. 157.
68 See p. 207.
69 Cf. Koehler–Baumgartner (³1967), 235.
70 Wellhausen, 84.
71 See p. 89.
72 See p. 156.
73 See pp. 149–51.
74 Noth, *World*, 192–93 [172–73].

preted as a promise of deliverance. A detailed exposition of the text in Amos then follows (CD 7.15b–19a):

> The books of the Torah are (meant by) "the booth [סוכת] of the king," just as he has said: "Then I will raise up the fallen booth of David." The "king" is [. . .] the congregation, . . . and the "Kêwān of the images" are the books of the Prophets whose words Israel has despised. And (by) the "star" is (meant) one who searches the Torah, the one who (then) enters Damascus, just as it is written . . . [a citation from Num 24:17 follows].[75]

CD 7.15–19 is thus a step–by–step interpretation of Am 5:26, in the course of which *M* "Sikkût" (CD 7.14) is read as *sûkkat* (סוכת), "booth" (CD 7.16), and explained on the basis of Am 9:11. It remains a contested issue whether "the land of Damascus" should be taken literally as a geographic locale, or rather understood as a cipher for the place of the congregation's sojourn in the wilderness of Qumran. The fact that the name "Damascus" from Am 5:27 is cited in CD 7.15 ("beyond the tents of Damascus") but, unlike the other key words in the Amos text, is not specifically interpreted, argues in favor of the first option.[76] The Essenes apparently understood Am 5:21–23 as an oracle of judgment against the Jerusalemite priesthood.

Aim

Speaking in the name of Yahweh, Amos threatens those in Israel who, while engaging in sacral festivities, have set aside the gift of justice.[77] The way in which the adopted rhetorical forms have here been elaborated and intensified indicates that Amos has not merely issued a cultic decision of limited applicability. On the other hand, neither has he undertaken to present fundamental deliberations on the cultus as such. It is precisely in his pointedly direct address that "the maximum possible for Amos in terms of basic principle"[78] is achieved. In 5:25–26 the Deuteronomist, arguing

on the basis of salvation history, then proceeds to offer general theological deliberations. Renouncing the gods crafted by human hands, he thus directs the text toward the New Testament renunciation of sacrifice as a human enterprise. Amos threatens the self–security of a congregation living within the confines of its orders of worship, confronting it with the inescapable reality of the living God who demands justice and righteousness and who announces his imminent intervention. "We are dealing here with the first radical critique of religion, which denounces it as spiritual alienation."[79]

Karth Barth, in his farewell lecture in the winter semester of 1961–62,[80] found it proper and necessary to relate our text also to "the 'temptation' encountering theology," which "is simply the event that God withdraws himself from the theological work of man."[81] The reader learned in Scripture will bypass Barth's exposition of this observation only to the detriment of himself and his social milieu. Barth describes what may become of our theological efforts in these words: "Everything is in order, but everything is also in the greatest disorder. The mill is turning, but it is empty as it turns. All the sails are hoisted, but no wind fills them to drive the ship. The fountain adorned with many spouts is there, but no water comes. Science there is, but no knowledge illuminated by the power of its object. There is no doubt piety, but not the faith which, kindled by God, catches fire. What appears to take place there does not really take place. For what happens is that God, who is supposedly involved in all theological work, maintains silence about what is thought and said in theology *about* him (rather than *of* him as its source and basis). It does happen that the real relation of God to theology and the theologians must be described by a variation of the famous passage in Amos 5: 'I hate, I despise your lectures and seminars, your sermons, addresses, and Bible studies, and I take no delight in your discussions, meetings, and

---

75 [Trans. of CD 7.13a–19a by Ed. Text: Chaim Rabin, *The Zadokite Documents* (Oxford: Clarendon Press, ²1958), 29, 31.] Cf. Eduard Lohse, *Die Texte aus Qumran: Hebräisch und Deutsch* (München: Kösel–Verlag, 1964), 80.

76 Cf. Paul Kahle, "Der gegenwärtige Stand der Erforschung der in Palästina neu gefundenen hebräischen Handschriften," *ThLZ* 77 (1952): 409; Johann Maier, *Die Texte vom Toten Meer*, vol. 2 (München: E. Reinhardt, 1960), 49–50; and Millar Burrows, *More Light on the Dead Sea Scrolls: New Scrolls and New Interpretations* (New York: Viking

Press, 1958), 219–27.

77 See p. 264.

78 Smend, "Nein," 414; see also Masao Sekine, "Das Problem der Kultpolemik bei den Propheten," *EvTh* 28 (1968): 605–9.

79 G. Casalis, *Göttinger Predigtmeditationen* 19 (1964–65): 335.

80 *Evangelical Theology: An Introduction*, tr. Grover Foley (New York: Holt, Rinehart and Winston, 1963), 133–44 [*Einführung in die evangelische Theologie* (Zürich: EVZ–Verlag, 1962), 146–58].

81 *Ibid.*, 134 [147].

conventions. For when you display your hermeneutic, dogmatic, ethical, and pastoral bits of wisdom before one another and before me, I have no pleasure in them; I disdain these offerings of your fatted calves. Take away from me the hue and cry that you old men raise with your thick books and you young men with your dissertations! I will not listen to the melody of your reviews that you compose in your theological magazines, monthlies, and quarterlies.'

It is a terrible thing when God keeps silence, and by keeping silence speaks. It is terrible when you or another theologian must notice or, at least, suspect that this occurs, and most terrible of all when many do not even seem to notice and perhaps not even suspect that this occurs. How horrendous it is for them when, pursuing their own carefree way, they fail to notice that theology and all its questions are called in question totally and radically by God. All theology is threatened finally and definitively by the temptation that comes from *him*!" [82]

82   *Ibid.*, 135–36 [148–49].

Woe to Those Who Are Secure!

Bibliography

Otto Eissfeldt
"Etymologische und archäologische Erklärungen alttestamentlicher Wörter," *OrAnt* 5 (1966): 165–76 (reprinted in *idem, Kleine Schriften* 4, 285–96).

Reinhard Fey
Amos und Jesaja: Abhängigkeit und Eigenständigkeit des Jesaja, WMANT 12 (Neukirchen–Vluyn: Neukirchener Verlag, 1963), 10–17.

See the bibliography for the "woe–cries," pp. 226–27 and 242 n. 99.

6

1 Woe [(to those) who are secure on Zion]ᵃ
  (to those) who are carefree on
  Mount Samaria,
    the (most) notable of the choicest
    of the nations!
    [And the house of Israel comes to
    them.]ᵇ

a The reference to Zion on the part of Amos presents grave interpretive problems. To be sure, Oettli (*Amos*, 72) has asked: "Why should not Amos, a Judean, be allowed in the course of his address to touch on his own homeland?" But the prophet never does so elsewhere, nor is such in keeping with his commission (7:15). Moreover, in this passage "those who are secure in Zion" are mentioned, not peripherally, but prominently in initial position. Consequently, interpreters have tried in various ways to relate the tone–setting first line to Samaria. Georg Fohrer ("Zion–Jerusalem in the Old Testament," *TDNT* 7, 295) supposes that Zion, in this instance, is "... a technical expression for the situation of the capital; Samaria is the 'Zion' of the Northern Kingdom." But such a usage would constitute a singular exception. Would it not have been ambiguous even in eighth–century Samaria? Is there ever an instance where Amos does not make it unambiguously clear to whom he is speaking? Sellin (KAT 12 [¹1922]) suggested we read בָּעִיר ("in the city") instead of *M*'s בציון ("in Zion"), thinking of the "capital city" as a synonymous parallel to "Mount Samaria" in v 1aβ (cf. עִיר in 6:8 and 1 Sam 27:5). This is particularly unlikely in the opening statement of an oracle, to judge by Amos' rhetoric elsewhere (3:9, 12; 4:1), and it lacks manuscript support. Thus Sellin himself subsequently returned to the transmitted text (KAT 12 [²1929, ³1930]). Weiser (*Profetie*, 229–31) tried to resolve the difficulty through an attempt to understand שאננים as parallel to בטחים, rendering "those who are proud of Zion." In support of this interpretation he adduced the historical memory of the battle at Beth–Shemesh, which led to the capture of Jerusalem in the beginning of the eighth century (Noth, *History*, 237 [217]). It is pride in this military victory which supposedly informs Amos' address. In Amos' time, however, this event lay some thirty years in the past; above all, שאן never means "proud of," but rather "carefree, secure." Furthermore, the parallelism

>Pass over to Calneh, and see;
  and thence go to Hamath[c] (the)
    Great;
      go down to Gath of the Philis-
        tines.
Are (you)[d] better than these kingdoms,
    or is their[e] territory
      greater than your[e] territory?<

of thought between בציון and בהר שמרון would be destroyed by Weiser's interpretation. Ehrlich (*Rand-glossen* 5, 243) proposed בְּגָאוֹן ("in pride"), in view of 6:8; following Ehrlich and Budde ("Amos," 121–23), Maag (*Text*, 37) reads בִּגְאוֹנָם ("those who are carefree" [Maag: "unsuspecting"] in their haughti-ness"). This proposal, like that of Sellin (בָּעִיר, see above) constitutes a wide departure from the trans-mitted consonantal text and completely destroys the parallelism between the names of cities. *G* (Οὐαὶ τοῖς ἐξουθενοῦσι Σιων), which nowhere else trans-lates שאנן in this way, apparently recognized the difficulty of this reference to Zion in the context of Amos' oracles and so interpreted "those who despise Zion," against the literal meaning of the Hebrew. Having thus examined all alternative suggestions, I am driven to a solution already anticipated by Marti in 1904. He regarded השאנגים בציון ו as a supplement added "by someone who wanted to have Amos take Judah into consideration as well," to whom we must then also attribute 2:4–5 and 3:1b, and the other supplementations which we have identified as Deuteronomistic. This explana-tion (cf. also Victor Maag, "Amosbuch," *RGG*[3] 1, 331), apart from the fact that all others remain un-satisfactory, is supported on the following grounds. 1) It avoids the need to attach an otherwise un-attested meaning to either שאנגים or "Zion." 2) The woe–cry here thus begins with a participle rather than an adjective; the initial participle after הוי, subsequently interchanged with finite verbs, is the rule which has no exception elsewhere in Amos (cf. 5:7, 10, 18 and the continuation 6:3–6). 3) Since v 1bβ is also difficult to incorporate into the context (see textual note "b"), v 1aβbα emerges as a clear bicolon with three stresses per colon. 4) The oracle opens with a designation of the primary addressee and so agrees with the usual style of Amos' procla-mation.

b   This word–group was already misunderstood by both *G* and *V*. *G* attached some of the words to the preceding sentence and some to the following; *V* renders *ingredientes pompatice domum Israhel* ("enter-ing with pomp [into the] house of Israel"). The diffi-culties found here have led to fantastic conjectures. Oettli (*Amos*, 72) proposed to read (הֵמָּה) וְכֵאלֹהִים בְּבֵית יִשְׂרָאֵל ("and like gods [they are] in the house of Israel"), a conjecture which has found adherents up to the present time (Robinson; Weiser; Maag, *Text*, 37), even though it requires changes of the consonantal text in at least four places and has no support from any ancient version. Ehrlich (*Rand-glossen* 5, 243) fully preserved the consonantal text of v 1bβ, but vocalized וּבָאוּ and took להם as referring to the preceding הגוים, thus creating here a tran-sition to v 2: "Go to them, house of Israel!" This incorrectly presupposes that v 2 belongs to the orig-inal woe–cry (see p. 274). Marti (199) took v 1bβ, which he read as וּבָאלֹהֵי בֵית יִשְׂרָאֵל, to be a gloss on v 1aβ: "those who rely upon the mountain of Samaria . . . and (thus) upon the gods of the house of Israel." He appealed to Is 10:9–11 (10!) for support. This proposal offers a closer interpretation of the consonantal text than does Ehrlich's. It is crucial to recognize that the sentence is only intelligible as a later addition. As such, however, it can be more easily explained as a Deuteronomistic gloss on v 1bα (הגוים; see above, Ehrlich!) than (with Marti) as a gloss on v 1aβ (cf. Josh 23:7; 2 Kgs 17:8, 11, 15, 33, etc.): "And the house of Israel came to them (the foreign nations)." The proposal to regard v 1bβ as a later Deuteronomistic interpretation has the following advantages: 1) The bold conjectures become unnecessary. 2) It deals with the objection that the sentence is much too pale to belong to an oracle of Amos (this being the only sentence in 6:1 + 3–6 which does not consist of a reproach against the ruling class), and it was precisely this objection which provoked the conjecturing of forced, ironical readings of the line (Amsler, 216 n. 2). 3) The sentence is prosaic and somewhat awkward syntactically, standing out clearly from the series of tightly constructed three–stress bicola in 6:1 + 3–6, while its structure is without parallel elsewhere in sequences of woe–cries. 4) The construction בוא ל is foreign to Amos, who rather construes the verb with the accusative (4:4; 5:5, 19), or אֶל (8:2), or עַל (4:2). בוא ל is quite rare in general (Jer 50:26), but it does appear in the Deuteronomistic History (1 Sam 9:12, and Josh 2:3 also in a gloss). 5) Since השאננים בציון in v 1aα has also been recognized to be a Deuteronomistic addition (see textual note "u" above), we thus find that the original text of Amos in v 1 exhibited a clear three–stress bicolon.

c   On the construct form which appears here, instead of the usual חָמַת, see Joüon, par. 131n.

d   The restoration of an explicit אַתֶּם (Oettli, *Amos*, 72; Weiser, *Profetie*, 232) seems unnecessary since those being addressed in the presence of the speaker are the subject of the sentence. We have here a single–element (Brockelmann, *Syntax*, par. 13b) or "unipolar" nominal sentence (Karl Oberhuber, "Zur Syntax des Richterbuches: Der einfache Nominalsatz und die sogennante nominale Apposition," *VT* 3 (1953): 3–8); cf. Ps 115:7.

e   Following Wellhausen, it has become common practice to interchange the pronominal suffixes, but it is more difficult to explain how the present text could have arisen secondarily than to interpret it as it stands in light of eighth–century history. "The utterance makes good sense if it is regarded as a quotation of those, addressed in v 1, who are ever so self–confident" (Maag, *Text*, 39).

f   For ל with the accusative, see Joüon, par. 125k.

g   The shift in *M* to direct address ("but you bring near") is surprising since this style does not appear in the context of the ancient woe–cries. (To be sure,

3

(Woe to those) who set aside[f] the evil
day,

but \<bring near>[g] the rule[h] of
violence;

4 who lie upon couches of ivory,
and sprawl[i] on their beds;

who eat lambs from the flock,
and calves from the midst
of the fattening–pen;

5 who howl to the sound of the lute,
and [like David][j]

invent for themselves instruments;

6 who [k]drink wine from basins,[k]
and anoint themselves
with the choicest oils.

>But over the ruin of Joseph
they are unconcerned.<

h The phrase שֶׁבֶת חָמָס remains difficult, since שֶׁבֶת
elsewhere in the Old Testament means "sitting
still" = "inactivity" (Ex 21:19; Prov 20:3). Nowack
and Weiser have proposed reading שֶׁבֶר וְחָמָס ("destruction and violence"); on the basis of 3:10, Marti
conjectured שֹׁד וְחָמָס ("devastation and [act of]
violence"); Koehler–Baumgartner (947), Maag
(*Text*, 37–38), and Amsler suggest שְׁנַת חָמָס ("year of
violence") as an appropriate parallel to יום רע in
the preceding colon. None of these emendations of
the consonantal text finds support in the ancient
textual traditions. G (σαββάτων ψευδῶν ["false sab-
baths"]) and V (*solio iniquitatis* ["throne of iniquity"]) confirm M. An attempt to interpret our passage along the lines of Prov 20:3 (שֶׁבֶת מֵרִיב "inactivity in the face of strife")—hence "inactivity"
[in the face] of violence" or the like—suffers not
only because the text lacks the privative מִן, but also
because the verbs lead one to expect a clear case of
antithetic parallelism between the cola in v 3. Joseph
Reider ("Etymological Studies in Biblical Hebrew,"
VT 2 [1952]: 113–30) has postulated (*ibid*, 122) the
meaning "assault" for שֶׁבֶת in our text, on the basis
of Arabic *waṭbat*. It suits the context excellently but
unfortunately does not find any support in the Old
Testament itself. It remains to consider the interpretation of Wellhausen (85), supported by V (*solio
iniquitatis*), which takes שֶׁבֶת to reflect ישׁב in its sense
"to occupy the throne" (with reference to a king or
judge); this would elicit in our text the meaning
"rule" or "reign" of violence.

i Literally those who "hang over, hang down" (used
with reference to blankets, Ex 26:12; to a turban,
Ezek 23:15; to a vine growing wild, Ezek 17:6);
here, then, the sense is "those who sprawl, lounge
about."

j G (ὡς ἑστῶτα ἐλογίσαντο καὶ οὐχ ὡς φεύγοντα ["as
permanent they have reckoned (them) and not as
fleeting"]) knows nothing of "David" here, with
only חָשְׁבוּ of M's text of the line being recognizable
in ἐλογίσαντο. Instead of כדויד, G perhaps presupposes כְּעָמֵד (cf. Zech 3:1 where G ἑστῶτα = עֹמֵד),
and in antithesis to this perhaps כְּשָׂרִיד (cf. Ob 14
where G τοὺς φεύγοντας ἐξ αὐτῶν = שְׂרִידָיו) instead
of כלי־שׁיר. Instead of לָהֶם, G assumes a negative.
Thus the sense of the line, which now speaks of
boasting with steadfastness, has been completely
obscured in G, in contrast to M which exhibits a
close parallel to v 5a. In favor of an original כדויד

it is also present in a woe–cry in 5:18b). If the second–person plural style were original here, however,
one would also expect to find it attested in the finite
verbs which follow (6:5, 6, 7). V already presupposes the second–person plural reading of v 3, but in
the participial translation of G there is no evidence
for the style of direct address. Probably וַיַּגִּישׁוּן was
the original reading, this having been altered (so M)
to conform to the second–person plural style of v 2
after the latter's inclusion in the context.

272

7 Therefore now!

They move along at the head of the exiles,
ᶦand suppressed is the spree
of the sprawlersᶦ

—<oracle of Yahweh
[God of Hosts]>.ᵐ

it must be noted that *G* already presupposes a similar group of consonants. Nevertheless, "like David" should be understood as a later addition. It not only overloads the line, breaking the otherwise regular pattern in this context of parallel three–stress cola, but the reference is also unlikely in an utterance of Amos addressed to the leaders of the northern kingdom. On the other hand, it can easily be understood as a postexilic addition, comparable to the statement in 5:22aα which points to the time of the Chronicler (see p. 295 n. "c").

k–k Literally "drink from bowls of wine"; the preposition ב as used here denotes the drinker's mouth laxly resting against the vessel's rim (cf. Gen 44:5 and Brockelmann, *Syntax* par. 106a).

l–l The translation is meant to reflect the alliteration of the three Hebrew words; more literally the line reads "And the revelry of those who are stretched out disappears." *G* (καὶ ἐξαρθήσεται χρεμετισμὸς ἵππων ἐξ Εφραιμ ["and the neighing of the horses is taken away from Ephraim"]) must have read סוּסִים instead of סְרוּחִים, which led to the peculiar translation ("neighing") of מרזח, elsewhere correctly understood in *G* ("screeching," see p. 277). "From Ephraim" would have arisen as an explanatory addition; cf. Karl Vollers, "Das Dodekapropheton der Alexandriner," *ZAW* 3 (1883): 268.

m Since in v 8 [אלהי צבאות] נאם יהוה is surely not original alongside נשבע יהוה ("Yahweh has sworn"), it is possible that it has been displaced from the end of v 7 to its present position through a copyist's error. It would be unusual if an oracular announcement of judgment by Amos were not explicitly designated as divine speech. Yet the oracle formula is absent from *G* in both places; see textual note "c" to 6:8. (On the expansion of the brief oracle formula, see pp. 287–88, on 6:14.)

Form

6:1 + 3–6a exhibits the basic form of the woe–cries.[1] At least the first colon of each bicolon begins with a participle in the plural. The woe–cry here assumes the function of the accusation in the prophetic judgment oracle, the second part of which, namely the announcement of punishment, is attached through לָכֵן ("therefore"), as often in Amos (3:11; 5:16; 7:17).[2] In contrast to the woe–cries, which are never designated as Yahweh's speech, the threat of punishment was probably concluded with the designation "oracle of Yahweh."[3] That 6:7 belongs to 6:1 + 3–6 is evidenced not only by the connecting לָכֵן but also by interlocking catchwords. Thus בראש in v 7a takes up the repeated [ו]ראשית of v 1bα and v 6aβ, and the very unusual סרוחים in v 7b recalls v 4aβ.[4]

6:6b departs from the basic bicolon structure of the pericope, and also exhibits its only negative statement. To be sure, the thematically related oracle in Is 5:11–13 also contains a negative sentence after a positively formulated woe–cry and this immediately before the threat.[5] There, however, the *parallelismus membrorum* is

---

1   See pp. 242–45. On 6:1, see textual notes "a" and "b"; on 6:5, textual note "j."

2   On 5:11, see p. 233.

3   See textual note "m" to 6:7.

4   Differently Weiser, *Profetie*, 229–48.

5   Cf. Fey, *Amos und Jesaja*, 12.

preserved even in the negative segment (Is 5:12b). In addition, it is noteworthy that in 6:6b Israel is called "Joseph," an identification found elsewhere in Amos only in 5:15.[6] We must observe above all, however, that just as 5:15 refers to the "remnant of Joseph," the reference is here to the "ruin of Joseph." Such a statement within an accusation leveled by Amos himself would be unusual. Stylistic, linguistic, and thematic observations therefore make it necessary to ask whether v 6b cannot be most easily explained as a supplement from a later time.

The same is true of 6:2. Its formulation as direct address (second–person plural imperatives in v 2a and questions in v 2b) interrupts the otherwise regular sequence of participial and third–person plural verbal forms appropriate to the original didactic style of the woe–oracle.[7] The series of three exhortations in v 2a also breaks the prosodic pattern. As to content, we note here the mention of precisely that Philistine city (Gath) missing in 1:6–8.[8] The disputational style reminds one of 5:14–15, a text which apparently reflects the rhetorical confrontation between one of Amos' disciples and residents of the northern kingdom.[9]

Setting

Indeed, the additions in 6:2 and 6:6b can be better understood when attributed to the circle of Amos' disciples than to the prophet himself. Calneh and Hamath were conquered in 738 by Tiglath–pileser III who, at the very same time, demanded tribute from the Israelite king, Menahem. In 734 Gath came under the hegemony of Assyria, either losing its independence or passing out of Judean control.[10] It is during this period, between 738 and 733,[11] the time of the impending "ruin of Joseph," that the woe–oracle against the self–reliant was most likely reinterpreted in the light of the contemporary political situation. The original woe–oracle, however, attacks an untroubled sense of security and was probably proclaimed by

Amos in Samaria itself.

Interpretation

■ 1 In the language of Amos, the verb בטח ("to trust") is used to connote a facile optimism and the sense of security as such. So too does proverbial wisdom characterize the confidence of the fool who lives a life of careless ease (Prov 14:16), or the self–assurance of one who considers himself secure on account of his riches (Prov 11:28). Thus the preposition ב ("in, on") does not necessarily introduce here that upon which the sense of security is based (as it does in Hos 10:13 and Dtn 28:52). The question as to whether the citadel of Samaria could easily be defended was not yet a relevant one in the days of Amos. Rather, the preposition here probably serves merely to introduce the location of the carefree, as in 4:1 (cf. 3:9); ב has the same function in the Deuteronomistic supplement in v 1a.[12] Nor in what follows is there allusion to any danger in the face of which one would have to rely on the advantageous location of the capital city. Those reproached by the prophet display a completely carefree arrogance; they deem themselves to be pre–eminently "notable." The fundamental meaning of the verb נקב is "to perforate" (2 Kgs 12:10; Is 36:6; Hag 1:6), and then derivatively "to determine, fix" something (such as the amount of someone's wages, Gen 30:28), and hence to accentuate or lift up something in either an honorific (Is 62:2) or derogatory manner (Lev 24:11, 16). In the latter cases the verb has to do with name and reputation. So too in Am 6:1 the passive participle of נקב expresses the notion of pre–eminence. In this context, of course, ראשית denotes not temporal primacy (Gen 1:1) but pride of rank or quality (as also in 6:6aβ!),[13] the self–acknowledged "choicest" stratum of society. Thus the carefree attitude of the elite class of Samaria is rooted in the sense of belonging to the patently superior people. It is this proud security which is the target of the woe–cry of funerary lamentation. The gloss in v 1bβ could

---

6   On "house of Joseph" in 5:6, see p. 240.
7   See pp. 243–45; on 6:3b, see textual note "g" to that verse.
8   See p. 158.
9   See pp. 108–11 and 250.
10 See p. 158.
11 See p. 277.
12 See textual note "a."

13 1 Sam 2:29; 15:21; the expression "foremost of nations" (ראשית גוים) also appears in Nu 24:20.

refer to the "(most) notable" (נְקֻבִים) and thus express in a loose way that the house of Israel depended on its leaders. Such a banal gloss would then have to be explained as due to unfamiliarity with the rare word נקבים. But are the people, in contrast to the leadership, called "the house of Israel" (בית ישראל)?[14] It seems more natural to regard "the nations" (הגוים) as the antecedent of the pronoun in v 1bβ, and consequently to see here expressed the Deuteronomistic notion that Israel had become a follower of the heathen nations.[15]

■ **2** One of Amos' disciples[16] reinterpreted the woe, which the prophet had raised over the self–assured in Samaria, for a later generation threatened by Assyria in the time of Tiglath–pileser III. Now specific peoples are adduced for comparison. Calneh (Is 10:9 Calno; Akkadian *Kullani*) was the capital city of a state in northern Syria;[17] in 738 it was conquered by Tiglath–pileser, just as was Hamath.[18] It remains uncertain whether the unusual construction "Hamath (the) Great" (חמת רבה) means the capital city Hamath or the great state of Hamath whose territorial claims had expanded considerably after 800 B.C. Philistine Gath is mentioned by Amos' disciple perhaps because of its proximity to the Judean border; after having belonged temporarily to Judah it eventually came under Assyrian hegemony.[19] It was Sargon II who, in 712–11, finally subjugated Gath,[20] as he had Hamath in 720 and Calneh in 717. But just as Tiglath–pileser had already reduced the territorial holdings of Hamath and Calneh to a minimum, while imposing tribute upon them, so it was his advance into the Philistine coastal plain in 734 which robbed the Philistine cities of their independence.[21] Similarly, Tiglath–pileser in 738 imposed tribute on "Menahem of Samaria" and in 733 he transformed Dor, Megiddo, and Gilead into Assyrian provinces, while reducing Israel to the status of a relatively limited vassal kingdom in the hill country of Samaria.[22] Thus if it was in the period between 738 and 733 that Amos' disciple addressed a group of north Israelites, perhaps on the occasion of some pilgrimage by them to the Beer–sheba sanctuary,[23] then the re-interpreted oracle was certainly designed to demolish whatever sense of security they may have retained. The question "Are you better than those kingdoms?" was probably aimed less at evoking a comparison of ethical qualities than of prowess and power to offer resistance (cf. Na 3:8). The other question—in its transmitted wording[24]—undercuts the carefree attitude of those who thought that Israel, in contrast to Hamath, Calneh, and Philistia, would be too insignificant to become a target of Tiglath–pileser's lust for conquest.

■ **3** Vv 3–6 develop the theme that the proud confidence of the leaders of Samaria makes them culpable. These leaders have excluded from consideration, at least as far as their own lives were concerned, the "evil day" which, according to Prov 16:4, threatens the wicked and which Amos had announced as the "Day of Yahweh" (5:18–20). נדה (pi'el) means "to banish, cast out hatefully" (Is 66:5). Amos could be thinking of the reaction triggered by his proclamation of approaching calamity. Regardless of whether his hearers wished to "conjure away by magical means, scare off" the evil day[25] as though it were some sort of evil spirit, or whether they merely tried to push it out of consciousness,[26] in either case they bring near "violence."[27] The latter may well refer primarily to the leadership's abusive treatment of the underprivileged as this is expressed in 4:1 and 3:9–10. The oppressed are made to suffer, while the oppressors loll about, indulging their appetites for food, wine, and frivolity.

14   See p. 164, and Hos 5:1; on the latter passage, see Wolff, *Hosea*, 97 [123].
15   See textual note "b" to 6:1.
16   See p. 274.
17   Cf. Noth, *World*, 261 [235]; and Martinus A. Beek, "Kalne," *BHHW* 2, 922.
18   Cf. A. Leo Oppenheim, *ANET³*, 282–83; and Kurt Galling, *Textbuch zur Geschichte Israels* (Tübingen: J. C. B. Mohr [Paul Siebeck], ²1968), no. 24.
19   On the location of Gath, cf. Hanna E. Kassis, "Gath and the Structure of the 'Philistine' Society," *JBL* 84 (1965): 259–71 (esp. 259–60); and Galling, *Text-buch*, no. 64 (probably ʿArâq ʾel-Menšîyeh).
20   A. Leo Oppenheim, *ANET³*, 286.
21   Galling, *Textbuch*, no. 25.
22   Cf. A. Leo Oppenheim, *ANET³*, 283–84.
23   See p. 239, on 5:5aγ.
24   See textual note "e" to 6:2.
25   So Maag, *Text*, 209.
26   Koehler–Baumgartner, 596: "refuse to think of."
27   On חמס ("violence"), see p. 194, on 3:10; on שבת ("rule") see textual note "h" to 6:3.

■ **4** This life of affluence is pictured here by Amos with unique concreteness. Other of the prophet's oracles call attention to the preference of the rich for plush furnishings,[28] ornamented with precious ivory inlays.[29] But now we glimpse their owners not merely lying indolently upon them but sprawled out in a stupor of satiation (v 4b) and drunkenness (cf. v 6a), no longer even able to control their own limbs.[30] Amos here employs in provocative fashion a word elsewhere used to describe loosely hanging textiles or the splayed tendrils of a wild vine, but which is never otherwise applied to human beings. They eat the young lambs from the flock, whose flesh makes for the tenderest meat. Then too this gourmet taste finds only veal acceptable from the herd, and even that from calves "set aside for fattening." רבק means "to bind tightly" (Arabic *rabaqa*); the מרבק is the enclosure where animals are restrained from moving about freely so that they can be fattened, hence "fattening-pen."[31] The prominent of society accept only selected meats.

■ **5** Feasting calls for music. The meaning of פרט has not yet been clarified. "Plucking" of strings has been proposed,[32] as has "improvising," which would seem to make an appropriate parallel to the use of חשׁב ("to devise, plan") in the following colon.[33] But עַל־פִּי (literally "over the mouth") hardly means "on the strings," and the expression here can more likely be rendered "to the sound of the lute."[34] This suggests for פרט a meaning like "wail" or "screech," hence we render "howl." The parallel colon, which speaks of the invention of musical instruments, points in the same direction. Since in v 5b the instruments are associated with song, it is probably singing to which the verb in v 5a refers (cf. 5:23). The כְּלֵי־שִׁיר are musical instruments which accompany the singing;[35] in 1 Chr 15:16 the expression denotes a general category, being here followed by specific references to lutes, zithers, and cymbals. In 1 Chr 16:42 and 2 Chr 5:13 trumpets and cymbals are mentioned before the כלי־שיר; in 2 Chr

23:13 they are associated—in contrast to the trumpets—with the singers. Thus we must suppose them to be typical instruments for the accompaniment of song, such as stringed instruments and timbrels (Ex 15:20; 1 Sam 18:6), of which many variant forms might be "devised" (חשׁב). Since in the Chronicler's time the orchestral institutions of the Jerusalem Temple were attributed to David's initiative—in 2 Chr 29:27 the instruments which accompany cultic singing are even specifically called "the instruments of David" (כְּלֵי דָוִיד; cf. 1 Chr 15:16)—there is good reason to suppose that "like David" (כדויד) in v 5bα is a late postexilic addition. Amos heard the sounds of dissolute, noisy improvising, which he found as indicative of careless self–confidence as the drinking that went with it.

■ **6** Intemperance abounds, as Amos at once harshly and pithily indicates when he labels the vessels from which the wealthy drink "wine–basins" (מזרקי יין). The verb זרק means "to splash," and describes, for example, the dashing of sacrificial blood against the altar (Ex 24:6, 8; 2 Kgs 16:13, 15). Consequently, מזרק must denote a wide–mouthed bowl which could hold the liquid for splashing.[36] Only in Amos are such bowls referred to as wine chalices. An ivory carving from Megiddo depicts a prince drinking from a bowl, while in front of him stand a servant and a lute player.[37] Such bowls apparently served as containers in which the wine was mixed with spices.[38] No doubt one normally drank from a "goblet" (כּוֹס) rather than from such a bowl. If the society accused by Amos nevertheless used bowls for drinking, its intemperance is thereby exposed. The teacher of wisdom also reproved uninhibited imbibing of wine,[39] and likewise associated the extravagant use of wine and oil (Prv 21:17). Amos has in mind oil which one rubs on (משׁח) in order to care for the skin and whose fragrance has an exhilarating effect (Song 1:3; 4:10, here also alongside reference to wine); anointing is among the exquisite pleasures of life (Eccl 9:8). Hence Amos is referring to the oil which promotes

---

28   On "couch" and "bed," see p. 198 on 3:12.
29   See p. 202 on 3:15.
30   On סרח ("to sprawl"), see textual note "i" to 6:4.
31   Maag, *Text*, 167–68.
32   Gesenius–Buhl, 659.
33   Koehler–Baumgartner, 778.
34   On נבל ("lute"), see pp. 263–64 on 5:23.
35   See p. 264.
36   Cf. A. M. Honeyman, "The Pottery Vessels of the Old Testament," *PEQ* 71 (1939): 76–90 (esp. 83–84 and pl. xix, fig. 6).
37   See James B. Pritchard, *Archaeology and the Old Testament* (Princeton: Princeton University Press, 1958), 34–35 and fig. 14.
38   Barrois, *Manuel* 1, 388.
39   Prv 20:1; 21:17; 23:20–21, 29–35; 31:4–7.

"well–being, high spirits, and joy."[40]

Ancient Near Eastern literature is familiar with festal banqueting; so, for example, the seventh–century Assyrian king Esarhaddon reports as follows on the dedicatory celebration in his newly constructed palace: "The nobles and the people of my land, all of them, I made to sit down therein, at feasts and banquets of choice dishes, and gratify their appetites. With grape–wine and sesame–wine I 'sprinkled their hearts,' with choicest oils I drenched their foreheads."[41] The nobility of Samaria were similarly satisfied with nothing less than "the choicest oils."[42] Nor do we lack pictorial representation of banquets replete with drinkers and musicians.[43]

In all probability v 6b is secondary, introduced into the text by the same disciple of Amos whom we met in connection with 6:2.[44] The "ruin of Joseph" alludes to Israel's condition which, between 738 and 733, became ever more precarious as the state came under the deepening shadow of the vast Assyrian empire, till at the end of the period it had lost most of its territorial possessions.[45] But all the while there remained those in the capital who, rather than being "troubled" (חלה nip'al, literally "become sick") by the demise of Israel, persisted in seeking security in personal well–being and pleasure.

■ **7** If the elaborate "woe" in 6:1 + 3–5 is impressive because of its detailed portrait of the elite's ill–boding behavior, comparably striking by reason of its very succinctness is the denouement of that woe, announcing "therefore now" their imminent fate. Exile is threatened.[46] The terse bicolon is so artfully crafted that the interconnection of guilt and fate is epitomized by giving an ironical twist to two key words in the preceding lines. Those who have deemed themselves "the choicest" among the nations and who demand for themselves "the choicest" in quality (vv 1b, 6aβ ראשית) will be granted primacy of place in the judgment as well—as they are marched off "at the front" (בראש) of those going into exile. And thus too those who formerly lolled about at their sumptuous banquets will experience the final "sprawl" of their way of life (סרחים of 6:4aβ is taken up in v 7b).[47] Especially this concluding utterance must have been engraved in the memory of the prophet's audience. מרזח ("spree") in later Phoenician and in Punic texts denotes cultic festivities.[48] In Jer 16:5 it has to do with rites of funerary lamentation. Otto Eissfeldt[49] has shown that the root רזח, which underlies the word, probably does not mean "to join, gather together" (רזח II), but "to shout, screech" (רזח I).[50] That which unites funerary lamentation and festal celebration is the loud shouting.

40 Ernst Kutsch, *Salbung als Rechtsakt im Alten Testament*, BZAW 87 (Berlin: A. Töpelmann, 1963), 5.

41 Esarhaddon, Prism A 6.34–40; tr. Daniel David Luckenbill, *Ancient Records of Assyria and Babylonia*, vol. 2 (Chicago, 1927), 269–70.

42 On ראשית ("finest, choicest, first") see p. 274 on 6:1b.

43 Cf., e.g., *ANEP*, fig. 637 (a relief from Carchemish from the second half of the eighth century); or the famous relief of Asshurbanipal's banquet in the vine pavillion: Andre Parrot, *The Arts of Assyria*, tr. Stuart Gilbert and James Emmons; The Arts of Mankind 2 (New York: Golden Press, 1961), fig. 60.

44 See pp. 273–75.

45 See p. 110.

46 Cf. 5:5, 27; and above, pp. 239–40, 266.

47 On the alliteration in v 7b, see textual note "l–l."

48 *KAI* 60.1; 69.16. [For additional texts and discussion of the *marzēaḥ* see now Bezalel Porten, *Archives from Elephantine: The Life of an Ancient Jewish Military Colony* (Berkeley and Los Angeles: University of California Press, 1968), 179–86; Patrick D. Miller,

Jr., "The *Mrzḥ* Text" in *The Claremont Ras Shamra Tablets*, ed. Loren R. Fisher; AnOr 48 (Roma: Pontificium Biblicum Institutum, 1971), 37–48; and Marvin H. Pope, "A Divine Banquet at Ugarit" in *The Use of the Old Testament in the New and Other Essays* (*Studies in Honor of William Franklin Stinespring*), ed. James M. Efird (Durham, N. C.: Duke University Press, 1972), 170–203 (esp. 190–94). Ed.]

49 "Etymologische und archäologische Erklärungen alttestamentlicher Wörter," *OrAnt* 5 (1966): 166–71 (= idem, *Kleine Schriften* 4, 286–90).

50 Cf. G χρεμετισμός ("neighing") and textual note "l–l" to 6:7.

The noise and the howling of the drinker will give way to the silent march into exile.

Aim

An unusual amount of space is devoted here to portraying the way of life of the Israelite leaders. The institution of the monarchy bred a class of courtiers and military officials who, together with the small group of major landowners, could enjoy a life of luxury. Not a syllable is uttered here about the God of Israel and his righteousness. That injustice is being perpetrated against others is only tersely mentioned in the original oracle (v 3b), though it is spelled out a bit more fully in the reinterpretation (v 6b). Rather it is the obverse side of Israel's culpability which comes into sharp focus here: a self–assured sense of security (v 1) whose pretense is that thoughts of the "evil day" (v 3) can be dispelled by banqueting on selected delicacies (v 4) to the accompaniment of boisterous singing and music–making (v 5), as well as unbridled imbibing and lavish use of perfumes (v 6). So the elite of Samarian society rehearse for their dismal role of leading the way into exile; so they themselves hasten the end of all their feasting.

Not many decades after Amos, those whose blindness had persisted could be confronted with a vision of their own ruin as prefigured in major political events of the time (vv 2, 6b). The woe–cry of Jesus in Luke 6:24–25 found in Am 6:1–7 the precedent for a broad indictment of the leading circles among God's people: "But woe to you that are rich, for you have received your consolation. Woe to you that are full now, for you shall hunger. Woe to you that laugh now, for you shall mourn and weep."

The Fall of the City

Bibliography

Godfrey Rolles Driver
  "A Hebrew Burial Custom," *ZAW* 66 (1955): 314–
  15.
Reinhard Fey
  *Amos und Jesaja: Abhängigkeit und Eigenständigkeit des
  Jesaja*, WMANT 12 (Neukirchen–Vluyn: Neukirchener Verlag, 1963), 48–49, 80–81.
Willy Schottroff
  *"Gedanken" im Alten Orient und im Alten Testament: Die
  Wurzel zākar im semitischen Sprachkreis*, WMANT 15
  (Neukirchen–Vluyn: Neukirchener Verlag, ²1967),
  250–51, 395.

6

8

Sworn has [the Lord]ᵃ Yahweh by his
life ᵇ
  [—utterance of Yahweh,
  God of Hosts]: ᶜ
I abhor the arrogance of Jacob.
  I hate his strongholds.
    I will deliver up ᵈall that is in the
    city. ᵈ

9

    And it will be (that) if ten men
    remain in one house, they (too)
    will die. ᵉ

a   אדני was not yet present in the text underlying *G*;
see textual note "o" to 1:8.

b   *G* (καθ' ἑαυτοῦ ["by himself"]) already presupposes
that נפש ("life") here has a reflexive meaning (as in
Prv 8:36; 19:8; and 1 Sam 18:1). But the facile
translation "by himself" does not adequately express the important nuances of personal volition and
intense purposefulness which נפש still conveys in this
usage; cf. Werner H. Schmidt, "Anthropologische
Begriffe im Alten Testament," *EvTh* 24 (1964):
374–88 (esp. 380–81). בנפשו ("by his life") is used
here by Amos with a sense very similar to that of
בקדשו ("by his holiness") in 4:2.

c   The expanded oracle formula in this position is not
yet attested in *G*. Perhaps the shorter version of it
belongs at the end of 6:7 (see textual note "m" on
6:7, and textual note "c" on 6:14). The formula is
attested in 6:8 by *V* (*dicit Dominus Deus exercituum*).

d–d Literally "the city and that which fills it." The *wāw
explicativum* (cf. Gesenius–Kautzsch–Cowley, par.
154a n. b) introduces an apposition, defining "city"
to include its populace (cf. הָאָרֶץ in 7:10!) and perhaps also its portable valuables (cf. also the statements about Gilgal and Bethel in 5:5, and Maag,
Text, 217).

e   *G* adds: καὶ ὑπολειφθήσονται οἱ κατάλοιποι ("but the
remnant [of them] will remain"). Weiser (*Profetie*,
215) takes this to be the translation of an original
וְנִשְׁאַר אַחֵר and thereby finds an antecedent for the
third–person singular pronominal suffix in 6:10aα.
But this does not do justice to the plural verb of *G*;
furthermore, *G* gives οἱ κατάλοιποι as the translation
of שְׁאֵרִית in 1:8 and 9:12, and of אַחֲרִית in 9:1 (cf.
M in 4:2!). If one seeks an antecedent for the suffixes
that follow, one could think of נִשְׁאַר שְׁאָר as the text
underlying *G*. But the textual difficulties in 6:10aα
cannot be removed so easily (see textual note "f").
We would expect to find in Amos an expression
about the remnant only in the stylistic form of the
"unreal *synchoresis*" (Gese, "Beiträge," 436; see p.
207, on 4:2). The text underlying *G* seems to intro-

10
And when ⟨someone⟩[f] lifts up
his[g] relative and is ⟨constrained⟩[h]
to take the corpses out of the
house, he will say to whomever
may be in the furthest recess of
the house, "Is there still anyone
with you?" He will say, "No
one!" and then he will say,
"Hush! For one must not
mention Yahweh by name."[i]

11
Indeed (it shall be) so!—Yahweh
commands:
He will smite the great house
into fragments[j]
and the little house into bits.[j]

duce a certain tempering of the harsh threat of disaster.

f   No sure textual base has as yet been found for the first three words of the Hebrew text. *M* ("his uncle and the one who burns him carries him") makes sense neither in relation to 6:9 nor in light of what follows in v 10. *G* (καὶ λήμψονται ["and they will take"]) presupposes וְנָשְׂאוּ. This obviates the question of finding an antecedent for the suffixed pronoun in the *M* reading. As the subject, we must assume an indefinite "one." To be sure, *G* finds the verb's subject to be דודו, which for the sake of agreement must be rendered as plural (οἱ οἰκεῖοι αὐτῶν ["their relatives/kinfolk"]).

g   Perhaps the suffix here refers to בית ("house"), understood in the sense of "family."

h   *G* (καὶ παραβιῶνται ["and they shall endeavor"]) probably presupposes וּפָצְרוּ (cf. Gen. 19:3, 9; 33:11; Ju 19:7; and 2 Kgs 2:17; 5:16), which makes the following infinitive construct intelligible. The connection with what follows remains unclear if the reading of *M* is accepted, i.e., the pi'el participle of an otherwise unattested סרף. (The latter form has been regarded as an erroneous or deliberate misspelling of שׂרף [Maag, *Text*, 164–67; a "Canaanitism," which designates "the closest living relative"]). The connection with the rest of v 10 is no clearer, even if one follows G. R. Driver ("A Hebrew Burial Custom," *ZAW* 66 [1955]: 314–15) in postulating a common Semitic root סרף with the meaning "to anoint, embalm." Cremation of corpses "was quite uncommon in Israel" (Ludwig Wächter, *Der Tod im Alten Testament*, Arbeiten zur Theologie 2/8 [Stuttgart: Calwer, 1967], 183). Even more drastic emendations of the consonantal text have commonly been proposed (cf. Weiser, *Profetie*, 215–16; Amsler; etc.).

i   Cf. Schottroff, *Gedenken*, 250–51, 395.

j   *G* (θλάσμασι—ῥάγμασιν) imitates the assonance of *M*.

Form

6:8 opens with a new oath by Yahweh.[1] In the portion which is divine speech, the judgment of guilt (v 8a) is closely connected with the announcement of punishment (v 8b). The oracle is quite complete as a unit of speech and as such needs no continuation.

Yet the transmitted text attaches in 6:9–10 a brief story which bears only a loose thematic connection with v 8. While it was the city with its populace that was threatened in v 8, it is the fate of the family of a single remaining house which is described in the continuation. To be sure, Amos is quite often inclined elsewhere to describe the eradication of even the final remnant (cf. 1:8; 2:13–16; 4:2; 8:10; 9:1–4). In all these instances,

however, the unity of the oracle in question is much more apparent than is the case with 6:8 and 9–10. The "and it will be" (והיה) could in itself already indicate a secondary linking (cf. 8:9); the connective "and when" (והיה אם), which one encounters in the continuation of the first vision report (7:2), is probably also a later addition.[2] Of weightier significance is the observation that *parallelismus membrorum* is no longer present in 6:9–10; instead, we find images syntactically entangled in a way otherwise unknown in Amos. Four different kinds of dependent clauses appear side by side: a conditional clause (v 9), a final infinitive clause (v 10aα), a relative clause (v 10aβ), and a motive clause (v 10bβ). We are dealing here with a purely prose account. The little parable in 5:19, which is functionally most closely related to our piece here, reveals precisely in its simple chain of short verbal sentences the stylistic difference involved. On the other hand, the threefold "and one/he says" (וְאָמַר) in v 10 corresponds to the reportorial style of the third and fourth vision reports (7:8–9; 8:1–2). The monotony of the narrative framework causes the stirring content of the speech fragments to stand out all the more glaringly. The greatest distinguishing feature of vv 9–10, as compared to v 8, is the fact that divine first–person speech is not only absent but also that Yahweh is even spoken of in the third person at the end in v 10bβ. The result of these observations is the likelihood that 6:9–10 must be differentiated from the rhetorical unit constituted by 6:8. Yet, it cannot be decided with certainty whether the brief story is a fragment of a different utterance of Amos or a recasting by Amos' school of some theme once treated by the prophet. The syntactically involved style (cf. 5:14–15 and 8:4–6) and the interest in specific cultic phenomena could speak in favor of the latter assumption.[3]

A further oracular fragment is attached in 6:11. The connective device in v 11a, "Indeed (it shall be) so!—Yahweh commands," is evidently the work of Amos' school (cf. 9:9). "The words of Amos from Tekoa" in chaps. 3—6 and the old cycles do not attest this sort of linking of oracles. In addition, a threat is here connected with a threat (cf. 9:8a, 9). V 11aα is also shown to be a secondary linking formula in that while it announces a command of Yahweh, it is followed not by an utterance of Yahweh himself but by a third–person report of what he will do (v 11aβb; cf. 9:9). The latter, in contrast to 6:9–10 but like 6:8, exhibits a prosodic structure of synonymous parallelism, and the assonance of the closing words of both cola again reveals the prophet's own imaginative use of language.[4] Thus it is precisely the harshness of the transition in v 11aα which prohibits our denying to Amos the authorship

of v 11aβb. Since no oracle of Amos begins with a perfect consecutive, while the announcements of punishment are quite often so introduced after a preceding demonstration of guilt,[5] we must here be dealing with a fragment. Thematically it goes well with 6:8; it is connected to 6:9–10 by the catchword "house" (בַּיִת).

Setting
6:8 may well have been proclaimed in Samaria. Which other city had strongholds? The attachment to the preceding oracle (6:1–7), which must certainly be assigned to Samaria, likewise speaks in favor of this setting. In the same way 6:11 (as 3:15) is best understood as having been addressed to residents of the capital city, where the officialdom lived in high style.

In the literary structure of the book, these three connected utterances appear near the end of the old collection of "the words of Amos from Tekoa" (chaps. 3—6). As our observations on 6:12–14 will confirm,[6] short utterances and oracular fragments were here gathered together by way of concluding the collection, presumably not without collaboration on the part of Amos' school.

Interpretation
■ 8 The accent falls increasingly on Yahweh's judicial intervention. Thus the verse directly opens with Yahweh's oath, a feature that, in 4:2, follows only after a detailed presentation of the guilt of those being addressed (4:1). Yahweh swears by "himself,"[7] since there is no higher authority for him to invoke. Perhaps the touching of the "throat" (נֶפֶשׁ), understood as a vital organ, was still known from ancient oath rituals as they are attested for Mari.[8] What Yahweh thus swears "by his life" is abhorrence and hatred. "To abhor" (תעב hitpa'el) and "to hate" (שׂנא) stand in parallelism already in 5:10; there they express human attitudes, here the attitude of Yahweh. The attestation here in *M* of תאב, in place of the usual תעב, is not

---

1 Cf. 4:2, and above p. 206.
2 See textual note "d–d" to 7:1.
3 See p. 110.
4 See pp. 96–97.
5 1:4, 7, 14; 2:2; 3:14bβ, 15; 5:27.
6 See p. 288.
7 See textual note "b" to 6:8.
8 Charles F. Jean, *Lettres diverses*, ARM(T) 2 (Paris:

Imprimerie Nationale, 1950), 77.2′-8′ (and p. 237 on *napištam lapātum* ["to touch the throat"]): In the report of treaty negotiations between Hammurabi and Zimri-Lim each is said to have touched his own throat, a gesture intimating that strangulation would be the fate of the one breaking the oath; see also 62.9′, etc. Cf. *AHW*, 535 (*lapātum* G 3a) and 738 (*napištu* A 1); and also J. M. Munn–Rankin, "Dip-

likely due to a mere copyist's error. Rather the unique writing quite probably originated as a conscious alteration, introduced into the text by some ancient scribe, affronted by the notion that Yahweh "abhors," a verb which usually expresses a human and often objectionable mode of behavior. Amos, however, was at home in the wisdom tradition where the "abhorrence / abomination of Yahweh" (תּוֹעֲבַת יהוה) is mentioned quite frequently (twelve times in Prv), including specific reference to his abhorrence of arrogance (Prv 16:5) and pride (Prv 6:16–17, where also "to hate" [שֹׂנֵא] parallels "abhorrence / abomination" [תּוֹעֵבָה]). It is the "pride" of Jacob which is the object of Yahweh's abhorrence in Amos. "Pride, arrogance" (גָּאוֹן) is cited in proverbial wisdom as being the way to destruction (Prv 16:18) and as being something which Yahweh "hates" (Prv 8:13). It is rare for Amos to reduce the guilt to one concept in this way; "arrogance" summarizes what is elsewhere characterized in specific detail as arbitrariness, injustice, luxurious living, and military self–confidence.[9] If "pride, arrogance" is here and in this whole group of oracles named as the only cause of Yahweh's rejection, then the aim is to expose the root of evil. "Haughtiness" (*superbia*) is *V*'s rendering of גָּאוֹן, and *hybris* (ὕβρις) is that of *G*. "Jacob" stands here (as in 3:13; 7:2, 5; [8:7; 9:8;] and Is 9:7 [8]; cf. Is 17:4) for the northern kingdom.[10] Perhaps the expression "arrogance of Jacob" is proverbial, in view of the traditions of the fathers taken up in Hos 12:3–4.[11]

For Amos this "arrogance" is manifest in the imposing "strongholds."[12] As the punishment, Yahweh will "deliver up" (סגר hip'il).[13] This word refers primarily to the giving up or abandoning of the populace, but an allusion to accumulated wealth may also be

intended.[14] Yahweh will abandon Jacob to the hands of strangers (cf. 5:27; 6:14). In view of the parallel reference to "strongholds," it is improbable that "city" (עִיר) should be understood here in a collective sense, similar to "the city" (הָעִיר) in 5:3.[15]

■ 9 The story that follows spells out the theme of total destruction in a most vivid manner, placing alongside the panoramic view of the abandonment of an entire city a close–up scene of the fate of a single household (cf. 2:13–16). To one family there is left only a remnant of ten people. But even of these few who have thus far been spared, it is laconically noted, "they (too) will die." What follows suggests that the thought here is of a pestilence, for it is not an enemy to whom they are handed over, but Yahweh himself (v 10bβ) who is feared.

■ 10 Somehow the corpses have to be removed from the house. If the uncertain attempt at reconstruction[16] is approximately correct, then some relative is compelled (by whom?) to perform the task. The masculine form עֲצָמִים (literally "bones"), as the word designating "corpses," is found only here; elsewhere the feminine form עֲצָמוֹת has this connotation.[17] The whispered conversation gives one an uncanny sense of the dread of death seeking out even the very last person. The one who fetches the corpses from the house directs his question into the darkness. The "furthest recess of the house" (יַרְכְּתֵי הַבַּיִת) designates the part of the house which is innermost (1 Kgs 6:16), least accessible (Ps 128:3), most hidden (cf. Jon 1:5).[18] It is not clear who is being asked, "Is there still anyone with you?" Is there still someone seriously ill yet alive among the dead? Is a second person also searching the nooks of the house? The further response to the query indicates that someone is still in danger, for it begins with the

---

lomacy in Western Asia in the Early Second Millenium B.C.," *Iraq* 18 (1956): 68–110 (esp. 89–90)

9   Am 2:6–8; 3:9–10, 15; 4:1; 5:7, 10–12, 21–23; 6:1, 3–6, 13–14.

10   The same may also be true in Hos 10:11; so Gunther Wanke, *Die Zionstheologie der Korachiten in ihrem traditionsgeschichtlichen Zusammenhang*, BZAW 97 (Berlin: A. Töpelmann, 1966), 56; differently Wolff, *Hosea*, 185 [240].

11   Cf. Am 8:7; Na 2:3 [2](?); and Ps 47:5 [4].

12   On the word, see p. 155; on the subject matter, cf. 3:9–11.

13   On this word, see p. 157 on 1:6.

14   Cf. 3:10, and see textual note "d" to 6:8.

15   See p. 281.

16   See textual notes "f," "g" and "h" to 6:10.

17   Gen 50:25; Ex 13:19; Ezek 6:5, etc.

18   יַרְכָה designates the "hinder portion" (*Rücken*); cf. Gen 49:13.

19   Hab 2:20; Zeph 1:7; Zech 2:17 [13]; Neh 8:11.

fearful cry urging silence, "Hush!" "Hush" (הס) is used elsewhere primarily to command silence in the sanctuary where Yahweh is immanent.[19] Here the dominant concern is that Yahweh's name might be mentioned, perhaps in an outcry of lamentation. "To mention" (זכר hip'il), which is perhaps a denominative of "remembrance, memorial" (זֵכֶר),[20] means the simple act of mentioning the name. The expression "to mention by name" (הזכיר בשם) appears, apart from our passage, in Josh 23:7 (with reference to foreign gods) and in Is 48:1 and Ps 20:8 [7] (with reference to the God of Israel). Undertones of magic accompany this expression, the notion being that to name Yahweh's name is necessarily to invoke the presence of Yahweh himself.[21] Given all that Amos has proclaimed, Yahweh's presence can only mean fatal danger (5:17; 9:4). The Assyrian king Enlil–nirāri (1326—1317) opens a decree concerning the procedures for reporting the death of someone among the members of the palace with the command "May the god by no means speak!"— probably reflecting an apotropaic expression.[22]

■ 11 The threat against the great and the little houses further supplements the oath of Yahweh against the city and its strongholds (6:8). It remains very uncertain whether the distinction between "great" and "little" houses is identical with that of summer and winter houses in 3:15. In connection with these "great" houses, one is better off thinking of the buildings of hewn stone in 5:11, while the "little" ones may perhaps be sought in the magnificently laid out vineyards.[23] But our harsh text does not intend to arouse curiosity over such questions; it rather wants to state that all houses, the great ones as well as the little ones, will crumble under Yahweh's blow. "To smite" (הִכָּה) probably envisions an earthquake (cf. 3:15; 9:1;

[2:13]), since the result is broken (רסס) and split (בקע) walls, or in other words a field of ruins.

Aim

This little series of utterances and oracular fragments is held together by Yahweh's threat against the "houses," probably above all the royal residence. Only proud arrogance is identified as the reason for Yahweh's abhorrence of the populace. This identification lays bare the underlying attitude which determines as guilt all the misdeeds that have been concretely described. "Arrogance" (גָּאוֹן) has displaced "right" (נְכֹחָה 3:10), "justice" and "righteousness" (מִשְׁפָּט and צְדָקָה 5:7, 24; 6:12). Therefore Yahweh's hatred delivers up the proud city to strangers. The populace is abandoned (6:8). Death slithers into the deepest recesses of the last house (6:9–10). Only a field of ruins remains (6:11). Not a single concrete reproach stands alongside these harsh announcements of punishment. In 6:1 + 3–7 the number of sentences establishing guilt exceeded by far the brief threat at the end. Elsewhere the two chief elements of the prophetic oracles of judgment—the accusation and the announcement of punishment—were generally held in balance. Only in 5:1–3 did the question of guilt recede completely, and there also death was explicitly mentioned. While 5:3 spoke of the army being decimated, 6:9 goes even farther; the human remnant must also die. Even the very last person, expiring in the furthest nook of the house, only whimpers with fear. The movement of the account reminds one distantly of the parable in 5:19: there is no escaping Yahweh's grasp. Untiringly Amos drives home the point that no self–built stronghold can provide security against the blow of the God of Israel.

---

20   Brevard S. Childs, *Memory and Tradition in Israel*,
      SBT 37 (London: SCM Press, 1962), 12; cf. Schott-
      roff, *Gedenken*, 244.
21   Cf. 1 Sam 20:42 and 2 Kgs 2:24; and also Hans
      Bietenhard, "ὄνομα," *TDNT* 5, 255.
22   Cf. Ernst Weidner, "Hof- und Harems–Erlasse
      assyrischer Könige aus dem 2. Jahrtausend v. Chr.,"
      AfO 17 (1954–56): 257–93 (esp. 270–71).
23   Weiser, *Profetie*, 201.

Distortion of the Natural Order

Bibliography

Friedrich Horst
"Recht und Religion im Bereich des Alten Testaments," *EvTh* 16 (1956): 49–75 (reprinted in *idem*, *Gottes Recht*, 260–91).

Hans Heinrich Schmid
Gerechtigkeit als Weltordnung: Hintergrund und Geschichte des alttestamentlichen Gerechtigkeitsbegriffes, BHTh 40 (Tübingen: J. C. B. Mohr [Paul Siebeck], 1968), 112–13.

Artur Weiser
Die Profetie des Amos, BZAW 53 (Giessen, 1920), 197–99.

6

12

**Do horses race over rocky terrain?
Or does one[a] plough ⟨the sea
with oxen⟩[b]?
Yet you turn justice into poison
and the fruit of righteousness
into wormwood.**

a The third–person singular here signifies the general subject "one." (Cf. textual note "g" to 4:2; Gen 11:9; and Brockelmann, *Syntax*, par. 36d.) It is superfluous to make a change to nipʻal יֵחָרֵשׁ with Wellhausen, Weiser and others, following Johann David Michaelis, *Deutsche Übersetzung des Alten Testaments*, vol. 1 (Göttingen, 1772).

b M ("Does one plough with oxen?") makes a self–evident observation which, in its context, is senseless. The preceding parallel leads one to seek a counterpart to the place designation בסלע ("over rocky terrain"). Thus בִּבְקָר יָם ("the sea with oxen") has found general acceptance since the time of Michaelis (see textual note "a"). To read a plural ("oxen") in the unvocalized consonantal sequence of בקרים was easy in view of the preceding plural form סוסים ("horses").

Form

The sapiential device of leading up to an insight by way of rhetorical questions is familar to us from 3:3–6 and 8.[1] The special feature of this short oracular composition lies in the antithetical relationship between the similies and that to which they are compared. Since the preceding questions require negative answers, the כי ("yet") has an adversative force in 6:12b, just as it usually does following negative statements. The images drawn of animal life compel human beings to acknowledge the perversity of their own contrasting behavior. Similar argumentations (although not formulated in interrogative style) are found in Isaiah (1:3) and Jeremiah (8:7)—where human wrongdoing is set over against the proper behavior of animals. The prosodic structure reinforces the sharp thrust of the aggressively direct address: two three–stress bicola, each with internal synonymous parallelism, are juxtaposed as antitheses.

Setting

This oracle could be a complete saying from one of the discussions about "justice and righteousness" (cf. 5:7, 24). That no threat of punishment is connected with it need not lead to the assumption that it is a fragment. However, it probably does derive from a setting in which other oracles of the prophet were also spoken. Being a particularly memorable formulation, it has here been appended, along with other brief utterances, to the basic collection of the prophet's "words."[2] Didactic style and theme preclude supposing that 6:12 originally formed a rhetorical unit with either 6:11 or 6:13–14, nor can it be convincingly demonstrated that 5:7, 10; 6:12; 5:11b; and 6:11 comprised an original unit of proclamation.[3]

Interpretation

The two rhetorical questions depict absurd situations in order to provoke. For the sake of their hoofs alone, horses naturally do not run over rocky terrain. The latter need not mean here only steep mountainsides and sharply jagged cliffs, but can also refer to generally rocky mountain area with its stony terrain (Is 42:11). For in Amos' day horses were employed only as draught–animals for chariots,[4] which operated primarily on the plains where beaten tracks made fast movement possible. Rocky terrain ruins the horse. And it would be complete folly—Amos pushes his comparison to the limits—to drive the ox not to the field but to the sea for plowing. The animal would drown and the field would remain unplowed. But it is precisely such insanity that is practiced by Israel when it perverts the order of justice, with the result that the life of a healthy society is killed as by poison, while behavior in communal affairs and in court ("the fruit of righteousness") is repugnantly bitter rather than benevolent.

Most of the words in 6:12b have already been treated in discussing 5:7.[5] A new feature here is the parallel to wormwood, namely "poison," which is elsewhere known in relation to berries (Dtn 32:32–33), roots (Dtn 29:17 [18]), and snakes (Dtn 32:24; Job 20:16). On "fruit of righteousness" (פרי צדקה) as the yield (result) of faithful behavior, compare the parallel concept "fruit (of wisdom)" in Prv 8:19, to which belongs "righteousness" (צדקה) according to Prv 8:18 and 20, and note also the contrasting concept, "fruit of lies" (פְּרִי־כַחַשׁ) in Hos 10:13.[6]

Aim

Amos exposes Israel's perversity in the light of the generally valid world order, an approach which is in keeping with his sapiential thinking. He saw Israel and the nations as in principle standing under the same law (1:3—2:8), and he illustrated his compulsion vis–à–vis his prophetic proclamation with the most varied series of cause–effect relationships (3:3–6, 8). In the same way he now shows that perversion of justice destroys that structure of order which prevails in other realms as a matter of course. What no animal and no handler of animals would ever do, that is what human beings do to one another when they bribe judges, intimidate witnesses, or in some other way abuse power. Such an embittering, even fatal propensity on Israel's part is sufficiently well illustrated in 2:6–8; 3:9–10; 4:1; and 5:10–12. The hearers would not even have to be "chosen" (3:2), they would merely have to be intelligent (Lk 16:8!) in order to perceive the insanity of their behavior.

---

1   See pp. 181–83.
2   See p. 281, on the "Setting" of 6:8–11.
3   *Contra* Weiser, *Profetie*, 196–202.
4   See pp. 171–72, on 2:15.
5   See pp. 245–46.

6   The latter expression forms a contrast with a probable "fruit of righteousness" (פְּרִי־צֶדֶק) in Hos 10:12 cj. See Wolff, *Hosea*, 180 [234], textual note "u" to Hos 10:12.

The Destruction of the Victor

Bibliography

Henning Fredriksson
Jahwe als Krieger: Studien zum alttestamentlichen Gottes-bild (Lund: C. W. K. Gleerup, 1945).

Martin Metzger
"Lodebar und der *tell el-mghannije*," ZDPV 76 (1960): 97–102.

A. H. van Zyl
The Moabites, Pretoria Oriental Series 3 (Leiden: E. J. Brill, 1960), 147–48.

6

13   . . ., who rejoice in Lo–debar,[a] who say: "Have we not by our own strength taken Karnaim[b] for ourselves?"

14   Indeed (it shall be) so! I am raising up against you, house of Israel [utterance of Yahweh, the God of the Hosts],[c] a nation that will oppress you from Lebo–Hamath[d] to the Brook of the Arabah.

a   G (ἐπ' οὐδενὶ λόγῳ ["over no word"]), σ' (ἀλόγως ["unspoken"]) and V (*in nihilo* ["in nought"]) translate M literally (so also Buber, *Kündung*, 645: "(at) no–thing, nonsense" [*Undings*]). However, the reference is to the place name attested in Josh 13:26 and 2 Sam 9:4, 5; 17:27.

b   Here also G (κέρατα) and V (*cornua*) interpret the place name literally as "horns" (so again Buber, *Kündung*, 645: "pair of horns" [*Hörnerpaar*]); cf. 1 Macc 5:26, 43–44 and 2 Macc 12:21, 26.

c   The expanded oracle formula is not reflected in the original text of G (see Ziegler, *Duodecim prophetae*, 197). Its position between the vocative "house of Israel" and the object "a nation" seems strange and is best explained as a secondary insertion. Did "utterance of Yahweh" (נאם יהוה) originally stand at the end of the oracle (see textual notes "m" to 6:7 and "c" to 6:8)? It is difficult to answer this question without knowing the opening of the oracle; see the excursus on p. 287.

d   G (τοῦ μὴ εἰσελθεῖν εἰς Εμαθ ["so that you shall not enter into Emath"]) misunderstands the geographical designation as a negative telic clause identifying the purpose of the oppression; σ' (ἀπὸ εἰσόδου) and V (*ab introitu*) already offer the correct interpretation, "from (the) entrance of (Hamath)."

Form

At least the beginning of this verse is transmitted only as a fragment. No oracle of Amos has so far begun with unaugmented participles.[1] A "woe" (הוי) may have stood at the beginning,[2] such as we found in 5:18 and 6:1 and conjectured in 5:7; yet our oracle does not show the regularity of the other woe–oracles. It is also possible that an exhortation to hear with a designation of the addressees (as in 4:1), or a different type of oracular opening (as in 5:12), preceded the participial characterization of those addressed. In any case the participial clauses serve, as always, the purpose of indicting. Deictic כי ("indeed") and the attention–getting הנה ("[it shall be] so!") with suffix and par-

---

1   See p. 141, on 2:7; p. 197, on 3:12; and p. 241, on 5:7.

2   So Maag (*Text*, 42) and Amsler.

ticiple[3] open the announcement of punishment, which is formulated as divine first–person address, proclaiming the imminence of Yahweh's action (v 14a) and its consequences (v 14b).

Yahweh (the) (God) of (the) Hosts
(יהוה [אלהי] [ה][צבאות)

The formula occurs nine times in the book of Amos: six times in the form יהוה אלהי צבאות ("Yahweh, God of Hosts" 4:13; 5:14, 15, 16 [+ אדני "the Lord"], 27; 6:8); twice as יהוה אלהי הצבאות ("Yahweh, the God of the Hosts" 3:13; 6:14); and once as אדני יהוה הצבאות ("the Lord Yahweh of the Hosts" 9:5). Apart from 5:14–15, these appellations always appear in structural formulas, namely in conjunction with נאם יהוה ("utterance of Yahweh" 3:13; 6:8,14), (כה) אָמַר יהוה ("[thus] Yahweh has said" 5:16, 27), and the refrain יהוה שְׁמוֹ ("Yahweh is his name" 4:13; cf. 5:27), and in the isolated opening piece in 9:5. In all instances more or less cogent reasons lead to the suspicion that the whole formula, or at least the expansion "[the God of the] Hosts" was added secondarily.[4]

It is striking, first of all, that the expression "Yahweh, [the] God of [the] Hosts," with its eight occurrences, is clearly the predominant form. It appears exclusively in chaps. 3—6, in the old corpus of "the words of Amos from Tekoa." The short form "[the Lord] Yahweh of [the] Hosts" has been appended only once, in 9:5, outside of this old corpus. However, one must be extremely cautious in drawing conclusions from this distribution in the book of Amos, since the formulas have already penetrated into the doxologies from the time of Josiah, while they are not represented in the Deuteronomistic and postexilic additions.

The dominant position of the longer form "Yahweh, [the] God of [the] Hosts" deserves special attention because this stands in contrast to the overall pattern of usage in the Old Testament. In addition to its eight occurrences in the book of Amos, the appellation is found only ten times in the rest of the Old Testament.[5] As is the case in the book of Amos, elsewhere as well the formula is frequently a later addition.[6] Thus the longer form is attested a total of eighteen times, for the most part in later additions. In contrast, the shorter form "Yahweh of Hosts," which appears in the book of Amos only in 9:5, occurs 267 times in all.[7] Thus the ratio between occurrences of the shorter and the longer forms is 15/1. Obviously the heaviest concentration of the longer form is to be found in the work of the redactors of the book of Amos (eight occurrences as enumerated above). Therefore we must not associate the redactional usage in the book of Amos with the very frequent occurrence of the short form "Yahweh of Hosts" in the books of Haggai, Zechariah, and Malachi.[8] The earliest approximately datable occurrence of the longer form is that in Jer 15:16, which comes from late monarchial times (probably during the reign of Jehoiakim), while the latest occurrence comes from the Baruch–reports in the book of Jeremiah. The doxologies incorporated into the book of Amos in the time of Josiah have been partially affected by the redaction which added "Yahweh of Hosts" (cf. 4:13 with 5:8 and 9:6),[9] but the doxologies in their original form are still clearly distinct from this redactional work, while the Deuteronomistic and postexilic strata appear completely untouched by it. Hence it seems highly probable that the redaction which introduced the epithet "[the] God of [the] Hosts" into the book of Amos must be contemporary with the promulgation of Jeremiah (c. 600).

What is the intent of this predication of Yahweh as "[the] God of [the] Hosts," and why this emphasis that it was precisely his word which the prophet proclaimed? In 5:27; 6:8, 14; and 9:5, the context clearly portrays Yahweh as the military commander who deploys Israel's enemies against his own people. Likewise at 3:13; 5:14–15; and 5:16 the context leads one to think of military action, and the redactor no doubt felt the same to be true of 4:13b.[10] Although "hosts" (צבאות) in the appellation "Yahweh of Hosts" could have been understood as an abstract plural connoting

---

3 See the excursus on p. 142.

4 See the textual notes to the passages cited.

5 2 Sam 5:10; 1 Kgs 19:10, 14; Hos 12:6 [5]; Jer 5:14; 15:16; 35:17; 38:17; 44:7; Ps 89:9 [8].

6 E.g., Hos 12:6 [5]; Jer 5:14; 2 Sam 5:10; Ps 89:9 [8]; and also in 1 Kgs 19:10, 14 according to *G*.

7 So Otto Eissfeldt, "Jahwe Zebaoth" in *Kleine Schriften* 3, 105. Cf. B. N. Wambacq, *L'épithète divine Jahvé S^{e}ba'ôt*, (Bruges: De Brouwer, 1947); and Wanke, *Zionstheologie*, 40–46.

8 Wanke, *Zionstheologie*, 42.

9 See textual note "b" to 4:13.

10 The situation may be understood similarly in 2 Sam 5:10; and in Jer 38:7 and 44:7.

"mightiness,"[11] the redactor of Amos nevertheless manifestly wished to characterize Yahweh as the "God of the armies" (even more precisely, of the enemy armies).[12]

The hypothesis that "the words of Amos from Tekoa" and the literary text of the two "cycles"[13] were not combined prior to the Deuteronomistic redaction can only with the greatest caution draw support from the fact that redactional supplements with "[the] God of [the] Hosts" are not found in chaps. 1—2 and 7—9 of the book of Amos. Nevertheless, it is surprising that our expansion does not appear in such places as 1:3ff; 2:16; 7:17; 9:1ff and 10, but does appear in 5:27; 6:8, 14, etc.; yet it is also lacking in 4:3 and 5:3. The "Bethel–Exposition" of the time of Josiah[14] already embraced chaps 3—9, though this does not necessarily presuppose the prior literary fixation of this material. Therefore the combination of "the words of Amos from Tekoa" with the text of the "cycles" may be attributed to the old school of Amos just as easily as to the Deuteronomistic redaction.

Setting

This oracular fragment belongs to the time after the successful military operations of Jeroboam II in the Transjordan which warded off the incursions of the Arameans (1:3) and the Ammonites (1:13).[15] Amos probably encountered Israel's military leaders in the royal capital of Samaria. Being fragmentary, this oracle together with the short supplementations in 6:9–12 concludes the longer and, on the whole, more completely preserved oracles assembled in the old collection of "the words of Amos from Tekoa." It is no longer possible to determine whether the fragmentary character of these final oracles, which is especially evident in the cases of 6:11 and 13,[16] derives from their first deposition in writing or whether it is to be traced to some later damaging of the document.

Interpretation

■ **13** We are probably to think of military victories as having occasioned the rejoicing over both Lo–debar and Karnaim. The former place name is variously written, with the vocalization לֹא דָבָר (lō' dābār) appearing only here.[17] This writing suggests an ironic twist of the name, hearing it as "No–thing,"[18] a pun which if not attributable to Amos himself[19] indicates that the old school of Amos continued his tradition of prophetic criticism. Lo–debar is very probably to be located at Tell 'el-Ḥammeh, which lies to the north of the Jabbok, where the river leaves the mountains and enters the broad rift of the Jordan.[20] The boundary described in Josh 13:26 places Lo–debar in the vicinity of Mahanaim (Tulūl 'ed-Dahab, located four kilometers east–southeast of Tell 'el-Ḥammeh). The archaeological data show that the site was occupied in the Iron Age.[21] Battles against the westward–pressing Ammonites (cf. 1:13) can easily be imagined as having occurred at this strategically important spot. In connection with Karnaim, on the other hand, one must think of battles with the Arameans (cf. 1:3). Karnaim was situated on a northern tributary of the middle Yarmuk and so was already deeply within the sphere of influence of Damascus. It is the modern Šēḫ Saʿd, some four kilometers north of Ashtaroth (Tell ʿAštarah). One of the Assyrian provinces which Tiglath–pileser III in 732 carved out of the defeated Aramean kingdom was named Qarnini after its capital city Karnaim.[22] The victors boast of their own military achievement ("by our own strength . . . for ourselves") in connection with the taking of this important city. The name Karnaim is a dual form of the word for "horn" (קֶרֶן); "horn" and pair of horns alike symbolized the strength of the bull and of world powers (Zech 2:4), and hence the very

---

11   Otto Eissfeldt, "Jahwe Zebaoth" in *Kleine Schriften* 3, 106–23 (esp. 120).
12   Cf. Fredriksson, *Krieger*, 50–55; and von Rad, *Theology* 1, 18–19 [32], with reference to 1 Sam 17:45.
13   See pp. 107–08.
14   See pp. 111–12.
15   See p. 89.
16   See pp. 281 and 286.
17   We find לֹא דָבָר in 2 Sam 17:27, and לוֹ דְבָר in 2 Sam 9:4 and 5. In Josh 13:26 the plane name appears as לִדְבִר which, with Noth (*Josua*, 76), we should probably read לִדְבָר; cf. also Karl Elliger,

"Lodebar," *BHHW* 2, 1101.
18   See textual note "a" to 6:13.
19   Cf. the place names in 1:5 and textual notes "i" and "j" to that verse.
20   Martin Metzger, "Lodebar und der *tell el-mghannije*," *ZDPV* 76 (1960): 97–102.
21   Nelson Glueck, *Explorations in Eastern Palestine, IV* (Part 1: Text), AASOR 25–28 (New Haven: American Schools of Oriental Research, 1951), 313.
22   Noth, *World*, 100–1 [92]; and Georg Sauer, "Karnaim," *BHHW* 2, 935.

name of the city may have led its conquerors proudly to voice their consciousness of military superiority. As far as Amos is concerned, such haughty expressions only testify to the guilt of these conquerors (cf. "arrogance" [גָּאוֹן] in 6:8).[23]

■14 Yahweh is already prepared to initiate the counterattack ("[it shall be] so! I . . ." [הנני with participle]). Just as Yahweh at one time raised up a deliverer for Israel (Ju 3:9), just as he raised up an adversary against Solomon (1 Kgs 11:14) and a king against the house of Jeroboam (1 Kgs 14:14), so now he "raises up" (קום hip'il) a nation against the state of Israel. He does not say which. He hardly means the Arameans here, who had just been defeated.[24] Eduard Meyer already warned against thinking only of the Assyrians, whom Amos never mentions; one could just as well imagine "a people thus far unknown, or perhaps Urartu."[25] Amos just as faintly hints at the identity of Yahweh's instrument—"a nation"—as he had previously spoken indefinitely of "an adversary" (3:11). Amos is a messenger, not of any particular world power, but of the one and only commander-in-chief of all powers, Yahweh. Besides his main task, namely that of proclaiming Yahweh's action, Amos considers the consequences for Israel as worth only one explicit sentence: "they will oppress you." The plural verb (לחצו) interprets the collective term "nation" to mean the troops of the superior power coming to "oppress" and "torment" Israel, just as Egypt once did.[26] The extent of the conquest is indicated by designating boundaries. "Lebo-Hamath" (לבוא חמת) is to be sought in the region of the Lebanon and the Anti-Lebanon, though it must remain an open question for the time being whether the reference here is to a specific locality or rather to a general strip of territory marking the boundary of the state of Hamath and thereby the access to its capital city on the Orontes.[27] Certainly the northern border of Israel is meant, as we can reliably gather from Nu 34:8, and Ezek 47:15–17 and 48:1. The "Brook of the Arabah" must then designate the southern border. It is to be sought in the vicinity of the northern end of the Dead Sea, which is often called "The Sea of the Arabah" (יָם הָעֲרָבָה Dtn 3:17; 2 Kgs 14:25; etc.). Usually the name designates the lower course of the *Wādī 'el-Qelt*, which opens into the Jordan rift from the west near Jericho,[28] but it may also refer to the *Wādī Kefrein* entering the rift from the mountains of the Transjordan.[29] The whole expression is strongly reminiscent of 2 Kgs 14:25, where a promise of the prophet Jonah is mentioned, according to which Jeroboam would restore Israel's border from Lebo-Hamath to the Sea of the Arabah. In his description of boundaries of the land to be conquered, it is not impossible that Amos alludes critically to this message of a contemporary prophet of weal.[30] Amos emphasizes once more, this time in geographic categories, the totality of the destruction of the northern kingdom.

Aim

This oracular fragment adds yet another touch to the picture of Israel's guilt. Proud self-assurance was already denounced in 6:8, and in 6:1 + 3–6 the "woe!"

23 On the function of quotations in the demonstration of guilt, see 4:1; and also Hans Walter Wolff, *Das Zitat im Prophetenspruch: Eine Studie zur prophetischen Verkündigungsweise*, BEvTh 4 (München, 1937), 15, 58, 74 (reprinted in idem, *Gesammelte Studien*, 43, 81, 94).

24 See the comments on 4:3 and 5:27.

25 *Geschichte des Altertums*, vol. 2/2: *Der Orient vom Zwölften bis zur Mitte des Achten Jahrhunderts* (Stuttgart and Berlin, ⁴1931), 358.

26 Cf. לחץ ("to oppress") in Ex 3:9 (E).

27 Cf. Karl Elliger, "Hamath," *BHHW* 2, 630; and the detailed discussion of the possible interpretations in Zimmerli, *Ezechiel*, 1213–14.

28 Albrecht Alt, "Das Institut im Jahre 1928," *PJ* 25 (1929): 57–58 ("Die Reise 'Bach in der Wüste'"); Galling, "Bethel I," 153; Koehler–Baumgartner, 733.

29 So van Zyl, *Moabites*, 147–48.

30 Cf. Otto Eissfeldt, "Amos und Jona in volkstümlicher Überlieferung" in ". . . und fragten nach Jesus." *Beiträge aus Theologie, Kirche und Geschichte (Festschrift für Ernst Barnikol zum 70. Geburtstag)*, ed. U. Meckert (Berlin: Evangelische Verlagsanstalt, 1964), 11–12 (reprinted in idem, *Kleine Schriften* 4, 140); and Hans Walter Wolff, *Studien zum Jonabuch*, BSt 47 (Neukirchen–Vluyn: Neukirchener Verlag, 1965), 14–15.

was aimed at the extravagant (victory?) celebrations. Here now are cited the pompous words by which one exalts one's own strength. Yahweh will make an end of this secure self–assurance. He who bases his future on his own strength will founder before the overwhelming power which Yahweh commands. Proverbial wisdom already taught: "The horse is made ready for the day of battle, but the victory belongs to Yahweh" (Prv 21:31). Amos has to proclaim that Yahweh will celebrate his victory in the total destruction of Israel.

No More Forgiveness

Bibliography

Gilbert Brunet
"La vision de l'étain: réinterprétation d'Amos 7:7–9," *VT* 16 (1966): 387–95.

Franz Hesse
Die Fürbitte im Alten Testament, Unpub. Diss. (Erlangen, 1949).

Delbert R. Hillers
"Amos 7:4 and Ancient Parallels," *CBQ* 26 (1964): 221–25.

Friedrich Horst
"Die Visionsschilderungen der alttestamentlichen Propheten," *EvTh* 20 (1960): 193–205.

Ernst Jenni
Die politischen Voraussagen der Propheten, AThANT 29 (Zürich: Zwingli–Verlag, 1956), 38–41.

Hubert Junker
"Text und Bedeutung der Vision Amos 7:7–9," *Biblica* 17 (1936): 359–64.

Julian Morgenstern
"Amos Studies I," *HUCA* 11 (1936): 68–130 (reprinted in *idem, Amos Studies,* 52–114).

Henning Graf Reventlow
Das Amt des Propheten bei Amos, FRLANT 80 (Göttingen: Vandenhoeck & Ruprecht, 1965), 30–56.

Ivar P. Seierstadt
Die Offenbarungserlebnisse der Propheten Amos, Jesaja und Jeremia (Oslo: J. Dybwad, 1946, ²1965), 52–59, 82–91.

Shemaryahu Talmon
"The Gezer Calendar and the Seasonal Cycle of Ancient Canaan," *JAOS* 83 (1963): 177–87.

John D. W. Watts
Vision and Prophecy in Amos (Grand Rapids: Eerdmans, 1958), 22–31.

Herbert Werner
Amos, Exempla Biblica 4 (Göttingen: Vandenhoeck & Ruprecht, 1969), 129–45.

Ernst Würthwein
"Amos Studien," *ZAW* 62 (1950): 10–52 (esp. 28–35).

7

1   Thus [the Lord]ᵃ Yahweh showed me:

There was someone formingᵇ a locust–swarm, just when the late–planting had begun to shoot up, and [here ᶜlate–planting (is that which) follows the

a   אדני is not yet reflected in *G*; see textual note "o" to 1:8.

b   *G* (ἐπιγονή ["offspring"], *T* (ברית ["formation"]), and *S* erroneously read יֵצֶר. *V* (*fictor locustae* ["former of locusts"]), as well as the corresponding participles in 7:4 and 7, support *M*.

c–c   *G* (βροῦχος εἷς Γωγ ὁ βασιλεύς ["one larva (was) Gog the king"]) read יֶלֶק (cf. Joel 1:4, "locust") instead of לקש, אֶחָד instead of אחר, and גּוֹג instead of גּוֹי; similarly *S*. The supplement (see textual note "d") thus seems to have been extant in a state that made its reading difficult.

king's mowings,^c 2/ and when]^d it was
about to finish off the herbage of the
land completely, I said: "My Lord Yah-
weh, do forgive!^e ^f"How is Jacob to
endure?^f For he is so small." 3/ Then
Yahweh repented concerning this.^g
"It^g shall not happen," Yahweh said.

4   Thus [the Lord]^h Yahweh showed me:

There was someone summoning <a rain
of fire>,ⁱ [the Lord Yahweh],^j and it

d   The purpose of the later addition in v 1b was to
define לֶקֶשׁ ("late–planting") more precisely. It was
probably this addition which introduced the cumbersome link with v 2 formed by the first two words
thereof. וְהָיָה ("and it will be") is inappropriate as a
continuation of the report (cf. the beginning of 7 : 4b,
and see above p. 280, on 6 : 9) and has therefore been
considered a misspelling of וַיְהִי (so Joüon, par.
119z). The conjunction אִם (with a following perfect) seems equally strange in light of the otherwise
paratactic style. Thus as the original continuation
of v 1a, preceding the introduction of the prophetic
speech, we should expect a simple וְכִלָּה ("when he
had finished"), corresponding to the form וַאּכְלָה
("and it devoured") in 7 : 4b before 7 : 5. The perfect
states the fact which elicits the prophet's objection.
Less in keeping with the style of the parallel second
report is the proposal to restore וַיְהִי הָא מְכַלֶּה
(Charles Cutler Torrey ["On the Text of Am 5 : 25;
6 : 1, 2; 7 : 2," *JBL* 13 (1894): 63], Wellhausen,
Sellin, and others).

e   See textual note "l" to 7 : 5.

f–f   Since "Jacob" is the subject of מִי יָקוּם, מִי ("who")
must be interpreted predicatively (as an accusative
of circumstance): "As who [= how] can Jacob
stand?" Giovanni Rinaldi ("*mj* [*mî*]," *Bibbia e
Oriente* 9 [1967]: 118) renders מִי here with *qualis*
("what sort of"); cf. Ruth 3 : 16 and Koehler–
Baumgartner, 518. *G* (τίς ἀναστήσει τὸν Ιακωβ ["who
will raise up Jacob?"]) read יָקִים, making "Jacob"
the object, and thereby avoided the unusual construction.

g   In conjunction with נחם ("repented"), the preposition עַל introduces not the reason for the reversal
but rather that which is reversed [i.e., "concerning
this" rather than "because of this"]; cf. Jer 18 : 8,
10; Joel 2 : 13; Jon 3 : 10; etc. The plan which is reversed is referred to with the neutral feminine forms
["this," "it shall . . ."] (Joüon, par. 152c). *G* (μετα-
νόησον . . . ἐπὶ τούτῳ ["repent . . . concerning this!"])
read נחם as an imperative, drawing v 3a into the
prophet's petition.

h   Here also, as in 7 : 1 (see textual note "a"), *G* originally had only a simple κύριος (cf. Ziegler, *Duodecim
prophetae*, 198).

i   While *M* ("to contend with fire") is already presupposed by the versions, the reading is nevertheless highly unlikely. רִיב ("to contend") belongs to
the language of legal controversy; a following בּ
always introduces the party being contended with
or accused (Gen 31 : 36; Ju 6 : 32; Hos 2 : 4 [2]). The
word order makes problematic the attempt to con-
strue בּ with קרא (rendering "call . . . upon [fire]"
or the like) rather than with the adjacent לָרֹב. One
expects a formulation parallel to 7 : 1, a participle
with an object. Hendrik J. Elhorst (*De profetie van
Amos* [Leiden, 1900]) suggested the reading לָהֶבֶת
אֵשׁ ("flame of fire," cf. Ps 29 : 7); a more familiar
idiom for this would be לַהַב אֵשׁ (Is 29 : 6; 30 : 30;

devoured the great abyss: and it was about to devour the acreage[k] 5/ when I said: "My Lord Yahweh, cease![l] [m]How is Jacob to endure?[m] For he is so small." 6/ Then Yahweh repented concerning this.[n] "That[n] too shall not happen," Yahweh [the Lord][o] said.

7   Thus ⟨Yahweh⟩[p] showed me:

There was [the Lord][q] standing on a wall [plumb–line],[r] and in his hand (he held) a plumb–line. 8/ Then Yahweh said to me, "Amos, what do you see?" I said, "A plumb–line." Then my Lord said to me, "Hence I am setting a plumb–line in the midst of my people Israel. I will no longer (benignly) pass him by."

Joel 2:5). Hillers ("Amos 7:4," 221–23) has recently taken up the proposal of Max Krenkel ("Zur Kritik und Exegese der kleinen Propheten," *Zeitschrift für wissenschaftliche Theologie* 14 [1866]: 271) to read אֵשׁ לִרְבִיב ("[calling] for a rain of fire"). That leaves the consonantal stock unchanged, the only alteration being in word division. Although the word itself is not there attested, Gen 19:24 and Ezek 38:22 offer such strong conceptual parallels that little hesitation remains in accepting this emendation. What hesitation does remain comes from the fact that, elsewhere in the Old Testament, this particular word for rain occurs only in the plural (רביבים). However, Ugaritic texts attest *rbb* in parallelism with "dew": *CTA* 19 (= *UT* 1 Aqht). 4; *CTA* 3 (= *UT* ʿnt). 2.39–40; *WUS*, no. 2480 ("Sprühregen" ["drizzling rain"]); cf. also Dtn 32:2 and Mi 5:6 [7]. In view of the rarity of the singular noun רְבִב ("rain"), it is understandable that the words were at some later time incorrectly divided, a more familiar word being read into the passage.

j   The awkward position of the appellation alone suffices to indicate that it is a later specification of the one who calls. (*G* attests only κύριος; *V* [*Dominus Deus*] presupposes *M*). Hillers ("Amos 7:4," 221) suggests a "vertical dittography" from 7:3.

k   *G*[BV] were first to add κυρίου (reading "the portion of the Lord [יהוה]"); the plus is not yet attested in *G*[W] (a manuscript from the third century A.D.).

l   *T* (שבוק כען לחובי שארה דבית יעקב ["Leave behind now for those who are guilty a remnant of the house of Jacob"]) supposes here the same imperative as in 7:2 (likewise *S*), but at the same time reinterprets the sentence.

m   See textual note "f" above.

n   See textual note "g" above.

o   See textual note "a" above, and cf. 7:3b as well as Maag, *Text*, 119.

p   *G*[B] (οὕτως ἔδειξέ μοι κύριος καὶ ἰδοὺ ἑστηκώς . . . ["Thus the Lord showed me, and behold one stood . . ."]) presupposes exactly the same introduction as in 7:1 and 4 (see textual notes "a" and "h" above), i.e. כה הראני יהוה והנה נצב. *V* (*haec ostendit mihi Dominus et ecce Dominus stans* . . . ["This (is what) the Lord showed me, and behold the Lord was standing . . ."]) confirms the first four words of this text; then, however, it presupposes (והנה אדני) with *M*. *G*[A], Origen, and other witnesses (see Ziegler, *Duodecim prophetae*, 198) supplement (ἰδοὺ) ἀνὴρ (ἑστηκώς) ["(behold) a man (was standing)"].

q   אדני is a later addition here, just as was אדני יהוה in 7:4aβ (see textual note "j" above); *G* does not yet presuppose it.

r   Following Oort ("Amos," 121), חוֹמָה ("wall") is frequently read here alone. Since אֲנָךְ ("plumb–line") appears three times in the immediately following context, it may have been erroneously introduced into the text at this point through scribal

Then the high places of Isaac[s]
shall be made desolate,
   the sanctuaries of Israel
   shall be shattered,
     and I will rise against
     the house of Jeroboam
     with the sword.

dittography, the construct form חומת being the result of subsequent smoothing. However, it is also possible that חומת אנך emerged from a misreading of an original חוֹמַת אֶבֶן ("wall of stone"), influenced by the following occurrences of אנך, since all of the ancient translations already presuppose M: G ἐπὶ τείχους ἀδαμαντίνου ("on a wall of brass"), α' γανῶντα ("shining"), θ' τηκόμενον ("molten"), and V super murum litum ("upon a plastered wall"); T דדין interprets אנך in all cases as "judgment" (דין).

s G (τοῦ γέλωτος) read שְׂחֹק ("laughter"); cf. Gen 21:6. σ' attests τὰ ὑψηλὰ τοῦ ιακωβ ("the high places of Jacob").

Form

The clause "Thus Yahweh showed me" (7:1) opens a completely new and different complex of tradition in the book of Amos. Since the same opening clause recurs in 7:4, 7, and 8:1, while 7:9 + 10–17 stand out as stylistically and thematically distinct from their context, one must see in 7:1–8 and 8:1–2 an original literary unit. Perhaps this unit was even continued in 9:1–4.

Both the style of the prophetic first–person report, common to this complex, and the content, which at first concerns only the prophet, suggest Amos as the author. It must remain an open question, though, whether he himself wrote down the account or whether he dictated it. The strictly regular form makes it unlikely that later hands committed to writing the prophet's free accounting of his experience.

The regularly repeated opening clause immediately characterizes the pieces as "vision reports" (*Visionsberichte*). They exhibit in their composition the typical form of autobiographical *memorabilia*.[1] Terse words sketch out unheard–of happenings. The dominating fact, towards which everything that is reported moves, is Yahweh's decision to bring about the end of Israel. 8:2 reveals that end, and 9:1–4 describes it in greater detail.

The reports of the first three visions in 7:1–8 lead up to this main point. The first two exhibit three formal elements. At the beginning stands the description of what was actually seen in the vision (vv 1–2aα, 4). In this connection, a participial form is used in each instance to introduce a certain person ("someone forming," "someone summoning"), a person who brings about something ("locusts," "rain of fire"[2]) which in each case has similarly devastating results

("to devour"). As a second element there follows the outcry of the prophet (vv 2aβb, 5), which is formally identical in the two accounts although the exact imperative used differs. The situation with respect to the third element, the decision of Yahweh (vv 3, 6), is similar. First a stirring of his compassion is reported, and then his decision is verified by his word. The only deviation in wording consists of the intensifying addition "that too" in the second account. This apparently insignificant expansion underscores the literary association of the first two vision reports.

That the third (7:7–8) and fourth (8:1–2) reports also belong in this same literary complex is shown not only by the common opening clause, but more particularly by the concluding sentence "I will no longer (benignly) pass him by"; the "no longer" (לא־אוסיף עוד) makes sense only with reference to the preceding decisions, reported in 7:3 and 7:6, to respond favorably to the prophet's supplication. The sentence indicates at the same time the decisive turn towards the chief proclamation of these *memorabilia*, a turn that is furthermore reflected in the different structure of the third and fourth reports, both of which have four constitutive elements. Apart from the opening clause, the first formal element already deviates from the corresponding element in the first and second reports, for it does not portray a scene (an event with its denouement) but rather describes isolated images (wall with plumb–line in 7:7, basket with summer fruit in 8:1). Secondly, there follows upon the viewing of these images, not a response by Amos, but a question of Yahweh, identically worded in both instances (7:8aα; 8:2aα). In the third formal element, Amos has only to fix in words what he has seen (7:8aβ; 8:2aβ). In the fourth and concluding element—a second divine utterance—

Yahweh interprets the images ($7:8b\alpha$; $8:2b\alpha$) and confirms that he will no longer hold back the punishment ($7:8b\beta$; $8:2b\beta$).

One cannot miss the fact that the form of reporting changes in the transition from the second to the third vision because of the differing content. The literary unity remains uncontestable nevertheless. Recognition of this necessitates our drawing 8:1–2 into view if we are to understand the facts reported in 7:1–8.[3]

With regard to the relation of the content of the visions and the indicated course of events, the cycle presents three different types of visions: the vision of an event (7:1–2, 4–5; 9:1–4),[4] the vision of a symbolic image (7:7–8),[5] and the vision involving a wordplay (8:1–2).[6]

The chief mark of poetic construction, *parallelismus membrorum*, is completely lacking in these *memorabilia*. Therefore at the outset it hardly seems promising to seek here a metric form.[7] That we are dealing with elevated, even finely polished prose is shown already by the paired structure, identical even down to the very wording, in 7:1–6 and in 7:7–8 and 8:1–2.

7:9, on the other hand, is set off from the vision reports by reason of its prosodic form alone. 7:9a exhibits a three–stress bicolon with synonymous parallelism (the subjects and predicates forming a chiasm); 7:9b, as the third colon bearing four stresses, intensifies and personalizes the threat by introducing Yahweh in the first person as the subject and the house of Jeroboam as the object.

Setting

7:9 is also clearly distinguished by its content from the third vision report. Nothing is left to remind one of the visionary scene. The sentence "I will no longer pass

him by" was an obvious conclusion to the vision report ($7:8b\beta$). Why was v 9 inserted here? Apparently this verse is to facilitate the transition to 7:10–17. Hence it makes explicit that the intervention of Yahweh, the inevitability of which had been confirmed for the prophet in the third vision (7:8), will mean the downfall of the "high places of Isaac" ("Isaac" is found elsewhere in the book of Amos only in 7:16b!), the "sanctuaries of Israel" ("sanctuary" elsewhere appears only in 7:13b!) and the "house of Jeroboam" ("Jeroboam" is elsewhere named in an oracle of Amos only in 7:11a!). On the other hand, this verse corrects the threat of death against Jeroboam in 7:11a by referring it to his house, since it was actually Jeroboam's son, Zechariah, who fell by the sword.[8] Thus we may suppose both 7:9 and 7:10–17[9] to be the work of Amos' school which combined the oral traditions of its master with his already extant literary legacy.[10]

It is easy to understand why 7:9–17 came to be inserted between 7:7–8 and 8:1–2: these texts interpret each other. The third and fourth visions explain for Amos' school how the experience described in 7:15 came about. On the other hand, the eviction from Bethel (7:12) explains why Amos wrote down his visions. In this connection the fifth vision (9:1–4) must be considered to have been included because of 7:9a and 16–17.

One can sense from these vision *memorabilia* that they were put down in writing at a time rather distant from the experiences described. At least such distance makes more understandable the uniform stylizing of the varied contents of the visions, as well as the structural relationship between this cycle and the cycle of oracles against the nations.[11] To whom did Amos entrust the literary record? Should we not think first of his disciples in his

---

1   See Wolff, *Hosea*, 10–11 [9–10], 57–58 [71–72].
2   See textual note "i" to 7:4.
3   See also pp. 94–95.
4   See pp. 297, 299.
5   See p. 300.
6   See pp. 318–19.
7   Georg Fohrer finds here what he describes as "short verse" [i.e., poetic lines lacking parallelism]: "Über den Kurzvers," *ZAW* 66 (1954): 199–36 (esp. 229–30) (reprinted in *idem, Studien*, 59–91 [esp. 85]). [Cf. Georg Fohrer, *Introduction to the Old Testament*, tr. David E. Green (Nashville and New York: Ab-

ingdon, 1968), 46–47; Ed.]
8   Cf. 2 Kgs 14:29 with 15:10.
9   See p. 108.
10 See pp. 108–10.
11 See pp. 107–08, 151.

Judean homeland who subsequently elaborated his oracles? If, after the abrupt end of his career in the northern kingdom, he had thus communicated to them the immense burden of Yahweh's demands, then it becomes clear why his reports mention neither a commissioning to proclaim nor the basis of Israel's culpability. His reports were not intended to justify his appearance before an Israelite audience, as was his oracle in 7:15–16, spoken in the presence of the priest Amaziah at Bethel. It is much more likely to suppose that Amos wanted to share with his confidants how the unheard–of and inescapable certainty of the complete and full end of Israel had come upon him, a certainty which at that time was surely without precedent in Judah no less than in Israel. Thus these *memorabilia* were probably written down after his return from Samaria and Bethel.

But to what time do the reported experiences themselves belong? Certainly one should not facilely label them "call visions."[12] After all, they do not recount a commissioning to proclaim, nor is it in the least improbable that the five encounters with Yahweh, presented to our view in a fairly uniform literary structure, took place at quite different times.[13] However, the reports give even less reason to suppose that the experiences which they relate occurred "sometime after his call."[14] Why is it necessary to think that someone must already have become a prophet before being able to voice on Israel's behalf petitions such as those in 7:2 and 5?[15] Amos himself says that his startling encounters with Yahweh gave rise to his petitions. Where have we evidence that he ever proclaimed anything other than doom concerning Israel, evidence on the basis of which we might distinguish phases of weal and woe in his prophecy?[16] Thus the hard road along which

Amos was led in the visions, unbroken till at least the third or fourth vision, must be considered the decisive preparation for his appearance in the northern kingdom. He must have been trembling still from the shattering impact of these insights, experienced in profound isolation, when at the time of his public appearance, he likened his compulsion to speak with the terror induced by a lion's roar (3:8), and when he announced to Amaziah that Yahweh had summoned him away from the flock to prophesy against Israel (7:15). The earliest redactors must have had these visions in mind when they specified that Amos' words were ". . . viewed concerning Israel two years before the earthquake" (1:1b).[17]

That Amos' deadly certainty may have ripened in him gradually can perhaps be concluded from the fact that some visions point to different seasons of the year.[18] He sees the locusts in late spring (7:1a), the season of "late–planting" to which the Gezer Calendar also refers (ירחו לקש ["the (two) months of late–planting"]).[19] The fire that dries out everything can be understood in terms of the mid–summer heat (7:4). Lastly, the basket with "summer fruit" (8:1) recalls the so–named final month of the agricultural year in the Gezer Calendar.[20] Nevertheless, it is the congruity of the experiences which is emphasized most by the form given the reports.

Interpretation

■**1** The semantic range of ראה (hip'il "to show") in the opening clause, "Thus Yahweh showed me," includes auditory as well as visionary phenomena. Hence the book's superscription appropriately refers to the "words" which Amos "viewed" (1:1). Likewise in the Mari prophetic texts ". . . no weight at all is placed on the difference between seeing and hearing."[21] There-

12 This point is correctly made by Robinson, Deden, and others.
13 Weiser, *Profetie*, 14.
14 Würthwein, "Amos–Studien," 29.
15 Cf. already Hesse, *Fürbitte*, 40–41.
16 On 1:3—2:16, see pp. 144–48.
17 See pp. 119–20.
18 Cf. Shemaryahu Talmon, "The Gezer Calendar and the Seasonal Cycle of Ancient Canaan," *JAOS* 83 (1963): 183–84.
19 *KAI* 182.2.
20 *KAI* 182.7.

21 Friedrich Ellermeier, *Profetie in Mari und Israel*, Theologische und orientalistische Arbeiten 1 (Herzberg am Harz: Jungfer, 1968), 90. Cf. especially Jean–Robert Kupper, *Textes divers*, ARM(T) 13 (Paris: Imprimerie Nationale, 1964), 112.1′-2′, which William L. Moran (*ANET*³, 624) renders: "He saw the following (dream): You (pl.) shall not (re–)build this *deserted* house."

fore both here and in 7:4 and 7 the opening clause
(כה הראני) must be read as an introduction not merely
to the immediately following visions but to complete
units, including the decisions uttered by Yahweh.[22]
It is curious that the "forming" figure seen at the outset
is not specifically identified, especially since it is the
formation of living creatures which is meant;[23] Amos
could have been referring to none other than Yahweh—
as his outburst in v 2 indicates. Yet the initial focus of
the report is on that which Amos sees being created:
the "locust–swarm." The term גבי used here is elsewhere attested only in Na 3:17;[24] it should not unduly
surprise the reader of Amos' visions to find unusual
terminology being employed.[25] Amos sees the locusts
coming forth at a time when they would pose an especially grave threat. The term לקש designates the
"late–planting" of the grain and perhaps beyond that
refers to the final seasonal growth of field and pasture
in late spring (during April, following the late rains),
before complete drought sets in for half a year.[26] The
supplement in v 1b[27] perhaps presupposes the king's
right to lay claim to the first cutting (cf. 1 Kgs 18:5?).
The term גז designates not only the "shearing" of sheep
but also the "mowing," harvesting or grazing away of
vegetation, and it can even refer to the mown fields
themselves (Ps 72:6).

■ **2** The swarm of locusts which Yahweh shows to Amos
is about to devour completely all vegetation. "Herbage" (עשב) includes seeded crops as well as wild growth;
locusts spare not even vines, fig trees or other fruit
trees.[28] Were locusts to consume all vegetation nour-
ished by the late spring rains, the resulting shortage of
grain and vegetables for human consumption and of
fodder for cattle would indeed be severe. Since what
Amos is here shown directly depicts the course of

things to come, we may typologically identify this as
an "event–vision."

Israel's future is endangered. Therefore Amos cries
out, "My Lord Yahweh!" The appellation אדני יהוה
is appropriate to the language of prayer,[29] especially
imploring lamentation,[30] and for this reason it may very
well be original here,[31] in contrast to the numerous passages in the book of Amos where "Lord" (אדני) is a later
addition.[32] This particular appellation ". . . uniquely
and simultaneously suggests both the absolute exalted-
ness of Yahweh and his close relationship with the
prophet."[33] "Do forgive!" is the prophet's plea. The
root סלח is etymologically related to Akkadian salāḫu,
"to sprinkle"; by way of the specialized meaning "to
sprinkle for the purpose of cleansing," it has developed
the only meaning attested for it in the Old Testament,
namely "to pardon, forgive."[34] Although no guilt is
in any way described, forgiveness is nevertheless the
decisive presupposition for an effective cessation of the
locust plague which is understood as punishment.
The report wastes not a word, not even to motivate the
plea except merely to affirm that Jacob by himself is
helpless.[35]

Why does Amos call Israel "Jacob" here? Does he
want to remind Yahweh of the election of the patriarch
who, after all, was considered the founder of the sanctuary at Bethel?[36] Or does the name "Jacob" include
acknowledgment of guilt for that Israel who haughtily
rebelled against Yahweh but nevertheless cannot escape
him?[37] The motivation clause merely points out that
Jacob is small and so in need of help; it calls to mind
the sapiential word of admonition in Prv 22:22: "Do
not rob the poor (דל), because he is poor (כי דל הוא),
or crush the afflicted in the gate."[38] Amos abstains
from any recalling of tradition; he cites neither promise

22 On the psychology of the visions, see p. 299 on 7:4.
23 Cf. Gen 2:19; on the word יצר ("to form"), see p. 223 on 4:13.
24 For the usual terminology, see pp. 27–28.
25 Cf. the use of רבב in v 4; see textual note "i" to 7:4.
26 Cf. Dalman, *Arbeit* 1/2, 411–12.
27 See textual note "d" to 7:1–2.
28 See Joel 1:4–7 and above, pp. 28–29.
29 2 Sam 7:18–20, 22, 28; Ju 6:22.
30 Josh 7:7; Jer 1:6; 4:10; 14:13; Ezek 4:14; 9:8; 21:5 [20:49].
31 On the other hand, cf. Baumgärtel, "Gottesnamen,"

1–29 (esp. 10–11).
32 See textual note "o" to 1:8.
33 Maag, *Text*, 119.
34 Cf. Johann Jakob Stamm, *Erlösen und Vergeben im Alten Testament* (Bern, 1940), 57–58; on Ugaritic *slḫ*, see Gordon, *UT*, 450, no. 1757.
35 On the sense of מי, see textual note "f–f" to 7:2.
36 Cf. Gen 28:10–22, and also p. 201 on 3:13.
37 Cf. Hos 12:3–5 [2–4], and also p. 282 on 6:8.
38 Cf. Wolff, *Amos the Prophet*, 70–72 [48–49].

nor election. Thus it remains questionable whether one should expect such an intercession in Israel only from the mouth of one who already holds office as a functionary of the cult.[39] It was both the coming devastation which Yahweh showed to him and his insight into the helplessness of the guilty that drove Amos to his pleading cry.

■ 3 How does Yahweh react? "To repent concerning" (נחם nip'al with על) designates a change of mind prompted by the emotions, a turning away from an earlier decision on the part of someone deeply moved. From the standpoint of the party directly affected by the altered decision, the change might as easily be unfavorable as favorable.[40] In itself, therefore, "to repent concerning" means neither forgiveness nor condemnation.[41] Here Yahweh is moved by the objection of the one to whom he has confided his intention in the vision.[42] Just what sort of change takes place within Yahweh is more precisely defined by the quotation "It shall not happen." In other words, the particular judgment here threatening Israel's future—the invasion of locusts—will not be carried out. A change of mind with respect to Israel is not recognizable insofar as the forgiveness requested is not expressly granted. In fact, by 7:5 such forgiveness is no longer even requested. The terse report merely conveys that the punishment shown shall not take place. In context this signifies initially no more than a postponement of punishment, or more precisely, a readiness to alter the sentence.[43] If one keeps the subsequent visions in mind, one is inclined to think here, not so much of forgiveness, but rather of Yahweh's offering an opportunity for selection of punishment (cf. 2 Sam 24:12ff).

■ 4 While the one who formed the locusts was already a supernatural being, the mythical features of the figure become even clearer in the second vision. Here too, of course, the early commentator captured the unexpressed view of Amos that Yahweh was the one issuing the summons;[44] the prophet, however, only focused attention on what was being summoned, namely a "rain of fire."[45] This conjectured reading, רְבָב אֵשׁ (which preserves the consonantal text of *M*), commends itself particularly in view of the reference to the "great abyss" (תהום רבה) being devoured by the fire. The heat of mid–summer is here concretized into streams of fire which consume the primeval waters and hence also the tillable land ("acreage"). Related traditions can be found in the Hittite myth of the dragon Illuyankas[46] and in the song of Ullikummis,[47] as well as in Hesiod's *Theogony*[48] and tangentially in Homer's *Iliad*.[49] The great primeval waters are to be thought of here as referring to the subterranean ocean that gives fertility and feeds all springs.[50] Ugaritic texts describe 'El as living "at the source of the streams, in the midst

---

39 Cf. Hesse, *Fürbitte*, 40–41; Würthwein, "Amos–Studien," 29 ("Only as a Nabi could he offer up such intercession."); and Reventlow, *Amt*, 34–56.

40 On the former, cf. Gen 6:6–7 and 1 Sam 15:11, 35; on the latter, 2 Sam 24:16 and Joel 2:13 par.

41 Cf. Koehler–Baumgartner, 608, and above, p. 49.

42 For the conceptual parallels, cf. Gen 18:17–32 and Ex 32:11–14.

43 Cf. Johann Jakob Stamm, *Erlösen und Vergeben im Alten Testament* (Bern, 1940), 113.

44 See textual note "j" to 7:4.

45 See textual note "i" to 7:4.

46 Albrecht Goetze, *ANET*³, 125–26.

47 *Ibid.*, 123 (II–c).

48 The scene in Amos' vision and that portrayed in the *Theogony*, 687–700, are surprisingly close, even in specific details. The latter passage depicts the battle of Zeus against the Titans:
    (687) Then Zeus no longer held back his might; but straight his heart was filled with fury and he
    (690) showed forth all his strength. From Heaven and from Olympus he came forthwith, hurl-

ing his lightning: the bolts flew thick and fast from his strong hand together with thunder and lightning, whirling an awesome flame. The life–giving earth crashed around in burning, and the vast wood crackled loud with fire
    (695) all about. All the land seethed, and Ocean's streams and the unfruitful sea. The hot vapour lapped round the earthborn Titans: flame unspeakable rose to the bright upper air: the flashing glare of the thunder stone and lightning blinded their eyes for all that they were
    (700) strong. Astounding heat seized Chaos. . . .
    (Hugh G. Evelyn–White, tr., *Hesiod, The Homeric Hymns and Homerica*, Loeb Classical Library [Cambridge, Massachusetts, and London, ³1936], 129–31. Cf. the reconstructed text and commentary of Martin Litchfield West, *Hesiodus. Theogony* [Oxford: Clarendon Press, 1966], 137, 349ff.) The themes of Amos' vision are fully present here: the rain of fire, its devouring fury, the great primeval waters and the life–giving soil. Hesiod belongs to the century of Amos. It is hard not to surmise that these contem-

of the riverbeds of the primeval waters (*thmtm*)," which probably means "in a cosmic paradise."[51] If all sources of water are consumed and all springs must therefore dry up, then the portion of land (חלק [here translated "acreage"]) allotted to the individual Israelite farmer is also devoured by the fire. Here also we are dealing with the type of the "event–vision." To be sure, the subject matter of the first and second visions has to do with concrete matters crucial to Israel's very existence; however, the content of these visions is not the stuff of everyday life, and hence the visions were not triggered by anything seen naturally.

This too is why Amos stresses, "Thus Yahweh showed me." Psychologically one is not to think here of a normal state of wakefulness, but of a heightened consciousness. This must be sharply distinguished from an ecstatic transcendence of individual consciousness, for otherwise the critical reaction manifest in the intercessory objections (7:2 and 5) would be inexplicable.[52]

■ 5 The new outcry is distinguished from that in the first vision by beginning with "cease!" (חדל־נא) instead of "forgive!" (סלח־נא). The verb חדל used absolutely means as much as "not to do."[53] Terrified by his vision of the fateful fire, Amos no longer dares to make petition for forgiveness, a petition which as such was not granted earlier.[54] Nonetheless, he does interject the plea that Yahweh should cease summoning the devastating rain of fire.[55]

■ 6 Likewise this form of punishment ("that too" [גם־היא]) is taken back.[56]

poraries owed the basic outlines of their respective depictions to the same Hittite–Anatolian source. (On the Hittite sources referred to in nn. 46 and 47 above, cf. Goetze, *Kleinasien*[2], 140, and also pl. 11 fig. 20 [an orthostat from Malatya, depicting in relief the weather–god armed with lightning as he dispatches the sea dragon Illuyankas]. Cf. also Ekrem Akurgal, *Die Kunst der Hethiter* [München: Hirmer, 1961], pl. 104 [lower register]; and Peter Walcot, *Hesiod and the Near East* [Cardiff: University of Wales Press, 1966], esp. 1–26.)

The encounter which Hesiod poetically elaborates as appropriate to "theogony" [genesis of the gods] Amos is compelled to recognize as Yahweh's activity against Israel. And how sparse in comparison is the prophet's description of the cataclysm! How different too is the emotional thrust of Amos' presentation, in which everything moves forward towards the dialogue with Yahweh! These differences must not be obscured by the fact that Hesiod also experienced a kind of prophetic call, which summoned him away from his flock:

And one day they [the immortal gods] taught
Hesiod the glorious song while he was shepherding his lambs under holy Helicon, and this word first the goddesses said to me—the Muses of Olympus, daughters of Zeus who hold the aegis:
  'Shepherds of the wilderness, wretched things of shame, mere bellies, we know how to speak many false things as though they were true; but we know, when we will, to utter true things.'

For Hesiod's commission did not pertain to the course of concrete human history; rather, he says:
  . . . [the Muses] bade me sing of the race of the blessed gods that are eternally, but ever to sing of themselves both first and last.
(*Theogony*, 22–28, 33f; tr. Evelyn–White, Loeb, 79–81 [modified].) This mandate to Hesiod, completely different from that received by Amos, clarifies the profound distinction between them. (On the comparison of Hesiod with the prophetic literature, see Uvo Hölscher, "Anaximander und die Anfänge der Philosophie (II)," *Hermes* 81 [1953]: 385–418 [esp. 410–13].)

49 *Iliad* 2.780–85; see also Hillers, "Amos 7:14," 223–25.
50 Cf. Gen 7:11 and 49:25; and also Westermann, *Genesis*, 145–46.
51 Otto Kaiser, *Die mythische Bedeutung des Meeres in Ägypten, Ugarit und Israel*, BZAW 78 (Berlin: A. Töpelmann, 1959), 45–49 (citation, 48); cf. Schmidt, *Königtum*, 7–8.
52 Cf. Ivar P. Seierstadt, *Die Offenbarungserlebnisse der Propheten Amos, Jesaja und Jeremia* (Oslo: J. Dybwad, [2]1965), 52–59, 82–91; and Hans Walter Wolff, "Hauptprobleme alttestamentlicher Prophetie," *EvTh* 15 (1955): 452–56 (reprinted in *idem*, *Gesammelte Studien*, 213–17).
53 Koehler–Baumgartner ([3]1967), 280.
54 See p. 298, on 7:3.
55 On the motivation clause, identical in its wording with that of 7:2, see pp. 297–98.
56 See the discussion above p. 298, on 7:3.

■ 7 There follows a scene which biographically may just as well be earlier as later than the material which precedes it, but which in either case is not out of the same mold as the first two visions. There appears no plague like locusts or fire, but rather a figure standing on a wall[57] with some implement (אֲנָךְ) visible in his hand. As the interpretation in v 8 shows, the focus is entirely upon this object alone. That the one whose hand holds it stands on a wall is therefore merely indicative of the object's function. The one who is seen can indeed only be carrying out the task of inspecting the wall. He is a master builder testing whether it is firm or ready to fall. Accordingly, אֲנָךְ would refer to a "plumb–line" being used as a testing instrument.[58]

Against this interpretation stands the expectation of finding here, just as in 7:1 and 4, some indication of a judgment being executed. It has therefore been argued that we should emend to read חַמַּת אֲנָךְ with the connotation "glowing lead" (the preceding נצב על then being supposed to mean "to stand near something").[59] Recalled in support of this interpretation is the form of capital punishment attested in Miš. Sanhedrin 7.2 which involved the pouring of molten lead into the mouth of the criminal so that his viscera were burned.[60] Yet the text as transmitted denies this, not only by attesting "wall," but also by describing the standing figure holding the אֲנָךְ "in his hand" (while according to the above interpretation he was supposed merely "to stand near it"). Equally problematic is the interpretation according to which אֲנָךְ is taken to mean "tin," understood as a substance indispensable for the production of weapons and as such supposedly synonymous with "sword."[61] Now Akkadian *anāku* can certainly mean both "tin" and "lead,"[62] and אֲנָךְ appears in the Old Testament only in this vision. But what are we to make of the occurrences, side by side, of a "tin wall"[63] and the "tin in his hand"? And why the term "tin" if "sword" were meant (cf. 9:1–4)? Even 7:9, which Brunet considers an integral part of the third vision report,[64] does not clarify this question. Furthermore, 7:9 must actually be detached.[65] Thus the very wording of the text must of necessity free exegetes from the misleading urge to find here some indication that a judgment is being carried out. Moreover, in the fourth report the envisioned scene itself (8:2a) does not yet portray the mode of judgment in the same way as do the scenes in 7:1 and 4. In the third report there is reference to a mode of judgment neither in the vision itself nor in its interpretation if we take אֲנָךְ, an object held by the figure standing upon the wall, to mean "plumb–line" as an instrument for testing, essentially parallel to the "plummet" (מִשְׁקֹלֶת) and "line" (קָו) referred to in Is 28:17.

■ 8 Immediately upon the vision proper there follows Yahweh's question concerning the vision, Amos' answer, and then Yahweh's explanation. This catechetical style reminds one of the didactic method in the instruction of the "wise."[66] The question shows Amos being addressed by his proper name, as is also the case in 8:2a and as happens to Jeremiah in a similar context (Jer 1:11; 24:3).[67] The relationship informing the encounter is revealed by the way in which the man Amos is taken aside by his God in the course of his preparation. Amos answers with the single word "plumb–line!" Not a syllable refers to the wall and the one who stands on it, or even to the hand that grasps the plummet. Such an economy of words characterizes a man who is most intently alert. What is the significance of the testing instrument? Is he already worried about the outcome of the test? In his decision (v 8b), Yahweh

---

57 See textual notes "q" and "r" to 7:7.
58 Cf. מִשְׁקֹלֶת ("plummet") in Is 28:17 and 2 Kgs 21:13.
59 Following van Hoonacker.
60 Hubert Junker, "Text und Bedeutung der Vision Amos 7:7–9," *Biblica* 17 (1936): 359–64.
61 Brunet, "Vision," 387–92.
62 *AHW* 1, 49; cf. Koehler–Baumgartner (³1967), 69.
63 Brunet ("Vision," 387) considers even אֲנָךְ in 7:7a to belong to the original text.
64 *Ibid.*, 393–94.
65 See p. 295.
66 Cf. Johannes Lindblom, "Wisdom in the Old Testament Prophets" in *Wisdom in Israel and in the Ancient Near East*, ed. Martin Noth and D. Winton Thomas, SVT 3 (Leiden: E. J. Brill, 1960), 192–204 (esp. 202).
67 Cf. the "son of man" form of address frequently found in Ezekiel, e.g., Ezek 2:1, on which see also Zimmerli, *Ezechiel*, 70–71.

states first of all that he is setting the plumb–line in the midst of his people Israel. In contrast to the first and second vision, this third one requires such an interpretive element. In contrast to the fourth vision, it reiterates precisely the same catchword (אנך) rather than introducing an assonantal wordplay. In an attempt to find the assonance type of vision also in 7:7–8, Friedrich Horst proposed reading אֲנָחָה ([ˀanāḥāh] ("sighing, groaning") in v 8b, supposedly anticipated by אנך ([ˀanāk] "plumb–line") in the same way that קַיִץ ([qayiṣ] "summer fruit") anticipates קֵץ ([qēṣ] "end") in 8:2: "The word that is portrayed should culminate in a word that is heard."[68] In this connection Horst cited Jer 1:11–12, 13–14; in Jer 1:13–14 at least one important element (צָפוֹן ["north"]) is identical in the scene as described and in the interpretive utterance, just as in the transmitted text of Am 7:8. Horst's proposed emendation in v 8b, as well as his reinterpretation of the vision proper, is based on the expectation that what is envisioned ought to relate immediately to punishment. However, by setting the plumb–line in Israel, Yahweh is first of all asking whether Israel is stable or ready to be torn down. Thus the third vision must be assigned to the type of the "symbol–vision" and thereby distinguished from both the first two, which are "event–visions," and the fourth, which is a "word-play–vision."

So here Yahweh himself for the first time poses—at least implicitly—the question of Israel's guilt. This is the issue which had been presupposed by Amos in his first intercession, "Do forgive" (7:2), but which he did not dare to repeat in the second vision. It is true that Yahweh had previously decreed certain punishments, but regarding an assessment of Israel he had uttered nothing. Precisely that, however, is the aim of the new vision. For the first time we hear the name of the one who is being tested: "my people Israel." "Israel" means here, as always in Amos, the northern kingdom.[69] Israel as the unified people of God would have

been called "Israel, my people" (ישראל עמי).[70]

In the compact style of the *memorabilia*, the outcome is attached immediately to the announcement of the test.[71] The expression "to pass him by no longer" at the same time definitively states just wherein Yahweh had let himself be persuaded in his "repenting" in response to Amos' intercession: he did not intervene with the threatened punishments (cf. 5:17). But neither did he grant the requested forgiveness. Had he done so, at least it ought to have been said that "he passed over [the] crime" עָבַר עַל־פֶּשַׁע, cf. Prv 19:11 and Mi 7:18. The expression "to pass by" (עבר ל) means simply "not to intervene (with punishment) against someone"; it corresponds exactly to the "it shall not happen" (לא תהיה) of 7:3 and 6. Thus the third vision shows no more than that Yahweh was ready for a new examination of the question of guilt. It reports no decision concerning the form of punishment, something that interpreters can only seek in vain here, but it does reject decisively the hitherto unanswered appeal for forgiveness (7:2b).

■ **9** For the sake of clarification, and in order to make the transition to 7:10–17,[72] a threat formulated as a speech of Yahweh is introduced which pertains to the sanctuaries and the royal house. It has the effect of being a summary of the developed oracles against the cult and the court circles (5:5, 21–23; 6:1, 3–6). The במות are the numerous "high places" in the land,[73] though it is also possible that Bethel is more specifically in view here.[74] The "high places" are threatened with destruction: "to be made desolate" (שמם nipʿal) can mean destruction (Joel 1:17; with reference to provisions) and also the desolation of places which, having been destroyed (Ezek 6:4; Am 9:14), become depopulated (Is 54:3; Jer 12:11). The expectation that the populace will be deported stands behind this threat (5:5, 27; 6:7; 7:11, 17). The reference to the high places of "Isaac" probably indicates that this oracle was addressed to those on pilgrimage to Beer–sheba

---

68 Horst, "Visionsschilderungen," 201.
69 Cf. "my people Israel" (עַמִּי יִשְׂרָאֵל) in 7:15 with "the land of Judah" (אֶרֶץ יְהוּדָה) in 7:12.
70 Maag, *Text*, 218–19.
71 On עבר ("to pass by"), cf. 5:17 and see also p. 249.
72 See p. 295.
73 Cf. Hos 10:8 and Wolff, *Hosea*, 176 [229].
74 Cf. 1 Kgs 12:31–32, and Horst Seebass, "Die Ver-

werfung Jerobeams I. und Salomos durch die Prophetie des Ahia von Silo," *WO* 4 (1968): 163–82 (esp. 170).

from the northern kingdom who claimed Isaac as their eponymous ancestor.[75] The use of "Isaac" as a designation for the inhabitants of the northern kingdom—which is an expression that Amos himself never employs—as well as the epitomizing in this oracle of an important part of the message of Amos, may well indicate the work of Amos' school. There is no basis in language usage elsewhere to support the view that "Isaac" here refers to a limited geographical region in the vicinity of Penuel–Mahanaim, or to the portion of the Transjordan controlled by the northern kingdom, distinct from "Israel" as a designation for the area west of the Jordan (7:16).[76] The "sanctuaries of Israel" (מקדשי ישראל) are probably the larger state sanctuaries, in keeping with the fact that Bethel is explicitly called a "sanctuary of the king" (מִקְדַּשׁ מֶלֶךְ) in 7:13. They, too, will be devastated by enemy invasion and depopulation. In the course of these events the royal house will fall prey to the sword, as indeed happened to Jeroboam's son Zechariah (2 Kgs 15:10).[77]

Aim

Looking back over the first three vision reports, one is initially surprised by how much remains unsaid. Neither times nor places are even so much as intimated for the events reported, nor in the first and second visions is there any mention of those whose doom is portrayed, while in the third they are mentioned only incidentally and generally. Absolutely nothing is said about the reason for Yahweh's intervention. In their details, too, these *memorabilia* are extremely terse, leaving many questions unanswered: What is covered by the assurance "It shall not happen" in 7:3 and 6? Why is the tillable land mentioned alongside the great primeval abyss in 7:4? How is the setting of the plumb–line in Israel related to the denial of further sparing? But the most difficult question is posed by the composition. The formulations are pointed in each case in such a way that they apparently aim in a precise direction.

Can that direction be recognized?

Sometime after the fact, Amos apparently tried to articulate the compulsion which led him to prophesy.[78] As one cast out and misunderstood, he entrusted to a circle of persons (who had no need to ask the more obvious questions that we posed above) those disclosures of Yahweh which had driven him into profound isolation. He had become accessory to the knowledge of his God's firm intention to destroy Israel. The prophet leaves no doubt that he, for his part, passionately suffered with Israel and, in solidarity with the helpless, strove with the Almighty on their behalf (7:2, 5). But he could not refuse to allow himself to be called by name (7:8aβ), and everything within him that was not prepared to repeat the one word naming that which Yahweh had shown him (7:8aβ) fell silent. These visions and dialogues, in which Amos, utterly alone, was embraced by the inescapable presence of his God, the God of Israel, brought suspicion and enmity for the prophet in their wake. But these too the prophet endured, precisely for the sake of that word, imposed upon him, which ultimately outlasted his skeptical opponents.

According to the reports of the first three visions, what was the word which he could no longer resist? The uniform literary structure seems to make it easy for the exegete to recognize clearly the decisive statement which the reports wish to convey. However, this same structure complicates insight into those confusing proceedings which, upon closer examination, are perceptible precisely behind the first three of the five visions. One could lament the fact that the original literary unity of the first four visions was interrupted by the insertion of 7:9–17. However, with this insertion the redactor–disciples of Amos direct the reader's attention to the stormy route which leads from the first to the third vision, at which point an important goal has apparently been reached. Above all, this redactional effort blocks a simplistic view such as might be inclined to see, behind the two similarly structured

75 See pp. 110, and 239 on 5:5aγ; also Alfred Jepsen, "Zur Überlieferungsgeschichte der Vätergestalten," *Wissenschaftliche Zeitschrift Leipzig* 3 (1953–54): 269–81.

76 Against Adriaan van Selms, "Isaac in Amos" in *Studies on the Books of Hosea and Amos* (*Die Ou Testamentiese Werkgemeenskap in Suid–Afrika, 7th and 8th Congresses* [1964–65]) (Potchefstroom: Rege–Pers

Beperk, 1965), 157–65.

77 See p. 295 ("Setting").

78 See pp. 295–96.

narrative reports, no more than a reduplication of one and the same pronouncement. Now it becomes necessary to perceive more sharply what is distinctive in each vision, and thus to recognize the agony of the way along which Amos was led. In all this the concern is nowhere for "knowledge of higher worlds," but rather for "coming events, . . . which were also to be concrete realities in the objective world." One has to marvel at "this massive concentration upon historical events" and "the complete absence of any sort of 'speculative' inclinations. . . ."[79]

The uniformity of the first two visions consists primarily in the fact that they both depict dangers which constitute a most serious threat to the future of Israel; locusts and drought make continued existence doubtful. But the crucial difference appears in the intercession. Against the background of the identity of the other words, the "do forgive!" of 7:2 contrasts all the more forcibly with the "cease!" of 7:5. The first petition aims at Israel's guilt, pleading that it be washed away and that all reason for the punishing intervention thus be removed. The second petition has in view only Yahweh's punishment in form of the rain of fire: may this precise form of destruction not occur! Only the recognition of this difference unlocks the meaning of the first pair of visions. On what is this crucial distinction grounded? On the fact that the petition for forgiveness as such is not granted.[80] There is no forgiveness of guilt; there is only delay of punishment. Amos wins forbearance, not pardon. Why otherwise would a second vision of terror have come upon him at all? Yahweh certainly promised nothing less than "It shall not happen" (7:3), but neither did he promise anything more. Only when one is cognizant of the deliberate reticence here does one appreciate the impact of the sole variation in the second outcry, "cease!" (7:5). After Yahweh's decision in 7:3, Amos *cannot* expect more. The slight expansion in the new decision of Yahweh—"That too shall not happen!"—confirms that it is not the guilt, but only the form of the punishment that has been annulled.

Thus it seems too simple merely to explain that Amos' petition was granted twice, but then no more.

Already between the first two visions lies hidden the unresolved question of guilt. The second vision largely destroys the hope which was alive in Amos' first outcry. The newly revealed punishment, the rain of fire, surely no less dangerous than the locusts, proves that there had been no forgiveness but only a cancellation of the first punishment. Amos grasps this and merely cries "cease!" And Yahweh's change of mind means only that "That too shall not happen!"

So far the question of guilt has been introduced only very indirectly by Amos' "Do forgive!" in 7:2. Only in the third vision, and no less indirectly, does Yahweh take up the question. The plumb-line is to test whether the wall that is Israel can stand, or whether it has to be torn down. The result is immediately clear: no further sparing of it is possible. The expression "I will no longer" (לֹא־אוֹסִיף עוֹד) in 7:8 is clear only when heard in conjunction with 7:3 and 6; it retroactively interprets the earlier decisions of Yahweh. So far only a delaying of punishment has been conceded. In the tersest of words, and yet clearly enough, Yahweh's final decision states that the testing of the guilty makes any further sparing impossible. Only in this negative way is the decision expressed. There is no mention at all in this vision of any concrete punishment, which constitutes the difference between this and the parallel fourth vision (8:1–2). In all this we must remember that the question of guilt was not introduced by Yahweh, but only in a veiled way by Amos with his plea for forgiveness (7:2). Material in the Old Testament comparable to the three stations on the path of lonely hearing and contending which these visions traverse is to be found only in the story of Abraham's contending with Yahweh for the sake of Sodom (Gen 18:17–33). The only Old Testament parallel to the alterations here in the form of punishment is found in the choice of three years of famine, three months of persecution, or three days of pestilence, which the prophet Gad offered to king David (2 Sam 24:13–15).

The result is important for our total understanding of the oracles of Amos. Yahweh's fundamental word is one of judgment. The question of guilt is introduced by Amos. Yahweh's compassion breaks through in for-

---

79 Von Rad, *Theology* 2, 59 [67].
80 See p. 298, on 7:3.

bearance, but the test with the plumb–line finally precludes his sparing. All preceding details in the *memorabilia* serve the purpose of highlighting the final decision in 7:8bβ. In 7:9 the disciples interpret the decision with an epitome of Amos' oracles.[81]

What is it that may discomfort the modern reader of Amos who looks beyond Hosea and Jeremiah to the New Testament, and from there to the present? Will it be recalled that the proclamation of Jesus, in spite of all his solidarity with transgressors, likewise knew of a "too late?" Or will the example of Amos open one's eyes to the new feature in God's Christ—that he not only cried out for those to whom punishment was decreed, but even stepped into their place? Be that as it may, does there not in any case remain one who stands on the wall and holds a plumb–line in his hand, testing whether the house still rises straight from its foundation or whether it has become ready for demolition?

81   See pp. 301–02.

The Accuser Is Condemned

Bibliography

Peter R. Ackroyd
"Amos 7:14," *ExpT* 68 (1956–57): 94.

Sebastián Bartina
"'Hiendo los higos de los sicomoros' (Am 7:14)," *Estudios Biblicos* 25 (1966): 349–54.

Eberhard Baumann
"Eine Einzelheit," *ZAW* 64 (1952): 62.

Simon Cohen
"Amos *Was* a Navi," *HUCA* 32 (1961): 175–78.

Gustaf Adolf Danell
"Var Amos verkligen en nabi?" *SEÅ* 16 (1951): 7–20.

Godfrey Rolles Driver
"Amos 7:14," *ExpT* 67 (1955–56): 91–92.

Antonius H. J. Gunneweg
"Erwägungen zu Amos 7:14," *ZThK* 57 (1960): 1–16.

Richard Hentschke
Die Stellung der vorexilischen Schriftpropheten zum Kultus, BZAW 75 (Berlin: A. Töpelmann, 1957), 149–52.

Albin van Hoonacker
"Le sens de la protestation d'Amos VII, 14–15," *Ephemerides Theologicae Lovanienses* 18 (1941): 65–67.

Arvid S. Kapelrud
"Profeten Amos og hans yrke," *Norsk Teologisk Tidsskrift* 59 (1958): 76–79.

Ludwig Keimer
"Eine Bemerkung zu Amos 7:14," *Biblica* 8 (1927): 441–44.

Sigo Lehming
"Erwägungen zu Amos," *ZThK* 55 (1958): 145–69.

J. MacCormack
"Amos 7:14," *ExpT* 67 (1955–56): 318.

Julian Morgenstern
"Amos Studies I," *HUCA* 11 (1936): 29–67 (reprinted in *idem, Amos Studies*, 13–51).

Henning Graf Reventlow
Das Amt des Propheten bei Amos, FRLANT 80 (Göttingen: Vandenhoeck & Ruprecht, 1962), 14–24.

H. Neil Richardson
"A Critical Note on Amos 7:14," *JBL* 85 (1966): 89.

Leonhard Rost
"Zu Amos 7:10–17" in *Festgabe für Theodor Zahn* (Leipzig, 1928), 229–36.

Harold Henry Rowley
"Was Amos a Nabi?" in *Festschrift Otto Eissfeldt*, ed. Johann Fück (Halle an der Saale: Max Niemeyer, 1947), 191–98.

Herbert Schmid
"'Nicht Prophet bin ich, noch bin ich Prophetensohn.' Zur Erklärung von Amos 7:14a," *Judaica* 23 (1967): 68–74.

Stanislav Segert
"Zur Bedeutung des Wortes *nōqēd*" in *Hebräische*

Wortforschung: *Festschrift zum 80. Geburtstag von Walter Baumgartner*, ed. Benedikt Hartmann, *et. al.*; SVT 16 (Leiden: E. J. Brill, 1967), 279–83.

Rudolf Smend
"Das Nein des Amos," *EvTh* 23 (1963): 404–23 (esp. 416–18).

Salomon Speier
"Bemerkungen zu Amos," *VT* 3 (1953): 307–10.

Hans Joachim Stoebe
"Der Prophet Amos und sein bürgerlicher Beruf," *WuD* N.F. 5 (1957): 160–81.

Ernest Vogt
"Waw explicative in Amos 7:14," *ExpT* 68 (1956–57): 301–02.

John D. W. Watts
Vision and Prophecy in Amos (Grand Rapids: Eerdmans, 1958), 9–12, 32–35.

Ernst Würthwein
"Amos Studien," *ZAW* 62 (1950): 16–24.

7

10 Then Amaziah the priest of Bethel sent to Jeroboam, king of Israel, the following (message): "Amos is instigating insurrection against you in the midst of the house of Israel; the land is no longer able to contain all his words. 11/ For thus Amos has said: 'Jeroboam shall die by the sword, and Israel shall depart into exile away from its land.'"[a]

12/ But to Amos Amaziah said, "Visionary, go! Flee away[b] to the land of Judah! Eat bread there! Prophesy there! 13/ But never again prophesy at Bethel! For here is the royal sanctuary, here the state temple."

14 Then Amos answered and said to Amaziah: "I (am)[c] no[d] prophet, nor (am)[c] I a prophet's disciple. I (am)[c] rather a livestock breeder[e] [f]and one

a   See textual note "i–i" below.

b   The dative (literally "flee for yourself") underscores the significance of the act for the person addressed (Gesenius–Kautzsch–Cowley, par. 119s).

c   *G* translates ἤμην ("I was"); it is only Chrysostom, and after him some few minuscule manuscripts, as well as the younger Greek translations (λ′) that have εἰμί ("I am"); see Ziegler, *Duodecim prophetae*, 199. *V* reads *sum* ("I am"). On the basis of 7:13a, a translation in the present tense would make sense; on the basis of 7:15, a translation in the past tense. The Hebrew nominal sentence in itself is neutral with respect to tense, which in each case must be determined from the context. On the subject matter, see pp. 312–13.

d   A decision in favor of the present–tense value of the nominal sentence has misled interpreters, on account of the tension arising with 7:15, to look upon the first לא as either a negative reply to the preceding speech of Amaziah (Cohen, "Navi," 177: "No! I am indeed a Navi, but not a Ben Navi") or as an asseverative, emphatic particle (H. Neil Richardson, "A Critical Note on Amos 7:14," *JBL* 85 [1966]: 89: "I am surely a Nabi, but not a member of the prophetic guild"); cf. already G. R. Driver, "Amos 7:14," *ExpT* 67 (1955–56): 91–92, and Peter R. Ackroyd, "Amos 7:14," *ExpT* 68 (1956–57): 94. But the parallelism between the first and the second לא can hardly be denied. On the problem of the interpretation as past or as present tense, see pp. 312–13.

e   *G* (αἰπόλος ["goatherd"]) is probably influenced by צאן ("flock") which follows in 7:15; α′, σ′, θ′, and ε′ correct this to βουκόλος ("[cattle] herdsman"). The basic meaning of בּוֹקֵר (as a substantivized participle, denominative from בָּקָר, "cattle") may indeed be "herdsman" (Rudolf Meyer, *Hebräische*

who slits mulberry figs.[f] 15/ But Yahweh took me from following the flock, and Yahweh said to me, 'Go, prophesy unto my people Israel!' 16/ Now therefore hear the word of Yahweh: 'You are saying, "Do not prophesy against Israel! Do not expatiate[g] against the house of Isaac!"' 17/ Therefore thus Yahweh has said:

'Your wife shall become
a harlot in the city;[h]
    Your sons and daughters
    shall fall by the sword.
Your land shall be parceled out
with the measuring–line;
    You yourself shall die
    on unclean land.
[i]And Israel shall depart into exile
    away from its land.'[i]"

Grammatik, vol. 2; Sammlung Göschen 764/764a/764b [Berlin: Walter de Gruyter, ³1969], par. 36.2), but since Amos, according to what follows, is primarily occupied with sheep and goats (צאן), the more comprehensive translation "livestock breeder" recommends itself. Both *G* (αἰπόλος) and the צאן of 7:15 argue against an original נֹקֵד here (against Maag, *Text*, 50), especially since this word seems to be unknown to *G* in 1:1 (see textual note "b" to 1:1). Of the ancient versions, only *T* renders נֹקֵד in 1:1 and בוקר in 7:14 by means of the same word (מרי גיתין), interpreting the prophet's former career as that of "cattleman" (literally "owner of herds").

f–f   *T* (ושקמים לי בשפילתא ["and I have sycamores in the Shephelah"]) lacks an equivalent for בולס ("one who slits, tends") but knowledgeably explains that the fruits in question grow only in the lowland. To this is added the interpretive plus מן קדם חובי עמי אנא מסגיף נפשי ("because of the sins of my people I expose my life to affliction").

g   *G* recognizes the basic meaning of נטף hip'il in 9:13 (ἀποσταλάξει ["shall drip"]) but in 7:16 renders the same word with ὀχλαγωγήσῃς ("to court a mob"). The use of נטף as "dribble, drip"—referring to slavering speech—struck *G* as being most peculiar. *V* uses a form of *stillare* ("to drop, drip") in both places.

h   On the basis of etymological investigation, Speier, "Bemerkungen," 308–10 (309 n. 1 citing the support of G. R. Driver) proposes the meaning "enemy" for עיר (from the root עור III "to be hot–tempered, aroused"). Cf. Wolff, *Hosea*, textual note "z" to Hos 11:9, and also זנה ב Ezek 16:17. But even though "in the city" might seem remarkably pale, one still needs to keep in mind that the usual reading of *M* is supported by *G* (ἐν τῇ πόλει), as well as the other versions.

i–i   The exact repetition of 7:11b strikes one as an interpretive addition to the preceding sentence, especially since the statement concerning all Israel stands isolated following the two bicola (exhibiting synonymous parallelism) which concern Amaziah. However, the repetition may well go back to that narrator to whom we owe 7:10–17. Rost ("Amos 7:10–17," 231ff) considers the sentence in v 17 to be original precisely because of מעל אדמתו ("away from its [i.e., Israel's] land") and posits for 7:11b an abbreviation, eliminating just this expression in order to create a three–stress line appropriate there to the bicolon: בחרב ימות ירבעם ישראל גלה יגלה ("Jeroboam will die by the sword // and Israel shall go into exile"). See pp. 315–16.

Form

This prose section is clearly set off not only from the preceding oracle in 7:9 (formulated as first–person address of Yahweh), but also from the wider context (7:1–8; 8:1–2), by the fact that someone other than Amos himself is the narrator. Moreover, the incident does not concern the prophet's direct experience of Yahweh, but rather relates how Amos had to stand up against Amaziah. Amaziah is the actual theme which unites the pericope in 7:10–17. Anyone who suspects that we have here a fragment from a biography of Amos must explain the lack of information at the beginning concerning the circumstances of Amos' appearance at Bethel, to say nothing of the fact that there is likewise missing at the end any report of the decision made by the royal court on the basis of the message from Bethel and of the course of action taken by Amos after his eviction by Amaziah.[1]

Once it is acknowledged that Amaziah, and not Amos, is the focus of this story, there is no longer cause to misunderstand it as a fragment of some prophetic biography. Instead we must recognize here the clear form of an *apophthegma* (*memorabile*), in which an historical episode is presented solely for the purpose of making intelligible a pointed prophetic oracle by explaining the circumstances of its origin.[2] Thus two brief scenes are initially sketched (vv 10–11 and vv 12–13) to prepare the reader for the great oracle of Amos, which dominates everything else in the pericope by reason of its extent and climactic position (vv 14–17). Accordingly, the two introductory pieces consist almost entirely of quotations (vv 10b–11, vv 12aβb–13); insofar as actions are reported (v 10a, v 12aα), they function merely to introduce words. In the first scene Amaziah reports to king Jeroboam what Amos has done (v 10bα) and what effect this has had (v 10bβ); he supports his statement by quoting a single oracle (v 11). The second scene concerns Amaziah's response to Amos. The priest issues some advice (v 12a), adamantly informing the prophet as to where his further activity may be possible (v 12b) and where it is not (v 13). In the first scene the priest reports the effrontery of the prophet to the king. In the second scene the priest counsels the prophet on the basis of the king's authority. Both scenes presuppose Amos' major oracle, in the first part of which the prophet makes a statement concerning his own person (vv 14–15), while in the second he deals with Amaziah (vv 16–17). The first part reports the most important biographical data, but apparently only in order to stress that it is really Yahweh (v 15), rather than Amos (v 14), whom Amaziah has denounced and rejected. Here, then, the issue of Amos' authority, which Amaziah skirted in his communications to the royal court and the prophet alike, is unequivocally addressed. (It is noteworthy that Amos does not mention the name of the king.) Thus in the second part of his response Amos can only confront Amaziah with an oracle of Yahweh, here a two–part judgment speech directed against an individual. In the first part, the basis for the judgment, guilt is established by means of a quotation (v 16), which v 13 has prepared us to understand. The announcement of punishment is once again explicitly introduced as an oracle of Yahweh by means of the messenger formula. Thus everything from v 10 on moves towards this oracle of Yahweh, and not towards the question of the prophet's own fate.

The narrator remained faithful to the commission of the prophet to speak for Yahweh and not for his messenger, to confront the hearer in Israel with the word of God rather than to play up the story of his spokesman.

Setting

To whom do we owe this account? Its author must have been a contemporary of Amos, personally acquainted with the proclamation of the prophet as well as with his experiences. The otherwise unknown figure of Amaziah, the priest of Bethel, as well as his actions, bears the mark of historicity. The same holds true, in light of its content and structure, of that which is preserved as the proclamation of Amos. Whether our author's information was gained while accompanying the prophet on his travels through the northern kingdom, or whether it stems from later reports by Amos himself or other companions, can no longer be determined. In any case, this pericope makes it necessary to suppose that already during the prophet's lifetime there had come into being a circle of disciples concerned to transmit the legacy of the master.

When this literary effort took place can be demonstrated with relative certainty. It could have begun only after the return of the prophet to the southern kingdom, as a number of factors indicate. In 7:10 Jeroboam is explicitly called "king of Israel"; an oracle of Amos himself, spoken in the northern kingdom, could dispense with such an epithet (7:11; cf. 7:9). Furthermore, this section presupposes the vision–cycle as an already completed literary unit; together with 7:9 it interrupts the connection between 7:8 and 8:1, interpreting in concrete terms what Yahweh's unsparing intervention means for the kingdom, the cultus and the people, and indicating the extent to which the end will affect all circles of the northern kingdom. At the same time, the context into which the circle of disciples has inserted its account gives sharp outlines to v 15, in that here is described how it happened that Yahweh took Amos away from following the flock. If our analysis of the superscription in 1:1 is correct,[3] then there is reflected already in its second relative clause a combination of the recorded cycles with "the words of Amos from Tekoa," preserved in chaps. 3—6. However, in that second relative clause in 1:1, in contrast to the language of the vision reports themselves, חזה is used for the "viewing" of the words. In keeping with that, it is only in the report here under discussion that Amos is called "seer" (חֹזֶה) by Amaziah (7:12). We can no longer distinguish between what Amos himself said and what the narrator considered appropriate, as far as the detailed formulation is concerned. (The nature of Amos' response in 7:14 tempts one to suppose that Amaziah addressed him as "prophet" [נביא].) Accordingly, Amos' school not only had available the recorded cycles but it combined with them "the words of Amos from Tekoa." Only thus do this school's supplementations in chaps. 3—6 also become understandable.[4]

Such supplementations have directed us to the fourth decade before the end of the eighth century, to the time around 735.[5] A distance of approximately twenty to thirty years from the appearance of the prophet in the northern kingdom allows, on the one hand, for a generation of auricular witnesses who still know precisely the facts and fundamentals of Amos' proclamation (which had already attained a high degree of literary fixity) and, on the other hand, for the supplements, including new and special formulations. To the latter belongs, with much greater certainty than can be claimed for the designation "visionary" (חֹזֶה) in 7:12, the designation of Israel in 7:9 and 7:16 as "Isaac,"

which is unattested elsewhere in the book of Amos. Since the name Isaac was attached predominantly to Beer–sheba,[6] and further, since the school of Amos established contacts with pilgrims to Beer–sheba from the northern kingdom,[7] the suspicion arises that our supplemental narrative had its setting at that place. A generation after the public appearance of its master, and at a time when the northern kingdom was in dire straights, the school of Amos announced to Israelite pilgrims traveling through Judah to Beer–sheba the imminent fulfillment of Amos' oracles. In the meantime the threat against Jeroboam had been fulfilled upon his son.[8] Substantially the same as in 7:9, in 7:10–17 both kingship (v 11) and cultus (vv 16–17) are attacked together. The words of Amos transmitted elsewhere use separate oracles to reject the two institutions, and unlike here they do not do so by singling out the official representatives of these institutions (Jeroboam and Amaziah).[9]

We can only guess at the time when the conflict with Amaziah here reported actually took place. Two clues are discernible. The wording of the message of Amaziah in 7:10–11 presupposes that the name of Amos was already known at the royal court (v 10bα) and that Amos had already proclaimed a significant number of oracles (v 10bβ). However, in Bethel these oracles have become so pointed that Amos' further activity now appears to be politically unbearable (v 11). These remarks from the priest's report indicate not only that the activity of Amos had been going on for a time, but further that it had already reached its high point, and this is confirmed by the counsel to flee which Amaziah addresses to the prophet himself (v 12).[10] Hence it is very probable that this incident at Bethel was intended by the narrator to preserve the record of the conclusion of Amos' activity in the northern kingdom.

For a picture of the overall activity of Amos, the hypothesis then suggests itself that he first proclaimed his message in the capital Samaria and lastly at Bethel.

---

1   Cf. Budde, "Geschichte," 66–67.
2   See Wolff, Hosea, 10–11 [9–10], 57–58 [71–72].
3   See pp. 117–21.
4   See pp. 109–10.
5   See p. 275 on 6:2, and p. 277 on 6:6b.
6   See pp. 301–02 on 7:9, and also Kurt Galling, "Das Gemeindegesetz in Deuteronomium 23" in Festschrift für Alfred Bertholet, ed. Walter Baumgartner, et al.

(Tübingen: J. C. B. Mohr [Paul Siebeck], 1950), 182–83.
7   See p. 239 on 5:5aγ, and pp. 331–32 on 8:14.
8   See our comments on 7:9.
9   On the stronger emphasis placed on cultic questions by the old school of Amos, see p. 110.
10 Note also the formulation "never again" (לא תוסיף עוד) in 7:13a which confirms Amos' prior prophetic

Doubtless some of the first and last oracles now in the collection of chaps. 3—6 were proclaimed in Samaria (3:9, 12; 4:1; 6:1!),[11] as very likely were others in the same collection which do not mention Samaria explicitly. It is not possible with equal certainty to localize at Bethel any one oracle from "the words of Amos from Tekoa." On the other hand, 7:10–17 affirms Amos' appearance at Bethel as very probably amounting to a second and final phase of his activity. There is some evidence to favor the assumption that the oracles against the nations (1:3—2:16) were delivered at the beginning of his activity in Bethel.[12] His personal threat against Jeroboam, and then also against Amaziah, could well have been the final act.

Interpretation

■10 Apparently the priest Amaziah was charged with supervisory functions at the state sancturay (cf. Jer 20:1–2 and 29:26).[13] We know that it was possible in the northern kingdom for a prophetic circle to instigate a revolt which could bring down an entire dynasty. The dynasty of Jehu, to which Jeroboam II belonged, had itself seized power with the help of the Elisha–group (2 Kgs 9:1–10). The same word used here to characterize Amos' action, קָשַׁר, is also used with reference to Jehu's revolt (2 Kgs 10:9; hitpaʿel 2 Kgs 9:14). It connotes conspiratorial[14] incitement to insurrection by a group whose aim is the forceful overthrow of those who rule.[15] A responsible cult official would certainly have reported any impulse toward insurrection, especially were it generated, as here, within the Israelite state by a Judean and not far from the border with Judah at that. Amaziah initially supports his charge against Amos by referring to "all his words." While the use of this expression does not allow us to assume that Amos engaged in extensive prophetic activity at Bethel,[16] still less does it support the thesis of a one–time appearance there. Amos had spoken often enough to have reached the limit of what was

tolerable. In employing the verb "to contain" (כּוּל hipʿil), Amaziah looks upon the country, namely its attentive populace, as a huge container able to hold only a limited measure (cf. 1 Kgs 7:26, 38).

■11 And now the decisive drop has fallen, causing the barrel to overflow: a threat of violent death has been made against the king. The disciple apparently preserved here the oracle of his master, even though it is likely that prior to the time of recording Jeroboam II had already died a natural death (2 Kgs 14:29).[17] This particular oracle is therefore preceded by an interpretive supplement referring it to Jeroboam's son, Zechariah (7:9: "house of Jeroboam" [בֵּית יָרָבְעָם]),[18] who did fall victim to a violent conspiracy (2 Kgs 15:10). It is rather unlikely that in a single brief oracle Amos himself would have threatened both the deportation of the populace and the death of Jeroboam. The narrator has Amaziah summarize the major unbearable declarations of the prophet. Unlike the first declaration, the second (Israel's exile) is very well attested. According to 6:7[19] Amos prophesied this in Samaria; there is no reason to doubt that he did so as well at Bethel (cf. 5:27 with 5:21–23 and 5:5).

■12 A messenger from Bethel would have had to travel a distance of more than fifty kilometers to reach Samaria. An answer could be expected only days later. Although it is not self–evident that Amaziah on his own would have dealt with Amos before the arrival of a royal decree, his subsequent words do indeed bear the marks of independent initiative. Is the priest wavering between the authority of the king and that of a prohpet of Yahweh? The vocative designation "visionary" (חֹזֶה) acknowledges a charisma.[20] In preexilic times this word was used much less frequently than "prophet" (נָבִיא). For example, it is applied to Gad in 2 Sam 24:11 ("Gad, the prophet, David's visionary" [גָּד הַנָּבִיא חֹזֵה דָוִד]) where it would seem to designate a specific office. It next appears in Isaiah (30:10) where "visionaries" (חֹזִים) is paralleled by "seers" (רֹאִים; cf. 1 Sam 9:9)

11 See p. 207.
12 See p. 149, and Rost, "Amos 7:10–17," 236.
13 Würthwein, "Amos–Studien," 19; and Lehming, "Erwägungen," 163.
14 The original meaning of קָשַׁר is "to bind (together)": Gen 38:28; Prv 3:3; and Gen 44:30.

activity at Bethel; cf. the use of the same language in 7:8bβ and 8:2bβ.
15 Cf. 1 Kgs 15:27; 16:9, 16, 20; 2 Kgs 12:21 [20]; 14:19; 15:10 etc.
16 Cf. Lehming, "Erwägungen," 62; against Wüthwein, "Amos–Studien," 21.
17 See p. 309.
18 See pp. 301–02.
19 Cf. 6:1 and p. 274.
20 On חזה see p. 124, and Maag, Text, 147.

and designates a group to which Isaiah knows himself to belong, which is not the case in Is 28:7 when reference is made to the priest and the "prophet" (נביא). In Mi 3:7 "visionaries" (חֹזִים) along with "diviners" are viewed in a negative light. In Is 29:10 and 2 Kgs 17:13 "visionary" and "prophet" are used synonymously, in both instances perhaps only at a redacted level of the text. The Chronicler is the first to make frequent use of the term "visionary."[21] From this we can conclude that the חֹזֶה was probably considered a "prophet" (נביא) in preexilic times, but that a "prophet" was not necessarily a "visonary." חֹזֶה is in any case the much rarer word. Whether Amaziah used this solemn title or the disciple of Amos placed it in his mouth, it indicates the priest's respect for Amos as an extraordinary charismatic. (Did Amos proclaim his oracles at Bethel as vision reports?[22]) Amaziah found himself caught in a conflict over authority. Only thus does the command to flee at this particular moment become intelligible—a command that he apparently issued to Amos not without a measure of personal good will ("flee away!" [בְּרַח־לְךָ]).[23] It may well be that in his official capacity Amaziah could evict Amos only from the temple precincts, but not from the country.[24] Yet he directs Amos "to the land of Judah." He says nothing whatsoever to Amos regarding the content of his proclamation, there being only an indirect allusion to this in the reference to the place of the prophet's appearance (7:13). To be sure, the report to the royal court had already emphasized that Amos carried on his activity "in the midst of the house of Israel" (7:10a) in a manner that "the land" could not bear (7:10b). Judah is mentioned by Amaziah, not because it was the homeland of the prophet, but because it was a political realm in which he might "support himself" unhindered.[25] Amos' prophetic activity should earn him a living as far as Amaziah was concerned. From the counsel of the priest it appears that only the location of the activity was subject to question. Thus he created the impression of wishing to direct Amos to a place where his proclamation would be feasible. "Prophesy there!" (וְשָׁם תִּנָּבֵא) means that in Judah he would be able to carry on unhindered his prophetic activity against Jeroboam and the northern kingdom. In this way, then, Amaziah tried to evade conflict. He did not dare prohibit Amos' prophesying, nor did he want to wait until he had received the king's decree; therefore he advised Amos to cross the border. Perhaps he thus intended to save the life of a messenger of Yahweh to whom the king would presumably not show any mercy.

■ **13** This latter possibility is suggested by the subsequent warning. It also indicates the only problem, as far as Amaziah was concerned—the *place* of the proclamation. Not wishing to deny that Yahweh had commissioned Amos, the priest granted in general terms his necessity as a "visionary" to engage in proclamation. But it was not possible for him to do so at Bethel, the "state temple" (בֵּית מַמְלָכָה) over which the king himself, as the chief authority, exercised supervision, and in which the king himself could perform cultic acts ("royal sanctuary" [מִקְדַּשׁ מֶלֶךְ]; cf. 1 Kgs 12:31–33). After all, it was established explicitly as the national sanctuary by Jeroboam I, in opposition to Jerusalem and the kingdom of Judah.[26] In Bethel Jeroboam II must not be threatened. Amaziah attempted to extricate himself from the conflict by recognizing both the right of Jeroboam in Bethel and the right of Amos to engage in proclamation. What was Amos' response to the compromise solution of a "change of venue"?

■ **14** The first part of his answer points out that neither his right to function as a prophet nor his right to earn a livelihood thereby is pertinent to the discussion; the sole issue is rather Yahweh's precise commission. The compromising cultic official had spoken only of the person of Amos and of his conflict with the king; he had not made any reference at all to the God of Israel. Amos, on the other hand, immediately sets the matter

---

21 Cf. Rolf Rendtorff, "נָבִיא in the Old Testament," *TDNT* 6, 810.

22 Cf. 9:1–4; and also 7:9 as a supplement to 7:7–8.

23 See textual note "b" to 7:12.

24 Cf. Herbert Schmid, " 'Nicht Prophet bin ich, noch bin ich Prophetensohn.' Zur Erklärung von Amos 7:14a," *Judaica* 23 (1967): 70–71.

25 On "eat bread" (אכל לחם), see Koehler–Baum-gartner (³1967), 44–45.

26 Cf. 1 Kgs 12:26–29, and Noth, *Könige*, 281–85; cf. also Horst Seebass, "Die Verwerfung Jerobeams I. und Salomos durch die Prophetie des Ahia von Silo," *WO* 4 (1968): 163–82 (esp. 169–74).

straight with a twofold response. First of all he decisively excludes his own person as the issue (in three short nominal clauses, each with the subject "I" [אָנֹכִי v 14]), and then, no less emphatically, he focuses attention upon the one under whose authority stand all concerned (in three longer verbal clauses, of which the first two have Yahweh as their subject [7:15a, 15b] while the third introduces the "word of Yahweh" [7:16a]).

Especially contested among interpreters is the question whether the nominal clauses in 7:14 refer only to the prophet's past, or whether they intend to say something about his present status as well. This is a heated discussion because it includes the question of the self–understanding of Amos, and thereby also the problem of distinguishing between independent and officially sanctioned prophetism.

The Vocation of Amos

This is the only statement in the book wherein the prophet himself sheds light on his vocation.[27] Let us first of all note what can be taken as assured.

1. Amos had been engaged in an occupation by which he could fully support himself, one that had nothing to do with prophetic activity (7:14).

2. The commission to prophesy marked a change in the course of his life, attributable neither to a decision of his own nor to other human influences, but which he could only trace to Yahweh's intervention (7:15).

3. The declaration in 7:14 is primarily meant to be understood as an answer to the advice of Amaziah, who did not want to deny Amos the possibility of earning his living ("eat bread" [אֱכָל לֶחֶם]) and functioning as a prophet ("prophesy" [תִנָּבֵא]), but who rather intended to assure the prophet's future by relocating his activity across the border (7:12b: "there ... there" [שָׁם ... שָׁם]).

4. The broader context in 7:14–15 indicates no interest at all in drawing a contrast between a then and a now in the life of Amos. However, the unmistakably emphasized juxtaposition of the threefold "I" in 7:14 with the likewise threefold "Yahweh" used as subject in 7:15–16 shows that the interest here is in a correction of Amaziah's assessment of the case at hand.[28]

5. According to the extant wording, Amaziah called Amos a "visionary" (7:12a) rather than a "prophet," yet he refers more than once to the function of prophetic proclamation ("to prophesy" [הִנָּבֵא] 7:12b, 13a; cf. v 16b).

These observations on the text can initially serve as the basis for answering those disputed questions relevant to the problem of whether the nominal clauses are to be rendered in the present or past tense.[29] Scholarly opinion has remained almost equally divided between these options.[30]

This problem of tense depends upon the following open questions:

a) Can a decision on the point of temporal reference here be made on the basis of syntactical rules?

b) What is the significance of Amos' separation from the flock (7:15a), and especially of his present execution of the commission "prophesy!" (הִנָּבֵא 7:15b) for the interpretation of the nominal clauses in 7:14?

c) Are the words "visionary" (חֹזֶה 7:12) and "prophet" (נָבִיא 7:14) identical or different in meaning?

In response to question a): Ordinarily the rule holds that a nominal clause describes a state of affairs contemporary with the time span defined by the verbal clause with which it is associated. Since the verbal clause in question, 7:15, reports events in the past, many have thus decided in favor of a preterite translation of 7:14 as well. Yet reasons to the contrary compel me to assume here an exception to the general rule. 1) As the opening of Amos' answer, 7:14a has to be understood primarily on the basis of the immediately preceding address by Amaziah.[31] In this particular context, the nominal clauses are of neces-

27   On 1:1, see pp. 123–24.
28   Cf. Watts, *Vision*, 11.
29   See textual note "c" to 7:14.
30   The present tense is preferred by Nötscher, Maag (*Text*, 51), Neher (*Amos*, 20–21), Baumann ("Einzelheit," 62), Deden, Fosbroke, Hentschke (*Stellung*, 149–52), Lehming ("Erwägungen," 145–69), and Smend ("Nein," 416–18); a preterite interpretation is advocated by H. H. Rowley ("Was Amos a Nabi?" in *Festschrift Otto Eissfeldt*, ed. Johann Fück [Halle an der Salle: Max Niemeyer, 1947], 194–95), Cripps, Würthwein ("Amos–Studien," 16–22),

Gottfried Quell (*Wahre und falsche Propheten: Versuch einer Interpretation*, BFChrTh 46/1 [Gütersloh: C. Bertelsmann, 1952], 139–40), Osty, Antonius H. J. Gunneweg ("Erwägungen zu Amos 7:14," *ZThK* 57 [1960]: 1–16), Ronald E. Clements (*Prophecy and Covenant*, SBT 43 [London: SCM, 1965], 36–37), Reventlow (*Amt*, 16–20), and Amsler.
31   See above, point 3.

sity heard as statements concerning the present status of the prophet. 2) In 7:14 we have not merely a simple introductory clause to the verbal sentence of 7:15, but a threefold nominal declaration which is significant in its own right and whose present subject is the thrice repeated "I" of Amos. 3) Resuming our line of argument begun in point 4 above, we must recognize that in 7:15 an event of the past is referred to solely because it determines the present. Were the purpose of 7:14 nevertheless to describe a state of affairs antecedent to the event, then one would expect the finite verb הָיִיתִי ("I was") in 7:14 (comparable to the use of הָיְתָה in Gen 1:2 preceding וַיֹּאמֶר in Gen 1:3).[32] Thus a more comprehensive assessment of the syntax favors a present-tense understanding of 7:14.

In response to question b): Can Amos deny that he is at present a "prophet" (נביא) if he has accepted and is carrying out Yahweh's command to "prophesy" (הנבא)? Many interpreters apparently assume that this question, based on 7:15b, promptly resolves our problem in favor of a preterite interpretation of 7:14. Reference is then also made to 3:7 and 2:11 where there are positive statements about the "prophets."[33] But these passages are secondary.[34] In the only other case where Amos himself says something about the subject, 3:8, he likewise employs only a verbal form (נבא nip'al) to characterize his activity. And it is precisely this oracle which informs that (prophetic) proclamation, as Amos understood it, was not dependent on the office of the prophet. The rhetorical question "If Yahweh has spoken, who will (then) not prophesy?" surely means that no Israelite, whoever he might be, could refrain from prophesying under such circumstances.[35] In 7:14 as well, Amos apparently intends to distinguish between the office and the act. "The contrast between the 'not a prophet' of v 14 and the 'prophesy' of v 15" has been "intensified almost to the point of paradox by the use of the same word stem."[36] Thus Amos' use of the verb "to prophesy" (נבא nip'al) cannot stand in the way of a present tense understanding of 7:14; it can only confirm such an interpretation.

In response to question c): Amaziah likewise employs the verb "to prophesy" (נבא nip'al)[37] but not the noun "prophet" (נביא), yet he still addresses Amos as "visionary." Does he thereby deny to Amos the rights of a "prophetic" office? Does he treat him as a

mercenary opportunist (cf. Mi 3:5–7), an accusation against which Amos would then have to stress that only in the past was he no "prophet" (נביא)? We have already demonstrated, however, that "visionary" (חֹזֶה) and "prophet" (נביא) were not always interchangeable concepts,[38] and that "visionary" here is rather to be considered a less customary term of dignity (Is 30:10; 2 Sam 24:11).[39] Amos, who can tell of his visions, does not reject this form of address. But he takes pains to indicate that he does not thereby also claim either the professional title "prophet" or membership in a prophetic group. Thus Amaziah's choice of words also makes the present-tense translation of 7:14 more meaningful than the preterite rendering.

From all this we conclude that Amos establishes a sharp contrast, as far as he himself is concerned, between a prophet by virtue of office (נביא) and one called by Yahweh, between a "prophet's disciple" (בן־נביא) trained by prophets and one sent by Yahweh, between a salaried cult official and his own independent activity sanctioned by Yahweh alone. As a vocationally independent man, one who neither was nor is a prophet, he must temporarily be Yahweh's messenger in Israel. He must thus perform for a time a function similar to that of an Ahijah of Shiloh, Micaiah ben Imlah, Elijah, or Elisha, but without occupying a continuing office or even being associated with a prophetic school, as was at least in part the case with these others. He had to affirm the directive "prophesy!" (הנבא), but he did not thereby become a "prophet" (נביא), even though one can appropriately call him a "visionary" (חזה).

When Amos therefore denies that he is a "prophet" (נביא), he consequently rejects an evaluation of his appearance that is based on vocational considerations. He does not have to make his living by means of this activity (7:12b), nor does he think of himself as committed to it for life, much less as being assigned to a particular sanctuary. He rejects just as strongly any classifying of himself as a "prophet's disciple" (בן־נביא), a label which is applied almost exclusively to the disciples of Elisha,[40] though it is also used to designate

---

32   Baumann, "Einzelheit," 62.

33   Reventlow, *Amt*, 17–19.

34   See pp. 181 and 141–42.

35   See p. 187.

36   Smend, "Nein," 417.

37   See above, point 5.

38   Hentschke, *Stellung*, 150.

39   See pp. 310–11.

40   2 Kgs 2:3, 5, 15; 4:1, 38; 6:1; 9:1.

the anonymous figure in 1 Kgs 20:35.[41] The prophet's disciple[42] does not receive words of God independently; he instead carries out commissions from the prophet (cf. 2 Kgs 9:1). Conceivably Amos could have been sent by a prophet from Judah, like the disciple of Elisha in the passage just referred to. But neither as a master nor as a disciple does Amos belong to any association. Above all, he is economically independent. As a livestock breeder he was probably among the well–off of his society. Besides a "flock" (צאן 7:15) of sheep and goats, he may also have owned some cattle.[43] He also has something to do with mulberry figs. The *ficus sycomorus* is dependent on a warm climate and prospers only in the lowlands—primarily in the Mediterranean coastal region and in the Jordan Valley—where it is very abundant (cf. 1 Kgs 10:27). It bears fruit three or four times a year.[44] "To slit" (בלס) designates the job of scratching the fruit, which is done with a nail or some iron instrument. Before it ripens, each fruit must be treated in this fashion for it to turn sweet. That was probably the work of poor people, entailing as it did much toil in comparison with a small reward. But that fact alone is not sufficient to regard Amos as a poor man.[45] The term appears only here. We do not know whether the compound expression בולס שקמים ("one who slits mulberry figs") designates only someone who actually performed the work or might also refer to someone who supervised such labor. It is certain, however, that Amos is here pointing out an additional source of income.

■**15** This man of secure means was "taken" one day by Yahweh, just as one "takes" (Gen 18:7) the defenseless young of an animal, "takes" subordinates into one's service (Ex 17:5), or "takes" a wife.[46] Amos is able to identify the place where this intervention into his life

occurred at the time he was "following the flock." That need not mean that he has now given up his vocation once and for all. Our understanding of 7:14 rather suggests the opposite. Along with the grasp of Yahweh came his command, "Go, prophesy unto my people Israel!"[47] Amos thus explains that Yahweh determined not only the content of his message, but also the place of his appearance. Hence Amaziah's compromise ("there . . . there" [שָׁם . . . שָׁם] 7:12b) constitutes a clear decision against Yahweh's instruction. The vision reports say nothing of such a command by Yahweh. Nevertheless, the balance of the evidence is in favor of the assumption that Amos perceived his commission in connection with the visions.[48]

■**16** After it has been made clear that Amaziah's concern should not be for the life of Amos but for the will of Yahweh (7:14–15), the "visionary" announces to the priest that word of Yahweh which pertains to him personally. The expression "the word of Yahweh" (דבר־יהוה) is not otherwise found in the authentic oracles of Amos,[49] much less the exhortation "Hear the word of Yahweh!" (cf. 3:1a). It is not necessarily to be expected at this point, since the word of Yahweh is not introduced with the messenger formula until 7:17. Perhaps the exhortation in v 16a was in common use in Amos' school (cf. Is 1:10 and 28:13, 14). What follows, however, is in full accord with the style of Amos. A quotation is introduced as the motivation for the threat in 7:17, and it is done here as in 4:1 and 6:13 by means of a participle, namely "You are saying" (אתה אמר). The citation lays bare the guilt of the priest. It is primarily this quote which will have brought about the report of the events that preceded the actual oracle of Amos. The context of the question corresponds primarily to 7:13a, but the intervening lines have shown the utterance of

41   Cohen, "Navi," 176.

42   בן ("son, disciple") indicates a status subordinate to the prophetic "father": 2 Kgs 2:12; 6:21; 13:14.

43   See textual note "e" to 7:14, and above pp. 123–24; Stoebe, "Amos," 117; and Segert, "nōqēd," 280–81.

44   Cf. the picture of a sycamore in Dalman, *Arbeit* 1/2, fig. 6.

45   Koehler, *Amos*, 37; Jehuda Feliks, "Maulbeerfeigenbaum," *BHHW* 2, 1177.

46   Gen 4:19; Ex 34:16; Hos 1:2; cf. Wolff, *Hosea*, 13 [12].

47   The use here of the preposition אל ("unto") seems

to be determined in part by the imperative לך ("go"); cf. 7:16b: לא תנבא על ("do not prophesy against"). While אל primarily introduces the goal of movement, על often introduces the target of hostile actions; cf. Brockelmann, *Syntax*, pars. 108a, 110b. On עמי ישראל ("my people Israel") as designation for the northern kingdom, see p. 301 on 7:8.

48   See pp. 295–96 on 7:1–8, "Setting."

49   On 8:11–12, see pp. 330–31.

Amaziah to be in direct opposition to Yahweh's mandate (7:15bβ). Instead of the preposition "unto" (אל) in 7:15b, now the antagonistic "against" (על) is employed, thereby characterizing Amos as an adversary of Israel.[50] In parallelism with "to prophesy" (נבא nipʿal) we find here the verb נטף (hipʿil), which literally means "to let flow."[51] The word describes the delivery of an impassioned discourse, with drops spraying from the mouth of the speaker or his saliva freely flowing. The verb need not always have a pejorative sense;[52] it can also be used to depict the vehement speaking of the prophet in the context of a commission from Yahweh.[53] Amaziah's manner of dealing with Amos personally, according to 7:12–13, does not justify our finding an overtone of contempt in the use of this word. Amaziah forbids the vehement, hostile (here also appears the preposition "against" [על]) speaking against the "house of Isaac."[54] Amos can merely state that the priest's proposed compromise (7:12–13) contradicts Yahweh's command which had even determined where the prophet was to appear (7:15b); because Amaziah had forbidden the prophet to speak at Bethel (7:13b), Amos in turn must declare him culpable.

■ **17** And so Yahweh's announcement of punishment is delivered to Amaziah, there thus being a second judgment speech against an individual added to that previously issued against Jeroboam (7:9b, 11a). The speech states precisely what Israel's conquest by an enemy and the resulting deportation will mean for an individual figure, in this case the priest of Bethel.[55] His family is included in the threat.[56] His wife will become a harlot. Usually "in the city" (בעיר) is taken to mean the place of her reprehensible activity. In this connection we may recall Dtn 22:23–24,[57] according to which a wife who submits to sexual intercourse with a stranger "in the city" without calling for help is deemed guilty of adultery; it would be otherwise (rape) were she overpowered "in the open field" (בַּשָּׂדֶה). This citation suffices to explain the expression "become a harlot in the city," even though the subsequent parallel statements presuppose an encounter with the enemy. An explicit reference to the "enemy" can be found in this passage only by positing a dubious etymology for עיר.[58] In any case the fate of Amaziah's wife corresponds to the fulfillment of a curse similarly articulated in ancient Near Eastern treaties.[59] Amos proceeds to threaten that Amaziah's sons and daughters will die "by the sword." Apart from this passage, "sword" (חרב) appears in announcements of punishment within authentic utterances of Amos only in the immediate context, namely in the fifth vision report (9:1, 4), in the oracle against Jeroboam (7:9, 11), and finally also in 9:10. Here there is not only denied a future for the priesthood in Bethel, but even any sort of continuance for the family of Amaziah. Alongside the shame of his wife and the death of his offspring, the loss of his property or his homeland constitutes the third element in the announcement of punishment. What does "your land" mean? אדמה elsewhere in Amos may designate the whole of the arable land in general (3:2), more particularly being used with reference to Israel's native soil (5:2; 7:11b, 17bβ; 9:8). Thus it is possible that Amos threatened the priest with the distribution of his entire homeland (by enemies to new settlers; cf. Mi 2:4–5). But such an interpretation is scarcely certain in as much as this threat is set between punishments affecting Amaziah quite personally (cf. v 17aα and v 17bα), and it may even be declared improbable in view of the singular pronominal suffix "your (land)." אדמה is also used in Amos to refer to an individual plot

---

50 Cf. Brockelmann, *Syntax*, par. 110b; and Amsler, "Amos," 325.

51 See textual note "g" to 7:16.

52 I.e., "slaver, drivel;" cf. Mi 2:6, 11; and also 1 QpHab 10.9: מטיף הכזב for the "lying prophet" (literally "the spewer of the lie").

53 Cf. Ezek 21:2 [20:46] and 21:7 [2]; and Zimmerli, *Ezechiel*, 464.

54 On this designation for "Israel" (cf. the parallel member!), see pp. 301–02 on 7:9.

55 See textual note "i–i" to 7:17bβ.

56 Cf. Hos 4:5–6, and Wolff, *Hosea*, 78 [95].

57 Cf. Seeligmann, "Gerichtsverfahren," 259.

58 See textual note "h" to 7:17.

59 Cf. the Asshur–nirâri treaty (rev. 9–11) and especially the following curse in the Sefîre I inscription (*KAI* 222A.40–41): "[And just as a pros]ti[tute is stripped naked] so may the wives of Matiʿel be stripped naked, and the wives of his offspring and the wives of [his] no[bles]" (as cited in Delbert R. Hillers, *Treaty–Curses and the Old Testament Prophets*, Biblica et Orientalia 16 [Rome: Pontifical Biblical Institute, 1964], 58–59).

of ground (3:5). Thus the possibility is not to be excluded that Amaziah, like the priest Abiathar in 1 Kgs 2:26–27 and the priestly family of Jeremiah according to Jer 32:6–15, possessed land of his own. (To be sure, in the two analogues just cited the word used is not "land" [אדמה] but "field" [שָׂדֶה].) One would have to think here of a "fief awarded him by the king by virtue of his office."[60] In any case, use will be made of a "measuring–line" to distribute the land anew, this time, of course, to foreigners. That the land is to be "parceled out with the measuring–line" would suit an interpretation of אדמה as referring to either the substantial holdings of an individual landowner or the total territorial possession of Israel (cf. Mi 2:4–5). The counterpart to Amaziah's land in the following parallel line is "unclean land." Israel's own land (cf. 5:2), once the gracious gift of Yahweh (2:9!), will fall into the hands of foreigners, while the priest must die in a place where worship of Yahweh will no longer be possible.[61] Thus does Amos specify in particular for the priest in Bethel a fate which corresponds to that announced for Israel as a whole in the threats of war and deportation.

Aim

This one time a disciple of Amos has preserved for us an utterance of the prophet within its dramatic context. We witness the confrontation scene which gives rise to the utterance, a confrontation that not only shapes the accusation (7:16) but also takes up the fundamental conviction of the prophet and applies it specifically to the life of the priest (7:17). The disputation speech (7:14–15) preceding the judgment speech gives us an insight into the unprecedented sense of sovereignty and authority of the man from Tekoa. When Yahweh took hold of the prophet, he conferred upon him at once a total freedom from and superiority to the local authorities and liberated him from dependence upon institutional prerogatives. Amaziah's report to the royal court (7:10–11), which precedes the prophetic utterance, and the advice which Amaziah gives to Amos (7:12–13), show that the whole scene is concerned with the question of who really instigated rebellion. When Amos is put on report as a rebel against Jeroboam, does this not mean the prophet has been totally misunderstood? In actuality it is the priest Amaziah who, in his eagerness to resort to compromise, is exposed as a rebel, specifically as a rebel against Yahweh, since he has denied to Yahweh's messenger the right to speak at the place designated by Yahweh. Thus the accuser is himself condemned, and the accused is the one who announces the sentence. In this way both sides of the issue come clearly into focus: Amos is a witness for the God of Israel, not by virtue of office but rather because of Yahweh's hold on him, Yahweh's commission, and his own unwavering obedience. Amos' disciple is not concerned to devote even a single sentence to the question of whether the subsequent course of events brings to fulfillment the word of the priestly antagonist or the message of the prophet, or both. He lets us know only so much as is really worthy of being transmitted. Thus he induces us to side with him who has said, "My food is to do the will of him who sent me, and to accomplish his work" (Jn 4:34).

---

60 Albrecht Alt, "Der Anteil des Königtums an der sozialen Entwicklung in den Reichen Israel und Juda" in *Kleine Schriften* 3, 360; *idem*, "Micha 2, 1–5 ΓΗΣ ΑΝΑΔΑΣΜΟΣ in Juda" in *Kleine Schriften* 3, 373–81; and also Noth, *Könige*, 35.

61 Cf. 2 Kgs 5:17, and Wolff, *Hosea*, 154–55 [199–200] on Hos 9:3–4.

The End Has Come

Bibliography

Walter Baumgartner
  "Die Etymologie von hebräischen $k^e l\bar{u}b$ Korb," *ThẐ* 7 (1951): 77–78.
Samuel E. Loewenstamm
  "כלוב קיץ (A Remark on the Typology of the Prophetic Vision [Amos 8:1–3])," [Hebrew] *Tarbiz* 34 (1964–65): 319–22 (English summary, ii).
Bruce D. Rahtjen
  "A Critical Note on Amos 8:1–2," *JBL* 83 (1964): 416–17.

See also the bibliography on 7:1–9, p. 291.

8

1 Thus [the Lord]ᵃ Yahweh showed me:

There was a ᵇbasket of ripened–fruitᵇ
2/ Then he said,ᶜ "Amos, what do you see?" I answered, "A basket of ripened–fruit."ᵈ Then Yahweh said to me, "The reaping–timeᵈ has come for my people Israel. I will no longer (benignly) pass him by."

3 Then the ⟨songstresses⟩ᵉ of the palace will wail.
  On that day [utterance of the Lord Yahweh]ᶠ there will be many corpses.ᵍ
  They will be castʰ everywhere.
  Hush!

a אדני was not yet present in the text underlying *G*. See textual notes "a," "h," and "q" to 7:1, 4, and 7 respectively.

b–b Literally "basket of summer–fruit." *G* (ἄγγος ἰξευτοῦ ["fowler's pouch"]) erroneously read כְּלִי מוֹקֵשׁ (cf. 3:5). α′ and σ′ understood rightly (κάλαθος ὀπώρας ["basket of tree–fruit"]) while θ′ entered an·explicit correction: ἄγγος ὀπώρας θερίνης ("pouch of summer tree–fruit").

c In accord with the reading in 7:8, *S* adds יהוה אלי ("Yahweh [said] to me"); *G* (καὶ εἶπε) confirms *M*.

d The Hebrew exhibits a wordplay: *qāyiṣ* (קַיִץ) "ripened–fruit" and *qēṣ* (קֵץ) "end," here rendered "reaping–time." It is uncertain whether these words were distinguished in pronunciation and orthography at the time of Amos; cf. Leonhard Rost, "Bemerkungen zu Sacharja 4," *ẐAW* 63 (1951): 216 n. 4; and Bruce D. Rahtjen, "A Critical Note on Amos 8:1–2," *JBL* 83 (1964): 416–17. In the Gezer Calendar (probably from the second half of the tenth century) the last month of the year is attested as ירח קץ, with קץ designating (as does קיץ in our text) the harvest of summer–fruit; see *KAI* 182.7, and p. 319 below.

e *M* שִׁירוֹת ("songs") is unlikely as the subject of "wail"; this plural form is unattested elsewhere, the expected form being שִׁירִים as is presupposed otherwise in the book of Amos as well (cf. 5:23 and 8:10). Thus an original שָׁרוֹת ("songstresses") was probably misread on the basis of 5:23 (שִׁירֶיךָ) and 6:5 (כְּלֵי־שִׁיר). Cornelis van Gelderen (*Het Boek Amos* [Kampen, 1933], 224–25) argues at length in support of *M*.

f The extended oracle formula נאם אדני יהוה appears three times in the oracles inserted between the fourth and fifth visions (8:3, 9, 11); elsewhere in the book of Amos it occurs only in 3:13 and 4:5. In 8:9 (cf. 8:13) the formula is likewise preceded by (וְהָיָה) ביום ההוא ("[and it will come to pass] on that day"), and in 8:11 it follows הִנֵּה יָמִים בָּאִים ("hence, days are coming"). See the excursus on p. 143.

g   פגר ("corpse") has a collective meaning here, as in 1 Sam 17:46 and Na 3:3. This clause, like those preceding and following, must be considered a verbal sentence, so that רב is to be taken as a third–person singular perfect of רבב, in keeping with the tense of the parallel verbs.

h   The third–person singular perfect must here express a general subject; so also in 4:2 and 6:12 (see textual note "g" to 4:2, and "a" to 6:12; cf. Brockelmann, *Syntax*, par. 36d).

Form

The report of the fourth vision (8:1–2) has the same structure as that of the third (7:8–9). It exhibits four elements: the vision proper (8:1), Yahweh's question concerning the catchword (8:2aα), Amos' answer (8:2aβ), and Yahweh's interpretation (8:2b).[1]

Only two variations are to be noted. In the report of what is seen והנה ("there was . . .") is followed immediately by the object being viewed, rather than by a participle describing someone's action, as in 7:1 ("forming"), 7:4 ("summoning") and 7:7 ("standing"). While this difference is characteristic it is also insignificant, since in the preceding visions as well the primary focus was on an object. Thus in the third vision the figure "standing upon a wall" (7:7a) and "his hand" (7:7b) are completely overlooked in favor of the "plumb–line" in Amos' response to the question of what he sees (7:8). In the fourth vision, attention is fixed from the outset on the crucial object, the "basket of ripened–fruit" (8:1). Perhaps the narrator has merely abbreviated his report in this way, just as the formulation introducing Yahweh's question is more sparing of words here than in the previous reports (cf. 8:2aα with 7:8aα).[2]

The other variant appears in the relationship of Yahweh's interpretation to the prophet's characterization of the visionary image. While in the third vision the name of the object seen and the word which is interpreted are fully identical (7:8), here we have to do with two different words merely resembling one another in pronunciation. The former may be classified typo-logically as a "symbol–vision"; our present text exhibits a "wordplay–vision" (cf. Jer 1:11–12).[3]

In 8:3, very much as in 7:9, a prophetic utterance of three clauses, beginning with a verb form in the third–person plural perfect consecutive, is attached to the vision report. It has been subsequently designated as an oracle of Yahweh,[4] even though it does not (in contrast to 7:9) present Yahweh as speaking in the first person.

Setting

It is difficult to determine the temporal framework for the fourth vision. If the reference to "late–planting" (לֶקֶשׁ) in 7:1 points to spring,[5] then the "basket of ripened–fruit" points to early autumn.[6] In the Gezer Calendar *lqš* designates the third month, and *qṣ* the eighth month of the year.[7] In that case an interval of half a year may have separated the beginning of the visionary cycle from its climax in the fourth vision. But who would want to say that what "Yahweh showed" is tied to the calendar?

The fourth report was certainly fixed literarily at the same time as those in 7:1–8, as the uniform style indicates.[8] 8:3 probably belongs to the same phase of redaction as 7:9; the manner in which the respective visions are followed by interpretation is comparable. In both cases orally transmitted materials of Amos (cf. 6:9–10) were subsequently appended by Amos' school.[9]

Interpretation

■1 Here too the starting point of the visionary process

---

1   See pp. 94–95 and 294–95 (on 7:1–9 "Form").
2   See also textual note "c" to 8:2.
3   Cf. Horst, "Visionsschilderungen," 201–02. Samuel E. Loewenstamm ("Remark," 319–22) cites the example in which Alexander the Great, in the course of the siege of Tyre, saw a dancing "Satyr" in his dream, and was told by way of interpretation σὴ τῦρος, "Tyre is yours."
4   See textual note "f" to 8:3.
5   See p. 296.
6   See p. 319.
7   *KAI* 182.2, 7.
8   See pp. 294–95.
9   See pp. 295–96.

is not some ordinary object as such, which anyone else present might also have seen. It is rather Yahweh who initiates the process by causing the object to be seen.[10] This is so even though in the abbreviated report there is no reference to any figure acting in the field of vision, as happens in 7:1, 4, and 7.[11] The כלוב must be a container; according to its probable etymology the noun should mean "wickerwork,"[12] whether a "cage" (for birds) as in Jer 5:27 or a "basket" as only here in the Old Testament. קיץ defines the basket with respect to its purpose; the word does not mean "summer" itself, but that which summer brings, namely the season of "ripened–fruit." קיץ occurs in Jer 40:10 and 12 as harvest–yield, which is ingathered along with wine and oil. In 2 Sam 16:1 one hundred pieces of קיץ are mentioned alongside two hundred loaves of bread, one hundred raisin cakes and one skin of wine; they are designated "for eating" (2 Sam 16:2), just like bread. The parallel to grapes and olives makes one think primarily of figs (and similar tree fruits that ripen at the same time, such as pomegranates). They are harvested in August / September.[13] Thus Amos probably views a basket of newly harvested figs.

■ **2** In what follows, however, the accent does not fall on this image at all; it falls exclusively on Amos' naming of the object viewed, even more precisely on the second word of the designation he utters: "ripened–fruit" (קיץ). For it is only this part which is taken up by the interpretive statement and then in the form of its homonym "end" (קץ).[14] The two words here utilized have different roots.[15] While קיץ ("ripened–fruit")

derives from the root קיץ,[16] קץ ("end") derives from קצץ ("to hew off").[17] With respect to persons, therefore, "end" (קץ) means the end of life, the "reaping" of death.[18] This end "has come" (בא)—that is what Yahweh lets Amos know. The threat which older prophets like Ahijah of Shiloh, Jehu the son of Hanani, Elijah, and Elisha brought against the royal houses of Jeroboam I (1 Kgs 14:10ff), Baasha (1 Kgs 16:2ff), and Ahab (1 Kgs 21:20ff; 2 Kgs 9:7ff), is now directed against Yahweh's people Israel.[19] While the third vision had explained why Yahweh would "no longer pass him by," this fourth vision shows the terrible consequence. Furthermore, we must assume that it was this vision which first impressed upon Amos that basic conviction which evoked his proclamation of Israel's death (cf. 5:2, 16–17; 6:9–10; 2:14–16). It was demanded of no one else that he convey the message of the end of Israel's life in so binding and unqualified a manner as Amos. However, we do find the prophet Ezekiel taking up the catchword "end" (קץ) and spelling out in detail the message of Israel's destruction.[20]

■ **3** The attached oracle is suited to illustrate that the "end" envisioned is the end of life. "To wail" is an aspect of funerary lamentation.[21] The funerary cries are intoned by those female singers[22] who on other occasions provide most pleasant enjoyment for the royal court. Whenever "songstresses" (שרות) are mentioned in the Old Testament they are associated with the royal court.[23] Along with silver and gold, male and female singers are precious treasures of the king (Eccl 2:8). According to 2 Chr 35:25 they intone funerary

---

10 Differently Weiser, *Profetie*, 11–12.

11 See pp. 294–95 ("Form").

12 The noun apparently must be derived, not from the root כלב "to seize" (cf. כֶּלֶב "dog" and Arabic *kalaba* "to grasp"), but from a root כבל < כלב "to bind, weave, braid" (cf. Ethiopic *karabō* and German *Korb*). So Walter Baumgartner (citing the lexica of August Dillmann and Jacob Levy): "Die Etymologie von hebräischen *kelūb* Korb," *ThZ* 7 (1951): 77–78.

13 Cf. Dalman, *Arbeit* 1/1, 7–8; and Donner–Röllig, *KAI* 2, 182.

14 See textual note "d" to 8:2.

15 Loewenstamm, "Remark," 319–22.

16 Cf. Arabic *qāṭa* ("to be very hot").

17 See Dtn 25:12, where the reference is to a cutting off of the hand; cf. Ugaritic *qṣ* ("to cut, slaughter";

WUS, no. 2434), and the Phoenician 'Ešmun'azar inscription (*KAI* 14.9–10, 22) where the root meaning is "to destroy."

18 Cf. Ps 39:5 [4]; Job 6:11; and Lam 4:18.

19 On the meaning of עמי ישראל ("my people Israel"), the northern kingdom, cf. 7:8 and 15, and see p. 301.

20 Cf. Ezek 7:2, 3, 6; and Zimmerli, *Ezechiel*, 169–70.

21 Cf. Jer 4:8; 25:34; 49:3; Ezek 21:17 [12]; Mi 1:8; and Zeph 1:11.

22 See textual note "e" to 8:3.

23 Cf. 2 Sam 19:36 [35]; 2 Chr 35:25; and Eccl 2:8.

lamentation over Josiah. Thus the word היכל used here probably refers to the royal "palace" and not to the temple.[24] The reason for the lamentation is stated by the two following lines: the multitude of scattered corpses. The burial grounds either cannot or shall not contain them; thus they are cast about everywhere.[25] The judgment of death is intensified by the shame of not being buried; the corpses are consequently consumed by dogs and birds (1 Kgs 14:11, etc.) or they lie about like dung, fertilizing the fields (Jer 16:4, etc.).[26] "Hush!" (הס), the exclamatory imperative demanding strictest silence, suggests the sinister way in which death makes its rounds.[27] Any sound might attract the enemy of the living.

Aim

In terms of its form, the fourth vision is almost completely parallel to the third;[28] in terms of its content, it carries us a step further. In the third vision the imagery of testing appeared; here now we find that the catchword conveys the judgment. The fourth vision is to the third as the announcement of punishment is to the accusation. Taken together they confirm that a stay of execution is no longer possible, that a last minute reprieve is not to be expected. While the first and second visions had already indicated specific types of destruction for Israel—types which were revoked, however—the fourth vision keeps its silence concerning the way in which the end of life will come upon Israel. The attached oracle (8:3), however, announces funerary lamentation over a horrible scene of mass dying. In a definite historical moment, at the end of his lonely wrestling with his God, a prophet has to arrive at a certainty regarding those of whom Yahweh himself says that they belong to his people: the end has come.

---

24 Cf. Akkadian *ekallu* (*AHW* 1, 191–92); and also pp. 78–79 above, and Noth, *Könige*, 100 (textual note "z" to 1 Kgs 6:17).

25 On שלך ("to cast"), see p. 207.

26 Cf. Wächter, *Tod*, 171–80.

27 See pp. 282–83.

28 See pp. 294–95.

Oracles Concerning the End

Bibliography

Sebastián Bartina
" 'Vivit Potentia Beer–Šeba!' (Amos 8:14)," *VD* (1956): 202–10.

Ernst Kutsch
" 'Trauerbräuche' und 'Selbstminderingsriten' im Alten Testament" in *Drei Wiener Antrittsreden*, ThSt 78 (Zürich: EVZ–Verlag, 1965), 25–42.

Michael Leahy
"The Popular Idea of God in Amos," *ITQ* 22 (1955): 68–73.

Julian Morgenstern
"The Loss of Words at the Ends of Lines in Manuscripts of Biblical Poetry," *HUCA* 25 (1954): 41–83 (esp. 41–55).

Frank J. Neuberg
"An Unrecognized Meaning of Hebrew *DÔR*," *JNES* 9 (1950): 215–17.

R. B. Y. Scott
"Weights and Measures of the Bible," *BA* 22 (1959): 22–40 (reprinted in *The Biblical Archaeologist Reader*, vol. 3; ed. Edward F. Campbell, Jr., and David Noel Freedman [Garden City, New York: Doubleday and Company, 1970], 345–58).

August Strobel
"Masse und Gewichte," *BHHW* 2, 1159–69.

8

4   Hear this (those of you)
       who trample[a] (the) needy,
       [b]and who put an end to[b] (the) op-
       pressed[c] of (the) land,

5   who say,[d]
       "When will the new moon be over
       that[e] we may sell [f]grain,

a   See textual note "k" to 2:7b. *G* (οἱ ἐκτρίβοντες ["those grinding down"]) presupposes הַשֹּׁ(א)פִים here as also in 2:7; cf. Job 9:17 and Horst, *Hiob*, 140 (textual note "c" to 9:17).

b–b *G* (καὶ καταδυναστεύοντες ["and who overpower"]) renders the Hebrew infinitive construct with ל as a participle, for the sake of syntactic parallelism with the preceding colon. *G* is thereby in accord with the sense of the Hebrew construction, in which the infinitive construct with ל is here coordinate with the preceding participle, its usual function of expressing aim or purpose having been contextually modified. This coordination of the participial and infinitival forms is established by the use before לשבית of the copula ו which must not be deleted (against Weiser, *Profetie*, 27); cf. also Jer 17:10; 44:19; Hos 12:3 [2]; Joüon, par. 124p; and Gesenius–Kautzsch–Cowley, par. 114p.

c   On the vocalization, see Delekat, "Wörterbuch," 46–47.

d   As 7:10 also shows, לאמר does not stand only after verbs of speaking (cf. 2:12 and 3:1).

e   The indirect cohortative after the preceding question expresses aim or purpose; cf. Is 41:26, and Joüon, par. 116c.

f   The object is derived from the same root as the verbal form. Such paronomasia suggests to the hearer

and the sabbath,
that we may offer wheat for sale
  <and may sell (the) refuse^q of (the)
  wheat,>^{h}
that we may measure with a small
ephah
  and weigh with a heavy shekel,
    and defraud with false balances,

6   that we may buy (the) poor for silver
  and (the) needy for a pair of sandals < >^{i}?

7   Yahweh has sworn by the pride of
Jacob:
  Never^j will I forget any of their
  deeds!

8   On this account should not the land
tremble,
  and everything mourn that dwells
  in it,
and all of it rise <like the river>^{k}
[and be tossed about]^l
  and <sink>^{m} like Egypt's river?

9   And on that day it will come to pass—
utterance of the Lord Yahweh—

  I will bring in the sun at noon
  and darken the earth in broad day-
  light.

10   I will turn your feasts into a time
of mourning
  and all your songs into lamentation.
I will bring sackcloth upon all loins,
  and baldness on every head.
I will make it^n like mourning
for an only son,^{o}
  and the end of it^n like a bitter day.

11   [Hence, days are coming, utterance of
the Lord Yahweh,
  when I will dispatch famine into the
  land,
    ^{p}not hunger for bread
      ^{q}and not thirst for water,^{q}
  but rather^p of hearing Yahweh's
  words.^{r}

12   They will totter from sea^s to sea,
  ^{t}from north to east they will
  rove about,^{t}
    ^{u}to seek Yahweh's word,^{u}
    but they will not find (it).]

that the matter is being carried to its natural conclusion; cf. Brockelmann, Syntax, par. 91.

g G (καὶ ἀπὸ παντὸς γενήματος ["and from every product"]) here erroneously read וּמִכָּל־.

h   For thematic and metrical reasons 8:6b should
probably be transposed to this position.

i   See textual note "h" above.

j   On the elliptical use of אם as an oath–particle, see
Brockelmann, *Syntax*, par. 170c.

k M כָאֹר ("like the light") is a misreading of כַּיְאֹר,
the latter being assured by its analogues in the parallel member and in 9:5bα. As the expression
יְאוֹר מִצְרַיִם indicates, יְאוֹר is not employed here as
a proper name; it is simply the designation for
"river." Thus G renders all three occurrences in
Amos with ποταμός; V similarly translates *fluvius*
and *rivus Aegypti* in 8:8b.

l   This is a supplemental gloss in M, which was not
yet present in the text underlying G; the gloss is
metrically superfluous, overloading the otherwise
parallel three–stress cola of v 8b.

m M Ketib (וְנִשְׁקָה ["and is given to drink"]) trans-
mits a copyist's error which introduced a familiar
root, though in a nip'al form never attested otherwise and which makes very little sense here. M
Qere' corrects to וְנִשְׁקָעָה, thereby restoring the verb
which, in accord with 9:5b, was original here; but
since the nip'al of this verb is elsewhere unattested,
we should probably read וְשָׁקְעָה (as in 9:5b).

n   Literally "I will make her . . . her end." The third–
person feminine singular pronominal suffixes in v
10bα–β are used neutrally, with reference to the
sequence of activity described in v 10a as a whole.

o   As a genitive object, the *nomen rectum* (יָחִיד) here
defines the particular character of the mourning; cf.
Brockelmann, *Syntax*, par. 77e, and Joüon, par.
129e.

p–p   Duhm ("Anmerkungen," 16) deletes the two antithetical clauses in v 11bα (לא . . . ולא . . .) and the
following כי אם־ as a gloss introduced into the text
by "some artless fellow" wishing to stress ". . . that
the famine of which Amos speaks should not be understood literally"; see p. 330.

q–q   Robinson (with the qualification "perhaps") and
Maag (*Text*, 54) suggest deleting the second antithetical clause which concerns thirst, because the
positive threat speaks only of hunger; see p. 330.

r G (λόγον κυρίου), S and V (*verbum Domini*) presuppose the more familiar singular form דְּבַר־יהוה
("Yahweh's word").

s G (ὕδατα ["waters"]) erroneously vocalized מַיִם.

t–t   Procksch (170) deletes v 12aβ; see p. 331.

u–u   The singular ("Yahweh's word"), which deviates
from 8:11b, can lead one to surmise that the infinitival clause might be a later addition to insure the
sense.

v   The gender of the verbal form is determined by the
feminine subject that immediately follows it, even
though the statement also pertains to the second,

13
On that day
the comely maidens will grow faint,[v]
as well as the young men, from thirst,[w]

14
those who swear by the guilt[x] of Samaria
and say, "As your god lives, Dan!"
and, "As the way[y] to Beer-sheba lives!"
They will fall and never rise again.

masculine subject; cf. Nu 12:1; Gen 33:7; and Joüon, par. 150q.

w   Sellin, Maag (*Text*, 54), and Morgenstern ("Amos Studies IV," 305) read הָאַמִּצִים, the young men thereby being called "strong" and creating an appropriate parallel to the "comely maidens." But *M* בצמא ("from thirst") supplies the reason why both "faint" (עלף hitpaʿel), and to eliminate it would also destroy the catchword link between 8:11–12 and 8:13. The emendation has no basis in the textual tradition; this is equally true of Morgenstern's proposal ("The Loss of Words at the Ends of Lines in Manuscripts of Biblical Poetry," *HUCA* 25 [1954]: 41–55, and "Amos Studies IV," 305, 327) that four words have been lost at the end of v 13. His reconstruction (based in part on Is 40:28–31) remains an unsupported conjecture.

x   It has been suspected (by Osty and others) that an original אַשְׁמַת has been revocalized as אַשְׁמַת in *M*. 2 Kgs 17:30 mentions a deity "'Ashima" (אֲשִׁימָא) venerated by settlers from Hamath in Syria, but there is no evidence for an earlier cult of the deity in Samaria. (Cf. the divine name אשמביתאל ['Ešembethel] in Elephantine Papyrus 22.124; A. E. Cowley, *Aramaic Papyri of the Fifth Century B.C.* [Oxford, 1923], 70; and *AOT*², 454. [On the name and text in question, cf. further Bezalel Porten, *Archives from Elephantine: The Life of an Ancient Jewish Military Colony* (Berkeley and Los Angeles: University of California Press, 1968), 160–73; Ed.]). Since there is evidence that an image of "'Asherah" (אֲשֵׁרָה) was set up in the northern kingdom, perhaps even in Samaria itself (1 Kgs 16:33 and 2 Kgs 17:16), Maag (*Text*, 55) and others have preferred to read here אֲשֵׁרַת, thereby departing from the consonantal text, however.

y   *G* (ὁ θεός σου ["your god"]) is obviously an accommodation to the preceding colon (v 14aβ). Sellin, Walther Zimmerli (*Geschichte und Tradition von Beerseba im Alten Testament* [Göttingen, 1932], 3 n. 5), Galling ("Bethel II," 38), Maag (*Text*, 55–56), Deden, and others read דֹּדְךָ, understanding דוד to be an epithet for the patron deity of the holy place (i.e., "your kinsman, tutelary-god" or the like). Yet this interpretation remains quite uncertain, finding support at best in a difficult reference in the Mešaʿ inscription (*KAI* 181.11–12) to the ʾrʾl dwdh ("the altar of her tutelary-god"?) taken by the Moabite king from the Israelite town of Ataroth (ʿṭrt); cf. Rudolf Meyer, "Die Bedeutung der linearen Vokalisation für die hebräische Sprachgeschichte," *Wissenschaftliche Zeitschrift der Karl-Marx-Universität, Leipzig* 3 (1953–54): 196 n. 3; Leahy, "Idea of God," 70; and Donner-Röllig, *KAI* 2, 175. (Cf. further Johann Jakob Stamm, "Der Name des Königs David" in *Congress Volume, Oxford 1959*, SVT 7 [Leiden: E. J. Brill, 1960], 172; and W. F. Albright, ANET³, 320). More recently the attempt has been made to interpret דרך in light of Ugaritic *drkt*

(Gordon, *UT*, 387, no. 702; and *WUS*, no. 792) as meaning "dominion, strength, might" (Cf., e.g., Sebastián Bartina, "'Vivit Potentia Beer-Šeba!' Amos 8:14," *VD* 34 [1956]: 202–10; and Koehler–Baumgartner [³1967], 223 דֶּרֶךְ no. 7; cf. also Wolff, *Hosea*, 181, textual note "w" to Hos 10:13.) In this connection reference is made to the fish–goddess, "Derkétô" of Ashkelon, whose cult is attested in the temple of the Nabateans at *Ḥirbet Tannūr* (Nelson Glueck, *Deities and Dolphins: The Story of the Nabataeans* [New York: Farrar, Straus and Giroux, 1965], 353–54, 381–83; and Jean Starcky, "Le temple nabatéen de Khirbet Tannur. A propos d'un livre récent," *RB* 75 [1968]: 228–29); Derkétô has been related to דרך באר־שבע of Am 8:14 (J. T. Milik, "Nouvelles inscriptions nabatéenes," Syria 35 [1958]: 238 n. 6). But who can say that דרך and *drkt* are equivalent, especially since in Hebrew the meaning "rule," particularly with reference to a deity, is not at all assured. Frank J. Neuberg ("An Unrecognized Meaning of Hebrew *DÔR*," *JNES* 9 [1950]: 215–17) has proposed the vocalization דֹּרֶךְ, the noun דּוֹר ("circle, assembly") here supposedly having the connotation "assembly of the gods," hence "your pantheon, Beer–sheba!" (So also Peter R. Ackroyd, "The Meaning of Hebrew DÔR Considered," *JSS* 13 [1968]: 4; cf. KAI 26.3.19 [*wkl dr bn ʾlm*,"and all the assembly of the sons of the gods / 'El"; Ed.]) But who in Israel would ever have so spoken? The attempt to find the same meaning in the consonantal text of Ps 84:11 [10]; 49:20 [19], and elsewhere, is not convincing.

Form

This group of oracles has been inserted between the fourth and fifth visions, just as 7:10–17 was placed between the third and the fourth. In the latter case we have a narrative account, reporting the consequences of Amos' oracle in 7:9 (which has been attached to the third vision); in 8:4–14 various oracles interpret the theme of the fourth vision, which is spelled out in 8:3: the end of Israel's life, and the mourning which that entails.

Five oracles can be distinguished here. Only the first (vv 4–7) contains a complete judgment speech, with a remarkably broad indictment (vv 4–6) and an announcement of punishment, equally remarkable by reason of its blandness (v 7). All the remaining oracles either lack the element of accusation altogether or encompass it within threats (v 14a) describing the form in which the end will come, in much the same way as is done in 8:3. In vv 7, 9–10, and 11–12 the threats

are formulated as speech of Yahweh. The oracle in v 8, a rhetorical question attached in an unusual way to the oracle in vv 4–7 by means of "on this account" (על זאת), elaborates upon the colorless threat of v 7b. The third oracle (vv 9–10) is attached to the series by means of the formula "and it will come to pass on that day" (והיה ביום ההוא), a much favored redactional device.[1] The fifth oracle (vv 13–14) is connected by means of the shorter formula ביום ההוא ("on that day").[2] These connecting formulas are never found at the opening of an oracle in the older oracular compositions in the book of Amos; the only other occurrence is in 9:11. "On that day, utterance of the Lord Yahweh" (ביום ההוא נאם אדני יהוה) has been inserted into 8:3, while "on that day—utterance of Yahweh" forms the conclusion in 2:16. Even more unusual is the introduction of the fourth oracle (vv 11–12) with "Hence, days are coming, utterance of the Lord Yahweh" (הנה ימים באים נאם אדני יהוה), a phrase that has its only parallel in the book of Amos in the later addition at 9:13, but which is attested with particular frequency in the book of Jeremiah.[3]

Corresponding to the unusual devices for linking oracles are other features which depart from the typical style of Amos' authentic oracles. Instead of "Hear this word!" (3:1; 4:1; 5:1; cf. "Hear and attest" in 3:13), the first oracle begins with "Hear this!" (v 4a). The chain of infinitives which follows in vv 5b–6a[4]—a construction unusual for Amos—occasions surprise, as does the atypical way of announcing punishment by means of a rhetorical question in v 8, the full explication of the mourning ritual in vv 9–10, the prolonged treatment of the theme of "hunger" in vv 11–12 (which has provoked many efforts at abbreviation),[5] and, in vv 13–14, the encompassing of the accusation (v 14a) by announcements of doom (vv 13, 14b).

Setting

The formal differences therefore pertain not only to the immediate context of the visions cycle, but beyond that to the manner of connecting the oracles and even to their very structure. From this we can draw a twofold conclusion. First, we must here posit a literary effort different from the one which produced the cycles and "the words of Amos from Tekoa" in chaps. 3—6. The parallelism between the insertions in 7:9, 10–17 and 8:3, 4–14 leads one to think of Amos' school as most likely responsible for both supplements.[6] It is thus that we can most easily account for the similar interruptions of the visions cycle—already extant in literary form at a prior stage—as well as the novel way of connecting the oracles. The literary remains of the school of Amos are noticeably distinct from the layers of material that go back directly to Amos himself.[7]

Furthermore, there are differences in the form and the content of the oracles which can be detected. To be sure, we initially notice the proximity to Amos which also characterizes the narrator of 7:10–17.[8] The accusation in 8:4–6, which details the reasons for the impending end, demonstrably takes up utterances of Amos, i.e., the use of language from 2:7a and 6b in 8:4 and 6. Minor variations in the vocabulary point to the freedom of oral transmission. The oath formula in 8:7a reminds one of 4:2 and 6:8. The announcement of funerary lamentation in 8:9–10 takes up not only the general theme of 5:1–2 and 16–17 but also the catchwords קינה ("lamentation") and אבל ("mourning").[9] In 8:13–14 we seem to have an obvious interpretation of the funerary lament in 5:2. The symbolic figure "virgin Israel" (בְּתוּלַת יִשְׂרָאֵל) who has "fallen, no more to rise" (נָפְלָה לֹא־תוֹסִיף קוּם), now achieves realistic contours in the "comely maidens and young men" (הבתולת היפות והבחורים) who ". . . will fall and never rise again" (ונפלו ולא־יקומו עוד). At the same time, "never . . . again" (לא . . . עוד) echoes the concluding words of the (third and) fourth vision (8:2bβ), which our sequence of oracles interprets. Those who formulated these oracles apparently (as in 7:14–17) still had Amos' own words ringing in their ears.

Yet as well as speaking differently than Amos,[10] they interpret his message in a new situation. On the whole it is impossible to say in each instance what is old and what is new. For example, it cannot be determined whether the descriptions of deceitful trade in 8:5 appropriate oral tradition of Amos (as can be demonstrated for 8:4 and 6) or whether we rather have here a creative application of prophetic ideas to other realms of illegal activity. The contempt for new moon and sabbath decried in 8:5a could well be imputed to a different audience than that of the zealous celebrants with whom the prophet conversed in 5:21–27. The detailed depiction of the mourning rites in 8:9–10 exhibits a somewhat keener interest in ceremony than we find in Amos' own oracles. If 8:14a should contain an allusion to idolatry in Samaria, Dan, and Beersheba, then we would find ourselves in closer proximity to the basic theme of Hosea than to that of Amos.

It is precisely the reference to Dan in 8:14aβ that

---

1 See p. 75, on Joel 4:18 [3:18].
2 Cf. the interchange between the shorter and the longer connecting formulas in Is 7:18, 20, 21, and 23.
3 Jer 7:32; 9:24 [25]; 16:14; see Mandelkern, 471. Cf. the different type of construction in the oracle of Amos in 4:2.
4 On v 4b, see textual note "b–b" to 8:4.
5 See textual notes "p–p," "q–q," "t–t" and "u–u" to 8:11–12.
6 See p. 318 on 8:3, and pp. 308–09 on 7:9 and 10–17.
7 See pp. 107–11.
8 See pp. 308–09.
9 Cf. already the appearance of אבל in 8:8.
10 See above ("Form").

warns us against dating these oracles too late. They must have been spoken before the invasion by Tiglath-pileser III in 733. We thus arrive at the same period to which 6:2 led us, the fourth decade of the eighth century.[11] The invocation of "those who swear by the way to Beer–sheba" presumably designates those same pilgrims from the northern kingdom which the expansion in 5:5aγ (of the oracle in 5:4–5) has in view. The manner of clothing a threat in the guise of a question for debate (8:8) is in keeping not only with the readiness to engage in disputation characteristic of the disciples of Amos, but also with their somewhat greater lack of self–assurance (cf. 5:14–15 and 6:2). In short, these supplementers have endeavored to communicate the older message of Amos (which to a large extent was already fixed in written form) as directly as possible to the pilgrims from the northern kingdom before the collapse of their state.

Quite likely only 8:11–12 derives from a later time. The introductory formula already points to the work of a different redactor.[12] By deleting 8:11b and 12b the attempt has been made to recover a core tradition concerned strictly with a natural crisis of famine.[13] However, it is not at all certain that Amos had expected this type of judgment, nor is there support in older textual witnesses for such an abbreviation. One cannot exclude completely the possibility that Amos, who had been restrained from proclaiming the word of Yahweh (7:16), subsequently threatened a hungering for precisely this word which would not be satisfied. It is more likely, however, that these theologically reflective sentences express the concerns of that Deuteronomistic preacher who has elsewhere so thoroughly deliberated upon the rejection of Yahweh's word (2:11–12; cf. 2:4). Could "from thirst" (בצמא) in 8:13b have sug-

gested the introduction at this point of 8:11–12?

Interpretation

■ **4** The first oracle opens with the simple call to attention.[14] "This" (זאת) as the designation for what is to be heard is also found in Mi 3:9 and in the developed call to receive instruction in Hos 5:1 and Joel 1:2.[15] Those addressed are immediately characterized in the vocative as oppressors of the poor.[16] The needy are trampled in order to suppress them.[17] Hosea uses "to put an end to" (שבת hip'il) in the same sense to depict the extermination of the Israelite royal house (Hos 1:4);[18] Ezekiel uses it in the context of his spelling–out the theme of the "end"[19] in relation to the destruction of all pride (Ezek 7:24). The oracle in Am 8:4–7 at first expresses only indirectly that those who destroy the oppressed hasten the end of the people of Yahweh.

■ **5** Before attention is directed again to the offenses against the helpless (8:6), a new theme is raised in v 5, namely that of deceit in the realm of trade. In this connection the total statement of 8:5 and 6 is introduced as a citation of the accused. In their own speech is to be found the proof of their injustice.[20] "When will the new moon be over . . . and the sabbath?" They pursue their evil dealings with such zeal that they begrudge the time taken away from business—the celebration of the new moon once every four weeks, and the sabbath every seventh day. They are no longer capable of sharing in the joy of these festive occasions.[21] It is especially the sabbath which is here (as elsewhere) regarded as strictly a day of rest. While in other societies there are taboos against work on the seventh day because it is market–day,[22] in Israel even such commercial activity is explicitly forbidden on the sabbath. Jer 17:21–27 warns against carrying burdens on the

---

11 See p. 275.
12 See p. 324.
13 So Marti.
14 Cf. 3:1; 4:1, and 5:1; see p. 175.
15 See p. 20.
16 On שאף ("to trample"), אביון ("needy"), and ענו ("oppressed"), see textual notes "a," "b–b" and "c" to 8:4, and pp. 165–66 on 2:6–7.
17 On the construction, see textual note "b–b" to 8:4.
18 See Wolff, *Hosea*, 17–19 [18–20].
19 See p. 319 on 8:2.
20 See p. 97.

21 Cf. 1 Sam 20:5; Is 1:13–14; Hos 2:13 [11], and Wolff, *Hosea*, 38 [45–46]. New moon and sabbath are also mentioned side by side in 2 Kgs 4:23 and Ezek 46:3.
22 Cf. Ernst Jenni, *Die theologische Begründung des Sabbatgebotes im Alten Testament*, ThSt 46 (Zollikon–Zürich: Evangelischer Verlag, 1956), 12–13.

sabbath, while in Neh 13:15–22 marketing is forbidden; there are even prohibitions against the gathering of wood (Nu 15:32–36) and the lighting of a fire on the sabbath (Ex 35:3). The injunction against marketing appears to belong to the older regulations concerning sabbath rest; the context in Am 8:4 and 6 suggests that the social concern of protecting slaves played a part in it (cf. Ex 23:12 and Dtn 5:14–15). Here, however, only the restriction upon trade itself is mentioned. שבר ("grain") and בר ("wheat") alike designate marketable cereal, the two words also being used interchangeably in Gen 42:1–3 and 25–26.[23] The verb שבר in the qal connotes the purchasing of such grain (e.g., Gen 42:2–3), and in the hip'il its sale (Gen 42:6; Prv 11:26). The verb פתח (literally "to open") leads one initially to expect as its object the "sack" which contains the grain.[24] Because the signification of the verb is here transferred to the contents of the "sack," it acquires the meaning "to offer (for sale)." The malicious side of the eagerness to do business is revealed primarily in the fact that not only good grain but even "refuse" is offered for sale.[25] מפל occurs only here with this meaning; it must designate a product of inferior quality which, having fallen to the ground, has become soiled and trampled.[26] When weights and measures are falsified the result is the complete perversion of the economic and social order. The ephah was a dry measure approximately equivalent to forty liters,[27] the reference here being to its use in measuring the grain being sold. If its full capacity is diminished, for example by placing something into it or changing its form, it is no longer a "just ephah" (אֵיפַת צֶדֶק Lev 19:36) but a "scant measure that is accursed" (אֵיפַת רָזוֹן וְעוּמָה Mi 6:10; cf. Dtn 25:14–15); the buyer receives too little. The shekel, on the other hand, desig-

nates the weight employed in weighing the purchasing price, the silver, before minted coins were in use; such weights probably consisted of limestone balls flattened at the bottom. The normal weight of the shekel was approximately 11.5 grams.[28] If the weights were enlarged in any way (i.e., made heavier) one could no longer call them "just weights" (אַבְנֵי צֶדֶק Lev 19:36); they had become "deceitful weights" (אַבְנֵי מִרְמָה Mi 6:11; cf. Dtn 25:13, 15), since using them fraudulently raised the purchase price. The standard weight was placed into one of the two bowls of the scales, which as a rule were used to measure the purchase price rather than the wares (Jer 32:10). Thus the merchant could cheat the buyer even with "just balances,"[29] though tampering with the scales themselves was a third way of perpetrating fraud, here described by the verb עות. This word means "to bend, distort," which in our context perhaps connotes not merely "falsifying" in general (e.g., by over–weighting the norm–bowl), but quite specifically "bending" out of shape the cross-beam of the balances. Thus the just balances became "false balances" (מאזני מרמה). The root רמה means "to cheat" and "to betray." The deceitful balances enable the seller to take advantage of the buyer through cunning fraud.[30] Proverbial wisdom strongly condemns the use of "false balances" (Prv 11:1; 20:23) and otherwise denounces such fraudulent practices (Prv 16:11; 20:10). In contrast, there is no reference to false balances in the legal tradition, though it does condemn the use of false weights and measures (Lev 19:35–36 and Dtn 25:13–15). In the great Hymn to Shamash (2.50–53) we also find a sapiential–didactic treatment of such practices:

---

23 See p. 247 on 5:11.

24 So Gen 42:27; 43:21; and 44:11.

25 On the transposition of 8:6b, see textual note "h" to 8:5.

26 In Job 41:15 [23] the noun denotes the "folds" of the crocodile's skin.

27 Cf. Barrois, *Manuel* 2, 247–52; Scott, "Weights," 29–31; Strobel, "Masse," 1163; and Zimmerli, *Ezechiel*, 1161.

28 Barrois, *Manuel* 2, 252–58; *BRL*, 187; cf. Scott, "Weights," 34–39; and Strobel, "Masse," 1166–67.

29 Cf. מאזְנֵי צֶדֶק in Lev 19:36; Job 31:6; and Ezek

45:10; and also מאזְנֵי מִשְׁפָּט in Prv 16:11.

30 Klopfenstein, *Lüge*, 310–14.

He who handles the scales in falsehood,
He who deliberately changes the stone weights
  (and) lowers [their weight],
Will make himself lie for the profit
  and then lose [his bag of weights].
He who handles the scales in truth,
  much [good fortune].[31]

Corrupt economic practices must have been widespread in the Israelite cities of the eighth century.[32] General instruction has been converted here into pointed accusation.

■ 6 It is not for the sake of trading in goods alone that those accused cannot wait for the holiday to end, but—even worse—because they are out to trade human beings. In 2:6b the evil practices of debt–slavery were condemned;[33] here now the reference is to the "purchase" (קנה) rather than the sale of the poor.

■ 7 The threat as an oath of Yahweh is introduced similarly to those in 4:2 and 6:8. But what is the meaning of "the pride of Jacob" by which Yahweh swears? In 6:8 "the arrogance of Jacob" (גאון יעקב) undoubtedly means the haughty pride of Israel.[34] If one assumes the same meaning here, then Yahweh would be swearing "sarcastically by this unalterable given."[35] Against this interpretation it must be noted that Yahweh otherwise always swears by himself. "The pride of Jacob" would thus have to be a predicate of Yahweh. Marti paraphrases the oath, "As truly as I am the pride of Jacob, I will never forget your deeds."[36] Read in this way, the speech sounds even more sarcastic, because he of whom Jacob is proud punishes his people harshly (cf. 3:2). This interpretation presupposes that "the pride of Jacob" was a known epithet of Yahweh. However, that is not the case at all. "The pride of Jacob" is found otherwise only in Ps 47:5 [4], where it means the land

of Israel (cf. Is 58:14). Only Mi 5:3 [4] ("in the majesty of the name of Yahweh" [בִּגְאוֹן שֵׁם יהוה]) can be adduced for further comparison. But in our passage the expression does not unequivocally designate Yahweh himself, and hence we must probably retain here the sense of 6:8.[37] This oath–formulation, departing as it does from those attested in Amos' own oracles in 4:2 and 6:8 (where Yahweh swears "by his holiness" and "by his life") can be attributed to the school of Amos, which in all likelihood was making creative use of 6:8. We might suppose in this case the meaning to be "Yahweh has sworn against the pride of Jacob"; but then the preposition ל would be expected.[38] Thus an ironic sense remains the most likely: Yahweh's oath is just as unalterable as Israel's haughty arrogance is beyond reform.

The language of the disciples is even more apparent in what follows. The oracles of Amos in 4:2 and 6:8 do not use the conditional particle,[39] and they announce very concrete punishments. Here, on the other hand, Yahweh announces—in an unusually pale and general way for Amos—that he "will never forget any of their deeds," which appropriates an expression quite commonly attested in songs of lament. For example, we find in Ps 74:19: "The life of your afflicted do not forget forever" (חַיַּת עֲנִיֶּיךָ אַל־תִּשְׁכַּח לָנֶצַח).[40] This threat almost sounds like an announcement of rejection within the cultus. In the days of Amos' disciples, two or three decades after the proclamation of the prophet, decades that had initially run a peaceful course for the northern kingdom, it would be acutely appropriate to remind the northern disputants "Yahweh will never forget any of your deeds!" Already the threat of Tiglath–pileser III draws ever nearer.[41]

■ 8 There follows a rhetorical question, posing for

---

31 Tr. Ferris J. Stephens, *ANET*[3], 388b (modified). Cf. Falkenstein–von Soden, *Hymnen*, 244.

32 Cf. Hos 12:8 [7]; Mi 6:10–11; and Wolff, *Hosea*, 214 [277–78].

33 See pp. 165–66.

34 See p. 282.

35 Wellhausen, 93.

36 Marti, 217.

37 Cf. Hos 5:5 and 7:10.

38 Gen 24:7; Dtn 2:14; 26:3; Ju 2:15; 2 Sam 3:9; Ps 132:11; etc. Cf. Sellin, 258.

39 See textual note "j" to 8:7.

40 Cf. Ps 13:2 [1]; 44:24–25 [23–24]; and 77:9–10 [8–9].

41 See p. 110.

discussion a judgment as the result of Yahweh's not forgetting.[42] One is immediately reminded of the earthquake to which reference was already made for dating purposes in the superscription,[43] that was also threatened in 2:13,[44] and finally to which witness was also given in the fifth vision (9:1), connection thus being made with the framework into which our oracular complex has been set. The quake is designated, not by a form of the root רעש (as in 1:1 and 9:1) but by a verbal form of רגז ("to tremble").[45] Perhaps this is a reminder of that earthquake which occurred shortly after the conclusion of Amos' ministry. Only here and in 9:5 is mourning identified as the human response to an earthquake. The series of oracles interprets "the end" of 8:2 in the direction laid out by 8:3. It is strange that an earthquake, in which several rocking impacts might follow one another within a few minutes, is compared to the Nile whose rising and falling extends over a period of months. Perhaps the addition "and be tossed about" (ונגרשה)[46] was meant as an interpretive correction, since the picture here is of waters in upheaval, just as גרש describes the tossing of the sea in Is 57:20.[47] Did the one who introduced the Nile simile "never witness the phenomenon himself"?[48] Did he "want to make use of his acquaintance with the wonders of the world"?[49] Or was the only point of the comparison to underscore the irresistible and far–reaching force of natural events which forebode an encroachment of chaos itself?[50] In any case, the presupposition here, as in Hos 4:1–3, is that anyone in Israel who tampers with the just orders of life draws the earth and its inhabitants into perdition

at the same time.[51]

■ **9–10** And not only is the earth affected as Israel's end draws near, but so is the rest of the cosmos as well. The sun darkens in midday; noon turns into night. Some have thought to find here a reference to the eclipse of the year 763; February 9, 784, had even brought a total eclipse. The uncanny feeling of such hours was probably told from generation to generation. In this context, however, the only thing to be said is that, on the day of the announced end of Israel, not only the female singers of the court (8:3) and all inhabitants of the earth (8:8), but even the heavens will join in the mourning (cf. Is 50:3). Indeed, the sun itself becomes the leader in the great funerary lamentation in Israel. By turning day into night, Yahweh transforms joyous feasts into ceremonies of mourning, and hymns of praise into funerary laments.[52] The place of the festal robe is then taken by the coarsely woven, dark loin cloth, which is merely draped around the hips.[53] The hair of the head is shorn off; apparently complete baldness is meant here (cf. Jer 16:16), while in Dtn 14:1 there is reference only to shaving the forelock and in Lev 19:27 to a bald edge shorn around the head.[54] The feminine singular pronominal suffixes in v 10b ("I will make her [שמתיה] . . . her end [אחריתה]") can scarcely be taken other than as neutral pronouns whose antecedent is the total situation described in v 10a. The extraordinary intensity of the mourning is epitomized by characterizing it as like that "for an only son"; such was indeed a most bitter form of mourning, for with the death of the only son the whole blessing of posterity

---

42 See p. 324 ("Form").

43 See pp. 120 and 124.

44 In 2:13 the announcement of the earthquake follows an accusation (2:4–6) quite closely related to that in 8:4–6; see p. 171.

45 Also used with reference to earthquakes in Joel 2:10; 1 Sam 14:15; and Hab 3:7; in Ps 77:19 [18] רגז and רעש appear in parallelism.

46 See textual note "l" to 8:8.

47 Cf. Josua Blau, "Über homonyme und angeblich homonyme Wurzeln," *VT* 6 (1956): 242–48 (esp. 245); differently Delekat, "Wörterbuch," 22–23.

48 Robinson, 102.

49 Wellhausen, 93.

50 Cf. Amsler.

51 Cf. Wolff, *Hosea*, 68–69 [85–86]; cf. also Jer 5:25–26 and 23:10. On יאור ("river"), cf. Zimmerli, *Eze-*

chiel, 707.

52 Cf. Jer 7:34; 16:9; 25:10; Ezek 26:13; and Lam 5:15. On קינה ("lament"), see p. 236 on 5:1; on אבל ("to mourn"), see pp. 249 on 5:16–17; on חג ("pilgrimage–feast") and שיר ("song"), see pp. 262–64 on 5:21–23, and p. 276 on 6:5.

53 Cf. Gen 37:34; Joel 1:8, 13; and above, pp. 29–30.

54 So according to Elliger, *Leviticus*, 261, and also Lev 21:5; differently Kutsch, "Trauerbräuche," 26.

was wiped out.[55] "The end," upon which nothing else follows, is like the "bitter day."[56] "Bitter" (מַר), the opposite of "sweet" with reference to the sense of taste (Is 5:20; Prv 27:7), and descriptive of wormwood,[57] designates primarily the bitterness of weeping (Is 33:7), of crying (Ezek 27:30), of funerary lamentation ("bitter mourning" [מִסְפֵּד מָר] Ezek 27:31), and of death (Eccl 7:26; Job 21:25; and 1 Sam 15:32, "bitterness of death" [מַר־הַמָּוֶת]). Here the climactic point would seem to be that at the end of the funerary lamentation with its heavy grief, "the bitter day" of death itself comes even for the mourners.

■ **11** An oracle is introduced by means of a formula differing from the language of Amos' school,[58] and whose theology points to a later time. Theological precision is more important to the oracle than stylistic consistency; there is mention of "Yahweh's words" (v 11b) and "Yahweh's word" (v 12b) even within first–person speech of Yahweh ("When I will dispatch" [וְהִשְׁלַחְתִּי] v 11a). The verb שׁלח occurs in the hip̄'il only five times in the entire Old Testament.[59] Yahweh is always the subject in these instances, while the object is a plague or disaster.[60] The hunger which Yahweh will send is immediately differentiated from the craving for even the most essential means of sustenance, bread and water. The nouns "hunger" and "thirst" are otherwise attested in the same context surprisingly seldom.[61] Thus it is understandable why some have suspected that the clause "and not thirst for water" might have been added later.[62] This reference, however, is better explained as reflecting vv 11–12 as a supplement to the oracle in 8:13–14; the point was not so much to en–large upon the threat of thirst in 8:13b (in which case the redactor should rather have stated at the outset of v 11 "I will send hunger *and thirst* into the land"), as it

was to clarify it in the light of a particular, well–known formulation. The new affliction of hunger and thirst about to come upon Israel was the longing "to hear Yahweh's words." The expression "to hear [all] the words of Yahweh" is found, apart from our passage, only in the narrative portions of Jeremiah (Jer 36:11; 37:2; 43:1), i.e., in proximity to Deuteronomistic activity, and furthermore only in contexts in which the hearers refuse to accept Yahweh's word. The notion that man lives by "that which proceeds from the mouth of Yahweh," and not "by bread alone," appears first in Deuteronomic preaching (Dtn 8:3; cf. 30:15–16 and 32:47), where it stands as ". . . an intentional fresh interpretation of the early tradition concerning man–na."[63] The addition uniquely proclaims that the longing "to hear Yahweh's words" is a famine decreed by Yahweh himself. Those who refused to hear the prophetic word (2:11–12; cf. 7:16) are punished by that very word being withheld from them.

■ **12** The distress thereby caused leads to desperate quests. In 4:8 "to totter" (נוע) describes the helter-skelter search for water of those parched with thirst; in Jer 14:10 it means greedily racing about, in Is 24:20 the uncertain staggering of intoxicated persons, and in Lam 4:14–15 the groping of the blind. In our context the word refers to agitated and aimless running to and fro in a state of distress. The parallel verb, שׁוּט (polel "to rove"), connotes a roaming over vast areas which is also a kind of seeking. It is used with reference to the eyes of God,[64] of Satan (in the qal, Job 1:7 and 2:2), but significantly also of those who seek to find the manna (Nu 11:8; cf. 2 Sam 24:2, 8). The range of the roaming is described in the most far–reaching terms. "From sea to sea" surely does not here mean from the Dead Sea to the Mediterranean,[65] but is intended to designate

---

55 Cf. Jer 6:26; Zech 12:10; and Wächter, *Tod*, 60.

56 On the force of the suffixes, see textual note "n" to 8:10.

57 Prv 5:4, with reference to the temptress: "But in the end she is as bitter as wormwood" (ואחריתה מרה כלענה).

58 See pp. 324–25.

59 In comparison with more than 500 attestations of the qal and considerably more than 200 of the pi'el.

60 Ex 8:17 [21] (J); Lev 26:22; 2 Kgs 15:37; and Ezek 14:13 (cf. 14:21) where the object of the verb is רעב ("famine") as in Am 8:11.

61 Dtn 28:48; Is 5:13; Neh 9:15; and 2 Chr 32:11.

62 See textual note "q–q" to 8:11.

63 Gerhard von Rad, *Deuteronomy: A Commentary*, tr. Dorothea Barton; OTL (Philadelphia: Westminster, 1966), 72 [*Das fünfte Buch Mose: Deuteronomium*, ATD 8 (Göttingen: Vandenhoeck & Ruprecht, 1964), 51].

64 Zech 4:10; 2 Chr 16:9; cf. Jer 5:1.

65 As is supposed by Harper. But cf. the more precise determinations in Joel 2:20; see p. 62.

the uttermost boundaries of the earth, as in Ps 72:8 and Zech 9:10. If the intention here were to delimit the boundaries of Palestine, one would not expect "from the north to the east" in the parallel colon. One must rather think here of those vast regions into which the people of God were scattered. The peculiar combination of north and east is most easily understood in this way.[66]

The purpose of all these laborious, far–flung quests is "to seek Yahweh's word" (בקש את־דבר־יהוה)—a formulation otherwise unattested in the Old Testament.[67] בקש portrays a searching for something lost which, being deemed essential to the very existence of the searcher, compels immediate action.[68] God's judgment renders the searching futile, a quest without a goal. Famishing after God's word and forced to roam vainly in search of it through the world—that is the end of Israel as the people of God. Thus in a unique manner this oracle interprets the fourth vision (8:2).

■ 13 In the wake of their master, the disciples of Amos offer a final oracle interpreting the "end" (8:2). In spite of all the problems which these terse declarations pose, the threat they carry is nevertheless unambiguous; the flower of youth is swept away, and therewith Israel is denied a future. The verb עלף (hitpaʿel) is used to characterize Jonah when he became completely enervated in the shadeless heat (Jon 4:8). One cannot call this a state of "unconsciousness" since he is still able to turn pleadingly to God, but it does mean utter weakness and feebleness. "To grow faint" is thus a close approximation of the meaning of the Hebrew word;

G translates similarly (ἐκλείψουσιν ["they shall faint"]). What in the case of Jonah is caused by heat is here, according to the transmitted text,[69] the result of thirst. Despite the similarity of 8:14b to 5:2-3, one is not to think here of death by the sword in battle, since beautiful maidens and vigorous young men alike swoon away.[70] The people fall victim to a great drought.

■ 14 Those in question have been found guilty of swearing falsely. One who swears by a god confesses loyalty to that god. The god is invoked as a witness who will be an enduring divine informant, able to watch and judge the fulfillment of the oath. To take an oath is thus to place oneself under the power of a god affirmed to be one who lives, thereby accounting for the oath formula "as [your god] lives" (חי).[71] "The oath sworn by other deities is certainly a sign of apostasy. . . ."[72] Since v 14a has to be understood as establishing grounds for punishment, swearing by the sanctuaries enumerated must be interpreted as defection from Yahweh. This would hold true even if the original text did not directly name foreign deities such as, for example, the ʾAshima or ʾAsherah of Samaria, or the "power," the "patron," or even the "pantheon" of Beer–sheba.[73] "The guilt of Samaria" could mean the national sanctuary at Bethel (7:13)[74] with its image of a young bull.[75] Yet this is doubtful. For, while Bethel is indeed missing from the list of explicitly enumerated sanctuaries, so too is Gilgal (cf. 4:4 and 5:5). Moreover, we are dealing here no longer with oracular material deriving ultimately from Amos himself but rather with an oracle of his disciples.[76] The disputants to whom it was addressed must surely

---

66 Maag, *Text*, 55.
67 On the subject matter, cf. Hos 5:6, 15 (also Wolff, *Hosea*, 100–1 [127–28]) and Jer 50:4; on the language, cf. Is 41:17 and Lam 1:11.
68 Cf. Song 3:1–2, and Westermann, "Fragen," 2–3.
69 See textual note "w" to 8:13.
70 On בתולה ("maiden"), see p. 236 on 5:2; on בחורים ("young men"), see p. 221 on 4:10.
71 Cf. Hans–Joachim Kraus, "Der lebendige Gott: Ein Kapitel biblischer Theologie," *EvTh* 27 (1967): 169–200 (esp. 175–76); and Joachim Becker, *Gottesfurcht im Alten Testament*, AnBibl 25 (Rome: Pontifical Biblical Institute, 1965), 94.
72 Friedrich Horst, "Der Eid im Alten Testament," *EvTh* 17 (1957): 366–84, quotation from 370 (reprinted in *idem, Gottes Recht*, 292–314 [297]); in this connection Horst cites the following passages: Dtn

6:12–13; 10:20; Ps 63:12 [11]; Jer 12:16; Josh 23:7; Am 8:14; Zeph 1:5; and Jer 5:7.
73 Cf. the discussion of proposals to emend the text in textual notes "x" and "y" to 8:14.
74 See p. 311.
75 Cf. Hos 8:5–6, and Wolff, *Hosea*, 140–41 [179–80].
76 See pp. 325–26.

have thought first of all of the capital city itself, all the more so since the existence of an official sanctuary in Samaria, devoted at least in part to the worship of Baal and 'Asherah, must certainly be assumed.[77] That the god by whom the oath is sworn is here labeled "the guilt of Samaria" is in keeping with the prophetic device of injecting a note of judgment into fictitious quotations.[78] It of course remains to be considered that the term "guilt" (אַשְׁמָה) is well–attested only in later language, especially in the Chronicler's History; yet Hosea employs the verb "to be guilty" (אשם) in his criticism of the cult of Baal (Hos 4:15; 13:1). Thus we must not preclude use of the substantival form by Amos' school. This attribution is even more likely in view of the fact that neither do the following oaths specifically invoke foreign gods. In the oath associated with Dan, the thrust of the criticism focuses precisely on the suffix "*your* god"; even though there may be allusion here to the image of the young bull (1 Kgs 12:28–29), the stress is on the cult's location. The same holds true for the third oath formula as well. The "way" to Beer–sheba must surely mean the pilgrimage to that place.[79] When viewed together, the common basis of defection from Yahweh informing the three oath–formulas becomes evident. It is not an apostate invocation of some foreign deity that is the primary issue in each case, but rather the emphatic insistence on the deity's localization at a particular sanctuary and on the religious practice of making pilgrimage there. In the fashion of the Canaanite cults, Yahweh has been fragmented into several gods, conceived as patron deities of territorial regions.[80] Hence this critique still follows the lead of Amos himself (4:4–5; 5:4–5, 21–23), even though it departs from Amos in treating the gods of the sanctuaries as self–evidently distinct from Yahweh.[81]

The concluding line, "They will fall and never rise again," completes the announcement of punishment begun in 8:13. Here the final clause of the fourth vision report (8:2bβ) is interpreted in light of the funerary

lament of Amos (5:2). Within the total scope of the oracle, therefore, the old prophetic proclamation of the end has thus been grounded anew by means of reference to false cultic practice, a reference quite understandable in the context of dispute with pilgrims to Beer–sheba from the northern kingdom.[82]

Aim

The collection of oracles in 8:4–14 takes its cue from 8:3, interpreting the "end" which Yahweh disclosed to Amos in the fourth vision as being the inevitable fate of Israel. The concluding line of the final oracle— "They will fall and never rise again" (8:14b)—shows most clearly, by way of continuing 8:2bβ and taking up 5:2, that nothing short of death can be expected; it precludes anticipation of any future. In keeping with this, the other oracles likewise follow 8:3, referring to mourning (8:8) and funerary lamentation (8:9–10). To be sure, the concrete cause for such reaction differs, which shows that this literary composition is compiled of material of diverse origins and varying proximity to Amos. The disciples of Amos portray for their readers several ways in which the end is approaching: by earthquake (8:8); by cosmic catastrophe, a vast scene of death (8:10) inaugurated by an eclipse (8:9); and by a fall drought which even the vigorous youth will be unable to survive (8:13–14). It seems as though these oracles derive from a comprehensive discussion concerned with the question of how the message of the prophet, delivered years earlier, would be realized in history. The disciples of the prophet and those with whom they converse are alike agitated.[83] Is it not apparent to them that the Assyrians Tiglath–pileser III, Shalmaneser V, and Sargon II, will pause only for a brief time before overwhelming the territory of Israel and the gates of its capital city?

Those who kept the word of Amos alive did not miss their chance to cite old and new reasons for the downfall of Israel. From the prophet himself derives the accu-

---

77 Cf. 1 Kgs 16:32–33, and the comments of Noth, *Könige*, 284, 355.

78 Cf. Hans Walter Wolff, *Das Zitat im Prophetenspruch*, BEvTh 4 (München, 1937), 46–47 (= *idem, Gesammelte Studien*, 70–71).

79 Cf. Galling, "Bethel II," 38–39. In light of Ps 139:24; Jer 2:23; 10:2; and 12:16, Ernst Würthwein wishes to interpret "way" (דרך) as referring

to "the practice of the cult" ("Erwägungen zu Psalm cxxxix," *VT* 7 [1957]: 173–74).

80 Cf. Leahy, "Idea of God."

81 Cf. Hos 4:15, and Wolff, *Hosea*, 90 [113–14].

82 See pp. 325–26.

83 On the interrogative style in 8:8, see pp. 328–29.

sation of social injustice (8:4, 6) and the reference to the haughty arrogance of Jacob (8:7a). The allusion to the mentality of the merchant, whose zeal for deceit provokes a cursing of the work–free days (8:5), may already be a new injustice, added to those indicted by the prophet. It is certain, however, that the manner in which the prophet's criticism of the cultus is expanded in 8:14 has been influenced by the accusation of unfaithfulness toward Yahweh which Hosea raised.

The message of Amos is thus brought home. Those who would gain life for themselves by oppressing the weak, by practicing deceit in the economic realm, or through cultic–political attempts to establish security will in one way or another surely lose the same.

The oracle in 8:11–12, which is very probably a later supplement,[84] expands particularly the material in 8:13–14, adding new dimensions to the proclamation. The prostrating physical thirst (v 13) now becomes the unquenchable longing for the word of Yahweh. The frantic activity in Samaria and from Dan to Beer–sheba in search of life secured by the gods of the sanctuaries becomes a searching of the whole earth for the saving word of God. The end is now described as the hour in which Yahweh is sought but can no longer be found (cf. Is 55:6). The people are caught up in world–wide commotion; they chase from sea to sea, and from the north to the east. Perhaps they lack not bread or water, but they certainly are in need of that one thing which they despised time and again. Now they sense that they can no longer live without hearing the word of Yahweh, the prophetically proclaimed word. This is a different sort of end from the one that Amos had seen and announced. Here there is neither life nor death but only an endless, desperate, and futile searching.

Thus this multi–level collection of oracles evokes the recognition that loss of life, and more than life, is threatened by the proclaimed word; the "more" is this word itself. It was not within Amos' purview to expect that the word which has power over life and death would, in the midst of Israel's end, enter anew into humanity. The oracle concerning Yahweh's lost, inaudible word is confronted by the quiet voice which says, "My food is to do the will of him who sent me, and to accomplish his work" (Jn 4:34). He carries the message of Amos (for example, 8:4–6, 14) even further beyond its formulation in 8:11–12. He unmasks the impudent challenge to make bread from stones as a tempter's scheme for world salvation. He overcomes the world's distress by working among us as the one who does not live by bread alone, but "by every word that proceeds from the mouth of God" (Dtn 8:3; Mt 4:3–4). Jesus thereby introduced for the whole of humanity that which Amos and his Old Testament successors could not envision for Israel. The word which had been rejected and could no longer be found allows itself to be found in his human form. A new life is opened up for those who had prepared themselves for the unavoidable end.

---

84   See p. 326.

None Will Escape

Bibliography

Reinhard Fey
Amos und Jesaja: Abhängigkeit und Eigenständigkeit des Jesaja, WMANT 12 (Neukirchen–Vluyn: Neukirchener Verlag, 1963), 49, 109–10, 114.

Friedrich Horst
"Die Visionsschilderungen der alttestamentlichen Propheten," *EvTh* 20 (1960): 193–205 (esp. 196–97).

Paul Joüon
"Notes de lexicographie hébraïque," *Biblica* 7 (1926): 165–68 (מוג).

Edwin C. Kingsbury
"The Prophets and the Council of Yahweh," *JBL* 83 (1964): 279–86.

Henning Graf Reventlow
Das Amt des Propheten bei Amos, FRLANT 80 (Göttingen: Vandenhoeck & Ruprecht, 1962), 48–51.

Samuel Terrien
"Amos and Wisdom" in *Israel's Prophetic Heritage: Essays in honor of James Muilenburg*, ed. Bernhard W. Anderson and Walter Harrelson (New York: Harper & Brothers, 1962), 108–15 (esp. 110–11).

Artur Weiser
Die Profetie des Amos, BZAW 53 (Giessen, 1929), 41–52.

See also the bibliographies on 4:4–13, p. 208, and 7:1–9, p. 291.

9

1

I saw my Lord
  standing on the altar.
< >ª <He smote>ᵇ the capitalᶜ
  so thatᵈ the thresholds shook.
<Then he said>,ª

a Following Paul Volz (Review of Hendrik Jan Elhorst, *De profetie van Amos* [Leiden, 1900], *ThLZ* 25 [1900]: 291), many interpreters (Marti, Robinson, Weiser [*Profetie*, 42], Amsler, and others) place ויאמר ("then he said") after הספים ("the thresholds"). For who is supposed to have been addressed by the "smite!" of the transmitted text? Can the hand of the prophet shatter the temple? "Later sensitivity could no longer tolerate this drastically anthropomorphic image and hence established the present form of the text" (Weiser, *Profetie*, 42).

b The reading of *M* ("smite!") probably arose from the erroneous transposition of ויאמר (see textual note "a"). To be expected here is the continuation of the vision scene (see p. 337, "Form"); thus perhaps וַיַּךְ ("and he smote").

c *G* (τὸ ἱλαστήριον ["the mercy–seat"]) read erroneously הַכַּפֹּרֶת, which occurs almost twice as often in the Old Testament as הכפתור.

d The proposal of Procksch (*BH³*, n. "c" to Am 9:1) and Weiser (*Profetie*, 42) to read an imperfect consecutive (וַ instead of וְ) cannot be adequately sup-

"<I will cleave>^e the head of them all,
   and I will slay their remnant
   with the sword;
None^f of them^g shall flee away,
   and the fugitive among them^g
   shall not escape.

2   If they break into Sheol,
     from there my hand will take them.
   If they climb up to heaven,
     from there I will bring them down.

3   If they hide themselves on the head
     of Carmel,
   I will search (them)^h out
     and take them from there.
   If they hide [from my eyes]ⁱ at the
   bottom of the sea,^j
     <there>^k I will command
     the serpent^l to bite^m them.

ported; the new clause is intended to report the result of the blow.

e   It is just as difficult to interpret this word as it is to improve upòn it. *M* must be read either as an imperative of בצע ("to cut off") with third–person plural suffix, or as a third–person singular perfect consecutive with third–person plural suffix. It is to be assumed that we have here a statement concerning Israel ("them all"), i.e., the transition from vision to audition. For that reason, ויאמר ("then he said") likely precedes this difficult word (see textual note "a"). Furthermore, the following parallel declaration (אהרג ["I will slay"]) leads one to expect a first person singular form of the verb. For all these reasons the proposal אֲבַצֵּע (Maag, *Text*, 45) seems plausible (cf. *G*⁴¹⁰ διακόψω ["I will sever"]). Yet the meaning ("to cut off, make an end to life"; cf. Is 38:12; Job 6:9; and Koehler–Baumgartner [³1967], 141) in combination with בראשׁ ("on the head") remains uncertain. Horst (*Hiob*, 196) reads וַאֲבַצְּעֵם and translates: "I will make an end of them all with poison." The parallel בחרב ("with the sword") speaks in favor of this interpretation, but the context provided by the visionary image is decidedly against it. This context has prompted other interpreters to change בראשׁ into ברעשׁ ("with quaking"; so Paul Volz, Review of Hendrik Jan Elhorst, *De profetie van Amos* [Leiden, 1900], *ThLZ* 25 [1900]: 291; Procksch, *BH*³, n. "d–d" to Am 9:1; Weiser, *Profetie*, 43–44; Amsler). Great uncertainty remains. We for our part consider the interpretation of *G*⁴¹⁰ relatively enlightening: διακόψω εἰς κεφαλὰς πάντων ("I will sever the heads of all").

f   The paronomasia of subject and predicate, in which the subject is formed by the participle of the corresponding verb, substitutes for, and clarifies, the indefinite pronoun. The clause reads literally: "Not will a fleer flee of them"; cf. Joüon, par. 155d, and Brockelmann, *Syntax*, pars. 37, 49a.

g   ל introduces the genitive here; cf. Gen 17:12; Jer 13:13; and Joüon, par. 130g.

h   חפשׂ is to be taken with לקח as a *verbum relativum*. Therefore only the dependent verb has the suffix: "I will catch them after a thorough search"; cf. Oskar Grether, *Hebräische Grammatik für den akademischen Unterricht* (München: Evangelischer Presseverband für Bayern, ²1955), par. 87i, k.

i   The plural עֵינַי ("my eyes") stands in tension with the singular עֵינִי in 9:4b. Furthermore, מנגד עיני ("from my eyes") makes the colon overly long in comparison with its parallel. Thus this phrase was probably an addition; it is found in the same form in Is 1:16 and Jer 16:17, in the latter instance also preceded by סתר nip'al ("be hidden, concealed").

j   *G* (εἰς τὰ βάθη ["into the depths"]) offers a plural rendering.

k   *G* (ἐκεῖ ["there"]) presupposes שָׁם, which is also in keeping with the sense of the sentence. *M* (משׁם ["from there"]) may have been filled in later after

4

And if they go into captivity
before their enemies,
<there>[n] I will command the sword
to slay[n] them.
I will fix my eye[o] upon them.
for evil and not for good."

5

[p][{Even the Lord, Yahweh of the Hosts}[q]
He who touches the earth [r]so that it
totters[r]
[s]and all who dwell in it mourn[s]
[t]{and all of it rises like the river
and sinks like Egypt's river}.[t]

6

He who builds his <upper chamber>[u]
in heaven,
founds his vault[v] on earth
[w]{who summons the waters of the sea
and pours them out upon the face
of the earth}[w]
Yahweh[x] is his name.][p]

---

the pattern of 9:2a, 2b, and 3a. However מִשָּׁם,
which is repeated altogether five times, may have
been original also in 9:3b and 4a. It would then
have to be understood in relation to the last verb in
each case (וּנְשָׁכַם ["that it bite them"] or וַהֲרַגְתֶּם
["that it slay them"]); it would emphasize in a stereotyped way the violent removal from every supposed place of refuge (cf. Amsler, 239).

l *G* does not here translate *M*'s נָחָשׁ with ὄφις, as it
usually does, but rather with δράκων (cf. Job 26:13),
i.e., the sea–serpent, in contrast to land–serpent; cf.
Oskar Grether and Johannes Fichtner, "ὄφις,"
TDNT 5, 572–73.

m Here and in 9:4a the imperfect "I will command" is
followed by a perfect consecutive; see Joüon, par.
177j.

n See textual notes "k" and "m" above.

o *G* (τοὺς ὀφθαλμούς μου ["my eyes"]) read עֵינַי, apparently having been inspired to do so by the insertion מִנֶּגֶד עֵינַי (ἐξ ὀφθαλμῶν μου) ["from my
eyes"] in 9:3.

p–p See pp. 111–12 and 215–17.

q A later interpretation anticipates the older refrain
of the hymn, יהוה שְׁמוֹ ("Yahweh is his name"
9:6bβ), plerophorically introducing the one who is
praised in the hymn. See the excursus on 6:14, pp.
287–88.

r–r Budde ("Amos II," 107) and Horst ("Doxologien,"
47 [*idem, Gottes Recht*, 158]) read וְתָמוֹג ("and it will
totter"). Such syntactical highlighting of the resulting event is conceivable, to be sure, but after a participle it hardly appears necessary, as 5:8b = 9:6b
shows. The imperfect consecutive in those verses
supports the reading of *M* here also. Unlike *M* and
V (*tabescet* ["it will melt"]), *G* (καὶ σαλεύων αὐτήν
["and he who makes it shake"]) sees here yet another act of Yahweh, rather than the result of his
work.

s–s The text of Mur xii (88) 8.15 here is precisely the
same as that [of M] in 8:8aβ [i.e., attesting the singular forms אבל ... יושב; there is a lacuna in Mur
xii at Am 8:8; Ed.] (see P. Benoit, J. T. Milik and
R. de Vaux, *Les grottes de Murabba'ât*, DJD 2/
Texte [Oxford: Clarendon Press, 1961], 183 and
188).

t–t This bicolon is apparently a later insertion of the
reading original at 8:8b (the identity of the preceding lines in 9:5aβ and 8:8aβ having given rise to
this harmonistic expansion). Lacking a participle
in the initial colon, the reading singularly violates
the pattern elsewhere exhibited by the hymnic
pieces; see p. 215–16.

u Mur xii (88) 8.16 (see note "s–s" above) already
attests the reading of *M*, מעלותו ("his ascents"),
while *G* (ἀνάβασιν αὐτοῦ) presupposes the singular
and, following Neh 3:31 and 32, could more easily
read עֲלִיָּתוֹ ("his upper–chamber"; cf. already
Nowack). The text of *M* arose through dittography
(the initial מ) and misreading of י as ו, no doubt

influenced by the fact that מַעֲלָה is a much more frequently attested noun than עָלֶיהָ.

v   G (τὴν ἐπαγγελίαν αὐτοῦ ["his promise"]) must have misunderstood the Hebrew term, deriving it from נגד hipʿil, which is rendered by the verb ἀπαγγέλλειν ("to proclaim") in 4:13; Hos 4:12; Is 44:8; 57:12; and Jer 16:10.

w–   This bicolon probably stood originally only in 5:8b;
w   see p. 216.

x   G (ὁ θεὸς ὁ παντοκράτωρ) presupposes the addition of אלהי צבאות ("God of Hosts") as in 4:13 and 5:8 (G).

Form

The vision report in 9:1–4 agrees formally with the preceding four reports in 7:1–8 and 8:1–2. It too exhibits the structure of an autobiographical *memorabile*, with the vision proper at the beginning, the verbal decree of Yahweh at the end, and the visionary act being introduced by the word "to see" (ראה, here qal). But the differences are even more apparent. Nothing stands between the vision proper and Yahweh's oracle of decision which interprets it; the element of dialogue between Yahweh and Amos has been omitted. In the initial line it is no longer Yahweh who makes the prophet see ("Thus Yahweh showed me" [7:1, 4, 7; 8:1]); instead, Yahweh himself is the one who is seen by the prophet ("I saw my Lord . . ."). If our reconstruction of the text is correct,[1] then we have three short lines describing where Yahweh stands, what he does, and the consequences thereof. The oracle of Yahweh, which immediately follows the vision, dominates the pericope, being six times as long as the vision report itself.

Yet the view that we have to do here with another vision report, albeit one in altered form, has been contested. In the transmitted text (M), the terse report of the vision of Yahweh standing over the altar is immediately followed by an oracle commissioning the prophet: "Smite the capital so that the thresholds shake!" The conclusion has been drawn from this that it is not essentially a vision report at all with which we are dealing here, but "merely the commission to perform a symbolic act."[2] The introductory sentence,

it is claimed, only testifies to the certainty of the presence of him who gives the commission. In addition to being based upon the transmitted text, this view is bolstered by the fact that many accounts of symbolic acts lack specific statements about their being performed.[3] Be that as it may, there are weightier arguments to the contrary.

First of all, such commissionings are not otherwise presented in the form of visions. As the only other example supporting his case, Reventlow[4] cites Ezek 3:22–27. There, however, the mandate to the prophet is clearly described at the very beginning of the pericope, before the report of his visionary experience, and afterwards there is a detailed and unambiguous account of how Yahweh will act through the prophet; moreover, it is not at all evident that what the prophet is commanded to do has the character of a symbolic act.[5]

Amos 9:1–4, exhibiting only one instance of imperative address to the prophet (and that one textually suspect!),[6] would therefore be quite unique as a commission to perform a symbolic act. But, secondly, we must also consider what the prophet is supposedly commanded to do. Is this a task which the prophet could be expected to execute? Would a human being be able to smite the capital of a column in such a way that the thresholds tremble? Is not the destruction of a sanctuary most peculiarly the business of Yahweh? Does not Yahweh's standing on the altar become meaningful only through his performing such an act himself? When one recalls that the altar of burnt offering was located some yards from the portal of the

---

1   See textual notes "a" and "b" to 9:1.
2   Reventlow, *Amt*, 49.
3   Georg Fohrer, "Die Gattung der Berichte über symbolische Handlungen der Propheten," *ZAW* 64 (1952): 115 (= *idem*, *Studien*, 107): "in more than half of the cases."
4   *Amt*, 50.
5   Cf. Zimmerli, *Ezechiel*, 106–11.

6   See textual note "b" to 9:1.

temple, the superhuman dimensions of the visionary figure become clear.[7]

Finally, this assessment is confirmed by the connection with the four preceding visions, sketched in our introductory comments above. The formal differences exhibited by the fifth vision, its final position and lack of a parallel following the earlier paired visions, and the considerable space now occupied by the oracular proclamation of Yahweh indicate that this is the climax of the series. The fifth vision is thereby set off from the first four in a manner similar to that in which the oracle against Israel is set off from the preceding oracles against foreign nations (1:3—2:16). In terms of its content, this final vision represents the essential capstone of the series. The fourth vision had announced only *that* the end would come; now we are told *how* the inevitable judgment will be effected. Now Yahweh's oracular address approximates the formal style of the prophetic messenger speech. Yahweh's address begins in v 1aα^3–b with two synonymous bicola. Then follow five parallel conditional sentences, each exhibiting internal synthetic parallelism, the length of the lines increasing from short two or three–stress cola (v 2) to three–stress cola (v 3), and eventually to two four–stress cola (v 4a). Thematically the first four sentences fit together in pairs; the fifth and longest sentence articulates a concretely historical threat. Thus in these five sentences the formal structure attested by the cycles or the five visions and the oracles against the nations is repeated *in nuce*. At the end of Yahweh's oracle there again appears a single three–stress bicolon (v 4b) which, in its brevity, forms a conclusion of striking impact.[8]

Setting

It is impossible to determine the temporal relationship between this fifth visionary experience and the preceding ones, since the author simply was not concerned with such biographical issues. Form and content merely permit the assumption that the fifth vision was also the last which Amos saw. Since Amos himself refrained from dating and localizing the visions, it is futile to speculate whether he received this fifth vision before his departure from Judah or only subsequently, in the immediate vicinity of the sanctuary at Bethel,[9] whether it occurred during a new year's festival,[10] or rather in solitude. That it took place in Jerusalem[11] cannot be supported.[12]

We can speculate somewhat more confidently about when and where the vision was recorded than we can concerning the time and place of the experience itself. The two sets of questions must, of course, be strictly separated.[13] The uniform stylizing suggests a considerable distance between the written form of the reports and the experiences as such, and it also necessitates the assumption of internal differences between what was actually experienced and what was written down. Especially in this fifth vision, the broadly developed speech of Yahweh leads one to suspect that much from the later history of the prophet's proclamation has been introduced into the report. In this way the proximity to the formal structure of the cycle of oracles against the nations as a whole becomes intelligible, as does, more particularly, the relationship of the speech of Yahweh in the fifth vision to the announcement of punishment in the oracle against Israel.[14]

The hymnic piece (9:5–6), as a judgment doxology, refers the vision of Yahweh to the destruction of the sanctuary at Bethel by Josiah.[15]

Interpretation

■1 If we had to assign the preceding visions to a psychological state of heightened consciousness,[16] then we must do so all the more here, since the Lord himself hardly comes under the rubric of things seen in everyday life. So too we should not suppose that, just because an altar is specified, the prophet was actually viewing a particular sacred precinct. On the other hand, neither

7   Cf. Amsler, 238–39.
8   On the form of the hymn in 9:5–6, see pp. 215–17.
9   Cf. Weiser, *Profetie*, 42.
10 Edwin C. Kingsbury, "The Prophets and the Council of Yahweh," *JBL* 83 (1964): 283.
11 Neher, *Amos*, 127; and René Vuilleumier–Bessard, *La tradition cultuelle d'Israël dans la prophétie d'Amos et d'Osée*, CTh 45 (Neuchâtel: Delachaux and Niestlé,
1960), 72.
12 Cf. Amsler, 239.
13 See pp. 295–96.
14 See p. 151.
15 See pp. 111–12 and 217–18.
16 See p. 299 on 7:4,5.

should it be denied that this visionary experience provided the foundation for Amos' certainty regarding the imminent destruction of the actual national sanctuary at Bethel, and above all of the congregation which gathered there (5:5; 7:17; cf. 3:14). And yet here interest centers not on the place but rather on the completely unusual happening perceived by the eye of the visionary. There is, first, the fact that the Lord stands "*on* the altar," just as that figure who did the testing in 7:7 stood "on the wall" (the formulation נצב על being used in both places).[17] The altar was that place of "slaughtering" (זבח) on which the great burnt offerings were offered;[18] it was situated in the outer court of the temple.[19] The figure of Yahweh, towering beyond all human dimensions (cf. Is 6:1), occupies this place in order to smite the capital with outstretched arm and strong hand.[20] The reference here must be to the capital of one of the columns which flanked the thresholds of the portal. Otherwise it would be impossible for the thresholds to shake as a result of the shaking of the foundations of the columns.[21] "To shake" (רעש) is otherwise used almost exclusively with reference to earthquakes (cf. 1:1; Ju 5:4; etc.) and to cosmic upheaval in general (Joel 2:10).[22] The quake thus envisioned must have been tremendous, since the "thresholds" of a sanctuary were usually of considerable dimension; according to Ezek 40:6, those of the Jerusalem sanctuary were six cubits in depth. Hence the temple smitten by Yahweh becomes the epicenter of a quake whose radiating shocks bring the inescapable end. The redactional dating in 1:1b is based

solely on this feature of the visions.[23]

In considering the question of the vision's type, it is of decisive importance to determine the relationship of the vision proper to the subsequent oracle of Yahweh. The uncertainty of the text[24] complicates the issue. בראש, which is securely transmitted and which in conjunction with כלם most probably means "on the head of them all," could be understood with reference to the capital (i.e., the "head" of the column) mentioned in the vision.[25] Were the same verb associated with "head" which in the visionary experience connotes the smiting of the capital (and had the vision not gone on to portray the quaking which resulted from that blow) we might have classified our vision as a "symbol–vision" (along with that in 7:7–8). But the necessary verbal correspondence is lacking. Thus we must type the vision before us here an "event–vision" analogous to those in 7:1–2 and 7:4–5. The brief scene of the vision proper portrays the opening act of a drama whose further course is outlined in the following oracle. The oracle, in other words, presents a continuation rather than an interpretation of the events seen by the prophet. בצע, as a technical term in weaving, designates basically the "cutting off" of the thread.[26] If a pi'el form is to be read as original here,[27] it has probably acquired the general sense of "to injure" (Ezek 22:12) or "to crush" (Job 6:9). It remains unclear whether the people are affected by the earthquake, either directly or indirectly, or whether they fall victim to additional acts. The context reminds one of 2:13–16, where also Yahweh starts out by initiating an earth-

---

17 In 2 Kgs 23:9 the priests of the high places did not ascend "*to* the altar of Yahweh" (אֶל־מִזְבַּח יהוה). However, of Jeroboam I it is said not only that "he ascended *on* the altar" (וַיַּעַל עַל־הַמִּזְבֵּחַ, 1 Kgs 12:33) but even that he "was standing *on* the altar" (עֹמֵד עַל־הַמִּזְבֵּחַ, 1 Kgs 13:1). The use of על therefore can include the notion of standing "before" the altar.

18 Cf. Rendtorff, *Studien*, 86–87.

19 In the case of Jerusalem, cf. 1 Kgs 8:64, and Noth, *Könige*, 191. For Shechem, cf. Lawrence E. Toombs and G. Ernest Wright, "The Third Campaign at Balâṭah (Shechem)," *BASOR* 161 (1961): 33 fig. 12; and *idem*, "The Fourth Campaign at Balâṭah (Shechem)," *BASOR* 169 (1963): 18 fig. 9. Cf. further Rudolf Smend, "Altar," *BHHW* 1, 63–65.

20 At least no implement is explicitly named; cf. Is

5:25; 9:11 [12]; Ps 136:12; Dtn 11:2; 26:8; etc.

21 On כפתור, cf. Leonhard Rost, "Kapitäl," *BHHW* 2, 932 with references and plates.

22 See p. 47.

23 See p. 120.

24 See textual note "e" to 9:1.

25 Cf. רָאשֵׁי הָעַמּוּדִים ("the heads of the pillars") in 1 Kgs 7:16!

26 Cf. Is 38:12, with reference to the thread of life; and Horst, *Hiob*, 104, on Job 6:9.

27 See textual note "e" to 9:1.

quake, and where then the consequence is depicted as being panicky flight without any possibility of escape.[28] The totality of annihilation is doubly emphasized here. After "the head of them all" has already been struck, there is mention—contrary to all expectation—of a "remnant" which is slain "with the sword" (cf. 4:2).[29] The fact that the sword is deliberately cited as an additional means of destruction strengthens the supposition that the preceding statement must be seen in conjunction with the earthquake initiated by Yahweh. The portrayal of hopeless flight in the final bicolon tersely states what 2:14–16 expansively develops. Just as in 9:1aβ so also here there is a double affirmation that not a single person will remain. At first it is said that no escape will be possible at all.[30] Then, surprisingly, there is a "fugitive" to be reckoned with after all, who believes that he can reach security.[31] But neither will he "escape" (מלט nip'al). The "end" announced in the fourth vision could not be more precisely and comprehensively interpreted. All thought of a remnant is thus most decisively rejected.

■ 2 Nevertheless, the following five conditional sentences (אם) again and in detail eliminate the various possibilities which an Israelite might have considered as ways of eluding Yahweh's grasp. Israelites might first of all have thought that in the underworld they could pass beyond the limits of Yahweh's sovereignty.[32] They could get there on their own only through strenuous effort, comparable to trying to "break through" (חתר) a wall into a practically inaccessible place.[33] It is different with Yahweh! When Amos speaks of Yahweh in this regard, he stands in the wisdom tradition, as Prv 15:11 shows: "Sheol and Abaddon lie open before Yahweh, how much more the hearts of men!" No less than all peoples of the world (cf. 1:3ff; 9:7), all of its

regions without exception are subject to Yahweh's sovereign authority. His "hand" means his power, which is superior to the "hand of the underworld" (Hos 13:14), "hand" being that part of the body which represents effectiveness and capability. To be "taken" (לקח) by Yahweh is something which Amos himself has experienced as irresistible (7:15); in 6:13 this verb is used to describe military conquest. With flight to the regions below is juxtaposed flight to the upper realms. "Heaven" (שמים) as the antithetic parallel to "Sheol, underworld" (שאול) is also found in Ps 139:8 where there is a following reference to the sea (v 9), just as in v 3b of our passage. In the same context Ps 139 also mentions futile flight from Yahweh into the remotest regions of the world (v 7).[34] Yahweh himself fetches the refugees down from on high, just as he retrieves them from the underworld.

■ 3 While 9:2 affirms that even the extreme opposite regions of the cosmos are alike accessible to the hand of Yahweh, v 3 continues with the thought that not even the most secluded hiding places can shield a fugitive from his eye. "To hide oneself" (חבא nip'al) is the goal of any who cannot manage escape to distant parts; this term is used of those in flight in Gen 31:27 and Dan 10:7, and in Gen 3:10 of Adam, who wishes to hide from Yahweh. The top of Mount Carmel is suited as a hideout not only because of its elevation (over 500 meters) but even more on account of its dense forests.[35] Perhaps there is also an echo here of the thought that Carmel belongs to the realm of a foreign god, Baal Carmel.[36] But the fact that Yahweh "searches out" (חפש pi'el) the mountains shows that it is the thought of hiding in the dense forest growth which primarily informs this attempt at escape. Yahweh's searching out leads here as well to his personally seizing and appre-

---

28 See pp. 171–72.

29 Cf. Gese, "Beiträge," 436–37, on the stylistic form of the "unreal *synchoresis*."

30 See textual note "f" to 9:1.

31 On פליט ("fugitive"), cf. Georg Fohrer, *TDNT* 7, 978–79.

32 Is 38:18; Ps 6:6 [5]; Job 14:13.

33 Cf. Ezek 8:8; 12:5, 7, 12; and Jon 1:13.

34 Cf. Kraus, *Psalmen*, 919.

35 See p. 125 on 1:2.

36 Cf. 1 Kgs 18:20–29, and Kurt Galling, "Der Gott Karmel und die Ächtung der fremden Götter" in

Geschichte und Altes Testament (Festschrift Albrecht Alt), ed. Gerhard Ebeling; BHTh 16 (Tübingen: J. C. B. Mohr [Paul Siebeck], 1953), 105–25 (esp. 119).

hending (לקח as in 9:2a).

In the sea, on the other hand, he makes use of a subordinate being. In naming as a hideout the "bottom of the sea" (קרקע הים),[37] a place of refuge is identified which is just as absurd as the underworld or heaven in 9:2.[38] In his description of extreme or even senseless attempts at escape, Amos apparently modified (much as has Ps 139:8–9) a traditional sapiential "four–part schematization of the universe" (*viergliedrige All-formel*).[39] The sea is often portrayed as the deified power of chaos,[40] while the sea dragon is the mythical embodiment of the sea's inimical power.[41] Amos treats the serpent as Yahweh's servant, receiving and carrying out his commands (cf. Job 9:13), its deadly bite felling those who believe themselves secure (cf. 5:19!).

■ **4** With the fifth condition, the oracle moves from the realm of the cosmos into that of human history. It is no longer some self–chosen route of escape which is in view but the forced march into captivity. "Before their enemies," driven on by overseers, the Israelites are forced to move off to distant lands as deportees.[42] Some in their despair may have magnified even this fate as a way to save their lives. But even they are pursued by Yahweh's sword. With the reference to the "sword," the oracle of Yahweh reverts to the beginning of the threat against any possible remnant (9:1aβ) and thereby recalls the purpose for summoning the sword: that it will "slay" them. The end will be nothing short of death itself; compared with such an end, exile would still be an escape. The political enemies actually appear as saviors compared with Yahweh, the truly destructive

enemy. The concluding sentence puts it in a nutshell: it is not Yahweh's absence, as one might think, but rather his presence that brings Israel to ruin (cf. 5:17b). Yahweh, whose eye had once fatally transfixed the Egyptians in order to save Israel at the Sea (Ex 14:24), now directs his destructive gaze against his own people. Yahweh as warrior has made a complete turnabout, his eye being fixed upon Israel no longer "for good" but rather "for evil."[43]

■ **5** The following hymnic strophe is introduced in the received text by an interpretive insertion identifying "the Lord" of the vision report in 9:1–4 as "Yahweh of the Hosts"; this is the old war god of Israel (2 Sam 6:2) who is praised in the song that follows. While there are eight occurrences in the book of Amos of the appellation "Yahweh [the] God of [the] Hosts" (יהוה אלהי [ה]צבאות), the abbreviated form here used by the redactor is unique (though the shorter formula without the definite article is otherwise far more frequently attested in the Old Testament than the longer version).[44] The first three words in v 5 therefore probably belong to the most recent stratum in the book of Amos.

The hymnic piece itself must be associated with those in 4:13 and 5:8.[45] It has been incorporated at this point in the text by reason of its function as *exhomologesis*, here a confession acknowledging personal guilt while simultaneously offering praise to Yahweh for having fulfilled his threatened destruction of the Bethel sanctuary. The seventh–century community may also have found an internal connection between the hymnic confession and the preceding pericope. While in 9:2

37 קרקע elsewhere always denotes the "floor" of a building: Num 5:17; 1 Kgs 6:15–16, 30; 7:7.

38 Cf. 9:1b where, after any chance of successful flight has already been precluded, an additional statement concerning futile efforts to escape is offered.

39 Job 11:8–9: heaven, underworld, earth, and sea (cf. Horst, *Hiob*, 170); a three–part schema is attested in Sir 1:3: heaven, earth, and sea.

40 Cf. Ps 74:13; 93:3–4; and Job 7:12.

41 Job 26:13; Is 51:9–10; and 27:1. Cf. *CTA* 5 (= *UT* 67).1.1–3
      [*ktmḫṣ . ltn . bṯn . brḥ*
      tkly . bṯn . ʿqltn
      šlyṭ . d . šbʿt . rʾašm
      "When you (Baʿl) smote Lôtān the primal serpent,
          dispatched the twisted serpent,

the seven–headed tyrant"; Trans. by Ed.]. Cf. also *CTA* 3 (= *UT* ʿnt).3.34–39, and Schmidt, *Königtum*, 44.

42 Cf. *ANEP*, figs. 10, 205.

43 Cf. J. Alberto Soggin, "Der prophetische Gedanke über den heiligen Krieg, als Gericht gegen Israel," *VT* 10 (1960): 79–83; and Hans Martin Lutz, *Jahwe, Jerusalem und die Völker*, WMANT 27 (Neukirchen–Vluyn: Neukirchener Verlag, 1968), 190–200.

44 The article may have been added to the formula in 9:5 under the influence of the full appellation, יהוה אלהי הצבאות, as it appears in 3:13 and 6:14; elsewhere in the Old Testament the full appellation is found only in Hos 12:6 [5]. Cf. the excursus to 6:14, pp. 287–88.

45 See the excursus, pp. 215–17.

there is reference to Yahweh's hand powerfully grasping human beings, here now are sung the praises of the one who merely needs to touch the earth to make it "totter." מוג takes up the earthquake motif (9:1), for in most instances the verb depicts cosmic upheaval instigated by Yahweh himself.[46] Even the earth trembles under Yahweh's gaze (cf. 9:4b with Ps 104:32). As the aftermath of the earthquake, the hymn then refers to the mourning of all who dwell on the earth. The God who causes the funerary mourning is honored in a judgment doxology (cf. "to slay" [הרג] in 9:1aβ and 4aβ). To those who inserted the hymnic strophe at this point in the text, its initial bicolon must therefore have seemed an appropriate response to the fifth vision, just as they found it appropriate to introduce praise of the one who treads upon the high places of the earth (4:13) following the allusions to the destruction of the sinful sanctuary of Bethel in 4:11–12 (cf. 4:4).[47]

■ 6 The ancients would also have found appropriate connections between the strophe's second bicolon and the preceding oracle of Yahweh. How could he who has built his upper chamber in heaven *not* reach those who seek refuge in heaven (cf. 9:2b)? The use of עליה[48] to designate Yahweh's heavenly dwelling and אגדה to refer to the "vault" of his abode, with its foundation on the earth, is unparalleled in the Old Testament, though the basic concept is elsewhere attested in biblical sources.[49] The idea is by no means specifically Israelite, however, having parallels in the surrounding cultures, just as do almost all the statements in the hymnic pieces in the book of Amos.[50] Thus Ishtar also makes the mountains quake,[51] and she too is "enthroned on high."[52] And of Shamash it is said that "he occupies an awesome throne in the ethereal sky" and "surveys the earth."[53] Whatever other peoples may say in praise of their deities, Israel must confess that Yahweh is the name of him who controls the cosmos and fills it with his presence.[54]

Aim

The fifth vision report makes concrete that message of Israel's end which had already been entrusted to Amos in the fourth vision. The third vision had earlier conveyed to him the decision resulting from a testing, namely that there was no longer any possibility of revoking the sentence of judgment as had been done after the first two visions. Yahweh first of all smites the sanctuary; radiating outward from this epicenter, the shockwave devastates the entire nation. The unusually detailed elaborations in the oracle of Yahweh have as their only aim the elimination of every last hope of flight. There is not a single escape route leading to a realm beyond the reach of Yahweh's hand, his eye, or his sword. The terrible truth, emphatically and precisely reiterated, is that even someone who imagines he might be escaping will inevitably be caught. Like all the prophetic visionaries, Amos foresaw not enduring stability but vast, even total permutation. Yet Amos' commission, like that of no other prophet, was to announce an upheaval which would mean the full end of the course of history preceding it. Hence it was essential that not a single route be left open which might lead into the future, bypassing Yahweh's judgment. Even the very last survivor would be delivered up to the divine presence.

In this message of the fifth vision is revealed a new dimension of Amos' universalism. Not only is Yahweh the lord of all nations,[55] his sovereignty is exercised on an even vaster scale extending over all realms of the cosmos. The underworld is not beyond his reach, nor

---

46 Cf. Joüon, "Notes," 165–68. In Na 1:5 מוג (hitpaʿel) is paralleled with רעש ("to shake"); cf. Ps 46:7 [6] and 75:4 [3].

47 On 9:5b, see textual note "t–t," and p. 329 on 8:8b.

48 See textual note "u" to 9:6.

49 So Gen 28:12 (E); 1 Kgs 8:12 (where Yahweh is said "to tent in thick-darkness"; see Noth, *Könige*, 181–82); Dtn 26:15; and Is 66:1.

50 See p. 217.

51 Falkenstein–von Soden, *Hymnen*, 260.

52 *Ibid.*, 336.

53 *Ibid.*, 317. On the typical Old Testament depiction of heaven, cf. Westermann, *Genesis*, 165. On 9:6bα, see textual note "w–w," and p. 241 on 5:8.

54 See pp. 223–24.

55 Certainly this aspect of the prophet's message (cf. 1:3—2:3; 3:9; and 9:7) can also be heard in 9:4a.

can the sea dragon refuse to obey him.

Thus the subsequently inserted hymn of praise is particularly well adapted to this form of the message of judgment. The community whose country has been shattered and whose sanctuary is destroyed acknowledges its guilt by praising the one who causes the earth to tremble and its inhabitants to mourn. As the builder of his heavenly sanctuary, it is he who is the sovereign judge over the earthly sanctuary.

Who Must Die?

Bibliography

Ephrem Florival
  "Le jour du jugement (Amos 9:7–15)," *BVC* 8 (1954–55): 61–75.
Emil Forrer
  "Aramu," *Reallexikon der Assyriologie*, vol. 1; ed. Erich Ebeling and Bruno Meissner (Berlin and Leipzig, 1932), 131–39.
Paul Volz
  "Zu Am 9:9," *ZAW* 38 (1919–20): 105–11.
Gerald Avery Wainwright
  "Caphtor–Cappadocia," *VT* 6 (1956): 199–210.

9

7 Are you not like the Cushites to me, sons of Israel?

—[a]oracle of Yahweh.[a]

Did I not bring up Israel from the land of Egypt
  and the Philistines from Caphtor[b]
  and Aram from Kir?

8 Hence the eyes of the Lord Yahweh (are directed) against the sinful kingdom.
I shall destroy it from the face of the earth.
And yet I will not absolutely[c] destroy the house of Jacob

—oracle of Yahweh.

9 Indeed (it shall be) so!
Now I will command
  and shake the house of Israel [among all the nations],[d]
as one shakes[e] with a sieve,
  so that not (even) a pebble[f] will fall to the earth.

10 All the sinners of my people will die by the sword,
    who say,
      "You are not leading up the evil,[g]
        nor are you bringing it close[h] to us."

a-a λέγει κύριος is lacking only in G^{62+147} (a sub–group of the Lucianic recension, dating to the eleventh and twelfth centuries; see Ziegler, *Duodecim prophetae*, 74, 203).

b *G* renders here καππαδοκία ("Cappadocia"), as in Dtn 2:23; so also α' and σ' in Jer 47:4.

c לא virtually always stands between the infinitive absolute and the finite verb (Gesenius–Kautzsch–Cowley, par. 113v; Joüon, par. 123o), the only other exception being Gen 3:4 (leaving aside the uncertain text of Ps 49:8 [7]). Apparently here, as in Gen 3:4, the unusual construction indicates that a prior oracular declaration is negated. If the infinitive absolute emphasizes the certain occurrence of something that has been announced (Brockelmann, *Syntax*, par. 93a), then לא in this position negates precisely that certainty.

d The transmission of this phrase is uncertain in *G* (ἐν πᾶσι τοῖς ἔθνεσι), with the Catena–group lacking an equivalent for הגוים ("the nations"). The phrase is not presupposed by the following simile; it may have been introduced as a gloss to interpret the "shaking" as a reference to the exile, perhaps also in recollection of 9:7. But it does break the older train of thought in vv 9–10, where the sole concern is for the internal sifting of Israel (see p. 349 on 9:10a).

e Literally "is shaken" (nip'al).

f *G* translates σύντριμμα ("fracture"), which is generally used to render שֶׁבֶר. Is it possible that the *Vorlage* of *G* could already have attested the latter (in the sense of "grain"), instead of the rare צרור? *G* would then have misunderstood the word שֶׁבֶר as "breaking." α' (ψηφίον) understood *M* as "pebble," as did *T* (אבן) and *V* (*lapillus*).

g If הרעה ("the evil") is taken to be the subject of the sentence, then the verbs must be read as תַּגִּשׁ (nip'al) and תְּקַדֵּם (Maag, *Text*, 60 [cf. RSV and NAB; Ed.]). To do so removes from the quotation its character as a protestation.

h The use of בַּעַד as a preposition here suggests the idea of surrounding someone, as in Lam 3:7; Ps 139:11; and Job 1:10.

Form

The group of oracles in 9:7–10, occupying a position between the fifth vision with its hymnic conclusion on the one hand and the oracles of weal in 9:11–15 on the other, appears to be a collection of partially fragmentary oracular utterances; various seams are evident where the individual pieces have been linked, and yet overall they have much in common. To the common features belong the formulation of the material as first–person speech of Yahweh, this being interrupted in the transmitted text only at v 8aα.[1] But the stylistic break evident in the transition from the third–person reference to Yahweh (v 8aα) to the divine first–person in v 8aβ is not the only one. Already within v 7 we find a shift from direct address (v 7a, "you" [plural]) to speech about Israel in the third person (v 7b). It is possible that two thematically related short oracles were combined here, with the concluding formula "oracle of Yahweh" (נאם יהוה) marking the division between the first and the second. The two are formally related by virtue of being rhetorical questions (each introduced with הלוא), but the parallelism extends no further. Nevertheless, the possibility of an original rhetorical unit here still remains worth considering. The transition from direct address to the indirect statement about Israel could have been conditioned by the adoption of the confessional formula (cf. 2:10a; 3:1b).

How are we to understand the stylistic break between v 8aα and that which follows? V 8aα can be interpreted as a redactional superscription, introducing the following messenger speech and emphasizing that it is spoken specifically "against the sinful kingdom." V 8aβ, the initial utterance, affirms the kingdom's destruction, whereas v 8b adds a qualification. It is apparent that a distinction is being made between those who are to be destroyed and those who are to be spared.

In vv 9–10, where the picture is precisely of sifting (which means screening), this becomes even clearer. Taking up the catchword "sin" (חטא) from v 8aα, v 10a

identifies those who are particularly affected by the judgment. The imagery of sifting presupposes as self–evident that not all will be so affected. One need only compare, as recipients of the judgment, the "all the sinners of my people" in v 10 with the "my people" in 8:2 (7:8, 15).

What conclusion is to be drawn from this configuration of stylistic breaks and thematic linkings? This oracular composition is best explained as the literary distillate of later discussion concerning the fifth vision. In this respect it resembles the material inserted between the fourth and the fifth visions (8:3–14), which interpreted more fully the prophet's message concerning the end. Subsequent discussion must likewise have been provoked by the fifth vision, for in it the fundamental theme of Amos' proclamation reached its climax: not even the most adept fugitive would be able to escape the grasp of Yahweh.

By its disputational style and its catchword associations with 9:1–4, our series of oracles shows itself to be the literary deposit of oral discussions. Lively controversy with opponents is directly revealed in the two questions in 9:7a and 7b: "Is it not so?" In terms of their content, these questions take up the protest against the announced reversal of the holy war,[2] their theme being the relationship of Yahweh to Israel and the nations. V 8aα repeats the catchword from the concluding declaration of the vision report: "I will fix my eye upon them . . ." (9:4b). The disputational style is exhibited by the transmitted text also in the transition from the first person of the messenger speech to the third person. In response to counter questions there is now offered a more precise argument concerning whom Yahweh transfixes with his judgmental gaze. In this connection a striking distinction is made between the kingdom, which will be destroyed (v 8a), and the house of Jacob, which will not be destroyed (v 8b). The derivation of the following oracle (vv 9–10) from the context of dispute is recognized most readily on the basis of its

---

1 Oort ("Amos," 140), Sellin, Robinson, and others. Maag (*Text*, 59, 118) and Amsler attempt to restore divine first–person speech in 9:8aα as well, by reading "my eyes" (עֵינַי) or "my eye" (עֵינִי) and omitting "the Lord Yahweh" (אדני יהוה) as an erroneous later interpretation. Even though the grounds for this conjecture may be found insufficient, one must acknowledge that taking "the sinful kingdom"

in v 8aα as the antecedent of the pronominal object (אתה "it") in v 8aβ does effect a linkage between these two clauses.

2 See p. 341.

conclusion. Here the protest is actually cited (v 10b): "You are not leading up the evil, nor are you bringing it close to us." This rejoinder has no better point of reference than the words of Yahweh uttered in the final vision. "The evil" (הרעה) takes up the crux of the concluding declaration in 9:4b: Yahweh's eye is fixed upon Israel "for evil" (לְרָעָה) and not for good.[3] But is the denial of Yahweh's impending judgment not also directed against the plethora of statements in 9:1–4, whereby each and every attempt at escape was declared futile? Before quoting the words of protest, our disputant recalls the repeated threat of the death–dealing sword (9:1a, 4a): they "will die by the sword . . ." (v 10a). But just as in v 8, those affected are now defined more closely as "the sinners of my people." Contrary to 9:1–4, and in keeping with v 8b, this interpretation presupposes—in conjunction with the preceding image of the "sifting"—that there are others who do not have to die. We cannot exclude the possibility that the statement concerning the "shaking" of the sieve (נוע hip'il v 9a, nip'al v 9b) may have been prompted by the vision of the quaking of the thresholds under Yahweh's blow (9:1aα).[4] Already the opening of the oracle, "now I will command" (הנה אנכי מצוה), can be recognized as an interpretation of the double "I will command" (אצוה) in 9:3bβ and 4aβ. Thus both the individual utterances and the overall composition of 9:7–10 are understandable as an answer to the protest evoked by message of the fifth vision.

Setting

What is the provenance of this discussion? Its nearness to Amos is just as obvious as its distance from him. On the whole it would seem most likely to suppose that this supplement, directly following the fifth vision, is the work of Amos' school, comparable to those we have previously found appended to the third (in 7:9–17) and the fourth (in 8:3–14) visions. Here as also in those cases Amos' own oracles are both recalled and de-

veloped further. Yet in the present case it is not merely the verbal correspondences with the fifth vision report, noted above,[5] that recall the speech of Amos himself. Rather we must also posit orally transmitted material which, in the context of the discussion, may have been altered to a degree that can no longer be exactly determined. Thus underlying the equation of Israel with the foreign nations in 9:7 we can recognize a proclamation which is distinctly Amos' own (cf. 1:3—2:16), just as we can in the threat against the kingdom in 9:8a (cf. 7:9b, 11a) and in the form of the simile in 9:9 (cf. 2:13; 3:12; 5:19). The use of a participle ([האמרים] "who say") to introduce the quotation in 9:10b is also reminiscent of Amos' style of speech (4:1; 6:13; 7:16; 8:14).[6] On the other hand, certain differences are not to be overlooked. The qualification made in the exceptive clause (9:8b), with its unusual introduction, is set off both formally and in terms of its content from the unqualified judgment of Amos, to say nothing of what might be meant by the "house of Jacob."[7] Of a piece with this is the definition of those condemned which 9:10a sets against the background of the "sifting" imagery. In this regard it is especially instructive to note that the adjective "sinful" (חַטָּא) occurs in Amos only in 9:8a and 10a; the only other derivative of that root is the noun "sins" (חטבות) in 5:12.[8] Amos never uses such a theological category for distinguishing between people. Likewise the word "kingdom" (ממלכה 9:8a) is otherwise attested only in statements deriving from Amos' school (6:2; 7:13). Whether the interrogative form in 9:7a and 7b also reflects the disputational language of the disciples of Amos—language such as we encountered in 6:2b and 8:8—must remain an open question. To be sure, Amos himself likes to pose questions, but they are more of a didactic–rhetorical sort (3:3–6; 6:12a) and less of factual judgment. Moreover, when in such cases Amos presses his audience with questions, he never does so—as here—in a messenger speech, but rather in a free witness speech (cf.

---

3   Cf. the resumption of 9:4bα (the first part of the same declaration) in v 8aα.

4   Is 6:4 also uses נוע to describe the quaking of the temple's thresholds, whereas Amos uses רעשׁ.

5   See pp. 345–46.

6   See p. 97.

7   See p. 248.

8   Cf. the excursus, pp. 152–53.

3:8; 5:18b, 20a).[9]

Thus it is impossible in detail to get down to the *ipsissima verba* of Amos by peeling away the accumulated rejoinders of his disciples. What definitely does remain, however, is the fact that, precisely in those sentences which stand out on stylistic grounds, the fundamental conceptual difference also becomes apparent. The unqualified pronouncement of judgment is reflected upon theologically and, in the process of being defined, is also qualified. Thus is advanced the course sketched out by the disciples of Amos in 5:14–15.

On the question of dating, we can here elaborate upon earlier observations[10] and point out that this defense of Amos' message was conducted at a time when it was possible to distinguish between the end of a "sinful kingdom" and the continued existence of the house of Jacob.[11] We are thus once again directed to the decade after the end of the "house of Jeroboam" (745).[12]

Interpretation

■ **7** The Egyptians likewise called "Cushites" those Nubian tribes in the area of the great "S"–shaped loop south of the second cataract of the Nile; they often include in this designation the Negroes who live even further to the south.[13] To compare the Israelites with the Cushites probably does not in itself mean to say anything disdainful, much less anything reprehensible, about them. They are mentioned simply as representative of foreign and remote peoples who live on the outermost periphery of the known world. If Israel is the same as they in the sight of Yahweh, then it cannot claim any kind of privileged position. Precisely that is what those who rejected the threats of Amos must have done. Having reckoned themselves foremost of the

noblest nations (6:1), they must suffer being equated with a people from the remotest part of the world. The interrogative form of the sentence presupposes that it was part of Israel's tradition to know that its relationship to Yahweh did not rest upon any special qualities or accomplishments of its own.

The second question demands in response the concession that Yahweh had not done anything unique for Israel simply by leading it out of Egypt. Certainly Yahweh had drawn Israel into a special relationship of trust (3:2a)[14] and had gained for the nation a land in the face of overwhelming enemy odds (2:9). In response Israel was certainly to stand in a relationship of grateful obedience to Yahweh. But Israel should not draw from this the conclusion that its God had guided only its history.[15] By paralleling the exodus from Egypt with the early history of the Philistines and the Arameans, Amos has deprived his audience of a last court of appeal against him. Israel is equated before Yahweh precisely with its two great arch–enemies.[16] This equation must be viewed in the context of the threatened punishment. The Philistines had been defeated by David (2 Sam 5:17ff), and the Arameans most recently by Jeroboam II.[17] Thus in Israel's case as well there could be objection to the reversal of holy war on the grounds that God had graciously guided its early history.[18] Yahweh's comparable role at the beginning of the histories of all these nations is noted in order to show that their contemporary destinies are also parallel.

Yahweh had led the Philistines out of "Caphtor." Where is Caphtor to be located? Following *G* ("Cappadocia"),[19] and on the basis of linguistic and archaeological evidence from the second millennium, some have recently sought to locate Caphtor on the southern coast of Asia Minor.[20] But it appears that, in the first

9   See pp. 93–94.
10   See p. 110.
11   See p. 348.
12   See pp. 301–02 on 7:9b, and p. 275 on 6:2.
13   Noth, *World*, 235–36 [211–12]. Cf. Gen 10:6; Is 11:11; and 20:3–5.
14   See pp. 176–77.
15   Cf. Martin Buber, *Israel und Palästina: zur Geschichte einer Idee* (Zürich: Artemis, 1950), 35. On the form of the exodus confession, see pp. 169–70 on 2:10.
16   See pp. 152–59 on 1:3–8.
17   See pp. 288–89 on 6:13b.
18   See p. 341, and cf. Is 28:21.
19   See textual note "b" to 9:7.
20   Gerald Avery Wainwright, "Caphtor–Cappadocia," *VT* 6 (1956): 199–210; cf. Friedrich Cornelius, "Genesis 14," *ZAW* 72 (1960), 5 n. 16.

half of the first millennium, Israel identified Caphtor with Crete. Thus Caphtor is called an island in Jer 47:4; the Philistines are called Cretans in Zeph 2:5 and Ezek 25:16, and in 1 Sam 30:14 the area of Palestine where they settled is called the "Negeb of the Cretans."[21]

The name "Arameans" appears for the first time in the fourth year of the reign of Tiglath–pileser I (1127).[22] They advanced from the southern Syrian–Arabian desert across the Euphrates and into the area of the mouth of the Ḥabur. That their original homeland was Kir is attested only by Amos (cf. also 1:5 and 2 Kgs 16:9); Is 22:6 mentions Kir along with Elam and Aram. We still do not know where within the vast region of the Syrian–Arabian steppe Kir should be sought.

■ 8 After the admonition that Israel should not self–confidently elevate itself above either a foreign and remote people or its arch–enemies, there follows a new oracle clarifying against whom Yahweh directs his judgmental gaze.[23] The problem for interpretation lies in the distinction between the sinful "kingdom" (ממלכה) and the house of Jacob. Since Amos otherwise condemns Israel without qualification, exegetes have supposed that "kingdom" means Israel in contrast to Judah, understood as the "house of Jacob."[24] Speaking against such an interpretation is the consideration that Amos nowhere else juxtaposes the northern and southern kingdoms in this way.[25] Moreover, we have already recognized as unusual the introduction of the exceptive clause with "and yet" (אפס כי),[26] and we have found its origin most explicable in the give and take of a discussion. Thus on the whole it seems better to assign this oracle to the disciples of Amos than to Amos himself. One could regard v 8b in isolation as a later ad-

dition informed by an eschatology of salvation, in which case it would have to be interpreted with reference to Judah.[27] But the presence of the appellation "[house of] Jacob," in current use by the circles of Amos, argues against that. How different is the vocabulary used by later hands to juxtapose Judah and Israel![28] Furthermore, this qualification is closely related to the notion of the sifting of the northern kingdom as expressed in 9:9–10. In the linguistic usage of Amos' school, ממלכה does not mean "kingdom," but rather "kingship" in the sense of "royal house," as 7:13 clearly shows. Set against that usage, then, the "house of Jacob" means specifically the people of the northern kingdom, as in 3:13 (cf. 7:2, 5; 6:8; 8:7). With respect to the whole people, destruction is not at all certain.[29] Thus the hope expressed in the exceptive clause transcends the "perhaps" of 5:15b. Did the disciples of Amos base their qualifying interpretation of the fifth vision on the recollection that the intercession of Amos for Jacob in the first two visions had halted the punishment? The school of Amos also employs "Jacob" as the name for Israel in 8:7. In any case, we have here a delimiting interpretation. It is noteworthy that the very same vocabulary of v 8aβ appears in connection with the "sin" of the house of Jeroboam in 1 Kgs 13:34: "to destroy [it] from the face of the earth" (לְהַשְׁמִיד מֵעַל פְּנֵי הָאֲדָמָה; cf. the different expression in Am 7:11). Whereas the visions did not specify any kind of guilt, here the theological point is made that death will strike the "sinner" (חטא), and him alone.[30]

■ 9–10 The first–person speech of Yahweh as found in 9:7, 8aβ, and 8b is also employed in the following oracle which, however, exhibits neither an introductory formula nor a concluding divine–oracle formula.[31] The disciples have adopted this speech as a self–evident

---

21 In the Ugaritic texts "Caphtor" (*kptr*) is given as the residence of the craftsman god *Kôṭar wa-Ḥassis*; *CTA* 3 (= *UT 'nt*).6.14–15. Cf. *WUS*, no. 1371; and, on the whole issue, Robert Bach, "Kaphtor," *RGG*³ 3, 1134. On "the Cherethites and the Pelethites" (הכרתי והפלתי) in 2 Sam 8:18; 1 Kgs 1:38, 44; etc., cf. Noth, *Könige*, 25–26.

22 Cf. Emil Forrer, "Aramu," *Reallexikon der Assyriologie*, vol. 1; ed. Erich Ebeling and Bruno Meissner (Berlin and Leipzig, 1932), 131.

23 See p. 341 on 9:4.

24 So from Wellhausen through Neher (*Amos*, 142).

25 On 9:11–12, see p. 353.

26 This expression occurs elsewhere only in Nu 13:28; Dtn 15:4; Ju 4:9; and 2 Sam 12:14. Instead of this, Amos himself employs בִּלְתִּי אִם in 3:3–4.

27 So, for example, Marti (224–25).

28 Cf. Am 2:4–5; 6:1a (see textual note "a" to 6:1); and 9:11–12.

29 On the unusual negation of the infinitive absolute, see textual note "c" to 9:8.

30 Cf. Ps 26:9 and 104:35; and Knierim, *Hauptbegriffe*, 73. On the house of Jeroboam as the probable referent of "sinful kingdom," see p. 347.

element of Amos' transmitted materials.[32] Nowhere else in the Old Testament do we find the image of shaking a "sieve" (כברה, a word not otherwise attested) for the purpose of screening, and for this reason alone the utterance may be assigned to the orally transmitted material which the disciples received from their master. There is some initial unclarity in the interpretation of this image, because "pebble" (צרור), understood as that which remains in the sieve, is also a rare word.[33] The textual *Vorlage* of G must have identified צרור as "grain."[34] This presupposes the idea that the matter remaining in the sieve, since it has not fallen to the ground, is of good quality (cf. 5:7b!). But this interpretation imposes a moralizing evaluation upon a procedure intended to explain a theological situation. We must rather think here of a sieve with coarse meshing, such as is used on the threshing floor; the grains fall through, but that which is useless—straw, stones, clods of earth—is retained. Thus צרור can only mean "pebble," as in 2 Sam 17:13 (where G also translates λίθος). Sir 27:4 confirms this view: "When a sieve is shaken, the refuse remains (בְּהָנִיעַ כְּבָרָה יַעֲמֹד עָפָר); so too a man's filth when he speaks." Thus the oracle intends to say that, in the convulsions accompanying the judgment, that which is useless will be retained in the sieve. From v 9a on, the emphasis rests upon the fact that the "sinners" will be shaken in the sieve.

Nevertheless, this is the first time in the book of Amos that Yahweh's punitive intervention is interpreted as a purifying judgment. The notion of a remnant, hinted at in 5:14–15, is developed further here. Using precise theological concepts, "death" and "sin" are now associated with one another (cf. the similar juxtaposition already in 9:8). The formulation "all the sinners of my people" resembles 9:8 in presupposing that Israel does not consist entirely of transgressors deserving death. An echo of the basic meaning of חטא, "to miss (the mark)," can still be perceived here.[35] For those threatened are defined more precisely by citing their own words.[36] They "miss" the prophetic message, insisting that the proclaimed destruction will not befall them (on "the evil" [הרעה], cf. 9:4). It has been suggested that we read קדם as a pi'el in place of the unique hip'il in *M*.[37] Yet it may be that the unusual form is meant to indicate an intensification; if נגש in the hip'il means "to lead up close," then קדם in the hip'il probably signifies direct confrontation, so "to allow to catch up with," or even "to allow to overtake" ("to lead to the fore"). The protest against the prophetic messenger was leveled in the form of direct address. It was contested that he, as the proclaimer, was ushering in that which he was proclaiming. Thus the old opponents of the prophet, who contradicted his words, are designated by the later interpreters as being precisely those against whom the fifth vision's threat of the sword was directed.

Aim

An interpretation of the prophet's oracle in the next generation does not merely repeat the old oracle. The message of Amos is upheld, namely that Yahweh directs the history of all nations, that Israel bears in itself no grounds for any sense of superiority, and that Yahweh on his own will indeed respond to the contempt for the prophetic word by sending the death–dealing sword. This message is modified in that the emphasis no longer lies on the totality of the destruction.[38] Instead, there is now reflection upon the theme of guilt bringing death in its wake. A distinction is drawn between those affected by the judgment and those not affected. Thus the judgment as a whole becomes a process of sifting out.

31 See p. 92.
32 On the linkage with the motifs and catchwords from 9:1–4, see pp. 345–46.
33 Cf. Paul Volz, "Zu Am 9:9," *ZAW* 38 (1919–20): 105–11.
34 See textual note "f" to 9:9.
35 Knierim, *Hauptbegriffe*, 56.
36 See p. 97.
37 Koehler–Baumgartner, 823.
38 See p. 342 on 9:1–4.

Beyond the End

Bibliography

Karl Cramer
Amos: Versuch einer theologischen Interpretation,
BWANT 51 (Stuttgart, 1930), 177–89.

Reinhard Fey
*Amos und Jesaja: Abhängigkeit und Eigenständigkeit des
Jesaja,* WMANT 12 (Neukirchen–Vluyn: Neu-
kirchener Verlag, 1963), 54–56.

Ephrem Florival
"Le jour du jugement (Amos 9:7–15)," *BVC* 8
(1954–55): 61–75.

Max Haller
"Edom im Urteil der Propheten" in *Vom Alten Tes-
tament: Festschrift Karl Marti,* ed. Karl Budde;
BZAW 41 (Giessen, 1925), 109–17.

Arvid S. Kapelrud
Central Ideas in Amos, SNVAO 1956/4 (Oslo: H.
Aschehoug and Co. [W. Nygaard], ²1961), 54–59.

Ulrich Kellermann
"Der Amosschluss als Stimme deuteronomistischer
Heilshoffnung," *EvTh* 29 (1969): 169–83.

Henning Graf Reventlow
Das Amt des Propheten bei Amos, FRLANT 80 (Göttingen: Vandenhoeck & Ruprecht, 1962): 90–110.

Edward Rohland
*Die Bedeutung der Erwählungstradition Israels für die
Eschatologie der alttestamentlichen Propheten,* Unpub.
Diss. (Heidelberg, 1956), 230–33.

Artur Weiser
Die Profetie des Amos, BZAW 53 (Giessen, 1929),
282–90.

9

11 [On that day
I will raise up the fallen[a] booth of
David,
    and repair ⟨its⟩[b] breaches,
      raise up ⟨its⟩[b] ruins,
      and I will build it as in days of old,

12 that they may possess[c] the remnant of
Edom[d] [e]and of all nations,[e] over whom
my name has been called

        —utterance of Yahweh who
does this.

a   The temporal sense of the attributive participle can
be determined only from the context (Joüon, par.
121 i). In the light of what follows, a reading in the
perfect, rather than in the present or even the future,
is clearly to be preferred.

b   *G* (τὰ πεπτωκότα αὐτῆς καὶ τὰ κατεσκαμμένα ["her
breaches and ruins"]) presupposes feminine singular pronominal suffixes: פִּרְצֶיהָ and הֲרִסוֹתֶיהָ. The
plural suffix with the former term in *M* reflects the
plural reading סֻכֹּת ("booths"), this being much
more frequently attested in the Old Testament than
the singular form of the noun; the plural noun is
also found in the history of David (2 Sam 11:11),
but above all it is the form commonly employed
with reference to the Feast of Booths (Lev 23:42–
43; 2 Chr 8:13; Neh 8:14–17). The plural subject
in 9:12 also presupposes a plural object in v 11.

c   *G* (ἐκζητήσωσιν ["they will seek"]) presupposes
יִדְרְשׁוּ as its *Vorlage.*

d   *G* (τῶν ἀνθρώπων ["of men"]) erroneously read אָדָם.

e–e *G* (καὶ πάντα τὰ ἔθνη) takes וכל־הגוים as a second,
independent direct object. Since there is here neither

13 Hence, days are coming, utterance of
Yahweh, when the ploughman ⌜shall
follow close behind⌝ the reaper
  and the treader of grapes
  him who sows the seed.
Then the mountains will drip with
juice,
  and all the hills will flow with it.

14 When I restore the fortunes of my
people Israel:
They will rebuild the ruined cities
and inhabit them,
  plant vineyards and drink their wine,
    make gardens and eat their fruit.

15 I will plant them in their land,
and they shall never again
be uprooted from their land which I
have given them

  —Yahweh, ⌜your God,⌝ has
said.]

a new *nota accusativi* nor a new verb (which would
clearly establish parallel statements), "and all the
nations" is more likely to be read as a second genitive, alongside אדום, dependent on שְׁאֵרִית.

f–f נגשׁ nip'al; literally "approaches."

g–g Instead of אלהיך, G (ὁ θεὸς ὁ παντοκράτωρ) here
presupposes אלהי (ה)צבאות, as also in 3:13; 4:13;
5:8 (*G*), 14, 15, 16, 27; 9:5, 6 (*G*).

Form

Two oracles are clearly marked off by introductory
and concluding formulas: 9:11–12 and 13–15. Whether
each represents a unit in itself is less clear. In the
first oracle, v 11 consists of an announcement of salvation (in four synonymously parallel declarations)
which v 12 would seem to presuppose, as the transitional particle לְמַעַן ("that") indicates. Yet several
factors suggest that v 12 could be secondary: 1) it
exhibits pure prose, lacking any trace of prosodic, parallel structure; 2) the plural subject of the main verb,
"they may possess" (יִדְרְשׁוּ), has no formal counterpart
in v 11; and 3) the content of v 11 is not obviously
presupposed by the consequences announced in v 12.
Nevertheless, these tensions do not justify the assumption that v 12 is literarily secondary in relation to v 11.
Since framework formulas and the particle לְמַעַן bind
the utterances together, it is rather to be assumed that
some author has combined heterogeneous traditional
materials. Thus we now have before us a two–element
unconditional oracle of weal, proclaiming in its first
part Yahweh's salvific deed and announcing in its
second part the consequences of that deed. For in v 11
Yahweh is the subject, whereas in v 12 those who receive
the promise become the subject, the first–person speech
of Yahweh being maintained throughout (v 12aβ:
"my name").

Tensions are evident also in the second oracle. After
the introductory formula, v 13 presents two bicola in
strictly synonymous parallelism (aβ // γ; bα // β). For

the most part these cola can be read as having three
stresses. Although introduced as a divine oracle, the
lines are concerned only with people and their land.
First–person divine speech then first appears in v 14
where it is announced that Yahweh will restore the
fortunes of his people. This announcement is explicated
in three longer cola, best read as having four stresses
each. While these cola also have persons as their subject, thereby depicting the consequences of Yahweh's
intervention, nonetheless they are completely different
in structure from the declamations of the two bicola
in v 13. Each of the three cola in v 14 describes a human
act and its successful outcome; here threats of futility
such as that in 5:11aβ are reversed, the actual wording
of the threats for the most part being taken up. The
change of fortunes announced at the outset is thus
concretely portrayed. In v 15 a purely prose statement
is attached, once again formulated as first–person speech
of Yahweh. Its content continues the notion of the
change of fortunes developed in v 14, though in such a
way that now the old threat of judgment is directly
negated. Thus vv 14 and 15 interpret in different forms
and by means of diverse themes the introductory statement of v 14aα, "I will restore the fortunes of my people
Israel." In both verses, however, salvation is depicted
as abrogation of judgment. A similar juridical background is not visible in v 13. Thus three types of statement are combined in vv 13–15, of which the second
and the third are most closely related thematically.
The framework formulas combine them into one un-

conditional oracle of weal. Here too, therefore, we can better posit the work of a single author who combined various forms and themes received from tradition than assume the presence of several literary strata.

Setting

These observations concerning the multi–layered form of the two oracles, which are without analogy in the work of Amos himself, should alone suffice to cast doubt on the opinion—still defended by some—that the prophet of the eighth century was their author. Too often the case has been argued without regard to the structure of the oracles, all attention being devoted to their startlingly new thematic content. It is claimed that Amos ". . . perceived the separate existence of the northern kingdom . . . as an arrangement which from the beginning violated Yahweh's order," a view which in no way precluded the awakening of a hope that the ". . . fallen kingdom as a whole might experience a time of salvation."[1] Where, however, does Amos so much as intimate that he condemns the northern kingdom on account of its secession from Jerusalem? Yet does not the "promise to Judah mean at the same time a judgment on the northern state"?[2] But 9:11–15 does not display the least polemic against the northern kingdom. So one is finally left with the desperate argument that while, admittedly, Amos would not likely have proclaimed these oracles of weal alongside the rest of his message, nonetheless he could well have included them here in written form.[3]

Simultaneous attention to the prophetic forms of speech, the tradition–history of the themes and the literary history of the prophetic books has led to the recognition that 9:11–15 is a later addition. Julius Wellhausen memorably characterized the enormous distance between this passage and the rest of the book of Amos: we find here "roses and lavender instead of blood and iron."[4] In considering more precisely the provenance of this later addition, we must ask whether one of the secondary interpretive strands already discovered in the book is here being continued. The school of Amos adheres more closely to the word of its master than do these oracles. Though it mitigates the sharpness of his threats, it never annuls them. The preachers from the time of Josiah relate their message strictly to Bethel and demand the acknowledgment that Yahweh's threats of judgment were there fulfilled. Besides, the improvement of Judean affairs under Josiah and the situation in Jerusalem at that time do not fit vv 11 and 14–15 in any case. Thus some have finally thought of the Deuteronomistic redaction.[5] The connection with the prophecy of Nathan (2 Sam 7:11–16) and the reference to the ruins of Jerusalem (v 11) and to the exile (v 15) could be cited as supporting evidence.

And yet this attribution does not stand up under closer scrutiny. Initially a redaction–historical investigation of the matter ought not to draw upon the whole breadth of Deuteronomistic literature for comparison, but should give primary attention to the specifically Deuteronomistic interpretations in the book of Amos. Such interpretations, however, are in all cases rather closely accommodated to the wording of their contexts.[6] In contrast, the isolated final position of 9:11–15 is in itself suspicious. The difference in thematic content is even more significant. The Deuteronomistic interpreters place particular emphasis upon the culpability of Yahweh's people as a whole, thereby accounting for the judgment against Judah no less than against Israel;[7] nowhere do they allow any hope for Judah to shine through. Furthermore, the Deuteronomistic preachers draw Edom as well as Judah into the judgment (1:11–12; 2:4–5), for they know of Edom's furious attacks against its kindred nation.[8] This does not accord well with the reference to the "remnant of Edom" in 9:12.

Therefore we have to think of a later level of redaction which gave its own conclusion to the book of Amos. This makes the following features more understand-

---

1 Maag, *Text*, 250; cf. Koehler, *Amos*.
2 Johannes Hempel, "Zwei wichtige Hilfsmittel für Forschung und Praxis," *ZAW* 68 (1956): 263; cf. Sellin, 271.
3 Deden, 118.
4 Wellhausen, 96.
5 Amsler, "Amos," 320; and Ulrich Kellermann, "Der Amosschluss als Stimme deuteronomistischer

Heilshoffnung," *EvTh* 29 (1969): 169–83.
6 Cf. 1:9–12; 2:4–5, 10–12; 3:1b, 7; 5:25–26; and 8:11–12.
7 See pp. 112–13
8 See p. 160.

able: 1) The form–critical and thematic contrast between 9:11–15 and the rest of the book of Amos, including the other secondary layers. 2) The concluding formulas which have no parallels elsewhere in the book of Amos ("utterance of Yahweh who does this" [9:12b], the only comparable passage being Mal 3:21 [4:3], and "Yahweh, your God, has said" [9:15], unparalleled in the prophetic books). 3) The redaction–historical parallels to the conclusions of other postexilic collections of prophetic oracles.[9] 4) The reference to a "remnant of Edom," nowhere else mentioned but most easily attributable to relatively advanced postexilic times;[10] in the fifth century Edom was probably weakened considerably by a coalition of Arabic tribes.

The few clues provided by our text do not allow us to fix its date more precisely. Yet we see here clearly enough the hand of a redactor not in evidence elsewhere in the book of Amos, whose talent it was to combine theological traditions with a firm determination to proclaim salvation. This later interpretation has not thoughtlessly appended its new note of assurance to the altogether different message of the prophetic book as received. Rather the additional oracles are formally attached by means of linking formulas in 9:11 and 13, taken up from 8:13 and 11 respectively; as to content, there is, for example, the antithetic interpretation of 5:11 in 9:14. Yet these are only the most striking points of contact between the supplement and the book as received.

Interpretation

■ **11–12** Perhaps the original expression "the fallen booth of David" already constitutes an antithetic link between this supplement and the oracle against the "sinful kingdom" (9:8) which, long after the Deuter-

onomistic precedent for doing so had been established, could have been interpreted with reference to Jerusalem (cf. 2:4–5), with the exile understood to be its fulfillment.[11] But we do not know for sure what is meant by this unusual expression. A reference to the Davidic dynasty could be supposed since the promise in v 11bβ ("I will build it as in days of old") recalls the prophecy of Nathan (2 Sam 7:11–16), although the catchword "to build" (בנה) [with the Davidic "house" as its object] does not occur there, appearing only in the following prayer of David (2 Sam 7:27). One could also suppose the reference to be to the southern kingdom of Judah as a destroyed state, forming a counterpart to the following designation of its malicious adversary Edom (v 12a).[12] But since in addition to Edom "all nations" are mentioned, it is also possible that the fallen empire of David was meant. According to our theologian, at the time of David Yahweh had called his name over the nations, thus declaring his suzerainty and ownership.[13] But perhaps our postexilic theologian saw the center of salvation within narrower limits. Because he explains the expression "booth" only by referring to breaches in a wall[14] and to ruins, one gains the impression that he had in view primarily the city of Jerusalem as the "booth of David." As one versed in scripture, he may have been influenced by Is 1:8. The ruins of Jerusalem's walls were a scandal until Nehemiah's days (cf. Is 58:12). In any case, this witness is dominated by the confident expectation that a Davidic imperium, long since demolished, would be the focal point of the coming global reign of Yahweh. The restored imperium would correspond in splendor to that of the empire "as in days of old" (כימי עולם) and would embrace the remnant of the arch–enemy Edom, but also of all the other nations.

---

9   Cf. especially Joel 4:18–21 [3:18–21] where reference is also made simultaneously to the future of Judah–Jerusalem, to Edom, and to flowing abundance; note even the verbal agreement between Joel 4:18a [3:18a] and Am 9:13b. Cf. further Ob 19–21 and Is 11:10–16, and also Ephrem Florival, "Le jour du jugement (Amos 9:7–15)," *BVC* 8 (1954–55): 71.

10 Cf. Hubert Grimme, "Der Untergang Edoms," *Die Welt als Geschichte: Zeitschrift für universal–geschichtliche Forschung* 3 (1937): 452–63; and also Ulrich Kellermann, *Nehemia: Quellen, Überlieferung und*

Geschichte, BZAW 102 (Berlin: A. Töpelmann, 1967), 170–72.

11 Cf. the Deuteronomistic gloss בכל־הגוים ("among all the nations") in 9:9 with כל־הגוים in 9:12; see textual note "d" to 9:9.

12 Cf. Lam 4:21–22, and also above, p. 160 on 1:11.

13 Cf. 2 Sam 12:28, and Kurt Galling, "Die Ausrufung des Namens als Rechtsakt in Israel," *ThLZ* 81 (1956): 65–70.

14 On פרצים ("breaches"), see p. 207 on 4:3.

■ **13** To this central restoration of the Davidic empire is linked in the new oracle the promise of a fertility such as had not hitherto been experienced. As a rule the task of plowing cannot be begun in Palestine until after the first autumnal rainfalls in October / November; almost half a year after the harvesting of the grain, which is largely carried out in April / May. The treading of the grapes follows upon the vintage in autumn, approximately in September, while the "drawing" of the seed grain through the furrows takes place mainly in November / December. But now ploughing and harvesting, grape treading and sowing are to follow immediately one upon the other. Thus is expressed in different terms a phenomenon similar to the one expected by Ezek 47:12 where, because of the water flowing from the sanctuary, the trees bear new fruit each month. Joel 4:18 [3:18] also announces paradisal fertility, brought about by the temple–fountain.[15] There is no reference to this fountain in v 13a. The following words (v 13bα), however, coincide verbatim with the initial statement in Joel 4:18 [3:18] and deviate from the wording of the subsequent statement there concerning the "hills" only in the use of the hitpaʿel of מוג ("to drip"). Exuberantly pictured in the mind's eye here is a "rippling" of wine across the slopes.[16] The Old Testament cannot more powerfully express the notion of abundance of grain and sweet wine, and thereby of the fullness of life itself.

■ **14** Like 9:11–12, what follows once again brings into view the drab political situation of the present, just as happens in Joel 4:19–21 [3:19–21]. The catchword expression of changed fortunes is also found in Joel 4:1 [3:1].[17] In terms of its content, this promise of a reversal is so articulated that now the rebuilding of the ruins (cf. 9:11) and the planting of vineyards and gardens (cf. 9:13) are parallel to one another. In terms of its form, the earlier threat of futile labor is here transformed into the proclamation of success. Obviously the threats of 5:11aβb[18] have been converted into diametrically opposite statements whose scope has even been expanded. Instead of individual houses of hewn stone, now cities are mentioned.[19] Thus the judgment threatened in terms of destruction and drought is fully cancelled (cf. 5:11; also 3:11, 15; 6:8, 11).

■ **15** The last verse goes even one step further by also reversing the threat of exile (4:2–3; 5:5, 27; 7:11, 17). In doing so, transmitted oracles of weal—distinctively like those found in the book of Jeremiah[20]—are developed. The new element here is the explicit assertion that the punishment of expulsion from the land will never again take place. This promise renews the original gift. It is the land, that "which I have given them," from which Israel shall never again be taken away. This linking of the element of hope with the ancient salvific gift connects the second oracle once again with the first one (cf. 9:11b "as in days of old" [כימי עולם]) and thereby suggests—as does already the linking of themes in 9:14—that we probably have before us in the two later additions the work of the same theologian.

Aim

The conclusion of the book witnesses to the assurance that the proclamation of Amos concerning the end of Israel was not God's last word. After 721 the incomparably harsh fate which the prophet of the eighth century had to proclaim to the people of the state of Israel belonged to history. New messengers had subsequently been sent to that part of God's people which had been preserved even during the exile. A new word of God had followed upon the now fulfilled prophetic word of judgment. Thus the old word was no longer to be transmitted without the new.

It is remarkable how little this final redaction's eschatology of salvation has penetrated the preceding book of Amos. The fulfilled word was left as the inviolate word of God. Not a single unconditional oracle of weal was inserted into the transmitted corpus; the terse reminders of the postexilic veneration of David and of the postexilic sacrificial cultus, which have been incorporated at 6:5b[21] and 5:22aα,[22] do more to heighten our amazement at this than they do to diminish it.

However, in the final analysis the oracle of weal sounds an extremely powerful note. No further accusatory word is uttered, not even an admonition to

---

15 See pp. 82–83.
16 Cf. Joüon, "Notes," 167.
17 On שוב שבות, see p. 76.
18 See p. 247.
19 With the supplemental clause mentioning tree–fruits, cf. Ezek 47:12.

repent or to renew faithfulness; no conditions whatsoever are laid down for the total reversal of fortunes. It is true that the accomplished fact of judgment clearly stands there in the background, at least in v 11 (booth–ruins–breaches), v 14 (reversal–ruined cities) and v 15 (exile). Dominating the foreground, however, is Yahweh's message that he himself will rebuild the fallen booth of David and will adjoin all nations to it, together with the remnant of the exilic enemy, Edom.[23] Also in the foreground is the promise that all futile labor in the field, in the vineyard, and in the rebuilding of the cities will give way to an unprecedented fullness of life and that the terrible judgment of expulsion from the land will never again come to pass. In effect, a truly new world is proclaimed to the disconcerted people. Yet this new world will correspond to the old salvific gifts; it is explicitly affirmed that the new booth of David will resemble the state of affairs pertaining under the ancient empire (v 11bβ), and that the new bestowal of the land will definitively bind the people to the land which had already once been given to Israel (v 15b). The new bestowal transcends the ancient gift, however, in that no judgment will ever again annul it and that the land will be far more fertile than heretofore. God's action alone effects this intensified renewal of the ancient salvific gift. It is not said that guilt is forgiven, much less that disobedience becomes obedience (cf. Jer 31:33–34). Yahweh, "who does this" (v 12b), "your God," establishes this new life for those who have been punished. The past is set aside. Only the judge can save.

The oracle concerning the rebuilding of the fallen booth of David preoccupied the Qumran community.[24] The New Testament treats the same text in broader scope, giving it a more comprehensive interpretation.

In Acts 15:16–17 we find as part of James' speech a citation combining Am 9:12 with 9:11; in as much as the *G* rendering of v 12 is followed, the rebuilding of the booth of David acquires as its immediate purpose "that the rest of humanity and all the nations" may seek the Lord. Am 9:11–12 therefore becomes a prophetic witness to the original intention of God to gain through Israel "a people for his name from among the nations" (Act 15:14)—here the new, world–encompassing congregation of Christ.

While the message of the conclusion to Amos has not only relegated to the past the prophet's word of judgment but has also renewed and intensified the ancient salvific gifts, the New Testament, with the help of the Septuagint rendering and on the basis of the message of Christ, goes one step further. The goal of God's saving activity on behalf of Israel is the new humanity, seen as the people of God. The old word, however, should warn the present congregation against missing its goal.

The juxtaposition of the prophetic word of death and the new promise of life, together with its more broadly developed but nonetheless still selective exegesis in Acts, must be taken to exclude every legalistic interpretation. The postexilic theologian, in any case, was asking what new word Yahweh was entrusting to his time. No generation, however, should fail to hear in his words the basic theme that the renewal of the fallen community is to be expected only on the basis of God's activity of building and planting. Only in this way will the new life surpass the old. Amos sufficiently drove home the point that, left to its own devices, humanity procures for itself only its demise. The promise which transcends this state of affairs applies only to those who have already been judged and condemned.

---

20 Cf. the contrast drawn between planting and uprooting in the oracles of promise in Jer 24:6; 31:28; and 42:10. Cf. also Robert Bach, "Bauen und Pflanzen" in *Studien zur Theologie der alttestamentlichen Überlieferungen* (*Festschrift für Gerhard von Rad zum 60. Geburtstag*), ed. Rolf Rendtorff and Klaus Koch (Neukirchen: Neukirchener Verlag, 1961), 7–32.

21 See p. 276.

22 See 259 n "c."

23 See p. 353.

24 In CD 7.16, Am 9:11 is cited to inform the interpretation of Am 5:26; see pp. 266–67. Am 9:11 is itself directly interpreted in 4QFlor (174) 1.12–13 (text: John M. Allegro, *Qumrân Cave 4*, vol. 1 [4 Q158—4 Q186] DJD 5 [Oxford: Clarendon Press, 1968], 53): ". . . just as it is written, 'Then I will raise up [והקימותי] the fallen booth of David'—that (means) 'the fallen booth of David' who will stand forth to deliver Israel" [Trans by Ed.]. Here the metaphor of the Davidic "booth" must be taken to mean the "Warrior Messiah" or the "Searcher of the Law"; cf. Herbert Braun, *Qumran und das Neue Testament*, vol. 2 (Tübingen: J. C. B. Mohr [Paul Siebeck], 1966), 319–20.

Bibliography
Indices

The following sections of bibliography are based on those which originally appeared in the author's *Dodekapropheton* vols. 1 and 2; they have been supplemented by the editor of this volume, especially with items published since 1963 on Joel and since 1966 on Amos.

1. Commentaries

a / Commentaries to the Twelve (Minor) Prophets

For additional literature on the Twelve Prophets, see Wolff, *Hosea*, 242–44.

Augé, Ramir
 Profetes Menors, La Bíblia versío dels textos originals i comentari pels monjos de Montserrat 16 (Barcelona: Monestir de Monserrat, 1957).

Bewer, Julius A.
 The Book of the Twelve Prophets, 2 vols.; Harper's Annotated Bible (New York: Harper & Brothers, 1949).

Bleeker, L. H. K.; and G. Smit
 De kleine Propheten, 3 vols.; Tekst en Uitleg (Gronigen; [1/1] 1932, [1/2] 1934, [2] 1926, [3] 1934.)

Coppens, Joseph
 Les douze petits Prophètes. Breviaire du Prophetisme (Bruges: Desclée de Brouwer; and Louvain: Publications Universitaires; 1950).

Deden, D.
 De kleine Profeten uit de grondtekst vertaald en uitgelegd, 2 vols.; BOT 12 (Roermond: Romen; [1] 1953, [2] 1956).

Deissler, Alfons; and Matthias Delcor
 Les petits prophètes, 2 vols.; La Sainte Bible 8 (Paris: Letouzey & Ané; [1] 1961, [2] 1964).

Duhm, Bernhard
 "Anmerkungen zu den Zwölf Propheten," *ZAW* 31 (1911): 1–43, 81–110, 161–204.

Idem
 The Twelve Prophets: A Version in the Various Poetical Measures of the Original Writings, tr. Archibald Duff (London, 1912) [*Die zwölf Propheten, in den Vermassen der Urschrift übersetz* (Tübingen, 1910)].

Ehrlich, Arnold B.
 Randglossen zur hebräischen Bibel: Textkritisches, Sprachliches und Sachliches, vol. 5: *Ezechiel und die kleinen Propheten* (Leipzig, 1912 = Hildesheim: Georg Olms, 1968).

Ewald, Georg Heinrich August von
 Commentary on the Prophets of the Old Testament, 5 vols.; tr. J. Frederick Smith (London, 1875–81) [*Die Propheten des Alten Bundes* (Göttingen, ²1867–68)].

Hitzig, Ferdinand
 Die zwölf kleinen Propheten, KEH 1 (Leipzig; 1838, ⁴1881 [with Heinrich Steiner]).

Hoonacker, Albin van
 Les douze petits Prophetes, traduits et commentés, ÉtB (Paris, 1908).

Jepsen, Alfred
 Das Zwölfprophetenbuch, Bibelhilfe für die Gemeinde (Leipzig and Hamburg, 1937).

Keil, Carl Friedrich
 Biblischer Commentar über die Zwölf Kleinen Propheten, BC 3/4 (Leipzig; 1866, ²1873, ³1888).

Laetsch, Theodore Ferdinand K.
 The Minor Prophets, Bible Commentary (St. Louis: Concordia, 1956).

Lehrman, Simon Maurice; S. Goldman; and Eli Cashdan
 The Twelve Prophets, The Soncino Books of the Bible 3/4 (London and Bournemouth: Soncino; 1948, ²1952).

Lippl, Joseph; Johannes Theis; and Hubert Junker
 Die Zwölf Kleinen Propheten, übersetzt und erklärt, 2 vols.; HS 8/3 (Bonn; [1] 1937, [2] 1938).

Marti, Karl
 Das Dodekapropheton erklärt, KHC 13 (Tübingen, 1904).

Mowinckel, Sigmund; and N. Messel
 De Senere Profeter, Det Gamle Testamente 3 (Oslo: H. Aschehoug & Co. [W. Nygaard], 1944).

Nötscher, Friedrich
 Zwölfprophetenbuch oder Kleine Propheten, Echter–Bibel (Würzburg: Echter, 1948).

Nowack, Wilhelm
 Die kleinen Propheten übersetzt und erklärt, HK 3/4 (Göttingen; 1897, ²1903, ³1922).

Orelli, Conrad von
 The Twelve Minor Prophets, tr. J. S. Banks (Edinburgh, 1893) [*Die zwölf kleinen Propheten*, Kurzegefasster Kommentar zu den heiligen Schriften Alten und Neuen Testamentes A/5/2 (München; 1888, ³1908).

Riessler, Paul
 Die kleinen Propheten oder das Zwölfprophetenbuch (Rottenburg, 1911).

Ridderbos, Jan
 De kleine Profeten, 3 vols.; Korte Verklaring der Heilige Schrift (Kampen; 1932–35, ²1952).

Rinaldi, Giovanni

I Profeti minori, 3 vols.; La Sacra Bibbia (Torino and Roma: Marietti; [1] 1952, [2] 1960, [3, with Ferdinando Luciani] 1969).

Robinson, Theodore H.; and Friedrich Horst
Die Zwölf Kleinen Propheten, HAT 1/14 (Tübingen: J. C. B. Mohr [Paul Siebeck]; 1938, ²1954, ³1964).

Schumpp, Meinrad, O.P.
Das Buch der zwölf Propheten, Herders Bibelkommentar 10/2 (Freiburg i. B.: Herder, 1950).

Sellin, Ernst
Das Zwölfprophetenbuch übersetzt und erklärt, 2 vols.; KAT 12 (Leipzig; 1922, ²1929, ³1930).

Smith, George Adam
The Book of the Twelve Prophets, 2 vols.; The Expositer's Bible (New York; [1] 1896, [2] 1898; revised edition 1929).

Vella, B. M.
Ἑρμηνεία Παλαιᾶς Διαθήκης, 5 vols. (Athens: Aster, 1947–50).

Weiser, Artur; and Karl Elliger
Das Buch der zwölf Kleinen Propheten, ATD 24–25 (Göttingen: Vandenhoeck & Ruprecht; [ATD 24] 1949, ⁵1967; [ATD 25] 1950, ⁶1967).

Wellhausen, Julius
Die kleinen Propheten übersetzt und erklärt, Skizzen und Vorarbeiten 5 (Berlin: Georg Reimer; 1892, ³1898 = 1963).

b / Commentaries to Joel

Allen, Leslie C.
The Books of Joel, Obadiah, Jonah and Micah, The New International Commentary on the Old Testament (Grand Rapids, Michigan: William B. Eerdmans, 1976).

Bewer, Julius A.
A Critical and Exegetical Commentary on Obadiah and Joel, ICC (Edinburgh: T. & T. Clark, 1911).

Bič, Miloš
Das Buch Joel (Berlin: Evangelische–Verlagsanstalt, 1960).

Brockington, Leonard H.
"Joel" in *Peake's Commentary on the Bible*, ed. Matthew Black and H. H. Rowley (London: Thomas Nelson and Sons, 1963), 614–16.

Couve de Murville, M. N. L.
"Joel" in *A New Catholic Commentary on Holy Scripture*, ed. Reginald C. Fuller, *et al.* (London: Thomas Nelson and Sons, 1969), 689–92.

Credner, Karl August
Der Prophet Joel übersetzt und erklärt (Halle, 1831).

Driver, Samuel Rolles
The Books of Joel and Amos, The Cambridge Bible for Schools and Colleges (Cambridge; 1897, ²1915 [with H. C. O. Lanchester]).

Edgar, S. L.
The Minor Prophets (excluding Amos, Hosea, and Micah), Epworth Preacher's Commentaries (London: Epworth, 1962).

Frey, Hellmuth
Das Buch der Kirche in der Weltwende: Die kleinen nachexilischen Propheten, BAT 24 (Stuttgart: Calwer; 1941, ⁴1957), 203–49 (Joel).

Haller, Max
Das Judentum. Geschichtsschreibung, Prophetie und Gesetzgebung nach dem Exil, SAT 2/3 (Göttingen; 1914; ²1925).

How, J. C. H.
Joel and Amos, Smaller Cambridge Bible for Schools (Cambridge, 1910).

Jones, Douglas Rawlinson
Isaiah 56–66 and Joel: Introduction and Commentary, Torch Bible Commentaries (London: SCM, 1964).

Kapelrud, Arvid S.
Joel Studies, UUÅ 1948/4 (Uppsala: A. B. Lundequist, 1948).

Keller, Carl A.
"Joël" in Edmond Jacob, Carl A. Keller, and Samuel Amsler, *Osée, Joël, Amos, Abadias, Jonas*, Commentaire de l'Ancien Testament 11a (Neuchâtel: Delachaux & Niestlé, 1965), 99–155.

Kennedy, J. Hardee
"Joel" in *The Broadman Bible Commentary*, vol. 7 (Hosea–Malachi); ed. Clifton J. Allen (Nashville: Broadman, 1972), 61–80.

Kutal, Bartholomaeus
Liber Prophetae Joelis, Commentarii in Prophetas Minores 2 (Olmütz, 1932).

Marti, Karl
"Der Prophet Joel" in *HSAT* 2, 23–29.

Murphy, Roland E., O Carm.
"The Book of Joel" in *The Interpreter's One–Volume Commentary on the Bible*, ed. Charles M. Laymon (Nashville and New York: Abingdon, 1971), 461–64.

Myers, Jacob M.
The Books of Hosea, Joel, Amos, Obadiah, and Jonah, The Layman's Bible Commentary 14 (Atlanta: John Knox, 1959).

Rinaldi, Giovanni M.
Il libro di Joele tradotto e commentato (Rapallo, 1938).

Rudolph, Wilhelm
Joel—Amos—Obadja—Jona, KAT 13/2 (Gütersloh: Gütersloher Verlagshaus [Gerd Mohn], 1971).

Schmalohr, Josef
Das Buch des Propheten Joel, übersetzt und erklärt, ATA 7/4 (Münster i.W., 1922).

Scholz, Anton
Kommentar zum Buche des Propheten Joel (Würzburg, 1885).

Thompson, John A.
"The Book of Joel: Introduction and Exegesis" in *IB* 6, 729–60.

Trinquet, Joseph
Habaquq, Abadias, Joël, SBJ (Paris: Les Éditions du Cerf; 1933, ²1959).

Wade, G. W.
The Books of the Prophets Micah, Obadiah, Joel and Jonah, Westminster Commentaries (London, 1925).

Watts, John D. W.
The Books of Joel, Obadiah, Jonah, Nahum, Habakkuk and Zephaniah, The Cambridge Bible Commentary on the New English Bible (Cambridge: University Press, 1975).

Widmer, Gottfried
Die Kommentare von Raschi, Ibn Esra, Radaq zu Joel: Text, Übersetzung und Erläuterung. Eine Einführung in die rabbinische Bibelexegese (Basel: Volksdruckerei, 1945).

Williams, Arthur Lukyn
Joel and Amos, The Minor Prophets Unfolded (London, 1918).

Wood, Geoffrey E.
"Joel" in *The Jerome Biblical Commentary*; ed. Raymond E. Brown, s.s.; Joseph A. Fitzmyer, s.j.; and Roland E. Murphy, O. Carm. (Englewood Cliffs, New Jersey: Prentice–Hall, 1968), I: 439–43.

Wünsche, August
Die Weissagung des Propheten Joel übersetzt und erklärt (Leipzig, 1872).

c / Commentaries to Amos

Amsler, Samuel
"Amos" in Edmond Jacob, Carl. A. Keller, and Samuel Amsler, *Osée, Joël, Amos, Abadias, Jonas*, Commentaire de l'Ancien Testament 11a (Neuchâtel: Delachaux & Niestlé, 1965), 157–291.

Baur, Gustav A. L.
Der Prophet Amos erklärt (Giessen, 1847).

Blechmann, Malke
Das Buch Amos im Talmud und Midrasch (Leipzig, 1937).

Budde, Karl
"Zu Text und Auslegung des Buches Amos," *JBL* 43 (1924): 46–131; 44 (1925): 62–122.

Burrons, W. O.
Amos (1898).

Canney, Maurice A.
"Amos" in *A Commentary on the Bible*, ed. Arthur S. Peake (New York, 1920), 547–54.

Cripps, Richard S.
A Critical and Exegetical Commentary on the Book of Amos (London: SPCK; 1929, ²1955 = 1960, 1969).

Driver, Samuel Rolles
The Books of Joel and Amos, The Cambridge Bible for Schools and Colleges (Cambridge; 1897, ²1915 [with H. C. O. Lanchester]).

Edghill, Ernest Arthur; and G. A. Cooke
The Book of Amos, Westminster Commentaries (London; 1914, ²1926).

Elhorst, Hendrik Jan
De profetie van Amos (Leiden, 1900).

Fosbroke, Hughell E. W.
"The Book of Amos: Introduction and Exegesis" in *IB* 6, 761–853.

Frey, Hellmuth
Das Buch des Ringens Gottes um seine Kirche: Der Prophet Amos, BAT 23/1 (Stuttgart: Calwer; 1958, ²1965).

Gelderen, C. van
Het boek Amos, Commentaar op het Oude Testament (Kampen, 1933).

Gressmann, Hugo
Die älteste Geschichtsschreibung und Prophetie Israels (von Samuel bis Amos und Hosea), SAT 3/1 (Göttingen; 1910, ²1921).

Guthe, Hermann
"Der Prophet Amos" in *HSAT* 2, 30–47.

Halévy, Joseph
"Recherches bibliques—Le Livre d'Amos," *Revue Sémitique* 11 (1903): 1–31, 97–121, 193–209, 289–300; 12 (1904): 1–18.

Hammershaimb, Erling
The Book of Amos: A Commentary, tr. John Sturdy (Oxford: Basil Blackwell, 1970) [*Amos Fortolket* (Kjøbenhavn: Nyt Nordisk; 1946, ²1958, ³1967)].

Harper, William Rainey
A Critical and Exegetical Commentary on Amos and Hosea, ICC (Edinburgh: T. & T. Clark, 1905).

Hauret, Charles
Amos et Osée; Verbum Salutis, Ancien Testament 5 (Paris: Beauchesne, 1970).

How, J. C. H.
Joel and Amos, Smaller Cambridge Bible for Schools (Cambridge, 1910).

Hyatt, J. Philip
"Amos" in *Peake's Commentary on the Bible*, ed. Matthew Black and H. H. Rowley (London: Thomas Nelson and Sons, 1963), 617–25.

King, Philip J.
"Amos" in *The Jerome Biblical Commentary*; ed. Raymond E. Brown, s.s.; Joseph A. Fitzmyer, s.j.; and Roland E. Murphy, O. Carm. (Englewood Cliffs, New Jersey: Prentice–Hall, 1968), I: 245–52.

Kraft, Charles F.
"The Book of Amos" in *The Interpreter's One–Volume Commentary on the Bible*, ed. Charles M. Laymon (Nashville and New York: Abingdon, 1971), 465–76.

Kutal, Bartholomaeus
Libri Prophetarum Amos et Abdiae, Commentarii in Prophetas Minores 3 (Olmütz, 1933).

McKeating, Henry
The Books of Amos, Hosea and Micah, The Cambridge Bible Commentary on the New English Bible (Cambridge: University Press, 1971).

Marsh, John
Amos and Micah: Introduction and Commentary, Torch Bible Commentaries (London: SCM, 1959).

Mays, James Luther

Amos: A Commentary, OTL (Philadelphia: Westminster, 1969).

Myers, Jacob M.
The Books of Hosea, Joel, Amos, Obadiah, and Jonah, The Layman's Bible Commentary 14 (Atlanta: John Knox, 1959).

Osty, Émile
Amos, Osée, SBJ (Paris: Les Éditions du Cerf, 1952).

Prager, Mirjam
"Amos, der Hirte aus Teqoa," *Bibel und Liturgie* 36 (1962–63): 84–96, 164–72, 243–55, 295–308.

Procksch, Otto
Die kleinen Prophetischen Schriften vor dem Exil, Erläuterungen zum Alten Testament 3 (Calw and Stuttgart, 1910).

Routtenberg, Hyman J.
Amos of Tekoa: A Study in Interpretation (New York, Washington, and Hollywood: Vantage, 1971).

Rudolph, Wilhelm
Joel—Amos—Obadja—Jona, KAT 13/2 (Gütersloh: Gütersloher Verlagshaus [Gerd Mohn], 1971).

Ryan, D.
"Amos" in *A New Catholic Commentary on Holy Scripture*, ed. Reginald C. Fuller, *et al.* (London: Thomas Nelson and Sons, 1969), 693–701.

Smith, Ralph L.
"Amos" in *The Broadman Bible Commentary*, vol. 7 (Hosea–Malachi); ed. Clifton J. Allen (Nashville: Broadman, 1972), 81–141.

Snaith, Norman H.
Amos, Hosea and Micah, Epworth Preacher's Commentaries (London: Epworth, 1956).

Idem
The Book of Amos, 2 vols. (London: Epworth, 1945–46).

Veldkamp, H.
Paraphrase van het boek van den profeet Amos en van het boek van den profeet Obadjah (1940).

Werner, Herbert
Amos, Exempla Biblica 4 (Göttingen: Vandenhoeck & Ruprecht, 1969).

Williams, Arthur Lukyn
Joel and Amos, The Minor Prophets Unfolded (London, 1918).

2. Select Monographs and Articles on Joel

a / General Studies on Joel

Ahlström, G. W.
Joel and the Temple Cult of Jerusalem, SVT 21 (Leiden: E. J. Brill, 1971).

Dennefeld, Ludwig
"Les problemes du livre de Joël," *Revue des Sciences Religieuses* 4 (1924): 555–75; 5 (1925): 35–57, 591–608; 6 (1926): 26–49.

Engnell, Ivan
"Joels bok" in *Svenskt Bibliskt Uppslagsverk*, vol. 1; ed. Ivan Engnell, *et al.* (Gävle: Skolförlaget, 1948), 1075–77.

Kritzinger, Johan Hendrik
Die profesie van Joël (Amsterdam, 1935).

Merx, E. O. Adalbert
Die Prophetie des Joel und ihre Ausleger von den ältesten Zeiten bis zu den Reformatoren. Eine exegetisch–kritische und hermeneutisch–dogmengeschichtliche Studie (Halle a. S., 1879).

Neil, William
"Joel, Book of" in *The Interpreter's Dictionary of the Bible*, vol. 2 (E–J); ed. George Arthur Buttrick, *et al.* (Nashville and New York: Abingdon, 1962), 926–29.

Preuss, G.
Die Prophetie Joels unter besonderer Berücksichtigung der Zeitfrage, Unpub. Diss. (Halle, 1889).

Weise, Manfred
"Joelbuch," *RGG*[3] 3, 800–02.

b / Textual Problems in Joel

Leibel, Daniel
"On יַעְבְּטוּן (Joel 2:7)," [Hebrew] *Lešonenu* 24 (1959–60): 253.

Loewenstamm, Samuel E.
"יַעְבְּטוּן = יְעֻתוּן?" [Hebrew] *Lešonenu* 24 (1959–60): 107–08.

Nestle, Eberhard
"(Miscellen, 1.) Zur Kapiteleinleitung in Joel," *ZAW* 24 (1904): 122–27.

Rahmer, M.
"Der hebräischen Traditionem in den Werken des Hieronymus. Zweiter Theil: Die Commentarien zu den XII kleinen Propheten, II. Joel," *MGWJ* 41 (1897): 625–39, 691–92.

c / Form and Tradition Criticism of Joel

Graetz, Heinrich
Der einheitliche Charakter der Prophetie Joels und die künstliche Gliederung ihrer Teile (Breslau, 1873).

Sievers, Eduard
"Alttestamentliche Miscellen (VI. Zu Joel)," *Berichte über die Verhandlungen der Königlich Sächsischen Gesellschaft der Wissenschaften zu Leipzig*, Philologisch–historische Klasse 59 (1907): 3–37.

Stocks, H. H. D.
"Der 'Nördliche' und die Komposition des Buches Joel," *Neue Kirchliche Zeitschrift* 19 (1908): 725–50.

d / Authorship and Origin of Joel

Amon, G.
Die Abfassungszeit des Buches Joel, Unpub. Diss. (Würzburg, 1942).

Birkeland, Harris
Zum hebräischen Traditionswesen. Die Komposition der prophetischen Bücher des Alten Testaments, Avhandlinger utgitt av Det Norske Videnskaps–Akademi i Oslo 2/1 (Oslo, 1938).

Holzinger, Heinrich

"Sprachcharakter und Abfassungszeit des Buches Joel," *ZAW* 9 (1889): 89–131.

Jensen, Kjeld
"Indledningsspørgsmaal i Joels Bog," *DTT* 4 (1941): 98–112.

Kessner, Georg
Das Zeitalter des Propheten Joel (Leipzig, 1888).

Lattimore, Ralph Edward
The Date of Joel, Unpub. Diss. (Southern Baptist Seminary, 1951).

Myers, Jacob M.
"Some Contributions Bearing on the Date of Joel," *ZAW* 74 (1962): 177–95.

Preuss, G.
Die Prophetie Joels unter besonderer Berücksichtigung der Zeitfrage, Unpub. Diss. (Halle, 1889).

Reicke, Bo
"Joel und seine Zeit" in *Wort—Gebot—Glaube. Beiträge zur Theologie des Alten Testaments (Walther Eichrodt zum 80. Geburtstag)*, ed. Hans Joachim Stoebe; AThANT 59 (Zürich: Zwingli, 1970), 133–41.

Rudolph, Wilhelm
"Wann wirkte Joel?" in *Das ferne und nahe Wort (Festschrift Leonhard Rost)*, ed. Fritz Maass; BZAW 105 (Berlin: A. Töpelmann, 1967), 193–98.

Stephenson, F. R.
"The Date of the Book of Joel," *VT* 19 (1969): 224–29.

Thompson, John Alexander
"The Date of Joel" in *A Light unto My Path: Old Testament Studies in Honor of Jacob M. Myers*, ed. Howard N. Bream, *et al.*; Gettysburg Theological Studies 4 (Philadelphia: Temple University, 1974), 453–64.

Treves, Marco
"The Date of Joel," *VT* 7 (1957): 149–56.

e / Individual Problems of Interpretation in Joel

Baumgartner, Walter
"Joel 1 und 2" in *Karl Budde zum siebzigsten Geburtstag*, ed. Karl Marti; BZAW 34 (Giessen, 1920), 10–19.

Bourke, J.
"Le jour de Yahvé dans Joël," *RB* 66 (1959): 5–31, 191–212.

Budde, Karl
" 'Der von Norden' in Joel 2:20," *OLZ* 22 (1919): 1–5.

Idem
"Der Umschwung in Joel 2," *OLZ* 22 (1919): 104–10.

Cannon, William Walter
" 'The Day of the Lord' in Joel," *Church Quarterly Review* 103 (1927): 32–63.

Chary, Théophane
Les prophètes et le culte à partir de l'exil autour du Second Temple. L'idéal cultuel des prophètes exiliens et post-exiliens, Bibliothèque de Théologie 3/3 (Tournai: Desclée & Cie, 1955).

Dahood, Mitchell J.
"The Four Cardinal Points in Psalm 75:7 and Joel 2:20," *Biblica* 52 (1971): 397.

Frankfort, Thérèse
"Le כִּי de Joël 1:12," *VT* 10 (1960): 445–48.

Haldar, Alfred O.
The Nature of the Desert in Sumero–Accadian and West–Semitic Religions, UUÅ 1950/3 (Uppsala: A. B. Lundequist, 1950), 56–59.

Knieschke, Wilhelm
Die Eschatologie des Joel in ihrer historisch–geographischen Bestimmtheit (Naumburg a. d. S., 1912).

Kutsch, Ernst
"Heuschreckenplage und Tag Jahwes in Joel 1 und 2," *ThZ* 18 (1962): 81–94.

Mariès, Louis
"A propos de récentes études sur Joël," *Recherches de Science Religieuse* 37 (1950): 121–24.

Milik, J. T.
"Notes d'épigraphie et de topographie palestiniennes," *RB* 66 (1959): 550–75 ("II. Torrent des Acacias. Joël, IV, 18," 553–55).

Müller, Hans–Peter
"Prophetie und Apokalyptik bei Joel," *Theologia Viatorum* 10 (1966): 231–52.

Plath, Margarete
"Joel 1:15–20," *ZAW* 47 (1929): 159–60.

Roth, Cecil
"The Teacher of Righteousness and the Prophecy of Joel," *VT* 13 (1963): 91–95.

Rudolph, Wilhelm
"Ein Beitrag zum hebräischen Lexicon aus dem Joelbuch" in *Hebräische Wortforschung. Festschrift zum 80. Geburtstag Walter Baumgartner*, SVT 16 (Leiden: E. J. Brill, 1967), 244–50.

Sellers, Ovid R.
"Stages of Locust in Joel," *AJSL* 52 (1935–36): 81–85.

Thompson, John A.
"Joel's Locusts in the Light of Near Eastern Parallels," *JNES* 14 (1955): 52–55.

f / The Theology of Joel

Gelin, Albert
"L'announce de la Pentecôte (Joël 3:1–5)," *BVC* 27 (1959): 15–19.

Kerrigan, Alexander
"The 'sensus plenior' of Joel, III, 1–5 in Act., II, 14–36" in *Sacra Pagina: Miscellanea Biblica, Congressus Internationalis de Re Biblica*, vol. 2; ed. J. Coppens, A. Deschamps, É. Massaux; Bibliotheca Ephemeridum Theologicarum Lovaniensium 12–13 (Paris: Librarie Lecoffre, J. Gabalda et Cie, 1959), 295–313.

Plöger, Otto
Theocracy and Eschatology, tr. S. Rudman (Richmond, Va.: John Knox, 1968), 96–105 [*Theo-*

kratie und Eschatologie, WMANT 2 (Neukirchen: Neukirchener Verlag, 1959), 117–28].

Rad, Gerhard von
> *Old Testament Theology*, vol. 2: *The Theology of Israel's Prophetic Traditions*, tr. D. M. G. Stalker (New York and Evanston: Harper & Row, 1965), 119–25 ("The Day of Yahweh") [*Theologie des Alten Testaments*, vol. 2: *Die Theologie der prophetischen Überlieferungen Israels*; Einführung in die evangelische Theologie 1 (München: Chr. Kaiser, ⁵1968), 129–33].

Idem
> "The Origin of the Concept of the Day of Yahweh," *JSS* 4 (1959): 97–108.

Wolff, Hans Walter
> *Die Botschaft des Buches Joel*, Theologische Existenz heute N.F. 109 (München: Chr. Kaiser, 1963).

3. Select Monographs and Articles on Amos

a / General Studies on Amos

Brillet, Gaston
> *Amos et Osée* (Paris: Les Éditions du Cerf, 1944).

Copass, Benjamin Andrew
> *Amos* (Nashville, 1939).

Cramer, Karl
> *Amos. Versuch einer theologischen Interpretation*, BWANT 51 (Stuttgart, 1930).

Desnoyers, Louis
> "Le prophète Amos," *RB* 26 (1917): 218–46.

Engnell, Ivan
> "Amos" and "Amos' bok" in *Svenskt Bibliskt Uppslagsverk*, vol. 1; ed. Ivan Engnell, *et al.* (Gävle: Skolförlaget, 1948), 59–61, 61–63.

Eybers, I. H.; F. Charles Fensham; J. J. Glück; C. J. Labuschagne; L. M. Muntingh; A. van Selms; B. J. van der Merwe; and H. S. Pelser
> *Studies in the Books of Hosea and Amos* (*Die Ou Testamentiese Werkgemeenskap in Suid–Afrika, 7th and 8th Congresses* [*1964–65*]) (Potchefstroom: Rege–Pers Beperk, 1965).

Fohrer, Georg
> *Die Propheten des Alten Testaments*, vol. 1: *Die Propheten des 8. Jahrhunderts* (Gütersloh: Gütersloher Verlagshaus [Gerd Mohn], 1974), 22–55 ("Amos").

Gunning, Johannes Hermanus
> *De Godspraken van Amos* (Leiden, 1885).

Haran, Menahem
> "Amos" in *Encyclopaedia Judaica*, vol. 2 (A–Ang) (Jerusalem: Keter, 1971), 879–89.

Hartung, Kaspar
> *Der Prophet Amos, nach dem Grundtext erklärt*, BSt (Freiburg, 1898).

Herntrich, Volkmar
> *Amos, der Prophet Gottes*, Wege in die Bibel 4 (Göttingen, 1941).

Kapelrud, Arvid S.

Central Ideas in Amos, SNVAO 2 1956/4 (Oslo: H. Aschehoug & Co. [W. Nygaard]; 1956, ²1961).

Koehler, Ludwig
> "Amos," *Schweizerische Theologische Zeitschrift* 34 (1917): 10–21, 68–79, 145–57, 190–208 (= *Amos* [Zurich, 1917]).

Krause, Hans Helmut
> "Die Gerichtsprophet Amos, ein Vorläufer des Deuteronomisten," *ZAW* 50 (1932): 221–39.

Kroeker, Jakob
> *Die Propheten oder das Reden Gottes (vorexilisch): Amos und Hosea*, Das lebendige Wort 4 (Giessen, 1932).

Löhr, Max
> *Untersuchungen zum Buch Amos*, BZAW 4 (Giessen, 1901).

Maag, Victor
> *Text, Wortschatz und Begriffswelt des Buches Amos* (Leiden: E. J. Brill, 1951).

Mitchell, H. G.
> *Amos: An Essay in Exegesis* (Boston; 1893, ²1900).

Moreno, C. A.
> "Amos," *Theología y Vida* 4 (1963): 23–35.

Morgenstern, Julian
> *Amos Studies*, vol. 1 (Cincinnati: Hebrew Union College, 1941 [= "Amos Studies I," *HUCA* 11 (1936): 19–140; "Amos Studies II," *HUCA* 12–13 (1937–38): 1–53; "Amos Studies III," *HUCA* 15 (1940): 59–304).

Idem
> "Amos Studies IV," *HUCA* 32 (1961): 295–350.

Neher, André
> *Amos. Contribution à l'étude du prophétisme* (Paris: J. Vrin, 1950).

Oettli, Samuel
> *Amos und Hosea. Zwei Zeugen gegen die Anwendung der Evolutionstheorie auf die Religion Israels*, BFChrTh 5/4 (Gütersloh, 1901).

Oort, Henricus
> "De profeet Amos," *Theologisch Tijdschrift* 14 (1880): 114–58.

Schmidt, Hans
> *Der Prophet Amos* (Tübingen, 1917).

Schottroff, Willy
> "Amos—Das Porträt eines Propheten (I–V)," *Stimme* 24 (1972): 113–15, 145–46, 193–96, 225–27, 289–92.

Smart, James D.
> "Amos" in *The Interpreter's Dictionary of the Bible*, vol. 1 (A–D); ed. George A. Buttrick, *et al.* (Nashville and New York: Abingdon, 1962), 116–21.

Sutcliffe, Thomas Henry
> *The Book of Amos*, Biblical Handbooks (London, 1939).

Touzard, Jules
> *Le livre d'Amos* (Paris, 1908).

Tweedie, Andrew
> *A Sketch of Amos and Hosea* (Edinburgh and London, 1916).

Valeton, J. J. P.

*Amos und Hosea. Ein Kapitel aus der Geschichte der
israelitischen Religion,* tr. Karl Echternacht (Giessen, 1898).

Vienney, Amos B.
Amos de Tekoa, son époque et son livre (Montauban,
1899).

Ward, James M.
"Amos" in *The Interpreter's Dictionary of the Bible,*
Supplementary Volume; ed. Keith Crim, *et al.*
(Nashville: Abingdon, 1976), 21–23.

Idem
Amos and Isaiah: Prophets of the Word of God (Nashville and New York: Abingdon, 1969).

Watts, John D. W.
Vision and Prophecy in Amos (Grand Rapids: William B. Eerdmans, 1958).

Weiser, Artur
Die Profetie des Amos, BZAW 53 (Giessen, 1929).

Wolfe, Rolland Emerson
Meet Amos and Hosea, the Prophets of Israel (New
York: Harper & Brothers, 1945).

Würthwein, Ernst
"Amos–Studien," *ZAW* 62 (1950): 10–52.

b / The Text of the Book of Amos

Arieti, James A.
"The Vocabulary of Septuagint Amos," *JBL* 93
(1974): 338–47.

Auer, Franz X.
*Vulgatastudien an Hand der Kleinen Propheten, I: Oseas
bis Micha,* Unpub. Diss. (Breslau, 1942).

Hirscht, Arthur
"Textkritische Untersuchungen über das Buch
Amos," *Zeitschrift für wissenschaftliche Theologie* 44
(1903): 11–73.

Howard, George
"Some Notes on the Septuagint of Amos," *VT* 20
(1970): 108–12.

Muraoka, Takamitsu
"Is the Septuagint Amos 8:12—9:10 a Separate
Unit?" *VT* 20 (1970): 496–500.

Oesterley, W. O. E.
*Studies in the Greek and Latin Versions of the Book of
Amos* (Cambridge, 1902).

Praetorius, Franz
Textkritische Bemerkungen zum Buche Amos, Sitzungs-
berichte der Preussischen Akademie der Wissenschaften zu Berlin, Philologisch–historische Klasse
(Berlin, 1918), 1248–62.

Rahmer, M.
"Die hebräischen Traditionen in den Werken des
Hieronymus. Zweiter Theil: Die Commentarien
zu den XII kleinen Propheten, III. Amos,"
MGWJ 42 (1898): 1–61, 97–107.

Robinson, Theodore H.
The Book of Amos: Hebrew Text (London, 1923).

Snaith, Norman Henry
Notes on the Hebrew Text of Amos (London: Epworth, 1945–46).

c / The Forms of Amos' Proclamation

Balla, Emil
Die Droh– und Scheltworte des Amos (Leipzig, 1926).

Baumann, Eberhard
Der Aufbau der Amosreden, BZAW 7 (Giessen, 1907).

Condamin, Albert
"Les chants lyriques des prophètes," *RB* 10
(1901): 352–76.

Farr, Georges
"The Language of Amos, Popular or Cultic?"
VT 16 (1966): 312–24.

Harper, William Rainey
The Utterances of Amos arranged strophically (Chicago, 1900) [= *idem, Biblical World* (Aug.–Nov.,
1898): 86–89, 179–82, 251–56, 333–38].

Hoffman, Hans Werner
"Form—Funktion—Intention," *ZAW* 82 (1970):
341–46.

Janzen, Waldemar
Mourning Cry and Woe Oracle, BZAW 125 (Berlin
and New York: Walter de Gruyter, 1972).

Lemcke, Günther
*Die Prophetensprüche des Amos und Jesaja metrisch–
stilistisch und literar–ästhetisch betrachtet* (Breslau,
1914).

Lewis, Ralph Loren
*The Persuasive Style and Appeals of the Minor Prophets
Amos, Hosea, and Micah,* Unpub. Diss. (University
of Michigan, 1959).

Lindblom, Johannes
*Die literarische Gattung der prophetischen Literatur.
Eine literargeschichtliche Untersuchung zum Alten Tes-
tament,* UUÅ 1924/Theologi. 1 (Uppsala, 1924),
66–97 ("Buch der Revelationen des Propheten
Amos").

Meinhold, Johannes; and Hans Lietzmann
Der Prophet Amos. Hebräisch und Griechisch, Kleine
Texte für theologische Vorlesungen und Übungen
15/16 (Bonn, 1905).

Praetorius, Franz
Die Gedichte des Amos (Halle, 1924).

Sievers, Eduard; and Hermann Guthe
Amos, metrisch bearbeitet, Abhandlungen der Sächsischen Gesellschaft der Wissenschaften 23/3 (Leipzig, 1907).

Staples, W. E.
"Epic Motifs in Amos," *JNES* 25 (1966): 106–12.

Stephany, A. T. M.
"Charakter und zeitliche Aufeinanderfolge der
Drohsprüche in der Prophetie des Amos,"
Christentum und Wissenschaft 7 (1931): 281–89.

Stuart, Douglas K.
Studies in Early Hebrew Meter, Harvard Semitic
Monographs 13 (Missoula, Montana: Scholars
Press, 1976), 197–213 ("The Poetry of Amos").

d / The Person of Amos

Bič, Miloš
"Der Prophet Amos—ein Haepatoskopos," *VT* 1

(1951): 293–96.

Budde, Karl
"Die Überschrift des Buches Amos und des Propheten Heimat" in *Semitic Studies in Memory of Rev. Dr. Alexander Kohut*, ed. George Alexander Kohut (Berlin, 1897), 106–10.

Cohen, Simon
"Amos *Was* a Navi," *HUCA* 32 (1961): 175–78.

Danell, Gustaf Adolf
"Var Amos verkligen en nabi?" *SEÅ* 16 (1951): 7–20.

Herntrich, Volkmar
"Das Berufungsbewußtsein des Amos," *Christentum und Wissenschaft* 9 (1933): 161–76.

Junker, Hubert
"Amos, der Mann, den Gott mit unwiderstehlicher Gewalt zum Propheten machte," *TrThZ* 65 (1956): 321–28.

Kapelrud, Arvid S.
"Amos," *BHHW* 1, 85.

Idem
"Profeten Amos og hans yrke," *Norsk Teologisk Tidsskrift* 59 (1958): 76–79.

Lehming, Sigo
"Erwägungen zu Amos," *ZThK* 55 (1958): 145–69.

Murtonen, A. E.
"The Prophet Amos—a Hepatoscoper?" *VT* 2 (1952): 170–71.

Reventlow, Henning Graf
Das Amt des Propheten bei Amos, FRLANT 80 (Göttingen: Vandenhoeck & Ruprecht, 1962).

Rothstein, Gustav
"Amos und seine Stellung innerhalb des Prophetismus," *Theologische Studien und Kritiken* 78 (1905): 323–58.

Rowley, Harold Henry
"Was Amos a Nabi?" in *Festschrift Otto Eissfeldt*, ed. Johann Fück (Halle a. d. S.: Max Niemeyer, 1947), 191–98.

Schmidt, Hans
"Die Herkunft des Propheten Amos" in *Karl Budde zum siebzigsten Geburtstag*, ed. Karl Marti; BZAW 34 (Giessen, 1920), 158–71.

Seierstad, Ivar P.
"Erlebnis und Gehorsam beim Propheten Amos," *ZAW* 52 (1934): 22–41.

Idem
Die Offenbarungserlebnisse der Propheten Amos, Jesaja und Jeremia (Oslo: J. Dybwad; 1946, ²1965), 52–59, 82–91.

Stoebe, Hans Joachim
"Der Prophet Amos und sein bürgerlicher Beruf," *WuD* N.F.5 (1957): 160–81.

Varadi, M.
Il profeta Amos (1947).

Watts, John D. W.
"Amos, The Man," *Review and Expositor*, 63 (1966): 387–92.

e / The Time of Amos

Cohen, Simon
"The Political Background of the Words of Amos," *HUCA* 36 (1965): 153–60.

Haran, Menahem
"Observations on the Historical Background of Amos 1:2—2:6," *IEJ* 18 (1968): 201–12 (=[Hebrew], *Yedi'ot* 30 [1966]: 56–59).

Idem
"The Rise and Decline of the Empire of Jeroboam ben Joash," *VT* 17 (1967): 266–97.

Peiser, Felix Ernst
"שְׁנָתַיִם לִפְנֵי הָרָעַשׁ. Eine philologische Studie," *ZAW* 36 (1916): 218–24.

Soggin, J. Alberto
"Amos 6:13–14 und 1:3 auf dem Hintergrund der Beziehungen zwischen Israel und Damaskus im 9. und 8. Jahrhundert" in *Near Eastern Studies in Honor of William Foxwell Albright*, ed. Hans Goedicke (Baltimore and London: Johns Hopkins, 1971), 433–41.

Idem
"Das Erdbeben von Amos 1:1 und die Chronologie der Könige Ussia und Jotham von Juda," *ZAW* 82 (1970): 117–21.

Tuschen, W.
Die historischen Angaben im Buche des Propheten Amos, Unpub. Diss. (Freiburg, 1951).

f / The Formation of the Book of Amos

Botterweck, G. Johannes
"Zur Authentizität des Buches Amos," *BZ* N.F.2 (1958): 176–89.

Budde, Karl
"Zur Geschichte des Buches Amos" in *Studien zur semitischen Philologie und Religionsgeschichte: Festschrift Julius Wellhausen*, ed. Karl Marti; BZAW 27 (Giessen, 1914), 63–77.

Caspari, Wilhelm
"Wer hat die Aussprüche des Propheten Amos gesammelt?" *Neue Kirchliche Zeitschrift* 25 (1914): 701–15.

Crüsemann, Frank
"Kritik an Amos im deuteronomistischen Geschichtswerk" in *Probleme biblischer Theologie (Gerhard von Rad zum 70. Geburtstag)*, ed. Hans Walter Wolff (München: Chr. Kaiser, 1971), 57–63.

Döller, Johannes
"Vom 'Überschüssigen' bei Amos," *Studien und Mitteilungen aus dem Benedictiner- und Cistercienserorden* 28 (1907): 413–15.

Gordis, Robert
"The Composition and Structure of Amos," *HTR* 33 (1940): 239–51.

Hobbs, T. R.
"Amos 3:1b and 2:10," *ZAW* 81 (1969): 384–87.

Hoffmann, Hans Werner
"Zur Echtheitsfrage von Amos 9:9f," *ZAW* 82 (1970): 121–22.

Horst, Friedrich
  "Die Doxologien im Amosbuch," *ZAW* 47
  (1929): 45–54 (= *idem, Gottes Recht*, ThB 12 [München: Chr. Kaiser, 1961], 155–66).
Jozaki, Susumu
  "The Secondary Passages of the Book of Amos,"
  Kwansei Gakuin University Annual Studies 4 (1956):
  25–100.
Kapelrud, Arvid S.
  "Amosbuch," *BHHW* 1, 85–87.
Kellermann, Ulrich
  "Der Amosschluß als Stimme deuteronomistischer
  Heilshoffnung," *EvTh* 29 (1969): 169–83.
Koch, Klaus
  "Die Rolle der hymnischen Abschnitte in der
  Komposition des Amos–Buches," *ZAW* 86
  (1974): 504–37.
Maag, Victor
  "Amos" and "Amosbuch" *RGG*³ 1, 328–30, 330–
  31.
Osswald, Eva
  *Urform und Auslegung im masoretischen Amostext. Ein
  Beitrag zur Kritik an der neueren traditionsgeschicht-
  lichen Methode*, Unpub. Diss. (Jena, 1951) [Review: *ThLZ* 80 (1955): 179].
Schmidt, Werner H.
  "Die deuteronomistische Redaktion des Amos-
  buches. Zu den theologischen Unterschieden
  zwischen dem Prophetenwort und seinem Samm-
  ler," *ZAW* 77 (1965): 168–93.
Wagner, Siegfried
  "Überlegungen zur Frage nach den Beziehungen
  des Propheten Amos zum Südreich," *ThLZ* 96
  (1971): 653–70.
Watts, John D. W.
  "The Origin of the Book of Amos," *ExpT* 66
  (1954–55): 109–12.
Willi–Plein, Ina
  *Vorformen der Schriftexegese innerhalb des Alten Testa-
  ments. Untersuchungen zum literarischen Werden der
  auf Amos, Hosea und Micha zurückgehenden Bücher
  im hebräischen Zwölfprophetenbuch*, BZAW 123 (Berlin and New York: Walter de Gruyter, 1971).
Winter, Alexander
  "Analyse des Buches Amos," *Theologische Studien
  und Kritiken* 83 (1910): 323–74.

g / Amos' Cultural Background

Bach, Robert
  "Gottesrecht und weltliches Recht in der Ver-
  kündigung des Propheten Amos" in *Festschrift für
  Günther Dehn*, ed. Wilhelm Schneemelcher (Neu-
  kirchen: Verlag der Buchhandlung des Erzie-
  hungsvereins, 1957), 23–34.
Brueggemann, Walter
  "Amos 4:4–13 and Israel's Covenant Worship,"
  VT 15 (1965): 1–15.
Collins, John J.
  "History and Tradition in the Prophet Amos,"

ITQ 41 (1974): 120–33.
Crook, Margaret B.
  "Did Amos and Micah Know Isaiah 9:2–7 and
  11:1–9?" *JBL* 73 (1954): 144–51.
Dürr, Lorenz
  "Altorientalisches Recht bei den Propheten Amos
  und Hosea," *BZ* 23 (1935): 150–57.
Fensham, F. Charles
  "Common Trends in Curses of the Near Eastern
  Treaties and *kudurru*–Inscriptions compared with
  Maledictions of Amos and Isaiah," *ZAW* 75
  (1963): 155–75.
Gottlieb, Hans
  "Amos und Jerusalem," *VT* 17 (1967): 430–63.
Junker, Hubert
  "Amos und die 'opferlose Mosezeit'," *ThG* 27
  (1935): 686–95.
Proksch, Otto
  Die Geschichtsbetrachtung bei Amos, Hosea und Jeremia,
  (Königsberg, 1901).
Rieger, Julius
  *Die Bedeutung der Geschichte für die Verkündigung des
  Amos und Hosea* (Giessen, 1929).
Robscheit, Hellmuth
  "Die thora bei Amos und Hosea," *EvTh* 10 (1950–
  51): 26–38.
Seilhamer, Frank H.
  "The Role of Covenant in the Mission and Mes-
  sage of Amos" in *A Light unto My Path: Old Testa-
  ment Studies in Honor of Jacob M. Myers*, ed. How-
  ard N. Bream, *et al.*; Gettysburg Theological
  Studies 4 (Philadelphia: Temple University,
  1974), 435–51.
Stoebe, Hans Joachim
  "Überlegungen zu den geistlichen Voraussetzun-
  gen der Prophetie des Amos" in *Wort—Gebot—
  Glaube. Beiträge zur Theologie des Alten Testaments
  (Walther Eichrodt zum 80. Geburtstag)*, ed. Hans
  Joachim Stoebe; AThANT 59 (Zürich: Zwingli,
  1970), 209–25.
Stuhlmueller, Carroll
  "Amos, Desert–Trained Prophet," *The Bible To-
  day* 1 (1962–63): 224–30.
Terrien, Samuel
  "Amos and Wisdom" in *Israel's Prophetic Heritage:
  Essays in honor of James Muilenburg*, ed. Bernhard
  W. Anderson and Walter Harrelson (New York:
  Harper & Brothers, 1962), 108–15.
Vollmer, Jochen
  *Geschichtliche Rückblicke und Motive in der Prophetie
  des Amos, Hosea und Jesaja*, BZAW 119 (Berlin:
  Walter de Gruyter, 1971).
Vuilleumier–Bessard, René
  *La tradition cultuelle d'Israël dans la prophétie d'Amos
  et d'Osée*, CTh 45 (Neuchâtel and Paris: Dela-
  chaux & Niestlé, 1960).
Wolff, Hans Walter
  Amos the Prophet: The Man and His Background, tr.
  Foster R. McCurley (Philadelphia: Fortress,

1973) [*Amos' geistige Heimat*, WMANT 18 (Neukirchen–Vluyn: Neukirchener Verlag, 1964)].

h / The Message of Amos

Amsler, Samuel
"Amos, prophète de la onzième heure," *ThZ* 21 (1965): 318–28.

Barackman, Paul F.
"Preaching from Amos," *Interpretation* 13 (1959): 296–315.

Barth, Karl
Church Dogmatics 4/2, *The Doctrine of Reconciliation*, tr. G. W. Bromily (Edinburgh: T. & T. Clark, 1958, 445–52 [*Die Kirchliche Dogmatik*, 4/2 (Zollikon–Zürich: Evangelischer Verlag, 1955), 502–09 ("Gerichtsbotschaft des Propheten Amos")].

Baumgartner, Walter
Kennen Amos und Hosea eine Heilseschatologie? Unpub. Diss. (Zürich, 1913).

Benson, Alphonsus
" 'From the Mouth of the Lion.' The Messianism of Amos," *CBQ* 19 (1957): 199–212.

Boehmer, Julius
"Die Eigenart der prophetischen Heilspredigt des Amos," *Theologische Studien und Kritiken* 76 (1903): 35–47.

Botterweck, Johannes
" 'Sie verkaufen den Unschuldigen um Geld.' Zur sozialen Kritik des Propheten Amos," *Bibel und Leben* 12 (1971): 215–31.

Bruston, Edouard
"Messages prophétiques: I. Le message d'Amos," *Études Théologiques et Religieuses* 7 (1932): 158–72.

Dijkema, F.
"Le fond des prophéties d'Amos" in OTS 2 (Leiden: E. J. Brill, 1943), 18–34.

Dumeste, M. L., o.p.
"La spiritualité des prophètes d'Israël (Le message du prophète Amos)," *La Vie Spirituelle* 74 (1946): 834–52; 75 (1946): 424–37.

Fendler, Marlene
"Zur Sozialkritik des Amos. Versuch einer wirtschafts– und sozialgeschichtlichen Interpretation alttestamentlicher Texte," *EvTh* 33 (1973): 32–53.

Feuillet, André
"L'universalisme et l'alliance dans la religion d'Amos," *BVC* 17 (1957): 17–29.

Hermann, Siegfried
Die prophetischen Heilserwartungen im Alten Testament: Ursprung und Gestaltwandel, BWANT 85 (Stuttgart: W. Kohlhammer, 1965), 118–26.

Howie, Carl G.
"Expressly for Our Time: The Theology of Amos," *Interpretation* 13 (1959): 273–85.

Humbert, Paul
"Un héraut de la justice, Amos," *Revue de Théologie et de Philosophie* n.s. 5 (1917): 5–35.

Hyatt, J. Philip

"The Book of Amos," *Interpretation* 3 (1949): 338–48.

Irwin, W. A.
"The Thinking of Amos," *AJSL* 49 (1932–33): 102–14.

Kapelrud, Arvid S.
"God as Destroyer in the Preaching of Amos and in the Ancient Near East," *JBL* 71 (1952): 33–38.

Idem
"New Ideas in Amos," *Volume du Congrès, Genève, 1965*, SVT 15 (Leiden: E. J. Brill, 1966), 193–206.

Laridon, V.
"Amos, genuinae religionis defensor ac propheta iustitiae socialis," *Collectiones Brugenses* 47 (1951): 405–10; 48 (1952): 3–7, 27–31.

Lattes, Dante
"Amos, prophète de la justice," *Madregoth* 1 (1940): 23–31.

Leahy, Michael
"The Popular Idea of God in Amos," *ITQ* 22 (1955): 68–73.

McFadyen, John Edgar
A Cry for Justice: A Study in Amos (New York, 1912).

Morgenstern, Julian
"The Universalism of Amos" in *Essays Presented to Leo Baeck on the Occasion of His Eightieth Birthday* (London: East & West Library, 1954), 106–26.

Mousset, Pazifique
"La pédagogie d'un prophète: Amos," *Catéchistes* 27 (1956): 267–73.

Oettli, Samuel
"Der Kultus bei Amos und Hosea" in *Greifswalder Studien. Theologische Abhandlungen (Festschrift Hermann Cremer)* (Gütersloh, 1895), 1–34.

Paton, Lewis Bayles
"Did Amos Approve the Calf–Worship at Bethel?" *JBL* 13 (1894): 80–91.

Prado, Juan
Amos, el Profeta Pastor (Madrid: El Perpetuo Socorro, 1950) [= " 'Emisiones Biblicas' de Radio Madrid," *Biblia y Predicación* 2 (May–June, 1944)].

Randellini, Lino
"Ricchi e Poveri nel libro del Profeta Amos," *Studii Biblici Francescani* 2 (1951–52): 5–86.

Rudolph, Wilhelm
"Gott und Mensch bei Amos" in *Imago Dei: Festschrift für Gustav Krüger*, ed. Heinrich Bornkamm (Giessen, 1932), 19–31.

Schrade, Hubert
Der verborgene Gott. Gottesbild und Gottesvorstellung in Israel und im alten Orient (Stuttgart: W. Kohlhammer, 1949), 157–63.

Smend, Rudolf
"Das Nein des Amos," *EvTh* 23 (1963): 404–23.

Spiegel, Shalom
"Amos vs. Amaziah" in *The Jewish Expression*, ed.

Judah Goldin (New York: Bantam Books, 1970), 38–65.

Steenbergen, Van
Motivation in Relation to the Message of Amos, Unpub. Diss. (Los Angeles, 1953).

Whitesides, R. A. D.
The Gospel according to Amos, Unpub. Diss. (Princeton, 1952).

Williams, Donald L.
"The Theology of Amos," *Review and Expositor* 63 (1966): 393–403.

Wolff, Hans Walter
Die Stunde des Amos. Prophetie und Protest (München: Chr. Kaiser, 1969).

i / Various Individual Problems of Interpretation

Albert, Edwin
"Einige Bemerkungen zu Amos," *ZAW* 33 (1913): 265–71.

Andrews, Mary E.
"Hesiod and Amos," *Journal of Religion* 23 (1943): 194–205.

Danell, G. A.
Studies in the Name Israel in the Old Testament (Uppsala: Appelbergs Boktryckeri, 1946), 110–36.

Driver, Godfrey Rolles
"Two Astronomical Passages in the Old Testament," *JTS* N.S. 4 (1953): 208–12.

Galling, Kurt
"Bethel und Gilgal," *ZDPV* 66 (1943): 140–55; [II] 67 (1944): 21–43.

Gese, Hartmut
"Kleine Beiträge zum Verständnis des Amosbuches," *VT* 12 (1962): 417–38.

Hoffmann, Georg
"Versuch zu Amos," *ZAW* 3 (1883): 87–126, 279–80.

Hoonacker, Albin van
"Notes d'exégèse sur quelques passages difficiles d'Amos," *RB* 14 (1905): 163–87.

Keller, Carl A.
"Notes bibliques de prédication sur les textes du prophète Amos," *Verbum Caro* 60 (1961): 390–98.

Lohman, Paul
"Einige Textkonjekturen zu Amos," *ZAW* 32 (1912): 274–77.

McCullough, W. S.
"Some Suggestions About Amos," *JBL* 72 (1953): 247–54.

Maigret, Jacques
"Amos et le sanctuaire de Bethel," *Bible et Terre Sainte* 47 (1962): 5–6.

Mamie, Pierre
"Le livre d'Amos. Les châtiments et le 'reste d'Israël'," *Nova et Vera* 37 (1962): 217–23.

Montgomery, James A.
"Notes on Amos," *JBL* 23 (1904): 94–96.

Oort, Henricus

"Het Vaderland van Amos," *Theologisch Tijdschrift* 25 (1891): 121–26.

Praetorius, Franz
"Bemerkungen zu Amos," *ZAW* 35 (1915): 12–25.

Idem
"Zum Texte des Amos," *ZAW* 34 (1914): 42–44.

Riedel, Wilhelm
Alttestamentliche Untersuchungen I. (Leipzig, 1902), 19–36 ("Bemerkungen zum Buche Amos").

Sant, C.
"Religious Worship in the Book of Amos," *Melita Theologica* 3 (1950): 75–93; 4 (1951): 34–48.

Seesemann, Otto
Israel und Juda bei Amos und Hosea (Leipzig, 1898).

Shoot, Frederick von Buegelow, Jr.
The Fertility Religions in the Thought of Amos and Micah, Unpub. Diss. (University of Southern California, 1951).

Speier, Salomon
"Bemerkungen zu Amos," *VT* 3 (1953): 305–10.

Idem
"Bemerkungen zu Amos, II" in *Homenaje a Millás–Vallicrosa*, vol. 2 (Barcelona: Consejo Superior de Investigaciones Científicas, 1956), 365–72.

Talmon, Shemaryahu
"The Gezer Calendar and the Seasonal Cycle of Ancient Canaan," *JAOS* 83 (1963): 177–87.

Weiser, Artur
"Die Berufung des Amos," *Theologische Blätter* 7 (1928): 177–82.

Whitford, John B.
"The Vision of Amos," *Bibliotheca Sacra* 70 (1913): 109–22.

j / Particular Passages in Amos

For additional literature on specific passages, consult the bibliographies in the text of the commentary.

Ackroyd, Peter R.
"Amos 7:14," *ExpT* 68 (1956–57): 94.

Ahlström, G. W.
"*Hammoreh liṣdāqāh* in Joel 2:23" in *Congress Volume, Rome, 1968*, SVT 17 (Leiden: E. J. Brill, 1968), 25–36.

Bartina, Sebastián
"'Vivit Potentia Beer–Šeba!' (Amos 8:14)," *VD* (1956): 202–10.

Barstad, Hans M.
"Die Basankühe in Amos 4:1," *VT* 25 (1975): 286–97.

Baumann, Eberhard
"Eine Einzelheit," *ZAW* 64 (1952): 62.

Baumgartner, Walter
"Amos 3:3–8," *ZAW* 33 (1913): 78–80.

Beek, M. A.
"The Religious Background of Amos 2:6–8" in OTS 5 (Leiden: E. J. Brill, 1948), 132–41.

Bentzen, Aage

"The Ritual Background of Amos 1:2—2:16" in OTS 8 (Leiden: E. J. Brill, 1950), 85–99.

Berg, Werner
Die sogennante Hymnenfragmente im Amosbuch, Europäische Hochschulschriften 23/45 (Bern: Herbert Lang; Frankfurt: Peter Lang, 1974).

Bertholet, Alfred
"Zu Amos 1:2" in *Festschrift G. Nathaniel Bonwetsch* (Leipzig, 1918), 1–12.

Bewer, Julius A.
"Critical Notes on Amos 2:7 and 8:4," *AJSL* 19 (1903): 116–17.

Boyle, Marjorie O'Rourke
"The Covenant Lawsuit of the Prophet Amos 3:1—4:13," *VT* 21 (1971): 338–62.

Brueggemann, Walter
"Amos' Intercessory Formula," *VT* 19 (1969): 385–99.

Brunet, Gilbert
"La vision de l'étain: réinterprétation d'Amos 7:7–9," *VT* 16 (1966): 387–95.

Budde, Karl
"Amos 1:2," *ZAW* 30 (1910): 37–41.

Condamin, Albert
"Le prétendu 'fil à plomb' de la vision d'Amos," *RB* 9 (1900): 586–94.

Coote, Robert B.
"Amos 1:11: *RḤMYW*," *JBL* 90 (1971): 206–08.

Crenshaw, James L.
Hymnic Affirmation of Divine Justice: The Doxologies of Amos and Related Texts in the Old Testament, Society of Biblical Literature Dissertation Series 24 (Missoula, Montana: Scholars Press, 1975).

Dahood, Mitchell J., s.j.
" 'To pawn one's cloak'," *Biblica* 42 (1961): 359–66.

Devescovi, Urbano
" 'Camminare sulle alture'," *Rivista Biblica* 9 (1961): 235–42.

Dobbie, Robert
"Amos 5:25," *Transactions of the Glasgow University Oriental Society* 17 (1959): 62–64.

Driver, Godfrey Rolles
"Amos 7:14," *ExpT* 67 (1955–56): 91–92.

Idem
"Difficult Words in the Hebrew Prophets" in *Studies in Old Testament Prophecy Presented to Professor Theodore H. Robinson*, ed. H. H. Rowley (Edinburgh: T. & T. Clark, 1950), 52–72.

Idem
"A Hebrew Burial Custom," *ZAW* 66 (1955): 314–15.

Elhorst, Hendrik Jan
"Amos 6:5," *ZAW* 35 (1915): 62–63.

Felsenthal, Bernhard
"Zur Bibel und Grammatik" in *Semitic Studies in Memory of Rev. Dr. Alexander Kohut*, ed. George Alexander Kohut (Berlin, 1897), 133–37 ("2. Zur Erklärung von Amos 6:10").

Fishbane, Michael
"The Treaty Background of Amos 1:11 and Related Matters," *JBL* 89 (1970): 313–18.

Flurival, Ephrem
"Le jour du jugement (Amos 9:7–15)," *BVC* 8 (1954–55): 61–75.

Freedman, David Noel; and Francis I. Anderson
"Harmon in Amos 4:3," *BASOR* 198 (1970): 41.

Gaster, Theodore H.
"An Ancient Hymn in the Prophecies of Amos," *Journal of the Manchester Egyptian and Oriental Society* 19 (1935): 23–26.

Glanzman, George S.
"Two Notes: Am 3:15 and Os 11:8–9," *CBQ* 23 (1961): 227–33.

Gunneweg, Antonius H. J.
"Erwägungen zu Amos 7:14," *ZThK* 57 (1960): 1–16.

Happel, Otto
"Am 2:6–16 in der Urgestalt," *BZ* 3 (1905): 355–67.

Hesse, Franz
"Amos 5:4–6; 14f," *ZAW* 68 (1956): 1–17.

Hillers, Delbert R.
"Amos 7:14 and Ancient Parallels," *CBQ* 26 (1964): 221–25.

Hogg, Hope W.
"The Starting–Point of the Religious Message of Amos" in *Transactions of the Third International Congress for the History of Religions*, vol. 1 (Oxford, 1908), 325–27.

Holladay, William L.
"Amos 6:1bβ: A Suggested Solution," *VT* 22 (1972): 107–10.

Idem
"Once More, 'ᵃnak = 'tin,' Amos 7:7–8," *VT* 20 (1970): 492–94.

Holwerda, Benne
. . . Begonnen hebbende van Mozes . . . (Terneuzen: D. H. Littoij, 1953), 31–47 ("Da exegese van Amos 3:3–8").

Hoonacker, Albin van
"Le sens de la protestation d'Amos VII, 14–15," *Ephemerides Theologicae Lovanienses* 18 (1941): 65–67.

Hyatt, J. Philip
"The Translation and Meaning of Am 5:23–24," *ZAW* 68 (1956): 17–24.

Junker, Hubert
"*Leo rugiit, quis non timebit? Deus locutus est, quis non prophetabit?* Eine textkritische und exegetische Untersuchung über Amos 3:3–8," *TrThZ* 59 (1950): 4–13.

Idem
"Text und Bedeutung der Vision Amos 7:7–9," *Biblica* 17 (1936): 359–64.

Kaupel, Heinrich
"Gibt es opferfeindliche Stellen im Alten Testament?" *ThG* 17 (1925): 172–78.

Keimer, Ludwig

"Eine Bemerkung zu Amos 7:14," *Biblica* 8 (1927): 441–44.

Leeuwen, C. van

"The Prophecy of the *Yōm YHWH* in Amos 5:18–20" in *Language and Meaning: Studies in Hebrew Language and Biblical Exegesis*, OTS 19 (Leiden: E. J. Brill, 1974), 113–34.

Limburg, James

"Amos 7:4: A Judgment with Fire?" *CBQ* 35 (1973): 346–49.

Loewenstamm, Samuel E.

"כלוב קיץ (A Remark on the Typology of the Prophetic Vision [Amos 8:1–3])," [Hebrew] *Tarbiz* 34 (1964–65): 319–22 (English Summary, ii).

Loretz, Oswald

"Vergleich und Kommentar in Amos 3:12," *BZ* N.F. 20 (1976): 122–25.

MacCormack, J.

"Amos 7:14," *ExpT* 67 (1955–56): 318.

Mackenzie, H. S.

"The Plumb–Line (Amos 7:8)," *ExpT* 60 (1948–49): 159.

Malamat, Abraham

"Amos 1:5 in the Light of the Til Barsip Inscriptions," *BASOR* 129 (1953): 25–26.

Marti, Karl

"Zur Komposition von Amos 1:3—2:3" in *Abhandlungen zur semitischen Religionskunde und Sprachwissenschaft. Wolf Wilhelm Grafen von Baudissin zum 26. September 1917*, ed. Wilhelm Frankenberg and Friedrich Küchler; BZAW 33 (Giessen, 1918), 323–30.

Metzger, Martin

"Lodebar und der tell el–mghannije," *ZDPV* 76 (1960): 97–102.

Mittmann, Siegfried

"Gestalt und Gehalt einer prophetischen Selbstrechtfertigung (Am 3,3–8)," *Theologische Quartalschrift* 151 (1971): 134–45.

Moeller, Henry R.

"Ambiguity at Amos 3:12," *The Bible Translator* 15 (1964): 31–34.

Neubauer, Karl Wilhelm

"Erwägungen zu Amos 5:4–15," *ZAW* 78 (1966): 292–316.

Neuberg, Frank J.

"An Unrecognized Meaning of Hebrew *DÔR*," *JNES* 9 (1950): 215–17.

Ouellette, Jean

"Le mur d'etain dans Amos, VII, 7–9," *RB* 80 (1973): 321–31.

Idem

"The Shaking of the Thresholds in Amos 9:1," *HUCA* 43 (1972): 23–27.

Paul, Shalom M.

"Amos 1:3—2:3: A Concatenous Literary Pattern," *JBL* 90 (1971): 397–403.

Rabinowitz, Isaac

"The Crux at Amos 3:12," *VT* 11 (1961): 228–31.

Ramsey, George W.

"Amos 4:12—A New Perspective," *JBL* 89 (1970): 187–91.

Reider, Joseph

"דמשק in Amos 3:12," *JBL* 67 (1948): 245–48.

Rendtorff, Rolf

"Zu Amos 2:14–16," *ZAW* 85 (1973): 226–27.

Richardson, H. Neil

"A Critical Note on Amos 7:14," *JBL* 85 (1966): 89.

Rinaldi, Giovanni

"Due note ad Amos," *Rivista degli Studi Orientali* 28 (1953): 149–52.

Rost, Leonhard

"Zu Amos 7:10–17" in *Festgabe für Theodor Zahn* (Leipzig, 1928), 229–36.

Rudolph, Wilhelm

"Amos 4:6–13" in *Wort—Gebot—Glaube. Beiträge zur Theologie des Alten Testaments (Walther Eichrodt zum 80. Geburtstag)*, ed. Hans Joachim Stoebe; AThANT 59 (Zürich: Zwingli, 1970), 27–38.

Idem

"Die angefochtenen Völkersprüche in Amos 1 und 2" in *Schalom. Studien zu Glaube und Geschichte Israels (Alfred Jepsen zum 70. Geburtstag)*, ed. Karl–Heinz Bernhardt; Arbeiten zur Theologie 1/46 (Stuttgart: Calwer ,1971), 45–49.

Idem

"Schwierige Amosstellen" in *Wort und Geschichte (Festschrift für Karl Elliger zum 70. Geburtstag)*, ed. Hartmut Gese and Hans Peter Rüger; Alter Orient und Altes Testament 18 (Kevelaer: Butzon & Bercker; Neukirchen–Vluyn: Neukirchener Verlag, 1973), 157–62.

Schmid, Herbert

"'Nicht Prophet bin ich, noch Prophetensohn': Zur Erklärung von Amos 7,14a," *Judaica* 23 (1967): 68–74.

Schmidt, Nathaniel

"On the Text and Interpretation of Am 5:25–27," *JBL* 13 (1894): 1–15.

Schoville, Keith N.

"A Note on the Oracles of Amos Against Gaza, Tyre, and Edom" in *Studies on Prophecy*, SVT 26 (Leiden: E. J. Brill, 1974), 55–63.

Schult, Hermann

"Amos 7:15a und die Legitimation des Außenseiters" in *Probleme biblischer Theologie (Gerhard von Rad zum 70. Geburtstag)*, ed. Hans Walter Wolff (München: Chr. Kaiser, 1971), 462–78.

Smythe, H. R.

"The Interpretation of Amos 4:13 in St. Athanasius and Dydimus," *JTS* N.S. 1 (1950): 158–68.

Soper, B. Kingston

"For Three Transgressions and for Four. A New Interpretation of Amos 1:3, etc," *ExpT* 71 (1959–

60) : 86–87.

Speiser, Ephraim Avigdor
"Note on Amos 5:26," *BASOR* 108 (1947) : 5–6.

Thomas, David Winton
"Note on נוֹעָדוּ in Amos 3:3," *JTS* N.S. 7 (1956) :
69–70.

Torczyner, Harry
"Dunkle Bibelstellen" in *Vom Alten Testament.
Karl Marti zum siebzigsten Geburtstage*, ed. Karl
Budde; BZAW 41 (Giessen, 1925), 274–80.

Torrey, Charles Cutler
"Notes on Am 2:7; 6:10; 8:3; 9:8–10," *JBL* 15
(1896) : 151–54.

Idem
"On the Text of Am 5:25; 6:1, 2; 7:2," *JBL* 13
(1894) : 63.

Tucker, Gene M.
"Prophetic Authenticity: A Form–Critical Study
of Amos 7:10–17," *Interpretation* 27 (1973) : 423–
34.

Vischer, Wilhelm
"Perhaps the Lord will be Gracious (A Sermon)"
(tr. Donald G. Miller), *Interpretation* 13 (1959) :
286–95.

Vogt, Ernest
"Waw explicative in Amos 7:14," *ExpT* 68
(1956–57) : 301–02.

Vriezen, Theodorus C.
"Erwägungen zu Amos 3:2" in *Archäologie und
Altes Testament. Festschrift für Kurt Galling*, ed.
Arnulf Kuschke and Ernst Kutsch (Tübingen:
J. C. B. Mohr [Paul Siebeck], 1970), 255–58.

Watts, John D. W.
"An Old Hymn Preserved in the Book of Amos,"
JNES 15 (1956) : 33–39.

Idem
"Note on the Text of Amos 5:7," *VT* 4 (1954) :
215–16.

Weiser, Artur
"Zu Amos 4:6–13," *ZAW* 46 (1928) : 49–59.

Wurthwein, Ernst
"Amos 5:21–27," *ThLZ* 72 (1947) : 143–52.

Youngblood, Ronald
"לקראת in Amos 4:12," *JBL* 90 (1971) : 98.

Zevit, Ziony
"A Misunderstanding at Bethel, Amos 7:12–17,"
VT 25 (1975) : 783–90.

Zolli, Eugenio
"Amos 4:2b," *Antonianum* 30 (1955) : 188–89.

Zolli, Israele
"Note Esegetiche (Amos 2:7a)," *Rivista degli Studi
Orientali* 16 (1936) : 178–83.

Review and Expositor 63 (1966) : 375–85.

Koehler, Ludwig
"Amos–Forschungen von 1917 bis 1932," *ThR*
N.F. 4 (1932) : 195–213.

Mays, James Luther
"Words about the Words of Amos. Recent Study
of the Book of Amos," *Interpretation* 13 (1959) :
259–72.

Seierstad, Ivar P.
"Amosprophetien i ljoset av nyare gransking,"
Tidsskrift for Teologi og Kirke 2 (1931) : 111–27.

k / Literature on Amos

Craghan, John F.
"The Prophet Amos in Recent Literature," *Biblical Theology Bulletin* 2 (1972) : 242–61.

Kelley, Page H.
"Contemporary Study of Amos and Prophetism,"

Indices*

1. Passages

a / Old Testament and Apocrypha

---

* Numbers and letters in parentheses following page citations for this volume refer to footnotes and textual notes.

Prv	
8:19	285
8:20	245, 285
8:36	279(b)
9:6	239
10:12	153
11:1	327
11:13	188(48)
11:27	250
11:28	274
12:1	246
13:5	246
14:16	274
14:31	206
15:10	246
15:11	340
15:16	193
16:4	275
16:5	282
16:11	327
16:18	245, 282
16:33	246
17:23	166
19:8	279(b)
19:11	301
20:3	272(h)
20:10	327
20:19	188(48)
20:23	327
21:3	245
21:31	290
22:22	166, 297
23:29–35	244
23:29–30	244
25:9	188(48)
26:28	246
27:7	330
28:8	247
29:10	246
29:26	246
30:1	143
30:18–19	138
30:27	29
30:29–31	138
31:9	165
31:20	206

Eccl	
4:1	190(f)
7:26	330
9:8	276
10:16	244

Song	
1:3	276
4:10	276
8:2	83(93)

Is	
1:3	284
1:8	353
1:13–17	264
1:13	262(22)
1:14	262
1:15	264
1:16	335(i)
1:21–22	236
1:21	245
1:23	248
2:1	118
2:4	76(12), 80
2:7	79
5:7	245
5:8–10	248(137)
5:8	244
5:11–13	273
5:11	244
5:19	244
5:20	244, 330
5:21	244
5:22	72(n), 244
5:23–24	244
5:23	248
5:25–29	218
6:4	246(4)
6:8–10	94
7:6	131(x)
8:18	81
8:9–10	80
8:18	76(12)
9:7–20[8–21]	218
9:11[12]	157
9:12[13]	220
10:2	166
10:9–11	271(b)
10:21	72(n)
11:2	66
13	43, 47
13:2ff	40
13:3	46, 73(r)
13:4	44
13:6	47
13:8	46
13:10	47
13:19	214, 218, 221(96)
13:20	85(109)
14:14	224(121)
22:6	348
23:1–14	22
23:7	23
24:20	330
25:4	81
27:13	43(29)

Is	
28:7	311
28:17	245, 300
28:21	34
29:10	311
30:10	310, 313
30:15	220
31:4	185
33:7	330
36:6	274
37:30	209(b)
37:31	169, 169(311)
38:12	339(26)
41:14–16	58
42:5	223
43:1	223
43:7	223
44:2–5	60
45:7	223
45:12	223
45:18	223
45:23	153(127)
48:1	283
49:26	83(93)
51:3	45
52:1	76(12), 82
55:11	154
57:19	70
57:20	329
58:12	353
61:5	32
62:2	274
66:5	275

Jer	
1:1	120
1:4–10	94
1:11	300
2:2	259(b)
4:4	228(o)
4:5–6	44
4:5	191
4:16	191
5:12	182
5:20	191
5:22	46
5:24	55(j)
5:27	319
6:4	79
8:7	284
9:14–15[15–16]	246
9:16–21[17–22]	236(32)
9:16[17]	243, 249
9:20–21[21–22]	237
9:21[22]	236
10:2	210(p)

4. Commentators and Modern Authors

Jenni, Ernst
  45(37),188(48),291,
  326(22)
Jensen, Kjeld
  62,76(25)
Jepsen, Alfred
  26,50(79,80),124(76),
  149(94),245(123),302(75)
Jeremias, Gert
  63,64(55)
Jeremias, Jörg
  115,118(12,13),121(46),
  125,236(34)
Jerome
  3(2)
Johnson, Aubrey R.
  158(182),162(238)
Joüon, Paul
  19(u),55(f),56(s),120(33),
  130(r),131(v),133(h),
  165(268),203(e),209(b,
  i),211(z),228(j,m),
  256(15),259(b),271(f)
  321(b,e),322(o),334,335(f),
  342(46),344(c),354(16)
Junker, Hubert
  179,183(14),258,291,300(60)

Kahle, Paul
  267(76)
Kaiser, Otto
  299(51)
Kapelrud, Arvid S.
  6(23,29),25(36),29(76),
  30(90).43(28),48(64),
  62(33,39),81(78),84(100),
  116(1),124(70),125(87),
  127,145(59),146(69),
  147,238(58),248(144),
  305,350
Kassis, Hanna E.
  275(19)
Keil, Carl Friedrich
  27(58,59),42(15),64(60),
  84(99),264(40)
Keimer, Ludwig
  305
Keller, Carl A.
  133(e)
Kellermann, Ulrich
  350,352(5),353(10)
Kerrigan, Alexander
  54
Kienitz, Friedrich K.
  4(12)

Kierkegaard, Søren
  252(178)
Kingsbury, Edwin C.
  334,338(10)
Kittel, Rudolph
  43(20)
Klopfenstein, Martin Alfred
  164(259),206(19),327(30)
Knierim, Rolf
  152(117,118),153(123),
  174,177(25),194(23),
  209(a),219(56),247(133),
  348(30),349(35)
Koch, Klaus
  50(80),254(7)
Koehler, Ludwig
  25(33),123(59),136(2,5),
  152(116),155,172(341),
  181(6),187(46),212,212(9),
  218(48),314(45),352(1)
Koehler-Baumgartner
  27(57),32(103),130(t),
  133(m),155(140),159(201),
  165(269),190(f),201(13),
  205(9),206(25),209(g),
  228(p),240(72),241(87),
  249(152),253(d),263(28),
  266(69),272(h),275(26),
  276(33),289(28),292(f),
  298(41),299(53),300(62),
  311(25),324(y),335(e),
  349(37)
Koenig, Jean
  39(n)
Kopf, L.
  160(208)
Kornemann, Ernst
  4(13)
Kosmala, Hans
  139(25)
Kraeling, Carl Hermann
  264(35)
Kraus, Hans-Joachim
  21(6),22(16),41(8),68(93),
  79(50),81(79),83(94),
  122,147(75,77),218(53),
  219(61),239(69),263(33),
  265(53),331(71),340(34)
Krause, Gerhard
  7(31),15(69),86(115),
  257(22)
Krenkel, Max
  293(i)
Kuhl, Curt
  82(91)

Kühnöl, Christian Gottlieb
  64(68)
Kupper, Jean-Robert
  296(21)
Kuschke, Arnulf
  82(83),123(62),155,
  166(284)
Kutsch, Ernst
  17,33(119),37,38(l),40(3),
  42(15),45(43),124(76),
  125(84),249(153),277(40),
  321,329(54)

Lapp, Paul W.
  123(62)
Lauha, Aarre
  62(33,39)
Lausberg, Heinrich
  183(15)
Leahy, Michael
  321,323(y),332(80)
Lehming, Sigo
  127,179,181(1,4),184(20),
  305,310(13,16),312(30)
Leibel, Daniel
  37,38(g)
Levy, Jacob
  319(12)
Lietzmann, Hans
  132(c)
Lindblom, Johannes
  122(51),125(88),148(87),
  300(66)
Loewenstamm, Samuel E.
  37,38(g),317,318(3),
  319(15)
Löhr, Max
  174(a),253(b)
Lohse, Eduard
  267(75)
Loretz, Oswald
  159(194)
Loud, Gordon
  264(34)
Luckenbill, Daniel David
  277(41)
Luther
  7(31),8(41),15,86(115),227
Lutz, Hans Martin
  341(43)
Lys, Daniel
  66(76),223(118)

Maag, Victor
  116(d),117(5),130(q),
  141(36),155,155(141,
  142),166(286),167(293),
  175(1),180(b),181(l),
  190(h),196(b),197(l),
  199(c),210(q),211(2),
  228(i,o,p),229(r),230(v,y),
  233(12),234(17),260(f),
  266(64),270(a,b),271(e),
  272(h),275(25),276(31),
  279(d),280(h),293(o),
  297(33),301(70),307(e),
  310(20),322(q),323(w,x,y),
  331(66),335(e),344(g),
  345(l),352(l)
McCarthy, Dennis J.
  145(58)
MacCormack, J.
  305
Maier, Johann
  267(76)
Malamat, Abraham
  127,129(j),156(157)
Mandelkern, Solomon
  213(16),325(3)
Marti, Karl
  44(34),72(o),84(99),
  129(g),134(r),140,144(50),
  174(a),180(b),181(l),
  183(14),199(c),204(k),
  234(17),260(f),265(54),
  266(65),270(a,b),271(b),
  272(h),326(13),328,
  328(36),334(a)
Meer, Petrus E. van der
  149(93)
Meinhold Johannes
  132(c)
Meissner, Bruno
  185(26)
Mendelsohn, Isaac
  157(163,167),158(172)
Merx, E. O. Adalbert
  12(59),38(j,k),54(a),
  57,76(22)
Metzger, Martin
  286,288(20)
Meulen, Daniel van der
  155(144)
Meyer, Eduard
  78(36),289
Meyer, Rudolph
  306(e),323(y)
Michaelis, Johann David
  284(a,b)

Scharbert, Josef
49(75)

Scheepers, Johannes H.
54,66(70,79)

Schmalohr, Josef
6(22),63(42)

Schmid, Hans Heinrich
245(123),284

Schmid, Herbert
305,311(24)

Schmidt, Hans
155,123(66)

Schmidt, Werner H.
43(27),80(67),82(83),
84(107),115,120(32),127,
140,140(33),142(41),
147(77),152(112,113),
174,175(4),179,180(b),
181(1,6),182(8),219(68),
223(113),258,262(16),
266(63),279(b),299(51),
341(41)

Schmökel, Hartmut
161(214)

Schnutenhaus, Frank
257(21)

Schottroff, Willy
159(192,193),279,280(i),
283(20)

Schrader, Eberhard
260(i)

Schult, Hermann
136(5)

Schunk, Klaus Dietrich
219(59,61),253,255(13)

Schwantes, Siegfried J.
203,207(26)

Schwarzenbach, Armin W.
76(23),264(44)

Scott, R. B. Y.
321,327(27,28)

Seebass, Horst
301(74),311(26),315(57)

Seeligmann, Isac Leo
189,194(23,27),247(128)

Segert, Stanislav
115,234(20),305,314(43)

Seierstadt, Ivar P.
291,299(52)

Sekine, Masao
258,267(78)

Sellers, Ovid R.
17,27,63(50)

Sellin, Ernst
6,6(27),17(e),18(i),21(5),
27(58),41(10),45(41),
48(63),55(e),57(z),59,
69(99),72(o,p),140,165(265),
181(1),183(14),190(h),
204(o),217,217(46),
222(102),228(o),230(v),
233(12),240,241(83),
253(b),260(f),264(40),
265(54),266(64),269(a),
270(a),292(d),323(w,y),
328(38),345(1),352(2)

Selms, Adriaan van
302(76)

Sethe, Kurt
144(53),146(65,68)

Sievers, Eduard
181(i)

Sinclair, Lawrence A.
174

Smend, Rudolf
149(89),177(27),181(6),
267(78),306,312(30),313(36),
339(19)

Smith, George Adam
228(q)

Snijders, L. A.
31(99)

Soden, Wolfram von
136(5),154(129,130),
196(b),239(64),248(142),
328(31),342(51,52,53)

Soggin, J. Alberto
79(57),341(43)

Speier, Salomon
115,123(66),203,206,227,
241(93),306,307(h)

Speiser, Ephraim Avigdor
258

Sprengling, M.
17,19(z)

Stählin, Gustav
29(84),236(32),249(153)

Stamm, Johann Jakob
297(34),298(43),323(y)

Starcky, Jean
76(19),324(y)

Steck, Odil Hannes
201(5)

Stephens, Ferris J.
248(142),328(31)

Steiner, Heinrich
57(5)

Stoebe, Hans Joachim
115,123(62),124(71),
306,314(43)

Storer, Tracey I.
27(55)

Strack, Hermann
30(89)

Strobel, August
321,327(27,28)

Talmon, Shemaryahu
291,296(18)

Terrien, Samuel
187(45),189,193(20),334

Theis, Johannes
27(58),41(9),181(1)

Thomas, David Winton
179,179(a)

Thompson, John A.
6(29),17,27,28(68),29
(75),32(103),41(11),
42(17),44(35),83(97)

Toombs, Lawrence E.
339(19)

Torczyner, Harry
230(aa),247(132)

Torrey, Charles Cutler
292(d)

Treves, Marco
4(9),71,76,82,84(107)

Trinquet, Joseph
21(5),55(e),72(o)

Usinger, Robert L.
27(55)

Vatke, Wilhelm
6

Vaux, Roland de
30,129(d),130(o),155,
155(139),177(21),202(20),
237(41),246(126),336(s)

Vernes, Maurice
6

Vila, André
144(53),145(54)

Vogt, Ernst
306

Vollers, Karl
273(l)

Volz, Paul
334(a),335(e),344,349(33)

Vriezen, Th. C.
68(94),176(17)

Vuilleumier–Bessard, René
208,338(11)

Wächter, Ludwig
280(h),320(26),330(55)

Wainwright, Gerald Avery
344,347(20)

Walcot, Peter
299(48)

Wallis, Gerhard
264(34)

Wambacq, B. N.
287(7)

Wanke, Gunther
227,242,242(99,106),
243(109),282(10),287(7,8)

Watts, John D. W.
208,215(31),227,229(s),
291,306,312(28)

Weidner, Ernst F.
145(58),283(22)

Weise, Manfred
79(56)

Weiser, Artur
6(29),17(e),24(26),32(103),
41(10),55(e),82(90),
117(5),119(18),121,
127,132(c),140,144,147,
148(82),149(89,90,92),
174(c),175(2),181(1,4),
183(14,17),185(31),
197(1),204(l),205(7),
209(a),211(2),212(8),
215(29),219(65),233(13),
234(18),237,237(44,46,47),
239(61),241(84,85),
253(b),260(f),264(40),
265,266(64),269(a),270(a,b),
271(d),272(h),273(4),
279(e),280(h),283(23),
284,284(a),285(3),296(13),
319(10),321(b),334,334(a,d),
335(e),338(9),350

Weiss, Meir
115,253,255

Wellhausen, Julius
38(g),56(p),72(o),83(95),
97(46),128(b),132(e),
140,144(51),159(199),
160,160(209),178(29),
191(l),210(m),211(1),
230(aa,cc),231(ii),240,
240(74),266(70),271(e),
272(h),284(a),292(d),
328(35),329(49),348(24),
352,352(4)

Werner, Herbert
291